ART and MUSIC

An Introduction

ART and MUSIC

An Introduction

Dale G. Cleaver □ John M. Eddins

University of Tennessee   *Southern Illinois University*

Harcourt Brace Jovanovich, Inc.

New York / Chicago / San Francisco / Atlanta

Cover photo: HENRI MATISSE, *Piano Lesson,* 1916. Oil on canvas, 8'$\frac{1}{2}$" x 6'11$\frac{3}{4}$". Collection, The Museum of Modern Art, New York. Mrs. Simon Guggenheim Fund.

ISBN: 0-15-503437-5
Library of Congress Catalog Card Number: 77-72026

Printed in the United States of America

Page 546 constitutes a continuation of the copyright page.

Preface

The successful classroom use of *Art: An Introduction* has led many instructors in the humanities to request an expansion of the book to include music. In response to this demand, we have produced *Art and Music: An Introduction,* which offers parallel approaches to these subjects. Part One discusses the visual, tactile, and aural materials, and the elements of form, design, technique, meaning, and value in music and the visual arts. Part Two presents a historical survey in which these elements and materials are utilized for stylistic analysis in discussions of painting, sculpture, architecture, and music.

Based on the Third Edition of *Art: An Introduction,* this expansion incorporates chapters on music that generally complement the chapters on art. Comparisons between the visual arts and music, however, have not been forced, and the uniqueness of the separate disciplines has been maintained. It is our belief that comparisons and analogies between the arts are best left to individual instructors and their students. At the present stage of criticism, relationships between the arts are a matter of individual judgment and insight.

This book offers generally accepted interpretations of the historically important periods, styles, artists, and composers of Western culture. Of necessity, the writing is condensed. The result is a core text that can serve as a structural basis for courses of varying aims and orientations. The book is intended to be used in conjunction with other material. To this end, selected bibliographies are provided with each chapter, and most of the music chapters also include listening lists. Many of the books and musical works cited here contain additional examples of the periods, artists, and composers covered, but further supplements may be desired for such specialized subjects as folk art and music, art and music from other cultures, and various fields of design. As an aid to the student's understanding and appreciation of music a separate recording is available, including complete performances of Beethoven's *Seventh Symphony*, second movement, Bach's *Brandenburg Concerto, Number I*, fourth movement, Debussy's *Prelude to the Afternoon of a Faun*, Berio's *Sinfonia*, Section I, and Bartók's *Music for Strings, Percussion, and Celesta*, first movement. These works are used throughout Part One to illustrate the various principles of music.

We would like to express our thanks to instructors of art history and music across the country for their interest. Their encouragement and insightful suggestions were very helpful during the genesis of this book. Although there are too many to thank individually, we are especially grateful for valuable suggestions in the art chapters to Richard McLanathan, Director of the American Association of Museums; for equally valuable suggestions in the chapter on photography and motion pictures to Diane Kirkpatrick of the University of Michigan and Allan Casebier of the University of California; and for their close reading of and perceptive comments on the music chapters, Maynard Anderson of Wartburg College and Gary Sudano of Illinois State University. We have a continuing debt to Rachael Young of the University of Tennessee for her considerable help with and close attention to the art chapters of this book. Nina Gunzenhauser, Abigail Winograd, and Sidney Zimmerman of Harcourt Brace Jovanovich deserve special appreciation for their editorial talents.

Dale G. Cleaver

John M. Eddins

Contents

ART and MUSIC

An Introduction

PART ONE
The Principles of Art and Music

To understand the art of our own time or that of other eras, it is necessary first to consider the nature of art and some of the principles by which it operates. Art has always outgrown the definitions imposed upon it; but, for our purposes, a work of art might be defined as an object or event created or selected for its capacity to express and stimulate experience within a discipline. The experience may range from the pity evoked by the face of a starving child to a revelation of order in architecture, from the pathos evoked by a skillful blues trumpeter to the beauty of design in a classical symphony. The discipline may vary from the strictest geometrical organization or regularity of rhythm pattern to a spontaneous irregularity that approaches the accidental, yet discipline provides for order, completeness, and intensity.

HSIA KUEI, detail from *River Scenes,*
Sung Dynasty. Collection of the
National Palace Museum, Taipei,
Taiwan.

All of the arts are based on sensory experience: In the visual arts these experiences are visual and tactile, in music they are aural. But not all sensory
experiences are art; the difference lies in human purpose. The artist or musician arranges an experience for us by selecting and manipulating, within the
limits of a discipline, such elements as line, shape, mass, value, texture, color,
and, in the case of music, sounds in time. Painters or sculptors may use these
elements to represent well-known objects from the everyday world and to suggest feelings about them, or they may create an entirely new world for our
contemplation. Architects are equally concerned with these elements, although
they are rarely inclined to depict objects in their art and must usually consider utilitarian functions such as shelter and useful space. Musicians use
sounds in time to evoke familiar symbols or associations, or to create new
worlds in sound. Whatever their field, artists create by choosing and composing the basic elements, and the word COMPOSITION is often used to denote a
work of art. In the visual arts the individual objects or parts are frequently
called FORMS, but the word FORM is also used in both music and art for the
total character or structure of a composition. The means of organizing these
elements is spoken of as FORMAL PROCESSES and the study of how these elements function in art and music is called FORMAL ANALYSIS.

Visual and Tactile Elements in Art

Line

Line may be thought of as the path of a moving point, as the edge of a flat shape, as the axis (dominant direction) of a shape, or as the contour of a solid object. Line may be of even or modulated (varied) thickness; and the range of personality it may express is wide: quick, slow, or still; nervous, majestic, or rigid. It can suggest mass, texture, light, and shadow; it can emphasize form or create mood.

In Picasso's pencil drawing of Dr. Claribel Cone (Fig. 1-1), the lines overlap and are modulated to suggest the roundness and heaviness of the body, but they become light and rippling to depict the ruffles of lace. In contrast, the drypoint, *Self-Portrait with Graver*, by Beckmann (Fig. 1-2) expresses a nervous, tense personality through its jerky, restless lines and their contrasting angles. Beckmann used *crosshatching* (superimposed sets of parallel lines) for the shadows that define the mass of the head.

Delacroix's painting (Plate 15) evokes line with short, curving brush strokes that occasionally establish

1-1
PABLO PICASSO, *Dr. Claribel Cone,* 1922. Pencil on paper, 25³⁄₁₆″ × 19½″ Cone Collection, Baltimore Museum of Art.

the contour of an object but more often blur the separations between the parts, move from the edges into the mass of the forms, and heighten the frenzied activity depicted. In the Chinese scroll painted by Hsia Kuei (pp. 2–3), vast scale is suggested by the contrast between clusters of precise linear details and areas left relatively empty. Men, plants, and surface textures are almost microscopic in a world of towering peaks and infinite, mist-filled space.

Line in sculpture may be seen as the edge of a form considered in silhouette, as incisions in the surface of the mass, or as the general directional thrust of a form. In all three types of line, the horseman carved by a Dogan tribesman of Africa (Fig. 1-3) has tense, straight sections enlivened by abrupt changes of direction. On the other hand, *The Assumption of the Virgin* by Cosmas and Egid Asam (Fig. 1–27) has a Delacroix-like activity in its complex twisting and curling edges.

In architecture, line may emphasize rigid simplicity and sharply defined edges, as in Santa Maria delle Carceri (Fig. 1-16). In contrast to the simple balance of vertical and horizontal lines in this church, a powerful

1-2 MAX BECKMANN, *Self-Portrait with Burin*, 1917. Drypoint, 11¾″ x 9⅜″. Collection, The Museum of Modern Art, New York (gift of Edgar Kaufman, Jr.).

1-3 DOGON TRIBESMAN, *Horseman*, late nineteenth century (?). Wood, 14¾″ high. Katherine White Collection.

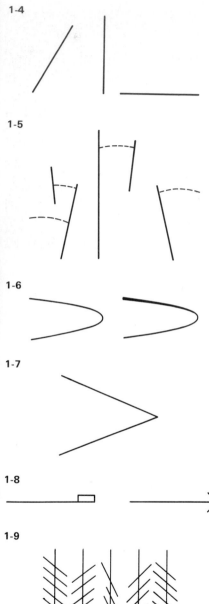

1-4

1-5

1-6

1-7

1-8

1-9

(a)

upward thrust is provided by the dominant vertical lines of Amiens Cathedral (Fig. 1-29).

MOTION IN LINE

To suggest or emphasize movement, as in the painting by Delacroix or in Amiens Cathedral, line may be used in at least two ways: It may represent or suggest things that we know are capable of motion, such as rippling waves, or it may imply motion by its form or by its relation to other lines. Our experience of gravity causes us to feel that vertical and horizontal lines are stable, whereas unsupported diagonal lines often seem to move in the direction in which they are leaning (Fig. 1-4). Grouped lines may suggest tensions between each other by the degree to which they seem to require or to provide mutual support (Fig. 1-5), an effect often utilized by Cézanne (see Plate 17). Curving lines tend to move in the direction of their greatest thrust; modulating the thickness of a line can accentuate this effect (Fig. 1-6 and Plate 28). An angle often seems to point toward its apex (Fig. 1-7), and a line may suggest motion by drawing the viewer's attention toward one end (Fig. 1-8 and Plate 3). The dynamic effect lines may have on each other is dramatically illustrated by several classic diagrams. The vertical lines in Figure 1-9a are actually parallel but appear otherwise because of the pushing forces of the diagonals. The horizontal lines in Figure 1-9b are of equal length but appear different because of the expanding and contracting qualities of the diagonals, whereas the verticals in Figure 1-9c seem to push the two diagonals out of alignment. These effects may be exploited deliberately or instinctively by the artist, architect, or designer.

LINE AND SPACE

The depth in Masaccio's *Tribute Money* (Fig. 1-10) is achieved partly by *linear perspective*, one means of

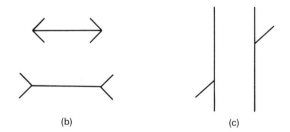

(b)

(c)

1-10 MASACCIO, *The Tribute Money, c.* 1425. Fresco, approx. 20′ × 8′ Brancacci Chapel, Santa Maria del Carmine, Florence.

creating the illusion of depth on a flat surface. To our eyes, parallel lines in a plane pointing into space appear to converge at a *vanishing point* (V. P.) on the horizon established by our eye level, or on a line perpendicular to the horizon (Figs. 1-11 and 1-12). Frequently, however, intervening objects hide the horizon. In Figure 1-11, the converging lines of Masaccio's building have been extended until they meet, thus revealing the vanishing point, the hidden horizon, and the eye level chosen for us by the artist. Masaccio used linear perspective also to emphasize the major figure in the composition, Jesus, by placing the vanishing point right behind his head. In choosing the eye level and hence the horizon, the artist may give us an ordinary view (Fig. 1-11), a worm's-eye view (Fig. 1-12), or a view from above (Fig. 1-13). When all converging lines focus on a single vanishing point, as in the Masaccio, we call it a *one-point perspective* system (Fig. 1-11). It is often desirable to have more than one vanishing point, as in Figures 1-12 and 1-13; an appropriate term is *multiple-point perspective*. The artist is not bound to restrict himself to a particular system. The various types of perspective—and there are others, which have not been mentioned here—are only devices that the artist may or may not wish to use. He may deliberately use two or more different eye levels in the same painting in order to emphasize certain objects or to create for the viewer an unusual experience of space (Fig. 1-14).

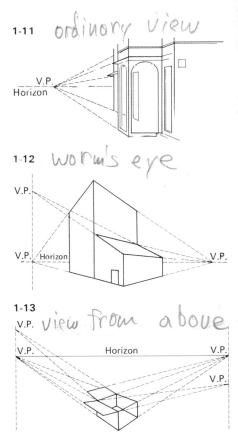

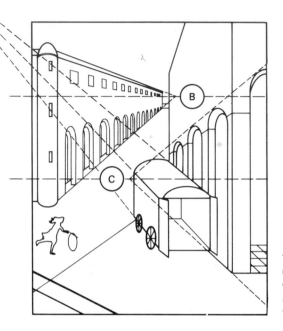

1-14

This diagram of a painting by De Chirico (Fig. 19-20) indicates vastly different eye levels, A, B, and C, for the two buildings and the trailer.

1-15

Diagram of *Decorative Figure on an Ornamental Background.*

Shape

A *shape* is an area or a plane with distinguishable boundaries. If we think of shape as having length and width only, then it is a more limited term than *form* and is distinguishable from *mass*, which requires depth as a third dimension (although it is possible to ignore the third dimension of a mass and consider it as a shape if we view it one surface at a time or see it in silhouette). Shape, like line, may have many personalities: rigid, flexible, precise, uncertain, calm, active, awkward, or graceful.

Picasso's *Three Musicians* (Plate 27) has shapes that tip, slide, bend suddenly, break up, and interweave in a staccato fashion; the total effect is one of great activity. In the *Decorative Figure on an Ornamental Background* (Plate 25), Matisse placed a massive, rigidly contoured figure in an environment of shapes that blossom expansively within loose-framing lines (Fig. 1-15). It is the room that is agitated; the woman seems motionless. This unusual effect comes partly from the orientation of the figure along vertical and horizontal lines, which seem stable compared with the diagonals of the floor and the irregular curves on the wall.

As we have seen, it is often necessary to ignore the third dimension when considering shape in sculpture and architecture. Although Egyptian sculpture derives much of its character from mass, it is helpful to consider the nature of shape in *Mycerinus and His Queen* (Fig. 7-8). The clearly delineated shapes present vertical and horizontal elements locked into a static, timeless rigidity. In contrast, the forms of the Asam composition (Fig. 1-27), if considered as shapes, have the restlessness of dried leaves in a wind. Similarly, the simple rigid shapes, organized by line, of Santa Maria delle Carceri (Fig. 1-16) contrast with the lilting and constantly interrupted shapes of San Carlo alle Quattro Fontane (Fig. 15-13), where multiplicity and changes of direction suggest flexibility and even metamorphosis.

1-16
GIULIANO DA SANGALLO,
Santa Maria delle Carceri,
Prato, Italy, 1485–92.

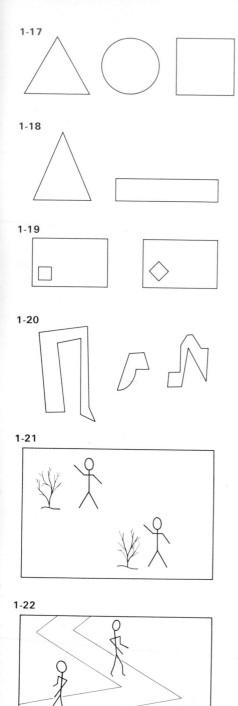

1-17

1-18

1-19

1-20

1-21

1-22

MOTION IN SHAPES

Static shapes maintain a rigid equilibrium within themselves and with their environment (Fig. 1-17). Shapes become more dynamic as they draw our attention in a specific direction. The triangle in Figure 1-18 pushes upward more than to the sides. The rectangle is relatively stable, but because of its width our attention is drawn along a horizontal axis. Even the stability of the square may be disturbed if we move it out of alignment with a stable environment (Fig. 1-19). Less regular shapes can suggest much more activity; Figure 1-20 shows several of the shapes in Picasso's *Three Musicians* (Plate 27). Their liveliness comes from irregularly expanding and contracting parts that draw our attention in several directions.

SHAPE AND SPACE

The illusion of depth on a flat surface may be produced simply by overlapping shapes, as in the Picasso painting and the landscape by Hsia Kuei on pages 2–3. Even the position of shapes on the picture surface can suggest space. In Figure 1-21 the upper figure appears to be farther away even though the two figures are equal in size. The assumption is easily made that the figures are standing on a plane that extends to an unseen horizon outside the picture. Diagonal lines or parallels that do not converge may strengthen the effect of depth (Fig. 1-22), but the illusion of space is strongest when linear perspective is employed. A size difference between similar or recognizable shapes may suggest distance between them because the effect implies linear perspective, as with the figures or the trees in Ghiberti's relief (Fig. 14-17).

Mass

Mass, or three-dimensional solidity, is used directly in architecture and sculpture but must be created by illusion in painting and drawing. The artist can produce the effect of thickness or roundness with highlights and shadows, as in Masaccio's *Tribute Money* (Fig. 1-10); with lines describing some forms pushing in front of others, as in Picasso's drawing of Dr. Claribel Cone (Fig. 1-1); with lines delineating the various sides of a three-dimensional object, either with linear perspective, as in Masaccio's *Tribute Money*, or without it, as in Davis'

1-23

PETER PAUL RUBENS, *Coup de Lance (The Crucifixion)*, 1620. Oil on canvas, 14' × 10'. Koninklijk Museum voor Schone Kunsten, Antwerp.

1-24

Diagram of *Coup de Lance*.

1-25

Diagram of *Supper at Emmaus*.

Something on the Eight Ball (Fig. 19-25); and with colors that advance or recede (see p. 19) to pull some parts of an object forward. Mass may express dynamic power, as in Rubens' *Coup de Lance* (*The Crucifixion*, Fig. 1-23), where the vast bulk, foreground placement, and twisting forms emphasize the dramatic violence of the subject (Fig. 1-24). Rembrandt reinforced the quiet equilibrium of his *Supper at Emmaus* (Plate 11) by aligning and framing the figure masses with the stable architectural forms and the rigid edges of the painting (Fig. 1-25).

Sculpture may emphasize or deny mass. The term *closed form* is used for sculpture, painting, or architecture that stresses impenetrable mass. The figures of *Mycerinus and His Queen* (Fig. 7-8) have simplified anatomical forms with broad surfaces of blocklike permanence. The mass is not opened up between the two figures or between their legs or their arms and their bodies. For more *open form* and more violent push-pull tensions, consider the Asam sculpture (Fig. 1-27). Some sculptors deny the importance of mass. Gabo, for example, prefers transparent plastics that seem to give order to space without displacing it, as in *Linear Construction* (Fig. 19-32).

Architecture usually employs mass to define interior space, and the character of architectural mass ranges from the quiet symmetry of Santa Maria delle Carceri (Figs. 1-16 and 14-29) to the swooping, turning liveliness of Notre-Dame-du-Haut (Figs. 19-50–19-52). In the Seagram Building (Fig. 19-49), glass and steel reduce the mass to thin, transparent, membrane walls.

Value

Variations in lightness and darkness, called variations in *value*, are used to define shapes, to suggest line, to create the illusion of mass and space on a flat surface, to emphasize certain parts, and to express feeling. Value changes define shapes in Picasso's *Three Musicians* (Plate 27). In Rubens' *Coup de Lance* (Fig. 1-23), he *modeled* (molded) solids with light and shadow, focused attention on Christ by floodlighting, and reinforced the dramatic quality of the scene with bold contrasts in value. Holbein clarified details and space relations with light and shadow in his *Ambassadors* (Fig. 14-52); but Rembrandt, in the *Supper at Emmaus* (Plate 11), obscured much of the detail in deep shadow, sacrificing clarity for an effect of soft glowing atmosphere and quiet drama. The light and shadow used to model form, as in the works by Rubens and Rembrandt, are often called by the Italian term *chiaroscuro*. Leonardo da Vinci, a pioneer in the use of chiaroscuro, often used *reflected light* to separate shaded surfaces. In Figure 1-26, the jaw of the pointing angel acquires solidity and moves out from the neck because the shaded area of the jaw receives reflected light from the lower neck and shoulder.

In sculpture and architecture, value contrasts are produced by different degrees of projection and recession in the masses and by use of different materials and colors, as in *The Assumption of the Virgin* (Fig. 1-27), where the contrasts of colors and of light and dark stone work with the light and shadow produced by bold recessions and deep hollows in the figure groups. The opposition of light and shadow is intensified by win-

1-26
LEONARDO DA VINCI, *The Madonna of the Rocks, c.* 1485. Oil on wood panel, approx. 6′ × 4′ Louvre, Paris.

dows directly overhead. Value contrasts dramatize the event and acquire Christian content—the Virgin ascends toward the light, which symbolizes God. In Frank Lloyd Wright's Robie House (Fig. 19-40), the hovering horizontals, which suggest shelter and align themselves sympathetically with the ground surface, are stressed by the value contrasts of brick and concrete and by highlights and shadows of projecting and receding parts.

VALUE RELATIONS

Our perception of the value, as well as of the size and color, of a given form may be affected by its environment through the principle of *simultaneous contrast*. Of

1-27
COSMAS DAMIAN and
EGID QUIRIN ASAM,
*The Assumption of the
Virgin,* 1718–25. High
altar, monastery church
at Rohr, Bavaria.

the two circles of equal white in Figure 1-28a, the top
one appears lighter because of its strong contrast with
its surroundings. In Figure 1-28b, the white circle tends
to appear larger because light areas seem to radiate and
expand against darker backgrounds or surroundings. In
the *Coup de Lance* (Fig. 1-23), such effects help create
the monumentality of the figure of Jesus, the glowing
flesh of Mary Magdalene at the foot of the cross, and
the malevolent eye of the warrior who thrusts the lance
into the side of Jesus.

VALUE CONTRAST AND SPACE

Value contrast can be used in painting to create the illusion of space by defining mass, which implies the space necessary to contain it; by separating planes or edges; and by sharpening or softening details. The illusion of deep space in the Chinese landscape (pp. 2–3) is achieved partly through a carefully adjusted sequence of overlapping masses and planes separated not only by line but also by value contrasts that become softer from foreground to background. *Aerial perspective* (or *atmospheric perspective*) is the term for the softening of value contrasts and details and the muting of colors to give the effect of distance. Aerial perspective is used by Giorgione in his *Pastoral Concert* (Plate 6) and by Masaccio in his *Tribute Money* (Fig. 1 10).

Texture

Texture is the quality of a surface: smooth, rough, slick, grainy, soft, or hard. In painting, it may apply both to the texture of the paint itself and to the textures that are depicted. The painter, the sculptor, and the architect frequently use texture for variety, focus, or unity. In Holbein's *Ambassadors* (Fig. 14-52), the smooth surface of the paint helps give unity to the work even while the painting gives the illusion of a great variety of textures in the different objects depicted. Delacroix was less interested in depicting a variety of textures in his *Lion Hunt* (Plate 15). He used the rough texture of the paint in undisguised brush strokes to stress the violence of the action and to unify the variety of shapes. In Gabo's *Linear Construction* (Fig. 19-32), space is articulated mainly by nylon strings that produce the illusion of grooved—that is, textured—surfaces. The Asam sculpture (Fig. 1-27) has a multiplicity of textures that increases the complexity of the composition but also helps to separate the figures from their setting. From a distance, the thousands of sculptured details on the surface of Amiens Cathedral (Fig. 1-29) give the cathedral a bristling roughness of texture that has great variety. The countless perforations in the stone façade accentuate the soaring lightness of the structure. Notre-Dame-du-Haut (Fig. 19-50), with its more asymmetrical form, attains some of its unity and massive strength from its relatively uninterrupted surfaces and the overall texture of the concrete.

Textural variation may be used in painting to give the illusion of space. The softening of focus in aerial

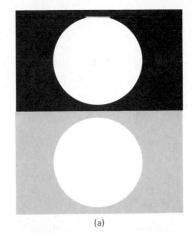

(a)

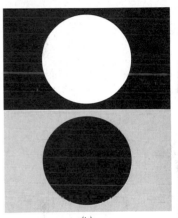

(b)

1-28

1-29
Robert De Luzarches, Amiens
Cathedral, thirteenth century
with later additions.

perspective involves the softening of textural qualities—
not only the depicted textures but the actual texture
of the paint. In sculpture and architecture, spatial effects
may be emphasized by using bold textures in the foreground and softer ones for more distant surfaces.

Color

Color is one of the artist's principal means of achieving
variety, emphasis, and unity; of creating the effects of
mass and space; and of expressing feelings. In Giorgione's *Pastoral Concert* (Plate 6), the focal color of the
red hat is set against the cool light green of the distant
meadow; the contrast of warm and cool colors works
with the contrast of values and aerial perspective to
create depth, and the total effect of serenity and elegance comes partly from the opulent but quiet colors.
Monet was fascinated by the shimmer of light and color
on the stone façade of Rouen Cathedral (Plate 18). Vibrating contrasts of blue and orange dance backward
and forward in accord with their brightness and warmth,
denying the mass of the stone and producing a luminous
vision. The colors in Matisse's *Decorative Figure on an
Ornamental Background* (Plate 25) are heavier and more
earthy, but they provide a rich and lively variety as they

change in modulations of reds, browns, blues, yellows, and greens.

Color in sculpture and architecture may come from the natural color of the materials or from paint, glaze, or chemical treatment (see Chapter 4). Color may complicate the form, or it may stress the point of central importance and even act as the axis of balance. Color can separate the various parts of a composition or pull the parts together by giving them a common characteristic. Architecture may be united with a landscape through the use of native wood or rock that repeats the colors of the setting, or the building may be separated from its environment by the use of "foreign" colors.

THE NATURE OF COLOR

Sunlight, or white light, contains the elements of all colors in such a mixture that each color is canceled. White light can be broken into its component colors by projecting it through a prism. An object is seen as a particular color because it absorbs some elements of white light and reflects others. That is, an apple is red when it reflects those elements of light that we have named red and absorbs the others.

The basic color that the artist chooses to give an object is called its *local color*. The artist may emphasize local colors, stress their modifications, or subordinate them to a general effect. The local red of an apple may be modified by reflections from a green tablecloth or by light coming through yellow curtains. By partly subduing local colors, Rembrandt achieved the overall effect of brown-gold light that characterizes many of his works, such as the *Supper at Emmaus* (Plate 11). Matisse, in contrast, retained more local colors (Plate 25).

The word *color* refers to a combination of *hue, saturation*, and *value*. Hue is the property that distinguishes one color from another, the property that enables us to name the color. Three hues are especially important because, in theory, they can be mixed to produce all the others. These are called the *primary colors*. Although there is some disagreement among scientists, for our purposes we may say that the primary colors in pigments are red, yellow, and blue. (In light, certain hues of red, green, and blue function as primaries.) The convenient arrangement called a color wheel (Fig. 1-30) places between each two primary colors the color made by mixing them. Thus orange, green, and violet are

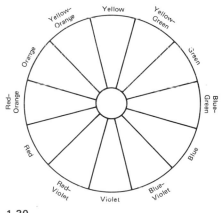

1-30

By mixing the primary pigment colors red, yellow, and blue, we obtain the secondary colors: orange, green, and violet. Each secondary is placed between the primaries that produced it. Each secondary may then be mixed with adjacent primaries to produce a third set of hues. In the resulting color wheel, complementary colors are opposite one another. Complementaries may be mixed to lower their saturation, to produce browns, or to produce a neutral gray.

called *secondary colors.* Mixing of primaries and secondaries produces additional colors; the mixing could go on indefinitely. Colors directly opposite each other on the wheel are called *complementaries.* Complementary colors dull or neutralize each other when mixed together. A small amount of green added to red will dull the red. A larger amount of green will convert the red to brown, and a very careful adding of still more green will usually turn the brown to neutral gray. The proportions required of red and green will depend on the purity of the hues employed; since absolutely pure hues do not exist in pigments, the theoretical relationships described here are flexible in practice. Complementary colors placed side by side usually intensify each other, depending on the sizes of the areas of color and the distance of the observer. This characteristic is basic to the intensity and spatial effect of Monet's blues and oranges (Plate 18) and the focal and spatial effects of the red hat in the Giorgione (Plate 6).

Saturation refers to the purity or vividness of a color. A strong red is said to be of high saturation. It is possible to lower the saturation of a color by adding its complement, by diluting it with white, or by darkening it with black.

The *value* of a color is its darkness or lightness. Colors at full saturation can be assigned positions on a value scale ranging from white to black. A bright yellow, for example, would have the value equivalent of light gray, whereas a red would be darker in value. Colors that are greatly diluted with white are called *tints;* colors rendered darker by the addition of black or a complement are called *shades.*

THE EFFECTS OF COLOR

For the greatest possible control over his medium, the artist must consider the effects of simultaneous contrast in colors. A neutral gray or white placed near a strong color will seem to acquire some of the complementary of the color. This effect also occurs with combinations of colors; for example, red next to yellow will assume a touch of yellow's complement, violet; the yellow will appear to have a tinge of red's complement, green.

Certain colors (yellow, red, orange, and often violet) are considered *warm,* while others (greens and blues) are considered *cool.* This classification is largely based on our association of certain colors with light and heat. Contrasts of warm and cool colors can be especially intense.

For some color phenomena, we do not have adequate experimental data to draw precise conclusions. The considerable variation in response to colors is apparently due to both physiological and emotional differences in observers. Warm colors may make an object seem larger, while cool colors often seem to diminish its size, but value and saturation differences can be manipulated to reverse this effect. For many observers, certain warm colors, especially when light and highly saturated, seem to advance toward the eyes, cool colors often seem to recede. The individual observer's color preferences, however, appear to be important in causing certain colors rather than others to advance. The old rule that warm colors always advance and cool colors always recede is not valid in all cases.

In a given culture, certain colors may be commonly understood as being expressive of particular feelings; we may speak of "seeing red" or "feeling blue." The artist may utilize this expressive potential, but it may not work for an observer from another culture.

Some theorists and researchers have attempted to equate colors with sounds or with tastes (*synesthesia*), but the results have been inconclusive.

Suggestions for Further Study

Albers, Josef. *Interaction of Color.* New Haven, Conn.: Yale University Press, 1963.

Ball, Victoria. "The Aesthetics of Color: A Review of Fifty Years of Experimentation." *Journal of Aesthetics and Art Criticism,* Vol. 23, No. 4 (Summer 1965), pp. 441–52.

Fisher, Howard T., and James M. Carpenter. *Color in Art.* Cambridge: Fogg Art Museum and Harvard University, 1974.

Hanes, Randall M. "The Long and Short of Color Distance." *Architectural Record,* Vol. 127, Pt. 2 (April 1960), pp. 254–56 and 348.

Libby, William Charles. *Color and the Structural Sense.* Englewood Cliffs, N.J.: Prentice-Hall, 1974.

Luckiesh, M. *Visual Illusions, Their Causes, Characteristics, and Applications.* Republication of the original edition of 1922, with a new introduction by William H. Ittelson. New York: Dover, 1965.

Norling, Ernest R. *Perspective Made Easy.* New York: Macmillan, 1939.

Sargent, Walter. *The Enjoyment and Use of Color,* rev. ed. New York: Dover, 1964.

Sloane, Patricia. *Color: Basic Principles and New Directions.* New York: Van Nostrand Reinhold, 1968.

White, Gwen. *Perspective: A Guide for Artists, Architects, and Designers.* London: Batsford; New York: Watson-Guptill, 1968.

Elements of Music: Time and Sound

Time

Music is sound and silence organized in time. Since sound is a form of energy, it always exists during a finite span of time. For this reason, time is an ever-present and indispensable element in all music. Time is equally indispensable to dance, theater, cinema, and television. It is an important element in the visual arts too, but on a less immediate level than in the musical and theatrical arts.

In music we are made aware of time when the sounds and silences follow each other in some ordered way. More fundamentally, our awareness is increased by sensing and comparing the intervals of time between individual sounds and the relative length of sustained sounds, silences, and larger sections. Musical time is organized at many levels, including single events, groups of events, patterns, and combinations of groups and patterns. When we are caught up in the flow of music, our enhanced sense of time often generates an intense self-awareness, and this certainly is one of music's primary attractions.

RHYTHM, PATTERN, AND MEASURE

Rhythm in music is a general term for the organization and control of time. Its two essential features are *succession* (how one sound follows another), and *duration* (how long sounds last). The word also is commonly used to mean a particular pattern or arrangement of sounds, motions, or visual events. In this more restricted sense we refer to patterns of sound in music as *rhythm patterns.*

We speak of measuring time when we compare the sequence and duration of events to a regular cycle of motion, such as the revolutions of the earth, or the movement of a clock. In music, too, the rhythm often is measured through simple periodic events, such as recurring patterns or groupings, and we call the most basic groupings *measures.*

Listen for about one minute to the beginning of Ludwig van Beethoven's Seventh Symphony, second movement (Ex. 1). The initial sustained sound has only a durational value, but the succeeding sounds produce a repeated pattern of *long*-short-short-*long-long,* which persists throughout much of the piece. Immediately after the fourth repetition of this pattern a brief silence occurs, which represents a sort of punctuation of, or conclusion to, what has happened so far. The musical material leading to this brief silence is called a *phrase*. We will label this first phrase A. If we disregard the introductory sustained sound, phrase A is a time frame constructed out of four repetitions of the rhythm pattern. Phrase A is followed immediately by a second phrase that we will call B, which differs from A in its particular combination of sounds, yet creates an identical time frame through repetition of the same pattern. Phrase B is then repeated exactly, except not as loudly. This gives us a section consisting of three consecutive phrases, all having equal length, with the third phrase repeating the second: A–B–B.

This section is the primary unit on which the rest of the composition is based; that is, its rhythmic organization pervades the entire piece. Listen to the whole example, paying particular attention to the persistence of the pattern of long and short sounds. The three-phrase, A–B–B, section is repeated three times after its first appearance, with new material added each time. It also recurs later, following other material obviously derived from it, but lacking its precise time frame. This recurrence of rhythm patterns, phrases, and sections unifies the rich diversity of sounds and musical ideas.

METER

If we "beat time" to Beethoven's Seventh Symphony, second movement (Ex. 1), we can sense regular pulses corresponding to the long sound of the *long-short-short-long-long* pattern. These regularly recurring pulses usually are called *beats*, in reference to the physical response they provoke. Some of the beats seem to be stronger than others, and this stress, or extra weight, applied to a sound is called *accent*. In this piece the accents usually occur with every other beat, causing us to sense the beats in groups of two: strong-weak, strong-weak, and so forth. Furthermore, we can respond to this music at a rate just twice as fast as the beats themselves, that is, in a two-to-one ratio. Two of these faster pulses, or subbeats, occur with each beat, so that groupings occur simultaneously at the level of the beat and at the level of the subbeat. A group of beats is called a *measure*, and we will call the group of subbeats a *subgroup*. Groups of two are commonly referred to as *duple*, and groups of three as *triple*. The particular relationship of groupings defines the *meter*; thus the meter of Example 1 consists of duple measures and duple subgroups.

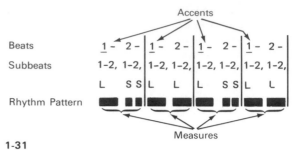

1-31
Metrical grouping in Beethoven's Seventh
Symphony, second movement.

We tend to organize sense data into the simplest
possible patterns. Thus, we tend to hear beats and
subbeats as recurring in groups of two or three; and we
may also perceive these groups simultaneously in larger
groups, such as two groups of three, three groups of
two, and so forth. This perceptual phenomenon is so
strong that the listener can easily supply such groupings, even when they are only implied by the organization of the musical sounds. If the groupings are not
regular, the listener will still tend to reduce them per-
ceptually into combinations of two and three. In Example 1, the music is designed to reinforce the perception
of its groupings. Regular groupings of this kind occur in
music on at least two levels simultaneously—the beats
and subbeats—and these groupings usually are propor-
tional to one another, in a ratio of either two-to-one or
three-to-one. This makes possible four basic meters:
two groups of two (as in Example 1), two groups of
three, three groups of two, and three groups of three.
   Johann Sebastian Bach's Minuet, Trio I, Polacca, and
Trio II from the first Brandenburg Concerto (Ex. 2) is
in reality four short pieces grouped together so that
the first one—the Minuet—is repeated after each of
the others: Minuet-Trio I-Minuet-Polacca-Minuet-Trio
II-Minuet. In each of the pieces meter is persistent and
quite regular. In all but Trio II the meter consists of
triple measures and duple subgroups; in Trio II both the
measures and the subgroups are duple.

COMPLEX METRICAL SYSTEMS

The metrical organization of time in music often involves much more subtle and complex relationships
than the four basic meters. Varied and complex meters
result from unbalanced or inconsistent groupings of
beats and subbeats, from their irregular recurrence, or
from disproportion in simultaneous levels. In general,

we can perceive and describe the results of these meters as various combinations of two and three, as in the basic meters.

Accents frequently occur out of phase, or in conflict with the prevailing metrical groupings—a technique called *syncopation.* Syncopation is extended further when a whole series of irregular patterns is crossed with a regular meter.

Occasionally two or more different meters occur simultaneously. Such crossed meters sometimes create an imprecise rhythmic blur, and at other times produce an exciting rhythmic tension. Beginning about midway through Example 1, Beethoven very unobtrusively introduces, in some of the parts, a meter comprised of triple subgroups, which sounds against the prevailing duple subgroups, sometimes almost completely subduing them, and at other times disappearing entirely. The result here is an example of the rhythmic blur mentioned above.

DURATIONAL TIME STRUCTURES

So far we have considered how a sense of time in music is created by repeated patterns and groupings. Pattern and repetition help to reinforce our perception of the *succession* of musical structures; at the same time, they enhance our sense of the *duration* of these structures. Our time sense depends on the duration of single sounds and silences, but it is also possible to sense the continuity of time over longer periods. In jazz and similar musical styles, for instance, the performers must anticipate how much material they can make up to fit within the available time frame while it is being created.

In both Examples 1 and 2, meter and recurring patterns clearly delineate the larger time spans. In Claude Debussy's *Prelude to the Afternoon of a Faun* (Ex. 3) and Luciano Berio's *Sinfonia,* Section I (Ex. 4), time is organized differently. Beats may be felt at times in the Debussy piece but they are not prominent, whereas, in the Berio piece, beats and meter seem irrelevant. Both composers effectively control succession and duration in large time divisions without relying on metrical procedures. Proportion and repetition are there, but not in the metrical sense. Sustained sounds, silences, and small segments of musical material are timed so that each is proportionate in length to the others, though the precise relationships are not obvious. Debussy tends to repeat small fragments, phrases, and larger segments of material, while Berio repeats single sounds and brief combinations. Berio

1-32

Cecil Payne, jazz musician. Jazz improvisation requires an acute sense of time and metrical relationships.

also uses prominent, controlled silences to create a sense of expectation. Both of these pieces tend to focus attention as much on the duration of sounds and musical structures as on the way the sounds and musical structures follow one another.

In recent years composers have begun to rely on external, mechanical means for controlling durations. The precise timing of taped electronic sounds can serve as an example. In some music, especially where improvisation and chance are employed, a conductor may control longer time spans in performance with the aid of a clock.

MUSICAL MOVEMENT

We generally describe the experience of the passage of time through the spatial analogy of "movement"; thus, we say that the music moves toward goals, that it moves fast or slowly, that it pauses or stops from time to time, and so forth. Furthermore, the rapidity and complexity of successive sounds and musical ideas combine to create a sense of speed, often called *tempo*. Musical *movement*, then, means the consciousness or awareness of time that music creates through succession and change, and *tempo* means the speed at which musical ideas occur. *Movement* also is used by musicians in another sense, to mean separate parts in a large musical work that are structurally complete in themselves; for instance, the Minuet, Trio I, Polacca, and Trio II of Example 2, and Example 1 in its entirety are all movements from larger works.

A sense of movement and tempo can be created by repetition or change of any aspect of the music, by the complex interplay of sounds or rhythm patterns, and by various devices which cause us to expect something to

1-33

A group of students perform a string quartet.

follow. Some kinds of music are characterized by con
sistent tempos, while others make use of changing
tempos. Ordinarily a regular meter with prominent
accents will produce a consistent tempo so long as most
other facets of the music occur at a regular rate.
Changes in meter, in the speed of the beat, or in the rate
at which prominent nonrhythm factors occur can all
result in tempo changes. Tempo change can be a powerful expressive device, because the sense of activity,
expectation, and involvement in the music—the *musical
energy*—is closely tied to musical movement.

In Beethoven's Seventh Symphony, second movement (Ex. 1) and Bach's Minuet, Trio I, Polacca, and
Trio II, from the first Brandenburg Concerto (Ex. 2), the
tempo is consistent throughout because of regular repetitions within the metrical scheme. In Debussy's *Prelude to the Afternoon of a Faun* (Ex. 3), the tempo is
less well defined, and it changes frequently, while in
Berio's *Sinfonia*, Section I (Ex. 4), the sense of movement almost stops during some of the silences, then
surges forward during the rapid bursts of activity.

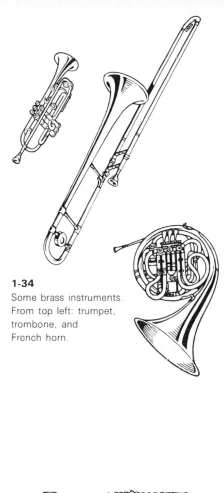

1-34
Some brass instruments.
From top left: trumpet,
trombone, and
French horn.

TIME AND FORM

Generally, we expect a piece of music to be a coherent
and unified entity—the parts should relate to each other
and to the whole. This means, among other things, that
every aspect of the music is timed so that it seems
neither too long nor too short within the given context.
It also involves a balance between continuity, through
repetition and return of familiar elements, and variety,
through change and contrast. Rhythm plays a major
role in creating continuity and variety; continuity is
created by meter and other repetitive techniques, and
variety is created by changes and surprises in pattern,
meter, and tempo. Cycles of tension and release are
closely bound up with musical movement and timing.
Measured silences also can serve effectively to mark
formal divisions in the music.

Sound Sources and Their Expressive Uses

Humans are capable of some very fine distinctions in
their perception of sound energy. We hear differences
among sounds in three ways, and we call these three
kinds of sensation *loudness, timbre,* and *pitch.* Though
all of these perceptual factors are interrelated, they are

1-35
Some woodwind instruments.
Top, flute; left, oboe; right, clarinet.

easy to distinguish by the listener, and musicians exploit them in different ways and in varying degrees. We will focus on loudness and timbre here, deferring consideration of pitch until Chapter 2.

LOUDNESS AND TIMBRE

Control of the degree of loudness in music is one of the simplest and most obvious means of musical expression. Musicians can change, contrast, and control loudness in five ways: (1) by choosing loud or soft instruments or voices; (2) by deciding on the number of instruments or voices; (3) by making loud or soft sounds; (4) by controlling gradual movement from soft to loud and loud to soft; and (5) by using electronic amplification and manipulation. Whereas only some of these techniques are evident in older music, today they are all exploited to a high degree—from complete and prolonged silence to electronic amplification loud enough to damage the inner ear.

Timbre is the way our ears respond to the whole complex structure of a sound. It is the distinctive quality that characterizes a particular sound—the means by which we can tell the sound of one musical instrument from another, or a musical instrument from a human voice. Differences in timbre provide a rich variety of musical possibilities. They are easy to perceive and constitute probably the most important source of music's attraction. Composers and performers today seem particularly interested in seeking variety in their music through experiments with new timbres.

1-36
Some string instruments. Above: left, violin; right, viola. Below, cello.

The combination and use of instrumental timbres for expressive purposes is called *orchestration*. There is no equivalent word for the use of vocal timbres, but composers may be equally sensitive to the variety of sounds possible with the human voice. Musicians use timbres in much the same way that painters use colors, and timbres in music are often called *tone colors*. Both the composer and the performer must be sensitive to the variety of sounds and their combinations and interactions in the music, and they must understand the physical, acoustical, and musical characteristics and limitations of a particular instrument or voice. The composer must consider the differences in sound sources, alone and in combination, as well as the many subtle nuances that a musical instrument can produce. The traditional system of musical notation is virtually incapable of indicating these nuances, and there are no names for specific timbres. Composers usually call for particular instruments or combinations and try to express verbally the manner of performance desired. This leaves considerable interpretative freedom to the performer, who must master the skills needed to produce and control the desired shadings of sound.

TRADITIONAL SOUND SOURCES

When we hear sounds we are sensing energy in the form of pressure waves in the atmosphere impinging on our eardrums. Anything capable of setting such energy in motion is a potential sound source. The traditional sources for musical sounds are, quite simply, various instruments and the human voice. The most common of these, aside from the voice, are wind, string, percussion, keyboard, and fretted string instruments.

The wind instruments produce sounds by means of a vibrating air column. They include the brass instruments (such as the trumpet, trombone, French horn, and tuba) and the woodwinds (such as the flute, oboe, bassoon, clarinet, and saxophone). Brass players and flutists control the vibrating air with their lips, tongue, and breath, while players of the other woodwinds use the vibrating cane reeds which are set in motion by the breath.

String instruments make sounds with vibrating strings, which are made of gut or wire, and which are set in motion by plucking or by rubbing with a bow of stretched hair. For most string instruments, the player makes higher and lower sounds by changing the active length of the strings with his or her fingers. Sounds are regulated on some of these instruments with frets—narrow strips under the strings that mark off where to place one's fingers. The violin, viola, cello, and string bass are bowed as well as plucked and have no frets. The guitar, lute, banjo, and mandolin have frets and are plucked. The harp is also plucked, but the length of the strings is altered with pedals instead of with the player's fingers.

The sounds of percussion instruments, for the most part, are made by striking or shaking them. Some, such as the kettledrums, marimba, xylophone, and chimes, produce clear tones, while others, such as the cymbals, wood blocks, tambourine, and various drums, make sounds of indefinite focus.

Instruments with keyboards can produce many sounds at once, providing the player with precise control and great versatility. In both the piano and the harpsichord the sounds come from vibrating strings; in

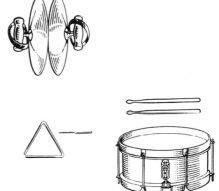

1-37
Some percussion instruments.
Above: top, cymbals;
left, triangle,
right, snare drum.
Below, kettledrum.

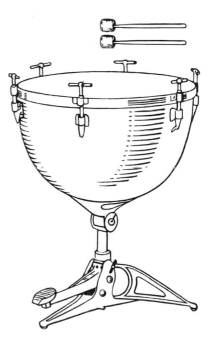

the piano the keyboard mechanism strikes the strings, while in the harpsichord the keyboard mechanism plucks them. The sounds of the pipe organ come from ranks of wind pipes through which air is blown, and in the electronic organ sounds are generated through electronic circuitry.

For many years the orchestra has provided composers with an extremely rich source of instrumental tone colors. The modern orchestra had its beginnings in the seventeenth century and reached its present makeup of about a hundred players near the beginning of this century. Families of similar instruments in an orchestra are normally grouped together, to take advantage of similarity and blend of timbres, as well as to stand apart as contrasting groups. The woodwind group is comprised of flutes, oboes, bassoons, clarinets, and some of their larger and smaller relatives. The brasses include trumpets, trombones, French horns, and tubas, and the strings include violins, violas, cellos, and string basses. Percussion instruments usually include kettledrums; the use of other percussion instruments varies with the music. Performances differ, but in general the strings are placed in front, the woodwinds in the middle, and the brasses and percussion instruments in the back of a concert hall stage.

The orchestra is built around the strings, which constitute about two-thirds of the players. The string instruments are capable of quite subtle nuances of tone color, and they also blend very well as a group. The

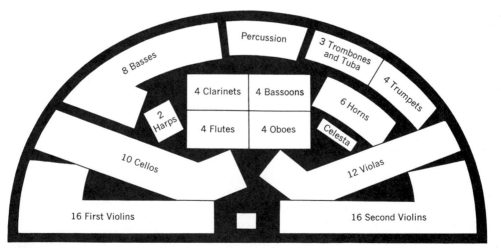

1-38 A seating plan of an orchestra.

woodwinds blend together too, but their individual sounds are rich and diverse, and they are often used for variety, especially as solo instruments. The brass instruments mix well together, and the French horns also mix with the woodwinds, but the brasses are most often used to add power and weight to the full orchestra. The percussion instruments produce the most diverse sounds of all. They are used especially to highlight rhythm patterns, to add force to climaxes, and to create special color effects.

NEW SOUNDS AND NEW SOUND SOURCES

In the past only those sounds regarded as characteristic and proper for the voice and for traditional instruments were considered musical. In recent years, however, there has been an accelerating tendency to experiment with new timbres, and the distinction between "noise" and "musical sounds" is now almost meaningless. A few novelties such as guns and wind machines, introduced into the orchestra for special effects during the nineteenth century, led more recently to the use of such sound sources as chains, anvils, whips, sirens, and automobile brake drums. Musicians have also sought new ways to produce sounds on traditional instruments: plucking or striking the strings inside a piano; "preparing" the piano by placing various objects inside it; playing strings with the wooden part of the bow; "flutter-tonguing" on flutes or brasses; humming one sound while playing another; and thumping, tapping, or scraping the body of an instrument. A corollary of this development has been experimentation with cluster effects, or "sound masses," in which individual sounds become submerged in a larger aggregate, thereby producing new composite timbres.

Recent attitudes toward new musical sounds and their uses found an ideal means of expression during the 1950's. At that time electronics technology became sophisticated enough to make possible the generation, alteration, manipulation, combination, recording, and playback of any conceivable sounds. Composers began using electronic devices for the entire process of creating, recording, and performing their music. In modern electronic studios, sounds are generated with oscillators or recorded live, altered and combined through the use of filters, ring modulators, echo and reverberation devices, and multichannel mixers, and stored on magnetic tape. Synthesizers are commonly used to generate, alter, manipulate, and place the sounds in sequence automat-

1-39
Producing electronic music on a synthesizer.

ically. Computers are also being used to create musical sounds.

THE SOUND ENVELOPE

All sounds begin with a rise of energy to a peak, are then either sustained or not, and end with a dying away of energy. Physicists and composers of electronic music refer to these three stages as *attack, steady-state,* and *decay.* The entire life of a sound as described here is called the *sound envelope.* The sound envelope can be shaped at will with electronics, but most musical instruments can produce only a certain kind of envelope, and the player can control only a limited part of that. Each instrument has its own techniques and possibilities, most of which affect the loudness or timbre of a sound during some part of the attack or steady-state phase. When the sound is made by plucking or striking, there is a sharp attack and then a decay, but no steady-state. The player can control the sharpness and loudness of the attack, and he or she can sometimes muffle or stop the decay. Instruments that use wind pressure or some other continuous energy source produce a steady-state, which the player often can control in addition to the attack, but he or she usually cannot control the decay. The human voice is one of the most flexible of all the instruments because it can control the entire envelope. Control of the sound envelope by the performer is frequently referred to as *articulation.*

SOME EXPRESSIVE USES OF
LOUDNESS AND TIMBRE

Loudness and timbre play major roles in music. The separate parts in a complex combination may be made to stand out independently through contrasting timbres. Particular timbres may be associated with particular recurring musical relationships or ideas, giving them a distinctive character, and these may be made prominent through loudness. Or, the recurring ideas may be the timbres themselves, such as the characteristic reappearance of particular instruments. Formal divisions in a piece often are marked by changes in loudness and in the number and kinds of instruments or voices. Changes in loudness usually accompany and support any changes in musical activity, thus enhancing the sense of movement and timing; it is commonplace for loudness to increase when the musical activity builds toward a climax. Sudden changes in loudness or timbre may be used to surprise the listener. Rich and varied timbres can be a source of purely sensuous pleasure, or they can at times evoke symbolic associations.

The initial four statements of the basic three-phrase segment (A–B–B), of Beethoven's Seventh Symphony, second movement (Ex. 1) reveals close attention to the gradations in loudness and the combinations of instruments. Woodwinds play the opening sustained sound, which diminishes from loud to soft, then the lower strings (a contrasting timbre) quietly begin the first statement of the A–B–B segment, playing the third phrase softer than the other two. More instruments join with each new statement of this segment—violins first, and, eventually, with the fourth statement, the whole orchestra. The addition of instruments increases the loudness of sound, but the performers also play with increasing loudness through the third statement, reaching a very loud level in the fourth statement, then diminishing rapidly at the end of the last phrase. Beethoven utilized all the means at his disposal for controlling loudness: number and kind of instruments, and instructions to the players specifying loudness levels and gradual changes. At the same time, his loudness gradations are simple and obvious, and they are used to outline the larger structure rather than for their own expressive potential. His choice of instrumental timbres relates directly to the structure of the phrases and sections and to the buildup of musical activity, but variety of timbre is not itself a significant source of interest.

By comparison, Debussy, in *Prelude to the Afternoon of a Faun* (Ex. 3), shows much more concern for the fine shadings of both loudness and timbre. His orchestra is larger and more varied than Beethoven's, but he exploits mostly the variety of timbres available from single instruments and unique combinations, rather than the massed sound of the full orchestra, which he only utilizes at climactic points. The flute solo that begins the piece can serve as an example. This is one of the primary musical ideas of the work, appearing three times in the first part and again near the end. It is a melody, but more important, it is a *flute* melody. To play it on any other instrument would alter its essential character. First we hear this melody alone, followed by the sustained sounds of oboes and clarinets played over a sweeping gesture on the harp, then two horns—and silence. The harp and the horns return, then the flute melody again, this time played over trembling, fluttering strings. Now the oboe takes over the flute melody, and this shift of timbre leads to a brief climax of sound by the whole orchestra, with loudness rising to a peak. The flute solo returns once more, this time with a harp and part of the strings. A second flute joins in, and together the two flutes expand the idea somewhat; then, a sudden new sound by the clarinet and muted horns introduces a new phase of the piece. The rest of the piece reveals a rich treasure of similarly subtle nuances of sound, with carefully controlled articulations and shadings of loudness. The piece unfolds as a series of related musical episodes based to a large extent on shifting orchestral tone colors.

Bach's Minuet, Trio I, Polacca, and Trio II from the first Brandenburg Concerto (Ex. 2) requires a small orchestra of two horns, three oboes, a bassoon, strings, and a harpsichord—about twenty players. The instruments differ in number and kind from movement to movement, but they remain constant within each movement. For the most part, loudness changes when the instruments change. The Minuet frames the other movements by returning after each one, and it is played by the whole orchestra, which emphasizes its primacy. By contrast, Trio I calls for two oboes and the bassoon, the Polacca requires the strings and the harpsichord, and Trio II is played by two horns plus the oboes. Especially in the two Trios, the timbres help to make the different parts stand out, and changes in loudness and timbre mark the separate movements.

In Examples 1 and 2, Beethoven and Bach use loudness and timbre to enhance sound structures based essentially on pitch and time. In Example 3, Debussy's tone colors are essential to the design and structure of the piece, but the sounds are manifested through organized pitch structures. However, in Berio's *Sinfonia*, Section I (Ex. 4), pitch relationships serve only as a minor adjunct to sound structures organized through loudness, timbre, and time. Extremes of variety and contrast seem to dominate this piece, yet a coherent sequence of events can be discerned. A gong opens the piece. There follow three units, or subdivisions, one minute, twenty-five seconds; two minutes, forty seconds; and two minutes, twenty seconds, respectively. The first subdivision uses sustained vowel sounds, spoken French words, a variety of instrumental sounds, and controlled silences, all clearly delineated and occurring sequentially in a sort of exposition of the available sound materials. The gong closes this first unit. In the next unit these materials are mixed, varied, and developed in a more complex fashion. The third subdivision utilizes instruments only. It begins with fragmented sounds from the piano, with frequent silences, to which are gradually added other instrumental sounds, producing a buildup of energy, which finally subsides to near silence, and the gong returns to end the piece as it began. Since loudness and timbre are the primary sources of interest, this music will not make sense if one listens for other kinds of relationships, such as those in Example 1. Berio exploits the emotive force as well as the rich variety of timbres in the sounds of spoken language.

Suggestions for Further Study

Baines, Anthony. *European and American Musical Instruments*. New York: Viking Press, 1966.

Bonnani, Filippo. *The Showcase of Musical Instruments*. New York: Dover Publications, 1964.

Bragard, Roger, and Ferdinand J. de Hen. *Musical Instruments in Art and History*. Translated by Bill Hopkins. New York: Viking Press, n.d.

Buchner, Alexander. *Musical Instruments Through the Ages*. Translated by Iris Urwin. London: Spring Books, 1956.

Creston, Paul. *Principles of Rhythm*. New York: Franco Colombo, 1964.

Donington, Robert. *The Instruments of Music*. New York: Barnes and Noble, 1962.

Lincoln, Harry B., ed. *The Computer and Music*. Ithaca: Cornell University Press, 1970.

Sachs, Curt. *The History of Musical Instruments*. New York: Norton, 1940.

Strange, Allen. *Electronic Music*. Dubuque: William C. Brown, 1972.

Winternitz, Emanuel. *Musical Instruments of the Western World*. New York: McGraw-Hill, n.d.

Suggestions for Further Listening

Bach, Johann Sebastian. One of the six Brandenburg Concertos. (Basic metrical regularity.)

Ligeti, György. *Atmosphères*. (Durational time control; sound masses.)

Penderecki, Krzysztof. *Threnody for the Victims of Hiroshima*. (Durational time control; sound masses.)

Strauss, Richard. One of the orchestral tone poems. (Metrical freedom; rich and varied orchestration.)

Stravinsky, Igor. *The Rite of Spring*. (Metrical irregularities; cluster sounds.)

Varèse, Edgard. *Ionisation*. (Metrical irregularities and durational controls; central focus on timbres.)

Chapter 2 Art

Functions
of
Design

Among the many sources of satisfaction that works of art offer are the experiences of order and variety. An artist may work consciously or unconsciously to create such experiences. Design is his organization or composition of the visual and tactile elements in a work of art. He may employ *rhythm*, a recurrence of variations—often in the form of accents and intervals—that have enough similarity to establish continuity and order. Rhythm may be extended indefinitely; it does not require limits. *Balance*, the equilibrium of opposing forces, does involve limits and provides self-sufficiency and unity. Balance may be *axial*, that is, organized on either side of an actual or implied axis that acts as a fulcrum (Fig. 2-1), or *central*, that is, radiating from or converging upon an actual or implied central point (Fig. 2-2). Axial balance may be *obvious* (symmetrical), having very similar or identical elements on either side of the axis (Fig. 2-1a, b, c), or it may be *occult* (asymmetrical), having an equilibrium of elements that are dissimilar in size or shape (Fig. 2-1d, e). Central balance

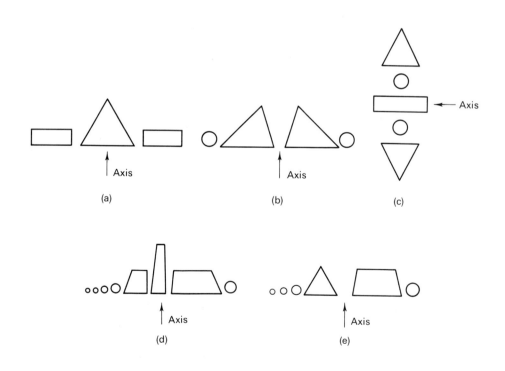

2-1 Types of axial balance: a, b, and c are in obvious axial balance; d and e are in occult axial balance.

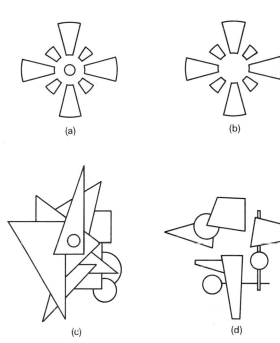

(a)

(b)

(c)

(d)

2-2 Types of central balance.

may also be obvious with similar elements in equilibrium around a center (Fig. 2-2a, b), or occult, using dissimilar elements (Fig. 2-2c, d). Axial balance and central balance usually become three-dimensional in sculpture, in architecture, and in painting that has the illusion of depth.

Different kinds of rhythm and balance, or the lack of them, can evoke strong reactions in the viewer of a work of art. Such reactions are in part due to the process of *empathy*, by which we identify with an object and tend to respond to it sympathetically. A statue of a man in an unbalanced or awkward pose may cause a sense of physical discomfort. Empathy is especially strong with images of our own species, but it also occurs in response to designs using forms that do not refer to nature.

Both rhythm and balance involve *proportion*, the size relationship of parts. It is partly because of proportion that some schemes of rhythm and balance are more satisfying than others. Throughout history, numerous theories have been proposed as bases for satisfying proportions. One of the most famous is that of the *Golden Mean*, whose mathematical ratio cannot be simply stated, though its proportions are easily found by using geometry (Fig. 2-3).

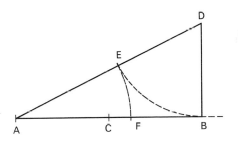

2-3
The Golden Mean. To divide line AB by the Golden Mean, first bisect the line (point C). At B, erect a perpendicular equal in length to AC. Complete the triangle ABD, and on the hypotenuse, AD, locate point E so that DE equals BD. Then locate point F on line AB so that AF equals AE. Line AB is divided by point F according to the proportions of the Golden Mean.

Repetition and Variation on a Theme

Several basic devices are used to achieve order and variety in art. One of these is repetition, the most elementary means of establishing order. We instinctively assume a relationship between similar or identical things. In the visual arts, repetition may appear in line, shape, mass, value, space, color, size, or even directional emphasis. At Moissac (Fig. 2-4), the sculptor used repetition to build an extremely symmetrical composition, or, more precisely, one of obvious axial balance. Such ritualistic formal order adds dignity to the subject. In Matisse's *Decorative Figure* (Plate 25), the scalloped shapes on the wall provide a theme or motif that is repeated with variations in the mirror, the plant, and the floor designs. Even the sturdy figure of the woman

2-4 *The Apocalyptic Christ,* twelfth century. 18'8'' wide, abbey church of St. Pierre at Moissac, France.

2-5 MICHELANGELO BUONARROTI, Tomb of Giuliano de' Medici, 1524–34. Marble, central figure approx. 6' high. New Sacristy, San Lorenzo, Florence.

is *modulated*, or modified, by curved drapery around the hips to conform to the other curved shapes. The rippling alternation of concave-convex shapes gives rhythmic vitality to the scene. Objects are further related by colors, such as the browns, greens, and yellows that are repeated with variations. Unlike the Moissac sculpture, Matisse's painting employs an occult axial balance. The figure is opposed by the potted plant and the diagonal floor lines, and the implied axis is a vertical line running through the knees of the figure to the bowl of fruit in the foreground.

In contrast, an obvious axial balance may employ repetition to unify opposing elements and to provide focus. For example, in Michelangelo's Tomb of Giuliano de' Medici (Fig. 2-5), the concave curves of the reclining figures are countered by the convex curve of the sarcophagus (Fig. 2-6). Within the obvious axial balance, symmetrical repetition of alternating curves leads our attention to the figure of Giuliano, who is given added importance by the buildup of repeated architectural forms.

The columns of the Parthenon (Fig. 9-10) create a rhythmic repetition of masses and spaces that adds variety to the rectangular building and enriches its symmetry. Subtle variation in the intercolumnar spaces helps to prevent monotony. The horizontals of the platform on which the temple sits are contrasted with repeated verticals in the columns and are echoed by horizontals in the roof, making an almost static balance with very sharply defined limits. In Amiens Cathedral (Fig. 1-29), a profusion of repeated vertical and horizontal elements frames variations on the theme of the pointed arch. The arches, in turn, frame circular or *foliated* (scalloped) openings and occasional standing figures. Complexity makes the compositional limits fuzzy, but order is achieved by repetition and variations on themes within the obvious axial balance.

Contrast

Contrast is basic to variation and important for visual interest. Contrast can be used to clarify or modify form, to create mass and space, to suggest activity, to provide balance, to express feeling, and to focus attention. The lively, aggressive personality of Picasso's *Three Musicians* (Plate 27) depends on contrasts in color, in value, and in shape. Contrast of direction gives the African sculpture (Fig. 1-3) its tense equilibrium, while contrasts

2-6 Diagram of the Tomb of Giuliano de' Medici.

of texture, value, and color emphasize the horizontals
of brick and concrete masses in the Robie House (Fig.
19-40).

Gradation and Climax

Gradation is smooth or step-by-step development that
usually suggests direction and builds to a climax. Any
of the visual and tactile elements may be treated in this
way. In the *Supper at Emmaus* (Plate 11), Rembrandt
developed a gentle gradation from shadow toward a
climax of light that emphasizes Jesus. The Asam
brothers used gradation and climax in light, in the
pyramidal buildup of figure groups, and in the architectural setting (Fig. 1-27). At Amiens Cathedral (Fig.
1-29), the gradation in the size of the three main doors
emphasizes the center one. Each entrance, in turn, is
the focus of a funnel-like gradation of arches of decreasing size.

Suggestions for Further Study

Arnheim, Rudolf. *Art and Visual Perception: A Psychology of the Creative Eye.* Berkeley. University of California Press, 1954.

Gombrich, E. H. *Art and Illusion: A Study in the Psychology of Pictorial Representation.* New York: Pantheon Books, 1960.

Kepes, György. *The Language of Vision.* Chicago: Theobald, 1944.

Lowry, Bates. *The Visual Experience: An Introduction to Art.* Englewood Cliffs, N.J.:
Prentice-Hall; New York: Abrams, 1961.

Moholy-Nagy, László. *Vision in Motion.* Chicago: Theobald, 1947.

Norberg-Schulz, Christian. *Intentions in Architecture.* Cambridge, Mass.: M.I.T. Press,
1965.

Pepper, Stephen C. *Principles of Art Appreciation.* New York: Harcourt Brace Jovanovich, 1949.

Pope, Arthur. *The Language of Drawing and Painting.* Cambridge, Mass.: Harvard
University Press, 1949.

Scott, Robert G. *Design Fundamentals.* New York, Toronto, and London: McGraw-Hill,
1951.

Seiberling, Frank. *Looking into Art.* New York: Holt, Rinehart and Winston, 1959.

Zevi, Bruno. *Architecture as Space: How to Look at Architecture.* Edited by Joseph
Barry, translated by Milton Gendel. New York: Horizon Press, 1957.

Elements
of
Music:
Pitch
Structures
and
Relationships

Melodies

Pitch is the way our ears respond to the frequency of sound-wave vibrations; a tone is a sound having a clear and constant pitch. We commonly speak of "high" and "low" tones, meaning those whose pitches result from faster or slower vibrations. Musicians have available to them many discrete pitches, which can be made to relate to each other in numerous ways, both as simultaneous combinations and as successive sound events.

A melody is a coherent succession of tones—what we call a "tune." We hear a series of tones as a melody, or tune, when we hear relatedness among the pitches and ordering in time. To describe a particular melody exactly, we have to define in some way the pitch and duration of each tone in the succession. The separate pitches are the materials that make up the melody, which in essence is perceived as an ongoing totality.

PERCEPTUAL QUALITIES OF MELODY

The most obvious feature of any melody is the amount, direction, and timing of its pitch changes. We customarily describe melodies as "lines," which is a visual-spatial analogy. The "rise" and "fall" of the successive pitches in a melody can be described as a linear "shape," or "curve," created by the direction and amount of pitch change, or "movement," within a given time frame. Our attention usually will be drawn to the highest pitches in the curve, and these may serve as peaks of tension.

A distance in pitch between two tones is called an *interval.* Small intervals often are called *steps,* while large intervals are called *skips,* or *leaps.* Although control of pitch relations depends on precise control of pitches and pitch intervals, the listener may only be aware of relative differences. In most melodies the pitch changes encompass a variety of intervals, but a preponderance of either steps or leaps may give a melody much of its particular character. In some styles of music, such as blues, the performers may fill in the intervals between the primary notes of a melody by "sliding" from one pitch to another. The *range* of a melody is the array of possible tones between its lowest and highest pitches. We usually define the range by the interval between these limits. Though there are many exceptions, melodies that move within a wide range of pitches are more apt to employ large leaps than are those with narrow ranges.

2-7
AUGUSTE RENOIR, *Lady at the Piano,*
c. 1875. Oil on canvas, 35⅞'' x 28⅛''.
Courtesy of The Art Institute of Chicago.
Mr. and Mrs. Martin A. Ryerson
Collection.

The flute melody that opens Debussy's *Prelude to the
Afternoon of a Faun* (Ex. 3) moves back and forth
through very small intervals within a narrow range,
while most of the pitches in the main melody at the
beginning of Beethoven's Seventh Symphony, second
movement (Ex. 1) do not change at all, but repeat themselves.

Some melodies are well suited for the voice, while
others are easier to play on instruments. The easiest
melodies to sing are those that move in comfortably
small intervals within a restricted range, with phrases
short enough to allow for normal breathing. On the
other hand, there are many interesting melodies designed to exploit the potentialities of a particular instrument. Wide and awkward leaps, wide ranges, extremely long phrases, rapid notes, and a variety of
articulations all are relatively easy to play on suitable
instruments, but generally they are quite difficult to
sing. Whether a melody is vocally or instrumentally
conceived may strongly affect the way we hear it.

FORMAL QUALITIES OF MELODY

The smallest coherent fragment of a melody is called a
motive. Some melodies are created by repetition of one

A Mexican-American musician performing on a homemade bamboo instrument. Each pipe produces a different pitch.

or two prominent motives, whereas other melodies grow out of successive new motives or display a minimum of motivic structure. Motives with distinctive rhythm patterns and pitch configurations are most apt to attract our attention, and a "catchy" tune usually is one with attractive motives. Musical structures may be expanded on a large scale by a variety of permutations and combinations of prominent motives, a process called *development*.

Melodies often seem to move forward toward goals. This directed motion may result from the repetition of motives or from movement away from and back to certain prominent pitches. The goals of this motion are called *cadences*, and a *phrase* is a segment of melody or other material that ends with a cadence. Cadences are analogous to punctuation in language; they define the phrases, and they vary in relative strength or prominence. Strong cadences often mark off formal divisions, while weaker cadences allow more continuity of movement from phrase to phrase.

In Bach's Minuet, Trio I, Polacca, and Trio II from the first Brandenburg Concerto (Ex. 2), the Minuet has a prominent melody with complex accompanying parts. Counting three beats to a measure, we will find a strong cadence at the end of twelve measures, which is the goal of all the material that precedes it. There are also weaker cadences at the ends of the fourth and eighth measures. This results in a twelve-measure section of three phrases, marked off by the strong cadence, which constitutes one fourth of the whole Minuet.

Melodies in which the pitches move in obvious relation to one another are most likely to produce an impression of coherent organization; yet careful listening may reveal subtle kinds of order in a series of seemingly unrelated pitches. Some modern composers even contend that we can impose our own order on any succession of sounds, whether random or preordered.

In the second movement of Beethoven's Seventh Symphony (Ex. 1) the main melody at the beginning is made up of motives using the pattern of *long*-short-short-*long-long*. All of the melodies in this piece exhibit strong goal-directed motion. Debussy's *Prelude to the Afternoon of a Faun* (Ex. 3) is rich in prominent melodies and melodic fragments that are frequently extended through motivic repetition. There are few obvious cadences, and a rather weak sense of directed pitch movement, yet the succession and repetition of melodic ideas keeps the music flowing. On the other hand, Berio's *Sinfonia*, Section I (Ex. 4) contains practically nothing that can be called melody except perhaps some of the fragmentary piano sounds near the end.

Textures

Melodies are prominent in most music, and they usually are accompanied by other musical sounds. For several centuries it has been a common practice in Western music to accompany melodies with other melodies, so that in much of the music we hear today the principal melody is accompanied by about three more-or-less subordinate melodies. There is also much Western music in which two or more equally important melodies accompany each other. Music composed of such simultaneous independent melodies is called *polyphony*, meaning "many voices." *Counterpoint* is the artistic discipline by which one learns to create polyphony. When used to describe music, counterpoint and polyphony mean the same thing and are important features of Western music rarely found in the music of non-Western cultures.

Figurative comparison of the interwoven melodies in polyphony with the interwoven threads of a fabric has led musicians to use the word *texture*. This term is used especially to distinguish among different polyphonic combinations. It is also used more generally, however, to mean the total effect created by the number, arrangement, and complexity of any simultaneous, interrelated musical sounds.

VARIETIES OF TEXTURE

Textural variety results from different kinds of simultaneous sounds and from the ways in which these sounds are combined. A piece of music may focus attention on melodies, rhythms, or timbres, yet all of these elements are interrelated and each is capable of almost endless variety. The essence of musical texture lies in our perceiving the many simultaneous sounds and their relation to each other.

The crowding together of separate sounds often is referred to as *density*. Textural density is produced by the number of different musical parts at a given moment, by the placement of their respective pitches, and by the number of performers producing each part. In electronic and some other recent music, composers have created sound masses out of solid "bands" of densely clustered pitches.

An important aspect of texture is the relative independence of the separate parts. The most intricate textures are polyphonic combinations of melodies having distinctive rhythms, timbres, and pitch contours. It is easiest to follow two or more simultaneous but different melodies in which the rhythms are perceptibly different if they are sounded by markedly different timbres and if their motive structures and general pitch movements are actively independent. In truly great polyphonic music all of this variety and independence can also be interrelated so as to produce a completely harmonious total effect.

In many textures, rhythmic independence is minimized in the accompanying parts, allowing one melodic line to dominate. Such textures are often called *homophonic,* as distinct from polyphonic. In Beethoven's Seventh Symphony, second movement (Ex. 1), the basic three-phrase segment (A–B–B) is first played by the lower strings in three parts, with several instruments per part. All parts move in the same rhythm, which minimizes their independence. Each part is actually a melody, but the upper part (violas) tends to stand out most prominently, so that the texture is homophonic.

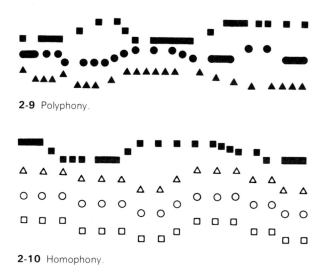

2-9 Polyphony.

2-10 Homophony.

With the first repetition of this segment, the second violins play the first melody at a higher pitch, while the violas and cellos introduce a second melody below the first, which moves in small intervals but is rhythmically independent. These two melodies and the bass part constitute a three-part polyphonic texture.

The segment is next repeated with the two melodies played still higher by the violins, and a new accompanying part is played by the violas and cellos, making a fourth part. Finally, as the full orchestra enters, the first melody is shared by the upper and lower woodwinds, the first violins play the second melody at a still higher level, and the lower strings add a fifth part, with triple subgroupings, against the prevailing duple groupings. The textural density is increased by expanding the range of all the sounds and by adding rhythmically independent parts and new timbres.

Texture is a primary source of contrast between the different movements of Bach's Minuet, Trio I, Polacca, and Trio II from the first Brandenburg Concerto (Ex. 2). The Minuet is the most complex. It consists of a four-part polyphonic texture with one prominent melody, plus a pattern of repeated notes in the two horns. Several instruments play each part. By contrast, two oboes and the bassoon together play three independent melodies in Trio I. The Polacca is in four parts and homophonic, and the texture reverts to three parts in Trio II, with the two horn parts moving together against a third part played by all three oboes.

In the Bach example, distinctive timbres are used to highlight the separate parts. On the other hand, in Debussy's *Prelude to the Afternoon of a Faun* (Ex. 3) and Berio's *Sinfonia*, Section I (Ex. 4), the textures seem designed to produce specific timbres. Density and independence are important in the Berio. Sometimes there is only one sound source, sometimes several, but generally each kind of sound stands out distinctly from the rest, with one performer producing each part. Certain discrete pitches are sustained from time to time, usually spaced well apart from each other. In the Debussy, many of the melodic ideas are inextricably bound with their associated instruments, and the textures consist of combinations of sounds chosen with sensitive regard for their particular timbres.

Béla Bartók's *Music for Strings, Percussion, and Celesta*, first movement (Ex. 5) is a study in polyphonic complexity and extremes of density. Beginning with a single part, the web of melodic lines thickens as more closely interweaving parts join in, and the increasing density is a primary factor in the buildup of tension toward the central peak.

POLYPHONIC DEVICES

Composers use a number of devices for altering and manipulating melodic ideas in a polyphonic texture.

Some of these are easy to perceive, while others may be altogether too complex or abstract to follow without intimate knowledge of the written musical score. Probably the most obvious device is *imitation*, where each part enters in turn with the same melody or portion of a melody. Other common devices include slowing a melody (*augmentation*), speeding it up (*diminution*), reversing intervals (*inversion*), changing pitch levels (*transposition*), and sometimes even sounding the melody backwards (*retrograde*).

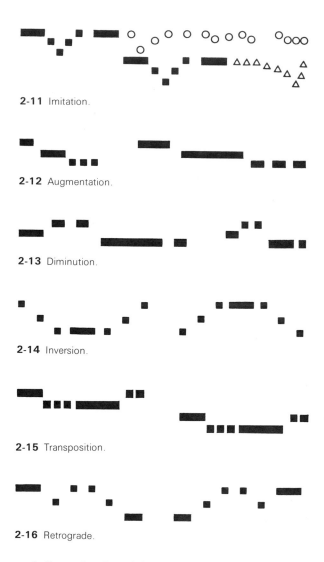

2-11 Imitation.

2-12 Augmentation.

2-13 Diminution.

2-14 Inversion.

2-15 Transposition.

2-16 Retrograde.

In Example 5 Bartók begins with a single melody in four unequal phrases. A second part then imitates this melody, while the first part accompanies it with new melodic material, making a two-part texture. More parts enter, one at a time, each imitating the original melody, which holds the listener's attention as the density of the texture increases. Beginning about half-way through the piece, careful listening will reveal the same melody appearing several times inverted, or "up-side down."

TEXTURE AND FORM

Musical texture may be a source of coherence and continuity as well as variety. Maintaining sameness of texture within a musical passage can be used to help set off sections of contrasting textures, as in the different movements of our selections from Bach's first Brandenburg Concerto (Ex. 2). Variety results when there are frequent changes in the number and relative independence of the parts. An increase in textural density will contribute to a buildup of musical energy, as in the first half of the Bartók (Ex. 5) and in the first four repetitions of the basic three-phrase segment of the Beethoven (Ex. 1).

Imitation of a melodic idea creates continuity because it is a form of repetition. The phrases in polyphonic music often begin with imitation, and sometimes a single melodic idea is imitated in the various parts or by voices and continually reappears throughout all or a considerable portion of a musical passage. Such a unifying melodic idea is called a *subject*. A complete piece structured on a recurring subject imitated in the different parts is a *fugue*, while a shorter passage of imitative polyphony sometimes is called *fugato*. About two-thirds through Example 1, Beethoven suddenly reduces the texture to two violin parts, one playing a derivative of the opening melody against a faster melody in the other. These parts are exchanged, then imitated in turn by the lower strings, while the increasingly dense texture leads to a return of the basic three-phrase segment by the full orchestra. This is a fugato passage.

In a fugue the subject may appear in numerous guises, such as inversion, augmentation, and diminution. A particularly effective treatment is *stretto*—the "piling up" of entries of the subject before other entries have been completed. The initial set of subject entries is called the *exposition*; passages from which the subject is absent are called *episodes*.

The Bartók piece (Ex. 5) is a fugue in which activity and tension build slowly to a central climax and then slowly subside. After the first few imitations, the sub-

2-17
Three musicians playing early brass instruments.

ject begins appearing in stretto, and it breaks down into a repeated motive just before the climax. The subject returns inverted in the latter part, in stretto, and it is combined with its own inversion several times, especially near the end.

When a melody is combined with itself in some particular, predetermined way throughout a piece of music, the process and the resulting piece are both called *canon*, meaning the "rule" that governs the polyphony. One of the simplest kinds of canon is a *round*, such as "Three Blind Mice," in which the entire melody accompanies itself as it is passed around (is imitated) from part to part. Though imitation is common in most canons, they also frequently employ inversion, transposition, augmentation, diminution, and other such devices.

Harmonies

When we sense relatedness among the constituent parts of something, we can say the parts are in "harmony." In music, the word *harmony* means relationships existing among the various pitches, whether considered simultaneously or successively.

SCALES, MODES, AND CHORDS

In most music the distinct pitches that make up the melodies and their accompaniments move within some system of harmonious relations. The simplest of these relations—known to Western culture as the "octave," but universally recognized and used throughout the world—results when one tone vibrates twice as fast as another. This is the starting point for most systems of pitch organization. When men and women sing the same melody they both seem to be singing the same pitches, yet with a difference. They are, in reality, singing an octave apart, always maintaining the same two-to-one ratio between their respective pitches.

Although the octave can be divided into any number of different pitches, most of the melodies in our culture use only a limited set of tones within the octave, customarily between five and twelve. We can extract the different pitches from a melody and arrange them sequentially to form a *scale*. The five-tone (pentatonic) and seven-tone (*diatonic*) scales contain the pitch materials for a large number of our melodies, although other systems, ranging up to twelve-tone (*chromatic*) scales are not uncommon. In most pitch systems the octave is divided into unequal parts, so that the distances, or intervals between the pitches, vary. This tends to focus our attention on those intervals that depart from the norm, and it causes one or more pitches to stand out from the rest.

Most traditional Western musical instruments can divide the octave into twelve equal parts. The smallest interval generated (a twelfth of an octave) is called a *half tone*, or *half step*. This is the interval marked off by the consecutive frets on a guitar fingerboard or by any adjacent keys on a keyboard. Two half steps make a *whole step*, and larger intervals can also be defined by adding half steps. The division of the octave in Western music can be seen in a diagram of the piano keyboard. Within the octave indicated in Fig. 2-18, the white keys constitute a diatonic scale. The black keys represent a pentatonic scale, and the black and white keys together make up a chromatic scale.

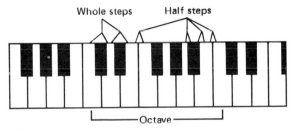

2-18 Intervals on the piano keyboard.

The particular arrangement of the intervals between the tones of a scale determines its character, or *mode*, and this produces certain kinds of melodic and harmonic effects. The two most common modes of the diatonic scale are called *major* and *minor*, though several other modes are possible. The determining factor in these modes is the placement of the two smallest intervals (half tones) in relation to each other and to one prominent tone. Western art music during the seventeenth through the nineteenth centuries used the major and minor modes almost exclusively, but other kinds of melody and harmony are common in older Western music, in the music of other cultures, in our own folk music, and in much music of the twentieth century.

When two or more pitches are combined to produce a single composite sound, we call the result a *chord*. Many chords have specific names; most of these contain three or four different pitches. The most common simple chord is called a *triad* and is composed of any three

2-19

PABLO PICASSO, *Mandolin and Guitar,*
1924. Oil with sand on canvas.
55⅜'' x 78⅞''. The Solomon R.
Guggenheim Museum, New York.

alternate tones in a diatonic scale. Any texture of more
than one part in which the sounds have perceptible
pitch will produce chords, but we are more aware of the
simultaneous pitch combinations in some textures than
in others. When the pitch relations change, the chords
also change. A simple accompaniment to a melody may
be entirely lacking in melodic interest, and so it can be
comprehended best as a series of chords. In more complex textures, and especially when there is polyphonic
independence, the listener may experience a bewildering array of harmonic combinations. In such textures
certain sonorities usually stand out more prominently
than others, and the intervening harmonies can be
regarded as connecting material. A student of counterpoint studies the intervals between the tones of simultaneous melodies, whereas the student of harmony
studies the more common chord types and the way they
succeed one another.

CONSONANCE AND DISSONANCE

Sounds can be combined in such a way as to seem
harmonious and complete (*consonance*), or they can be
combined to produce a feeling of tension, excitement,
and need for release (*dissonance*). Dissonant sounds
produce suspense or expectations; consonant sounds act
as foils to the dissonances and usually fulfill the
aroused expectations. In much Western music the relationships among chords and among the successive
pitches in a melody or a polyphonic texture have been
the chief means for creating consonance and disso-

nance. Fluctuations of dissonance may occur in music at several levels, producing cycles of suspense and resolution, sometimes over long time spans. Our perception of consonance and dissonance is influenced considerably by the context of pitch relations in which they occur. Furthermore, rhythm, loudness, and timbre may be used in such a way as to enhance or subdue the effects of harmonic dissonance.

One of the composer's chief concerns in writing counterpoint is control of the dissonant relationships among the tones that make up the musical texture. These dissonances are the primary pitch relations that help, along with variety of rhythm and timbre, to maintain independence among the melodies. Carefully constructed counterpoint can be quite satisfying harmonically, while still producing many dissonances, especially when the exchange between dissonant tension and consonant release are balanced.

TONALITY

Very often the pitches used in melodies and their accompaniments are related within a hierarchy. One pitch, called the *tonic*, acts as the focus toward which the other pitches tend, in varying degrees, to gravitate. Such a system is called *tonality*, in reference to the tonic pitch. It may include few or many pitches, and it may be either obvious or subtle to the listener. We refer to the specific pitch of the tonic in a piece of music as the *key* of the piece; for example, "key of A." In melodies with a strong sense of directed motion, the succession of tones tends to enhance the tonic pitch as well as one or two other pitches that act as foils to the tonic. The more equally the various pitches are treated, the weaker will be the tonal orientation.

The pitch of the tonic may change within a piece, a process called *modulation*. The complete process begins with the establishment of the initial tonic and ends in the confirmation of a new tonic with a cadence. Often there is a suspension of tonal focus during the course of a modulation. Ordinarily, tonally oriented music begins and ends with the same tonic, while interior departures provide contrast.

Tonality often is closely associated with cycles of dissonance. The way the pitches are made to relate to each other can lead us to expect movement toward the tonic; satisfaction of these expectations produces a strong sense of consonance.

2-20

An illustration of a performer playing on an early harpsichord.

TONALITY AND MUSICAL DESIGN

Composers often have used tonality to provide both variety and coherence and to control continuity and overall timing in musical design. Control of dissonance-consonance fluctuations and tonal relations produces a sense of movement. Cadences punctuate the stages in this process, thus helping to delineate the overall timing. They may confirm the tonic or they may suspend it, leading us to expect a later confirmation. Usually, the cadences are the high points of dissonance-consonance polarity; they employ dissonances to set up the expectation of a tonic, which are resolved into consonances when the expected tonic arrives. Each modulation within a piece leads toward a possible cadence and the opportunity to present a whole new section with new material. Since many successive modulations may occur before a return to the original tonic, the possibilities for expansion of the musical design are almost limitless.

In Bach's Minuet, Trio I, Polacca, and Trio II from the first Brandenburg Concerto (Ex. 2), the Minuet consists of two distinct sections, both of them repeated when the Minuet is first played. Each section contains three phrases and ends with a strong cadence (the phrases are twelve beats long). The sections can be represented schematically as follows: A–cadence; A–cadence; B–cadence; B–cadence; or simply, AABB. The sense of a tonic pitch is strongest at the cadences that end the sections and most elusive in the middle of the phrases. It can be heard best if one concentrates on the bass, or lowest pitches. A modulation occurs in the third phrase of both sections so that the cadence at the end of section A confirms a different tonic than the cadence that ends section B. All of the movements of Example 2 are designed in a similar way.

The chord changes occur quite regularly throughout the opening passage of Beethoven's Seventh Symphony, second movement (Ex. 1), and the overall mode is minor. In the basic three-phrase segment (A–B–B), the first phrase modulates to a new key, the second modulates back to the original key, and the third is a repetition of the second. Not only does the cadence that ends phrase A confirm a new tonic pitch, but the mode also changes momentarily to major. Following the repetitions of this segment there is a passage in the major mode, which proceeds for the most part over a single repeated bass tone instead of regular chord changes. This passage also modulates away from, then back to, its starting key. Both passages are used again, in addition to the short *fugato* passage mentioned earlier.

HARMONIC COLOR

Chords may have dissonant or consonant qualities when they relate to each other within a system of tonality. Chord changes in such a context produce a sense of *harmonic motion*. However, individual chords have unique sound qualities, and chord changes may simply produce various and contrasting sounds. Such usage of chords is sometimes called *harmonic color*. Composers often exploit harmonic color in conjunction with unique combinations of instrumental or vocal timbres. A texture of coloristic harmonies may produce little or no harmonic motion, in which case the terms *dissonance* and *consonance* may become meaningless.

In his *Prelude to the Afternoon of a Faun* (Ex. 3), Debussy uses harmonic color to enhance and complement the orchestral timbres; thus, a specific combination of pitches played by a specific combination of instruments is chosen to produce each effect. This considerably weakens the sense of tonality (though it is still present), but greatly enhances the expressive power of the orchestra. The sequence of events derives much of its logic from successive shadings of timbre, rather than from harmonic pitch successions.

In Berio's *Sinfonia*, Section I (Ex. 4), there is careful control of pitches despite the evident focus on loudness, timbre, and measured durations. The sustained sounds are carefully arranged and combined to create unique colors. Continued emphasis on certain sustained pitches may even be heard as a sort of fleeting tonality.

By contrast, the primary focus in Bartók's *Music for*

2-21
Music is a shared experience in a
neighborhood arts program.

Strings, Percussion, and Celesta, first movement (Ex. 5) is
on the manipulation of pitch relations through a polyphonic texture of combined melodies and on the resulting harmonic combinations. All twelve tones in the
octave are used so freely that any sense of a central tone
is momentary at best, though a consistent logic to the
use of the tones can be discovered with careful study.
Variances in the level of tension and activity, however,
are directly related to changes in density and to dissonance-consonance fluctuations.

HARMONY AND MUSICAL STYLE

The system of pitch relationships in a piece of music is
an important facet of its style. From about 1650 to 1900
composers of Western music utilized a clear and comprehensive system of tonality. In much music from this
period tonality unifies the overall structure, and variations in rhythm, loudness, timbre, and other factors
help to delineate the progress of the tonal relationships.
For this kind of music, the listener's perception of
formal continuity in a piece is enhanced by his or her
sensitivity to the composer's manipulation of tonality.

For the past five centuries composers have exhibited an ever-increasing tolerance for extremes of dissonant fluctuation and of sustained dissonance, and since about 1900 many composers have begun to ignore or to avoid tonality. Some have altogether abandoned familiar pitch combinations and relations, giving equal emphasis to all of the traditionally available tones. Most recently, especially since the advent of electronic means for manipulating sounds, musicians have begun to use the full spectrum of audible pitches. Often these sounds are produced with no reference at all to the older concepts of pitch relationships, or they de-emphasize pitch relations in favor of timbre and time. Meanwhile, most popular music has retained the tonal relationships common to the music of the past.

Suggestions for Further Study

Bamberger, Jeanne Shapiro, and Howard Brofsky. *The Art of Listening: Developing Musical Perception,* 3rd ed. New York: Harper and Row, 1975.

Boyden, David D. *An Introduction to Music,* 2nd ed. New York: Knopf, 1970.

Copland, Aaron. *What to Listen for in Music,* rev. ed. New York: McGraw-Hill, 1964.

Moore, Douglas. *Listening to Music,* rev. ed. New York: Norton, 1963.

Sessions, Roger. *The Music Experience of Composer, Performer, Listener.* Princeton, N.J.: Princeton University Press, 1971.

Wink, Richard L., and Lois G. Williams. *Invitation to Listening: An Introduction to Music.* Boston: Houghton Mifflin, 1972.

Suggestions for Further Listening

Bach, Johann Sebastian. One or more fugues from the *Well-Tempered Clavier.* (Polyphony; fugue.)

————. Second chorale verse from Cantata No. 140, *Wachet auf* (''Sleepers wake''). (Polyphonic texture; distinctive melodic contours.)

Beethoven, Ludwig van. First movement from Symphony No. 5. (Motivic development; tonality; goal-directed dissonance.)

Palestrina, Giovanni Pierluigi da. A motet or mass section. (Polyphony; dissonance-consonance fluctuation.)

Wagner, Richard. ''Prelude'' and ''Liebestod'' from *Tristan und Isolde.* (Sustained dissonance, resolutions avoided; chromatic harmony and polyphony.)

Webern, Anton. Symphony for small orchestra, Op. 21. (Atonality; fragmented melodies.)

Chapter 3 Art

Subject Matter

Subject matter is most simply defined as the recognizable objects depicted by the artist; yet subject matter acquires meaning on different levels and can be employed in different degrees.

Levels of Meaning in Subject Matter

Factual meaning in subject matter is established through identification of objects. Understanding the significance of the subject matter, however, frequently involves more than recognizing the objects. An inventory of the subject matter in Jan van Eyck's portrait of the Arnolfinis (Plate 4), for example, does not explain why the couple is so formally posed in the privacy of a bedroom; nor does a description of objects in Raphael's *Madonna of the Meadow* (Fig. 3-1) convey its content to a person unfamiliar with Christian scripture. Factual meaning is often supplemented or supplanted by meaning on other levels.

CONVENTIONAL MEANING

Certain objects, actions, and even colors acquire special meaning for a particular culture. In our culture, for example, the cross stands for Christianity, red suggests life or danger, and white is associated with purity. To understand the conventional or generally accepted symbolism of other cultures or historical periods, it is often necessary to do research. In the Van Eyck portrait, a number of symbols would be missed by the casual observer today. The painting is a testament to the marriage vow. The lone candle symbolizes the all-seeing Christ; the fruit on the window sill refers to the state of innocence before the Fall of Man; the mirror and the crystal beads are symbols of purity; the wooden shoes recall the command of God to Moses on Mt. Sinai to take off his shoes when he stood on holy ground; the dog stands for marital fidelity; and the back of the chair by the bed is carved in the image of St. Margaret, the patron saint of childbirth. The study of such conventional symbols is called *iconography*.

Some of the most pervasive symbols in Western art derive from the Christian tradition. The following are only a few of the hundreds of symbols used in Christian religious art, and for these only the more frequent meanings are included. The iconography of other cultures will be considered in the historical chapters in Part II.

3-1
RAPHAEL SANZIO, *Madonna of the Meadow*, 1505. Panel, approx. 4' × 3'. Kunsthistorisches Museum, Vienna.

APPLE Tree of Knowledge in the Garden of Eden, hence evil. An apple held by Jesus or Mary means salvation from sin.

CARNATION Red means pure love; pink stands for marriage.

CAT Laziness, lust.

CHALICE Last Supper. A chalice with serpent identifies St. John the Evangelist. A chalice with wafer identifies St. Barbara. A broken chalice indicates St. Donatus.

COLUMBINE Holy Ghost.

CROSS The Latin cross (tall post with short crosspiece) refers to Jesus; the Greek cross (equal arms) stands for the Christian Church; an X-shaped cross refers to St. Andrew the Apostle.

DOVE Holy Ghost, peace, purity.

EAGLE St. John the Evangelist. Resurrection. Generosity.

EGG Resurrection, source of life.

EWER AND BASIN Purity, cleanliness.

FISH Christ, since the five letters for the Greek word for *fish* form the initials of the words: "Jesus Christ, God's Son, Savior."

FOUNTAIN Mary, seen as the "fountain of living waters" (Song of Solomon 4:12ff. and Psalms 36:9) because she was the mother of Christ the Savior. Medieval and Renaissance Christian art often interpreted Old Testament passages as predictions of New Testament events.

GARDEN, ENCLOSED Mary. A symbol of the Immaculate Conception of Mary (Song of Solomon 4:12).

GLOBE Earthly or spiritual power, held by God, Jesus, or a monarch.

GRAIN Body of Jesus (bread in Holy Communion).

GRAPES OR GRAPEVINE Christ as the "true vine" of which his followers are the branches (John 15:1, 5, 8). Blood of Jesus (wine in Holy Communion).

GRIDIRON St. Lawrence, who was martyred on a grid over a fire.

HALO Saintliness. A round halo is most common. A triangular halo reflects the Trinity; a square halo refers to living persons.

HAMMER Instrument of the Passion, used in the Crucifixion.

INRI The initials of the Latin words for *Jesus of Nazareth, King of the Jews*, which appear on the Cross of Jesus.

IRIS Sorrow and purity of Mary. The bladelike leaf is associated with a sword and alludes to the suffering of Mary.

KEY St. Peter, a reference to Christ's giving the keys of the kingdom of heaven to Peter (Matthew 16:19).

LADDER Instrument of the Passion, used in the Crucifixion.

LAMB Jesus, the sacrificial lamb of God. The sinner saved by Jesus the Good Shepherd. St. John the Baptist. St. Agnes. St. Clement.

LAMP Wisdom.

LIGHT Christ.

LILY Purity, Mary.

LION Jesus. St. Mark the Evangelist. St. Jerome. Majesty.

MANDORLA Almond-shaped radiation of light surrounding the whole body of Jesus or Mary and signifying divinity.

MOON Mary, who is identified as the woman with the moon under her feet (Revelations 12:1).

NAILS Instruments of the Passion.

OINTMENT BOX Mary Magdalene, a reference to her anointing of Christ.

OLIVE Peace.

OX OR BULL St. Luke the Evangelist. The Jewish Nation. Patience.

PALM Victory.

PEACOCK Vanity. Immortality, because of the ancient belief that the flesh of the peacock does not decay.

PILLAR Instrument of the Passion (the pillar to which Christ was tied while he was whipped).

RIVERS The four rivers of Paradise, thought to flow from the same rock, symbolize the four Gospels, which had their source in Jesus.

ROSE Red for martyrdom, white for purity.

SCALES Equality and justice. The Archangel Michael is often shown with scales for the weighing of souls.

SCOURGE Instrument of the Passion.

SHIP The Christian Church, referring to the ark of Noah and the Church as means of salvation.

SKULL The vanity of earthly life (often shown with St. Jerome). A skull at the foot of the Cross refers to Adam and indicates the Cross as a means of salvation from man's original sin.

SPEAR Instrument of the Passion.

SPONGE Instrument of the Passion.

STAR Divine guidance, as in the journey of the Magi. One star is also the symbol of Mary. Twelve stars stand for the Apostles or for the twelve tribes of Israel.

SUN Mary (Revelations 12:1).

SWORD A symbol of martyrdom by the sword, often shown with St. Paul, St. Peter, St. Justina, St. Agnes, and many others.

THORNS Sin, grief. Instrument of the Passion (Christ's crown of thorns).

TOWER Identifies St. Barbara, who was confined in a tower.

WATER OR A WELL Purification, baptism, rebirth.

WHALE A symbol of the Devil or of the story of Jonah.

WHEEL Identifies St. Catherine, who was tortured on a wheel.

XP The Greek letters *Chi* and *Rho*, the first two letters in the Greek word for Christ. They are often super-imposed:

A society often modifies its iconography according to changes in the prevailing thought of a period. The study of factors causing changes in iconography and the interpretation of such changes within the history of thought is called *iconology*.

SUBJECTIVE MEANING

The individual artist may consciously or unconsciously employ a private symbolism based on an association of certain objects, actions, or colors with past experiences, a temporary state of mind, or an adopted world view. Similarly, the observer tends to interpret art according to his own associations, and over this interpretive activity the artist never has complete control. In a sense, therefore, a work of art is re-created anew each time it is experienced by an observer. Dali (Fig. 3-2) paints objects in such a way as to encourage a wide range of individual interpretation. So did Kandinsky (Plate 23), who felt that painting should make its appeal on the same nonrepresentational basis as music. Mondrian (Fig. 3-3) argued that recognizable objects were impurities that distracted the observer from the essential quality in art: a unique equilibrium of line and color. Thus his work can be described as the most "subjectless," that is, the least encouraging to associational meaning.

3-2 SALVADOR DALI, *The Persistence of Memory*, 1931. Oil on canvas, 9½″ × 13″. Collection, The Museum of Modern Art, New York. Given anonymously.

Degrees of Subject Matter

Writers on art generally employ three terms to classify works according to degree of subject matter. These categories overlap somewhat, but the terms are worthwhile if they are used cautiously. *Representational* art has clearly recognizable objects (Fig. 17-7); *abstract* art has a basis in identifiable objects (Plate 27); and *nonobjective* art has no direct reference to such objects, that is, no subject matter (Fig. 3-3). These terms may be applied from either the artist's or the observer's standpoint, with possible disagreement. The artist may work so abstractly that the observer finds no apparent subject matter and assumes the painting to be nonobjective; conversely, the artist may work nonobjectively, but the observer may see recognizable objects in the work and consider it to be abstract. It is important to recall that recognizing objects in representational or abstract art is not necessarily grasping its content. Content in both representational and abstract art is an interaction of subject matter with the interpretive qualities of the visual and tactile elements. In fact, subject matter may acquire meaning on different levels if it is present in any degree.

3-3
PIET MONDRIAN, *Composition with Blue and Yellow*, 1932. Oil on canvas, 16¼" × 13". A. E. Gallatin Collection, Philadelphia Museum of Art.

Suggestions for Further Study

Ferguson, George. *Signs and Symbols in Christian Art.* New York: Oxford University Press, 1961.

Gilson, Étienne. *Painting and Reality.* New York: Meridian Books, 1959.

Ogden, C. K., and I. A. Richards. *The Meaning of Meaning.* New York: Harcourt Brace Jovanovich, 1959.

Panofsky, Erwin. *Gothic Architecture and Scholasticism.* New York: Meridian Books, 1957.

———. *Meaning in the Visual Arts: Papers in and on Art History.* Garden City, N.Y.: Doubleday, 1955.

———. *Studies in Iconology: Humanistic Themes in the Art of the Renaissance.* New York: Oxford University Press, 1939.

———, and Dora Panofsky. *Pandora's Box: The Changing Aspects of a Mythical Symbol,* rev. ed. New York: Pantheon Books, 1962.

Pierce, James Smith. *From Abacus to Zeus: A Handbook of Art History.* Englewood Cliffs, N.J.: Prentice-Hall, 1968.

Chapter 3 Music

Musical Meaning and Musical Ideas

Except for the rare use of familiar sounds, such as thunder or birdcalls, music has no parallel to the depiction of familiar objects in the visual arts. Musical meaning functions most often on an abstract level, as time-sound constructs that have no external references. Meaning in music, however, can also operate on the level of conventional or private symbols and associations. Any configuration of musical sound, such as a motive, melody, rhythm pattern, timbre, or chord may be referred to as a *musical idea.*

Symbolic and Subjective Meaning

Musicians sometimes employ conventional symbols so that certain musical sounds in a given style may be commonly associated with particular ideas or emotions. Where words are sung or spoken, their meaning may be enhanced by associated musical figures (for instance, "waves" or "water" by an undulating pattern; "rising" or "increasing" by a rising melody). More often, musical symbols acquire conventional meaning through usage, as with certain harmonic colors and instrumental timbres that have come to be associated with specific dramatic situations.

Music listeners as well as those who create music may perceive and interpret particular timbres, melodies, or rhythms in terms of their personal experiences and associations. Just as in the visual arts, these private symbols and associations may be different for the composer than for the listener. Composers may design their music to encourage or discourage such associative meaning. When the musical structure is meant to express nonmusical ideas or events, composers may verbally reinforce or control their musical symbols through printed programs given to the listener; this is called *program music.*

Debussy's *Prelude to the Afternoon of a Faun* (Ex. 3) is a musical paraphrase of a poem by Stéphane Mallarmé. It seems to have been conceived as a musical accompaniment to a dramatic reading of the poem, possibly with mimed acting, so the poem itself would have served as the "program." In the poem a faun awakens from a drunken sleep and tries to recapture his erotic dreams as poetic fantasies. The poem is a study in levels of consciousness and is full of obscure symbolism. According to his own statement, Debussy intended the music to be a free interpretation of the poem, not an explicit synthesis; however, the faun, in the poem, translates his fantasies into music by playing the flute, thus the prominent flute melody is an obvious musical symbol.

Nonreferential Meaning

Many composers conceive their music purely as time-sound constructs. Such music is called *pure, absolute,* or *abstract,* as opposed to program music. Considered in this way, music has meaning for us when we associate the successive musical ideas and changing levels of activity with our own experiences of time and motion. In other words, the meaning of abstract music is in its formal structure. This kind of meaning exists in all music, regardless of any symbolic and subjective factors. Its most obvious manifestations are the experience of continuity, order, and variety, and of the organic growth and the sequence of musical ideas. Formal processes in music yield aesthetic experiences, which are types of life experiences onto which we project meanings. These meanings may be verbalized or left unspoken, but they are never identical to verbal expression. The meaning expressed by program music can be translated into verbal equivalents; the meaning of abstract music cannot.

Beethoven's Seventh Symphony, second movement (Ex. 1), Bach's Minuet, Trio I, Polacca, and Trio II from the first Brandenburg Concerto (Ex. 2), and Bartók's *Music for Strings, Percussion, and Celesta,* first movement (Ex. 5) are all instances of abstract music. Each in

3-4
Vaslav Nijinsky as the Faun, in a poster by Léon Bakst for the 1912 Ballets Russes production of *Prelude to the Afternoon of a Faun.*

3-5
VASSILY KANDINSKY, *Delicate Joy,* 1927. Gouache, 8'' x 7¼''. The Solomon R. Guggenheim Museum, New York.

3-6

A portion of Luciano Berio's score for *Sinfonia*, Section I. In his notes to the singers, Berio requests at times that they produce "random sounds simulating very fast speech." These sounds are indicated in the lower half of the score reprinted here.

its own way creates an aesthetic experience through self-evident formal processes, with no other meaning intended. Berio's *Sinfonia*, Section I (Ex. 4) is abstract music, but it also seems to invite private associations. Fragments and components of the spoken langauge are presented in such a way that the listener never quite hears the text as having verbal meaning; the human vocal sounds are integrated with the instrumental sounds, and the piece displays a continuity and an order that is purely musical. At the same time, the fragments of speech are particularly provocative because they suggest verbal meanings and associations for the listener.

Levels of Musical Understanding

Whether one experiences music as a composer, a performer, or a listener, musical understanding may occur at several levels: a direct response (one beats time, hums a melody, and so forth), a conscious association, and a consciousness of musical details and relationships.

The degree of one's musical awareness and understanding depends on the degree of direct involvement in and empathy with the music, conscious attention to details, prior experience with the characteristics expected from a given style, knowledge of symbolic possibilities, self-awareness, and a general aesthetic sensitivity. Musical experience involves an interplay between perception and cognition, and an interplay between heard sounds and imagined possibilities, together with their associated emotional responses. Time and memory are crucial factors, since order and coherence result from our recognition of similar events when they recur. Passive absorption of "background" music, without active attention and involvement, is not musical understanding.

Suggestions for Further Study

Coker, Wilson. *Music and Meaning: A Theoretical Introduction to Musical Aesthetics.* New York: Free Press, 1972.

Dewey, John. *Art as Experience.* New York: Capricorn, 1959.

Epperson, Gordon. *The Musical Symbol.* Ames, Iowa: Iowa State University Press, 1967.

Ferguson, Donald. *Music as Metaphor: The Elements of Expression.* Greenwich, Conn.: Greenwood, 1973.

Hanslick, Eduard. *The Beautiful in Music: A Contribution to the Revisal of Musical Aesthetics,* rev. ed. Translated by Gustav Cohen. New York: Da Capo, 1974.

Ives, Charles. *Essays Before a Sonata and Other Writings.* Edited by Howard Boatwright. New York: Norton, 1961.

Langer, Susanne K. *Philosophy in a New Key: A Study in the Symbolism of Reason, Rite, and Art,* 3rd ed. Cambridge, Mass.: Harvard University Press, 1957.

Lockspeiser, Edward. *Debussy: His Life and Mind.* 2 vols. London: Cassell, 1962. Volume 1, pp. 150–159.

Meyer, Leonard B. *Emotion and Meaning in Music.* Chicago: University of Chicago Press, 1956.

Chapter 4 Art

The content of a work of art depends in varying degrees on its visual and tactile elements, which in turn depend on the materials and techniques used. A particular material, along with the technique appropriate to it, is often called the *medium* (plural, *media*) *of expression.* We can better understand a composition if we know something of the problems and possibilities inherent in the medium. Today artists often combine many media in one work; the result is often referred to as *mixed media.*

Techniques

Drawing

Though generally identified with line, drawing is a term used so broadly that it often overlaps the realm of painting. A drawing may be a *study*, an investigation of a certain detail of what may become a more extensive work; it may be a *sketch*, the quick notation of the general organization and effect of a composition; or it may be a *cartoon*, a full-size composition meant to be transferred to another surface for a finished work.

In *pencil drawing*, a wide range of values is possible with *leads* (graphite) of differing hardness. Hard lead on a smooth surface is good for a precise light line, such as that in Picasso's drawing of Dr. Claribel Cone (Fig. 1-1); soft lead applied to a rough surface gives a dark line with grainy texture. If the lead is sharpened to a wedge shape, it can be twisted to create a line with considerable modulation.

In *ink drawing*, great variety is possible through the use of colored inks, colored papers, inks of differing degrees of opacity, and different pen points. Formerly pens were made by splitting quills or reeds; nowadays pen points of many shapes and sizes are available in steel. Modulation in line depends on the point's width and on its flexibility, which governs the spreading of the split point. Today pens with felt-tip points add to the range of possibilities.

Charcoal varies in hardness; it can be used directly for crisp lines, or it can be rubbed to produce soft grays. Large areas can be covered quickly in a variety of values characteristic of painting. Charcoal does not adhere well. Soft paper with considerable *tooth* (texture) takes it best, and smearing is minimized if the drawing is sprayed with a *fixative* (thin varnish).

Chalk and *pastel* are made of powdered pigments (coloring matter) mixed with glue and formed into sticks. *Crayon* is made of pigment mixed with wax; it adheres well but does not lend itself to rubbing for soft gradations. Pastels and chalks are more powdery because of their weak glue binder. They have the advantages and disadvantages of charcoal and require a fixative.

Brush drawing—application of ink or watercolor with a brush—is often used in combination with pen-and-ink or pencil. In *dry brush drawing*, ink or watercolor is used dryly, permitting great detail and easy correction. In *wash drawing*, watercolor or ink diluted with water is used for flowing transparent washes, and correction is more difficult. In brush drawing of both types, usually only one or two colors are used. The color limitation differentiates brush drawing from watercolor painting.

Printmaking

A *print* is a work of art produced by a duplicating process. It is considered an original rather than a reproduction because the artist works toward the print as the end product. For this reason the print has been called a multiple original. Many artists perform the whole process themselves; some prepare the printing surface and have special printers make the prints; still others create the composition only and have specialists transfer it to a printing surface and make the prints. In any case, the artist must understand the printing process to be used if he is to exploit its possibilities effectively. The total number of prints is called an *edition*. After the edition is printed, the printing surface is usually destroyed or *canceled* (x'd out with lines). The edition is thus limited, and the prints are more valuable to collectors. Today the artist frequently signs each print in pencil on the margin and uses a fraction to indicate the place of that particular print in the total edition; the number 6/45 would mean the sixth print in an edition of forty-five. Trial prints made during the preparation of the printing surface are called *artist's proofs*. Different stages of the composition (often indicated by artist's proofs but sometimes carried out even during the printing of the edition) are called *states*. A composition may have one or many states. An artist might make a number of prints of a landscape and then decide to add a cloud in the sky. Prints without the cloud would be first-state; prints with the cloud would be second-state.

The many processes used in printmaking may be grouped in four broad categories, although the contemporary tendency to mix techniques within each of these general groups sometimes makes it difficult for the observer to know how a print was produced.

RELIEF PROCESSES

In a *relief process*, the artist cuts away parts of the printing surface. The parts of the surface left raised (*in relief*) are inked, and the ink is then transferred to paper.

For *woodcuts*, a piece of wood is cut or gouged to leave the design in relief. Prints may be made with a press or by placing paper over the inked block, and rubbing it with a spoon or other smooth instrument. Color woodcut prints traditionally are made with a separate block for each color. Careful *registration* is necessary to ensure that each color is printed exactly in the proper area. Transparent colors may be overlapped to produce additional colors, and colored paper may be used. Woodcut lends itself to bold lines and large areas of light and dark. Sometimes the grain of the wood or the texture of the paper will be evident in the print.

In *wood engraving*, a hard end-grain (grain at right angles to the surface) block is used, allowing easy cutting in any direction. *Burins* (cutting tools) of various shapes and sizes are employed, and great detail is possible.

For *linoleum cuts*, linoleum mounted on a wood block is cut in the same manner as a woodcut. The surface is soft, and there is no wood grain to exploit. Like a woodcut, the linoleum cut does not encourage great detail.

In a *metal cut*, metal is cut away with engraving tools, or the surface is lowered with punches; or the design may be drawn with acid-resistant material and the rest of the plate eaten (*etched*) with acid, leaving the design in relief.

INTAGLIO PROCESSES

In *intaglio processes*, the low parts, rather than the relief parts, of the printing surface carry the ink. The lines of the design are cut or eaten into a metal plate (usually copper). Ink is forced into these lines, and the surface

4-1 Relief printing.

of the plate is wiped clean. A high-pressure press forces dampened paper against the surface and into the depressed lines. Often the dried ink can be felt standing in relief on the surface of the finished print. Unless the plate is larger than the print paper, the pressure of the press mashes the paper down around the edges of the plate and makes an indented *plate mark*, which may later be cut away. Since the pressure of the press slowly breaks down the edges or ridges between the intaglio lines, the size of an edition is limited (unless the copper plate is electroplated with a firmer metal), and early prints in an edition are generally valued more highly than later ones. As in the relief processes, a separate plate is employed for each color.

The sunken lines that hold the ink in an intaglio plate may be produced in several ways. In the *drypoint* process, a sharp point is used to scratch lines into the soft copper plate. Tiny ruffles of displaced metal (*burr*) pile up along the sides of each scratch. The ink held by the burr creates slightly fuzzy lines that can be used very effectively by the artist (Fig. 1-2). The burr quickly wears off, however, and drypoint editions are small.

For *metal engraving*, burins are used to cut out the metal, rather than to push it aside as in drypoint (a drypoint plate with the burr worn off produces the same effect as an engraved plate). Great sharpness and precision are possible. Engraving is often used in combination with etching.

In the process of *etching*, a copper plate is coated with acid-resistant material (*ground*) through which the lines of the design are easily drawn. The plate is then immersed in acid, which eats into the metal wherever lines have been scratched through the ground. Thus the artist does not fight the resistance of the metal, and lines are produced more easily than in drypoint or engraving. Some lines may be etched a longer time than others to obtain greater depth; these hold more ink and provide greater darkness of line in the print. Etched lines are generally softer and freer than engraved lines. In *soft ground etching*, the ground is so soft that lines drawn on a paper placed on the plate pick up the ground when the paper is pulled away from the plate. The plate is then etched. Fabrics and other materials may be pressed into the soft ground and lifted off. The ground is pulled away where the texture of the material pressed into it, and the texture of the material can then be etched into the plate. *Aquatint etching* produces soft sandy or speckled areas. It is done by sifting resin powder onto a heated plate. The resin melts partially and sticks to

4-2 Intaglio printing.

4-3

GOYA, *Love and Death* from the *Caprichos* series, 1797–98. Etching with aquatint, approx. 8½ × 6⅛". Clarence Buckingham Collection. Courtesy of The Art Institute of Chicago.

the plate. Acid attacks the metal exposed between the resin particles and produces thousands of tiny pits that hold ink and create speckled areas on the print. The evenness and darkness of the aquatint will depend on the amount of resin sifted onto the plate, the size of the resin particles, and the length of time the plate is exposed to acid. Although resin is sifted over the whole plate, the aquatint effect is limited to chosen areas by *stopping out* other areas with acid-resistant varnish.

PLANOGRAPHIC PROCESSES

As the name implies, these methods print with a level rather than a raised or lowered surface.

The *monotype* process produces only a single print. Inks or paints are brushed, dripped, or rubbed on a smooth glass or metal plate. A paper is laid over the plate and rubbed. Wide varieties of superimposed colors and textures are possible with this procedure.

For *lithography*, the printing surface is traditionally fine-grained limestone, but in commercial lithography metal plates are used. The drawing is done with grease-containing crayons, pencils, or inks; the surface is then treated chemically to make it reject ink except where the greasy substance has established the drawing. Printing is done with a special press.

STENCIL PROCESSES

One of the most important stencil processes is *silk-screen*, often called *serigraphy*. Many methods are used. Basically, the idea is to fill or cover the pores of the silk (stretched on a frame), leaving them open only in the shape of the design. Colored inks are then rolled or scraped across the silk and penetrate to form a print of the design on paper or cloth underneath.

4-4 Lithographic stone being inked for printing.

Painting

Oil paint, watercolor, crayon, and pastel can all be made from the same pigment. The differentiating factor is the *binder* (the substance that holds the color particles together and makes them adhere to a surface). The word "paint" is normally applied to media that are used in liquid or paste form. The immediate surface that receives the paint is called the *ground* (an entirely different meaning, obviously, from an etching ground). For watercolor, the ground is usually the surface of the paper.

For many paints applied to wood or canvas, intervening substances such as *sizing* and *priming* must be applied to limit the absorption of the base material. Then the panel or canvas becomes the *support,* and the preparatory coating becomes the ground. Paint may be applied in a single layer (*alla prima*) or in many layers. Transparent layers are called *washes* in watercolor and *glazes* in oil paint. Opaque color can be rubbed or dragged loosely over previous colors to modify them without obscuring them, a process called *scumbling.* Paint applied very thickly is called *impasto.*

TEMPERA PAINTING

In *tempera* painting, the binder is an emulsion (a mixture of oil and water) that may include casein, glue, gum, egg, or egg and oil. The advantages of tempera are its quick drying ability, its potential for precise detail, its resistance to yellowing and darkening with age, its relative insolubility when dry, and—for some types of tempera—the convenience of taking a water thinner. The disadvantages are the brittleness of some tempera formulas, the difficulty in blending it smoothly, some change in color and value as it dries, and the impossibility of creating impasto textures.

WATERCOLOR PAINTING

The binder in watercolor is an aqueous solution of gum. For whites, transparent watercolor depends on the whiteness of the paper, and colors are lightened by thinning with water. The quality of the paper is very important because yellowing can spoil the colors as well as the whites. Advantages of watercolor are the cheapness and lightness of the materials, the quickness with which large areas can be covered with washes, the rapid drying time, and the lively sparkle of transparent washes over the white ground. Disadvantages of transparent watercolor are the difficulty of correction, the change in value during drying, and the necessity of working from light to dark. Opaque watercolor, or *gouache,* sacrifices transparency and quick washes for greater ease of correction and the possibility of using light colors over dark ones.

OIL PAINTING

The most common binder in oil paints is linseed oil. Most supports (wood, canvas, or synthetic materials) require a ground of oil or synthetic primer. For glazing purposes, complex thinning mixtures are used to increase transparency, to add flexibility, or to speed drying. The advantages of oil paint are its permanence and durability, its range of textural effects from light scumble to heavy impasto, the ease with which it can be manipulated and corrected, and the fact that colors do not change in drying.

FRESCO PAINTING

True fresco, or *buon fresco*, is done with pigments combined with just a water "binder." The ground is wet lime plaster, usually on a wall. The paint becomes part of the ground and is very permanent. The mat, or dull, surface of fresco allows the painting to be seen easily from all angles without disturbing reflections. *Fresco-secco* is painting on a dry plaster surface, and a variety of media—tempera is common—may be used.

ENCAUSTIC PAINTING

The binder used in *encaustic* painting is refined beeswax with additives. Paints are mixed on a heated *palette* (mixing surface) and applied quickly to a rigid surface, usually a wood panel; in classical antiquity, encaustic was sometimes used on sculpture. A heat source (today, an electric coil) is then passed over the surface to "burn in " the wax. The inconvenience of heating is compensated for by the extraordinary range of effects from transparency to impasto, the quick drying time, and the permanence of the colors.

OTHER MEDIA

Casein paints, with a casein glue binder, harden to a water-resistant but brittle surface, requiring a rigid support. They have the conveniences of taking a water thinner, drying rapidly, and producing a mat finish, which does not create annoying light reflections as does a shiny surface. Modern science has developed synthetic binders such as acrylic resin and polyvinyl acetate that are also fast-drying and have a mat finish. With some such paints, water can be used for thinning and the dried surface is water-resistant. Heavy impasto is not possible with many of these paints unless they are combined with pastes or paints that have been specifically developed for impasto effects.

Stained Glass

Designs or pictures in colored translucent glass became especially important in the Medieval period. The basic color of each piece of glass came from chemicals, mainly metallic oxides, added in a molten state. The glass was blown to produce sheets from which pieces were cut for the design. Details were painted on the surface with a mixture of powdered glass and lead or iron oxides and fused by firing (see Fig. 13-26).

Sculpture

Sculpture may be freestanding or in relief (projecting from a background). Relief sculpture may be *high relief*, such as Ghiberti's *Sacrifice of Isaac* (Fig. 14-17), with high projections from its background, or *low relief*, with forms projecting only slightly.

MODELING AND CASTING

Modeling is an additive process of building up a sculpture from plastic material such as clay or wax. A wire, pipe, or wood *armature* (frame) can be used inside the work to prevent sagging (Fig. 4-5). No tools are necessary for modeling, although wooden spatulas with wire loops at one end are convenient for shaping and cutting. For permanence, natural clay can be *fired* (baked) in a *kiln* (oven), but it then cannot contain an armature, since shrinkage of the clay during firing would cause cracking, nor can it be of vastly different thicknesses. *Ceramic glazes* (a fine clay or glass coating) may be fired on the clay work, making possible a variety of textures and transparent or opaque colors. All fired clay may be called *terra cotta*, but the term refers more precisely to a brown-red unglazed clay.

Another way that clay sculpture may be given permanence is to cast it in plaster. A plaster mold is made while the clay is still wet. The mold is removed and oiled, soaped, or treated in some other way so that new plaster will not stick to it. After the mold has been reassembled and sealed, it is filled with plaster. Small sculptures may be cast solid; larger ones should be hollow. After the plaster has set, the mold is pulled or chipped away. This type of mold is called a *waste mold* because it is usually destroyed to free the cast within; for more than one cast a rubber or gelatin mold

4-5 An armature.

may be used. Plaster may be colored to make it resemble metal or stone.

Both cast plaster and fired clay are breakable; for the greatest permanence in sculpture, the traditional materials are stone and bronze. In the *sand mold* process of bronze casting, *French sand* (a mixture of clay, silica, and alumina) is pressed around a plaster cast of the work to form a mold. The parts of the sand mold are fitted into a *flask* (iron holder), and a core of French sand is made to fill the sand mold except for a one-eighth to one-quarter inch air space all the way around. The core is suspended inside the sand mold and flask by metal rods. Holes are made in the mold so that air can escape as molten bronze is poured into the air space between the core and mold. After the bronze has cooled, the mold is removed and the core is dug out. The hollow bronze cast needs much cleaning up before special workers (*patineurs*) can give the cast its *patina* (color) by acid baths and heat treatment. In the *lost wax* (*cire perdue*) method of bronze casting, the following procedure is one of several that may be used. A gelatin mold and a plaster shell to support it are made from the sculptor's plaster cast of the original clay work. On the inside of the gelatin mold, layers of wax are built up to the desired thickness of the bronze. The gelatin is removed, and the hollow wax replica is filled with a

4-6
THEODORE ROSZAK, *Whaler of Nantucket*, 1952. Steel, approx. 3' x 4'. Edward A. Ayer Collection, Art Institute of Chicago.

core of heat-resistant material. This material is also used to form a mold around the outside of the wax. Metal rods hold the core inside the mold, and vents are made in the mold to allow the melted wax to drain away when the assembly is heated. The air space left between the core and the mold by the removal of the wax is filled with bronze. The mold and core are taken away, and the finishing process begins.

Today the sculptor may do *direct sand casting* by working negatively, that is, creating the mold directly in a special sand mixture. Iron and aluminum are frequently used for the cast.

Another material common today is *cast stone*. A heavy reinforced plaster or gelatin mold is made from the original clay work, and a mixture of stone dust, pigment, sand, and cement is poured or packed into the mold. Sometimes an armature is included to reinforce the cement. After several days of drying, the mold is pulled or chipped away, and the cast can be finished by filing or carving.

CARVING

The carver must have foresight, since the subtractive process does not allow for addition if too much is cut away. The most common materials, stone and wood, have different kinds of textures and grains that have aesthetic potential for the sculptor. The stone carver uses hammers, picks, drills, and toothed chisels to rough out the form. Chisels and abrasives are used for finishing. The wood carver works with chisels, gouges, files, and sandpaper. Frequently the sculptor does the final work from a smaller preliminary model. A *pointing machine* may be used to transfer the proportions of the model to a larger block.

CONSTRUCTION

Constructed sculpture, of which Gabo's *Linear Construction* (Fig. 19-32) and Roszak's *Whaler of Nantucket* (Fig. 4-6) are examples, has become increasingly important during the twentieth century. The sculptor uses any materials or ready-made objects to build his composition, often soldering or welding them. The strength of metals and plastics has made possible very open forms. Different colors are obtained by the use of different metals, by painting, or by controlled oxidation. *Kinetic sculpture*, or mobile sculpture, utilizes air currents or motors to bring actual movement into the composition.

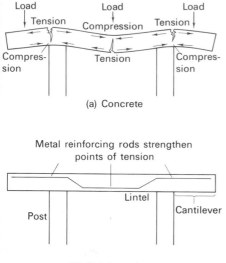

Load — Tension — Load — Compression — Load — Tension

Compression — Tension — Compression

(a) Concrete

Metal reinforcing rods strengthen points of tension

Lintel

Post

Cantilever

(b) Reinforced concrete

4-7 Post and lintel construction.

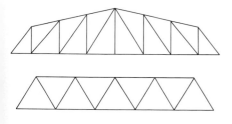

4-8 Trusses.

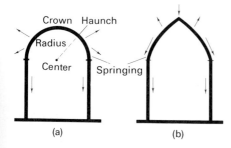

Crown — Haunch

Radius

Center — Springing

(a)   (b)

4-9 The dynamics of arches.

Architecture

The basic diagrams of architectural design are *perspective views, plans,* and *elevations.* A perspective view shows how the building will appear in three dimensions. A plan shows the two-dimensional distribution of interior spaces, walls, windows, and doors. An elevation shows the side of a room or a building without perspective distortion. Other kinds of diagrams, such as *cross sections, longitudinal sections,* and *orthographic projections* are also used to clarify spatial and structural relationships in architecture.

Traditional architectural materials are wood, mud brick, plaster, concrete, stucco, and masonry of stone or fired brick. More recent materials are iron, steel, aluminum, glass, reinforced concrete (ferroconcrete), plywood, and plastics. The strength of reinforced concrete has made it possible for floors, roofs, or ramps to twist, turn, and thrust out into space with very few points of support. Prestressed concrete is particularly strong; here the concrete is allowed to harden around stretched steel cables, or cables are run through the concrete in tubes and anchored under tension at each end. The result is a built-in compression that offsets the weakness of concrete under tension.

POST AND LINTEL

The simplest type of structure is post and lintel, a combination of uprights (*posts*) supporting a crosspiece (*lintel*). Columns, such as those of the Parthenon (Fig. 9-10), often serve as posts. The span between posts is severely limited by the strength of the material in the lintel. In the twentieth century, steel, reinforced concrete, and prestressed concrete have made possible very wide spans (Fig. 4-7). A lintel that extends beyond its supports (Fig. 4-7b) is called a *cantilever.* Lintels are frequently made in the form of *trusses,* very strong but light frameworks made of small pieces fastened together in such a way that they brace each other (Fig. 4-8). Special strength is provided by the perfect rigidity of a triangle.

ARCH

An arch diverts the load—the weight sustained—to the sides as well as down toward the vertical, making possible wider spans than does a post and lintel system in the same material; the arrows in Figure 4-9 show the forces exerted by weight and the tendencies of the

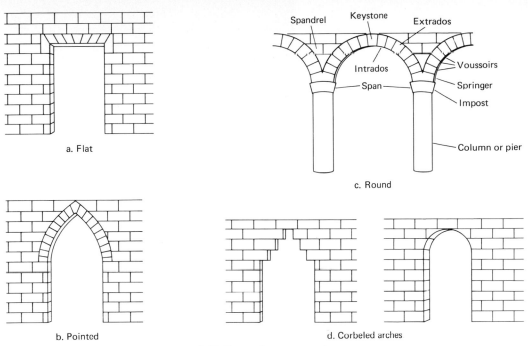

a. Flat

Spandrel · Keystone · Extrados

Intrados

Span

Voussoirs

Springer

Impost

Column or pier

c. Round

b. Pointed

d. Corbeled arches

4-10 Types of masonry arches.

arch to fall in and the walls to buckle out. Until the nineteenth century and the development of steel and ferroconcrete, the most common arch was the masonry arch, a structure of wedge shaped blocks spanning an opening. True arches have several forms. One, the flat masonry arch (Fig. 4-10a), resembles the post and lintel. The steep sides of a pointed arch divert the load more directly toward the ground (Fig. 4-10b) and require less outside *buttressing* (bracing) than the round arch (Fig. 4-10c). A *corbeled arch* (Fig. 4-10d) is not a true masonry arch; it sacrifices strength to avoid the more precise cutting required in the wedge-shaped blocks of the true arch (Fig. 4-10a, b, c). A masonry arch is supported during the course of its construction by a wooden scaffolding called *centering*.

VAULT AND DOME

Vaulting is arched roofing of stone, brick, or concrete. The *tunnel, barrel,* or *wagon vault* is an extension of a round arch (Fig. 4-11). It requires continuous buttressing along the sides. In Medieval masonry, the common solution to the buttressing problem was thick walls. Windows were infrequent and kept below the level of the *springing* (the beginning of the curve of the arch) to avoid weakening the vault (Fig. 4-12). The inte-

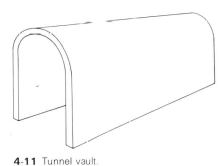

4-11 Tunnel vault.

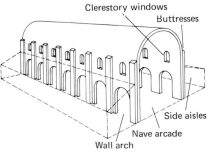

Clerestory windows

Buttresses

Side aisles

Nave arcade

Wall arch

4-12 Tunnel vault on a Romanesque church.

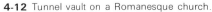

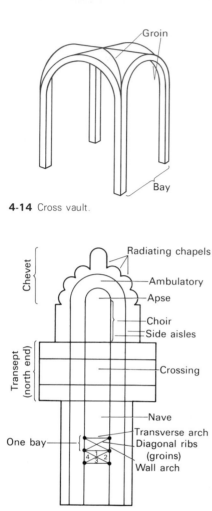

4-14 Cross vault.

4-15 Robert De Luzarches, plan of Amiens Cathedral.

Labels in 4-15: Radiating chapels, Ambulatory, Apse, Choir, Side aisles, Crossing, Nave, Transverse arch, Diagonal ribs (groins), Wall arch, One bay, Chevet, Transept (north end)

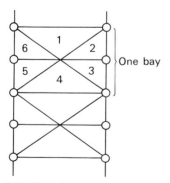

4-16 Plan of a sexpartite vault.

Labels in 4-16: One bay

4-13 Interior of St. Sernin, Toulouse, France.

rior view of St. Sernin (Fig. 4-13) shows how Medieval vaults were often divided into *bays* (sections) by *transverse arches* (arches at right angles to the length of the vault that have the appearance and sometimes the function of reinforcements). The bay division was often continued all the way down to the floor by *engaged columns* (columns partially buried in the wall). In Medieval architecture, vaulting is so important that it is often indicated on floor plans. The plan of St. Sernin (Fig. 13-10) shows the transverse arches in dotted lines.

Greater strength and flexibility are obtained if two vaults are crossed at right angles (Fig. 4-14). The *cross vault*, or *groin vault*, focuses the load on four legs and allows the sides to be opened up. The exterior indentations where the vaults meet are the *groins*. On the interior the groins project as ridges. From directly above or below, the groins form an X-shape between the transverse arches and are so indicated on the plans (Fig. 4-15). When the groins are emphasized by moldings or *ribs* on the interior, the vault is called a *ribbed cross vault*, a series of which can be seen over the nave of Amiens Cathedral (Fig. 13-30). It is thought that in Medieval architecture the ribs were often built first, as a skeleton to shape the vault, and panels of stone were filled in between ribs and side arches. Since the X formed by the ribs divides the vault into four parts, it is called a four-part, or *quadripartite*, vault. Sometimes an additional transverse arch was added in the center of the X, creating a six-part, or *sexpartite*, ribbed cross vault (Fig. 4-16). Figure 4-14 shows the intersecting tunnel vaults, wherein the height of the arches and the ribs is kept level. Semicircular ribs, however, would create a domical form (Fig. 4-17) since the ribs have a much longer diameter than that of the wall arches. The level *crowns* (tops) of the vaults in Figures 4-14 and 4-17b are made possible by depressing the ribs to less than semicircles, but depressed arches are weaker than semicircular ones. A level effect can be achieved without sacrificing strength if the principle of the pointed arch is applied to the vaulting. The pointed ribs and arches are easily adjusted to different heights by varying the degree of pointedness (Fig. 4-17c), as was done at Amiens Cathedral (Fig. 13-30). The pointed ribbed cross vault, like the pointed arch, can be built higher with less buttressing. As the height of Medieval vaults increased, *flying buttresses* (arched segments carrying the thrust from vaults to vertical buttresses) were developed to help bear the load by transferring the thrust of the vaults to buttresses along the outer walls (Fig. 4-18).

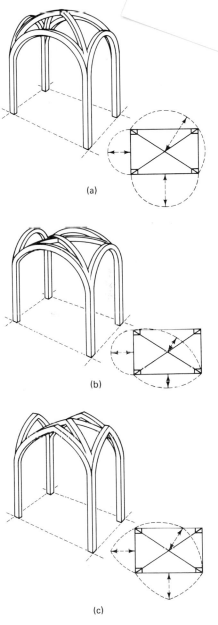

(a)

(b)

(c)

4-17 Ribbed cross vaults.

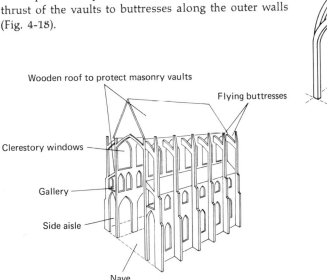

Wooden roof to protect masonry vaults

Flying buttresses

Clerestory windows

Gallery

Side aisle

Nave

4-18 Section of a Gothic cathedral.

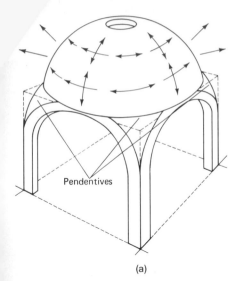

Pendentives

(a)

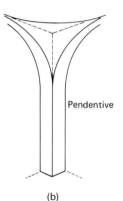

Pendentive

(b)

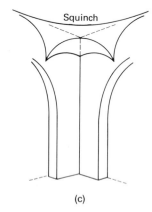

Squinch

(c)

4-19 The dome and its supports.

Domes may be hemispherical, less than hemispherical (like the depressed arch), or pointed. The problem of buttressing varies accordingly. To hold in the outward buckling tendency, large domes may be made of massive thickness or have circling bands of chain or wood buried in the masonry or concrete (modern domes may be made of ferroconcrete). Unlike the arch, the dome is not weakened by an opening in the crown, because the inward leaning only wedges the circular form more tightly together, and the load forces pushing inward are converted to an outward buckling tendency (Fig. 4-19a). Openings in the sides of a dome, however, tend to destroy the circular system of self-support and require special buttressing. The use of a dome over a square room requires a transition to the round base of the dome. Two solutions have been widely used: the *pendentive* and the *squinch*. The pendentive cuts off or fills in the corners of the square with curved triangular fillets (Fig. 4-19b). The squinch provides a more abrupt transition by arching over the corners to form an octagonal base, which is easily accommodated to the circular dome (Fig. 4-19c).

Two of the more striking forms developed in recent years are the *geodesic dome* and the *hyperbolic paraboloid.* The geodesic dome utilizes the geometry of the tetrahedron to create a light structure of enormous strength (Fig. 4-20). Buoyant spacious effects are possible with the hyperbolic paraboloid, where straight members can be used to construct a curved surface of great strength (Fig. 4-21).

4-20 Geodesic dome.

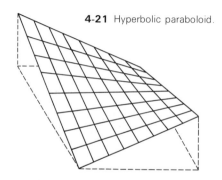

4-21 Hyperbolic paraboloid.

Suggestions for Further Study

DRAWING

Collier, Graham. *Form, Space, and Vision: Discovering Design Through Drawing.* Englewood Cliffs, N.J.: Prentice-Hall, 1963.

Kaupelis, Robert. *Learning to Draw: A Creative Approach to Expressive Drawing.* New York: Watson-Guptill, 1966.

Moskowitz, Ira, ed. *Great Drawings of All Time.* 4 vols. New York: Shorewood, 1962.

Nicolaïdes, Kimon. *The Natural Way to Draw.* Boston: Houghton Mifflin, 1941.

PRINTMAKING

Biegeleisen, J. I., and M. A. Cohn. *Silk Screen Techniques.* New York: Dover, 1958.

Brunsdon, John. *The Technique of Etching and Engraving.* London: Batsford; New York: Reinhold, 1965.

Hayter, S. W. *About Prints.* London: Oxford University Press, 1962.

Heller, Jules. *Printmaking Today: An Introduction to the Graphic Arts.* New York: Holt, Rinehart and Winston, 1958.

Ivins, William M., Jr. *How Prints Look: Photographs with a Commentary.* Boston: Beacon Press, 1958.

PAINTING

Doerner, Max. *The Materials of the Artist and Their Use in Painting,* rev. ed. Translated by Eugen Neuhaus. New York: Harcourt Brace Jovanovich, 1949.

Mayer, Ralph. *The Artist's Handbook of Materials and Techniques,* rev. ed. New York: Viking Press, 1957.

SCULPTURE

Clarke, Geoffrey, and Stroud Cornock. *A Sculptor's Manual.* London: Studio Vista; New York: Reinhold, 1968.

Gross, Chaim. *The Techniques of Wood Sculpture.* New York: Arco, 1965.

Hale, Nathan Cabot. *Welded Sculpture.* New York: Watson-Guptill, 1968.

Lynch, John. *Metal Sculpture: New Forms, New Techniques.* New York: Viking Press, 1957.

Norman, P. Edward. *Sculpture in Wood.* New York: Transatlantic Arts, 1966.

Rich, J. C. *The Materials and Methods of Sculpture.* New York: Oxford University Press, 1947.

ARCHITECTURE

Collins, Peter. *Concrete: The Vision of a New Architecture.* London: Faber & Faber, 1959.

Giedion, Sigfried. *Space, Time, and Architecture,* 4th ed. Cambridge, Mass.: Harvard University Press, 1962.

Gropius, Walter. *Scope of Total Architecture* (World Perspectives, Vol. 3). Edited by Ruth N. Anshen. New York: Harper & Row, 1955.

Hamlin, Talbot. *Forms and Functions of Twentieth-Century Architecture.* 4 vols. New York: Columbia University Press, 1952.

Wright, Frank Lloyd. *Frank Lloyd Wright: Writings and Buildings.* Edited by Edgar Kaufmann and Ben Raeburn. New York: Meridian Books, 1960.

Musical Form

Musical Design, Form, and Composition Techniques

Form in a piece of music refers to those qualities that give the piece coherence and cause us to perceive it as a unified whole. It is the result of the organization of all musical factors at all levels, especially in terms of the overall structure. A work of art is always more than the sum of its parts, and the essense of a piece of music is the interrelationships of the sound materials, acting in time as an organically coherent whole; in other words, its form.

Loudness, timbre, melody, texture, and tonality all help to create form, but our perception of musical form ultimately depends on our memory, since the musical events take place within a time continuum. We compare what we hear at one time with what we hear at another, and we are led to expect certain sound possibilities yet to come; thus, proper timing is the very essence of musical form.

MEANS OF FORMAL DESIGN

Musical form results from the organization or design of the elements of time and sound. One of the simplest ways to create form is to control the ebb and flow of sounds, thereby producing a sense of an overall "shape" to the piece. Any and all elements of the music can contribute to the level of musical energy by the amount of physical sound energy present, by the complexity of the musical ideas to be perceived, and, especially, by creating in the listener the anticipation of events. All of this is inexorably bound up with the way the music creates an awareness of time in the listener.

Another formal technique of musical design, common to much of the music in Western culture, is the repetition or return of the familiar, combined with contrasting elements. The form in some pieces may consist of simple patterns of repetition, contrast, and return within the motives or phrases of the melody. In larger forms, repetition and contrast usually pervade all elements of the music, but the overall formal organization generally focuses on one element. In much of the music written between 1650 and 1900, and especially during the eighteenth century, this element is tonality. The tonal center unifies, and departures from it provide variety, while the melodies, rhythms, and variations in loudness and timbre all act together with the manipulation of tonality to produce an integrated form.

In some twentieth century music the organization of pitches may not produce tonality and directed motion, and continuity may result from the way successive rhythms or timbres relate to each other. Some recent composers have even challenged the aesthetic necessity of continuity and controlled succession, leaving much of what happens to chance.

When musical form is created by the simple alternation of different musical ideas, the tendency is to produce a sequence of parts or sections—*sectional addition*; however, continuity often is effected in a large portion of a piece through the growth and development of musical ideas—*continuous expansion*. Either process may dominate the formal design of a piece of music, though both usually are evident to some extent.

Sometimes the structure and sequence of events in a piece of music are determined by nonmusical considerations, such as a text, a visual film sequence, or a dance (though, more often, the music determines the structure of a dance). In program music, the formal design is expected to be in some way analogous to the ideas, events, or poetic symbols expressed in the printed program, which may help the listener to follow the structure and form of the music. Or, the musical design may help to "depict" or "express" the content of the program.

In spite of its programmatic aspects (see pp. 62–63), Debussy's *Prelude to the Afternoon of a Faun* (Ex. 3) displays considerable formal interest. Continuity and connected movement are created by the repetition of motives, the succession of ideas, subtle shadings of timbre, and changes in density. There is some expansion and growth of the opening flute melody, but motivic development is minimal. This melody reappears several times, and there are other contrasting melodic ideas and fragments. Also, in spite of the vague sense of tonality, there are some definite cadences, which help to delineate stages in the formal process. Essentially, the music unfolds through continuous expansion; however, the last part of the piece is related to the first by the return of the opening flute melody.

COMMON MUSICAL FORMS

Certain kinds of formal structure have been employed so frequently by composers that we can regard them as common, or "standard" forms. Some of these are limited to particular kinds of music, while others have been used more widely. The simpler, shorter forms usually

4-22 Young musicians rehearsing.

are created by sectional addition, while the longer, more complex forms generally require the techniques of expansion and development to give them continuity.

One of the simplest sectional designs is the *three-part form*. This form results when an initial section, A, returns following an intervening, contrasting section, B, comprising an A–B–A scheme. The source of contrast in the B section may be any one or more aspects of the music, such as different melodies, textures, harmonies, or instruments.

Other simple uses of sectional addition include recurring refrains, alternating or repeated phrases, and *strophic* songs, where the separate stanzas of a poem are set to the same melody.

The three-part form can be expanded symmetrically by adding material or sections that return in reverse order, such as A–B–C–B–A or A–B–C–D–C–B–A. In a similar procedure called *rondo*, the opening material returns periodically as a refrain, which alternates with contrasting material. This may result in a scheme such as A–B–A–C–A, but most rondos have the symmetrical structure A–B–A–C–A–B–A.

Contrast produced through changes of the tonal center (modulation) usually results in a continuous process with great potential for expansion. At its simplest, the tonal design may consist of a movement away from the tonic to a cadence in a contrasting key, then a return and a cadence in the original key, comprising a two-way tonal movement. Such a structure is called a *two-part* form. Although both parts often are repeated, neither one constitutes a complete section, since the second part must finish the tonal movement commenced by the first part. As a result, the two-part form is a continuous and unified structure.

Each of the separate movements in Bach's Minuet, Trio I, Polacca, and Trio II from the first Brandenburg Concerto (Ex. 2) is a two-part form (see the discussion of tonality and modulation in this work on pp. 52–53). The additive principal also applies to the order of the movements, with the Minuet beginning and ending the set and returning after each of the other movements.

Composers in the eighteenth century developed a major expansion of the two-part form, called *sonata form*, which has proven to be one of the most cohesive of all musical designs and is susceptible of almost limitless extension. It has been utilized often as a structural procedure during the last two hundred years.

Bartók's *Music for Strings, Percussion, and Celesta*, first movement (Ex. 5) unfolds through continuous expansion based on the textural and harmonic potential of the opening melody (the fugue subject). The piece is constructed in one continuous shape, in which textural density and loudness gradually increase to a central peak, then slowly subside. The unique pitch relations in the piece also contribute to its structure. The fugue subject exploits all of the half tones within a narrow range of about half an octave. It enters alternately above and below the starting pitch, first successively, then in stretto. The range of pitches broadens so that as more lines are added to the texture, the pitch combinations become increasingly dissonant. At the central climax the violins and violas play a single tone, exactly half an octave from the starting pitch, in stark contrast to the dense texture immediately preceding. The tonal processes of the first part are reversed in the latter part. This is underlined by inversions of the subject. As the piece ends, a fragment of the subject sounds simultaneously with its own inversion, moving out a half an octave in both directions and returning to the beginning tone. This final phrase sums up the symmetrical half octaves out of which the form of the piece grows.

VARIATIONS ON A THEME

The modification of ideas is one of the most frequent formal processes in music. It provides a means for expanding and developing ideas without destroying their identity. This process is usually called *variation*, and its uses range from the creation of a melody by varied repetitions of a motive to the design of large musical structures.

Often a basic musical idea, or "theme," goes through a series of modified repetitions, or "variations," a formal procedure called *theme and variations*. The theme may range from a short musical idea to a complete unit, which could stand alone as an independent piece. In the latter case, the word *theme* refers to the structure of the entire unit, including its melody, rhythm, harmony, timbres, and form. Any one or combination of these may be retained intact, or at least remain recognizable, while others are modified or completely altered in the variations. As a formal procedure, theme and variations can sustain interest particularly well because it presents repetition and contrast both simultaneously and periodically.

Generally, when the theme itself is a complete unit, each variation is an equivalent unit, and the successive variations are separated by cadences and complete breaks in the music. This procedure, called *sectional variations*, is the usual structure of pieces called "Themes and Variations," or "Variations on a Theme." When the theme is only a short idea, however, it usually is repeated continuously, and the music unfolds without pauses or breaks. Structures of this type are called *continuous variations*. Composers do not always restrict themselves to one variation technique, but may employ several within the same composition.

In strict sectional variations, the form of the theme, including its harmonic structure and usually its length, are retained in the variations, while other elements are subject to modification. A well-known type of sectional

4-23
The guitar is one of the most popular instruments today.

4-24
JEAN AUGUSTE DOMINIC INGRES.
Paganini, 1819. Drawing, approx. 12″ x 8″
Louvre, Paris. Paganini was a famous violin
soloist. Many of his compositions were
themes and variations, which showed off his
playing ability.

variation is the classical structure of jazz, where the soloists improvise variations against the form, length, and chord changes of a popular song or blues melody.

In continuous variations the unifying theme usually is a short melody or a series of harmonies designed to be repeated in a continuous cycle. A melodic fragment or phrase repeated persistently and unchanged is called an *ostinato.* Ostinatos are particularly effective for measuring off a repeated time frame.

When the theme is a repeated melody, it is most likely to appear as the bass, or lowest part, since in this way it also strongly affects the harmonies; however, such repeated melodies also appear in other parts. When it is restricted to the bass part, such a theme is called a *ground bass.* Ground basses that are repeated exactly are ostinatos, but this is not always the case.

Although the mere succession of variants may suffice to unify a piece, composers usually arrange the structure and succession of variations in relation to each other in an overall plan, such as a gradual rise or fall in the level of activity from one variation to the next. It is a common practice to restate the original theme after the last variation.

Beethoven's Seventh Symphony, second movement (Ex. 1) begins as a set of strict sectional variations and then alternates sectional and continuous techniques. The opening three-phrase group (A–B–B) is the theme, and the three repetitions that follow are strict sectional variations. The next part is a free, or continuous, variation in the contrasting major mode, unified by a bass tone repeated in a *long*-short-short pattern reminiscent of the theme. A short connecting passage leads back to a new sectional variant of the theme, with the original melody now in the bass parts. Shorter connecting material leads into the *fugato* passage—a free variant of the original melody, which reaches a climax on a restatement by the full orchestra of the first phrase, A, of the theme. The second part (the major mode played over repeated bass tone) returns, followed by a final statement of the theme, heard in fragments scattered throughout the orchestra. The wind instruments end the piece with the same sustained chord with which they began it.

Formal Scheme of Beethoven's Seventh Symphony, Second Movement

(Sustained chord, wind instruments)
Theme (A–B–B)
Variations 1, 2, 3 (sectional)
Variation 4 (continuous, over repeated bass tone)
Variation 5 (sectional)
Variation 6 (continuous, *fugato*)
Variation 7 (sectional, first phrase only)
Variation 8 (continuous; return of Variation 4)
Variation 9 (sectional)
(Sustained chord, same as beginning)

The sectional variants act as unifying refrains, the free variants provide diversity and contrast, and the chord that opens and closes the piece adds a feeling of

4-25

GERALD TER BORCH, *The Suitor's Visit,*
c. 1658. 31½'' x 29⅝''. National Gallery of Art, Washington, D.C. Andrew Mellon Collection. Music was a popular form of entertainment in the home during the seventeenth century.

overall symmetry. There is continuity in the total design, and there is both order and variety at all levels.

Musical Composition

To "compose" means to form or organize something by putting together various elements or parts. Composers of music organize sounds and silences in sequences, durations, and combinations. The creation of musical works involves three phases: initial conception, composition, and realization. A composer may begin with a subjective experience that he or she wishes to translate into music; he or she can also begin with a formal idea (a melody, motive, rhythm pattern, organizing principle, or performance situation). Once the initial idea is conceived, the composer must decide on the best medium for the realization of his or her conception. Before starting the actual composition, the composer decides on the formal structure, length, and technical demands of the work.

As the work proceeds, the composer constantly makes decisions as to how to present and develop ideas, whether to add new ideas, what to keep, and what to change or discard, always striving for a coherent formal design. Much of this proceeds by trial and error, with the judgments made according to the composer's original intentions, but finally tempered by an intuitive sense of what is aesthetically "right."

A composition is realized when the composers' ideas are translated into sound. If composers must rely on others to perform their works, they must communicate their intentions accurately. This usually is done through a set of written instructions for performing the piece, called a *musical score.* Many composers specify in great detail how they want their music performed, while others prefer to give few instructions, so as to encourage freedom of interpretation by the performers. In some types of music the performers are, in effect, composers, improvising as they perform; while at the other extreme, some music is now being synthesized electronically, so that the composer can bypass the performer altogether and largely determine how the music will be realized.

In the recent past, composers of Western music worked within generally accepted aesthetic conventions, which allowed them freedom to make certain kinds of intuitive choices and also left some freedom of interpretation to the performer. For most present-day

4-26

Changes and deletions from the original score of Beethoven's *Moonlight Sonata,* first movement.

composers these conventions have been challenged and greatly extended. Decisions about how a piece will finally sound may be made prior to or during composition or during performance. These decisions may all be made by the composer or they may be made partly by the performer, and they may be made intuitively, by some arbitrary formula, or even by chance. Many composers today regard music as a process of working out the possibilities inherent in a given set of materials, so that each piece becomes a unique creation.

Berio conceived his *Sinfonia,* Section I (Ex. 3) as an abstract structure of time and sounds whose form derives from the nature of the materials. He chose a medium of eight voices and an orchestra, and he concentrated on the effects produced by various mixtures of fragmentary vocal sounds. By breaking down verbal structures into their components (phonemes, syllables, and random words) he destroyed the symbolic meaning of the language used, while at the same time he freed listeners to form their own private associations, triggered by the verbal sounds. Berio most likely developed his musical ideas intuitively, since no predetermined "system" is evident, but he expressed his intentions precisely in the score. The formal process is essentially continuous, with the events following each other according to their own logic. Distinct phrases or sections are discernible, created by the gong that opens and closes the first section as well as the whole piece, by the use of instruments alone in the last part, and by silences that serve to bracket the sections.

Suggestions for Further Study

Copland, Aaron. *Music and Imagination* (Charles Eliot Norton Lectures: 1951–1952). Cambridge, Mass.: Harvard University Press, 1952.

Green, Douglass M. *Form in Tonal Music: An Introduction to Analysis.* New York: Holt, Rinehart and Winston, 1965.

Hindemith, Paul. *A Composer's World: Horizons and Limitations* (Charles Eliot Norton Lectures: 1949–1950). Cambridge, Mass.: Harvard University Press, 1952.

Leichtentritt, Hugo. *Musical Form.* Cambridge, Mass.: Harvard University Press, 1951.

Stein, Leon. *Structure and Style: The Study and Analysis of Musical Forms.* Evanston, Ill.: Summy-Birchard, 1962.

Stravinsky, Igor. *Poetics of Music in the Form of Six Lessons* (Charles Eliot Norton Lectures: 1939–1940). Translated by Arthur Knodell and Ingolf Dahl. Preface by George Seferis. Cambridge, Mass.: Harvard University Press, 1970.

Tovey, Sir Donald Francis. *The Forms of Music.* Preface by Hubert J. Foss. New York: Meridian, 1956.

Suggestions for Further Listening

Bartók, Belá. Second movement from *Concerto for Orchestra.* (Three-part form, based on contrast of timbres.)

Brahms, Johannes. *Variations on a Theme by Joseph Haydn.* Op. 56a. (Sectional variations on binary theme, continuous variations on repeated melody.)

Coleman Hawkins Quartet. *The Man I Love* (The Smithsonian Collection of Classical Jazz). Washington, D.C.: The Smithsonian Institution; distributed by W. W. Norton, New York. (Improvised sectional variations.)

Hubbard, Freddie. "Delphia," from *Red Clay.* (Improvised sectional variations.)

Mozart, Wolfgang Amadeus. First and second movements from Symphony No. 40. (First movement: sonata form, motivic development; second movement: three-part form as composite of two-part forms, sectional addition.)

Palestrina, Giovanni Pierluigi da. "Agnus Dei" from the *Pope Marcellus Mass* and Motet, *Sicut Cervus Desiderat.* (Continuous expansion.)

Chapter 5
Art and Music

Problems
of
Value
Judgment

Problems of Objectivity and Subjectivity

Value judgment in art and music involves factors of varying degrees of subjectivity. The most obvious objective factors seem to miss the point. Physical permanence—that is, the artist's skill in producing a work that does not deteriorate—can be measured easily but is of little value unless the art object is worth preserving; the same can be said of musical works that continue to be performed. Some objectivity is possible in measuring the artist's skill in depicting recognizable objects when doing so seems relevant to the work, but such mechanical aptitude alone does not guarantee significant content. We may judge with some objectivity the extent to which the artist or musician has exploited the expressive possibilities of his or her medium; yet the range of colors in a painting, the modulation of line in a drawing, the variety of texture and color in a work of architecture, or the selection of instruments in a piece of music may have been deliberately limited. Furthermore, limitations may have been imposed upon the artist or musician by his or her time and place. The artist of ancient Egypt did not have the technical knowledge available to the artist of the nineteenth century, but we do not assume that, for this reason, any work produced by a competent nineteenth-century artist is superior to the best work of the older culture. The quality of artistic achievement has not progressed in an ascending spiral as Western technology has. Clearly, quality means more than technical virtuosity. Art goes beyond the skillful description of facts and feelings to the more subtle and subjective realms of expression and evocation. In this realm the artist and musician require not just an imitative facility but a special sensitivity to the visual, tactile, and aural elements. He or she may also need sensitivity to human experience, a capacity for empathy, an agile imagination, and an understanding of the symbols and associations that will be meaningful to other people. Such things would be hard enough to measure even if they were not interpreted by individual observers and listeners, whose capacities to respond may vary widely.

Criteria of formal analysis produce varied judgments because the individual's sensitivity to the visual, tactile, and aural elements depends partly on the natural sensitivity of his or her sensory perceptions and partly on training. Variations among individuals may therefore lead to disagreement about the total effect of an artistic or musical work. The breadth of the observer's or listener's experience is important. A person accustomed only to the flowing harmonies of paintings like Raphael's *Madonna of the Meadow* (Fig. 3-1) might find the relative dissonance and liveliness of Picasso's *Three Musicians* (Plate 27) lacking in unity. The same might be said of the color harmonies in a comparison of Rembrandt and Matisse (Plates 11 and 25). A musical work such as Berio's *Sinfonia*, Section I (Ex. 4) will have little meaning to a listener accustomed only to the kinds of melody, harmony, and metrical rhythm that characterize Bach's Minuet, Trio I, Polacca, and Trio II from the first Brandenburg Concerto (Ex. 2). The observer's or listener's response also rests on his or her sensitivity and understanding of human experience. A child might respond with great sensitivity to Rubens' *Coup de Lance* (Fig. 1-23), but more mature experience would deepen the content for him or her. In the visual arts, the observer's response may be limited if he or she has no understanding of relevant iconography.

Because of the tremendous stylistic variety encountered in examining even one medium, such as oil painting or vocal music, and because of the many subjective factors we have described, the major problem in art and music criticism is to find measurable standards. Most critical statements can be subsumed under the broad demands for *unity, variety, intensity of experience,* and, in music, *control.* These are qualities we value because they enable us to experience life more completely by developing the sensitivity and subtlety of our perception, imagination, and understanding. Yet it is obvious that no fixed proportion of these qualities would make an ideal formula for more than one piece of music or art; nor is it easy to agree upon a measurement for such things in a given work of art or music.

Aesthetic Theories of Value Judgment

Aesthetics, the branch of philosophy that deals with the nature of beauty, has described many different attitudes toward value judgments. These attitudes, which may be conscious or unconscious, may be classed broadly in three overlapping areas.

OBJECTIVISM

The most extreme objective attitude assumes unchanging standards by which absolute judgments can be made for the art of any time and place. An example is the Neoclassic art theory of the eighteenth and nineteenth centuries, which held that the painting, sculpture, and architecture of any culture should be measured against Greek or Roman art. A comparable attitude about music held that correct harmonic, melodic, and rhythmic principles were derived from natural laws, which were propounded by the ancient Greeks. Such an attitude tends to reject the art of many cultures and to deny variability in concepts of aesthetic value. A more flexible objective position argues that such qualities as unity, variety, and intensity—developed in varying degrees and proportions according to the nature of the art object—give the object aesthetic value not only for its own culture but also for others. In musical aesthetics, objectivism of this kind usually concentrates on such factors as movement, tension, and repose, characteristics regarded as analogous to life experiences common to all people. The capacity of the observer or listener to judge will vary with his or her sensitivity and understanding, but value resides in the art object itself. Changes in the history of taste therefore do not prove changes in value, but only in preference, and preference is not the same as evaluation; a person may prefer one work to another but concede that the second has a higher aesthetic value.

SUBJECTIVISM

Subjective theories consider the judgment of art and music to be purely personal; each individual uses different criteria, and all criteria are equally valid. The aesthetic value of an art object rests not in the object but in the response of the observer or listener, who may grant or deny such value to any object.

RELATIVISM

Relativist views hold that value arises from an interaction between participant and art object. According to the relativist position, there are objective standards that can be valid for the members of a particular culture, but each culture forms its own standards. When judging art or music from another culture, an observer or listener should attempt to escape the prejudices of his or her own culture and judge the work on the basis of the criteria of the culture that produced it. Historical perspective or cultural differences may enable the outsider to comprehend the standards of a foreign culture more objectively than would its own members. Relativist views make value judgments between art objects from different cultures difficult or undesirable. One aspect of relativism is the attempt to understand the artist's or composer's intention and then to judge to what extent his or her aim was achieved. One may use *internal* evidence (evidence within the art object or other works by the same artist or composer) and *external* evidence (such as statements by the artist or composer about his or her own work). In this regard, many contemporary composers and artists attempt to make each of their works unique, so that even stylistic norms are not relevant criteria. It is conceivable that a work might have high aesthetic value even if the artist's or composer's intention was not fulfilled; conversely, if the intention was fulfilled, we are left with the need for a decision about the aesthetic value of the intent. Which is better, a superficial success or a magnificent failure?

Suggestions for Further Study

Babbitt, Milton. "Who Cares if You Listen?" *High Fidelity,* Vol. 8, No. 4 (February 1958), pp. 38–40 and 126–27.

Beardsley, Monroe C. *Aesthetics: Problems in the Philosophy of Criticism.* New York: Harcourt Brace Jovanovich, 1958.

———, and Herbert M. Schueller, eds. *Aesthetic Inquiry: Essays on Art Criticism and the Philosophy of Art.* Belmont, Calif.: Dickenson, 1967.

Bell, Clive. *Art.* New York: Putnam, 1958.

Berenson, Bernard. *Aesthetics and History.* Garden City, N.Y.: Doubleday, 1954.

Boas, George. *Wingless Pegasus. A Handbook for Critics.* Baltimore. The Johns Hopkins Press, 1950.

Fry, Roger. *Vision and Design.* New York: Meridian Books, 1956.

Graf, Max. *Composer and Critic: Two Hundred Years of Musical Criticism.* New York: Norton, 1971.

Heyl, Bernard. *New Bearings in Esthetics and Art Criticism.* London: Oxford University Press; New Haven, Conn.: Yale University Press, 1943.

Langer, Suzanne. *Feeling and Form: A Theory of Art.* New York: Scribner's, 1953.

Meyer, Leonard B. *Explaining Music: Essays and Explorations.* Berkeley: University of California Press, 1973.

Mitchell, Joyce. "Aesthetic Judgment in Music." *Journal of Aesthetics and Art Criticism,* Vol. 19, No. 1 (Fall 1960), pp. 73–82.

———. "Criteria of Criticism in Music." *Journal of Aesthetics and Art Criticism,* Vol. 21, No. 1 (Fall 1962), pp. 27–30.

Read, Herbert. *The Meaning of Art,* 6th rev. ed. Baltimore: Penguin Books, 1959.

Rosenberg, Jacob. *On Quality in Art: Criteria of Excellence, Past and Present* (Bollingen Series No. 35). Princeton, N.J.: Princeton University Press, 1967.

Rosenfeld, Paul. *Discoveries of a Music Critic.* New York: Vienna House, 1972.

Schoenberg, Arnold. *Style and Idea: Selected Writings of Arnold Schoenberg.* Edited by Leonard Stein. New York: St. Martins, 1975.

Slonimsky, Nicolas. *Lexicon of Musical Invective: Critical Assaults on Composers since Beethoven's Time,* 2nd ed. Seattle: University of Washington Press, 1969.

Walker, Alan. *An Anatomy of Musical Criticism.* Radnor, Pa.: Chilton, 1968.

Worringer, Wilhelm, *Abstraction and Empathy: A Contribution to the Psychology of Style.* Translated by Michael Bullock. London: Routledge & Kegan Paul, 1953.

Bison, from the cave at Altamira, Spain, *c.* 13,540 B.C. 8¼" long.

PART TWO
The History of Art and
Music in Western Culture

The beginnings of art and music precede written records. The most prolific time for prehistoric art seems to have been the LATE PALEOLITHIC *or* LATE OLD STONE AGE, *which lasted from approximately 30,000* B.C. *to 10,000* B.C. *Particularly in the period between 15,000* B.C. *and 10,000* B.C., *men painted and scratched animals, hunting scenes, and geometric designs on the walls of caves and rock shelters. The artist sometimes painted with charcoal and colored earths with a binder of animal grease and sometimes spread the grease on the wall and blew powdered colors against it from a hollow bone tube. Many cave paintings have been found in France and northern Spain; some of the most remarkable are in the caves of Altamira in Spain and Lascaux in France. In these works modulated contours and modeling in light and dark create the illusion of mass in the bodies of bison, horses, and cows. A keen understanding of anatomy is combined with a sensitive expression of an animal's speed, ferocity, or gentleness. Paleolithic artists did not include landscape backgrounds, and each image or group of images is an isolated scene rather than one episode within the time sequence of a story; human figures were shown infrequently and often simplified, with single lines for torso and* limbs. The frequent representation of animals pierced by arrows or spears, the casual overlapping of images, and the frequent location of paintings in almost inaccessible parts of caves all suggest that the making of pictures was a magic ritual to ensure success in the hunt. A purely aesthetic impulse might be evidenced by the geometric designs, but these too could have had magical properties. Paleolithic artists not only painted but also modeled in soft earth and carved bone, tusk, and antler. Here too, animals and the hunt were the preferred subjects, but we have found female statuettes that may have been intended to increase the fertility of the clan. Some of the characteristics of these paintings and carvings are found in the art of primitive cultures today.

While discoveries of prehistoric art were once difficult to authenticate, it is now possible to be more certain. One method used for dating objects relies on STRATIGRAPHY; an object is dated according to the age of the earth stratum in which it is found. A more precise method is that of CARBON 14 measurement. While it is living, each organic substance maintains a known amount of radioactive carbon 14. After the substance ceases to live, the carbon 14 begins to lose its radioactivity at a constant rate. Thus the amount of radioactivity allows us to determine the age of the organic substance.

We know from surviving musical instruments that music existed since prehistoric times, but because there is no way to recreate the music itself, we can only speculate as to its nature and uses. Music was undoubtedly a powerful source of magic, and it probably developed as an integral part of ritual, as is still true in many cultures. Musicians, dancers, and musical instruments are frequently depicted in ancient art, and music figures prominently in legends and sacred writings of the oldest civilizations. Musicians of Mesopotamian, Egyptian, and other Near Eastern cultures used mathematics to explain some basic properties of musical sounds. Music itself could not be preserved, however, until the relatively recent development of musical notation.

The concept of STYLE is fundamental to an understanding of art and music, for the subtle differences in style reveal changing ideas of the beautiful or the significant. Style is a characteristic manner of expression and the kind of content that goes with it. It exists on several levels. PERIOD STYLE is the composite of very general characteristics that may be common to much work at a given time or cultural phase. Sometimes, especially in the nineteenth and twentieth centuries, a number of contrasting stylistic tendencies exist simultaneously, making it difficult or misleading to speak of a period style. REGIONAL STYLE may be detected in the work of various artists and musicians working in the same country or area, if there has not been too much influence from other regions. INDIVIDUAL STYLE is seen in the work of a particular artist or musician, whose style may change several times in the course of his or her career.

Chapter 6 Art

Ancient Near Eastern Art:

4000–330 B.C.

Of all the ancient Near Eastern cultures, that of Egypt has been most excavated and is best known; yet recent discoveries suggest that the Tigris-Euphrates Valley, in Mesopotamia, was slightly ahead of Egypt in developing an urban society and a form of writing. Political instability, frequent warfare, a lack of natural boundaries, and a constant mixing of different peoples all complicate our efforts to understand this area.

For a short survey, the developments might be grouped into three successive and overlapping cultures: (1) Sumerian-Akkadian-Babylonian, from about 4000 to 1594 B.C. and 612 to 539 B.C. (Neo-Babylonian); (2) Assyrian, from about 900 to 612 B.C.; and (3) ancient Persian, from about 1000 to 330 B.C. This simplified classification neglects many cultural groups about which we presently know very little, such as the Hittites in Asia Minor, the Mitanni in northern Mesopotamia, and the Aramaeans and Phoenicians in northern Syria. Persian culture itself was so varied that, for the purposes of this introduction, we will consider only its culmination under the Achaemenian kings (550–330 B.C.), whose era ended with the Persian surrender to Alexander the Great.

The major Sumerian city-states, such as Uruk, Eridu, and Ur, were near the Tigris-Euphrates Delta on the Persian Gulf. Each city had its patron god (represented by the local king), in addition to a common pantheon of nature gods including Enlil, the storm god; Anu, the sky god; Ea, the water god; and Eanna, the Great Mother or Lady of Heaven, who was later known as Ishtar, goddess of love, fertility, and war. The temple was the religious and administrative center for each city-state, handling the distribution of labor and food. The Sumerians eventually came under the domination of a Semitic people from the north, the Akkadians, whose great leader, Sargon of Akkad (*c.* 2340–2305 B.C.), established a centralized government and the concept of a god-king as central ruler to whom local god-kings were subject. The Akkadians adopted much from Sumerian culture, including the Sumerian script in *cuneiform* (a form of writing employing different combinations of wedge shapes). The Akkadian control was broken by the Gutti people, who were, in turn, overthrown by Sumerians. The Neo-Sumerian period (2125–2025 B.C.) was particularly productive during the Third Dynasty of Ur. Invasions by Elamites and Amorites led to the collapse of central government and the rise of another era of independent city-states, the Isin-Larsa period (2025–1763 B.C.). Central control was revived during this period by Hammurabi of Babylon (1792–1750 B.C.). Despite these violent disruptions, there is a discernible cultural continuity.

As the Assyrian Empire expanded from Assur, Nimrud, and Nineveh (c. 1350–612 B.C.) to absorb Mesopotamia, Egypt, Asia Minor, and Persia, the Assyrians also adopted much from Sumerian culture, including a number of gods. The Assyrian state-god, Assur, is a version of Enlil. The Assyrians, however, unlike the Sumerians, thought of their gods as remote from man. Assyrian art shows no confrontation of god and man as it is portrayed in the earlier cultures. The history of Assyria is one of incessant war, and its art expresses an obsession with physical power.

The Persian Empire grew out of the conquest by the Medes of Nineveh in 612 B.C. and Babylon in 539 B.C. In 550 B.C., Cyrus, a Persian, became king of the Medes and Persians, two related tribes on the Iranian Plateau. From Persian centers at Pasargadae, Susa, Persepolis, and Babylon, expansion swallowed up Syria, Asia Minor, and Egypt. The religion of the Persians evolved from the worship of fire to the worship of Ahura Mazda, god of light. The Persian king was the earthly representative of the god. Impetus came from the religious teacher, Zoroaster.

Sumerian (c. 4000–2340 B.C.)
Akkadian (c. 2340–2180 B.C.)
Neo-Sumerian (2125–2025 B.C.)
Isin-Larsa, Babylonian (2025–1594 B.C.)
Neo-Babylonian (612–539 B.C.) *Periods*

ARCHITECTURE

Temples and palaces received greatest emphasis. Stone and timber were scarce in the south; the major building material was sun-dried mud brick, which accounts for the scarcity of ruins.

The exterior appearance of the buildings was that of a cubic, closed form. Mass, rather than space, was the major expressive element. Mud brick walls gained visual interest from the play of light and shadow over alternating niches and buttresses and from whitewash, relief sculpture, and color in the form of inset shells, colored stones, terra cotta cones, and glazed brick.

Imported wooden roof beams were covered with reed mats and earth. Arches were used in doorways, and corbeled stone vaults have been found in the royal tombs at Ur. Large brick *piers* (vertical supports, usually square in section and more massive than single columns) and occasional wooden columns provided interior supports.

The major temple was usually placed on a mound of earth, providing either token elevation or considerable height. While such mounds were produced automatically by repeated reconstruction of ancient mud brick cities (city mounds are called *tells*), it is probable that the temple mounds were deliberately constructed. Sumerian religious thought stressed the mountain as the home of the gods and as a link between the earthly and the divine. During the Neo-Sumerian period, the temple mounds evolved into *ziggurats* (Fig. 6-1). In addition to the elevated temples, there were, from the Neo-Sumerian period on, low temples without terraces but with impressive tower-flanked entrances.

Temple plans usually consisted of a rectangular *cella* (sacred room; plural, *cellae*) with a niche for a cult statue at one end, an offering table, and an entrance at one side. There was a long-lasting tendency to use a *bent-axis* approach to important spaces: Doors were set off, and entries required one or more turns, forcing an indirect approach to the area. In time, however, the bent axis was replaced by a *direct axial* plan, wherein the entrance led directly to the focal point of the interior space. The general evolution of temple-building was toward thicker walls and more secluded cellae; anterooms and courtyards lengthened the approach to the place of worship. There was a tendency, especially after the beginning of the Akkadian period, to divide the cella into two parts: the antecella and the main cella. Often the entrance was at the center of a long side, and the altar and niche were placed at the center of the opposite wall, producing an oblong cella with stress on the short axis.

Palaces consisted of combinations of a basic unit: rectangular rooms opening onto a courtyard. The dwelling areas and the rooms for official ceremonies were distinctly separated. The houses of the people ranged from reed huts to mud brick structures having two floors of rooms facing an inner court.

Tombs were modest compared with those in Egypt. The most impressive ones found thus far are the royal tombs at Ur, where stairways of fired brick set in bitumen lead to underground vaulted rooms arranged somewhat like a private house.

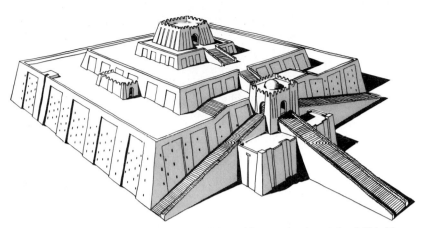

6-1 Reconstruction of the ziggurat at Ur. (Adapted from a drawing at the British Museum, London.)

Ziggurat at Ur (*c.* 2100 B.C.). The king Ur-Nammu built this, the best preserved of the ziggurats (Fig. 6-1). It is a mud brick mass with a facing of fired bricks in the form of niches and buttresses. The first level is 50 feet high, and the corners were oriented to the points of the compass. The closed form, with its simple masses, obvious axial balance, and gradation toward the summit of the temple, made a striking interruption in the stark plains. Interior space was limited to the gate, which functions as a kind of halfway house on the flights of stairs, and to the temple at the top; exterior space was organized by the stairways, which led the worshiper from height to height. A physical pilgrimage and ascent was intended to produce a spiritual parallel. Conversely, the god could descend to earth by way of the man-made mountain.

SCULPTURE

Sculpture served both religious and commemorative purposes. Statues of the gods were apparently used in the niches of the temple cellae, and statues of priests and worshipers were placed in temples to perform as "stand-ins" for their donors, insuring continuous obeisance to the deity. Relief sculpture was carved or modeled on votive plaques, stone maces, cult vessels, *steles* (upright slabs or pillars), *cylinder seals* (small stone rollers carved to produce a continuous relief design when rolled on soft clay or wax), and walls. Materials include a variety of stone, ivory, shell, clay, gypsum, bronze, gold, silver, and electrum (an alloy of silver and gold), often used in combinations for contrasts of color and texture. Subjects depicted include deities, sacrifices, cult processions, religious epics, military victories, hunts, animals, and hybrid creatures. Generalizations about style must be cautious because of the limited material presently available from excavations.

Throughout Mesopotamian art, a concern for the physical appearance of men and animals runs in contrast to a love of fantasy and lavish abstract ornament. Neither relief sculpture nor the few surviving fragments of wall painting show any desire to suggest the illusion of deep space. The human body was usually represented by a general type with massive and simplified anatomy. Enlarged inlaid eyes and prominent noses are common, but individual features occur occasionally. In Sumerian figures, the body from the waist to the calf was hidden by a full skirt, often embellished with a surface pattern suggesting fringe and tufts of hair or wool. During the Akkadian period, the clothing fitted more closely and revealed the body, which appeared to be softer and more flexible. Rigidity returned in later periods. Repeated linear motifs in hair, beards, and garments express a love of decorative pattern.

Statuettes from Tell Asmar (ancient Eshnunna) (c. 2700–2500 B.C.). This group of marble figures (Fig. 6-2) was found under the floor of a temple. Identification is uncertain, but the subjects are probably priests and worshipers.

6-2
Statuettes from the Abu Temple, Tell Asmar, c. 2700–2500 B.C. Marble, tallest figure approx. 30" high. Iraq Museum, Baghdad, and Oriental Institute, University of Chicago.

The tallest figure has been identified as Abu, the god of vegetation, although he lacks the horned hat normally worn by that god. The cups that he and the woman beside him hold in their hands may contain offerings or refer to the celebration of a cult marriage between earth and heaven. The hypnotically intense eyes, closed forms, full skirts, angular elbows, and tensely clasped hands are common to figures from the Sumerian and Neo-Sumerian periods.

PAINTING

Painting is found on walls, pottery, and sculpture. A dynamic style employing expansive abstract animal motifs and geometric designs enlivens the surfaces of pottery. The fragments of wall painting available to us indicate that painting followed the style of relief sculpture and depicted the same kinds of subjects. Painting was done on mud plaster or gesso (a mixture of plaster and glue) surfaces. There are no examples of the illusion of depth or mass modeled in light and shadow. Instead, flat, outlined shapes form lively geometric designs and figurative scenes.

Assyrian Art: 900–612 B.C.

ARCHITECTURE

Excavations have not yet produced sufficient evidence to establish a clear understanding of Assyrian architecture. It certainly borrowed from the Sumerians and may owe much to the Hurrians and the Mitanni. Stone was more plentiful in the north, and the basic mud brick was supplemented by stone blocks in lower walls and around gates. Glazed brick provided color. Wall paintings and reliefs decorated interiors. The power of the empire made possible a new grandeur of scale and elegance expressing the divinity of the monarch and his relation to the other gods. Emphasis continued to be placed on temples and palaces. The ziggurat was sometimes freestanding, sometimes paired, and sometimes built into a temple and palace complex. Temple and palace entrances were centrally placed and flanked by a pair of towers. Typically, temples used oblong antecellae and cellae, and palaces employed combinations of the traditional units of rooms grouped around courtyards. A new motif in planning was a rectangular room with a pillared entrance, actually an enlarged

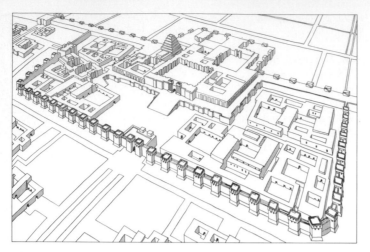

6-3
Reconstruction drawing of the
citadel of Sargon II,
Khorsabad, *c.* 720 B.C.

entry to a passageway leading to an interior court.
Sargon's records refer to this as a *bît hilani*, a borrowing
from Hittite architecture. Its origins seem to be in Syrian
architecture of the second millennium B.C., and it bears
a striking resemblance to the Greek *megaron* (Fig. 8-2).

Citadel of Sargon II at Khorsabad (ancient Dur Sharrukin) (*c.*
720 B.C.). The palace-temple complex (Fig. 6-3) covered
25 acres and was built into the city walls. Tower-flanked
gates with relief carvings of human-headed bulls wearing the horned crown indicating deity opened into the
courtyard of the lower level, from which a ramp led
to the upper palace. A number of temples were built
into the complex, as was a ziggurat with a spiral ramp
leading to a summit that was originally about 140 feet
high. The 209 rooms and courts of the palace provided
a political, military, and religious center for the empire.
Like earlier Mesopotamian palaces, the plan is an
aggregation of rooms around courtyards. Roofs may
have been barrel vaults. Interiors were ornamented with
paintings and reliefs glorifying the king as hunter,
warrior, and conqueror of evil.

SCULPTURE

The Assyrians produced a great deal of relief sculpture
but apparently had little interest in freestanding statues.
Palace walls were covered with reliefs depicting the king
participating in sacred rituals, festivals, wars, and hunts.
In major palaces, the deeds of the god-king eclipsed
those of the other gods, whose images are more plentiful in the provinces. Assyrian art continued the double
interest in decorative pattern and physical appearance,
but there was an increased study of animal behavior
and anatomical detail. Muscle structure was empha-

6-4

*Assurbanipal Killing
a Lion,* from Nineveh,
c. 650 B.C. Gypseous
alabaster, approx. 63¼"
wide. British Museum,
London.

sized; physical force was important. Yet even the taut
muscles and tendons are reduced to conventional forms
and used as motifs in linear patterns. Decorative richness and subtly modulated surfaces produce the effect
of opulence, even in the most brutal battle scenes. Relief
backgrounds are usually neutral, and, especially in ritual
scenes, cuneiform inscriptions may flow across both
raised figures and backgrounds. However, from the
ninth through the seventh centuries, there are frequent
scenes of battles and hunts with detailed, panoramic
landscape settings. Here, the earlier compulsion to
attach figures to *ground lines* (the horizontal bottom
edge of the composition) eases, and depth is occasionally suggested by the placement of objects one
above the other and by increased overlapping of figures.

Assurbanipal Killing a Lion, from Nineveh (British Museum,
c. 650 B.C.). This section of a *frieze* (a horizontal band
of designs) from the palace at Nineveh (Fig. 6-4) demonstrates the combination of violence, admiration for
physical power, and love of richly ornamented surfaces
that is characteristic of Assyrian art. The king is depicted with conventional body and face. More landscape
detail and suggestion of depth are found in some of the
other Nineveh reliefs from the reign of the same king.

PAINTING

The small number of surviving paintings show the same
subjects and stylistic character as the reliefs. Pigments
were mixed with some fatty binder, which has now

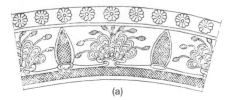

(a)

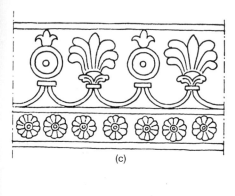

(b)

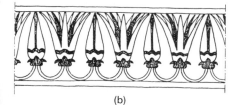

(c)

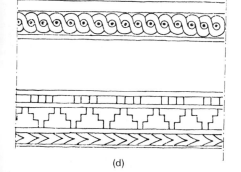

(d)

6-5

Mesopotamian decorative motifs:
(a) rosettes, palmettes, and pine cones;
(b) lotus flowers and buds;
(c) rosettes, palmettes, and pomegranates;
(d) guilloche, meanders, and chevrons.

disappeared, and were applied in flat shapes to walls that had been mud-plastered and whitewashed. Paintings in Sargon's palace at Khorsabad were done in black, red, brown, blue, and green. Assyrian design motifs include pine cones and lotus blossoms (derived from Egyptian lotus bud and blossom designs), palmettes (from Egypt), rosettes and guilloches (from Egypt or Chaldea), pomegranates and stepped pyramids (probably Chaldean), and chevrons (Fig. 6-5). Many of these forms occur with variations in Cretan art and, later, in Greek and Roman work.

Achaemenian Persian Art: 550–330 B.C.

ARCHITECTURE

Persian architecture during the Achaemenian period found its highest accomplishment in palaces. Though the Persians were eclectic, their borrowings were amalgamated into a distinctive style. Plans tended to be very open, and columns were used more extensively than in previous cultures in the Mesopotamian and Iranian areas. The typically three-part palace plan included a gatehouse, an *apadana* (a rectangular or square *hypostyle* [colonnaded] hall, probably derived from Egypt), and living quarters. These basic parts, as well as necessary storerooms, were often multiplied as successive rulers added to a palace (Fig. 6-8). The parts were sometimes widely separated, as at Pasargadae (sixth century B.C.), recalling the tent-cities of the Persian nomads, and sometimes loosely joined, as at Susa and Persepolis (both sixth to fourth centuries B.C.). The buildings were elevated on one or more terraces and often enclosed by a perimeter wall.

The most unusual element was the apadana. It had three to four colonnaded porches and entrances on four sides. The gatehouse was also rectangular or square and stood separately as a monumental entry. It was often given a bent-axis alignment with the apadana, producing a delayed confrontation with the sacred, or a ritualistic pilgrimage, as is suggested in many Mesopotamian temple plans and in the spiral ramp of Sargon's ziggurat. Columns were made of stone or wood, and wood shafts were often surfaced with plaster and painted with geometric designs. Shafts were both *fluted* (having vertical channels all the way around) and plain. Column designs (Fig. 6-6) reveal the influence of Egypt and of Ionia, the Greek territory in Asia Minor, areas from which the Persians imported skilled carvers. Wall surfaces were decorated with colored and glazed brick reliefs and stone relief sculpture. The Achaemenians worshiped outdoors; temple architecture was not of major importance. Most Achaemenian royal tombs were carved in the face of a cliff and given the form of a Greek cross (equal-armed). The horizontal arm contains a centrally placed door flanked by *engaged columns* (columns emerging from the wall as does relief sculpture) supporting a carved lintel. The upper part of the cross presents several *registers* (bands) of relief sculpture. Interiors are simple shallow spaces probably filled, at the time of burial, with royal furnishings.

Palace at Persepolis (6th–4th cens. B.C.). The whole palace complex (Figs. 6-7 and 6-8) stands on an irregularly shaped terrace that is 40 feet high, about 900 by 1500 feet in plan, and set against a mountain range. There is uncertainty about whether or not the whole area was originally surrounded by a high mud brick wall. The terrace is approached by a stairway at the gatehouse; and, from the gatehouse, a ninety-degree turn is necessary to face the main stairway to the apadana. The apadana, or audience hall of Darius, is 250 feet square and originally had a roof about 60 feet high supported by thirty-six stone columns. These columns are complex, both in form and cultural allusion. The fluted shafts and parts of the base seem to have come from Ionia. The *capitals* (the top or crowning element of the column) often begin with a ring of drooping petals and

6-6 Columns at Persepolis.

6-7 Stairway to the Royal Audience Hall, Persepolis, *c.* 500 B.C.

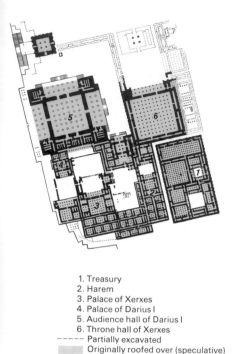

1. Treasury
2. Harem
3. Palace of Xerxes
4. Palace of Darius I
5. Audience hall of Darius I
6. Throne hall of Xerxes
----- Partially excavated
░░░ Originally roofed over (speculative)

6-8 Plan of the palace at Persepolis.

flaring papyrus blossoms that can be traced to Egypt. Above these is a vertical block with double *volutes* (scrolls) that are found, in various forms, throughout western Asia. These parts were used without additions or with pairs of griffins (winged, eagle-headed lions), bulls, human-headed bulls, or horned lions. Near the audience hall, a hundred-column throne hall was added later by Xerxes and his son, Artaxerxes. Behind the halls were living quarters, treasuries, and storerooms. Massive stone window and door frames survived the destruction of the palace by Alexander the Great, but mud brick walls have disappeared. Sculptural decoration was concentrated around stairways, gates, and columns; it was used to ornament the architecture rather than for its own sake. The total effect of Persepolis, even in ruins, is an expression of power, wealth, and regal ceremony.

SCULPTURE

Achaemenian sculpture was primarily the relief embellishment of architecture. Almost no freestanding statues have been found. The Assyrian interest in narration of battles and hunts is absent, although Assyrian influence is evident in the Persian love of linear patterns, and, specifically, in the human-headed bulls at the Persepolis gatehouse, which repeat those at Khorsabad. Assyrian violence is recalled by the motif of a lion biting a bull at Persepolis, but this may have been a symbolic action

6-9

Procession of Medes and Persians, detail from the eastern stairway to the Royal Audience Hall, Persepolis, *c.* 500 B.C. Black limestone, entire relief approx. 268'3" wide.

for the Achaemenians. Basically, subject matter consisted of real and fantastic animals and processions of retainers, warriors, or subjects. At Susa, relief was executed in richly colored glazed brick; at Persepolis, reliefs were carved in stone and originally painted. The carvings depict processions of soldiers, bearers of tribute from twenty-three nations of the empire, members of the court, guards, and scenes of the king giving audience and offering prayers, all parts of the Achaemenian New Year's festival celebrated at Persepolis. Another outlet for Persian talent in sculptural design was finely wrought gold, silver, and bronze metalwork ranging from cups and vases to jewelry and weapons.

Procession of Medes and Persians, eastern stairway of the audience hall of Darius (Persepolis, *c.* 500 B.C.). In this detail of the reliefs shown in Figure 6-9, the *Immortals* (imperial guards) are shown in alternation with Medes, who are clearly indicated by round hats and smooth clothing. Persian costumes are embellished with drapery folds in elegant, symmetrical patterns. The widespread sources of Persian art are revealed by this drapery, influenced by sixth-century Greece, and in the rosettes, taken from Egyptian and early Mesopotamian art. The distinctively Persian quality comes from the combination of repetitive processional compositions, neutral backgrounds, low but round relief modeling, and the love of opulent decorative patterns.

Suggestions for Further Study

Frankfort, Henri. *The Art and Architecture of the Ancient Orient* (Pelican History of Art). Baltimore: Penguin Books, 1955.

Ghirshman, Roman. *The Arts of Ancient Iran* (The Arts of Mankind). Translated by Stuart Gilbert and James Emmons. New York: Golden Press, 1964.

Mootgat, Anton. *The Art of Ancient Mesopotamia.* London and New York: Phaidon Press, 1969.

Porada, Edith. *The Art of Ancient Iran* (Art of the World). New York: Crown, 1962.

Parrot, André. *The Arts of Assyria* (The Arts of Mankind). Translated by Stuart Gilbert and James Emmons. New York: Golden Press, 1961.

Scranton, Robert L. *Aesthetic Aspects of Ancient Art.* Chicago: University of Chicago Press, 1964.

Strommenger, Eva, and Max Hirmer. *5000 Years of the Art of Mesopotamia.* New York: Abrams, 1964.

Chapter 7 Art

Egyptian Art:

3200–30 B.C.

Ancient Egyptian history falls into three major periods, which are further divided into dynasties (ages during which a single family provided the succession of rulers). The *Archaic* period and the *Old Kingdom* may be considered together as the first major period, which began with the unification of northern and southern Egypt, saw the establishment of Memphis as a cultural center, and ended with the decline of central power and an era of confusion and civil war. Order was restored during the *Middle Kingdom*, but in a feudal system that weakened the authority of the *pharaoh* (king). This kingdom eventually collapsed under the burdens of civil war and invasion by the Hyksos (probably Canaanites and Anatolians), who exacted tribute from much of Egypt until they were expelled by princes from Thebes. Thebes became a major center for the *New Kingdom* or *Empire*, the period that brought Egypt to its greatest power. We may group the Empire with the less important periods that followed and with the age of defeats that ended Egypt's leading role in ancient history. She was invaded by Assyrians in the seventh century B.C., by the Persians in the sixth century B.C., and by the Macedonians in 332 B.C.; finally, in 30 B.C. Egypt became a Roman province.

Egyptian civilization began as a series of independent city-states, each with its own patron god. The unity of these parts was always precarious, as Egyptian literature and art reveal; for example, the pharaoh is sometimes depicted wearing the crown (with a flat top and a raised portion at the rear) of northern or Lower Egypt, sometimes wearing the crown (shaped like a bowling pin) of southern or Upper Egypt, and occasionally wearing a combination of both crowns. Life depended on the rhythmic cycles of the Nile River, whose floods enriched the bottom lands but necessitated the frequent resurveying of fields; hence the Egyptians quickly developed a practical mathematics as well as astronomy and a rational calendar.

Egyptian society consisted of the nobility, which owned much of the land; the middle class, which consisted of merchants, artists, civil servants, and—in the Empire—soldiers; and the serfs, who formed the bulk of the population. By the end of the Empire, the power of the nobility had been partially taken over by the growing priesthood and by the increasing number of civil servants.

All Egyptian culture was pervaded by a complex religion that stressed a life after death; therefore, most of the painting, sculpture, and architecture was religious and sepulchral. Egyptian art presents a bewildering variety of gods—male and female human figures and combination animal-human creatures such as the sphinx. Some of the more important gods were Osiris, lord of the underworld (often shown as a swathed mummy); Anubis, the jackal-god of embalmment; Nut, the sky goddess (a human form arched over the earth); Hathor, the goddess of love and joy (usually shown with cow's horns); Horus, one aspect of the sun god (often shown as a hawk); and Re, or Ra, the sun god who traveled across the sky in his sun-ship during the day and through the underworld during the night. The pharaoh himself was believed to be a god. Many of the gods assumed each other's forms or evolved in form and name during the course of Egyptian history. The most striking development in this history was the effort of the XVIIIth-Dynasty king Akhenaten to establish a monotheistic religion founded on the worship of the sun god.

Archaic Period: 3200–2680 B.C., Dynasties I Through III, and Old Kingdom: 2680–2258 B.C., Dynasties IV Through VI

ARCHITECTURE

The palaces of the nobility and the homes of the wealthy were built either of wood frames with walls of colored reed mats or of mud brick with plaster or stucco surfacing decorated with paintings; more modest dwellings were probably made of reed mats plastered with mud. Such impermanent materials have left few remains. The Egyptians concentrated their efforts on tombs and temples, built to serve the deceased or the gods and to defy time and the destructive power of nature. Stone and brick were used for this more permanent architecture, but because the stone and brick sometimes encased only a rubble filling, the wall was not always as permanent as it might have been. The arch was known but rarely used; the basic structural system was post and lintel.

Egyptian architecture emphasizes mass and employs simple, rigid contours. Interior spaces are usually small in proportion to the masses enclosing them and are placed in a mazelike succession, with dead ends or roundabout connections. One of the basic tomb types

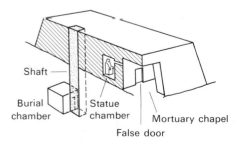

7-1 Cross section of a mastaba.

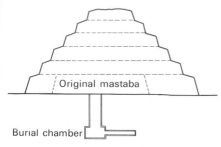

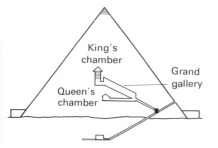

Burial chamber

7-2 Step-pyramid of Zoser.

7-3 Cross section of the pyramid of Khufu.

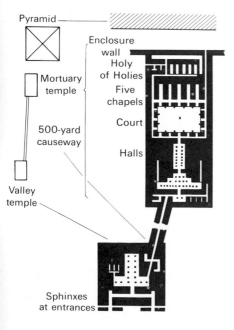

7-4 Pyramid of Khafre, Giza.

is the *mastaba* (Fig. 7-1), originally a rectangular block with *battered* (sloping) sides and more mass than enclosed space, though later mastabas are less regular in form and enclose more space. The basic parts are (1) the burial chamber, reached by a vertical or sloping shaft; (2) the statue chamber, a walled-up room containing a statue substitute for the body; (3) a mortuary chapel, where offerings could be left for the deceased; and (4) a false door through which the spirit of the dead was to have access to the offerings. Often the statue chamber has a peephole leading to the chapel. The statue chamber and burial chamber with its entry shaft are often encased in hard stone, meant to improve durability and to discourage tomb-robbers, who were attracted by the treasures buried with the dead. The mastaba was thought of as a house for the dead, and groups of mastabas formed cities of the dead (*necropolises*). It is conjectured that the *pyramid* tomb may have evolved from stacked-up mastabas of decreasing size, as in the tomb of King Zoser (Fig. 7-2).

Such a step-pyramid could have led to the true pyramid form, which protects its burial chamber and treasures under a mountain of stone (Fig. 7-3). The basic parts of an Old Kingdom pyramid complex are: (1) the pyramid, (2) a mortuary chapel or temple beside or against the pyramid, (3) a causeway leading from the mortuary temple to (4) a valley temple close to the Nile (Fig. 7-4). The huge pyramids only inspired greater efforts by tomb-robbers, however, and in later periods smaller tombs were built. For their post and lintel structures, the Egyptians derived column designs from plants and from construction methods in wood; some columns imitate a papyrus stalk and blossom; others imitate the form of bundles of palms tied together for strength. Polygonal fluted stone columns, like the later Doric columns of Greece, may imitate wooden palm bundles plastered with mud. Capitals atop the columns resemble lotus buds, papyrus blossoms, palm leaves, or leafy blossoms (Fig. 7-5).

Step-pyramid of Zoser (Saqqara, Dyn. III). The first large Egyptian architecture in stone, this 195-foot-high mass (Fig. 7-2) seems to have developed from an original mastaba by added stages. Around the pyramid, a wall originally enclosed a funerary community with chapels, palaces, and temples. Bundle, fluted, and papyrus blossom columns are used. The architect was Imhotep, one of the few Old Kingdom architects whose name is known to us.

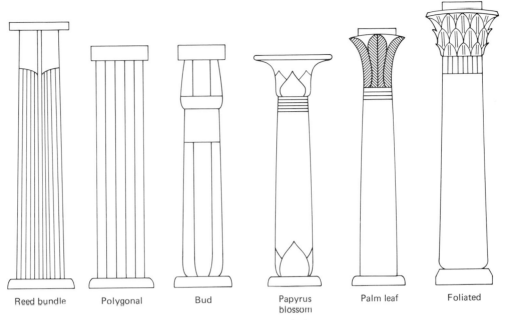

Reed bundle   Polygonal   Bud   Papyrus blossom   Palm leaf   Foliated

7-5 Egyptian column designs.

7-6 Great pyramids of Giza: Menkure, *c.* 2575 B.C., Khafre, *c.* 2600 B.C.; Khufu, *c.* 2650 B.C.

7-7 Victory palette of Narmer, front and back, from Hierakonpolis, *c.* 3000 B.C. Slate, 25″ high. Egyptian Museum, Cairo.

Pyramids of Khufu, Khafre, and Menkure (Giza, Dyn. IV). These largest of Egyptian tombs (Fig. 7-6) are in true pyramid form and were originally encased in polished limestone. The largest of the three, that of Khufu, has a base about 750 feet square and was originally about 475 feet high. The method of construction is not known with certainty; the mammoth stones may have been pulled on sledges up ramps of earth that were raised with each level of the structure. The massive, stable geometric form and the simple surfaces are characteristic of monumental architecture in Egypt.

SCULPTURE

Egyptian sculpture ranges from colossal statues to delicate goldsmith's work. The most significant pieces were done for tombs or temples. For large work, hard stones such as granite, diorite, or basalt were preferred. Softer alabaster was exploited for its translucence, and sandstone, limestone, and wood sculpture was often surfaced with plaster and painted. Small sculpture, or inlay work in large sculpture, might consist of gold, silver, electrum, lapis lazuli (a semiprecious, azure-colored stone), and enamel.

Relief sculpture, generally low relief consisting of sharp-edged, relatively flat forms, has some of the abstract symbolic character of Egyptian hieroglyphic writing. The human body is portrayed by conventionalized forms developed early in Egyptian history. A frontally seen eye, for example, is combined with a profile face, frontal shoulders, and profile hips and legs; the artist seems to have thought through an action step by step and shown these steps as in a diagram. The standardized bodies occasionally depict age, but otherwise the passage of time is ignored, for the sharp edges and angular poses tend to freeze any suggestion of motion. Motion implies time as mass implies space; neither is an element of Old Kingdom relief sculpture. Some overlapping of flat shapes suggests a very shallow space, but massive forms and a perspective illusion of space are not found. As a result, the reliefs do not weaken the mass of the wall or the *stele* that carries them.

In freestanding sculpture, the standard poses are free from the wall, but they may be attached to a supporting back-slab (Fig. 7-8). Much Egyptian sculpture retains the massive four-sidedness of the block from which it was carved, and the mass contributes to the impression of durability. Closed form is typical. Anatomy is simplified in the direction of geometric shapes, so that the figures assume the rigidity and static permanence of Egyptian architecture. Individuality is concentrated in the face, which is often alert in expression but motionless. It should be noted, however, that the art of the different areas of Egypt varies in its adherence to the conventional forms. The functions of the various statues, as votive images to the gods or as images of servants meant to serve the deceased in his afterlife, also influenced the style of the work.

Victory palette of Narmer (Dyn. I, slate, 25″. Egyptian Museum, Cairo). This elaborate version of the palettes used for mixing eye paints (Fig. 7-7) commemorates the subjection of northern Egypt by the South. On one side, King Narmer, wearing the tall crown of the South, is about to strike a northerner. A hawk holds captive a plant with a human head, probably the papyrus symbol of the delta region. Above, the symbol for Narmer is framed by a small palace. On either side of this is a human head with cow's horns, the symbol for Hathor. On the other side of the palette, Narmer, wearing the crown of northern Egypt, surveys decapitated enemies. At the bottom, he is seen as a bull knocking down the walls of a city. Typically, the artist shows the figures in "elevation," standing on base lines that establish different registers in the composition, until a different point of view is needed to convey the information he is giving. The artist changes to an aerial view to show the number of slain enemies. Scale expresses importance; therefore, the king acquires giant stature.

Mycerinus and His Queen (Dyn. IV, slate, 54½″ high. Museum of Fine Arts, Boston). The king wears a ceremonial false beard; the queen wears a wig (Fig. 7-8). The individual facial features are somewhat simplified, and yet they contrast with the more generalized treatment of the bodies. The pose is typical for standing figures. Closed form and anatomy reduced to geometric rigidity give a timeless dignity to the couple.

PAINTING

Papyrus was occasionally used by the Egyptians for painting, as well as for writing, but the most important paintings are on the walls of tombs and temples. Paint was also often used to enhance relief or freestanding sculpture. Grounds are smoothed stone or a coating of stucco, plaster, or mud and straw. Pigments made from powdered natural substances, such as soot, copper

7-8 Mycerinus and His Queen, Kha-Merer-Nebty II, from Giza, Dyn. IV, 2599–2571 B.C. Slate schist, 54½″ high. Museum of Fine Arts, Boston. Harvard-Boston Expedition.

7-9 Detail from *Geese of Medum, c.* 2600 B.C. Dry fresco, entire fresco approx. 18″ high. Egyptian Museum, Cairo.

compounds, or earth colors, were mixed with a binder of water and gum and were applied to a dry ground.

Old Kingdom painting, like the sculpture and architecture, shows a preference for rigidly imposed rectilinear order and a limited number of standard forms. During the millennia of Egyptian history, the striking quality of all the arts is not the subtle change or occasional rebellion against the standard forms but rather their continuity. Old Kingdom painting was often applied to relief sculpture; it was left to later ages to stress painting as an independent art. Like relief, painting uses sharp-edged flat shapes, and the diagrammatic poses symbolize activity rather than express it. Spaces between figures are often filled with hieroglyphics, which counter any slight illusion of depth that might come from overlapping shapes. Typical forms and actions of animals are keenly observed, but the repetition of shapes and details within shapes imposes a regimented order upon the variety of nature. Subject matter comes from mythology, ritual, biography, or daily activities. Symbolism is pervasive. Many of the activities, such as sowing, reaping, and offering prayers and food, were apparently intended to "serve" the deceased in his afterlife. As in the reliefs, scenes are organized in registers. While overall symmetry was valued, each picture seems to function as an isolated unit, and the accretion of these units gives the painting some of the additive character of the architecture.

Geese, from the mastaba of Itet at Medum (Dyn. III, approx. 1′ x 6′. Egyptian Museum, Cairo). Though this is one section from one register in a large wall painting, the composition works effectively as an isolated unit (Fig. 7-9). The colors and the poised strutting of the geese are quite natural, but a typically severe order is evident in the symmetry of the poses and in the crisp patterns of the feathers.

7-10
Interior of the tomb of Amenemhat I,
Beni Hasan, *c.* 1975 B.C.

Middle Kingdom: 2134–1786 B.C., Dynasties XI and XII

ARCHITECTURE

The Middle Kingdom produced smaller tombs and tomb-temple combinations. This resulted in part from a smaller concentration of wealth; it may also be explained by the growth of the Osiris cult, which stressed an afterlife in the underworld rather than in the tomb. Many small stone-faced brick pyramids and mastabas have crumbled, but more permanent tombs, cut into the rock of the cliffs along the Nile Valley at places like Beni Hasan, still remain.

Rock-cut tomb of Amenemhat I (Beni Hasan, Dyn. XII). Here (Figs. 7-10 and 7-11) typical features of the rock-cut tombs are seen: the modest size, the courtyard, pillared portico, the main room supported by fluted columns (sometimes called Proto-Doric because of their resemblance to later Greek Doric columns), and the shrine. Such tombs generally contained a simple grave pit for the body. The walls are painted with subjects in the tradition of the Old Kingdom; and the ceiling is decorated with geometric designs that probably imitate textiles.

SCULPTURE

Much Middle Kingdom sculpture was destroyed by the Hyksos and by New Kingdom rulers. What remains varies from crude to highly finished carving. The growing middle-class patronage and the dispersal of wealth

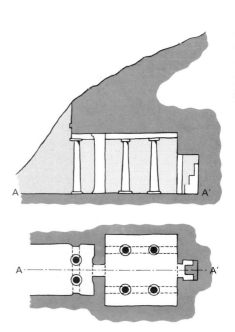

7-11 Plan and section of a rock-cut tomb. (After Sir Banister Fletcher.)

7-12 Relief on the sarcophagus of Mentuhotep's wife Kawit, Dyn. XI. Egyptian Museum, Cairo.

among the nobles seem in many works to have resulted in the sacrifice of quality for quantity. Frequent use was made of the cheaper method of *sunken relief*, in which the outlines of objects are cut into the wall and the form within the outlines is carved so that most of it is below the surface of the untouched background. Its style owes much to the Old Kingdom, although poses are often more affected. Freestanding sculpture developed even simpler bodies than in the Old Kingdom. Forms are either sleek and flowing or heavy, brutal, and blocky. Many seated figures have arms folded over drawn-up knees; such a statue was simply a modified block surmounted by a head and therefore involved a minimum of carving. The most distinctive feature of Middle Kingdom sculpture is the cynicism and careworn weariness in many of the faces, a quality that is echoed in Middle Kingdom writings. This detailed realism is often in striking contrast to the simplified bodies. Middle Kingdom servant statues tend to be of cheaper materials and cruder execution than earlier examples.

Relief on the sarcophagus of Mentuhotep's wife, Kawit (Dyn. XI, limestone, originally painted. Egyptian Museum, Cairo). Quite unlike earlier work, this sunken relief (Fig. 7-12) exemplifies the sleek, suave contours and rather precious poses characteristic of some Middle Kingdom sculpture.

7-13 *Sesostris III or Amenemhat III, c.* 1850 B.C. Obsidian, approx. 4" high. C. S. Gulbenkian Foundation, Lisbon.

Sesostris III or Amenemhat III—identity uncertain (Dyn. XII, obsidian, 4" high. National Gallery of Art, Washington, D.C.). The tired, lined face illustrates a Middle Kingdom tendency toward greater detail and more distinctly individualistic portrait features (Fig. 7-13). The small scale and hard stone demanded considerable skill.

PAINTING

The Middle Kingdom employed painting extensively, perhaps partly because painting was cheaper than relief. One of the chief sites for Middle Kingdom painting is the rock-cut tombs of Beni Hasan. The paintings are typically done in soft, subtle colors applied to broad, simple shapes that sometimes contrast with areas of meticulous detail.

Dancing Girls, from the tomb of Antefoker (Thebes, Dyn. XII, approx. 37" x 67"). The mild value contrasts, bland colors, simple shapes, and wirelike outlines seen in Figure 7-14 are typical of much Middle Kingdom painting. The costumes are also representative of the period. The outstretched forefingers of the dancers on the right may be ritualistic gestures or a method of counting the steps of the dance.

7-14 *Dancing Girls,* from the tomb of Antefoker, Thebes, Dyn. XII.

7-15 Court and pylon of Rameses II, *c.* 1290 B.C., and court and colonnade of Amenhotep III, *c.* 1390 B.C., temple of Amen-Mut-Khônsu, Luxor.

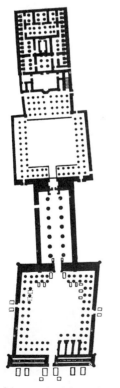

7-16 Plan of the temple of Amen-Mut-Khônsu.

New Kingdom (Empire) and Later Periods: 1570–30 B.C., Dynasties XVIII Through XXXI

ARCHITECTURE

Thebes is the center for the important remains of New Kingdom architecture. In the cliffs on the western side of the river are two desolate rock-strewn valleys: the Valley of the Tombs of the Kings and the Valley of the Tombs of the Queens. Here many of the New Kingdom rulers had themselves buried in hidden mineshaft-like tombs. While these cannot really be considered as architecture, they were lavishly decorated with paintings and sculpture. When the tombs became secret, the mortuary temples occupied more convenient locations near the city. Mortuary temples and temples to the gods became especially large during the New Kingdom and later periods (Figs. 7-17–7-19). Both kinds were built in the same general plan: (1) entry through a massive sloping façade called a *pylon*, (2) an open *courtyard*, (3) a *hypostyle hall*, and (4) a sacred *inner sanctum*. The basic parts could be multiplied, and temples to more than one god might have several sanctums. From entry to inner sanctum, the progression is from larger to smaller spaces, the plan being essentially an elaboration of the Middle Kingdom rock-cut tomb. The temples were often enlarged by a process of accretion over the centuries, and the resulting labyrinthine complexity, which does not lend itself to an easy comprehension of the whole interior, provided effective settings for the processionals so important in Egyptian worship.

Our knowledge of New Kingdom domestic architecture would be greater had not later generations carried away much of the stone from Akhenaten's new capital at Amarna. His North Palace has an extensive symmetrical plan organized around a large pool and tightly enclosed behind thick walls. Typical materials for such architecture were mud brick and stone.

Temple of Amun-Mut-Khônsu (Luxor, mainly Dyns. XVIII and XIX). This enormous temple (Figs. 7-15 and 7-16) was not for mortuary offerings but for the glory of the god Amun (whose identity merged with that of Re), his wife Mut, and their son Khôns. The basic temple parts have been multiplied. From the great pylon and the first court, built under Rameses II (Dyn. XIX), one enters the XVIIIth-Dynasty parts of the building: a double row of 52-foot-high papyrus blossom columns, a second court (bud columns), a hypostyle hall, smaller halls, and two sanctums. Originally, two *obelisks* (tapered shafts with pointed tips) stood in front of the temple. One remains; the other now adorns the Place de la Concorde in Paris. The total length of the structure is about 835 feet.

7-17 Temple of Horus, Edfu, mainly 237–212 B.C.

7-18 Temple of Horus, hypostyle hall from the court.

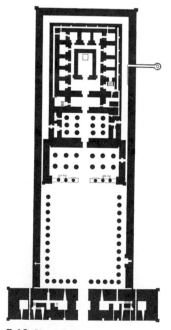

7-19 Plan of the temple of Horus.

Temple of Horus (Edfu, mainly 237–212 B.C.). The building (Figs. 7-17–7-19) comes from the Ptolemaic era, which followed the Macedonian conquest. It is notable for its well-preserved state and for its exemplification of the basic Egyptian temple unobscured by proliferation. The pylon (145′ x 250′) and massive exterior walls enclose court, vestibule, hypostyle hall, storage rooms, and inner sanctum. The plan indicates a characteristic axial progression to smaller and darker spaces. The columns typify the late period in the use of a variety of palm and foliated capitals.

SCULPTURE

Increasing prosperity during the Empire greatly encouraged artistic activity. Tomb statues were often carved in the living rock of the shaft tombs, and quantities of votive statues and reliefs decorated the temples. Sunken relief is common. Middle Kingdom style continued for a time, but the expansion of the Empire brought increased awareness of other peoples, and conventional forms soon relaxed to allow more representation of different racial types. The reign of Akhenaten marked a stylistic change toward more action, greater casualness in pose, increasing complexity in costume and accessory detail, a softening of body forms, and more accurate indication of age. The king's heavy lips, pendulous jaw, long neck, and sagging stomach were stressed to the point of caricature in portraits that he must have encouraged. The royal features soon set the style, and portraits of other people acquired his "ideal" form. The old conventions were modified rather than abolished. Soon after the death of Akhenaten, the old canons returned, but with slightly softer contours in some works and more open form.

Akhenaten or Amenhotep IV (Dyn. XVIII, sandstone with coloring, 13' high. Egyptian Museum, Cairo). Although the traditional pose is taken, the features of face and body on this sculpture (Fig. 7-20) make a striking contrast to Old Kingdom statues like *Mycerinus and His Queen.*

Nefertiti, wife of Akhenaten (Dyn. XVIII, painted limestone, with eyes—one missing—of inlaid rock crystal, approx. 20" high. Staatliche Museen, Berlin). This bust (Fig. 7-21), found among the remains of a sculptor's studio, served as a model. Suggestions of fleshy softness under the chin and around the eyes and mouth lend a flesh-and-blood reality to the regal poise of the queen.

PAINTING

The best-preserved examples of Egyptian painting come from the highly decorated walls of the New Kingdom. Those from the beginning of the period are characterized by stiff poses and vivid opaque colors, with wide use of blue backgrounds. Later came a change to more graceful poses and more delicate transparent colors applied with brushwork that is occasionally loose and sketchy. The reign of Akhenaten produced startling changes in painting as well as in sculpture. When he moved the capital from Thebes to Amarna, he had his palace there decorated with paintings of landscapes and animal life, all done with a new concern for continuity of all the parts. The direct visual experience of nature breaks through the old symbolic concepts. Human forms acquire the casual poses, soft bodies, and elongated faces common to the sculpture of the period. This so-called *Amarna Style* died shortly after Akhenaten, but its influence is seen in the occasional flashes of individuality and naturalism that lighten later art. For the most part, later painting, in answering the demands for ostentatious elegance, tends to be repetitious, garish in color, and technically mediocre.

7-20 *Akhenaten or Amenhotep IV,* from a pillar statue in the temple of Aton, Tell el-Amarna, *c.* 1375 B.C. Sandstone, approx. 13' high. Egyptian Museum, Cairo.

7-21 *Nefertiti,* from Tell el-Amarna, *c.* 1360 B.C. Limestone, approx. 20" high. Staatliche Museen, Berlin.

7-22 *Fowling Scene*, from the tomb of Amenemheb, Thebes, Dyn. XVIII. British Museum, London.

Fowling Scene, from the tomb of Amenemheb (Thebes, Dyn. XVIII, 2'10" high. Fragment in the British Museum, London). The artist gives us considerable information about types of fishes, birds, and plants, as well as methods of hunting—note the hunting cat (Fig. 7-22). The compositional arrangement of figures, boats, and papyrus is an ancient one for hunting scenes. The small scale of the hunter's companions indicates their lesser importance. The object on the head of the standing woman is a lump of perfumed ointment.

Wall paintings in the tomb of Nakht (Thebes, Dyn. XVIII). Nakht was a priest of the god Amun. The paintings (Fig. 7-23) describe offerings made at the painted false door of the chapel, the procedures of farming, and dancers and musicians entertaining guests at a feast. Here also the style indicates the period before Akhenaten, but the freedom of brushwork and the delicate color indicate the period just after the tomb of Amenemheb. Traditionally, men were given a darker skin color than women. The small but well-preserved chapel shows the typically sparkling decorative effect of the many flat shapes used in Egyptian painting.

7-23 Wall paintings in the tomb of Nakht, Thebes, c. 1450 B.C. Roar wall 55" x 60".

Suggestions for Further Study

Aldred, Cyril. *The Development of Ancient Egyptian Art from 3200–1315 B.C.* London: Tiranti, 1952.

Desroches-Noblecourt, Christine. *Ancient Egypt: The New Kingdom and the Amarna Period.* Greenwich, Conn.: New York Graphic Society, 1960.

Edwards, I. E. S. *Pyramids of Egypt,* rev. ed. Baltimore: Penguin Books, 1963.

Frankfort, H. A. G. *Arrest and Movement.* Chicago: University of Chicago Press, 1951.

Lange, Kurt, and Max Hirmor. *Egypt: Architecture, Sculpture, Painting in Three Thousand Years,* 4th rev. and enl. ed. Translated by R. H. Boothroyd, Judith Filson, and Barbara Taylor. London: Phaidon Press, 1968.

Mekhitarian, Arpag. *Egyptian Painting.* (Great Centuries of Painting). Translated by Stuart Gilbert. Geneva: Skira, 1954.

Smith, E. Baldwin. *Egyptian Architecture as Cultural Expression.* New York: Appleton-Century-Crofts, 1938.

Smith, William Stevenson. *The Art and Architecture of Ancient Egypt* (Pelican History of Art). Baltimore: Penguin Books, 1958.

Woldering, Irmgard. *Gods, Men, and Pharaohs: The Glory of Egyptian Art.* New York: Abrams, 1967.

Chapter *8 Art*

Aegean Art:
2800–1100 B.C.

Aegean art comes from three main areas: Crete, the Cycladic Islands, and the mainland that later became Greece. On Crete, major sites are Knossos, Phaistos, Hagia Triada, Gournia, Mallia, Palaikastro, and Zabro; of the Cycladic Islands, Melos, Naxos, Paros, and Syros are especially important; on the mainland, the many sites include Mycenae, Tiryns, Pylos, Lerna, Orchomenos, and Iolkos. By 2800 B.C., the use of bronze was ending *Neolithic* (New Stone) Age culture and opening the *Bronze Age.* Cretan culture (often called *Minoan,* after the one or more ancient kings named Minos), Cycladic culture, and, on the mainland, pre-Greek culture (referred to as *Helladic*) have been divided chronologically into *early* (2800–2000 B.C.), *middle* (2000–1550 B.C.), and *late* (1500–1100 B.C.) periods, corresponding roughly to the Old, Middle, and New kingdoms in Egypt. Further subdivisions are used by experts, but because the three geographical areas did not develop technologically at the same pace the subdivisions are somewhat arbitrary. Dates for Egypt are more certain, and Egyptian artifacts found among the remains of other cultures allow dating by relation to Egyptian chronology.

By 1550 B.C., Cretan art was a dominant influence both on the mainland and in the Cyclades. There is evidence of widespread destruction in Crete about 1700 B.C. and of much rebuilding around 1550 B.C. In 1450 B.C., more serious destruction befell the island, probably as a result of the eruption of the volcano on the nearby island of Thera (modern Santorin). After this, the Cretans seem to have been ruled by the Mycenaeans from the mainland until about 1200 B.C., when a period of war and dissolution was followed by the conquest of both Crete and the mainland by the Dorians (later to become the Greeks). It was during this confused period between 1200 and 800 B.C. that the Homeric epics, the *Iliad* and the *Odyssey,* came into being.

Cretan culture grew in the environment of a temperate climate, fertile soil, and a protective sea. The Cretans benefited as well from their position at a trade crossroads; there is evidence of contact with Egypt and Mesopotamia. Notable in Cretan architecture and art is the absence of fortifications and military subject matter. Early hieroglyphic scripts, inspired by Egypt, overlapped the use of two later scripts, Linear A and Linear B. Only Linear B has been completely deciphered; it is a form of early Greek and was used mainly for inventories. Thus far, there are more questions than answers about Cretan government and religion. Government was apparently decentralized, and religion viewed nature as a friendly force. Public worship was held in caves and on mountain tops; private worship was performed in small chapels in houses and palaces. It is not known whether Cretan religion was monotheistic or not. Apparent deities are most frequently female, and it is possible that the various representations are all of a single goddess shown in different forms and functions. Donkey-headed and bull-headed creatures with human bodies (minotaurs) were apparently considered as demons. Sacred objects were special columns, trees, and double-bladed axes. Life in Crete seems to have been colorful, nature-oriented, and relatively secure, despite the occasional devastations apparently caused by earthquakes.

Our knowledge of Cycladic culture is meager. Cretan influence was strong, and the Cyclades prospered from resources of gold, silver, copper, marble, and emery. On the mainland, hilltop fortresses such as Mycenae and Tiryns bespeak a much less carefree life than that of the islands. Graves contain weapons, bodies mummified in the Egyptian manner, and Cretan objects. Mycenae's wealth of gold may have come as payment for mercenary service in Egyptian battles against the Hittites. The art and the tombs reveal influence from Egypt and Crete. Mycenaean power reached its apex between 1400 and 1200 B.C.

ARCHITECTURE

Cretan architecture took the form of town houses, country villas, palaces, market halls, and tombs. Temples apparently were not needed. Plans for buildings and towns often had a north–south orientation in their long axis. Houses were built of brick, stone, and wood, had symmetrical façades, and consisted of several floors built around an interior courtyard. Palace plans were irregular, labyrinthine, and organized around rectangular inner courts. Royal apartments, storage magazines, and audience chambers have been identified. Although palace entrances were not stressed, the west façade was usually built first, given special ornamental emphasis, and confronted by an exterior courtyard. Walls were of mud brick, rubble masonry, and plaster; stone blocks were used in corners and in frames for doors and windows. Roofs were flat, resting on wooden beams and wooden columns that carried brightly painted cushion-shaped capitals and had shafts that tapered downward. Interior palace floors were of gypsum; exterior floors were made of limestone. Interior walls were often frescoed. Tombs were emphasized only in the early period, when circular stone structures, some probably vaulted, served the whole community.

Our sparse information about Cycladic architecture indicates that it was much like that of Crete; but mainland architecture included fortified citadels, the most famous being at Mycenae and Tiryns. Thick walls of huge stones encircled hilltop clusters of small houses and palaces with plans that developed around the *megaron*, a rectangular hall with central hearth, anteroom, and pillared porch. Such compressed quarters did not compare with the luxury of Cretan palaces, although mainland ruins reveal gypsum floor slabs and plastered walls with painted designs. Pit and shaft tombs in the early period and the first part of the middle period were replaced, at least for royalty, by round conical tombs with corbeled stone domes and ornaments of carved and painted stone as well as attached metal objects. Earth was piled over the tomb exteriors, obscuring everything but the *dromos*, a stone-lined approach to the entrance.

Palace at Knossos (*c.* 1600–1400 B.C.). The ruins of Knossos, the largest of the Cretan palaces, are those of the new palace, built some time after the destruction

8-1

Plan of the palace at Knossos.

 1. West porch
 2. Corridor of the Procession
 3. South propylon
 4. Central court
 5. "Theater area"
 6. North propylon
 7. Pillar hall
 8. Magazines
 9. Throne room
10. Palace shrine and lower verandas
11. Stepped porch
12. Grand staircase
13. Light area
14. Hall of the Colonnade
15. Hall of the Double Axes (principal reception room)
16. Queen's Megaron

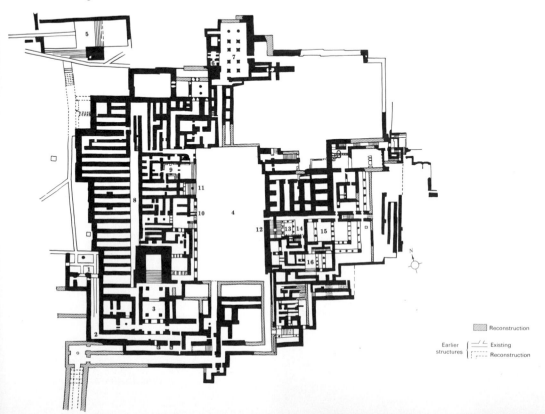

Reconstruction

Earlier structures { Existing / Reconstruction

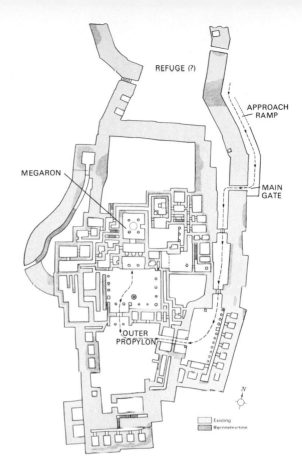

REFUGE (?)

APPROACH RAMP

MEGARON

MAIN GATE

OUTER PROPYLON

N

Existing
Reconstruction

8-2 Plan of the citadel at Tiryns,
    c. 1400–1200 B.C.

of about 1700 B.C. The complex, additive, asymmetrical character of the plan (Fig. 8-1) is typical, as are the indirect entrances on each side. The western half of the palace is divided by a long corridor into magazines (storage chambers) on one side and a complex of official rooms, including a throne room, on the other. The eastern half is divided into a northern section of workshops and a southern section of living quarters and reception rooms. Parts of the structure were three stories high, and interior staircases were built beside light wells. Beneath the palace, terra cotta pipes provided an efficient drainage system. Columns had the typical Cretan cushion capital and downward-tapering shaft. Colorful frescoes showing scenes of processionals and bull games adorned the walls.

Citadel at Tiryns (Peloponnesus, *c.* 1400–1200 B.C.). This small, heavily fortified hilltop (Fig. 8-2) is better preserved than the fortress at Mycenae. The Greeks believed that Tiryns was the birthplace of Hercules. Although it has none of the expansiveness of Cretan

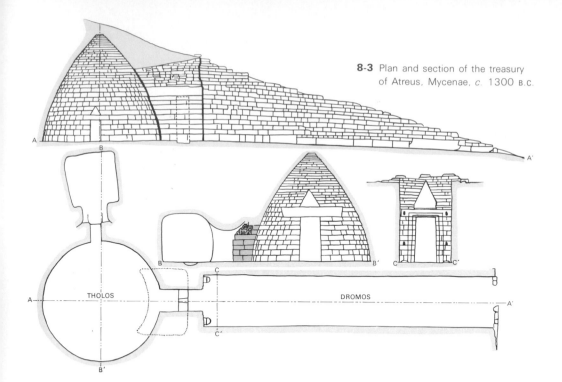

THOLOS

DROMOS

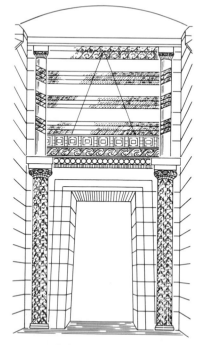

8-4 Relieving arch.

palaces, it suggests more careful planning. The focus is the megaron, which may have its source in Hittite architecture (see p. 60). Huge, rough-cut stones form massive walls that contain passageways with corbeled vaults.

Treasury of Atreus (Mycenae, c. 1300 B.C.). Of the nine *tholoi* (round tombs; sing., *tholos*) at Mycenae, this one (Fig. 8-3), mistakenly called the treasury of Atreus by its discoverer, Heinrich Schliemann, is the most impressive. Its diameter is 47′7″ and the top of the corbeled dome is 43′4″ from the floor. The span of the dome is the largest until the Roman Pantheon in the second century A.D. (see p. 126). The finely cut stones were buttressed and protected by the mound of earth that covered the exterior. The lintel over the door is protected from or relieved of the weight of the dome by a corbeled *relieving arch* (Fig. 8-4), originally filled by a decorated stone slab. Red and green marble embellished the entrance. Designs contained the running spiral, chevron, and petal forms characteristic of Cretan art, but these were used within more rigidly constricted framing shapes. Since the tomb was emptied in antiquity, we may never know who its original occupant was.

PAINTING

In Crete, the only painting that has been found in any quantity from the early and middle periods is on pottery. Stripes and soft mottled shapes were painted in red-brown or black on a lighter red-brown background. Toward the end of the early period, white designs were applied on a red-brown or black background. In the middle Minoan period (*c.* 2000–1550 B.C.), design motifs became bolder in contrast, surer in execution, and more varied. Running spirals, wavy lines, rosettes, lilies, palm trees, fish, seaweed, and net designs in white, red, orange, yellow, and black explode over the surfaces. The best examples are called *Kamares ware,* after the cave on Mt. Ida in which they were found. Late Minoan pottery painting exhibits several trends, some of which (the *Floral Style* and the *Marine Style*) continue the vitality of the earlier Kamares ware. Another style uses the same yellow, red, white, and black for more restrained, tightly grouped, and precisely repeated forms. This trend is also reflected in the so-called *Palace Style,* examples of which have been found only at Knossos and which represent the period of Mycenaean occupation rather than an indigenous Cretan art. Most of the Cretan wall paintings known to us come from the new palace at Knossos (*c.* 1600–1400 B.C.), and even these are fragmentary. As with the pottery, exuberance is combined with delicacy in drawing and color. True fresco is used; the images are of Cretans engaged in sports, processions, and ceremonies.

In the Cyclades, the style changes in pottery painting are similar to those of Crete, but they display less variety and sensitivity. Fragments of frescoes portraying plant and animal life in spontaneously painted flowing forms recall the art of Crete.

During the early and middle periods the mainland also developed pottery painting similar in style to that of Crete, but inferior in quality. The late period produced the ornate Palace Style, which the Mycenaeans carried to Crete. Fresco painting on the mainland was strongly influenced by Crete but tended toward rigid and static forms.

Bull Games, from the palace at Knossos (*c.* 1500 B.C., fresco, approx. 32″ high including border. Archeological Museum, Herakleion). A small room in the east wing of the palace was decorated with a sequence of scenes (Fig. 8-5) depicting a sport often shown in Cretan art. Male (red-skinned) and female (white-skinned) athletes grasp the

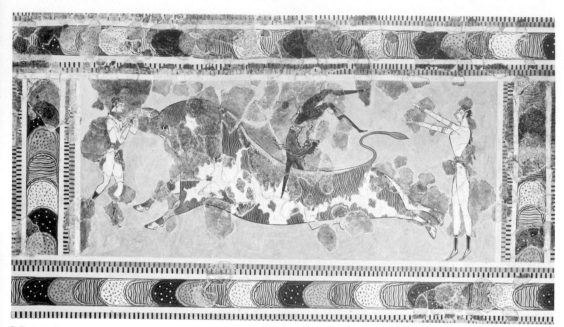

8-5 *Bull Games,* from Knossos, *c.* 1500 B.C. Fresco, approx. 32″ high including border. Archeological Museum, Herakleion.

horns of a charging bull and somersault over its back. Blue and yellow alternate as background colors. The light colors, supple curves, and wasp-waisted figures are typical of Cretan art.

Octopus Vase (Palaikastro, *c.* 1500 B.C., approx. 10″ high. Archeological Museum, Herakleion). The lively patterns and references to nature that characterize so much of Cretan art are displayed in this example of the late Minoan Marine Style (Fig. 8-6).

SCULPTURE

Although there is some evidence that the Cretans carved life-sized statues in wood, the only sculpture now known to us is less than three feet high. Idols, worshipers, children, animals, athletes vaulting over bulls, and individual limbs used as *ex-votos* (thank offerings for cures) were modeled, cast, or carved in terra cotta, glazed clay, bronze, ivory, or gold. From the early and middle periods come terra cotta figures found in communal tombs and mountain-top sanctuaries. These are severely simplified female images with full, bell-shaped skirts, and nearly nude males with the narrow waists and broad shoulders depicted in the later frescoes. As

8-6
Octopus Vase, amphora from Palaikastro,
c. 1500 B.C. Approx. 10" high.
Archeological Museum, Herakleion.

in Egypt, male skin was red and female skin was white
or pale yellow. More anatomical and decorative detail
is shown in the figures made of *faïence* (glazed clay)
and in those of ivory with gold fittings. Jewelry and
stamp-seal engravings of subjects ranging from geometric designs to animals and hieroglyphics reveal great
skill in miniature sculpture. The engravings were made
with stamp seals like those of Egypt rather than cylinder
seals like those of Mesopotamia.

Cycladic tombs have yielded up hundreds of slablike
marble statues varying in height from several inches
to life size. These so-called *Cycladic idols* are very
simplified human forms with the main body divisions
indicated by grooves or ridges. In silhouette, many
resemble a violin shape. Chronology is still in question,
but most seem to come from the early period.

On the mainland, there is little life-sized sculpture
preserved, but dimensions are more ambitious than in
Crete. Gravestones bore geometric designs and hunting
scenes in relief, and architecture apparently carried
sculptural reliefs, concentrated at major entrances.

Earth-Goddess with Snakes (Knossos, *c.* 1600 B.C., faïence,
11½" high. Archeological Museum, Herakleion). This small
Middle Minoan figure (Fig. 8-7) is one of two found

8-7 *Earth-Goddess with Snakes,* from Knossos,
c. 1600 B.C. Faïence, approx. 11½" high.
Archeological Museum, Herakleion.

8-8
Lion Gate, Mycenae,
c. 1300 B.C. Limestone,
relief panel approx.
9½'' high.

in stone-lined pits in the palace. Although we are not certain that she is a goddess, her deity is assumed on the basis of other Cretan art depicting females in control of animals and nature. These may all be different forms of a single mother-goddess. The jackets, bare breasts, and full, ground-length skirts seem to have been standard costume for religious festivals.

Lion Gate (Mycenae, *c.* 1300 B.C., limestone, triangular slab approx. 9½' high). The relief fits within an opening formed by the corbeled relieving arch above and the lintel below (Fig. 8-8). The column symbolized the strength and unity of Mycenae; the base may have served as an altar. The heads of the powerfully modeled lions were attached separately and were turned to confront the visitor approaching the gate. The approach ramp lies within the protection of the city wall.

8-9 *Vaphio Cups, c.* 1500 B.C. Gold with repoussé decoration, approx. 3½″ high. National Museum, Athens.

Vaphio Cups, from a tholos tomb at Vaphio (*c.* 1500 B.C., gold, approx. 3½″ high. National Museum, Athens). Each of the pair of cups (Fig. 8-9) is made of two sheets of gold, the outer sheet worked in repoussé (hammered out from the back) and lined with a smooth inner sheet. The reliefs depict the trapping of bulls in a net by men with Cretan bodies and costumes. The cups could be Cretan work or Mycenaean art under the influence of Crete. The action, anatomy, and foliage reveal careful observation of nature.

Suggestions for Further Study

Blegen, Carl W., and Marion Rawson. *The Palace of Nestor at Pylos in Western Messena.* Published for the University of Cincinnati. Princeton, N.J.: Princeton University Press, 1966.

Branigan, Keith. *The Foundations of Palatial Crete: A Survey of Crete in the Early Bronze Age.* New York: Praeger, 1970.

Demargne, Pierre. *Aegean Art: The Origins of Greek Art* (The Arts of Mankind). Translated by Stuart Gilbert and James Emmons. London: Thames and Hudson, 1964.

Hafner, German. *Art of Crete, Mycenae, and Greece.* New York: Abrams, 1968.

Hutchinson, Richard Wyatt. *Prehistoric Crete.* Baltimore: Penguin Books, 1962.

Marinatos, Spyridon, and Max Hirmer. *Crete and Mycenae.* New York: Abrams, 1960.

Palmer, Leonard Robert. *A New Guide to the Palace of Knossos.* New York: Praeger, 1969.

Vermeule, Emily. *Greece in the Bronze Age.* Chicago: University of Chicago Press, 1964.

Chapter 9 Art

Greek Art:
1100–100 B.C.

About 1100 B.C., the Dorian invasions seem to have been the final step leading to the amalgamation of peoples that became the basis for Greek culture. By 100 B.C., Greece was part of the Roman Empire. In the intervening years, the underlying theme of Greek culture was man and his rational faculty for understanding and perfecting himself and nature. The mild climate favored outdoor activity, influencing architecture directly and painting and sculpture indirectly. The periodic Olympic games (first recorded in 776 B.C.) reflected the Greek interest in the physical life and the human body. Yet the Greeks grew even more interested in the development of the mind, especially the power of reason, and in the conception of ideal forms for all things. Perfection was sought within carefully chosen limits or rules. The conviction that man is the measure of all things was basic to this culture, and even the gods were seen in the image of man, with few combinations of man and animal like those found in Egyptian religion. For art the most important Greek gods are (1) Zeus (Jupiter to the Romans), lord of the sky and supreme ruler, who wielded thunderbolts; (2) Hera (the Roman Juno), wife and sister of Zeus and goddess of marriage; (3) Poseidon (the Roman Neptune), god of the sea, recognized by his trident spear; (4) Athena (the Roman Minerva), originally a goddess of war but more commonly the patroness of civilized life and wisdom; (5) Artemis (the Roman Diana), huntress and patroness of wildlife and the young, often shown with bow and arrows; (6) Apollo (known by the same name to the Romans), god of poetry, music, truth, prophecy, and—in later mythology—god of the sun (sometimes shown with a lyre or with bow and arrows); (7) Aphrodite (the Roman Venus), goddess of love and beauty; (8) Hermes (the Roman Mercury), messenger of the gods and patron of commerce (shown with winged sandals and a wand with entwined serpents); (9) Dionysus (the Roman Bacchus), a latecomer to Greek mythology, god of wine and feasting; (10) Pan (reflected in the Roman god Faunus), god of shepherds and flocks, a mischievous creature largely in human form but with horns and goat's legs; (11) satyrs (also found in Roman mythology), who look like Pan and seek all sensual pleasures; and (12) centaurs, who are half man, half horse and are considered (with the exception of Chiron) to be savage creatures. The most common idea of life after death was that of a gray world of drifting spirits, and in contrast to the Egyptians, the Greeks emphasized life, an earthly life of balanced attainments, based on the idea that the complete man is one governed by reason and enlightened by wide interests. Consequently Greek tombs and burial customs were simple.

Geometric (1100–700 B.C.) and Archaic (700–500 B.C.) Periods

SCULPTURE

Greek sculpture was mainly religious. Of the works preserved from the Geometric period, many are small bronze votive statuettes dedicated to the gods. During this period, copper and fired clay were also common materials, and it is probable that there were large-scale wooden statues that have disappeared. Some of the metal statuettes were made of sheet metal riveted together; others were cast using a sand mold or the lost-wax process. Divisions between the parts of the body tend to be exaggerated, and some parts are modified according to the sculptor's instinct for design. The result is usually a rigid schematic form that resembles Egyptian art. This strict geometric order is the basis for the name given to the period. The stylistic trend during the Geometric period is toward more flowing transitions between body parts and more natural human form.

After the middle of the seventh century B.C., life-sized stone sculpture became more common, and the geometric rigidity of the earlier period slowly softened. Nudity, so rare in Egyptian art, occurs early in Greek sculptures of the male body. We have found many statues of young men (*kouroi;* sing., *kouros*) sculpted in the seventh and early sixth centuries B.C.; their frontal poses, stiff joints, and symmetrical hair and musculature recall Egyptian sculpture. It is rarely clear whether they were meant to be gods or mortals. A few works are signed, but little is known of sculptors from the Archaic period. A number of standing maidens (*korai;* sing., *kore*) have also been discovered. Their pose and clothing (female nudity was not represented until much later) have the same strict order as that of the male figures. On many kouroi and korai the corners of the mouth are turned up in the so-called Archaic smile.

Apollo (*c.* 7th cen. B.C., bronze, 8″ high. Museum of Fine Arts, Boston). This Archaic work (Fig. 9-1) remains Geometric in style and has an inscription on the thighs dedicating the image to Apollo. The words ("Mantiklos dedicated me to . . .") reveal that the Greeks assigned an independent life to each work of art.

9-1 *"Mantiklos" Apollo,* from Thebes. *c.* 700 B.C. Bronze, approx. 8″ high. Museum of Fine Arts, Boston (Frances Bartlett Fund).

Standing Youth, from Attica (late 7th cen. B.C., marble, 78"
high. Metropolitan Museum of Art, New York). This Archaic
kouros statue (Fig. 9-2) reveals its ancestry in the Geometric style. The frontal pose and the insistent symmetry are similar to Egyptian work, but there is no
back-slab, and the arms are separated from the body,
slightly opening up the form.

PAINTING

Greek painting of the Geometric and Archaic periods
is known to us only through vase decoration, but vase
painting was an important medium until the fourth
century B.C. Early Geometric painting consists of geometric shapes in registers. When the human body began
to be depicted, it was reduced to sharply divided and
simplified parts. The basic colors were provided by
painting with a thinned mixture of brown-black clay
on the body of red-brown clay, but other colors and
white were sometimes added. The technique employing
black shapes on the lighter reddish background is called
black-figure vase painting.

Black-figure painting continued through most of the
Archaic period and into the third quarter of the sixth
century B.C., when it began to give way to *red-figure*
painting, a technique in which the background is filled
in with brown-black, leaving a base color of red-orange
or warm tan for the figures. During the Archaic period,
the figures became more lifelike, and geometric ornament was reduced. Scenes depict events from mythology, and ornament includes animals and floral motifs.
Anatomy acquired more flexibility and naturalness of
shape and proportion, but conventional formulas still
dominated the forms. Beginning in the second quarter
of the sixth century B.C., Athens was the center of great
activity in vase painting. Both potters and painters began
to sign their work (sometimes one man did both vase
and painting).

Athenian grave vase (8th cen. B.C., 61" high. No. 804,
National Museum, Athens). The geometry of the figures
in this funeral scene (Fig. 9-3) places it easily in the
large expanse of purely geometric decoration. One of
the most common geometric patterns looks like a row
of key ends standing upright; this is called the *Greek
key* or *fret* and is still in use today. Many such grave
vases have been found in the Dipylon Cemetery in
Athens. They are often from 5 to 6 feet high, and some
have perforated bottoms through which liquid offerings
could drip onto the grave.

9-2 *Standing Youth,* kouros from Attica,
late seventh century B.C. Marble, 78" high.
Metropolitan Museum of Art, New York
(Fletcher Fund, 1932).

Ajax and Achilles Playing Draughts (550–525 B.C., vaso 24"
high. Vatican Museums, Rome). This black-figured scene
(Fig. 9-4) decorates an *amphora* (tall vase with two
handles) and was done by Exekias, one of the outstanding Archaic vase painters. Geometric ornament is
sparse. The frontally seen eye is still used with the
long-nosed profile of earlier work, and taut, flat shapes
seem to bend stiffly at the joints (compare this with
Archaic sculpture). Figures are anchored to a common
base line; there is no effort to suggest round mass or
deep space. The curve of the men's backs repeats the
curve of the base. The diagonals of the spears intensify
the focus of attention on the game—the center of the
obvious axial balance—and relate the composition to
the handles of the vase, which seem to continue the
lines of the spears.

ARCHITECTURE

Our knowledge of architecture from the Geometric and
Archaic periods is incomplete. The most important
buildings seem to have been temples to the gods and
treasuries to hold offerings. Prior to 650 B.C., the Greeks
built with wood and sun-dried brick; hence we have
few remains that date from before that time. As the
use of stone increased, some of the wooden structural
forms were imitated in stone and became decorative
rather than structural. Limestone was the usual material,
and it was sometimes covered with a white stucco made
of marble dust. Roofs were tile, with colored clay ornaments along the tops and edges. The basic structural
system was post and lintel. The dominant plan for
temples and treasuries was rectangular; from a stepped

9-3 *Dipylon Vase,* Geometric amphora,
eighth century B.C. Approx 61"
high. National Museum, Athens.

9-4 EXEKIAS, *Ajax and Achilles
Playing Draughts,* vase
painting, 550–525 B.C. Vatican
Museums, Rome.

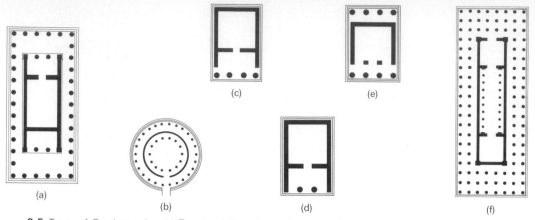

9-5 Types of Greek temples. (a) Temple of Hephaistos, Athens: peripteral temple (surrounded by colonnade) with cella in antis at both ends. (b) Tholos, Epidauros: tholos (round temple). (c) Temple B, Selinus, Sicily: prostyle temple (columns in front of antae). (d) Athenian Treasury, Delphi: temple in antis (columns set within antae). (e) Temple of Athena Nike, Athens: amphiprostyle temple (prostyle at both ends). (f) Temple of Zeus Olympios, Athens: dipteral temple (double colonnade) with cella prostyle at both ends.

base, windowless walls rose to enclose one to three cellae (Fig. 9-5a, c, d, e, f). A *peristyle* (a covered colonnade that surrounds a building or a court) was common. A second type of temple was the *tholos*, which was circular in shape and usually had a peristyle (Fig. 9-5b). The rhythmic alternation of columns and spaces gives the exterior of most Greek temples a lighter, more open

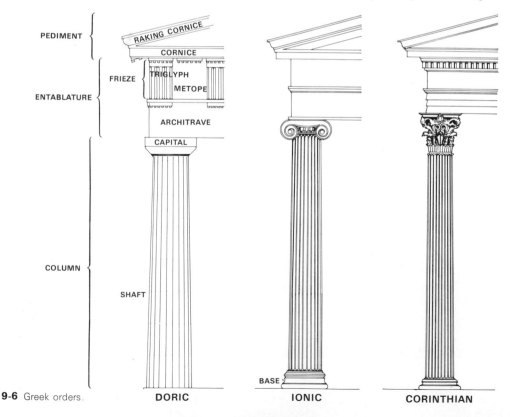

9-6 Greek orders.

PEDIMENT

RAKING CORNICE

CORNICE

FRIEZE

TRIGLYPH

METOPE

ENTABLATURE

ARCHITRAVE

CAPITAL

COLUMN

SHAFT

BASE

DORIC   **IONIC**   **CORINTHIAN**

form than that of Egyptian architecture. The modest
scale, simplicity, and clearly defined limits of Greek
buildings focus attention on the proportions and the
relationship of the parts to the whole form, which
normally uses obvious balance, either axial or central.
Two of the three basic types of Greek columns were
developed during the Archaic period: the Doric and the
Ionic, the latter being more prevalent in Ionia in Asia
Minor. These columns each had a special *entablature*
to match. The combination of column and entablature
is called an *order* (Fig. 9-6).

Temple of Ceres (Paestum, late 6th cen. B.C., limestone,
approx. 48' x 108'). Only the peristyle remains from
this Doric temple (Fig. 9-7) built in the Greek colony
at Paestum on the Italian peninsula. The ponderous
proportions of the pediment and the abrupt mush-
rooming of the capitals are typical of Archaic temples
and indicate some awkwardness on the part of the
provincial builders.

Fifth Century B.C.

ARCHITECTURE

Despite the wars with Persia, the Athenian struggle for
empire, and the Peloponnesian War, the fifth century
B.C. showed remarkable activity in the arts. Of the many
types of buildings, temples and treasuries continued to
be most important. These are often found in sacred
precincts such as Delphi, Aegina, Olympia, and the
Acropolis at Athens. Although systematic city planning
appeared in the fifth century, vast schemes of axial

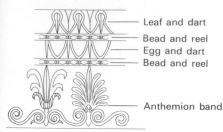

— Leaf and dart
— Bead and reel
— Egg and dart
— Bead and reel

— Anthemion band

9-8 Greek moldings.

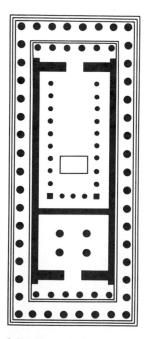

9-9 Plan of the Parthenon.

planning with space and mass were not developed until much later by the Romans; the sacred precincts of the Greeks are, by comparison, more freely arranged. The Athenian Acropolis presents some alignment of parts, however, and contains the most celebrated examples of fifth-century architecture. The major buildings, which owe their beginnings to the statesman Pericles, date from the second half of the century. Marble was used instead of the more economical limestone, and extraordinary efforts were made to achieve the most satisfying proportions and the highest quality of stone carving in both Ionic and Doric temples. The Doric order (Fig. 9-6) received a subtler *entasis* (the slight outward curving of the shaft) than in either the previous or the succeeding century, and the capital became a smoother transition between the vertical shaft and the horizontal entablature. In the most refined Doric temples, the temple platform is slightly domed and all columns lean inward almost imperceptibly, giving the building a more compact, self-contained unity that reinforces the stable equilibrium of vertical and horizontal lines. Unlike the Doric, the Ionic order employed a very slender shaft (sometimes with very slight entasis), a base between shaft and stylobate, a three-part architrave, and usually a continuous frieze instead of the Doric metopes and triglyphs (Fig. 9-6). The third Greek order, the Corinthian, appeared in the second half of the century. It differed from the Ionic only in its leafy capital. The use of two or three orders in the same building became common toward the end of the fifth century. Temples were richly decorated with sculpted moldings (Fig. 9-8) and figure sculpture. Major sculptural compositions were placed in the *pediments* (the triangular gables at the ends of the building), in the frieze area, and sometimes on the outside of the cella walls. As with sculpture, parts of Greek architecture were painted. Blue was common for pediment backgrounds and for Ionic friezes; red was often used as a background for metope sculpture and for capitals and architraves.

Parthenon, built by Ictinos and Callicrates (Acropolis, Athens, 447–432 B.C., marble, approx. 228' x 104' with columns approx. 34' high). The Parthenon (Figs. 9-9 and 9-10) has the most subtle proportions of all Greek Doric temples and has long been considered the high point of Greek architecture. It is the major building on the Acropolis, was dedicated to Athena, patroness of Athens, and formerly sheltered a colossal gold-and-ivory statue of the goddess. Originally, the Parthenon

9-10 ICTINOS and CALLICRATES, Parthenon, Acropolis, Athens, 447–432 B.C. Marble, approx. 228′ x 104′ with columns approx. 34′ high.

had sculpture in the pediments, in the metopes (Fig. 9-19), and in a frieze around the outside of the cella wall.

Erechtheum, built by Mnesicles (Acropolis, Athens, 420–409 B.C., marble, approx. 80′ x 90′)   This irregularly shaped temple (Fig. 9-11) is famous for the subtle proportions and precise carving of its Ionic order and for its porch with *caryatids* (columns in the form of female figures).

SCULPTURE

For sculpture, as for architecture, the fifth century was a time of brilliant activity. Sculpture was present in public places, in sacred precincts, and on temples. Bronze and marble were the main materials. Subjects

9-11 MNESICLES, Erechtheum, Acropolis, Athens, 420–409 B.C. Marble, approx. 80′ x 90′

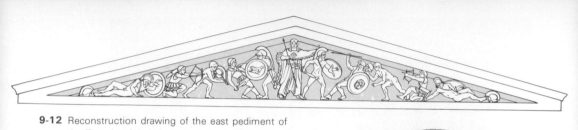

9-12 Reconstruction drawing of the east pediment of
the Temple of Aphaia at Aegina, *c.* 490 B.C.

9-13 *Fallen Warrior,* from the east pediment of the Temple of Aphaia at Aegina.

were usually taken from mythology, although there are
occasional portraits, figures of athletes or heroes, and
representations of animals; rather than depicting specific
historical events, the Greeks used allegory that borrowed themes from mythology. Early fifth-century
sculpture represents ideal youthful bodies with simplified, symmetrical anatomy. Proportions are more natural than in earlier work, but action is still slightly stiff,
and the musculature is hard. Toward the middle of the
century, the work of the great sculptor Myron shows
a slight softening and increased flexibility in pose. After
mid-century, Phidias started a trend toward more active,
flexible poses and more expression of emotion, only
to change in his later work to more restrained action
and a calmer, poised equilibrium of pose. His rival,
Polyclitus, also concerned himself with ideal form,
monumental dignity, and the rhythmic grace of the
contrapposto pose (in which the body relaxes with the
weight on one leg, and the tilt of the hips is countered
by the tilt of the shoulders). Late fifth-century sculpture
worked toward the suggestion of softer flesh and more
flexible poses. Throughout the century, however, space
remains strictly limited. In reliefs, a blank background
restricts action to a shallow layer of depth; in freestanding statues, the form opens predominantly in two
dimensions—shallow crates would suffice for packing
the works—and there is almost no spiral twisting of
the torso.

Pediment sculptures, from the Temple of Aphaia at Aegina (marble with traces of paint, slightly less than life size. Glyptothek, Munich). Three sets of pedimental sculpture were found in debris at the base of the temple, apparently dating from 510 to 490 B.C. Scenes of the Trojan War are depicted, but the exact composition of the pediments is not certain. The reconstruction of the east pediment (Fig. 9-12) utilizes obvious axial balance in poses and actions within the triangular pediment. From the tall figure of the goddess Athena, action diverges until it is countered by movements converging from the corners. The poses are more open and active than those in Archaic work, and the anatomy shows more observation of nature; there is, however, still some stiffness of pose and hardness of flesh. The pose of the *Fallen Warrior* (Fig. 9-13), for example, is complex and generally natural; yet some details, such as the misplaced navel, indicate reliance on earlier stylistic conventions rather than on observation of nature.

Artemision Statue (c. 460–450 B.C., bronze, eyes formerly inlaid, 6'10" high. National Museum, Athens). One of the finest of the votive statues that have been found, this work (Fig. 9-14) was discovered in the sea off Cape Artemision. The right hand originally held an object that is now lost, possibly a thunderbolt (indicating Zeus) or a trident (for Poseidon). The musculature and pose show the degree of flexibility, vitality, and poise characteristic of work just before mid-century. The composition opens mainly in two dimensions, with severely limited depth.

9-14 *Artemision Statue,*
c. 460–450 B.C. *Bronze,*
6'10" high.
National Museum, Athens.

9-15 Reconstruction drawing of the west pediment of the Temple of Zeus at Olympia, 465–456 B.C. Approx. 91' wide.

9-16 *Apollo,* from the west pediment of the Temple of Zeus at Olympia. Marble, over life size. Archeological Museum, Olympia.

9-17
MYRON, *Discus-Thrower* (*Discobolus*), Roman marble copy after a bronze original of *c.* 450 B. Life size. Museo delle Terme, Rome.

Pediment sculptures, from the Temple of Zeus at Olympia (465–456 B.C., marble, central figures approx. 10′ high. Archeological Museum, Olympia, and Louvre, Paris). The eastern pediment showed the preparation for the chariot race between Oenomaus and Pelops; the western pediment depicted Apollo observing the battle between the Lapiths and centaurs (Figs. 9-15 and 9-16). Stylistically, the work is close to the *Artemision Statue.*

Discus-Thrower, by Myron (c. 450 B.C., reconstruction of a Roman copy, 4′6″ high. Museo delle Terme, Rome). Myron chose to depict the moment of equilibrium before the forward swing of the throw (Fig. 9-17). The symmetry of the musculature continues to suggest ideal form, and the composition is very limited in depth, but the pose is more complex than that of the *Artemision Statue.*

Spear-Bearer, by Polyclitus (450–440 B.C., Roman marble copy, 6′6″ high. Museo Nazionale, Naples). Polyclitus was known for his theories of ideal proportions. The muscular figure (Fig. 9-18) attains flexibility through its contrapposto pose. However, the hips and shoulders are aligned in the same shallow space, and the only strong three-dimensional extension is the forward-reaching arm. The hair is organized in groups of wavy lines, and the face is simplified in broad planes. The musculature is still quite firm in the torso, but increasing softness and detail are evident in the arms, hands, and knees.

Lapith Fighting with Centaur (447–432 B.C., marble, 3′11″ x 4′ 2″. British Museum, London). The Parthenon metopes, of which this (Fig. 9-19) is an example, were probably carved under the direction of Phidias. Here

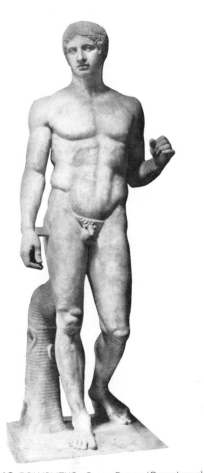

9-18 POLYCLITUS, *Spear-Bearer (Doryphorus),* Roman marble copy after original of *c.* 450–440 B.C. 6′6″ high. Museo Nazionale, Naples.

9-19 *Lapith Fighting with Centaur,* metope from the Parthenon. Marble, 4′8″ high. British Museum, London.

the rhythmic curves of the cloak unite and soften the divergent thrusts of the bodies. The blank background, which limits spatial extension, is typical of Greek reliefs. Despite the weathering of the stone, the carving still suggests the softness of skin overlying the bone structure of the ribs and the muscles of the abdomen.

PAINTING

We must turn again to vases, for the celebrated wall paintings of Polygnotus and Zeuxis are lost. Descriptions by ancient writers indicate that the wall paintings contained some illusion of depth and that theories of perspective had been formulated. The growing interest in depth may have contributed to the decline, after the fifth century, of the importance of vase painting, for depth in vase painting works against the form of the vase by denying its surface. Although red-figure painting continued, there was an increasing tendency to use delicate colors and light linear drawings on vases with white grounds. Figures became rounder, softer, and more flexible as contours overlapped to indicate folds in the flesh. Objects were drawn with more *foreshortening* (as though extending diagonally into space); the eye appears in profile for the first time.

Athenian mixing bowl, from Orvieto (475–450 B.C., approx 21″ high. No. G 341, Louvre, Paris). This work (Fig. 9-20) is traditional in its red-figure technique, but it demonstrates the increasing interest in natural anatomy, mass, and space. It depicts warrior heroes (perhaps the Argonauts) in casual poses freed from a common base line; the figures are placed at various levels, suggesting different degrees of depth. Overlapping contours and foreshortening imply mass in space.

9-20 Athenian mixing bowl, from Orvieto, 475–450 B.C. No. G 341, Louvre, Paris.

Fourth Century B.C.

ARCHITECTURE

Defeat in the Peloponnesian War put an end to Athens' leadership in architecture. During the fourth century, many important buildings were produced in cities like Delphi, Tegea, Epidauros, and—in Asia Minor—at Priene, Ephesus, and Halicarnassus. Efforts spread to a wider variety of types of buildings, many of them secular: *Stoas* (colonnaded, open-fronted sheds used in city centers as promenades and shopping areas), theaters, council halls, and tombs all received special attention, although they had prototypes in earlier centuries. All types of architecture used one or more of the three orders. The Corinthian capital shifted from interior to exterior use, and there was widespread development of the Ionic temple, particularly in Asia Minor. Theaters usually consisted of a slightly more than semicircular area of tiered seats set into a hillside, a round central space (orchestra), and a structure consisting of a raised stage and a building that provided an architectural background and housed dressing rooms and properties. Council halls were oval, square, or rectangular, often with tiered seats around a central altar. The tholos temple reached a height of subtlety and richness of design, and tomb architecture acquired monumental scale.

Mausoleum (Halicarnassus, 360–350 B.C., 136' high). The building (Fig. 9-21) is no longer extant, and its exact form is uncertain. Standing on a rectangular base, it had an Ionic peristyle and was topped by a stepped pyramid and a *quadriga* (chariot pulled by four horses). The structure served as a tomb for Mausolus, a satrap of the Persian kings. In antiquity, it was considered one of the Seven Wonders of the World.

Choragic monument of Lysicrates (Athens, 334 B.C., limestone and marble, 54' high). This monument (Fig. 9-22), developed from the tholos form, was built to commemorate a victory in a choral contest. It seems to be the earliest example of the exterior use of Corinthian columns. The small size recalls the decrease in monumental building in Athens after the defeat in the Peloponnesian War in 404 B.C.

SCULPTURE

Trends that began in the late fifth century grew more evident during the fourth century. Stone and bronze took on the softness of flesh, contrapposto poses became more pronounced, and poses opened up three-dimensionally, with more spiral twisting in the torso. Stone surfaces were polished until the details softened, as though seen through a veil. The famous Praxiteles led these developments in the mid-fourth century. In some work, the serene poise of earlier Greek art gave way to representations of violent motion; and deep-set eyes and beetling brows created an expression of suffering or consternation.

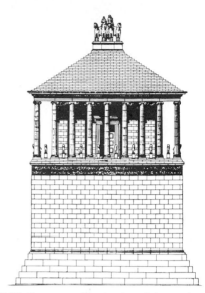

9-21 Reconstruction drawing of the tomb of Mausolus (Mausoleum) at Halicarnassus, 360–350 B.C.

9-22 Choragic monument of Lysicrates, Athens, c. 334 B.C.

Hermes with the Infant Dionysus (c. 350 B.C., marble, 6'11"
high. Archeological Museum, Olympia). The group (Fig.
9-23) may be an original by Praxiteles. Hermes, whose
divine powers were of a particularly intellectual bent,
was shown teasing the young god of wine, who often
represented human passions, by holding some grapes
beyond the child's reach. The cloudlike softness of the
modeling, the three-dimensional extension of the arms,
the spiral twist of the body, and the relaxed contrapposto pose are typical of later work.

Battle of Greeks and Amazons, from the east frieze of the
Mausoleum at Halicarnassus (c. 350 B.C., marble, 35" high.
British Museum, London). Ancient writers say that the
east frieze of the Mausoleum was carved by Scopas,
one of the most famous sculptors of the time. In the
surviving fragments of the frieze (Fig. 9-24) tense poses
and contorted faces express a physical and emotional
violence quite unlike the characteristic poise and equilibrium of earlier work. Scopas reveals an interest in
depicting the inner man; his style is characterized by
deep-set eyes and expressions of anguish.

Hellenistic Period: 323–100 B.C.

The Greeks called themselves Hellenes, and their culture is often called *Hellenic.* With the conquests of
Alexander the Great, Greek culture, modified by local
cultures, spread over the civilized world. This international Greek-inspired culture is called *Hellenistic.* Various dates are given for the Hellenistic period, but 323
B.C., the year of Alexander's death, and 100 B.C., a year
well after Rome had conquered Greece and had begun

9-23 PRAXITELES, *Hermes with the Infant
Dionysus, c.* 350 B.C. Marble, 6'11"
high. Archeological Museum, Olympia.

9-24
SCOPAS (?), *Battle of
Greeks and Amazons,*
from the east frieze
of the Mausoleum at
Halicarnassus, 359–
351 B.C. Marble, 35"
high. British Museum,
London.

9-25 West front of the Altar of Zeus and Athena, Pergamon (restored). Staatliche Museen, Berlin.

to transform Hellenistic art into Roman art, can be considered the approximate beginning and end dates.

ARCHITECTURE

The Hellenistic period saw the rise of important art centers in places far from Greece, such as Pergamon, Rhodes, Tralles, and Alexandria. An increase in the wealth of many cities led to larger *agoras* (city centers) with more elegant surrounding stoas. A grid plan of rectangular blocks and intersecting streets gave order to some cities. As in the fourth century B.C., there was a wide variety of building types. Town houses often had two stories built around a central court, and, in better houses, the court eventually acquired a peristyle. Stone, mud brick, and wood were enhanced by stucco and painted walls. In temple-building, the Doric order became less popular. When it was used, columns were more slender and wall surfaces more ornate; semicircular extensions (*apses*) sometimes emphasized one end of the cella interior. Ionic and Corinthian temples were occasionally raised on high platforms, prefiguring later Roman temples. Some of the Ionic temples were *pseudo-dipteral* in plan; that is, the inner peristyle of the *dipteral* plan (Fig. 9-5f) was omitted, leaving a deep porch around the cella.

Altar of Zeus and Athena (Pergamon, 180–150 B.C., marble; no longer extant except in reconstruction). The altar was

9-26 Temple of Zeus Olympios, Athens, planned *c.* 174 B.C.

a U-shaped *peripteral* building (one surrounded by columns, as in Fig. 9-5a) on a base 17′6″ high and about 112′ x 120′ wide (Fig. 9-25). The order was Ionic, and the base was heavily decorated with sculpture, typifying the increasing complexity and variety of architectural shapes and the tendency to cover more of the surfaces with decoration.

Temple of Zeus Olympios (Athens, marble, begun in 174 B.C. from the designs of the Roman architect Cossutius, and completed in 132 A.D. under the reign of the Roman Emperor Hadrian). The temple (Fig. 9-26), which measures 135′ x 354′, demonstrates the increasing interest in the ornate Corinthian order. The unusually thick columns are over 55 feet high, and their capitals influenced Roman architecture in Italy. The group of thirteen columns still standing at one corner of the temple is evidence of its original vastness.

SCULPTURE

Hellenistic sculpture, like Hellenistic architecture, was produced at creative centers far from the Greek mainland. Because artists moved from one center to another, it is hard to assign local styles to the different areas. Most sculpture of this period was not architectural but set in open spaces, in freestanding figures or groups. Portraits and specific historical events were common subjects and encouraged a detailed realism, as did the developing taste for *genre* subjects (scenes from everyday activity), which were sometimes humorous, undignified, or pathetic, and often revealed human character. Proportions became more elongated, figures became taller and more slender, poses were restless and required more three-dimensional space, and surfaces were treated with greater refinement than previously.

Apoxyomenos, by Lysippos (original done *c.* 320 B.C., Roman marble copy 6'9" high. Vatican Museums, Rome). Lysippos, court sculptor to Alexander the Great, preferred slender proportions and poses that expand in all three dimensions and consume a comparatively great volume of space. The *Apoxyomenos* (Fig. 9-27) is an athlete scraping the sand of the arena from his body. He is in the process of shifting his weight from one leg to the other, creating a more dynamic version of the contrapposto pose.

9-27 LYSIPPOS, *Apoxyomenos,* Roman marble copy, probably after a bronze original of *c.* 320 B.C. 6'9" high. Vatican Museums, Rome.

9-28
Winged Victory (Nike) of Samothrace, *c.* 190 B.C. Marble, approx. 8' high. Louvre, Paris.

Winged Victory, from Samothrace (250–180 B.C., marble, approx. 8' high. Louvre, Paris). The goddess (Fig. 9-28) is of the "nike" type; that is, she commemorates a military victory. The "wet drapery" effect reveals the Greek interest in the body, and the delicate carving of drapery details reveals an interest in the refinement of surfaces. Although the weight is supported by both legs, the body twists in space. The lines of the wind-whipped costume break the large masses into a restless complexity of lights and shadows.

Aphrodite, from Melos (late 3rd or early 2nd cen. B.C., marble, 6'8" high. Louvre, Paris). This statue (Fig. 9-29) is popularly known as the *Venus de Milo.* After the fifth century, Greek sculpture included more female nudes. In the extreme softness of modeling, the proportions of small head, narrow shoulders, and wide hips, and the

9-29 *Aphrodite of Melos,* late third or early second century B.C. Marble, approx. 6'8" high. Louvre, Paris.

9-30 *Laocoön and His Sons,* first century B.C. Marble, 8' high (partially restored). Vatican Museums, Rome.

pose with contrasting diagonals or spiral axes, this is one of the finest examples of Hellenistic work.

Laocoön and His Sons (1st cen. B.C., marble, 8' high. Vatican Museums, Rome). Laocoön, with his sons, is being slain by serpents for his disobedience to the gods. The present restoration (Fig. 9-30) is probably incorrect; the right hand of Laocoön should be closer to the head, thus completing the oval outline of the group. Although the composition has shallow depth, the intricate, restless, open form, the emphasis on anatomical detail, and the portrayal of mental and physical anguish are typical of late Hellenistic sculpture.

Suggestions for Further Study

Bieber, Margarete. *The Sculpture of the Hellenistic Age,* rev. ed. New York: Columbia University Press, 1961.

Blümel, Carl. *Greek Sculptors at Work.* Translated by Lydia Holland. London: Phaidon Press, 1955.

Boardman, John, José Dörig, Werner Fuchs, and Max Hirmer. *Greek Art and Architecture.* New York: Abrams, 1967.

Charbonneaux, J., R. Martin, and F. Villard. *Classical Greek Art, 480–330 B.C.* Translated by Peter Green. New York: Braziller, 1973.

Havelock, Christine Mitchell. *Hellenistic Art.* Greenwich, Conn.: New York Graphic Society, 1970.

Holloway, R. Ross. *A View of Greek Art.* Providence: Brown University Press, 1973.

Lawrence, Arnold W. *Greek Architecture* (Pelican History of Art). Baltimore: Penguin Books, 1957.

Lullies, Reinhard, and Max Hirmer. *Greek Sculpture,* rev. ed. Translated by Michael Bullock. New York: Abrams, 1957.

Pollitt, J. J. *The Art of Greece, 1400–31 B.C.* (Sources and Documents). Englewood Cliffs, N. J.: Prentice-Hall, 1965.

Richter, Gisela M. A. *Archaic Greek Art Against Its Historical Background: A Survey.* New York: Oxford University Press, 1949.

———. *Attic Red-Figured Vases: A Survey,* rev. ed. New Haven, Conn.: Yale University Press, 1958.

———. *A Handbook of Greek Art,* 2nd rev. ed. London: Phaidon Press, 1959.

———. *The Sculpture and Sculptors of the Greeks,* rev. ed. New Haven, Conn.: Yale University Press, 1950.

———. *Three Critical Periods in Greek Sculpture.* Oxford: Clarendon Press, 1951.

Robertson, Martin. *Greek Painting* (Great Centuries of Painting). Geneva: Skira, 1959.

Chapter 9 Music

Music in the Ancient World:

500 B.C.–300 A.D.

Ancient Greek music probably was not much different from the music of other civilized people at that time, and the few remaining fragments of Greek music tell us little of substance. However, Greek ethical and aesthetic theories about the nature and function of music have had a profound and lasting influence on Western society. The Greeks conceived of music as a reflection of order and proportion in the universe. They were particularly interested in the acoustical and mathematical principles that define the basic pitch relationships. The word *music* referred to any of the concerns of the *muses*, the sister goddesses responsible for poetry, drama, choral dance, astronomy, and history. Melody was integral to the singing of poetry and to choral dancing, but it was only one aspect of music understood in its larger meaning, which involved thought, speech, action, and time in the expression of universal truth and beauty. In its narrow sense, however, music also referred to melody, but the distinction between the broad and narrow senses is not always clear.

About 500 B.C. Pythagoras described how the division of a string into halves, thirds, and other simple ratios produced the octave and the other most common pitch intervals; ideas he probably acquired from the Egyptians. This was seen as proof that the universe is ordered according to simple proportions. The Greeks sought to create perfect form in the arts by establishing the proper ratios of the parts to the whole and by relating all elements to a basic unit of measure, as for example, to a rhythmic unit in music. Later theoretical explanations of Greek pitch systems, as well as Greek ethical theories concerning the proper use of music in society, made frequent references to a fundamental order expressed by simple ratios and proportions.

Treatises describing the various Greek pitch systems exist from as early as the fourth century B.C. These do not adequately explain musical practice, and there are conflicting interpretations of their meaning. Medieval music theorists, however, were strongly influenced by these treatises, both in their attempts to systemize and explain the music of the early Christian church and in their notion that such theoretical explanations were important. The tendency of present-day theories to explain music essentially in terms of pitch probably reflects the continuity of Pythagorean concepts.

According to the Greeks, music, taken in its higher meaning, reflected order in the cosmos, and hence it also reflected on a lower level order in human affairs. From this the Greeks developed the doctrine of *ethos*, asserting that music is a force capable of determining

9-31
Woman pouring libation while
playing the lyre. Ceremonial bowl,
c. 460 B.C. Delphi Museum,
Athens.

character and social behavior. Aristotle held that music
represents affective states, such as joy, anger, hate, love,
fear, and courage, which are transferred to the listener,
thereby molding his or her character. Both Aristotle and
Plato were concerned that the young be exposed only to
music conducive to forming good character. Their ideal
education included the study of music and gymnastics,
bringing soul and body into harmony with the universe.
Aristotle's theory of the affective states was the basis for
seventeenth-century musical aesthetic theories. The
idea of music as a moral force in society still persists.

Almost no examples of Roman music survive. The
practical Romans apparently regarded music as a performing art to be used for entertainment, and they were
little concerned with aesthetic or ethical theories. The
importance of music in Roman life is verified by many
references in literature and art to its military functions,
its use at public spectacles, and its performance for
private entertainment. The Romans undoubtedly borrowed Greek music along with the other Greek arts, but
practically no original Roman contributions to the art of
music are known to us.

Suggestions for Further Study

Aristotle. *Politics,* Book VIII.

Lippmann, Edward A. *Musical Thought in Ancient Greece.* New York: Da Capo, 1975.

Plato. *Republic,* Books III and IV.

————. *Timaeus.*

Chapter 10 Art

Etruscan Art:

700–41 B.C.

The origins of Etruscan culture are still unclear. It either arose from an existing *Villanovan* culture (named after a site near Bologna) or was the result of an infiltration and reformation of an older culture by a new people. Greek and Roman authors spoke of the Etruscans as immigrants from Asia Minor. It is clear that Villanovan culture changed suddenly between 700 and 675 B.C. under the influence of new ideas and perhaps the influx of a new population. Tumulus-covered tombs appeared (*tumuli* are earth mounds), some filled with a mixture of Villanovan, Greek, and Near Eastern objects; two different sculptural styles developed, one geometric and one Near Eastern in character; and new wealth is evident. By the late seventh century B.C., the two sculptural styles had fused into one, and a unified culture had formed.

The Etruscan culture existed as a group of independent city-states that generally had republican governments by the late fifth century B.C. In spite of various alliances between the city-states, rivalry prevented any lasting unity. Some of the major cities were Veii, Caere (modern Cerveteri), Tarquinii (modern Tarquinia), Perusia (modern Perugia), and Volsinii (modern Orvieto). Ancient Etruria spread from the areas of Tuscany, Umbria, and Latium as far north as the Alps. The land and sea power of the Etruscans reached its height in the seventh and sixth centuries B.C. Etruria profited as an intermediary in trade between continental Europe and the Mediterranean countries, and the Etruscans' wealth was supplemented by their widely feared piracy. The Tyrrhenian Sea took its name from the ancient name for the Etruscans, the Tyrsenoi; the Adriatic was named after Hadria, an Etruscan colony. Although Rome often warred against Etruscan cities and eventually absorbed them, Rome was ruled by Tarquinian Etruscans from 615 to 510 B.C. Etruscan power declined during the fifth and fourth centuries B.C., and Rome defeated Perusia, the last Etruscan stronghold, in 41 B.C.

The Etruscans borrowed the Greek alphabet and became literate in the mid-seventh century B.C., but only about a hundred words of Etruscan have been deciphered. A considerable literature has been lost; only funerary and ritual inscriptions remain.

Religion was important to the Etruscans. Their gods were of three kinds: those inherited from pre-Etruscan Italic cultures; native Etruscan gods later identified with Greco-Roman deities; and gods adopted from the Greeks.

Although there are different points of view, the

major periods of Etruscan art may be classified as follows: *Archaic* (including pre-Etruscan Villanovan geometric styles, the new Near Eastern or Orientalizing elements, and their merger by the late seventh century B.C.), *c.* 900–470 B.C.; *Classic* (with much Greek influence), *c.* 470–300 B.C.; and *Hellenistic* (continuing Greek influence), *c.* 300–41 B.C.

ARCHITECTURE

Remains are sparse because the Etruscans preferred wood and unbaked brick, and the Romans destroyed or built over much Etruscan work. Houses, known to us chiefly through the forms of cinerary urns, apparently ranged from *wattle and daub* huts (those having walls of woven saplings plastered with mud) to elaborate town houses of the Roman atrium type (see p. 119).

Tombs are the best-preserved remains of Etruscan buildings because they were built of stone blocks or carved from *tufa*, an easily worked stone that hardens when exposed to air. Cemeteries were arranged with grid plans as necropolises, and one tumulus might contain one or several rectangular tombs. The common tomb plan consisted of a rectangular room, with occasional subsidiary rooms, and a pitched roof rising to a ridge beam. When interior supports were used, they had the form of square piers with block capitals into which were incised *volutes* (spirals) that seem to be Asian rather than Greek in origin. Tomb interiors contain the best examples of Etruscan painting—murals depicting mythological scenes, feasting, and sports. Some tomb interiors seem to have imitated house interiors, even to the extent of having household utensils carved on the walls.

Until about 600 or 550 B.C., when temples began to be constructed, Etruscan religious ceremonies were apparently conducted at open-air sanctuaries consisting of platforms within sacred precincts. Although there are no remains that rise much above the stone foundation level, the Roman architect Vitruvius left a description of an Etruscan temple (Fig. 10-1). Its deep porch and three parallel cellae produce an almost square foundation. Widely spaced columns and overhanging eaves offer a topheavy façade. Vitruvius (1st cent. B.C.) probably would have known only late examples. Excavated foundations reveal variations in his plan, one of which may have evolved from the megaron. The decoration of pediments, ridgepoles, cornices, and roof edges with colorful clay sculpture is attested to by numerous frag-

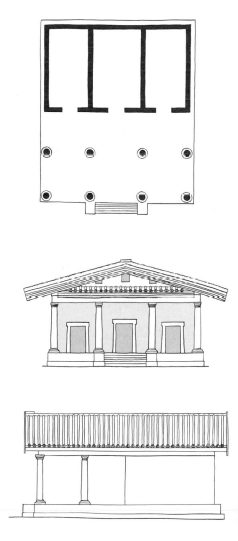

10-1 Plan, section, and elevation of an Etruscan temple. (After Vitruvius.)

ments found at temple sites. The Etruscans used an occasional corbeled dome in tombs and employed the corbeled arch. Their use of the true arch may have come from the Romans, who, in turn, had taken it from Greece or the East. The Porta Augusta in Perugia is a city gate with a true arch and was probably the result of Roman influence. By the second century B.C., Etruscan architecture had largely been absorbed by Roman and Hellenistic Greek forms.

Tomb of the Painted Reliefs (Caere, 5th–4th cens. B.C.). The necropolis at Caere consists of tumuli containing tombs carved and constructed of tufa. This single-chamber tomb (Fig. 10-2) imitates the beamed and pitched roof of a house, although a house would have used supports under the ridgepole, if at all. Here, the piers, carved from tufa left in place, have typically voluted *Aeolic*

10-2 Tomb of the Painted Reliefs, Caere, fifth to fourth centuries B.C.

capitals. The reliefs, both carved and modeled from stucco, depict weapons, household utensils, and even pets.

SCULPTURE

Etruscan sculpture took the form of cinerary urns, sarcophagus effigies, pottery, reliefs, freestanding statues, architectural ornaments, furniture decorations, bronze mirrors, containers, and jewelry. While they used a wide variety of materials, the Etruscans were especially renowned for their technical skill with clay and bronze. They were less interested in stone and used it principally for funerary sculpture. Villanovan or pre-Etruscan sculpture was geometric in style and had descended from Neolithic cultures. Circles, spirals, triangles are often combined with severely simplified images of men and animals. From 675 to 600 B.C., Oriental or Near Eastern elements appeared in the form of sphinxes, hawks, and other gods from Egypt, and winged lions and fertility goddesses from Assyria. Greek influence is also evident and continued to be important throughout Etruscan history. The geometric patterns in hair and drapery, the almond eyes and straight-ridged nose, and the stiff poses of Greek Archaic sculpture mixed with Oriental motifs in Etruria. During subsequent centuries, Etruscan sculpture, like that of Greece, moved toward greater flexibility in pose and naturalness in anatomical detail; yet the Etruscans never lost a suggestion of tenseness in the joints and musculature of the figure, a kind of aggressive awkwardness that is emphasized by large proportions in head, hands, and feet. In spite of Etruscan interest in effigies of the deceased on sarcophagi and cinerary urns, only a specific type of personality and age was expressed until about 300 B.C., when highly individualistic portraiture was imported from Greece.

Apollo of Veii (c. 510 B.C., clay, 69" high. Museo di Villa Giulia, Rome). This life-sized god (Fig. 10-3) was one of four deities originally placed at the ridgepole of the tile roof of a temple at Veii. The figures enacted the contest between Hercules and Apollo for the sacred hind. Greek influence is evident in the Archaic features of face, hair, and clothing. The taut leg muscles and the awkward forward movement are typical of Etruscan art.

Sarcophagus, from Caere (c. 520 B.C., clay, approx. 6'7" long. Museo di Villa Giulia, Rome). Such sarcophagi

10-3 *Apollo of Veii, c. 510 B.C. Clay, approx. 69" high. Museo di Villa Giulia, Rome.*

10-4 Sarcophagus from Caere, c. 520 B.C. Clay, approx. 6'7'' long. Museo di Villa Giulia, Rome.

(Fig. 10-4) provided images of the deceased, just as did many cinerary urns. In this period, the faces, with their abruptly changing planes and Archaic smiles, had little portrait character beyond an indication of age.

PAINTING

Of the paintings on vases, clay plaques, and tomb walls, the tomb murals are the most rewarding. Mineral and vegetable pigments were applied directly on the stone walls or on a plaster ground. Only a few tombs remain from the Orientalizing period. The flowering of tomb painting seems to have come in the second half of the sixth century B.C. Until the mid-fourth century B.C., subjects were generally happy depictions of hunting, feasting, dancing, and funeral games. The flatly painted, unmodeled images are placed on a base line against a neutral background. Human musculature is inflated and tense. By the mid-fourth century, subjects were more somber, depicting underworld scenes or mythical scenes of death and suffering. Proportions and musculature are more natural and mass and depth are suggested by overlapping shapes and outlines. The development parallels that in Greek art, which also expresses a greater awareness of tragedy and of mass in space during the Hellenistic period.

10-5 *Pipe-Player and Birds,* from the tomb of the Triclinium, *c.* 470 B.C. Museo Nazionale Tarquiniense, Tarquinia.

Pipe-Player and Birds, from the tomb of the Triclinium (*c.* 470 B.C. Museo Nazionale Tarquiniense, Tarquinia). The unmodeled figure, base line, and neutral background (Fig. 10-5) are typical of Etruscan painting of this period, but such delicacy of line, shape, pattern, and movement is unusual. The carefree nature of the subject was to change in the following century. Greek influence is evident, especially in facial profile and drapery.

Suggestions for Further Study

Bloch, Raymond. *The Ancient Civilization of the Etruscans.* Translated by James Hogarth. New York: Cowles, 1969.

———. *Etruscan Art* (Pallas Library of Art). Greenwich, Conn.: New York Graphic Society, 1965.

Mansuelli, G. A. *The Art of Etruria and Early Rome* (Art of the World). Translated by C. E. Ellis. New York: Crown, 1965.

Pallottino, Massimo. *The Etruscans.* Translated by J. Cremona. Harmondsworth, Eng.: Penguin Books, 1955.

Richardson, Emeline Hill. *The Etruscans, Their Art and Civilization.* Chicago: University of Chicago Press, 1964.

Spiteris, Tony. *Greek and Etruscan Painting* (History of Painting). Translated by Janet Sondheimer. New York: Funk and Wagnalls, 1965.

Chapter *11* *Art*

Roman Art:

200 B.C.–*330* A.D.

Roman art emerged with distinctive traits during the last two centuries before Christ. In style it persisted until perhaps 500 A.D., but its subject matter was reoriented by Christianity long before then. The year 330 A.D., when Constantinople was dedicated as the new capital of the Roman Empire, can thus be considered the end of the Roman period.

The major sources of Roman culture are the Greek and Etruscan civilizations. Like the Greeks, the Romans had little interest in an afterlife; they focused their attention on the organization and exploitation of the physical world, and this is evident in their art. But the Romans considered the manual arts of painting and sculpture less dignified than the arts of music and poetry. Roman art and literature took Greek works for their models, and Greek gods reappeared in Roman culture with Latin names. The Romans, however, were more concerned than the Greeks with historical documentation; Roman historical writings are paralleled by Roman history-recording art.

Second and First Centuries B.C.

ARCHITECTURE

Remarkable engineering skill was applied by the Romans to a variety of building types, most of which received their basic forms in this period. Materials were wood, mud brick and fired brick, stone, stucco, and concrete. The Romans were the first to use concrete extensively; they reinforced it with rubble and often concealed it behind a veneer of stucco, brick, marble, or travertine (a hard, light-colored limestone). The Romans did not limit themselves to the post and lintel system but went far beyond their predecessors in the development of the arch, the vault, and the dome. The semicircular *Roman arch* (Fig. 4-10, p. 43) could be extended in depth to form a *tunnel vault* (Fig. 4-11, p. 43). From this, the Romans created *cross vaults* (Fig. 4-14, p. 44) as early as the beginning of the second century B.C. Roman architecture used elaborated and modified basic Greek forms, including the three orders. Whereas the Greeks used columns as structural members, the Romans frequently added them as decoration without structural function. Greek column shafts are made with drums (cylindrical sections) placed one on top of the other and fastened with interior metal clamps; Roman shafts are generally monolithic.

Round Roman temples were inspired by the Greek tholos. Rectangular temples have the high base, frontal steps, and deep porch of pre-Roman Etruscan temples, but the Romans used Greek columns and modified Greek proportions in the entablature and pediment (Fig. 11-2). The wider Roman cella often has engaged columns, a device used less frequently by the Greeks. The most common form of Roman monument was the *triumphal arch* (Fig. 11-15 shows a late example), a freestanding structure with inscriptions and relief sculpture describing the event commemorated. One type of Roman building most influential for later architecture is the *basilica*, a rectangular structure with an apse at one or both ends and entrances in the sides or at one end (see the basilica part of Fig. 11-9). Columns divided the interior into center and side aisles. The roof (usually wooden) of the center aisle is higher than that of the sides so that *clerestory* windows (windows looking out over a lower roof) provide direct lighting for the center. Basilicas functioned as law courts, public halls, and audience chambers for rulers. The masses of the urban population lived in multistory tenements, usually built of mud brick and wood, but private city houses were also built, simple or complex according to the builder's financial means (Fig. 11-1). Larger houses occupied the center of a block and were insulated from the street by shops around the perimeter; therefore, all efforts at impressive architecture were concentrated on the interior of the home. The front door opened into a vestibule that led to the *atrium*, a receiving hall. In the center of this room was a pool into which water drained from an opening in the roof (the *impluvium*). The atrium ended in the *tablinium*, where family statues were kept. One then entered the peristyle, a colonnaded walkway around an open court (adapted from Hellenistic houses). Typically, a strong axis from front to back gave order to the progression of interior spaces.

House of Menander (Pompeii). The plan (Fig. 11-1) is typical in allowing a spatial vista down the major axis and in its alternation of small and large spaces. The high ceilings and the free passage of air from garden to front door helped to cool the house.

Maison Carrée (Nîmes, completed in 16 B.C., 59' x 117'). This small provincial temple (Fig. 11-2) is very well preserved. It exemplifies the Roman love of the Corinthian order and the high base, frontal steps, and deep

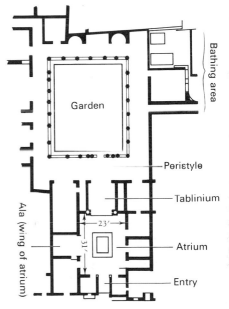

11-1 Plan of the House of Menander, Pompeii. Only the central portion is shown.

porch inherited from the Etruscans. It is one of the few Roman temples having some of the refinements of proportion found in the best Greek work. The *rinceau* (band of scroll-like vine ornament) in the entablature frieze was widely used in Roman architecture.

SCULPTURE

Roman sculpture owes much to the Etruscans and the Hellenistic Greeks. In spite of extensive importation of Greek sculpture and the demand for copies of famous Greek originals, the Romans developed certain types of sculpture that are distinctly expressive of Roman culture. The Roman interest in the actual world is reflected in the rise of portraiture as a major field. The custom of making wax images of dead ancestors, the love of factual documentation, and the late Hellenistic tendency toward realism in portraiture all helped to mold the Roman desire for absolute fidelity to physical appearance. Such realism was countered, however, by occasional periods of interest in the idealism of earlier Greek sculpture. Particularly in certain portraits of Augustus as Emperor, the idealistic simplification and strengthening of basic features can be seen. Relief sculpture became the other important form for the Romans and was used chiefly to commemorate events from Roman history. Roman sculpture went much further than Hellenistic sculpture in depicting specific events with specific details in face, costume, and environment. In place of the blank background of earlier Greek relief, the Romans tried for the illusion of infinite space by graduating the relief from high projection in the foreground to fainter projection for distant objects,

11-3 *Augustus*, from Primaporta, *c.* 20 B.C. Marble, 6'8'' high. Vatican Museums, Rome.

and by using diagonally receding forms. When occasional allegorical scenes make broader reference to Roman history, more general features reminiscent of earlier Greek art appear. Basic materials of Roman sculpture are wax, terra cotta, stone, and bronze. Parts of stone sculpture were sometimes painted.

Augustus, from Primaporta (*c.* 20 B.C., marble, 6'8" high. Vatican Museums, Rome). Individualism is veiled by the interest in ideal form (Fig. 11-3); much detail was omitted in the face, and the large planes are emphasized (note the brows). The visionary stare of the softly carved pupils contrasts with heroic body proportions, a pose of authority, and allegorical scenes on the breastplate referring to the exploits of Augustus. The Cupid and dolphin beside the right leg symbolize Aeneas, the half brother of Cupid and the divine source of the Julian family. The statue thus presents the emperor as a divinity.

Ara Pacis or **Altar of Peace** (Rome, completed in 9 B.C., marble, processional panels 63" high). The relief sculpture decorates a walled enclosure for the altar (Fig. 11-4). On two walls, a procession of Augustus with his family and retinue is depicted. An end wall shows an allegorical scene in which Tellus (Mother Earth) is surrounded by symbols of the abundance that Augustus brought to the Empire. There is marked contrast between the detailed portraiture of the procession and the ideal figures of the allegory, although the latter has specific details in plants and animals. The illusion of infinite space is present throughout. The lower part of the walls is covered with crisply carved symmetrical vine ornament.

11-4 *Tellus Relief,* from the Ara Pacis Augustae, Rome, 13–9 B.C. Marble.

Portrait of a Roman (1st cen. B.C., terra cotta. Museum of Fine Arts, Boston).   Suffering and disillusionment are nakedly revealed by the sagging muscles of the eyes and mouth (Fig. 11-5). The lifeless hair plastered over the wrinkled forehead gives an added feeling of dejection to the figure.

PAINTING AND MOSAICS

Our knowledge of Roman painting comes largely from wall paintings found in three cities buried by an eruption of Mt. Vesuvius in 79 A.D.: Pompeii, Stabiae, and Herculaneum. On such a limited basis, generalization must be tentative. We may assume probable influence of the lost paintings of the Hellenistic age, however, because imported Greek artists were responsible for some of the Roman paintings, as is evidenced by Greek signatures and inscriptions. Wall painting of the second century B.C. consisted of rectangular panels of color, often imitating marble. This *First Style* was succeeded around 60 B.C. by a *Second Style* depicting landscapes, figures, and architectural vistas. For the illusion of deep space, a makeshift system of linear perspective was devised, which consisted of different horizon lines and thus varying eye levels. Effects of light and shadow, aerial perspective, and convincing anatomy were achieved. The wall paintings seem to have been done in tempera with a binder of lime emulsion. Encaustic was used for a few colors. The ground was made with three coats of sand mortar and three of fine-grained plaster, often mixed with marble dust. The plaster was polished before the paint was applied. The permanence of such work has been remarkable. Sometimes wood

11-5 Portrait of a Roman, late first century B.C. Terracotta, 14″ high. Museum of Fine Arts, Boston. Purchased by contribution.

11-6 *Ulysses in the Land of the Lestrygonians,* from *The Odyssey Landscapes, c.* 50–40 B.C. Vatican Library, Rome.

panels were given the plaster ground and utilized as supports for paintings, but most of these panels have perished. Mosaics were widely used, both on floors and on walls. In both mosaics and painting, the style indicates a strong interest in the visual experience of the physical world.

Odyssey Landscapes (*c.* 50–40 B.C. Vatican Library, Rome). These Second Style paintings (Fig. 11-6) were discovered in the ruins of a house on the Esquiline Hill in Rome. Eight episodes from Books X and XI of the *Odyssey* are shown in a continuous landscape (44′ x 5′) divided only by a painted architectural framework. Lively figures are placed in a world of shimmering light and space. Shadows are used to define the ground plane and to locate objects on it. Aerial perspective creates depth. The breathtaking effects of color and light seem to be achieved without effort.

Mosaic showing street musicians (Museo Nazionale, Naples). The Greek Dioskourides of Samos signed this work (Fig. 11-7), probably during the period of the Second Style. The everyday subject, the characterization in faces and gestures, and the factual treatment of light and shadow—qualities first developed in late Hellenistic painting—are typical of much Roman painting. The handling of color is particularly subtle, and shadow areas are enlivened with reflected lights.

11-7
Mosaic showing street musicians, probably first century B.C. Museo Nazionale, Naples.

11-8 Colosseum, Rome, 72–80 A.D.

First Century to 330 A.D.

ARCHITECTURE

The Roman Empire reached its height in the second century A.D., and its power and wealth are reflected in architectural design. Vast size and lavish decoration are typical of the period from the first to the fourth centuries. Roman architects tended to impose a scheme of order upon the whole site, arranging landscape as well as spaces and masses to achieve effects of gradation and climax. Plans often used obvious axial balance. Examples may be found in the *forums* (civic centers for Roman towns), where temples, government buildings, and commercial houses were organized around an open space (Fig. 11-9). The forum has its sources in pre-Roman Etruscan town plans and in the Greek agora. Of the three Greek orders, the Romans preferred the most ornate, the Corinthian. From this they derived the *composite* capital by adding Ionic *volutes* (spirals) to the Corinthian capital. In addition they developed the *Tuscan order*, using a base, an unfluted shaft, a derivation of the Doric capital, and an entablature without frieze ornament. It was Roman architecture that established the system of superposed orders for buildings of several stories. Doric or Tuscan was used on the ground floor, Ionic on the next, and Corinthian above. These post and lintel forms were often combined with the arch, as in the *Roman arch order*, an arched opening framed by engaged columns or *pilasters* (flattened column shapes that project as planes from the wall) and an entablature. The Romans also adopted and elaborated Greek architectural moldings (Fig. 9-8, p. 98).

For an understanding of Roman culture, it is significant to note that wealth was spent not just on temples but on monuments to Roman leaders, on palaces, and on places of public entertainment such as baths and amphitheaters. For the late period, public entertainment was very important to Roman politics. The amphitheaters (as distinct from theaters, which followed the Greek form) were built for athletic or gladiatorial contests. The tiered seats surrounded an elliptical arena, and the exterior might be banked earth or arcaded galleries. Some of the largest Roman buildings were the public baths (*thermae*), which served as community centers with lecture halls, libraries, lounges, and outdoor playing fields in addition to bathing pools of various temperatures. All was planned around dramatic axes of interior and exterior spaces. Statues and mosaics decorated the interior; walls and mammoth cross vaults were veneered with sumptuous marble. The populace enjoyed these elegant public facilities and found them a relief from the apartments (mostly of concrete by the first century A.D.) in which many Romans led crowded lives.

Colosseum (Rome, completed *c.* 80 A.D. and frequently restored, elliptical, approx. 620' x 513'). This vast area (Fig. 11-8) seated 50,000 spectators. Tunnel and cross vaults were used in corridors and stairways. The core is concrete, and the façade is faced with travertine. The arcades of the façade employ the Roman arch order with engaged columns in the following sequence: Doric, Ionic, and Corinthian. The fourth level has Corinthian pilasters.

Forum of Trajan, designed by Apollodorus of Damascus (Rome, completed *c.* 113 A.D., central square approx. 300' x 350'). The Roman preference for grand organizations of spaces and masses is exemplified here (Fig. 11-9). The symmetrical order moves along the axis from the front gate, through the main forum space, into the basilica, past the column dedicated to Trajan's wars, to the climactic temple of the deified emperor.

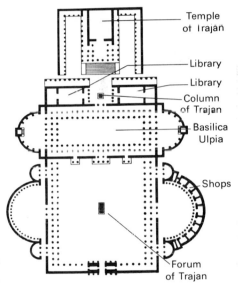

Temple of Trajan

Library

Library

Column of Trajan

Basilica Ulpia

Shops

Forum of Trajan

11-9 Plan of the Forum of Trajan.

11-10 Pantheon, Rome, 118–25 A.D.

11-11 GIOVANNI PAOLO PANNINI, *Interior of the Pantheon, c.* 1750. National Gallery of Art, Washington, D.C. Samuel H. Kress Collection.

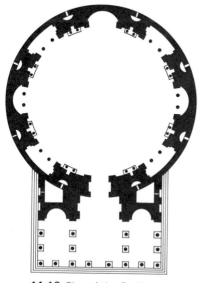

11-12 Plan of the Pantheon.

11-13 Basilica of Constantine, Rome, *c.* 310–20 A.D.

Pantheon (Rome, mainly built 118–25 A.D.). The concrete and brick core of this building (Figs. 11-10–11-12) formerly had a marble and stucco veneer. The dome (142 feet in diameter) was the most celebrated in ancient architecture. The concrete ranges in thickness from six to twenty feet, and the interior of the dome has *coffering* (an excavated grid effect), a device often used in vaulting by the Romans to lighten the structure without weakening it. Aside from the main door, the only light source in the Pantheon is the *oculus* (a round opening in the center of the dome). The dramatic lighting and the vast scale make the much-copied Pantheon one of the supreme examples of effective use of interior space.

Basilica of Constantine (Rome, completed *c.* 320 A.D., after having been started by Emperor Maxentius in 310, 265′ x 195′). Most basilicas had wooden roofs, but vast concrete tunnel and cross vaults were used here in one of the largest vaulted interiors of the ancient world (Figs. 11-13 and 11-14). Formerly huge columns were part of the decorative veneer. The effect was more like that of the great hall of a Roman bath than the hall of a basilica. The building provided a grandiose setting for the ritual of Roman government.

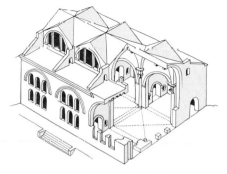

11-14 Reconstruction drawing of the Basilica of Constantine.

11-15 Triumphal Arch of Constantine, Rome, 312–15 A.D.

Triumphal Arch of Constantine (Rome, *c.* 312 A.D.). The three arches, the quantity of sculpture (some of it borrowed from earlier monuments), and the decorative Corinthian columns all break up the surfaces and create a sumptuous and dramatic play of light and shadow on the structure (Fig. 11-15).

SCULPTURE

During this period the other-worldly interests of Christianity began to undermine the Roman world of fact, flesh, and blood. In portrait sculpture, the third century brought increased animation in the twist of the head and the turn of the eyes, and the bust-type portrait came to include the shoulders and often one or both arms;

but by the fourth century, the eyes had become large and preoccupied, the carving crude or summary, and the forms more stereotyped. Historical and mythological reliefs, used on triumphal arches, commemorative columns, altars, and sarcophagi, became, during the late second and third centuries, more compressed into shallow foreground space, more complex in parts, and less definite about the climactic centers of the composition. By the fourth century, representations of specific events acquired the effect of scenes staged with dolls; the episode became ritual. The figure functioned somewhat abstractly as a symbol for man and for his role in a social or divine order. Heads were shown disproportionately large, without much variety in features or expression; costume folds were indicated by quickly carved grooves, poses were more rigid, and abrupt modeling created sudden dark shadows that tended to isolate the many parts.

Reliefs on the Arch of Titus (Rome, 81 A.D., marble). The arch was built to celebrate the subduing of Jerusalem by Titus. The reliefs (Fig. 11-16) depict a triumphal procession carrying booty (note the seven-branched candelabrum). Diagonal masses and increasingly faint

11-16 *Spoils from the Temple in Jerusalem,* relief on the Arch of Titus. Marble, approx. 7' high.

11-17 Reliefs on the Column of Trajan, Rome, 113 A.D.

relief suggest atmospheric perspective and deep space. The factual detail expresses the disorder of the event without the theme and variations of line and shape that would lend subtle harmony to a Greek interpretation of a similar subject.

Column of Trajan (Rome, completed *c.* 113 A.D., marble, 125' high). The column is divorced from its structural role to become a monument. A spiral relief 656 feet long and 50 inches high winds from bottom to top depicting Trajan's Dacian Wars (Fig. 11-17). Architecture and landscape are reduced to undersized stage settings in order for the figures to present clearly the historical narrative.

Julia Domna, wife of Septimius Severus (early 3rd cen. A.D., marble, 26" high. Metropolitan Museum of Art, New York). The animated turn of head and eyes and the inclusion of the body almost to the waist are typical of much third-century portraiture (Fig. 11-18).

Constantine Addressing the Senate, frieze on the Arch of Constantine (Rome, early 4th cen. A.D.). The style in Figure 11-19 reflects the development of late Roman sculpture, in which the depicted object was becoming an abbreviated symbol. The roughly carved, doll-like figures are shown with enlarged heads and repetitive poses; they provide a striking stylistic contrast with the relief medallions right above, which are from the second century.

PAINTING AND MOSAICS

In wall painting a *Third Style* seems to have prevailed from 20 B.C. to 60 A.D. Here, the wall was treated more flatly but illusional paintings of columns and moldings of delicate proportions were used. Monochrome landscapes were often added to suggest panel paintings hung on the walls. A *Fourth Style,* between about 60 and 79 A.D. in Pompeii, again opened up the wall with palatial,

11-18 *Julia Domna* (wife of Septimius Severus), early third century A.D. Metropolitan Museum of Art, New York

11-19 *Constantine Addressing the Senate,* frieze on the Arch of Constantine.

11-20 Third Style wall painting, from Pompeii, *c.* 20 B.C.–60 A.D. Museo Nazionale, Naples.

11-21 Fourth Style wall painting, from Herculaneum, *c.* 60–79 A.D. Museo Nazionale, Naples.

11-22 Portrait of a man, from Faiyum, second century A.D. Encaustic on wood panel, approx. 13¾″ x 8″. Albright-Knox Art Gallery, Buffalo (Charles Clifton Fund).

theatrical architecture, landscapes, cityscapes, and mythological scenes. It pushes illusionism even further than before. From Lower Egypt, during the period of Roman occupation, come a number of portraits on panels that have been preserved by the dry climate. These were attached to mummies. The technique is encaustic, and the style is similar to that of some miniature portraits painted on glass medallions during the third century A.D., probably in Italy. There is some evidence that painters (particularly those working for Christians), like sculptors, became less interested in accurate appearance by the fourth century and turned increasingly to flat, schematic shapes whose power lay in their symbolic content rather than in their imitation of physical reality.

Third Style wall painting, with monochrome landscape (*c.* 20 B.C.–60 A.D. Museo Nazionale, Naples). The scenery is presented as a monochrome panel, emphasizing the flat surface of the wall (Fig. 11-20). Illusionistic space is kept shallow, and the painted columns and moldings are delicate and slender, decorated with plant ornament.

Fourth Style wall painting, from Herculaneum (c. 60–79 A.D. Museo Nazionale, Naples). Delicate motifs from the Third Style are combined with bold architecture and deep space (Fig. 11-21). Curtains and an actor's mask give the effect of stage decoration.

Portrait of a man, from Faiyum (2nd cen. A.D., 13¾″ x 8″. Albright-Knox Art Gallery, Buffalo). Encaustic on wood was used here (Fig. 11-22) for the type of portrait that was attached to mummies. Individual features are rendered in somewhat stereotyped forms by an artist accustomed to working quickly and producing in quantity.

Suggestions for Further Study

Boethius, Axel. *The Golden House of Nero: Some Aspects of Roman Architecture.* Ann Arbor: University of Michigan Press, 1960.

Brilliant, Richard. *Roman Art from the Republic to Constantine.* London: Phaidon, 1974.

Brown, Frank E. *Roman Architecture* (Great Ages of World Architecture). New York: Braziller, 1961.

Hanfmann, George M. A. *Roman Art: A Modern Survey of the Art of Imperial Rome.* Greenwich, Conn.: New York Graphic Society, 1964.

Kähler, Heinz. *The Art of Rome and Her Empire* (Art of the World). New York: Crown, 1963.

Maiuri, Amedeo. *Roman Painting* (Great Centuries of Painting). Translated by Stuart Gilbert. Geneva: Skira, 1953.

Nash, Ernest. *Pictorial Dictionary of Ancient Rome.* 2 vols. New York: Praeger, 1961–62.

———. *Roman Towns.* Locust Valley, N.Y.: Augustin, 1944.

Pollitt, J. J. *The Art of Rome, c. 753 B.C.–337 A.D.* (Sources and Documents). Englewood Cliffs, N.J.: Prentice-Hall, 1966.

Richter, Gisela M. A. *Roman Portraits.* New York: Metropolitan Museum of Art, 1948.

———. *Three Critical Periods in Greek Sculpture.* Oxford: Clarendon Press, 1951.

Rivoira, Giovanni T. *Roman Architecture and Its Principles of Construction Under the Empire.* Oxford: Clarendon Press, 1925.

Robertson, Donald S. *A Handbook of Greek and Roman Architecture.* New York: Cambridge University Press, 1954.

Strong, Mrs. Arthur. *Roman Sculpture from Augustus to Constantine.* New York: Scribner's, 1907.

Vermeule, Cornelius C. *Roman Imperial Art in Greece and Asia Minor.* Cambridge, Mass.: The Belknap Press of Harvard University Press, 1968.

Chapter 12 Art

Early Christian and Byzantine Art:

100–1453

One of the most far-reaching changes in Western thought came through the impact of Christianity upon the Roman world. Late Roman history reveals an increasing interest in foreign religions, such as the worship of Isis (Egypt) or of Mithras (Persia), but Christianity won out and provided the basis for a new world view. For the Christian, reality was the drama within, the struggle of good against evil, the salvation of the soul, and the attainment of life after death; the physical world was inimical, irrelevant, or symbolic of the inner reality. As reality became less materialistic, the role of art became more complex.

Long before the legalization of Christianity by Constantine in 313, paintings with Christian subject matter were done on the walls of *catacombs* (underground passageways with niches used for burial by Christians). Thus the period of Early Christian art overlaps that of Roman art. The term *Early Christian art* refers not so much to a certain style as to a period, from about 100 to 500, and to art with Christian subject matter within that period. The term *Byzantine* refers not only to the geographical area of the Eastern Roman Empire, with its capital at Constantinople (the ancient Byzantium), but also to particular stylistic features common to much art of that region from about 500 until the fall of Constantinople to the Turks in 1453. There is, however, no sharp dividing line between Early Christian and Byzantine art. Important art centers were Rome, Constantinople, Antioch, and Alexandria. Much of the Byzantine painting and sculpture was destroyed and its stylistic development affected by *iconoclasm*, a controversy between the *iconophiles*, who wanted religious images, and the *iconoclasts*, who felt that images were idols and that religious art should present symbols rather than images of sacred persons. The battle began with an edict from the Eastern emperor in 726 prohibiting figurative images and ended with the victory of the iconophiles in 843.

Early Christian Period: 100–500

ARCHITECTURE

Early Christian architecture inherited the techniques and the forms of Roman building, but aims had changed and form was modified accordingly. Early Christian builders concentrated on churches, *martyria* (buildings marking the tomb of a martyr or the site of his death, or containing a sacred relic), and baptisteries. They did not seek the earthly grandeur of Roman temples but stressed instead a withdrawal from the physical world and a mystical experience of salvation for the worshiper. Exteriors were left starkly simple; in interiors glittering mosaics and Greco-Roman colonnades, arcades, or masonry piers (often made of columns taken from the ruins of Roman temples) were arranged for effects of gradation and climax that focus on the altar. Plans are of two basic types, the *longitudinal* and the *central,* both having roots in Roman architecture. The longitudinal type was a modified Roman basilica plan and is therefore called a basilica (Fig. 12-1). From an entry gate, one passes through the *atrium* (open court) into the *narthex* (vestibule), where one can see the altar at the far end of the nave. By means of these spaces, which provide progressive degrees of withdrawal from the outside world, the altar gains significance. The longitudinal axis, which lends itself so well to dignified processionals, is sacrificed in the central type of building. In the fourth century, the central plan was generally used for martyria, but it soon appeared in churches as well. Although the central space receives the major emphasis, a slight axis may be suggested by placing the altar just off center against an apse. Central plans have a variety of forms, especially in Syria and Armenia, ranging from circular to square or Greek cross (arms of equal length) within a square. Other variations were developed in the Byzantine period. Central churches often had vaulting or domes of stone or brick. Large basilicas were usually roofed with timber, although tunnel vaults were frequently used over side aisles; smaller basilicas, particularly in Syria and Asia Minor, used stone and brick vaulting.

Old Basilica of St. Peter (Rome). This old basilica (Fig. 12-1) was destroyed to make room for the Renaissance structure, but the original is known through drawings and descriptions. Built over the tomb of St. Peter between 324 and 354 by order of Constantine, it exemplifies an early but fully developed basilica plan. The nave was roofed with timber and the outer side aisles with tunnel vaults. Although in later Christian churches the main entrance was traditionally placed at the west, Old St. Peter's had its entrance at the east end.

Santa Costanza (Rome). The central building (Fig. 12-2) was ordered by Constantine in 324, possibly as a mausoleum for a member of his family, and was converted

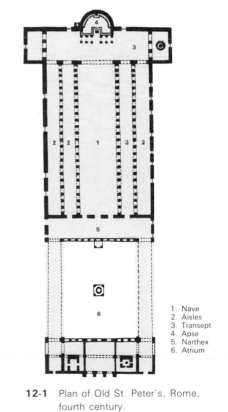

1. Nave
2. Aisles
3. Transept
4. Apse
5. Narthex
6. Atrium

12-1 Plan of Old St. Peter's, Rome, fourth century.

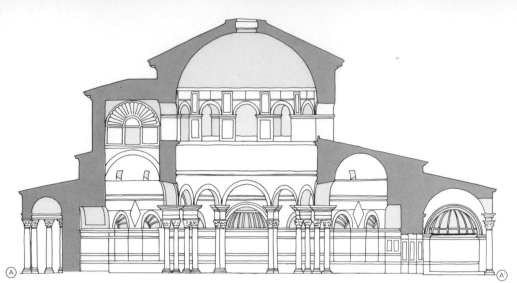

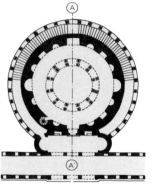

12-2 Plan and section of Santa Costanza.

to a church in the thirteenth century. The central space, about 40 feet in diameter, is covered by a dome on a drum that rests on arcades carried by twelve pairs of columns. Around the central space is a circular side aisle with a tunnel vault and mosaics. The building was originally peripteral. It is an important prototype for later central churches.

PAINTING AND MOSAICS

Painting was done on walls and panels and in book illustrations. Tempera, encaustic, and fresco-secco were employed. The earliest Christian painting is found in the catacombs in Rome. These fresco-secco works depict praying figures and episodes of miraculous salvation taken from the Old and New Testaments. The scenes are reduced to the minimum essentials; the figures are sketchily painted and have large heads, staring eyes, and doll-like bodies. There is little interest in landscape or depth, but the abbreviated episodes are sometimes set into painted geometric designs. The effect is that of brief pictorial prayers. Few catacomb paintings were done after the fifth century.

Until the development of the printing press during the Renaissance, books were copied and illustrated by hand. These *illuminated manuscripts* were at first in the *rotulus* form, following the Roman scroll books; rather than using separate pages bound at one side, the text was written on a continuous band held on two rollers, and the reader unrolled one side as he rolled up the other. Between the first and the fourth centuries, the rotulus type was slowly replaced by the *codex* form that we use today. Parchment (made from animal skin) was common for centuries; paper was not used until after the eleventh century. The painted illustrations in the Early Christian manuscripts showed varying degrees of naturalness, modified by a tendency to harden into conventional shapes that were repeated without direct observation of nature. They are often characterized by flat figures, abrupt modeling, and fanciful colors; the rigid boldness and intensity of these partially abstract and highly symbolic works made them an effective expression of Early Christian theology. A similar stylistic tension between nature and symbol is evident in the mosaics. Generally it is felt that, like Christianity itself, the tendency toward flat symbolic forms had its origin in the Near East.

The Good Shepherd and **The Story of Jonah** (Rome, 4th cen.). The painting is on a ceiling in the catacomb of Saints Pietro and Marcellino (Fig. 12-3). Within a simple geometrical design in obvious central balance, Christ as the Good Shepherd is shown in a landscape with two sketchily painted trees and several sheep. From the central scene radiate episodes from the story of Jonah done in a quick, abbreviated manner. Between the episodes, praying men hold out their hands to heaven. Some of the contrapposto poses echo pre-Christian Roman art, but the sketchiness and the disregard of scale relationships between Jonah, the ship, and the whale reveal a declining interest in the observation of the physical world.

12-3
The Good Shepherd and
The Story of Jonah, from
the catacomb of Saints
Pietro and Marcellino,
Rome, fourth century.

SCULPTURE

Sculpture showed a remarkable decline in importance, partly because of the Biblical injunction against idols and partly as a reaction against the widespread use of idols in Roman temples. It was generally confined to small-scale work, such as sarcophagi, metal plates and chalices, *reliquaries* (elaborate containers for sacred relics), and ivory carvings. What portraits there were showed less and less interest in specific details of physical appearance. Christian sarcophagi of the fourth and fifth centuries are *frieze-type*, with episodes carved in an unbroken frieze along the sides, or *columnar-type*, with scenes divided by engaged columns. Sometimes double registers were used. As in the catacomb paintings, favorite subjects included such miracles as Jonah and the Whale, the Raising of Lazarus, the Sacrifice of Isaac, Daniel in the Den of Lions, the Healing of the Blind, and Moses Striking Water from the Rock.

During the fourth century, sculptural style moved closer to that of the doll-like figures and repetitious poses on the Arch of Constantine. The declining interest in the physical world, the increasing love of flat geometric or floral decoration, and the inclination toward abstract symbols—such as the Cross instead of the figure of Jesus, or the monogram made by superimposing X and P (Chi and Rho), the first letters of Christ's name in Greek—grew from the other-worldly emphasis and the symbolic character of Eastern thought and art. Long before the time of Jesus, Persian art stressed flat patterns and nonfigurative designs. In Constantinople, Christian-Roman culture had been transplanted into the midst of ancient Eastern culture. Thus the more abstract

12-4 Sarcophagus of Junius Bassus, *c.* 359. Marble, 3'10½'' x 8' Vatican Grottoes, Rome.

sarcophagi generally come from Constantinople and other Eastern centers or from artists trained in those areas. The same might be said for the style of the ivory carvings. *Consular diptychs* (two-part ivory plaques celebrating election to the office of consul) from Rome show more interest in anatomy and natural drapery than those carved in Constantinople, even though the Roman work reflects the changes seen in the sculpture on the Arch of Constantine.

Sarcophagus of Junius Bassus, from St. Peter's (Rome, *c.* 359, marble, 46½" x 96"). This fine double-register columnar sarcophagus (Fig. 12-4) mixes Old and New Testament episodes without regard for chronology. Each episode was an abbreviated symbol for the initiate. In the center of the top register, the enthroned Jesus is giving missions to Peter and Paul. At his feet is the head and wind-blown canopy of Cailus, a Roman sky god. Directly below, the Entry into Jerusalem is flanked by Adam and Eve and Daniel in the Den of Lions. In the spandrels of the lower colonnade, lambs are used to represent episodes ranging from Moses Striking the Rock to the Raising of Lazarus. Much natural detail is retained in faces, poses, and costumes, but legs are shortened and heads are enlarged. Compared with earlier sarcophagi, the architecture here is smaller in scale and has more surface decoration.

Byzantine Period: 500–1453

ARCHITECTURE

Long before the time of Christ, the dome had been used as a symbol of the heavens and as a covering for sacred places or objects. The domed central plan is particularly characteristic of Byzantine churches; in Constantinople and surrounding regions, however, the central and longitudinal plans are often fused in the form of short, wide, domed basilicas. Domes, usually over square spaces, are supported by pendentives, which were probably developed in Syria, or squinches, which may have originated in Armenia (Fig. 4-19, p. 46). Domes were sometimes constructed of porous stone or hollow pottery in order to reduce weight and avoid the need for heavy buttressing. Byzantine architecture tends to conceal structural masses with flat mosaic decoration and multicolored marble veneer. Domes and walls appear to be eggshell thin, and capitals of supporting

12-5
Sant' Apollinare in
Classe, Ravenna,
530–49.

12-6
Interior of Sant' Apollinare
in Classe, view toward apse.

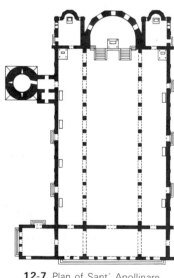

12-7 Plan of Sant' Apollinare
in Classe.

columns are perforated in basketlike designs that make
them look hollow and delicate. The supernatural qualities of the sacred place are expressed in the seeming
weightlessness and the shimmering color of walls and
domes.

Sant' Apollinare in Classe (Ravenna, 530–49). The
three-aisled basilica has a characteristically plain exterior (Fig. 12-5) with one of the earliest *campanili* (bell
towers). Inside (Figs. 12-6 and 12-7), the raised altar receives additional focal emphasis from the framing of

12-8
Hagia Sophia, Constantinople,
532–37.

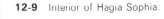
12-9 Interior of Hagia Sophia.

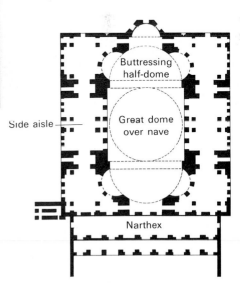

12-10 Plan of Hagia Sophia.

the apse and the concentration of the mosaics. Byzantine patronage is evident not only in the mosaics but also in the nave columns; the soft, spongy-appearing capitals are an abstraction from the crisp, leafy, Corinthian form.

Hagia Sophia (Constantinople, 532–37). Emperor Justinian commissioned this domed basilica (Figs. 12-8 and 12-9) during the first golden age of Byzantine art. A short basilica plan (Fig. 12-10), similar to that of the Basilica of Constantine, is combined with a central

12-11
San Vitale, Ravenna, 526–47.

12-12   Interior of San Vitale.

dome inspired by the Pantheon; but the effect of this dome (180 feet high) on pendentives is quite different from that of its prototype. The blossoming of light from windows around its base makes the Byzantine dome seem to be a hovering canopy. The delicately perforated capitals, the flat shapes in the mosaics, the concealment of the massive supports in the architecture, and the location of the windows all deny the physical weight of the structure and create the effect of a glittering vision, an expressive symbol of heaven.

San Vitale (Ravenna, 526–47). This polygonal central church (Figs. 12-11–12-13), built under the patronage of Justinian, shows both the direct influence of Constantinople and its more distant ancestry in buildings like Santa Costanza. The central space is scalloped by semicircular niches in the side aisles and gallery. The lightweight dome is constructed of pottery and mortar, allowing large clerestory windows in the drum. Mosaics cover the interior walls, and the capitals (Fig. 12-14) have intricate Byzantine basketwork weaving.

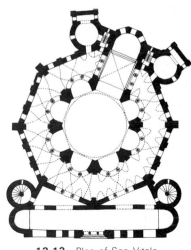

12-13 Plan of San Vitale.

PAINTING AND MOSAICS

By the sixth century, Western (Roman) and Eastern qualities had fused in much of the art produced in and around Constantinople. The resulting style combines frozen figure poses, a disregard for natural scale relationships, and a love of sumptuously decorated flat surfaces. Thus rigid formality is joined with sensuous luxury of design. This style, called Byzantine (after the Byzantine Empire of Constantinople), was not a stable formula, however. Periodic revivals of interest in Greco-Roman art, particularly during the tenth and twelfth centuries, complicated the stylistic development between 500 and 1453. Wall paintings and mosaics in Italian churches range from the worldly interests of ancient Roman painting to the symbolism of Byzantine art. Eastern influence is especially strong in the mosaics at Ravenna, one of the main outposts of the Byzantine Empire on Italian soil during the sixth century. The iconoclasm of the eighth and ninth centuries brought to Rome the talents of displaced Byzantine artists. Christian painting in Syria and Egypt (except for Alexandria) shows much Byzantine character, although Christian art was interrupted in these areas by Moslem conquests in the seventh century. After the iconoclast period, the second golden age of Byzantine art, lasting roughly from the ninth to the twelfth centuries, brought

12-14 Capital from San Vitale.

12-15 *St. Apollinaris,* apse mosaic from Sant' Apollinare in Classe.

a number of stylistic changes. More expression of emotion, more massiveness, and more natural anatomy appear, but the formal order of Byzantine art never relinquishes its hold on movement, costume, and figure.

In the decoration of Byzantine churches, subjects tend to be located according to order of importance. The dome was reserved for Christ as Judge, the drum and pendentives for angels and Evangelists, the vault of the apse for the Virgin, and the other regions of the walls for the Twelve Feasts of the Church (Annunciation, Nativity, Presentation, Baptism, Transfiguration, Raising of Lazarus, Entry into Jerusalem, Crucifixion, Harrowing of Hell, Ascension, Pentecost, and Death of the Virgin) and other scenes from the lives of Jesus and Mary. The west wall often showed the Last Judgment.

In manuscript illumination, as in other painting, the anthropomorphic symbolism, landscape interest, mass, space, and natural poses of the old Roman style— sometimes called the Latin style—were affected in varying degrees by the Eastern influence. The stylistic heritage of a painting is sometimes revealed by details; a bearded Christ or one riding sidesaddle into Jerusalem denotes an Eastern background, while a beardless Christ or one riding astride the donkey denotes a Latin source.

St. Apollinaris, apse mosaic from Sant' Apollinare in Classe (Ravenna, 533–49). This (Fig. 12-15) is one of the most striking examples of Byzantine art on the Italian peninsula. St. Apollinaris, who was martyred in Ravenna, is shown as an imitator of Christ's martyrdom. Above the saint, the Transfiguration of Christ is symbolized by the vision of the Cross between Moses, Elias, and three lambs representing disciples. The severe symmetry of the flat shapes and their exotic colors emphasize the symbolic nature of the event.

Justinian and Attendants, mosaic from San Vitale (Ravenna, c. 547). The Emperor, accompanied by his representative in Ravenna, Maximianus, carries an offering to Christ (Plate 1 and Fig. 12-16). The solid, individually detailed portrait heads contrast with the flat shapes of the costumes, and depth is further negated by the brilliant warmth of the gold background. The artist's indifference to weight and space left him free to allow the feet of several figures to stand upon each other. The ritualistic formality of the staring, symmetrically placed images conveys the hypnotic fascination of Byzantine art. The wall on the opposite side of the altar carries a similar composition depicting Justinian's wife, Theodora, with attendants.

12-16 *Justinian and Attendants,* mosaic from San Vitale.

12-17 *Crossing the Red Sea,* page from the *Paris Psalter,* tenth century (?). Bibliothèque Nationale, Paris.

12-18 *Madonna Enthroned,* thirteenth century. Panel, 32″ × 19½″. National Gallery of Art, Washington, D.C. Andrew W. Mellon Collection.

Crossing the Red Sea, a page from the *Paris Psalter* (Bibliothèque Nationale, Paris). The *Paris Psalter* (Psalm book) contains fourteen full-page illuminations on parchment, one of which is shown in Figure 12-17. The distortions in scale and anatomy and the schematic treatment of costume reveal Byzantine interests. The modeled roundness of some forms, the relatively natural musculature of the nude sea gods and goddesses, and the landscape setting are debts to earlier Roman art. The use of human figures for nature divinities, such as the sea gods and the figure of night (in upper left with canopy), is also characteristic of earlier Roman art. The date of the *Paris Psalter* is uncertain; it may come from the tenth century.

Madonna Enthroned 13th-cen. panel painting, 32" x 19½".
(National Gallery of Art, Washington, D.C.). Standard forms
are used in the costume folds and in the flat modeling
of the faces (Fig. 12-18). Repetition and variation occur
in thematic shapes, such as the radiating highlights in
the clothing. Mass, depth, and natural effects in proportion and drapery are sacrificed for stern order and
elegant formality. The result is a symbolic image that
stands outside the realm of the everyday world.

SCULPTURE

There was very little monumental sculpture in the
Byzantine Empire during the Byzantine period; the case
is quite different in northern Italy and in Europe, as
we shall see in the next chapter. Sarcophagi produced
in Constantinople or in its spheres of influence show
variations of the Byzantine style. Most of the ivory
consular diptychs in the Byzantine style seem to come
from the area of Constantinople and to date from the
sixth century. Icons or reliquaries combine small-scale
relief sculpture, often in gold, with enamel painting.
Their portability helped to spread the influence of
Byzantine art.

Sarcophagus of Theodorus, from Sant' Apollinare in Classe
(Ravenna, 7th cen., marble, 39½" x 81"). The Byzantine
tendency to use symbols rather than literal description
is well illustrated here (Fig. 12-19). The peacocks were

12-19 Sarcophagus of Theodorus, from Sant' Apollinare in Classe, seventh century. Marble.

symbols of immortality; the grapevines referred to the wine of the Eucharist. In the center and on the lid, the Chi-Rho symbol is hung with Alpha and Omega, the first and last letters of the Greek alphabet, standing for the all-inclusiveness of Christ. The symbols are framed by wreaths of victory. There is little interest in the natural detail of the vines or animals and no illusion of depth. The forms have little modeling and appear as shallow layers applied to a flat surface.

Diptych of Anastasius (dated 517, ivory, each leaf 14″ x 5″. Bibliothèque Nationale, Paris). The two halves of a diptych frequently carried approximately the same scene. Here (Fig. 12-20) the newly elected consul, Anastasius, is

12-20 Diptych of Anastasius, 517. Ivory, each leaf 14″ x 5″. Bibliothèque Nationale, Paris.

shown in the official act of throwing down the *mappa* (a piece of cloth used as a signal to start the games in an arena). He is surrounded by winged goddesses of victory. The disregard for natural scale relationships between the figures, the preference for flat ornate surfaces rather than mass and the illusion of deep space, the stiff frontal pose, and the masklike faces are all characteristic of Byzantine art.

Suggestions for Further Study

Ainalov, D. V. *Hellenistic Origins of Byzantine Art.* Translated by E. Sobolevitch and S. Sobolevitch. New Brunswick, N.J.: Rutgers University Press, 1961.

Beckwith, John. *The Art of Constantinople: An Introduction to Byzantine Art, 330–1453.* London: Phaidon Press, 1961.

Demus, Otto. *Byzantine Mosaic Decoration.* London: Routledge & Kegan Paul, 1941.

Du Bourguet, Pierre. *Early Christian Art.* Translated by Thomas Burton. New York: Reynal, 1972.

Grabar, André. *Byzantine Painting* (Great Centuries of Painting). Translated by Stuart Gilbert. Geneva: Skira, 1953.

————. *Byzantium from the Death of Theodosius to the Rise of Islam* (The Arts of Mankind). Translated by Stuart Gilbert and James Emmons. London: Thames and Hudson, 1966.

————. *Early Christian Art* (The Arts of Mankind). Translated by Stuart Gilbert and James Emmons. New York: Braziller, 1968.

Krautheimer, Richard. *Early Christian and Byzantine Architecture* (Pelican History of Art). Baltimore: Penguin Books, 1965.

Mathew, Gervase. *Byzantine Aesthetics.* New York: Viking Press, 1963.

Morey, Charles R. *Early Christian Art,* 2nd rev. ed. Princeton, N.J.: Princeton University Press, 1953.

Rice, David Talbot, and Max Hirmer. *The Art of Byzantium.* New York: Abrams, 1959.

Strzygowski, J. *Origin of Christian Church Art.* Translated by O. M. Dalton and H. H. Braunholtz. Oxford: Clarendon Press, 1923.

Swift, Emerson H. *Roman Sources of Christian Art.* New York: Columbia University Press, 1951.

Volbach, W. F., and Max Hirmer. *Early Christian Art.* Translated by Christopher Ligota. New York: Abrams, 1962.

Von Simson, Otto G. *The Sacred Fortress: Byzantine Art and Statecraft in Ravenna.* Chicago: University of Chicago Press, 1948.

Weitzmann, Kurt. *Illustrations in Roll and Codex: A Study of the Origin and Method of Text Illustration.* Princeton, N.J.: Princeton University Press, 1947.

Chapter *13* Art

Medieval
Art
in
the
North:
400–1400

Early Christian and Byzantine art is often considered the Mediterranean branch of Medieval art. *Medieval* and *Middle Ages* are both vague and unsympathetic labels invented by scholars who thought of the years between the decline of Rome and the beginning of the Renaissance as a barren transitional period. Today we are more appreciative of the age, but the labels remain standard terms. The beginning and end dates of the Medieval period vary with different interpretations. This text will follow one widespread practice in using the term Medieval with particular emphasis on Europe north of Rome during the period between 400 and 1400.

While Early Christian and Byzantine culture was developing in the Mediterranean area, cultures developed to the north in areas that now include France, Germany, Scandinavia, the Netherlands, Belgium, and the British Isles. The Celto-Germanic people inhabiting these areas, called Barbarians by the Greeks and Romans, had an indigenous art before their widespread conversion to Christianity during the third to the tenth centuries. Celto-Germanic art slowly changed through the influence of the Early Christian and Byzantine art brought north by missionaries. Art in the northern countries may be divided into at least four periods: *Celto-Germanic art* (400–800), *Carolingian art* (750–987), *Romanesque art* (mainly eleventh and twelfth centuries) and *Gothic art* (overlapping the Romanesque in the twelfth century and extending in some areas into the sixteenth century). The terms Romanesque and Gothic are also misleading and are retained only because of entrenched usage. Romanesque, or "Roman-like," is an inadequate description of eleventh- and twelfth-century art, just as Gothic, originally meant to imply the barbarism of the Gothic tribes, is a pathetic misnomer for such things as the thirteenth-century French cathedrals.

The greatest efforts of Medieval art were in the service of Christianity, the unifying element in a very divided Europe. The modern distinction between artist and craftsman did not exist; the best talent was often employed to design liturgical equipment, furniture, or jewelry. Since individual identity and originality were not so highly valued as they are today, many works were unsigned and stylistic change was generally gradual. The spread of stylistic influences can be traced along trade routes, the Crusade routes, and the pilgrimage routes. From the sixth century on, pilgrims traveled from northwest Europe to three major destinations: Rome, the Shrine of St. James at Santiago de Compostela in Spain, and the Holy Land.

The art of the first three periods developed mainly in the monasteries. Gothic art was more urban and came from the cathedral centers developed by the *secular clergy* (clergy who did not withdraw from lay society to live by rigid rules, as did the regular or monastic clergy). The word *cathedral* comes from the cathedra, the throne of the bishop, placed in the main church of the bishop's diocese.

Celto-Germanic and Carolingian Art: 400–987

METALWORK

Many of the earliest remains from the Celto-Germanic period are metalwork of bronze or gold decorated with enamel. Bracelets, brooches, armbands, swords, and purse covers are typical. The style combines lively, intricate, geometric designs with fantastic animal and human forms. Constantly expanding and contracting shapes, sudden changes of direction, and amazing intricacy account for the vitality and richness of the work. There is no illusion of mass or space.

Purse cover, from the Sutton Hoo ship burial (British Museum, London). This enamel and gold purse cover (Fig. 13-1) came from the grave of an East Anglian king who died in 654. It is a fine example of early Celto-Germanic metalwork. The style may have been brought to western Europe by migrating tribes from central Asia; it resembles the abstract animal style of nomadic art from southern Siberia and northern Persia.

13-1 Purse cover, from the Sutton Hoo ship burial, before 655. Gold and enamel. British Museum, London.

PAINTING

The most significant painting of the Celto-Germanic period that has been preserved from northwestern Europe is in illuminated manuscripts from the British Isles; the style is called *Hiberno-Saxon* or *Celtic* after the Celts of ancient Ireland. Monasteries became centers of learning where the manuscripts, mainly of the Scriptures, were copied and illuminated. Colors with gum, glue, or gelatin binders were used on parchment or *vellum* (calfskin or kidskin). Like the metalwork, the illuminations employ intricate spiral designs, interlaced shapes in *strapwork* (flat bands resembling cut leather), and fantastic animals. The Celto-Germanic style was characteristic of Hiberno-Saxon painting until the ninth

13-2 Detail from the initial page (XPI) of the *Book of Kells*.

13-3 *St. Matthew,* from the *Gospel Book of Archbishop Ebbo of Reims,* Épernay, c. 816–35. Bibliothèque Nationale, Paris.

century. The style slowly changed, however, under the influence of Byzantine paintings and ivories brought from the south by Christian missionaries, and the Hiberno-Saxon illuminations developed various mixtures of abstract Celto-Germanic design and the relatively more static and representational Early Christian and Byzantine art. During the Carolingian era (750–987), important centers of manuscript illumination were established on the Continent under the patronage of Charlemagne, and different styles evolved in different geographical areas. In the Carolingian Empire, as in the British Isles, Celto-Germanic stylistic traits were increasingly modified by the influence of Early Christian and Byzantine art. In addition, Carolingian painting shows contact with older Roman art; poses, drapery, and landscape sometimes are closer to Roman art than to the Early Christian and Byzantine styles that intervened.

Initial page (XPI) of the *Book of Kells* (8th cen., $12\frac{5}{8}$″ x $9\frac{1}{2}$″. Trinity College Library, Dublin). The manuscript was probably made at the monastery of Kells in Ireland or at that of Iona in Scotland. It contains tables of references, prefaces and summaries, the Gospels, and part of a glossary of Hebrew names. Here Celto-Germanic art serves Christianity. Intermingled with the interlaces and spiral designs are human heads and animals. Other pages in the book depict more of the human figure, but this illumination of the sacred initials of Christ (Plate 2 and Fig. 13-2) illustrates the typical shapes and the swirling dynamism of line that modified Roman, Early Christian, and Byzantine elements to form Medieval art.

St. Matthew, from the *Gospel Book of Ebbo of Reims* (Épernay, 9th cen., $6\frac{7}{8}$″ x $5\frac{9}{16}$″). The so-called Reims School (a regional style) of Carolingian illumination had classicizing tendencies; that is, the pose, costume, massiveness, facial type, and sketchy brush strokes all reflect the influence of ancient Roman art. The Carolingian painter intensified the nervous activity of the lines here (Fig. 13-3) to give the image considerable dramatic vitality.

ARCHITECTURE

Celto-Germanic and Carolingian architecture made extensive use of wood. *Half-timber* construction consisted of a carefully joined wood frame filled in with mud or plaster on reed mats called wattle and daub. Sometimes walls were *palisades* (logs planted vertically side by side, as in a stake fence). Norsemen built frame houses around a central pole resembling the mast of a ship. Such *mast construction* was often covered with vertical wood sheathing. Carolingian builders used stone only for important buildings. The little that remains of their architecture reveals a strong interest in longitudinal plans. The basilica plan was elaborated to create more space for altars, reliquaries, and worshipers. An *ambulatory* (aisle around the outside of the apse) was added (for a Gothic example, see Fig. 13-31); secondary chapels were provided by *radiating apses* around the outside of the ambulatory or by *apses in echelon* (apses placed beside the main apse or on the arms of the transept); and the main apse was separated from the transept by a nave extension called the *choir* (see Fig. 13-31), which allowed space for the clergy choirs. Under the raised choir and apse, a *crypt* provided space for special tombs of local saints and founders of the church or for relics. A Carolingian basilica might be a *double-ender*—that is, it might have an apse at the west end as well as at the east—or it might have a *westwork*, a high, blocklike enlargement giving the effect of a west transept and containing a narthex on the ground level and a chapel above. Carolingian basilicas had timber roofs and many towers; a tower over a westwork and flanking towers at the sides would be echoed by a tower over the *crossing* (where the transept crosses the nave) with flanking towers at the sides. Central-form churches might be octagonal, with tunnel and cross vaults, or a combination of the apse-buttressed square and cross-in-square, four-column type. Such central churches show Byzantine influence in their form and in the rich, flat patterns of decorative details, which were sometimes imported from Italy.

Palatine Chapel of Charlemagne (Aachen, Aix-la-Chapelle). The major extant example of Carolingian architecture is this central church (Figs. 13-4 and 13-5) designed by Odo of Metz and dedicated in 805. It reveals Charlemagne's admiration for Byzantine culture because the polygonal plan and the general form come from San Vitale in Ravenna. Marble columns, a mosaic, and bronze fittings were imported from Italy. The central octagonal space is covered by a domical vault instead of a true dome, and is surrounded by a cross-vaulted side aisle and a gallery with special tunnel vaults. The chapel, which also served as a tomb for Charlemagne, was originally part of a palace complex and contained a throne in its westwork.

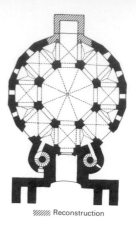

13-5 Restored plan of the Palatine Chapel of Charlemagne.

////// Reconstruction

13-4 Interior of the Palatine Chapel of Charlemagne, Aachen, 792–805.

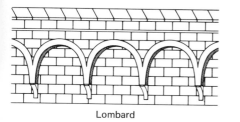

Lombard

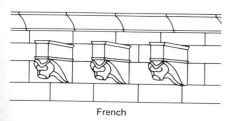

French

13-6 Types of corbel tables.

Romanesque Art: 1000–1200

ARCHITECTURE

The Romanesque period produced more buildings, greater variety, and more advanced masonry techniques than the Celto-Germanic and Carolingian periods. The wooden roofing used over the naves of many basilicas from Early Christian through Carolingian times—a roofing that invited disastrous fires—was slowly replaced by fireproof stone vaulting. Ancient Roman features, such as massive walls, vaults, engaged columns, and pilasters, were used, but with significant changes. Unlike Roman concrete construction, Romanesque building is of masonry, and Romanesque cross vaults have ribs (see pp. 44–45). The leading construction of ribbed cross vaults over the nave occurred in the early twelfth century in Durham Cathedral (Anglo-Norman England), in St. Étienne at Caen (Normandy), and in Sant' Ambrogio at Milan (Lombardy).

Despite its variety, much Romanesque architecture is characterized by: (1) fortresslike massiveness; (2) Roman arches; (3) two or more towers; (4) *splayed openings*—doorways or windows formed by layers of increasingly smaller arches producing a funnel effect (for a Gothic example, see Fig. 13-27); (5) *blind arcades*—arcades attached to a wall for decoration or for buttressing rather than to create openings; (6) *corbel tables* (Fig. 13-6)—a *stringcourse* (horizontal band or molding) supported in the Lombard type by a row of

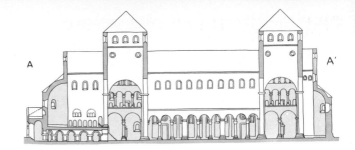

continuous small, blind arches, and in the French type
by small brackets projecting from the wall; and (7) *wheel
windows*—round windows divided into sections by
stone dividers radiating from the center like the spokes
of a wheel. The use of *Lombard pilaster strips* (slender
pilasters) spread northward along the trade routes to
Germany, as did the exterior arcaded galleries developed in Tuscany and Lombardy, while the Lombard
porch, supported by two columns resting on the backs
of lions, did not find wide acceptance elsewhere. Tuscan
churches employed the Early Christian basilica plan,
with the entrance at the west end and the apse at the
east; they were often decorated with patterns of different
colors in stone veneer. In Germany the double-ender
plan was often employed, while in France, in addition
to the pilgrimage church type (see p. 157), some basilicas were built in the form of *hall churches*, where
the side aisles are as high as the nave, and the nave
arcade rises to the springing of the vaults. Some of the
most unusual examples of French Romanesque architecture are the domed churches in Aquitania; their
source would seem to be Byzantine architecture, perhaps by way of St. Mark's in Venice. The pointed arches
that occur occasionally in Romanesque buildings and
are typical of later Gothic work appear to have their
source in Islamic architecture.

Church of St. Michael (Hildesheim). This church (Figs.
13-7 and 13-8) was built under the direction of Bishop

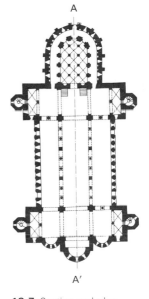

13-7 Section and plan
of St. Michael's.

13-8 Abbey church of St. Michael, Hildesheim,
c. 1001–33 (restored).

13-9 St. Sernin, Toulouse, eleventh and twelfth centuries.

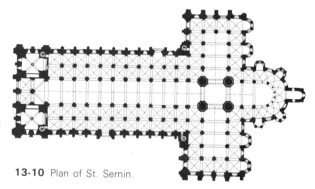

13-10 Plan of St. Sernin.

13-11 Interior of St. Sernin (view toward apse).

Bernward and completed in 1033, during the period of the Ottonian emperors in Germany. Carolingian architecture had provided all the basic elements. St. Michael's is a double-ender with a second transept, a choir, an apse, a crypt, and a crypt ambulatory in the west end. The nave roof is of wood. The entrances are at the sides of the nave, partly sacrificing the axial emphasis of a basilica plan. Towers over the crossings of both transepts and at their ends produce an almost equal exterior balance of east and west. The church was severely damaged in the Second World War.

St. Sernin (Toulouse). The church (Figs. 13-9–13-11) was begun in the eleventh century and finished in the twelfth, with the exception of the upper part of the crossing tower (thirteenth century) and the west façade, which was never completed. The twelfth-century

architect was Raymond Gayrard. St. Sernin is a pil
grimage church and one of the largest surviving Romanesque churches in France. It illustrates the elaboration of the basilica plan by means of choir, ambulatory,
apses in echelon, radiating apses, double side aisles,
and aisles around the transept. The high nave arcade
rests on *compound piers* (piers of several parts, here
having the form of superimposed pilasters and engaged
columns) and is topped by a gallery, which provides
more room for the congregation. There is no clerestory,
for the heavy tunnel vault needs the abutment of the
gallery vaults to sustain it. The bays are clearly marked
by the transverse arches resting on engaged columns
rising all the way from the floor. The columns break
through the horizontal lines to establish a vertical emphasis that suggests the Gothic architecture to come.
The exterior exhibits round-arched windows, French
and Lombard corbel tables, and blind arcades.

St. Étienne (Caen, 11th–12th cens.). The west façade (Fig.
13-14) of the Norman basilica has a strong relationship
to the interior (Figs. 13-12 and 13-13). The three divisions on the horizontal plane reflect the interior divisions into nave and side aisles; the three divisions from
the bottom to the base of the towers echo the three-
part elevation of the nave within. The Gothic steeples
must be ignored; the towers were originally flat. An
eleventh-century wooden roof over the nave was re-

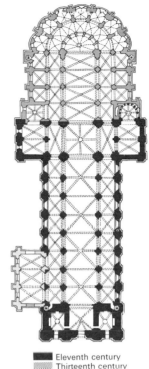

Eleventh century
Thirteenth century
Fourteenth century

13-12 Plan of St. Étienne.

13-13 Interior of St. Étienne, vaulted *c.* 1115–20.

13-14 West façade of St. Étienne, Caen, begun *c.* 1067.

13-15
Sant' Ambrogio, Milan, late eleventh
to early twelfth centuries.

13-16
Interior of Sant' Ambrogio.

placed in the twelfth century by six-part ribbed cross
vaults (Fig. 4-16, p. 44). To avoid a domical effect, the
diagonal ribs were depressed to less than a semicircle
(Fig. 4-17b, p. 45). Every other compound pier is given
extra engaged elements that rise to support the ribs and
transverse arches. This creates an *alternating system* of
supports in the nave arcade. The vaulting of St. Étienne
places its Norman builders among the pioneers of
Romanesque architecture. The *chevet* (the apse, ambulatory, and radiating chapels) is thirteenth-century
Gothic.

Sant' Ambrogio (Milan)   Construction on the cathedral (Figs. 13-15–13-17) extended from the ninth to the twelfth century, with the ribbed four-part cross vaults dating from the early twelfth century. The exterior is massive and simply decorated with pilaster strips and Lombard corbel tables. There are two towers of unequal height beside the narthex and a low polygonal tower over the octagonal domed vault at the crossing. From the atrium, one passes through the narthex to a nave of three low, dark bays. A domical effect comes from the cross vaults because the bays are square, and the ribs and transverse arches are semicircular (Fig. 4-17a, p. 45). An alternating system of piers divides each bay into two nave arches and two gallery arches. The gallery vaults buttress the nave vaults and leave no room for a clerestory. The side aisles terminate in apses in echelon beside the main apse. There is no ambulatory and only the suggestion of a choir. The nave vaults of this Lombard church place it beside St. Étienne in France and Durham Cathedral in England (built under Norman occupation) as a leader in Romanesque vaulting.

Durham Cathedral (England, 11th–12th cens., with later additions such as 13th- and 15th-cen. towers).   Durham Cathedral (Figs. 13-18–13-20) is a basilica 469 feet long with a large crossing tower and a square east end. An alternating system of supports is used in the nave, and the heavy round columns that constitute the secondary supports are carved with bold geometric decoration. Some authorities believe that Durham was more important than St. Étienne in Caen or Sant' Ambrogio in Milan for the development of ribbed cross vaults. Norman craftsmen were imported for the construction of Durham, however, so its inspiration came from Normandy, which, in turn, may have owed much to the Lombard builders of Sant' Ambrogio. The somber darkness of the Italian church is avoided at Durham,

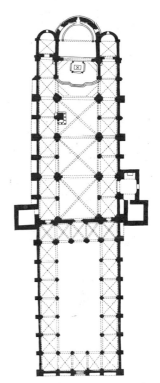

13-17 Plan of Sant' Ambrogio.

13-18 West façade of Durham Cathedral, eleventh and twelfth centuries.

13-19 Nave of Durham Cathedral, begun c. 1093.

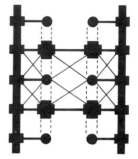

13-21 Plan of the vaulting in Durham Cathedral.

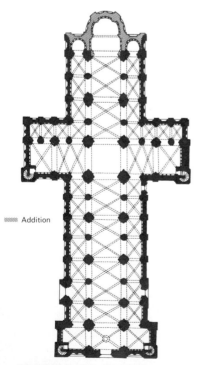

13-20 Plan of Durham Cathedral.

where clerestory windows flood the vaults with light. The segmented domical effect of the bay vaults in Sant' Ambrogio gives way to a level roof ridge formed by the *crowns* (the highest point in an arch or vault) of the vaults in the English church (the Durham vaults are 73 feet high). The level vaulting is achieved by employing pointed arches in the transverse and side arches so that they reach the height of the semicircular diagonal ribs. (Fig. 4-17c, p. 45, shows how this can be done with the exclusive use of pointed arches.) Durham's nave vaults are distinctive in their use of two sets of diagonal ribs for each bay (Fig. 13-21). Like the church of La Trinité in Caen (the sister church to St. Étienne), Durham has flying buttresses that support the wall at clerestory level, although these buttresses are hidden under a shed roof. Both in vaulting and buttressing, Durham provided an important basis for Gothic architecture.

SCULPTURE

The main sources for Romanesque sculpture are Celto-Germanic art, Roman art, and Early Christian and Byzantine art. The Carolingian period had shared the Byzantine preference for miniature sculpture. The revival of monumental sculpture came with the Romanesque period, although even then many large sculptural compositions were based on small ivory carvings or on manuscript illuminations. Romanesque sculpture is generally found around the entrances to churches, that is, on the *jambs* (layers of the splayed opening) of the door, in the *tympanum* (framed surface over the door), and on the *trumeau* (center post) of a double door; on columns, piers, and capitals; on altars and baptismal fonts; and on tombs. Subjects came from the Old and New Testaments, the Apocrypha, the lives of the saints, the labors of the months (a visual calendar of man's duties in the husbandry of the land), allegorical figures representing the Virtues and the Vices or the liberal arts, and the signs of the zodiac. There are also fantastic animals, which may have personified evil, and geometric or floral designs. Such elements suggest the influence of Celto-Germanic art. The capitals of columns may have been modifications of Greco-Roman forms, geometric ornament, or narrative relief. A number of pre-Christian Roman symbols are woven into the Christian subjects, as in Byzantine art. Romanesque sculpture has considerable regional variation ranging from angular, jerky, stiff figures in crowded linear designs (Fig. 2-4) to relatively massive calm forms. The more massive work is found in southern France and in Italy, where the tradition of ancient Roman art was strong. The beginnings of individual artists' styles can be seen in the work of some of the sculptors whose names have been preserved, such as Gislebertus of France (Cathedral at Autun), Antelami of Italy (Fidenza Cathedral), and Renier of Huy of Belgium (Baptismal Font at St. Barthélemy, Liège).

Adam and Eve Reproached by the Lord, panel from the doors of Hildesheim Cathedral (bronze, each panel 23″ x 43″). This example of Ottonian bronze casting (Fig. 13-22), done about 1015, was probably inspired by sculptured doors

13-22
BISHOP BERNWARD, *Adam and Eve Reproached by the Lord,* from the bronze doors of St. Michael's, Hildesheim, c. 1015. Approx. 23″ x 43″.

13-23 Detail from *The Apocalyptic Christ* at Moissac.

that Bishop Bernward had seen in Rome; it was originally made for the Church of St. Michael. Each of the two doors is divided into eight panels. The subjects depicted are the advent of sin and the means of salvation; the left door deals with the Fall of Man and the Murder of Abel, and the right door tells the story of Christ from the Annunciation to the Ascension. As in Ottonian manuscripts, the abrupt angularity of the figures, the active poses, and the severely simple backgrounds create dramatic intensity.

The Apocalyptic Christ (Moissac, 12th cen., 18′ 8″ wide). St. John's vision in Revelations and an illumination in the *Beatus Commentary on the Apocalypse* were the sources for this tympanum composition (Fig. 2-4) depicting Christ surrounded by the symbols of the Evangelists (a man for Matthew, a lion for Mark, a bull for Luke, and an eagle for John), angels, and the Elders. The overlapping layers of *plate drapery* are characteristic of the Languedoc region. The sharp edges of the plate folds make linear patterns of repeated and varied shapes that turn and twist with jerky vitality. The scene is framed at the sides by a twisted ribbon design and at the bottom by a lintel carved in delicate *rosettes* (round flower shapes), all having their origins in Greco-Roman architectural ornament. A powerful effect of gradation and climax comes from the enlarged scale of the central figures and their position at the apex of the tympanum and at the center of the obvious axial balance.

Sculpture from the west entrances ("royal portals") of Chartres Cathedral (1145–70). The twelfth-century façade (Fig. 13-24) is attached to a thirteenth-century church because a fire destroyed all but the façade of the twelfth-century structure. The center tympanum shows Christ and the symbols of the Evangelists, while the surrounding arches are carved to represent the Elders. The Apostles are represented on the lintel. The right tympanum contains the Madonna and Child, and the lintel, in two registers, shows the Nativity and the Presentation in the Temple. The arches personify the liberal arts. The left tympanum depicts the Ascension; the lintel contains angels and Apostles. The arches carry the signs of the zodiac and the labors of the months. The jambs beside all three doors carry large figures that seem to portray the kings, queens, and prophets of the Bible. The capitals of the engaged columns have reliefs depicting the lives of Christ and Mary. The sculpture of Chartres-west is sometimes called early Gothic; however, it is much

easier to understand as late Romanesque. A new clarity of parts is combined with the rigid poses and linear design of previous work.

13-24 West ("royal") portals of Chartres Cathedral, *c.* 1145–70.

PAINTING

During the eleventh and twelfth centuries, Romanesque painting, like Romanesque sculpture, proliferated in many regional styles, but its geographical bases were more widespread and its subject matter more varied. The term Romanesque was invented with architecture in mind, and it would be unrealistic to attempt a sharp distinction between Carolingian and Romanesque painting. During this period, the general tendency in the north was toward flat shapes and more insistence on line, line that is more active in its twisting and looping than the line in Byzantine art. Later twelfth-century work becomes more sculptural but often less lively. Byzantine influence is often evident in geometric drapery panels. Italian painting has Byzantine qualities but often loosens up Byzantine formality by means of more natural poses and more sculpturesque form.

St. Peter Receiving the Keys, from the *Book of Pericopes of Henry II* (Staatsbibliothek, Munich, 10⅜" x 7½"). This eleventh-century work (Fig. 13-25) is from Reichenau, a school known for illuminations depicting figures with large, dark, staring eyes, bold gestures, and slightly modeled but strongly outlined forms. The bodies here are crowded into spaceless groups and placed against

13-25 *St. Peter Receiving the Keys,* from the *Book of Pericopes of Henry II,* eleventh century. Staatsbibliothek, Munich.

13-26 Detail from the *Ascension* window of Le Mans Cathedral, *c.* 1150. Stained glass, 45″ x 74″.

a simple flat background; nothing detracts from the focus on the central action.

Sections from an Ascension scene, stained glass in Le Mans Cathedral (*c.* 1150, 45″ x 74″). Originally, this Romanesque window (Fig. 13-26) depicted Mary and the twelve Apostles watching the Ascension of Jesus; however, the figure of Christ has been lost, and the proper arrangement of the surviving panels is uncertain. The colors are blue, red, yellow, purple, green, and white. The thin figures and the linear drapery designs link the style to that of sculpture and manuscript illumination of the period.

Gothic Art: 1150–1400

ARCHITECTURE

In the mid-twelfth century, the first churches that are called Gothic appeared in the Ile-de-France region—north-central France, with Paris as its center. From France the Gothic style spread to other countries, where it acquired regional characteristics. The major features of Gothic architecture are height, open walls, and complex linear design, all of which are integrated into a vast system of theological symbolism. The basilica plan attained grand proportions. To its longitudinal focus was added a vertical emphasis achieved through the use of ever higher nave vaults, the pointed arch, and dominating vertical lines in interior and exterior design. The trend toward greater height, complexity, and openness in walls is illustrated by a number of major French cathedrals such as St. Denis, Noyon, Laon, Paris, Chartres, Reims, Amiens, and Beauvais. Late Gothic work of the fifteenth and sixteenth centuries elaborated the pointed arch and the *tracery* (intricate stone carving within a window) in flamelike curves and is therefore known as *flamboyant Gothic*. Examples may be found in the cathedral and the small church of St. Maclou in Rouen. As Gothic architecture developed, Romanesque massiveness disappeared (Figs. 1-29, 13-30, and 13-31); walls became perforated screens for the glowing colored light from stained glass. In Medieval theology, this light was a symbol for God. As walls became more open, mass was further denied by an increase in delicate sculptural detail, which gave a total effect of line rather than mass. On the interior, the stone vaults floated like canopies anchored by engaged columns and thin ribs over the clerestory windows. On the exterior, the openness of the forms, the vertical lines, and the fragile silhouette suggested a weightless vision of soaring splendor. During the Gothic period, the French cathedral became a complex symbol for the City of God; this was expressed not only by architectural form but by the extensive iconography presented in sculpture and stained glass windows.

Early English Gothic stressed length in plan and elevation, the major exception being an occasional tall spire or tower over the crossing. Few flying buttresses were needed. Late English Gothic emphasized height and opened the walls for more glass. Thus it is called the *Perpendicular period*. Typically English is the multiplication of vault ribs into an intricate network. The basilica plan in England tends to be rambling, with several transepts and frequently a square east end.

Germany was slow to turn to Gothic architecture but eventually was influenced by the French style. German Gothic made effective use of the hall church.

Cathedral of Notre Dame (Paris, 1163–1250). The Gothic façade (Fig. 13-27) here has more openings in the masses, more elaborately carved splayed openings, and more consistent use of the pointed arch than does earlier architecture. Open arcades and delicate detail soften the limits of the forms. The rose window shows the evolution from the wheel window as the sections became petal-like. Verticality is more insistent, although the three-part division from side to side and from the bottom to the base of the towers is still evident, as it was at Caen. The west towers are woven into an intricate geometric organization that integrates the sculpture and

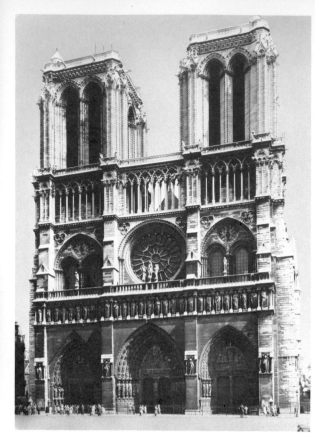

13-27 Notre Dame, Paris, 1163–1250.

13-28 Nave and choir of Notre Dame.

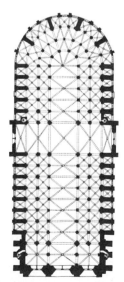

13-29 Plan of Notre Dame.

the architecture. Over the crossing, the tower used in earlier churches has been replaced by a tall, thin spire. The six-part ribbed and pointed cross vaults (Fig. 13-28) reach a height of 108½ feet and are supported on the outside by flying buttresses. The pointed arch allows the necessary flexibility for level crowns in the vaults (Fig. 4-17c, p. 45). Because of the six-part vaults, a typical bay of the nave elevation would include two arches of the nave arcade, two sets of gallery arches, and two sets of clerestory windows, each set consisting of two *lancets* (bullet-shaped windows) and a rose. The plan (Fig. 13-29) has a long choir, double side aisles, and a double ambulatory.

Amiens Cathedral, by Robert de Luzarches (13th cen., with later additions, such as 14th- and 15th-cen. towers and 16th-cen. rose window in west façade). The façade (Fig. 1-29) shows a further dissolution of solid wall into superimposed layers of meshlike openings and sculpture. The splayed openings no longer seem to be cut out of the wall; they are extended in the form of porches. Again we find the three-part divisions of the façade, but these have become more complex. The increased perforation and lightness of the walls match the ever more insistent vertical emphasis. The interior vaults (Figs. 13-30, 13-32) reach 139 feet above the floor. From compound columns with leafy capitals, the soaring engaged columns rise through a foliage stringcourse and a plain stringcourse to the four-part vaults above. A typical bay elevation consists of one arch in the nave arcade, two compound arches (each with three arches and a trefoil) at the gallery, which has now become a shallow passage, and a clerestory of four lancets and three roses. There is some variation, however, in the elevation in different parts of the church. A forest of flying buttresses provides exterior support. Although Amiens no longer has its original stained glass, the celebration of light and the double directional emphasis—toward the altar and toward the heavens—are dramatically evident.

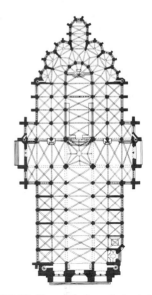

13-31 Plan of Amiens Cathedral.

13-30 ROBERT DE LUZARCHES, interior of Amiens Cathedral.

13-32 Choir vaults of Amiens Cathedral.

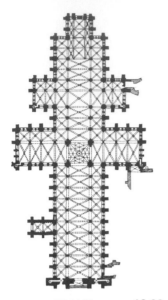

Salisbury Cathedral (begun *c*. 1220). Verticality is stressed only in the tower and spire over the crossing. The façade (Fig. 13-34), heavily sculpted but with many horizontal lines, does not have the lightness and openness or the three-dimensional complexity of French Gothic. The length is the same as that of Amiens (450 feet), but Salisbury's interior (Figs. 13-33 and 13-35) seems much longer because of the narrower nave, lower vaults (about 81 feet), and emphatic horizontal lines. Few flying buttresses are needed. The cathedral has a three-level nave elevation and four-part ribbed and pointed cross vaults. The crossing has an elaborate *star vault* (multiple ribs suggesting superimposed star shapes). The plan is typical in its square east end and secondary transept.

▨ Additions   **13-33** Plan of Salisbury Cathedral.

13-34 West façade of Salisbury Cathdral, begun *c*. 1220.

13-35 Nave of Salisbury Cathedral.

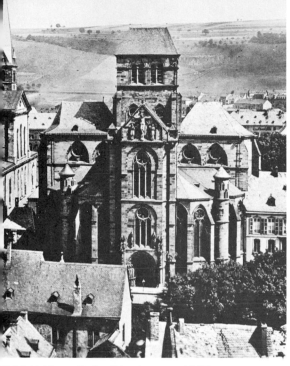

3-36 Liebfrauenkirche, Trier, begun c. 1227.

13-37 Interior of Liebfrauenkirche.

Liebfrauenkirche (Trier, c. 1227–43). The central plan is an exception to the predominance of the basilica in German Gothic architecture. Radiating chapels fill in the corners of a Greek cross plan that has an extended choir and apse for some longitudinal emphasis. The exterior (Fig. 13-36) illustrates the German reluctance to leave Romanesque forms; round arches and fortress towers are mixed with large pointed windows. Inside (Figs. 13-37 and 13-38), the arms of the cross have high ribbed and pointed four-part vaults. The elevation is in two levels: a high arcade and a clerestory of two lancets and a rose. Because the clerestory area is partly covered by the roofing of the outside chapels, however, the lancets had to be filled in until only curved triangular windows remained.

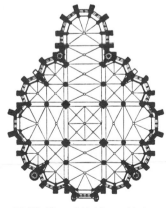

13-38 Plan of Liebfrauenkirche.

SCULPTURE

The beginnings of Gothic sculpture may be placed in the second half of the twelfth century. At this time, drapery and poses became calmer, and forms became somewhat less entangled. Figures began to pull away from their architectural backgrounds. In the early thirteenth century, bodies acquired more three-dimensional mass, more flexibility, more natural poses and drapery, and more individual faces. However, faces and figures retained some simplification and emphasis on large planes. Considerable stoniness and restraint of emotional expression are found in the important figures, giving them a more-than-human dignity and permanence. Later thirteenth-century sculpture gave up this monumental power for more specific anatomy, actions, and emotions; the development produced the effect of the superhuman descending to the human level (Fig. 13-41). Plants and animals were also depicted more naturally and less imaginatively. Late fourteenth-century work continued in the direction of greater mass and more portrait detail in faces. Stylistic development was quite uneven, and considerable variety may often be seen in the sculpture of one church because it was done by traveling sculptors from different regions or in different periods over a wide time span. In Italy, the remains of ancient Roman sculpture fostered an interest not only in mass but in certain facial types, poses, and methods of draping costumes. Classicizing tendencies may be seen in the work of men like Nicola Pisano.

By the thirteenth century, France had organized the involved subject matter of earlier sculpture into a complete world view including the hierarchy of heavenly beings, the role and duties of man, and the history of the world from events in the Old Testament to the Last Judgment (Fig. 13-40). So equipped with sculpture (and stained glass), the French Gothic cathedral, more than that of any other country, is a remarkable monument to its age.

St. Theodore, from south transept portal of Chartres Cathedral (c. 1215–20). The figure (Fig. 13-39), holding a spear and sheltered under a stone canopy, is quite distinct from its supporting column. The more human presentation is carried through in the naturalistic facial features and body proportions. Large, simple planes in the face and figure provide both a sense of monumental strength and a modification of the earthly reality implied by the image.

13-39 *St. Theodore,* from the south transept portal of Chartres Cathedral, *c.* 1215–20.

Plate 1
Justinian and Attendants, detail of an apse mosaic from San Vitale.

Plate 2

Initial page (XPI) of the *Book of Kells*, eighth century. Reproduced by permission of The Board of Trinity College, Dublin.

Plate 3
GIOTTO, *Lamentation, c.* 1305. Fresco. Arena Chapel, Padua

Plate 4
JAN VAN EYCK, *Arnolfini and His Bride,* 1434. Oil on wood panel, approx. 32'' x 22''.
Reproduced by courtesy of the Trustees, The National Gallery, London.

Plate 5
PIERO DELLA FRANCESCA, *The Annunciation,* c. 1455. San Francosco, Arezzo.

Plate 6
GIORGIONE DA CASTELFRANCO, *The Pastoral Concert*, c. 1508. Oil on canvas, approx.
43" x 54". Louvre, Paris.

Plate 7
TITIAN. *Danaë, c.* 1545 Oil on canvas, approx. 4′ x 6′. Museo di Capodimonte, Naples.

Plate 8
EI GRECO, *The Crucifixion*, 1584–90. Oil on canvas, approx.
10' x 6'. Prado, Madrid.

Plate 9
DIEGO VELÁZQUEZ, *The Maids of Honor* (*Las Meninas*), 1656. Oil on canvas, approx.
10'5'' x 9'. Prado, Madrid.

Plate 10
PETER PAUL RUBENS and assistants, study for *The Reception of Marie de' Medici at Marseilles, 3 November 1600*. Oil on wood, approx. 26″ x 19½″. Alte Pinakothek, Munich.

Plate 11
REMBRANDT VAN RIJN, *Supper at Emmaus, c.* 1648. Oil on panel, approx. 27″ x 26″
Louvre, Paris

Plate 12
JAN VERMEER, *Young Woman with a Water Jug, c.* 1665. Oil on canvas, approx.
18″ x 16″. Metropolitan Museum of Art, New York (gift of Henry G. Marquand, 1889).

Plate 13
JOSEPH MALLORD WILLIAM TURNER, *Rain, Steam, and Speed*, 1844. Oil on canvas,
3' x 4'. Reproduced by courtesy of the Trustees, The National Gallery, London.

Plate 14
CAMILLE COROT, *Souvenir de Mortefontaine,* 1864. Oil on canvas, 25¼″ x 34½″. Louvre, Paris.

Plate 15
Eugène Delacroix, *The Lion Hunt*, 1861. Oil on canvas, 30½″ x 38½″. Art Institute of
Chicago, Potter Palmer Collection.

Plate 16
EDGAR DEGAS, *Ballerina and Lady with a Fan, c.* 1885. Pastel on paper, 26″ x 20″.
Courtesy of the John G. Johnson Collection, The Philadelphia Museum of Art.

The Last Judgment, from central portal of west façade of Amiens Cathedral (c. 1220–30). In the lower register of this portal sculpture (Fig. 13-40), the dead arise from their tombs to be judged on the scales of St. Michael. Above, the Damned and the Elect are going to their respective rewards; and, at the top, Christ is surrounded by Mary, John, and angels bearing the instruments of the Passion. The splayed arches that frame the tympanum depict the Elect with angels, Martyrs and Confessors, the Wise and Foolish Virgins, the Elders, the Tree of Jesse (to represent the genealogy of Christ), and the Partriarchs of the Old Law. On the jambs below are larger-than-life-size figures of the Prophets and Apostles, each identified by some attribute indicating the instrument of his martyrdom or symbolizing his role. Below these statues are quatrefoil medallions with relief sculpture depicting prophecies, Virtues, and Vices. The trumeau statue, known as *Le Beau Dieu*, represents Christ. The sizes of the figures in the tympanum and surrounding arches vary according to their importance in the hierarchy. The large scale of the jamb statues and their nearness to entering worshipers give them special grandeur and visually strengthen the supporting columns for the whole portal. Anatomy in faces and nude figures still has austere simplicity, and drapery is arranged in orderly cascades or pleated folds; yet the total effect is so natural that the turning and twisting Apostles and Prophets seem to converse with each other.

13 40 *The Last Judgment,* from the central portal of the west façade of Amiens Cathedral, *c.* 1220–30

13-41
Vièrge Dorée (Golden Virgin), from
the south transept trumeau of Amiens
Cathedral, *c.* 1250–70.

13-42
Crucifix from St. Marie im Kapitol, Cologne,
1304. Wood, 57" high.

Vièrge Dorée (Golden Virgin), from south transept trumeau of Amiens Cathedral (*c.* 1250–1270). This popular statue (Fig. 13-41) took its name from the gilt paint originally used in the costume. The austere strength of earlier work is here replaced by extreme gracefulness and human emotion. Although the bulky garment obscures the lower body, the three-dimensional folds seem convincingly activated by a contrapposto pose.

Crucifix (Pestkreuz), from St. Marie im Kapitol (Cologne, 1304, wood, 57" high). The emaciated body in Figure 13-42 is shown with harsh angularity and much detail in the bleeding wounds and the sores that suggest that Jesus has suffered from disease and will be sympathetic to the pleas of the sick. The symmetry and orderly repetition of forms in the crown of thorns and the ribs make the wounds and the convulsed hands more shocking by contrast. The hands and arms indicate the increasing study of nature that characterizes much Gothic sculpture.

The Well of Moses, from former Monastery of the Chartreuse de Champmol (Dijon, 1395–1406, stone, Prophets approx. 72" high). This (Fig. 13-43) is the sculpture of Claus Sluter, who came from Holland to the court of the Dukes of Burgundy at Dijon. The well is surmounted by a badly preserved crucifix placed on a base containing the figures of six Prophets from the Old Testament. In accordance with a Medieval passion play, the Prophets are depicted as judges who decide that Jesus must be crucified for the sake of mankind. Each Prophet holds a scroll that contains a quotation from the Old Testament predicting the sacrifice. The massive forms, with their deeply cut depressions, the realism of costume detail, and the individualized faces of Sluter's style forecast the Renaissance, but the slightly exaggerated rhythmic curves in some sections of the drapery relate it to the late Medieval period.

PAINTING

As walls became more open, Gothic painters in the North had less wall surface on which to work. Their talents were employed in designing stained glass, which in turn affected the style in manuscript illumination. Thirteenth-century illuminations often depict slender, willowy figures in gracefully curving and folding costumes, all within the architectural frame of a cathedral window. The modeling of the objects is counteracted by strong, flattened contours. Space around objects is often denied by the use of flat gold backgrounds. By the fourteenth century, illuminations make less use of the window framework and close observation of nature is evident. Jean Pucelle, in Paris, placed paintings at the

13-43
CLAUS SLUTER, *The Well of Moses,*
1395–1406. Figures approx. 72″ high.
Chartreuse de Champmol, Dijon.

top and bottom of a page and surrounded the intervening text with elaborate decorative plants, animals, and geometric shapes. The most pioneering Gothic painting was done by the Italian Giotto di Bondone (1267?–1337). Under the influence of thirteenth-century sculpture, Giotto broke with Byzantine traditions to obtain massive bodies and more natural drapery. Landscape, architecture, and figures are severely simple. The directional movements of all his forms give ponderous dignity to the restrained gestures and facial expressions. The massiveness, the more individualized faces, the more natural poses, and the convincing but underplayed emotions all bring a new humanism to Medieval art. Yet Giotto's painting was not fully appreciated by his immediate successors, and it was only with the Renaissance that his interests were developed further. Duccio de Buoninsegna of Siena (about 1255–1319) made a more gentle break with Byzantine style.

13-44 Detail from the *Good Samaritan* window of Chartres Cathedral, early thirteenth century. Stained glass.

The *Good Samaritan* **window,** Chartres Cathedral (early 13th cen., stained glass). Chartres has one of the best-preserved sets of stained glass windows. The *Good Samaritan* window is a tall lancet contributed by the shoemakers of the town. Three medallions (circular clusters of scenes), one above the other, are separated by sets of three scenes each. The detail here (Fig. 13-44) shows only the central medallion and parts of the scenes above and below it. The compositions are read from the bottom up. The lower third of the window tells the story of the traveler's departure from Jerusalem, of his being robbed, beaten, and left along the road, and of his rescue by the Good Samaritan. The medallion in our reproduction begins an interpretation of the parable, depicting, in the bottom portion, the traveler in bed receiving care. The other scenes represent the creation of Adam (left) and Eve (right) and God's warning not to eat the fruit of the Tree of Knowledge (top). The top third of the window continues with the story of the Fall of Man and culminates with the figure of Jesus. Thus, Jerusalem represents Eden, the story of the traveler is related to the Fall of Man, and the Good Samaritan for all men becomes Jesus the Savior. The types of figure and drapery patterns, as well as the abbreviated symbols for trees and architecture, are artistic conventions of the time. The theological significance of light is enhanced by the glowing colors of the stained glass, colors that were projected in mottled hues onto the interior columns and floors.

Illuminated page from the *Psalter of St. Louis* (Bibliothèque Nationale, Paris, *c.* 1260, approx. 5″ x 4″). The illumination (Fig. 13-45) depicts Nahash the Ammonite threatening the Jews at Jabesh. Compared with most Romanesque work, the human figures here are natural in proportion and flexible in pose; but less important items, such as the horses (or architecture in other scenes), are given a diminished scale. Light and shadow are used sparingly to create a roundness that is countered by strong outlines. Depth is canceled by the gilt background. Shapes are filled with strong, relatively unmodulated colors, with blues and reds predominating. In each illumination in the psalter, the upper area is treated like a set of stained glass windows set into a Gothic building.

Lamentation, by Giotto, (Arena, or Scrovegni, Chapel, Padua, fresco, part of a series of paintings done in 1305-06, 7′7″

13-45 *Nahash Threatening the Jews at Jabesh,* illuminated page (I Kings 11:2) from the *Psalter of St. Louis, c.* 1260. Bibliothèque Nationale, Paris.

13-46 GIOTTO, detail from *Lamentation* at the Arena (Scrovegni) Chapel, Padua.

x 7'9"). The significance of the event is expressed here (Plate 3 and Fig. 13-46) not through awe-inspiring otherworldly images, but through massive human forms whose actions have solemn dignity. The drapery is simplified and used not to reveal the body but to emphasize the major movement of each figure. As the figures focus on Christ, so does the diagonally descending landscape. Giotto's emphasis on three-dimensional mass and his use of more normal human proportions constituted a new concept of reality in painting and broke with the conventions of Byzantine art. For this reason, Giotto is often seen as a forerunner of the Renaissance. His major frescoes are in Santa Croce in Florence and in the Arena Chapel in Padua.

Christ Entering Jerusalem, by Duccio (from the *Maestà Altarpiece,* Siena Cathedral, 1308–11, tempera on wood, detail 40" x 21"). The great altarpiece depicts, on the front, a Madonna enthroned and, on the back, scenes from the life of Christ. Compared with Giotto's work, Duccio's use of human proportions and flat shapes (Fig. 13-47) was a much less radical departure from Byzantine traditions. Rigid Byzantine drapery patterns appear in certain instances, particularly when Duccio shows Christ in less natural states—during the Transfiguration, for instance, or after the Resurrection. However, the details in gestures and faces have a delicate expressiveness and reflect a keen observation of nature. Duccio did not use a consistent system of linear perspective. The architecture is miniature in scale and may have been influenced by stage sets for religious drama.

13-47 DUCCIO. *Christ Entering Jerusalem,* detail from the *Maestà Altarpiece,* 1308–11. Siena Cathedral.

Conant, Kenneth J. *Carolingian and Romanesque Architecture: 800–1200* (Pelican History of Art). Baltimore: Penguin Books, 1959.

Decker, Hans. *Romanesque Art in Italy.* Translated by James Cleugh. New York: Abrams, 1959.

Dupont, Jacques, and Cesare Gnudi. *Gothic Painting* (Great Centuries of Painting). Translated by Stuart Gilbert. Geneva: Skira, 1954.

Frankl, Paul. *Gothic Architecture* (Pelican History of Art). Translated by Dieter Pevsner. Baltimore: Penguin Books, 1962.

Gardner, Arthur. *Medieval Sculpture in France.* New York: Macmillan, 1931.

Grabar, Arthur, and Carl Nordenfalk. *Early Medieval Painting from the Fourth to the Eleventh Century* (Great Centuries of Painting). Translated by Stuart Gilbert. Geneva: Skira, 1957.

——————. *Romanesque Painting* (Great Centuries of Painting). Translated by Stuart Gilbert. Geneva: Skira, 1958.

Katzenellenbogen, Adolf. *The Sculptural Programs of Chartres Cathedral: Christ, Mary, Ecclesia.* Baltimore: The Johns Hopkins Press, 1959.

Landolt, Hanspeter. *German Painting: The Late Middle Ages (1330–1500).* Translated by Heinz Norden. Geneva: Skira, 1968.

Mâle, Émile. *The Gothic Image: Religious Art in France in the Thirteenth Century.* Translated by Dora Nussey. New York: Harper & Row, 1958.

Meiss, Millard. *French Painting in the Time of Jean de Berry.* 2 vols. New York: Phaidon Press, 1967.

Panofsky, Erwin. *Gothic Architecture and Scholasticism.* New York: Meridian Books, 1957.

Pope-Hennessy, John. *An Introduction to Italian Sculpture,* Vol. 1. New York and London: Phaidon Press, 1955.

Porter, Arthur Kingsley. *Medieval Architecture: Its Origins and Development.* 2 vols., reprint of the 1909 ed. New York: Hacker Art Books, 1966.

——————. *Romanesque Sculpture of the Pilgrimage Roads.* 10 vols. in 3, reprint of the 1923 ed. New York: Hacker Art Books, 1966.

Rickert, Margaret Josephine. *Painting in Britain: The Middle Ages* (Pelican History of Art). Baltimore: Penguin Books, 1954.

Saalman, Howard. *Medieval Architecture: European Architecture, 600–1200* (Great Ages of World Architecture). New York: Braziller, 1962.

Stone, Lawrence. *Sculpture in Britain: The Middle Ages* (Pelican History of Art). Baltimore: Penguin Books, 1955.

Von Simson, Otto G. *The Gothic Cathedral: Origins of Gothic Architecture and the Medieval Concept of Order.* New York: Pantheon Books, 1956.

Webb, Geoffrey. *Architecture in Britain: The Middle Ages* (Pelican History of Art). Baltimore: Penguin Books, 1956.

White, John. *Art and Architecture in Italy, 1250–1400* (Pelican History of Art). Baltimore: Penguin Books, 1966.

Witzleben, Elizabeth von. *Stained Glass in French Cathedrals.* Translated by Francisca Garvie. New York: Reynal, 1968.

Medieval Music: 1000–1450

Western art music began with the development, in sacred vocal music, of controlled polyphony and a system of written notation. These developments centered in the region of modern France and were encouraged by the medieval fondness for logical systems and theoretical speculation.

Musical notation began with attempts to preserve the sacred liturgical melodies, or *plainchants*, that had developed over several centuries. At first only the pitches were shown. Two melodies that were to be sung simultaneously are indicated in some manuscripts from about the eleventh century. The practice of singing two melodies at the same time was probably widespread. In order to control the simultaneous movement of the two voices, a system for indicating rhythm was developed, and this in turn opened the possibility of three and four part music. By the early thirteenth century polyphonic sacred music was being performed extensively in France, Spain, Italy, and England, the most important center being the Cathedral of Notre Dame in Paris, and this type of music had become a significant element in French cathedral art.

The most important form of medieval polyphony was the *motet*, a composition in several parts with two or more texts sung simultaneously. Motet texts often were secular and probably were meant for performance outside of the church, representing an early move toward the composition of polyphonic secular music. Composers showed a strong interest in complex rhythms, canons, and musical puzzles and enigmas. Motets in three parts with the top voice the most active became standard, and by the fourteenth century composers were applying this texture to French secular poetic forms.

During the early fifteenth century there was considerable musical activity at the court and chapel of Philip the Good, duke of Burgundy. The arts flourished in an international, cosmopolitan atmosphere under the duke's patronage. French, Flemish, and English composers all contributed to the Burgundian musical style, which formed the basis for the music of the sixteenth-century Renaissance. Their most original contribution was in the style of the *chanson*, which was the name given to any polyphonic setting of French secular poetry. Typical Burgundian chansons consisted of a florid vocal solo accompanied by two instrumental parts of contrasting timbres. Harsh medieval harmonies began to be replaced by pleasing chord sounds, an English contribution, and music was designed for direct sensual appeal.

13-48

The Burgundians generally wrote sacred music in the chanson style, though they began to make some distinctions between sacred and secular styles around the middle of the century. They wrote motets, the word having come to mean a polyphonic setting of any sacred text, and they wrote settings of the sung portions of the Mass, or service of Holy Communion. Out of the portion of the Mass that was performed at every service, called the Ordinary, musicians often set the texts of five parts. The *Kyrie*, a prayer for mercy, is in Greek, whereas the other parts are in Latin. The *Gloria* is a hymn of praise. The *Credo*, or Creed, is a recital of Christian beliefs and is the longest part. The *Sanctus*, *Benedictus*, and *Hosanna* together are part of the ritual blessing of the consecrated bread and wine. The *Agnus Dei* is a prayer for mercy and peace. Though there had been earlier precedents, the Burgundians were the first to consistently set these five parts of the Mass to polyphonic music. They typically unified the whole with musical material common to all the parts.

Guillaume de Machaut (France, *c.* 1300–77). Machaut, who was a poet and cleric as well as a musician, was one of the earliest masters of polyphonic secular music. He set some of his secular poems to a three-part texture which anticipated the Burgundian chanson, and he is the first composer known to have made a complete and unified polyphonic setting of the Ordinary of the Mass. His penchant for lively cross-rhythms, polyphonic independence, and musical puzzles may be seen in his three-part setting of the text, "My end is my beginning and my beginning my end . . ." ("*Ma fin est ma commencement . . .*"). The upper line is the same as the middle line backwards, and the second half of the lower line is the reverse of its first half.

John Dunstable (England and France, 1380/90–1453). Dunstable was musician to the duke of Bedford at Paris while the duke was regent of France. He probably

13-49
Miniatures showing thirteenth century performers. In **13-48** they are playing cymbals; in **13-49** they are playing a rebec and a lute. From the *Cantigas* of Alfonso the Wise.

13-50 Medieval notation of a poem by Guillaume de Machaut. The modern staff of five lines dates from the thirteenth century. Earlier staves did not use a set number of lines.

influenced Binchois and Dufay, who admired the simple rhythms and pleasing harmonies of the English style. In his three-voice motet, "*Quam pulchra es*," all of the voices move according to the rhythm of the words, and polyphonic independence is subordinated to the harmonic sound of triads, with dissonances rarely used. Dunstable's most significant works were sacred motets of this type.

Gilles Binchois (Flanders, *c.* 1400–60). Binchois spent the latter half of his life as a musician to the Burgundian court, where he was the leading composer of chansons.

In these works the intimate scale of his music matched the courtly love poems that were the usual texts. His chanson *"De plus en plus"* is typical. The poem follows a rather complex scheme of meter and rhyme, with portions returning as refrains, and the music fits this scheme. The words are given to the upper line—a gentle, lyric melody that a soloist probably would have sung to the accompaniment of two instrumental parts.

Guillaume Dufay (Flanders and France, *c.* 1400–74). Dufay was one of the most prominent and influential musicians of his day. He traveled widely, spending considerable time in Italy, and his musical style was a synthesis of Franco-Flemish, Italian, and English influences that reflected the transition from medieval to Renaissance styles. Italian and English traits show in his fluid melodies and triadic harmonies. Though he usually maintained independence among the polyphonic lines, his rhythms were less complex than in medieval music. In his Masses, the polyphony often was designed around a borrowed melody, maintained throughout by the tenor voice. Such melodies frequently were secular songs, such as the melody of Dufay's own chanson, *"Se la face ay pale,"* which he used to unify his Mass of the same name. His Masses were written for four voices instead of three, as was customary for chansons.

Suggestions for Further Study

Grout, Donald Jay. A History of Western Music, rev. ed. New York: W. W. Norton, 1973. Chapters III–V.

Seay, Albert. *Music in the Medieval World.* Englewood Cliffs, N.J.: Prentice-Hall, 1965.

Suggestions for Further Listening

Binchois, Gilles. *"Adieu, m'amour et ma maistresse."*

————. *"De plus en plus."*

Dufay, Guillaume. *"Se la face ay pale."* (Chanson.)

————. *"Se la face ay pale."* (Mass.)

Dunstable, John. *"O Rosa Bella."*

————. *"Quam pulchra es."*

Machaut, Guillaume de. *"Messe de Notre Dame."*

Chapter **14** *Art*

Renaissance Art:

1400–1600

The term *Renaissance* implies a rebirth, and the period is often thought of as a rebirth of the glory of ancient Greek and Roman culture; yet the Renaissance involved much more than imitation of the past. It was a time of emphasis on the importance of the individual, of interest in the physical characteristics of man and nature, and of search for rational order and ideal form in the arts. The period saw widespread geographical exploration, much activity in scholarship, a rapid growth in the sciences, reformation in religion, and broad changes in the arts. These trends had been gathering momentum since the twelfth century, with the exchange of ideas fostered by the Crusades, the emergence of free cities, the rise of the universities, and the developing interests in nature and antique art during the Gothic period. Furthermore, some of the climactic effects of Renaissance trends occurred only afterwards, in the seventeenth century. Thus the beginning and end dates for the period are rather arbitrary markers in the continuous stream of history.

Our concepts of Renaissance art are based primarily on Italy, for it was here that the trends were most distinct. The period from 1400 to 1500 in Italy is called the *Early Renaissance*, the years from about 1500 to 1520 are considered to be the *High Renaissance*, and the remainder of the sixteenth century may be termed *Late Renaissance*. The urbanization that took place in the Gothic period made the cities important centers for the growth of Renaissance ideas and the patronage of art. Artists often joined the courts of nobles and received sustenance and salary in return for painting, sculpture, and design ranging from architecture to theatrical costumes. Florence played the major role in the fifteenth century but was superseded in the sixteenth century by Rome and Venice. Outside Italy, the most productive geographical area for the arts in the fifteenth century was the region of present-day Belgium, with the major centers at Tournai, Bruges, Ghent, Brussels, Louvain, and Antwerp. In Burgundian France, Dijon was an important art center until 1420, when the court of the Dukes of Burgundy was moved to Flanders. Paris continued to be important, along with Fontainebleau in the sixteenth century. In the Germanic areas, Cologne, Nuremberg, Vienna, and Basel were especially significant. London was the center of a tardy development of the Renaissance in England.

During the Renaissance, the Church continued to be an important patron of the arts, but the aristocracy and the growing merchant class commissioned art for themselves as well as for the Church. The Visconti and Sforza families in Milan, the Gonzaga family in Mantua, the Este family in Ferrara, and the Medici family in Florence, all powerful families, earned places in history through their patronage. The new individualism stimulated the quest for renown—for accomplishments in the earthly life—and architecture, painting, and sculpture could be seen as permanent monuments to the patron's importance. The desire to live fully was expressed in the concept of the universal man, the man of many abilities and interests as inspired by Greek thought and described in Baldassare Castiglione's sixteenth-century book, *The Courtier*.

Breadth of interests affected not only the patronage of art but also the attitude of the artist; Michelangelo was poet, painter, architect, and sculptor, and Leonardo da Vinci was artist, scientist, and engineer. The social status of the artist rose during the fifteenth and sixteenth centuries. By the sixteenth century, the craftsman-artist, trained in a *bottega* (shop) under the the apprentice system and the strict rules of a guild, had become the artist-genius, trained in an academy; he was a scholar and a fit companion for princes, a person emancipated from the regulations of the guilds.

During the fifteenth century, the development of the graphic arts in Germany made art in the form of prints available to a larger segment of the population, extending patronage and broadening the artist's audience. Woodcut, wood engraving, and metal engraving were the important media.

The Fifteenth Century

PAINTING IN THE NORTH

In the countries north of Italy, fifteenth-century painting is sometimes considered to be late Medieval rather than Renaissance because it shows little interest in ancient Greco-Roman art and does not portray man so heroically in scale, proportions, and action as does the painting of fifteenth-century Italy. Northern painting does intensify the late Gothic study of nature by adding deeper space, more convincing illusion of mass, more flesh-and-blood anatomy, and precise details and textures. Nevertheless, body proportions and drapery effects are conventional. The persistently thin bodies, large heads, narrow shoulders, angular drapery lines, and crowded landscape or architectural settings give much Northern painting of the fifteenth century the total effect of a miniature, no matter how large the actual work (see Plate 4). The intricate physical detail was frequently given spiritual meaning by the elaborate symbolism inherited from the Middle Ages. Painters obtained transparent color through the increased use of oil glazes employed alone or in combination with the more traditional egg tempera.

Robert Campin, probably identical with the **Master of Flémalle** (Flanders, 1378?–1444). Campin, one of the first painters to use oil paint extensively, had his studio in Tournai. The new realism of his style combines deep space created by means of exaggerated linear perspective, crowded objects, the typically rich color and angular drapery of fifteenth-century Northern art, and both private and conventional Medieval symbolism. His *Virgin and Child Before a Fire Screen* (Fig. 14-1), one of the earliest paintings to show a city view outside the window, presents the Madonna in a comfortable contemporary Flemish house. The fire screen suggests the shape of a halo behind her head, and the chalice (probably a later addition) by her elbow suggests the celebration of the Mass and hints at the future sacrifice of Christ.

14-1 ROBERT CAMPIN, *Virgin and Child Before a Fire Screen,* c. 1425. Panel, 24″ x 19¼″. Courtesy of the Trustees of the National Gallery, London.

Jan van Eyck (Flanders, c. 1390–1441). This pioneer in Northern painting worked for Count John of Holland and Philip the Good of Burgundy and finally died in Bruges. He was honored by the rulers and sent on a diplomatic mission to Portugal. *Arnolfini and His Bride* (Plate 4) has typically Northern features, such as the fragile bodies, angular drapery, miniature quality, and pervasive symbolism (see p. 26). The converging lines of the architecture effectively establish depth; but they are instinctive rather than systematic, for they meet at several different horizon levels. Two natural light sources admit a crossing light that shortens the shadows cast so that even the grain of the floorboards at Arnolfini's feet is not hidden. Although the woman's face has the smooth, wide, oval form and tiny mouth found in much Northern painting of the period, the striking individuality of Arnolfini's face is undeniable. The entire painting demonstrates remarkably careful observation, from the stubble on Arnolfini's chin to the transparent beads on the wall. The round mirror reveals the artist's interest in optical problems: It shows a wide-angle view of the room, the backs of the couple, and two spectators (perhaps including the artist) in the doorway. The mirror frame contains tiny round scenes of Christ's Passion. The most famous work by Van Eyck is the *Ghent Altarpiece* (Fig. 14-2), which carries the names of Jan and his brother Hubert. There is uncertainty about which parts were done by each and whether or not we have any other paintings by Hubert.

Rogier van der Weyden (Flanders, *c*, 1400–64). Rogier probably studied under Robert Campin at Tournai before becoming the official painter of Brussels. About 1450, he traveled through Italy. Whereas Van Eyck's compositions lead our attention smoothly from foreground to background, Rogier's paintings tend to locate the major figures in a shallow foreground space, and the background serves only as a backdrop. Moreover, the faces in Rogier's paintings convey greater emotional intensity than do the faces painted by Van Eyck. These characteristics are evident in *The Descent from the Cross* (Fig. 14-3), an early work. Other major works attributed to Van der Weyden include *Christ Appearing to His Mother* (*c*. 1440–45, Metropolitan Museum of Art, New York) and the *Portrait of Lionello (or Francesco?) d'Este* (*c*. 1450, Metropolitan Museum of Art, New York).

14-2 JAN and HUBERT VAN EYCK, *God,* a panel from the *Ghent Altarpiece, c.* 1432. St. Bavo, Ghent.

14-3 ROGIER VAN DER WEYDEN, *The Descent from the Cross, c.* 1435. Tempera on wood panel, approx. 7'3" x 8'7". Prado, Madrid.

14-4 JEAN FOUQUET, *Étienne Chevalier and St. Stephen*, c. 1450. 36½'' x 33½''. Staatliche Museen, Berlin.

Jean Fouquet (France, *c.* 1420–81). Fouquet was born at Tours, and it is thought that he may have attended the University of Paris, since Parisian buildings often appear in his later book illustrations. If so, he undoubtedly saw there the work of Flemish artists, but his paintings contain Italianate elements, which are best explained by a trip to Rome in 1445. After his return to France, he established himself in Tours, although his activity was not limited to this area. During the period between 1450 and 1460, Fouquet painted the *Portrait of Charles VII* (Louvre, Paris) and the *Pietà of Nouans* (Nouans). The portrait of Charles VII's minister of finance, Étienne Chevalier, with his patron saint, Stephen (Fig. 14-4), originally formed the left wing of the *Diptych* (two-part altarpiece) *of Melun;* the two figures were presented as worshipers of the Madonna and Child depicted in the right wing, which is now in the Antwerp Musée Royal des Beaux-Arts. (The face of the Madonna is thought to be a portrait of Agnes Sorel, the mistress of Charles VII.) The left wing reveals Italian influence in the perspective of the architecture, the amplitude of the massive bodies, and the equivalent scale of man and saint—even though the saint's head is given a traditionally higher position than the head of the man. Having served the court of Charles VII, Fouquet, in 1475, was made court painter to the king by Charles' successor, Louis XI.

Hugo van der Goes (Flanders, 1440–82). Van der Goes died in a monastery near Brussels after having spent most of his life in Ghent. His work often has a strange tenseness derived from sharp contrasts in directional forces and between sparse and crowded areas, passive and active attitudes, and concentrated and distracted attention. His major work is the *Portinari Altarpiece* (*c.* 1476), done for the Italian representative of the Medici banking interests in Bruges. The central panel of this *triptych* (three-part altarpiece) shows *The Adoration of the Shepherds* (Fig. 14-5). The disparity between the size of the Madonna and that of the angels echoes the Medieval lack of concern for physical reality, while the deep space and realistic detail are characteristically Renaissance. The perspective lines of the architecture converge toward a vanishing point behind the head of the Madonna and emphasize her importance. The foreground symbols include a cast-off shoe as a sign of a holy event, wheat as a reference to the bread of the Eucharist, scattered anemones as a symbol of sorrow and sacrifice, an iris (sword lily) as a symbol of the Madonna's suffering during the Passion of Christ, a lily

14-5 HUGO VAN DER GOES. *The Adoration of the Shepherds,* central panel of the *Portinari Altarpiece. c.* 1476. Galleria degli Uffizi, Florence.

as a symbol of sacrifice and chastity, and columbine as a symbol of the Holy Ghost. On the basis of the Portinari painting, a number of other stylistically similar works have been attributed to Van der Goes.

Hieronymus Bosch (Holland, *c.* 1450–1516). The extraordinary fantasies of Bosch seem closer to the grotesqueries of the Middle Ages than to the rational order of the Renaissance; yet even the Greeks had their Dionysiac Mysteries, and Bosch painted his visions with a control of deep space that is one hallmark of the Renaissance. His religious scenes and representations of proverbs and fables, which often contain moral lessons, are portrayed through strange combinations of men, plants, and animals; and interpretation is sometimes difficult. Bosch is often cited as a precursor of twentieth-century Surrealism. The much-copied *Temptation of St. Anthony* (Fig. 14-6) is a perfect subject for his imagination. The creatures of hell swarm from earth, sky, and water to torment the saint, whose body is almost lost, even in the very center of the composition. His other works include *The Garden of Earthly Delights* (*c.* 1500, Prado, Madrid) and *The Hay Wain* (*c.* 1485–90, Prado, Madrid).

14-6 HIERONYMUS BOSCH, *The Temptation of St. Anthony,* c. 1500. Museu Nacional de Arte Antiga, Lisbon.

PAINTING IN ITALY

While conservative Italian painting continued the traditions of Byzantine and late Gothic art, the new painting was molded by the major Renaissance interests: individual man, nature, and ancient Greco-Roman art. The scattered remains of antique sculpture had encouraged the love of mass in Medieval Italian sculpture. It was Medieval sculpture that helped shape the art of Giotto, which in turn became a source for the new fifteenth-century painting (Figs. 1-10 and 1-26). Increased efforts were made to duplicate the visual experience of the physical world: Linear and aerial perspective were used to create space; natural light (from direct sources and from reflecting surfaces) was studied as a means of suggesting mass; land forms, plant life, and animal and human anatomy were observed in detail; and natural posture as well as convincingly natural movement became important to the new concept of what was "real." For all of this, clarity was considered to be essential, but, at the same time, the attempt to achieve clarity led to conflicts. Clarity called for sharply outlined edges that contradicted the roundness of the form, and the insistence on mass sometimes made a painted face seem more like stone than flesh. Only late in the century were deep shadows allowed to obscure parts of the composition in the interests of strong focus (Fig. 1-26). Portraiture, nature study, Greco-Roman architecture and mythology, and traditional Christian subject matter were often mixed; an Adoration of the Christ Child might be depicted with ancient ruins or with Roman sarcophagi adorned with mythological reliefs, while portraits of the artist's contemporary patrons might be found among the Three Kings and their retinue. The confidence in the importance and capabilities of man was expressed by some artists in dignity of pose, emotional restraint, and boldness of masses (Fig. 1-10), all producing a kind of monumentality. Much fifteenth-century Italian painting has a breadth of form and a largeness of scale quite unlike the miniature quality of most Northern work. Flemish painting was admired by Italians, however, and its landscape backgrounds had some effect on Italian art. The major media for the period were fresco, tempera, and occasional oil glazing.

Fra Angelico (Florence, 1387–1455). Guido da Vicchio probably studied under Lorenzo Monaco before joining the Dominican Order and taking the name of Fra

14-7 FRA ANGELICO, *The Coronation of the Virgin.* c. 1435. Panel, 44⅛″ x 45″. Galleria degli Uffizi, Florence.

14-8 MASACCIO, *The Holy Trinity*, 1428(?). Fresco, 21'10½" x 10'5". Santa Maria Novella, Florence.

14-9 PIERO DELLA FRANCESCA, *Portrait of Battista Sforza, Duchess of Urbino*, 1472(?). Tempera and oil on panel, 18½" x 13". Galleria degli Uffizi, Florence.

Angelico. His early style, which lasted from 1418 into the 1430's and is illustrated by such works as *The Coronation of the Virgin* (Fig. 14-7), was Gothic in its slender figures, delicate textile patterns, and paradisaical settings. From 1435 to 1445, in such works as the frescoes in San Marco in Florence, his figures became more solid, the settings more earthbound, the color more restrained, and the drapery more massive. His late paintings have simpler, more massive bodies and deep perspective vistas framed by grand architecture.

Masaccio (Florence, 1401–28). *The Tribute Money* (Fig. 1-10) reveals Masaccio's use of aerial and linear perspective (see p. 6) and his modeling with light and shadow to create the illusion of mass. The linear perspective used systematically here was invented by his architect friend Filippo Brunelleschi, who was also an admirer of ancient Roman architecture. Brunelleschi probably encouraged Masaccio to use Roman architecture as a setting for his painting *The Trinity* (Fig. 14-8). The massiveness of Masaccio's figures owes much to the painting of Giotto, and the poses indicate the influence of the sculptor Donatello. Masaccio's greatness lies in the gravity, poise, and depth—the monumentality—he gave to his humanistic vision of man. These qualities stem from his combination of eloquent but restrained facial expressions, a stately rhythmic accord between the lines of poses and drapery, and the suppression of detail where necessary to strengthen the masses. Certainly the grandeur of scale and mass in the ruins of Roman architecture and sculpture was a formative influence.

Piero della Francesca (central Italy, 1415/20–92). Piero was primarily a painter, but he was also a Renaissance humanist scholar who wrote on perspective and was active as a poet, cosmographer, mathematician, and architect. In painting, his major technical interest seems to have been the effect of light on color and three-dimensional form. His painting often has the quality of bright, diffused luminosity. He brought simple massive figures into alignment with their architectural settings to produce an architectonic stability that reinforces the dignity of the persons portrayed. He owed much to Masaccio's painting and to Donatello's sculpture. Piero's major fresco cycle depicts *The Legend of the Holy Cross* (from the thirteenth-century *Golden Legend* by Jacopo da Voragine) on the walls of San Francesco at Arezzo (*c.* 1458–66). *The Annunciation* (Plate 5) from San Francesco shows Piero's subtle treatment of color

14-10 GIOVANNI BELLINI, *St. Francis in Ecstasy*, c. 1480. Panel, 48¾" x 54". Frick Collection, New York.

and light in addition to typically Renaissance architecture, perspective, and three-dimensional forms. His fresco work includes *The Resurrection* (1460, Town Hall, Borgo San Sepolcro). His panel paintings of the Duke and Duchess of Urbino (1472[?], Uffizi Gallery, Florence) are fine examples of fifteenth-century profile portraiture stressing individual features and meticulous detail.

Giovanni Bellini (Venice, 1430?–1516). Probably the most significant fifteenth-century Venetian painter, Giovanni was one of three famous painters bearing the Bellini name. He received his early training from his father, Jacopo, and from Andrea Mantegna. Giovanni was also influenced indirectly by Flemish painting, particularly in the use of color. His early style is represented by *St. Francis in Ecstasy* (Fig. 14-10). Sharp, intricate details reveal a kind of microscopic appreciation of nature. Later, possibly under the influence of his student, Giorgione, Giovanni's style changed to one using softer light, subordination of detail to large masses, and more emphasis on a general color effect rather than on local color.

14-11
ANDREA MANTEGNA, *San Zeno Altarpiece*, 1456–59. Each panel, 87″ x 45½″. San Zeno, Verona.

Andrea Mantegna (northern Italy, 1431–1506). Mantegna was apprenticed to Francesco Squarcione in Padua, but it was Donatello's sculpture in Padua that influenced Mantegna's love of statuesque figures with brittle, clinging drapery and highlights of stony or metallic character. Precise detail and settings with architectural reliefs and deep rocky landscapes are typical. In 1459, Mantegna became court painter to the Gonzaga family at Mantua, where he painted wall and ceiling frescoes in

14-12
ANDREA MANTEGNA, *The Dead Christ*, c. 1501. Tempera on canvas, 26¾″ x 31⅞″. Pinacoteca di Brera, Milan.

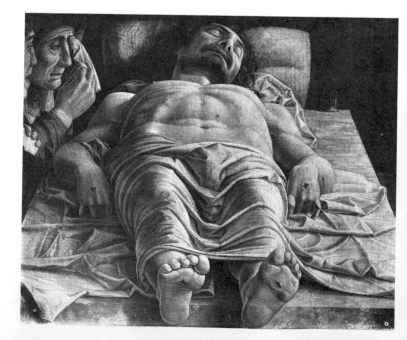

the palace. In the *San Zeno Altarpiece* (Fig. 14-11), the traditional triptych format acquires an architectural frame inspired by Roman work. This actual architecture is continued by the illusionistically painted architecture within the panels, architecture covered with reliefs that recall the sculpture of Donatello. The figures of the Madonna and saints reveal the painter's interest in three-dimensional form. *The Dead Christ* (Fig. 14-12) is a dramatic example of Mantegna's interest in spatial illusion; the body is daringly *foreshortened* (the effect of spatial recession obtained by drawing the object as a series of overlapping or successive masses). Mantegna's statuesque figures, his use of Roman architecture and sculpture, and his interest in illusionistic space had wide influence in northern Italy.

Sandro Botticelli (Florence, 1444–1510). Under the influence of his teacher Fra Filippo Lippi, Botticelli developed a style of knobby, jointed figures and rippling, linear drapery folds. He was patronized by the Medici family, and his *Adoration of the Magi* (1476–78, Uffizi Gallery, Florence) portrays members of the family as the Magi and their followers. His best-known paintings are *The Birth of Spring* (c. 1478) and *The Birth of Venus* (Fig. 14-13), both in the Uffizi Gallery. Both paintings exhibit Botticelli's use of sweeping linear curves and convolutions, his preference for lean figures with enlarged joints, and his use of repetition and variation in richly ornate patterns. In 1481, Botticelli was called to Rome to do one of the frescoes on the walls of the Sistine Chapel. In his later work, Botticelli turned in-

14-13
SANDRO BOTTICELLI, *The Birth of Venus, c.* 1480. Tempera on canvas, approx. 5'8" x 9'11". Galeria degli Uffizi, Florence.

14-14
SANDRO BOTTICELLI, *Lamentation, c.*
1500. Tempera on panel, 55'' x 81½''.
Alte Pinakothek, Munich.

creasingly to religious subject matter, and it is thought that his work was influenced by the emotional preaching of Savonarola. The *Lamentation* (Fig. 14-14) has only traces of his former delicacy of line, now imprisoned within harsh angular forms, and the expressions of the participants convey anguish.

Pietro Vannucci, called **Perugino** (central Italy, 1445?–1523). Perugino worked in Perugia in the region of Umbria except for his trip to Rome in the 1480's to paint *The Handing of the Keys to St. Peter* (Fig. 14-15) in the Sistine Chapel. Single-point perspective and a symmetrical composition focus on the central event, connect it to the building in the background, and imply that this building is the physical expression of the Church, whose earthly leadership Jesus is entrusting to Peter. Perugino simplified the parts and the action in his compositions, employing serene landscapes, figures and drapery with gently curving rhythmic lines, and passive faces with small, buttonlike eyes and delicate mouths. He was the teacher of Raphael.

Leonardo da Vinci (Florence, Milan, and Amboise, 1452–1519). Leonardo was born near Florence and sent at an early age to be trained in the studio of Andrea del Verrocchio. Leonardo's wide interests ranged from engineering to botany, and his notebooks are famous as records of a many-sided genius. *The Madonna of the*

14-15
PERUGINO, *The Handing of the Keys to St. Peter*, 1481–83. Fresco. Sistine Chapel, the Vatican, Rome.

Rocks (Fig. 126) reveals not only his interest in anatomy, geology, and botany, but qualities that forecast the sixteenth century: a conscious effort to perfect nature through concepts of ideal form and a desire to go beyond surface appearances to express the working of the mind or a condition of the spirit. While Leonardo was not the first to have these concerns, he faced them more deliberately than his contemporaries did and went further in seeking pictorial means for their expression. Sixteenth-century painting was influenced by his triangular figure groupings and his ideal facial type—the softly modeled oval with slender nose and delicately curved mouth. Unlike most fifteenth-century painters, he no longer felt the need for clarity in all parts. In *The Madonna of the Rocks* (Louvre version), he subordinated local colors to a total color effect and used strong chiaroscuro, leaving parts of the painting in obscurity but providing powerful focus. The highlighted fingers of the Madonna's outstretched hand create a startling illusion of depth; they hover over the head of Jesus and suggest a halo or a crown of thorns. The angel's hand points to the other child, who will become John the Baptist and recognize Jesus as the Christ. The tense concentration of attention between the two children is softened by the meditative gaze of the Madonna, while the angel seems more aware of the spectator. The jagged rocks and delicate plants do not seem to be included merely to demonstrate technical virtuosity or to establish physical reality, as they do in much fifteenth-century work. Instead, the powerful contrasts of light and shadow, of wild nature and soft flesh create the dramatic intensity of a mystery play or a sacred ritual. From 1483 to 1500, Leonardo worked in Milan for the Sforza family and painted, in addition to *The Madonna of the Rocks*, *The Last Supper* in Santa Maria delle Grazie, where again the total composition is expressive of mental drama. In Florence once more from 1503 to 1506, he painted the *Mona Lisa* (Fig. 14-16). After a trip to Rome in 1513 and more time in Milan, he accepted the invitation of Francis I to come to Amboise in France, where he remained until his death. The variety of Leonardo's interests and his tendency to leave projects unfinished have left us few paintings; his drawings and notebooks contain anatomical and botanical studies and inventions ranging from hydraulic engineering to flying machines. His late painting of John the Baptist (Louvre, Paris) has definite Manneristic traits (see p. 200) and influenced the Mannerist painter Parmigianino.

SCULPTURE IN ITALY

Florentine sculpture led the movement toward the consolidation of mass, contrapposto poses, studied anatomical detail, naturalistic drapery, and portraiture, all inspired by the growing interest in Roman art, the physical world, and man. The first freestanding nude figures since Roman times were produced, and relief sculpture exploited the illusion of depth. As in painting, the desire for clarity often resulted in a linear inscribing of detail on the masses. The range of sculpture widened in subject matter and in function. Human heroes, both contemporary and Biblical, were frequently chosen as subjects, and Greco-Roman mythology and secular allegory appeared more often than before. Enthusiasm for small bronze antique statuettes led Renaissance sculptors to take up this art, often borrowing subjects from mythology. Sculptures of the Madonna and of saints acquired portraitlike individuality. Relief sculpture served to emphasize focal points in the church, such as pulpits, *cantorias* (galleries for singers), and bronze doors. The relief on *tabernacles* (devotional centers ranging in size from small plaques to large wall niches) employed striking single-point perspective views surrounded by elaborate architectural frames using variations of ancient Greco-Roman moldings (Fig. 9-8, p. 98). The Renaissance appreciation of the individual is evidenced in the increased number of portrait busts after

14-16 LEONARDO DA VINCI, *Mona Lisa, c.* 1503–05. Oil on panel, approx. 30″ x 21″. Louvre, Paris.

LORENZO GHIBERTI, *The Sacrifice of Isaac*, from the *"Gates of Paradise,"* 1425–52. Bronze, 21" x 17½". Baptistery, Florence Cathedral.

the middle of the century. Like old Roman portraits, they contained much detail, yet the sculptor was capable of ennobling the subject by dignity of pose or alertness of expression. The ancient Roman equestrian statue of Marcus Aurelius in Rome inspired similar monuments for fifteenth-century Italians. The desire to perpetuate a name also asserted itself in the Renaissance wall tomb, built into the side of a church. The tombs present Roman pediments, columns, pilasters, moldings, and Roman figure types such as *putti* (Cupids or cherubs) and Greco-Roman winged victory goddesses.

Lorenzo Ghiberti (Florence, 1378?–1455). Ghiberti's two sets of bronze doors for the Florentine Baptistery show the transition from late Gothic to early Renaissance style. The *Sacrifice of Isaac* panel, done as an entry in the competition for the first set of doors (1401–02), is spatially shallow and crowded. The same subject done for the second set of doors (Fig. 14-17), the so-called *Gates of Paradise* (1425–52), is set in a spacious landscape with deep space created by a suggestion of linear perspective in the lines of trees and an effect of aerial

14-18 DONATELLO, *Young John the Baptist,*
c. 1455. Marble, entire figure
approx. 6' high. Museo Nazionale,
Florence.

perspective in the contrast of high relief in the foreground and faint relief in the background. Typical of the age are the drapery folds that emphasize the flexible poses of the bodies. Ghiberti's freestanding statue of St. Matthew (1420) for the Or San Michele adopts the mass, pose, and drapery forms of ancient Greco-Roman statues of orators. In his *Commentaries,* Ghiberti wrote about the lives of great artists and the theory of art, seeking in this way to establish his own place in the history of art.

Donatello (Florence, 1386–1466). The most significant fifteenth-century Italian sculptor was Donatello, who learned bronze casting under Ghiberti and traveled to Rome with the architect Brunelleschi to study ancient art. Donatello worked in marble, bronze, and occasionally wood and *stucco* (a fine plaster or cement). His first bronze statue of David (1430–32, Bargello, Florence) appears to have been the first freestanding nude since Roman times. Donatello also did relief sculpture, advancing its illusionistic possibilities by suggesting deep space and a variety of spatial relationships without using high relief for the foreground. He often combined his subtle low relief, called *schiacciato,* with architectural settings in single-point perspective; the effect is much like that of a drawing. Poses are active, and drapery breaks into a complexity of nervously rippling linear folds. Donatello's art reflects the growing importance of the individual not only in the use of specific features and expressions but also in the choice of human heroes such as David, Judith, and "Gattamelata" (Erasmo da Narni, a Renaissance general) as frequent subjects. Most amazing is his ability to express convincingly a wide range of human emotions, from the brutal confidence of a military leader (*The Gattamelata,* Padua) to the contemplative aloofness of *Young John the Baptist* (Fig. 14-18). Realism of form is accompanied by the realism of bared feelings. Strangely enough, Donatello, unlike other sculptors, did not show great interest in the portrait bust.

Andrea del Verrocchio (Florence, 1435–88). Verrocchio was first trained as a goldsmith and then may have worked with Desiderio da Settignano. Only one painting, *The Baptism of Christ* (*c.* 1472, Uffizi Gallery, Florence) is attributed with certainty to Verrocchio; his main interest was sculpture. He worked in terra cotta, stone, and bronze, with subjects ranging from saints and portrait busts to tomb designs and the equestrian statue of Bartolomeo Colleoni (Fig. 14-19). The *Colleoni,* a monument to a military leader, has much greater tension in both horse and rider than does its inspiration, Donatello's *Gattamelata*. Verrocchio's style is characterized by much hard-edged detail, bulbous anatomy, and distinct individuality in the faces. He taught Leonardo da Vinci.

ARCHITECTURE IN ITALY

The Renaissance man saw a sharp contrast between Gothic architecture, with its soaring verticals, irregular expansion, and complex geometric proportions veiled by lavish surface detail, and the remains of ancient Roman architecture. The Roman work, long since shorn of its decorative veneer, revealed a basic symmetry and a logical clarity in its proportioning that were simple enough to be quickly felt and comprehended, and the Renaissance scholar eagerly noted the static balance of vertical columns and horizontal architraves, the simple curve of the round arch, and the massive permanence of the walls that related to the rational structure of Greco-Roman literature and philosophy. Some fifteenth-century architects merely applied Roman pilasters, columns, and moldings in Gothic profusion, but the leaders sought to understand principles rather than to imitate details, and significant early Renaissance buildings, such as the Pazzi Chapel in Florence (Figs. 14-20–14-22) and Santa Maria delle Carceri in Prato (Figs. 1-16, 14-28, and 14-29) display a severe clarity of plan and elevation. The calculated simplicity and the linear outlining of each part call attention to the proportion of the parts to the whole, and the resulting diagrammatic effect is reminiscent of the insistence on linear clarity in much fifteenth-century Italian painting and sculpture. Studies of proportion in Roman architecture were intensified by the discovery, in a Swiss monastery in 1414, of the writings of Pollio Vitruvius, a Roman architectural theorist of the first century A.D., although difficulties in translating the work somewhat restricted its influence until the sixteenth century.

Florence contained the first early Renaissance architecture, the Foundlings' Hospital and the Pazzi Chapel. Other northern Italian cities, such as Rimini and Mantua, also became important. In Venice, the Renaissance came late and was mixed with strong Gothic and Byzantine traditions. Balconies and arcades kept walls light and open; Venetian politics were less violent than those of Florence, and the massive, fortresslike character of Florentine palaces was less necessary in Venice. Rome was also slow in developing the new style, partly

14-19
ANDREA VERROCCHIO, *Bartolomeo Colleoni*, c. 1483–88. Bronze, approx. 13' high. Campo dei Santi Giovanni e Paolo, Venice.

14-20 BRUNELLESCHI and GIULIANO DA MAIANO, Pazzi Chapel, c. 1440–61.

14-22 Interior of Pazzi Chapel, Florence.

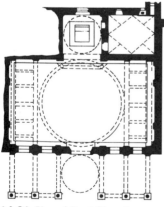

14-21 Plan of Pazzi Chapel.

because few buildings were completed during the century. When Renaissance elements appear, as in the Cancelleria (begun in 1486), the most evident source of inspiration is the architecture of Leon Battista Alberti.

Filippo Brunelleschi (Florence, 1377–1446). Brunelleschi's aspirations as a sculptor may have been crushed by his loss to Ghiberti in the competition for the reliefs on the Florentine Baptistery doors. Brunelleschi turned to architecture and was the first to make accurate measurements of Roman ruins. He was the first to use the rediscovered Roman architectural motifs consistently and to combine them with a new sense of spatial unity based on mathematical proportions. For example, his Florentine Church of San Lorenzo (designed in 1418) used a bay in the side aisle as a module that, in different multiples, governs the proportions of all the other spaces in the plan. Although Gothic architecture was often based on mathematical proportions and multiples of a chosen unit of measurement, its complexity does not allow the spectator to sense the relationships of basic proportions as he does in Brunelleschi's buildings. Brunelleschi's design (1417) for a dome on the unfinished cathedral of Florence revealed his engineering genius. Brunelleschi's surviving buildings include the Foundlings' Hospital (designed in 1419), the Church of Santo Spirito (designed in 1436), and the Pazzi Chapel, all in Florence. In the small Pazzi Chapel (Figs. 14-20–

14-22), the altar is set into a niche opposite the
entry and across the short axis of a simple rectangular
plan. Walls and vaults are divided by dark stone pilasters and moldings into distinct geometric areas. The
low relief of these details gives the effect of a linear
diagram. A Roman dome covers the center of the space,
and the unfinished porch, probably by Giuliano da
Maiano, employs the Corinthian order and a *broken
architrave* (architrave interrupted by an arch) in the
Roman manner. Roman moldings, pilasters, and columns organize mass, planes, and spaces with the self-
contained stability and dignity that Renaissance men
associated with ancient Roman architecture. Brunelleschi
is credited with painting two panels that demonstrated,
for the first time, a consistent system of linear perspective, a major step in the Renaissance search for pictorial
means of conveying the experience of space.

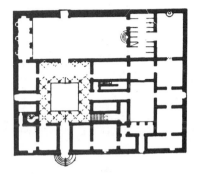

14-23 Plan of Medici-Riccardi Palace.

Michelozzo di Bartolommeo (Florence, 1396–1472). To
his contemporaries, Michelozzo was second only to
Brunelleschi as a pioneer in the new architecture.
Michelozzo became a favorite of Cosimo de' Medici,
and the Medici-Riccardi Palace (Figs. 14-23 and 14-24)
is the best-known work by the prolific architect. Roman
details compose the arches, moldings, and *cornices*
(terminating moldings that project at the top of a wall
or building), but the windows of the palace are connected by only a stringcourse, and no attempt was made
to proportion the floors with vertical dividers in the
form of pilasters or columns. The linear quality of the
design is modified by heavy *rustication* (rough stonework) on the ground floor, which changes to boldly
jointed but finished stone above and finally to smooth
masonry in the top floor. The design is powerful but
less subtle and less completely integrated in all its
parts than works by Brunelleschi. Michelozzo did re-
storing and additional building for San Marco and the
Palazzo Vecchio in Florence, and he designed the Medici
Bank and probably did the drawings for the Portinari
Chapel (Sant' Eustorgio), both in Milan. After the death
of Brunelleschi, Michelozzo was put in charge of the
Cathedral Workshop in Florence. Although occasional
use of Gothic arches links his work to the past,
Michelozzo helped to spread the basic elements of early
Renaissance architecture to Milan and even to Dalmatia.

Leon Battista Alberti (Florence, 1404–72). Alberti was
born in Genoa to an exiled Florentine family and was
educated at the universities of Padua and Bologna. He

14-24 MICHELOZZO DI BARTOLOMMEO,
Medici-Riccardi Palace, Florence,
begun 1444.

14-25 LEON BATTISTA ALBERTI, Sant´ Andrea, Mantua, c. 1470.

14-27 Interior of Sant´ Andrea.

14-26 Plan of Sant´ Andrea.

became a universal man of the Renaissance—a humanist scholar, painter, sculptor, mathematician, poet, and architect. His *Ten Books on Architecture*, like the treatises of Vitruvius, had wide influence, and he succeeded Brunelleschi as the leader in Renaissance architecture. The outstanding example of Alberti's church structures is Sant' Andrea in Mantua (Figs. 14-25–14-27). The façade combines the forms of a Roman temple and a triumphal arch. The height of the façade equals its width, although to achieve this perfect square, the façade was made lower than the rest of the church. The colossal pilasters on the façade, which rise more than one floor, are the same height as those within, and the nave is as wide as the whole façade. A vast barrel vault intersected by barrel vaults over the chapels on a lower level recalls the massive scale and structural features of the Basilica of Constantine (p. 127). Alberti held that numerical ratios were the source of visual and structural harmony. Sant' Andrea influenced much later work, including the plans for St. Peter's by Bramante and Michelangelo.

Giuliano da Sangallo (Florence, 1445–1516). Giuliano came from a family of celebrated artists and was trained as sculptor, engineer, and architect. His sphere of activity extended from Naples to Milan and into southern France, where he served Cardinal Giuliano delle Rovere in Lyons. Giuliano's Santa Maria delle Carceri (Figs. 1-16, 14-28, and 14-29) came late in the fifteenth century; its central Greek cross plan accords with Alberti's argument that the four-sided symmetry of a central plan expressed divine reason in its unity and harmony. Both Sangallo and Alberti forecast the sixteenth-century interest in central plans. The dome over the crossing of Sangallo's church, the linear framing of dark against light, and the low relief of pilasters and moldings all reveal the influence of Brunelleschi. The pilasters and dark bands on the exterior emphasize the proportions and suggest structural framing without destroying the flatness of the wall surface, while the nature of the interior spaces is clearly revealed by the flatness and simplicity of the enclosing walls. Giuliano's career extended into the sixteenth century, and, in later life, he was appointed to serve with Raphael in carrying on the construction of St. Peter's in Rome.

The Sixteenth Century

PAINTING IN ITALY

Italian painting of the High Renaissance period (1500–20) developed different aims from those of fifteenth-century art and should therefore not be thought of simply as a culmination of less successful fifteenth-century efforts. The earlier emphasis on the exploration of the physical world was superseded by a general effort to transform and transcend surface appearance without sacrificing its physical qualities. The artist sought to perfect nature according to preconceived ideal forms; faces were generalized to present types of humans rather than individuals, and there was less depiction of contemporary costume and more simplification of drapery folds for broad, sweeping, directional emphasis. The linear clarity of fifteenth-century work gave way to fuller masses; softer lighting often produced a dense atmospheric effect (called *sfumato*) that contrasted with the sharp airless space of much fifteenth-century painting. Individual actions formed a more flowing, harmonious, rhythmic pattern, and chiaroscuro provided dramatic focus and contrast. All this was part of a concept of the Grand Manner, by which the artist transformed nature and made it expressive of ideal form and inner experience, a concept possible only with the increased tendency to consider the artist as a divine genius rather than a mere craftsman. In the second half of the fifteenth century, many of the High Renaissance qualities had already been developed in

14-28
GIULIANO DA SANGALLO, interior of Santa Maria delle Carceri, Prato, 1485–92.

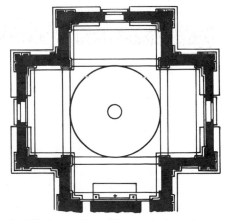

14-29 Plan of Santa Maria delle Carceri.

the art of Leonardo da Vinci. As a result, he is often considered a High Renaissance painter, even though most of his pioneering works were done in the fifteenth century. It is more helpful to see him as a bridge between the two centuries.

Florence was the seedbed for High Renaissance painting, not only because of Leonardo's work or the intellectually inquisitive and experimental background there, but because Raphael and Michelangelo painted their first mature works in that city. However, the blossoming occurred in Rome with the work of both these artists. In northern Italy, Venetian painting moved away from the sharp detail of the Early Renaissance toward fuller and less detailed masses, and the suppression of local colors for an overall color effect (Plate 6). Soft atmospheric effects were easier to achieve with oil paint, and in the sixteenth century the technique of oil on canvas supplanted the traditional tempera on wood panels that had been used for easel paintings (portable works). Fresco techniques continued to be used for mural painting, although during the sixteenth century use was made of oil on canvas applied to the wall. Venetian painters used oil paint opaquely and in glazes for textural and color effects of great richness.

Italian painting in the Late Renaissance (1520–1600) manifested several stylistic trends, sometimes within the work of a single artist. While High Renaissance concepts continued to shape the art of some leaders, a second trend, known as *Mannerism*, rejected the clear underlying order of High Renaissance painting and replaced it with ambiguity in spatial relations, mood, and even subject matter. Elongated figures with narrow shoulders, wide hips, tapering hands and feet, and self-consciously affected gestures were composed with a lack of central focus and deliberately inconsistent scale in crowded spaces. A third trend may be called *Proto-Baroque* because it forecasts the violent activity, dramatic lighting, great complexity, and breathtaking illusionism that were to become important devices in seventeenth-century Baroque art.

Michelangelo Buonarroti (Florence and Rome, 1475–1564). As a youth, Michelangelo was taken from his birthplace, Caprese, to Florence, where he studied painting with Domenico Ghirlandaio and sculpture with Giovanni Bertoldo. Although his real love was sculpture, Michelangelo was forced by papal and financial pressures to do painting and architecture as well. The only easel painting that is known with certainty to be his is *The Holy Family* (1504–06, Uffizi Gallery, Florence); the rest of his painting is mural work done in fresco. One of the greatest monuments of the High Renaissance is his series of frescoes on the ceiling of the Sistine Chapel in the Vatican, done between 1508 and 1512 at the insistence of Pope Julius II. Between 1536 and 1541, he painted *The Last Judgment* on the end wall of the Sistine Chapel, and from 1542 until his death he worked in the Pauline Chapel in the Vatican. Michelangelo concentrated on the human figure, often to the near exclusion of setting, and his concept of ideal form led him to paint figures of awesome bulk and musculature in active or restless poses. The Sistine ceiling boils with writhing giants enacting the Creation of the World, the Creation and Fall of Man, the story of Noah, and numerous secondary stories and allegories, all organized within a painted architectural framework. One of the few relaxed figures is that of Adam as he receives life from the outstretched hand of God, whose body ripples with energy. Typically, *The Creation of Adam* (Fig. 14-30) is divided into only two large groupings: that of Adam with the vaguely suggested mound of earth, and that of God and surrounding angels framed by the billowing cloak. The two groupings focus on the almost-touching fingers of God and Adam. In many other scenes, the extraordinary physical power of the bodies is countered by expressions of mental attitudes ranging from contemplation to consternation and anguish. Michelangelo's art and poetry indicate an increasing disillusionment with the search for physical beauty. The overpowering scale and activity in his painting forecast the Baroque art of the seventeenth century.

14-30 MICHELANGELO BUONARROTI, *The Creation of Adam*, detail from the ceiling of the Sistine Chapel, the Vatican, Rome, 1508–12.

14-31 GIORGIONE DA CASTELFRANCO, *The Tempest (The Soldier and the Gypsy)*. *c.* 1504. Oil on canvas, approx. 30" x 29" Galleria dell' Accademia, Venice.

Giorgione da Castelfranco (Venice, 1478–1510). The plague cut short the brilliant career of Giorgione, one of Titian's fellow apprentices in the studio of Giovanni Bellini. Scanty documentation has resulted in much discussion about the identification and dating of authentic paintings by Giorgione. Generally accepted works are the *Castelfranco Madonna* (Castelfranco), *The Tempest* (Fig. 14-31), *The Sleeping Venus* (Dresden Gallery), and *The Pastoral Concert*, although the latter has sometimes been questioned. The intended subject of *The Tempest* is, thus far, an unsolved mystery. This work was an innovation in Italian painting because of the importance of its landscape elements and its stress on mood. In *The Pastoral Concert* (Plate 6) the nude women may personify the subject of the music played by the young men. The nude bodies are painted as heavy three-dimensional forms with soft edges, generalized anatomy, and delicate nuances of light and color. The foliage masses and the lavish costumes have equally full forms and subtle textures. The painting is organized in alternating areas of light and dark that move back step by step from foreground to background; and the colors become cooler and less saturated as they move from the red hat of the central youth into the distance. The forms complement each other in graceful consonance; for example, the tree trunk on the left flows into

the vertical arm of the standing woman and also bends
to meet the curve of her back, while the leaning position and the rounded forms of the seated woman are
echoed in the foliage of the central tree. With his use
of soft light, quiet, graceful masses, bold simplification
of light and dark areas, and glowing color, Giorgione
exemplifies the High Renaissance in Venice. His style
may be seen as a bridge between the late work of Giovanni Bellini and the painting of Titian.

Tiziano Vecelli, called **Titian** (Venice, 1477/90–1576). As
a pupil of Giovanni Bellini and an admirer of Giorgione,
Titian acquired a love of soft, light, warm color effects,
which subordinated local colors, and massive simplified
forms. He enjoyed the lavish textiles and elegant costumes of the wealthy Venetian society and incorporated
these into his painting. His ideal for the female figure
is admirably presented in the Naples *Danaë* (Plate 7).
The breadth of the forms, the division of the composition into a few large parts, the subordination of details
to large areas of light and dark, and the preference for
spiral torsion in the poses probably owe something to
the art of Michelangelo, but Titian's color is richer and
his forms are softer. Titian achieved depth and a variety
of subtle textures by building up oil glazes of warm
and cool colors along with areas of impasto. His preference for dynamic grouping and powerful chiaroscuro
manifests itself in early works, such as *The Assumption
of the Virgin* (1516–18) and the Pesaro Madonna
(Fig. 14-32), where figures and areas of contrasting value
are grouped as counterbalancing diagonals. His late
work, such as *Christ Crowned with Thorns* (Fig. 14–33),
developed even greater dramatic contrast in the chiaroscuro and heavier impasto. Titian's fame spread, and
his energies were prodigious; in addition to religious
subjects and mythological themes, he painted many
portraits, including those of Pope Paul III and the Emperor Charles V.

Raphael Sanzio (Florence and Rome, 1483–1520). After
studying with Perugino in Umbria and revealing his
precocious talent, Raphael went to Florence (1504–08),
where he painted portraits and Madonnas. The *Madonna of the Meadow* (Fig. 3-1) is typical. The feeling of
gentle, sweet serenity is expressed not only through
faces and gestures but through the whole compositional
structure. The stable triangular group of figures works
with the quiet landscape to form an obvious axial balance. The large triangle provides an effect of gradation

14-32 TITIAN, *Madonna of the Pesaro
Family*, 1519–26. Oil on canvas, approx.
16' x 9'. Santa Maria dei Frari, Venice.

14-33 TITIAN, *Christ Crowned with Thorns*,
c. 1573–75. Oil on canvas, 9' x 6'. Alte
Pinakothek, Munich.

14-34 RAPHAEL SANZIO, *The School of Athens*, 1509–11. Fresco. Stanza della Segnatura, the Vatican, Rome.

and climax at the head of the Madonna, while the head of Jesus receives similar emphasis through the triangular shape formed by his body and the cross. The triangular groupings are softened by a modification of bodies and garments to produce variations on ovoid curves. Every part joins the gentle curvilinear harmony and fits into the underlying geometric structure. The face of the Madonna, the triangular grouping, and the sfumato effect owe much to Leonardo. In 1509, Pope Julius II called Raphael to Rome to paint a fresco series in several rooms of the Vatican. *The School of Athens* (Fig. 14-34), in the Stanza della Segnatura, combines Roman architecture on a vast scale, an ideal concept of human form, and individual portraits of the great minds of various ages. The many figures are organized in large, symmetrically balanced groups by geometric systems of sweeping curves, triangles, and vertical and horizontal lines. Restrained emotions, clear serene order, and exhilarating breadth dignify the grand symbolic program. We seem to witness the apotheosis of man. Some of the bodies in the Vatican paintings suggest the physique and poses of the figures in Michelangelo's contemporary frescoes in the Sistine Chapel. Raphael's earlier

Vatican works are the epitome of High Renaissance art; the later ones reveal Manneristic qualities.

Antonio Allegri, called **Correggio** (Parma, 1494–1534). Correggio's art indicates an acquaintance with the painting of Leonardo, Michelangelo, and the Venetians. His *Madonna of St. Jerome* (Fig. 14-35), like his frescoes in Parma Cathedral (1526–30), has the spiral poses, fluttering drapery, bold dark and light contrasts, and avoidance of stable verticals and horizontals that forecast much seventeenth-century painting; yet Correggio held the activity within large areas, and the compositions do not figuratively break through their architectural frame. His late work combines saccharine smiles and sensual fleshiness with Manneristic poses.

Francesco Mazzola, called **Il Parmigianino** (Parma, 1503–40). Parmigianino, a leading representative of Mannerism, was influenced by Correggio before coming to Rome (1524–27), where he attempted to achieve the dramatic lighting effects of Leonardo, the restless poses of Michelangelo, the rhythmic grace of Raphael, and the sensuality of Correggio. Parmigianino's *Madonna del Collo Lungo* (*Madonna with the Long Neck*, Fig. 14 36) shows the sinuous elongation and the ambiguity in space, scale, and emotions that are typical of the Mannerist aesthetic.

Jacopo Robusti, called **Tintoretto** (Venice, 1518–94). Tintoretto, one of the giants of Venetian painting, was an admirer of Titian and Michelangelo. His paintings include scenes from the life of St. Mark done for the School of St. Mark (1547–66), scenes from the life of Christ done for the School of San Rocco (1560–87), and religious and mythological subjects for the Doge's Palace (1577–78), all in Venice. Tintoretto's series were often elaborate in concept and grand in scale. His powers are summarized in the late painting of *The Last Supper* (Fig. 14-37), which makes a startling contrast with the same subject treated by Leonardo. Tintoretto grouped the active disciples along a table that pushes diagonally back into space. Halfway down the length of the table, the dazzling *nimbus* (glowing halo) around the head of Jesus provides the major light source in the dark room. Small nimbuses glow around the heads of all the disciples, a foreground lamp seems to radiate sparks, and transparent angels swoop down toward Jesus. This remarkably dramatic interpretation did much to inspire seventeenth-century art.

14-35 CORREGGIO. *Madonna of St. Jerome.* 1527–28. Galleria Nazionale, Parma.

14-36
IL PARMIGIANINO. *Madonna del Collo Lungo (Madonna with the Long Neck),* c. 1535. Oil on canvas, approx. 85'' x 52''. Galleria degli Uffizi, Florence.

14-37
TINTORETTO, *The Last Supper,* 1592–94.
12′ x 18′8″. San Giorgio Maggiore, Venice.

14-38
PAOLO VERONESE, *The Feast in the House of Levi,* 1573.
Oil on canvas. 18′2″ x 42′. Galleria dell' Accademia, Venice.

Paolo Veronese (Venice, 1528–88).   At the age of twenty-seven, Veronese came from Verona to establish himself as a portrayer of the material wealth of Venice. His selection and interpretation of Biblical subjects was governed by his love of lavish costumes, ornate architecture, and elegant table settings. *The Feast in the House of Levi* (Fig. 14-38) is typical in its grand scale. Veronese's interest in decorative details sometimes weakens the expressive power of the figures, but his technical facility, his use of silvery color, and the exuberance of his composition compensate for his shortcomings.

SCULPTURE IN ITALY

High Renaissance sculpture, like the painting of the period, sought ideal form, the Grand Manner that involved nobility of action and scale, ideal shapes and proportions, and depth of feeling. Some sculptors employed the serene equilibrium and smooth transitions seen in much of Raphael's painting; others chose the twisting poses and more tense vitality of Michelangelo's painting and sculpture. Both these facets of High Renaissance style contributed to the Late Renaissance trends: Mannerism and the Proto-Baroque. The serpentine curves and self-conscious elegance of a Mannerist figure might be derived from Raphael's suave harmonies or might be a softened version of the torsion and heroic musculature in Michelangelo's art. The bold contrast, dramatic action, and powerful focus of Proto-Baroque sculpture were inspired particularly by Michelangelo.

Portrait sculpture tended throughout the sixteenth century to express social position and physical or mental types rather than the sharply individual traits seen in fifteenth-century works. Sixteenth-century wall tombs were often larger and more complex than their fifteenth-century forerunners. The architectural frame developed greater spatial variety in different planes of projecting and receding parts. High Renaissance tombs usually have a smooth integration of figures and architecture, while Late Renaissance tombs may combine Manneristic figures with the lavish materials and bold contrasts that forecast the Baroque. The love of contrast sometimes led the designer to set figures and architecture sharply apart through changes in values, colors, shapes, or scale. The most important source for Late Renaissance tombs was Michelangelo's design for the tombs of the Medici (Fig. 2-5). Only in the Late Renaissance was the fountain developed as a public monument, one that could combine freestanding sculpture, relief sculpture, and water in movement. Fountains tended to become more complex, and relief sculpture gave way to more and more sculpture in the round (freestanding). Mass became more open, and dark and light contrasts became more extreme.

The major centers for the development of sixteenth-century sculptural style were Florence and Rome; Venice, Milan, and Naples were secondary. The sculptors, like the painters, often were active in several cities in the course of their careers.

Michelangelo Buonarroti. Michelangelo's early sculpture, such as *The Battle of the Centaurs,* done under the patronage of the Medici family in Florence, already showed the artist's preference for the nude, muscular body and active intertwining masses. Michelangelo's life was constantly upset by the conflicting demands of various patrons, and many of his sculptural projects remained unfinished or were finished in a compromise with original plans. This is the case with the tombs of Giuliano and Lorenzo de' Medici (Fig. 2-5), which underwent many changes and were left unfinished when Michelangelo departed for Rome. For the tomb of Giuliano, the wall emphasizes the climatic figure of Giuliano seated in a niche above the sarcophagus. Value contrasts stress the framing effect of the architecture, and the triangular grouping of the figures (Fig. 2-6, p. 24) integrates them with the geometry of the wall in spite of their restless poses and precarious positions; they were obviously designed to rest on horizontal surfaces. As in his painting, Michelangelo created muscular giants; he admitted that the central figure bore little resemblance to the face or body of Giuliano. Michelangelo saw his task not as the accurate portrayal of physical appearance but as the creation of a monument expressive of leadership. The female figure of Night and the unfinished male figure of Day seem to be grieving for Guiliano. The torso of *Day* reveals the influence of the *Belvedere Torso,* a fragment of a Roman copy of a Hellenistic Greek work that was known to Michelangelo. In view of his style, it is not hard to understand that Michelangelo's favorite ancient sculpture was the then newly discovered (1506) *Laocoön* (Fig. 9-30, p. 110), whose muscular power and dynamic pose suggest the source of Michelangelo's concept of ideal form. The artist's grandest tomb design, that for Pope Julius II (Fig. 14-39), suffered endless changes during forty years of struggle for funds and conflict with other projects. The result, in San Pietro in Vincoli, is a sadly heterogeneous collection of parts.

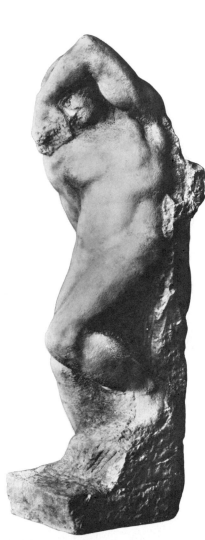

14-39 MICHELANGELO BUONARROTI, *The Young Slave* (for the Tomb of Pope Julius II), 1530–34(?). Marble, *c.* 8' high. Accademia delle Belle Arti, Florence.

Benvenuto Cellini (Florence, Rome, and France, 1500–71). Cellini was trained as a goldsmith and worked mainly in Rome from 1519 to 1540 as a medalist, that is, doing metal medallions with portraits in low relief. His skill is evident in the gold *Saltcellar of Francis I* (Kunsthistorisches Museum, Vienna), finished during a sojourn in France from 1540 to 1545. It was then that Cellini produced his first large-scale sculpture, using Mannerist proportions that suggest the influence of Francesco Primaticcio, Cellini's rival at the court of Francis I. Cellini's masterpiece was the *Perseus* (Fig. 14-40), done after his return to Florence. The Greek hero holds the severed head of the Medusa and is posed without twisting or violent action, showing more sympathy with Raphael than with Michelangelo. The intricate details reveal the goldsmith's art, and the only Manneristic elements are in the sculpture on the base. Cellini's autobiography is a major sourcebook for the Renaissance.

Giovanni da Bologna (Florence, 1529–1608). Giovanni da Bologna grew up in Flanders, traveled to Rome, and settled in Florence about 1556. Some of his works are Manneristic in their soft anatomy and effeminate poses. However, *The Rape of the Sabine Women* (Fig. 14-41) is more Proto-Baroque than Manneristic. The complex outline of the open forms, the intertwining organization, and the dramatic action forecast seventeenth-century art. He was the first sculptor since the fifteenth century to produce equestrian statues, but his work in this area is very restrained in style and close to its fifteenth-century prototypes. His activity was restricted to the area of Florence, but his influence was widespread.

ARCHITECTURE IN ITALY

The High Renaissance in Italy saw the creation of more effects derived specifically from Roman architecture. Closer attention was paid to Roman proportions, and walls were treated more as sculpted mass, resulting in stronger contrasts of light and shadow. Further study of Roman art revealed a concern for shaping not only mass but space, and High Renaissance architects turned to the possibilities of using mass to shape space not only inside but outside, between buildings in a group, for more comprehensive schemes of order. Architecture, like painting, strove for the effects of equilibrium and monumental scale that were so evident in the ruins of Roman architecture. Details were used with restraint in order to stress the largeness of the forms.

14-40
BENVENUTO CELLINI, *Perseus*, 1545–54. Bronze, 10'6'' high without base. Loggia dei Lanzi, Florence.

14-41

GIOVANNI DA BOLOGNA, *The Rape of the Sabine Women,* completed 1583. Marble, approx. 13'6" high. Loggia dei Lanzi, Florence.

Late Renaissance architecture is often characterized by features comparable to Mannerism in painting and sculpture: unexpected contrasts, deliberately crowded forms, fantastic shapes that suggest plants, animals, or men, and ambiguity in structural functions; a column might be robbed of its supporting role by undercutting its base, and an arch might be designed with its keystone slipping precariously out of place. Proto-Baroque tendencies also began to grow in architecture after 1520. Quiet equilibrium and clarity of parts were sacrificed for powerful focal effects, dramatic contrasts, and dynamic forms, such as concave-convex walls and expanding-contracting spaces. Surfaces were broken up with decorative elements in a great variety of depths.

Donato Bramante (Milan and Rome, 1444–1514). Bramante turned to architecture after beginning as a painter. His early buildings are in Milan and include the remodeling of Santa Maria presso San Satiro (begun *c.* 1479), where he used illusionistic perspective relief to make the choir seem deeper; and the choir and dome of Santa Maria delle Grazie (begun in 1492). The early work often shows a typically northern Italian tendency toward rich surface decoration, but there is already some subordination of details to large framing elements, the sign of bolder, grander systems of proportions. Bramante's mature style developed in Rome after 1500, where he was the leader of High Renaissance architecture. The Tempietto (Fig. 14-42), a chapel built on the spot of Peter's crucifixion, is based on the Greco-Roman tholos temple and typifies the High Renaissance interest in central buildings. The peristyle employs the Roman Doric order with triglyphs and metopes from the ancient Greeks (Figs. 9-5 and 9-6, p. 96), and the dome is a heightened version of the low Roman saucer dome seen on the Pantheon (Fig. 11-10). The wall was treated as a sculptural mass with projecting and receding parts; the light, delicate precision of earlier work has given way to a new monumentality. For the new church of St. Peter's, Bramante aimed at the magnificence of mass and space that still could be seen in the ruins of Roman baths. He turned back to the old Roman material, concrete, and drew a plan based on a Greek cross within a square (Fig. 14-43). The arms of the cross were to terminate in apses and be roofed with barrel vaults. The crossing would be covered with a great dome inspired by the Pantheon. Bramante's death put the construction into the hands of a succession of architects, and the present church (Fig. 14-45) owes its form mainly to three men: Michelangelo, who planned a Greek cross as Bramante had but made the masses bolder and more active; Carlo Maderna, who lengthened one arm to create a basilica plan and designed the façade; and Gianlorenzo Bernini, who planned the frontal square and its enclosing colonnades. Since Maderna and Bernini did their work in the seventeenth century, St. Peter's can hardly be considered simply as a Renaissance building. Bramante's plan for the Belvedere Court in the Vatican was realized somewhat more fully. Here he used massive walls and grand scale to mold the courtyard space into a focal apse. The boldness of mass, space, and scale set the key for High Renaissance architecture.

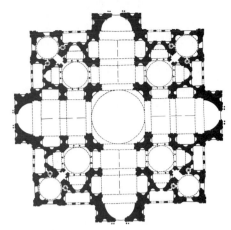

14-43 DONATO BRAMANTE, plan of St. Peter's, Rome, 1505.

14-42 DONATO BRAMANTE, Tempietto, San Pietro in Montorio, Rome, c. 1502–03.

14-44 MICHELANGELO BUONARROTI, vestibule of the Laurentian Library, Florence, begun 1524. Stairway designed 1558–59.

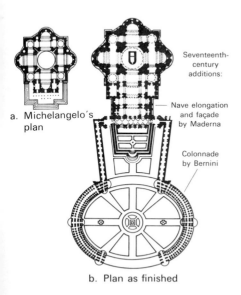

a. Michelangelo's plan

Seventeenth-century additions:

— Nave elongation and façade by Maderna

Colonnade by Bernini

b. Plan as finished

14-45 MICHELANGELO BUONARROTI, plan of St. Peter's, Rome.

Michelangelo Buonarroti. Michelangelo's first major architectural design, the Laurentian Library in Florence (1524), sacrificed the quiet equilibrium and logical clarity favored by Bramante. In the vestibule of the library (Fig. 14-44), the pilasters have an inverted taper, from small base to wide top, and engaged columns are denied their supporting role by being placed on console brackets extending from the wall. The pilasters, columns, and windows are crowded close together, and a staircase of expansive, curved steps dominates the room. This dramatic intensity disturbed some of Michelangelo's contemporaries, but it is considered today to be a Manneristic quality. In the 1530's, Michelangelo redesigned the Campidoglio (the Capitoline Hill) in Rome. A trapezoidal piazza flanked by two palaces focuses on the Palace of the Senators at the wide end. The piazza is filled by an oval pavement that radiates from the ancient equestrian statue of Marcus Aurelius. This dynamic space is enclosed by façades of strongly three-dimensional design, bold value contrasts, and *colossal orders* (columns or pilasters more than one floor high). Michelangelo's plan for St. Peter's provided walls of alternating angular and curved projections (Figs. 14-45a and 14-46), making the form complex to understand, somewhat restless in its movement, and powerful in value contrasts. To avoid weakening and cluttering the great masses of the building, Michelangelo used colossal orders to pull together the levels between base and attic. Such complexity, restlessness, and contrast may be considered Proto-Baroque.

Andrea Palladio (Vicenza, 1518–80). The most influential architect of the second half of the century was Palladio, an admirer of Vitruvius as well as of Alberti, a student of Roman ruins, and a writer on architectural theory. Palladio's structures were built in the region of his native Vicenza, but his influence was international, partly because of his *Four Books of Architecture* published in 1570. Many of Palladio's designs seem conservative in comparison with those of Michelangelo. A Roman dome and identical Ionic porches grace the simple square block of the Villa Rotonda (Figs. 14-47

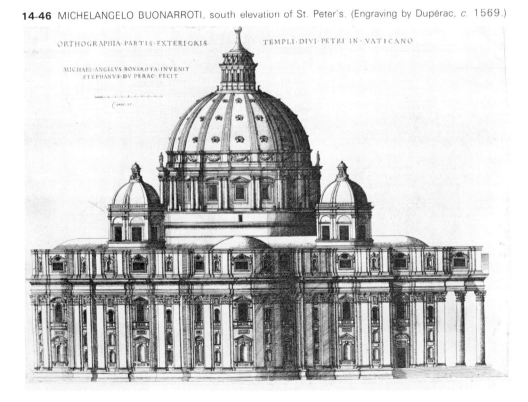

14-46 MICHELANGELO BUONARROTI, south elevation of St. Peter's. (Engraving by Dupérac, c. 1569.)

14-47 ANDREA PALLADIO. Villa Rotonda. Vicenza, begun 1550.

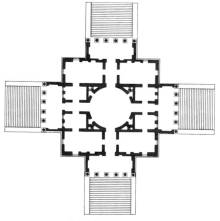

14-48 Plan of Villa Rotonda.

and 14–48). From any one of the façades, designed in obvious axial balance, one quickly comprehends the whole exterior form. Each part has a beginning, a middle, and an end—that is, a base, a main part, and a termination. Minor parts, such as pediments over windows and doors, build toward focal points like the pediments on the porches. Proportions are clearly marked by simple moldings. Inside, an equally severe clarity is felt in the obvious central balance of the plan. Such design fits the concepts of High Renaissance architecture. Touches of Manneristic enigma are found in his Palazzo Thiene, however, where windows are framed by columns imprisoned in large blocks and topped by flat arches, the keystones of which break into a pediment above. And his Loggia del Capitaniato bristles with crowded surfaces and complex three-dimensional variations, all heralding the Baroque age to come. One of Palladio's favorite devices, often called the *Palladian motif* (Fig. 14-49), was used frequently in seventeenth- and eighteenth-century architecture.

PAINTING IN THE NORTH

By 1520, Manneristic Italian elements had begun to appear in the work of many Northern artists. We find imaginative constructions of antique architecture, heroic proportions, broad, full masses, and the occasional use of chiaroscuro and sfumato. In Flanders, Antwerp became a prolific center for paintings in an exaggerated

Michelangelesque style imported from Rome. The intricacy of fifteenth-century work was retained in another type of Antwerp painting, done for export to other European countries: small religious scenes containing weird combinations of Italianate architectural parts and elongated figures in self-conscious poses and fantastic costumes. The term *Antwerp Mannerism* is sometimes applied to both trends. Antwerp and Brussels were both important for landscape and *genre* (scenes from everyday life) painting. Landscapes were panoramic, with delicate detail and subtle color; genre subjects, often including still life, tended to have sharply defined shapes in complex compositions.

In Germany, Austria, and Switzerland, the Medieval love of intricate active line on the one hand, and flat patterns of clearly edged shapes on the other, modified the ideas that came from Italy. While religious, mythological, and portrait subjects predominated, landscape painting was developed by painters working in the vicinity of the Danube River. Their so-called *Danube Style* created visions of icy peaks, winding valleys, and feathery evergreens or clawlike branches, all in delicate detail.

Sixteenth-century French painting centered on the Palace of Fontainebleau, where Francis I, Henry II, and Henry IV gathered native and foreign artists. The leaders were Italian Mannerists.

In sixteenth-century England, portraiture was the major interest, and leadership came from foreigners such as Hans Eworth of Flanders and Hans Holbein the Younger of Switzerland. Typical stylistic features are brilliant detail in costume and accessories and containment of details within larger areas with sharply defined edges.

Matthias Neithardt-Gothardt, called **Grünewald** (Germany, 1470/80–1528). Grünewald may have been born in Würzburg; little is known of his life. Between 1508 and 1514, he was court painter to the Archbishop-Elector and then to the Elector of Mainz. Grünewald's major work is the large, many-paneled *Isenheim Altarpiece*, commissioned for a church at Isenheim. The central panel (Fig. 14-50) depicts the torn body of Jesus on the Cross, flanked by the Madonna, John, Mary Magdalene, and John the Baptist. Like many German Medieval artists, Grünewald preferred harsh, jagged, and twisted forms. His sense of deep space and natural light, however, link him with the Renaissance.

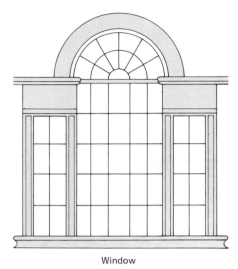

Window

Opening

14-49 The Palladian motif.

14-50 GRÜNEWALD, central panel of the *Isenheim Altarpiece, c.* 1510–15. Approx. 8'10'' x 10'1''. Musée Unterlinden, Colmar.

Albrecht Dürer (Germany, 1471–1528). Dürer began training as a goldsmith in Nuremberg but turned to painting and studied under Michael Wohlgemuth, a painter of altarpieces in the late Gothic style. Yet Dürer's fame spread more because of his engravings and woodcuts than because of his paintings. The woodcut of *The Four Horsemen of the Apocalypse* (Fig. 14-51) rivals wood engraving in its detail and demonstrates Dürer's love of intricate, boiling line. In an eruption of seething activity, the Four Horsemen—War, Sickness, Famine, and Death—ride down their helpless victims. This print is part of Dürer's *Apocalypse* series, based on the Revelations of St. John. The artist also designed a series of woodcuts on the life of Mary (1504–05) and others on the Passion of Christ: the *Great Passion* in woodcuts (1500–10), the *Little Passion* in woodcuts (1509–10), and a *Passion* in prints from metal engravings (1508–12). For the woodcuts, Dürer did the drawings, and expert cutters prepared the wood blocks. One of the best-known of Dürer's individual metal engravings is the *Adam and Eve*, done between 1504 and 1514. Although he traveled to Italy and the Netherlands, most of Dürer's work retained the gnarled forms and intricate line characteristic of German Medieval art; but his landscape and anatomical studies, his observation of textures and of light effects, his use of aerial and linear perspective, and his interest in portraiture all link him to the Renaissance. Dürer used the chiaroscuro and sfumato that had been developed in Italy; occasionally he employed simplified massive cascades of drapery that are reminiscent of Italian art.

Hans Holbein the Younger (Germany, Switzerland, and England, 1497–1543). Holbein grew up in Augsburg and established himself in Basel as a muralist, woodcut designer, and portraitist, but he found his greatest success as a portrait painter in England at the court of Henry VIII. In *The Ambassadors* (Fig. 14-52), Renaissance interests are apparent in the depiction of individual facial character and in the array of different forms and textures carefully situated in space and rendered in natural light. Like many Italian painters of the preceding century, he was not above using some illusionistic trickery to display his conquest of the physical world: When the long bony form in the foreground is viewed from the proper angle (hold the page against your face

14-51
ALBRECHT DÜRER, *The Four Horsemen of the Apocalypse*, 1497–98. Woodcut, 15½″ x 11″. Metropolitan Museum of Art. New York (gift of Junius S. Morgan. 1919)

14-53
HANS HOLBEIN THE YOUNGER, *Henry VIII*, 1536–37. Oil and tempora on oak panel, approx. 11″ x 8″. Thyssen-Bornemisza Collection, Lugano.

14-52
HANS HOLBEIN THE YOUNGER, *The Ambassadors*, 1533. Oil and tempera on wood, approx. 7′ x 7′. Courtesy of the Trustees of the National Gallery, London.

14-54 FRANÇOIS CLOUET, *Elizabeth of Austria*, 1571. Louvre, Paris.

and sight along the length of the object), it becomes a skull. Like many of his contemporaries, Holbein was intrigued by the idea of death, and he designed woodcuts portraying the figure of Death coming to claim men of various social levels. His portrait of Henry VIII (Fig. 14-53) is a remarkably frank expression of luxury and crafty cupidity, yet underlying the bulk of the head and costume are the typically Medieval silhouetted shapes and flat backgrounds.

François Clouet (France, 1500?–72). François was trained by his father, Jean Clouet, and succeeded him as court painter to Francis I. François Clouet's earliest known portraiture shows Italian influence in pose, setting, and massiveness. Later portraits belong to an international portrait style of the second half of the sixteenth century, a style that owes much to Holbein as well as to Italian painting. Standard poses and accessories are combined with elaborate costume detail, which is treated rather flatly. Clouet's chalk portraits achieve some of Holbein's conciseness of characterization, and his portrait of Elizabeth of Austria (Fig. 14-54) reflects Holbein's ability to depict character as well as an orchestral range of textures.

Pieter Bruegel the Elder (Flanders, 1525–69). Although Bruegel may have been born in the Netherlands, his career is part of Flemish art. After registering with the painters' guild in Antwerp in 1551, he traveled in Italy and then returned to Antwerp to work as an engraver. After 1563, Bruegel lived in Brussels. An intellectual, he was a friend of leading humanists in his region. His paintings suggest his philosophical position and often are subtly satirical. *The Wedding Feast* (Fig. 14-55) exemplifies his leadership in genre painting. The rounded, knobby forms, small scale, and jerky movements of the

14-55
PIETER BRUEGEL THE ELDER, *The Wedding Feast, c.* 1565. Panel, approx. 4' x 5'. Kunsthistorisches Museum, Vienna.

countless little people are in jolting contrast to sixteenth-century Italian style, but they are a logical outgrowth of fifteenth-century Flemish art. Although the individual figures are rounded and the space is deep, the contrast of local colors and values gives the effect of a complex, richly varied patchwork of flat shapes. Bruegel's best-known works include a series done in 1565 representing the seasons: *The Harvest* (Metropolitan Museum of Art, New York), *Hunters in the Snow, Dark Day,* and *The Return of the Cattle* (all in the Kunsthistorisches Museum, Vienna).

ARCHITECTURE IN THE NORTH

In northwestern Europe, the Gothic style lingered into the fifteenth and sixteenth centuries. Renaissance details slowly infiltrated Gothic detail until at last the basic structure changed and an integrated Renaissance style was formed. The change occurred first in France, the Renaissance influence coming from northern Italy in the early sixteenth century because of French military campaigns there. The importation of Roman moldings, pilasters, columns, arches, and floral ornament is evident in churches such as St. Eustache in Paris and in the châteaux of the Loire Valley, where Medieval forms are given Renaissance decorative details. The Palace of Francis I at Fontainebleau demonstrates various phases of Renaissance architecture during his reign and afterward. Of considerable influence were the writings of the Italian Sebastiano Serlio, who was called to France by Francis I in 1540. Typical sixteenth-century Northern features are steeply pitched roofs and ornate gables. As in painting, the northerners often applied Italian Renaissance motifs in a spirit of fantasy and profusion that suggests the Middle Ages.

Pierre Lescot (France, 1510/15–78). Lescot came from a wealthy family and received a broad education. His architectural style was formed before he traveled to Italy, although he undoubtedly knew the standard sourcebooks for Renaissance and antique architecture. Most of Lescot's work has been changed or destroyed. The most complete remaining structure is the façade of the square court of the Louvre (Fig. 14-56), in which the major horizontal and vertical dividing lines are broken at intervals, and the small size of columns and pilasters, along with the ornamental breakup of the surfaces, creates richness rather than the monumental grandeur of Italian design.

14-56
PIERRE LESCOT, square court
of the Louvre, Paris, begun
1546.

SCULPTURE IN THE NORTH

In the North, sculpture, like painting and architecture, clung to the Gothic style until well into the sixteenth century. The fifteenth century had nurtured increasing portraiture in tomb sculpture, the use of standard types in faces portrayed in religious and mythological scenes, and both the smoothly flowing drapery common to late Gothic French art and the crackling angular drapery of the Lowlands and the Germanic areas. Sixteenth-century sculpture produced more portraiture, more anatomical detail, and more interest in landscape and deep space in relief compositions. Countries with the tradition of angular drapery and thin figures turned to fuller masses and curving forms. French sculpture was strongly affected by the Italian Mannerist sculptors serving Francis I, and Renaissance concepts were introduced to England after 1512 by the Italian sculptor Pietro Torrigiano.

Jean Goujon (France, ?–1567). Although Goujon was one of the major sculptors of his day, little is known of his life. By 1540, he had developed a Renaissance style based on a knowledge of both Italian and antique art. His *Pietà* from St. Germain l'Auxerrois (1544–45) reveals Manneristic poses and proportions. Both the *Pietà* and the relief panels of nymphs from the Fontaine des Innocents (Fig. 14-57) have a delicate flowing harmony in the thin linear drapery folds that seems peculiar to Goujon's style.

14-57
JEAN GOUJON, nymphs from the Fontaine
des Innocents, Paris, 1548–49.

Suggestions for Further Study

Benesch, Otto. *The Art of the Renaissance in Northern Europe: Its Relation to the Contemporary Spiritual and Intellectual Movements,* rev. ed. London: Phaidon Press, 1965.

Blunt, Anthony. *Art and Architecture in France: 1500–1700* (Pelican History of Art). Baltimore: Penguin Books, 1953.

————. *Artistic Theory in Italy: 1450–1600.* New York: Oxford University Press, 1956.

Cuttler, Charles D. *Northern Painting from Pucelle to Bruegel.* New York: Holt, Rinehart and Winston, 1968.

De Tolnay, Charles. *Michelangelo.* 5 vols. Princeton, N.J.: Princeton University Press, 1943–60.

Freedberg, Sydney J. *Painting of the High Renaissance in Rome and Florence.* 2 vols. Cambridge, Mass.: Harvard University Press, 1961.

Gilbert, Creighton. *History of Renaissance Art: Painting, Sculpture, and Architecture Throughout Europe* (Library of Art History). New York: Abrams, 1973.

Gombrich, Ernst Hans Josef. *Norm and Form: Studies in the Art of the Renaissance.* London: Phaidon Press, 1966.

Hartt, Frederick. *History of Italian Renaissance Art: Painting, Sculpture, and Architecture.* New York: Abrams, 1969.

Krautheimer, R., and Trude Krautheimer-Hess. *Lorenzo Ghiberti.* Princeton, N.J.: Princeton University Press, 1956.

Lassaigne, Jacques. *Flemish Painting.* 2 vols. Translated by Stuart Gilbert. New York: Skira, 1957.

Müller, Theodor. *Sculpture in the Netherlands, Germany, France, and Spain: 1400–1500.* (Pelican History of Art). Baltimore: Penguin Books, 1966.

Murray, Peter. *The Architecture of the Italian Renaissance.* New York: Schocken Books, 1963.

Osten, Gert von der, and Horst Vey. *Painting and Sculpture in Germany and the Netherlands: 1500–1600* (Pelican History of Art). Baltimore: Penguin Books, 1969.

Panofsky, Erwin. *Early Netherlandish Painting: Its Origins and Character.* 2 vols. Cambridge, Mass.: Harvard University Press, 1953.

————. *Renaissance and Renascences in Western Art.* Stockholm: Almqvist and Wiksell, 1960.

Pope-Hennessy, John. *An Introduction to Italian Sculpture.* 3 vols. New York and London: Phaidon Press, 1955–62.

Seymour, Charles, Jr. *Sculpture in Italy, 1400–1500* (Pelican History of Art). Baltimore: Penguin Books, 1966.

Stechow, Wolfgang. *Northern Renaissance Art, 1400–1600: Sources and Documents.* Englewood Cliffs, N.J.: Prentice-Hall, 1966.

Vasari, Giorgio. *The Lives of the Painters, Sculptors, and Architects.* Edited by Betty Burroughs. New York: Simon and Schuster, 1959.

Wittkower, Rudolf. *Architectural Principles in the Age of Humanism,* 3rd rev. ed. London: Alec Tiranti, 1962.

Wolf, Robert Erich, and Ronald Millen. *Renaissance and Mannerist Art.* New York: Abrams, 1968.

Chapter 14 Music

Renaissance Music:
1450–1600

Musicians during the Renaissance had no direct knowledge of ancient Greek and Roman music, but they did accept the humanistic view that art should serve to enrich life through a harmonious and rational order. A musical style capable of satisfying this ideal first developed in northern France and Flanders around the mid-fifteenth century, soon spread to Italy, and finally to Germany, Spain, and England. This international style was characterized by a polyphony of equal voices in harmonious blend and perfect balance.

Secular patronage accorded music an equal place with the other arts, and the Franco-Flemish musicians were eagerly sought after, particularly in Italy. Their style was adopted by musicians everywhere, but, by the mid-sixteenth century, local and national traits had begun to emerge, especially in Italy, and later in England.

Music was first published by Ottaviano Petrucci at Venice in 1501, and music printing became widespread during the sixteenth century. Accurate copies of the music of the best composers became available to a large public, helping greatly to extend their fame and influence.

Franco-Flemish Music: Late Fifteenth and Early Sixteenth Centuries

The musical style of the Renaissance originated during the late fifteenth century in the music of the Burgundian and French courts, chapels, and churches. Though political boundaries were unstable, the culture of the area was essentially French. By the middle of the century Dufay and other Burgundian composers had adopted certain new techniques in their sacred works, and a distinct, sacred style emerged in the motets and Masses composed during the latter half of the century. A rather thick texture of four equal, homogeneous vocal parts became standard, with complex rhythmic interplay and some rudimentary imitation among the voices. Johannes Ockeghem was the leading composer of this period.

The Renaissance style appears fully developed by the beginning of the sixteenth century in the music of Josquin des Prez and his contemporaries. Textures are more open, with the voices moving within a wider range. Persistent imitation of the parts is the rule, and the lines flow smoothly with supple rhythmic interplay. The sound of the triad, along with carefully controlled dissonances, is the harmonic norm. The voices usually reach a cadence at different times, and the resulting overlap helps to maintain a continuous forward motion. Although instruments were frequently used in performance, most music was conceived as being ideally suited for human voices. Renaissance humanism is reflected in more careful attention to the relation between words and music.

The most conservative style of Renaissance music appeared in settings of the Mass, partly due to the problems inherent in its fixed text and liturgical requirements. On the other hand the motet offered fewer restrictions. It had a single, unified text that the composer could set as he saw fit, and it was here that the most progressive stylistic developments took place. For their Masses, composers commonly borrowed melodies and whole polyphonic textures from both sacred and secular sources, using these materials in all of the sections to unify the music. The use of devices from secular music in the Mass frequently was criticized by Church authorities. The chanson was the principal form

14-58

Allegory of Music. from northern Italy, late fifteenth or early sixteenth century. Bronze relief, approx. 4½" x 3". National Gallery of Art, Washington, D.C. Samuel H. Kress Collection.

14-59

Page from *Harmonice Musices Odhecaton A* published by Ottaviano dei Petrucci in Venice, 1501. This is the first publication of music using modern printing techniques.

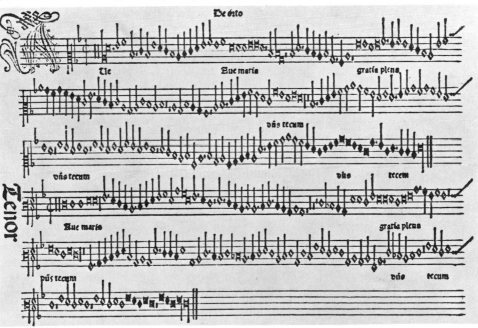

of secular music of the early sixteenth-century Franco-Flemish composers. Essentially they transferred the new motet style to the texts of French popular songs and poetry, which ranged in subject matter from courtly love to bawdy humor, from beauty in nature to human comedy. Composers developed many clever musical ways to reflect the words of the text. Chansons were extremely popular, appearing in many printed collections. They often were performed with instruments, especially in Italy, where they were called *canzoni.*

Johannes Ockeghem (Flanders and France, *c.* 1420–95). Ockeghem was born in the Netherlands but spent over half his life in the service of French kings. He studied with Dufay and probably with Binchois and was the teacher of many famous musicians. He is best known for his Masses. In works such as his *"Missa Mi-mi"* the separate polyphonic lines retain their independence, yet fuse into a whole fabric. Four equal voices make up the texture, and there is some use of imitation. Ockeghem showed a marked tendency to write specifically for human voices, yet he often seemed unconcerned with the rhythm, sound, and meaning of his texts. He retained a medieval fondness for canons and musical puzzles, as in his *"Missa prolationum,"* in which two separate canons are sung at the same time by two pairs of voices.

Josquin des Prez (Flanders, Italy, and France, *c.* 1445–1521). Josquin was born in Hainaut, was a choirboy at St. Quentin, and probably studied with Ockeghem. He was a musician at several Italian courts, sang in the Papal choir, and later served Louis XII of France. Josquin was recognized as the greatest composer of his day. In his Masses, motets, and chansons he imbued the techniques of equal-voice polyphony with a balanced, harmonious beauty, firmly establishing the polyphonic techniques characteristic of most Renaissance music. Polyphony and the flow of melodies always governed the music, but within these constraints he took care to set the word rhythms properly and to make his texts intelligible, a concern with words that was generally absent among his predecessors. The best examples of his style are his motets. His *"Ave Maria . . . benedicta tu"* is a setting of the prayer to the Virgin Mary, "Hail, Mary, full of grace. . . ." Each phrase of the text begins a new melodic idea, which is imitated by each of the four voices. Entry of the voices in imitation not only gives them independence, but, since they rarely reach a cadence at the same time, there is a continuous flow of music. The first phrases are long and are imitated at some distance. As the piece progresses the phrases get shorter, producing more frequent overlap of voices and changes in the texture. Rhythmic intensity builds slowly from the very calm beginning to a climax and cadence on the words, *"Jesus Christus Filius Dei vivi"* ("Jesus Christ, son of the living God"), where the flowing lines break up into short repeated motives. A contrasting section follows, in triple meter, then the original duple meter returns for the brief final section in the full four-voice texture.

Franco-Flemish, Italian, and English Music: Late Sixteenth Century

Throughout the sixteenth century the Franco-Flemish composers continued to transmit their polyphonic vocal style to the churches and courts of Europe. At the same time Italian composers absorbed the style and adapted it to their own idioms, and by the end of the century Italian influence had reached as far as Germany, Spain, and England. The last composers of Latin Masses and motets in the Renaissance style included the Fleming Roland de Lassus, the Italian Giovanni Pierluigi da Palestrina, and the Englishman William Byrd.

Italian musicians, always a little uncomfortable with complex polyphony, stressed simplicity and the meaning of the words. These tendencies characterized their secular part songs, which frequently moved in homophonic chordal textures, making the words easy to understand, and were structured in simple, repetitive verse forms. Influenced by the style of the motet and the chanson, these works evolved into the *madrigal*, which soon became the most influential and progressive type of Renaissance music. Madrigals were polyphonic settings of Italian poetry, intended to be sung by several soloists, typically four or five. Composers used a free version of the motet technique, influenced by traditions of Italian secular music. Eventually this led to a sacrifice of musical continuity in favor of sudden contrasts of rhythm and texture, abrupt harmonic changes, freer dissonance treatment, and extensive use of harmonic color. Madrigals of this kind became common by the end of the century, and they anticipated some of the major developments of the early Baroque. They can

14-60

HIERONYMUS BOSCH, detail from *The Garden of Earthly Delights, c.* 1505. 86½" x 36". Museo del Prado, Madrid.

properly be called *Manneristic,* reflecting parallel trends in the visual arts. Most composers, including the Flemish, wrote Italian madrigals. They were brought to England late in the sixteenth century, and this led to the development of English madrigals during the Elizabethan period.

Dominance of the polyphonic vocal ideal during the Renaissance often obscures the popularity of instrumental music in church and social uses. Wind instruments and viols were particularly favored, and solo works were developed for the lute, harpsichord, and organ. The lute was the most popular social instrument. It was used alone, with other instruments, and to accompany voices. The most common wind instruments included the recorder, a wooden flute with a whistle type mouthpiece; the shawm, an ancestor of the modern oboe; the cromorne, or krummhorn, a curved tube with a reed enclosed in a cap; the cornetto, or zink, a flared wooden or ivory tube with finger holes; the sackbut, or ancient trombone; and various trumpets, which were metal tubes without finger holes. The cornetto, sackbut, and trumpet were blown with a cup mouthpiece similar to modern brass instruments. The viols were bowed string instruments with frets, which produced a much softer tone than the modern violin family. All of these instruments blended well with the human voice. Most were made in different sizes and were often grouped in

14-61

A sixteenth-century woodcut showing a music room at court. We can see an organ, harp, drums, sackbut, lute, recorders, krummhorn, cornetto, viol, and spinet. The Metropolitan Museum of Art, New York. Harris Brisbane Dick Fund, 1888.

14-62

LUCAS VAN LEYDEN, *David Playing for Saul*. Engraving. The Metropolitan Museum of Art, New York. Rogers Fund, 1918.

families of like instruments corresponding to choirs of voices.

Renaissance instrumental music can be classified according to three general types; dance music, free improvisations for solo instruments, and pieces based on vocal polyphony. Although dance music often was performed by small instrumental groups, it was developed to its fullest in solo pieces for lute and harpsichord. These pieces typically were structured in repeated sections, with two or three complementary dances grouped together. The practice of varying the repetitions of the sections led composers, such as William Byrd in England, to create sets of sectional variations for the harpsichord based on entire dances. Solo pieces also were written for the lute, harpsichord, and, especially, the organ in the style of free improvisation. These were variously called *fantasias, preludes, ricercars, toccatas,* and other less common names.

The sound of most Renaissance instruments blended well with the human voice, and instruments commonly were used in the performance of vocal polyphony, either to reinforce the voices or to substitute for them. Choices in the use of instruments were made by the performers, not the composer. Often whole polyphonic pieces were performed with instruments; thus, motets were transferred to the organ, and chansons were played on the lute or harpsichord or with small instrumental groups. The Italian name for chanson is *canzona*, and Italian composers soon began writing canzoni specifically for instrumental performance.

The wealth, political power, and independence of Venice encouraged extensive patronage of music. Ceremonial processions with much pomp and display were held frequently on the piazza outside of St. Mark's Cathedral. The church itself had a long and distinguished musical tradition. Its vast interior is circular, with two organs in choir lofts on opposite sides, making it particularly suited to spatial distribution of performing groups. The use of divided choirs of singers and instrumentalists became a specialty of Venetian composers. Their interest in the interplay and opposition of contrasting sound blocks represents the beginning of the concerted style, which became an important feature of Baroque music. The concerted style stressed contrasting textures and timbres and opposition of large and small groups with combinations of different voices and instruments, often physically separated in performance. Textures tended toward chordal harmonies, which governed the movement of the melodic lines, as opposed to the polyphonic style, where movement of the lines determined the harmonies. With its emphasis on massive power and bold contrasts, the Venetian concerted style may be seen as a manifestation of the Proto-Baroque.

Giovanni Pierluigi, called **da Palestrina** (Italy, 1525–94). Trained as a choirboy in his home town and in Rome, Palestrina spent most of his career as a church musician in the Roman basilicas of St. Peter's, St. John Lateran, and Santa Maria Maggiore. He was one of the last and greatest composers of sacred music in the style of Franco-Flemish polyphony. He produced many motets and other sacred works, but his highest achievement was in his Masses. His style was dignified, restrained, and impersonal. He avoided emotional extremes, seeking instead to create a serene beauty through smooth-flowing lines and perfectly balanced textures. His melodic lines gently rise and fall within a comfortable singing range, and the interplay of parts creates subtle variations in rhythmic tension. A strong sense of tonal continuity adds to the effect of balance and repose. Imitative entries create continual changes of texture, and the various groupings and combinations of the voices produce contrasting vocal colors. His *Pope Marcellus Mass*, written for a choir of six parts is typical. In the *Sanctus* contrasts between high and low registers are prominent, and the independent motion of the lines is enhanced by frequent rising and falling motives. Imitative entries are not particularly conspicuous. The *Hosanna* begins with the voices moving in the same rhythm, but soon returns to a full polyphonic texture similar to the *Sanctus*. The *Benedictus* calls for four parts, the two bass parts being omitted, producing a timbre of high voices only. It is constructed much like a motet, with persistent imitation, new motives with each new phrase of the text, and a tendency to group the voices in pairs. The first *Agnus Dei* returns to the six-part texture, with imitation in all parts. The full range of sonorities is used to maximum effect in the shifting combinations of vocal color. The final *Agnus Dei* is written for seven parts, three of which proceed throughout in strict canon.

Roland de Lassus, also called **Orlando di Lasso** and **Orlandus Lassus** (Flanders, Italy, and Bavaria, 1532–94). Lassus was born in Mons, where he was a choirboy. He held several musical positions in Italy during his youth and spent the latter part of his life at the Bavarian court in Munich. He was a prolific and cosmopolitan composer, known and respected throughout Europe, whose works represent the peak of the Franco-Flemish style. He wrote Latin Masses and motets, Italian madrigals, French chansons, and German polyphonic vocal works, in which he freely adapted elements from all idioms as appropriate to each work. Lassus's Latin motets were his greatest achievement. *"Tristis est anima mea"* is typical. It is for five voices, which allows considerable scope for variety in the spacing and combination of the parts. Imitation occurs but is not pervasive. Melodic flow of the voices is enhanced by rich, resonant harmonies and shadings of vocal color produced by changes in the texture. Though Lassus generally stayed within the bounds of the polyphonic style, his representation of texts often was vivid and dramatic, showing the influence of the Italian madrigal. The chanson, *"La nuict froide et sombre,"* is a setting of a poem by Joachim Du Bellay describing the cold and darkness of night, followed by the miracle of the dawn. Lassus does not begin with imitation; instead, the four voices together express the gloom of night by dwelling on the initial chord sounds, sung in a low register. There is little movement, which enhances harmonic color. The word *skies* is set apart by a cadence to a major chord sung by the upper three parts only. As dawn comes, the voices become

14-63

A Renaissance sketch of a group playing the viol, flute, and lute. The viol performer is pointing to the score from which the others are playing.

more active and move into higher registers. There is increasing imitation of motives in all of the parts and a climax of activity as the new day arrives.

William Byrd (England, 1543–1623). Byrd studied under the composer Thomas Tallis, probably as one of the choirboys at the Chapel Royal. At age twenty he became the organist at the Lincoln Cathedral, and at twenty-nine was made a Gentleman of the Chapel Royal, where he later shared the post of organist with Thomas Tallis. Byrd remained high in the favor of Queen Elizabeth I throughout her reign. He wrote Catholic music, including Latin Masses and motets, as well as considerable music for Anglican worship. He was one of the last great composers of Latin church music in the sixteenth-century polyphonic style. His secular compositions include madrigals, solo songs for voice and viols, instrumental ensemble pieces, and numerous keyboard works. Byrd essentially founded the tradition of English keyboard music. Many of his keyboard works appear in manuscript collections of music for the *virginal,* or harpsichord. The most common pieces in these collections are dances and sets of variations based on folk melodies or dance tunes. His "The Carman's Whistle" is a set of nine variations on a folk song. The initial statement of the theme consists of four eight-beat segments. The succeeding variations include only the second, third, and fourth segments. The outline of the melody, considerably embellished, always can be heard in the upper voice. The metrical groupings never change, and the essential tonal and harmonic structure is the same in all of the variations. Variety is achieved through elaborate ornaments and melodic figurations, changes of texture, and rhythmic interplay among the parts.

Giovanni Gabrieli (Italy, 1557–1612). Gabrieli studied with his uncle Andrea Gabrieli, one of the organists at St. Mark's Cathedral in Venice, and he possibly studied with Lassus in Munich. He was second organist at St. Mark's for the last twenty-seven years of his life. Famous and influential throughout Europe, he had many students, the most renowned being the composer Heinrich Schütz. Gabrieli wrote a considerable number of madrigals and significant works for the organ, but his fame rests on his large festive pieces for multiple choirs of voices and instruments in as many as twenty parts in concerted style. In these works he replaced Franco Flemish polyphony with a homophonic chordal texture. The different choirs were separated spatially in performance to produce echo effects and increase sonorous contrasts. Instrumental pieces designed in this way were called "canzoni" or "sonatas." His "Canzona in the Seventh and Eighth Tones for Twelve Parts," from Part Three of the *Sacrae Symphoniae Ioannis Gabrielii* (1597), calls for three four-part choirs of equal weight. The instruments are not specified, but exchange of the same materials among all three choirs strongly suggests a different basic timbre for each, such as brasses and loud reeds, recorders and soft reeds, strings, or organ. Though many of Gabrieli's canzoni use imitative polyphony, recalling their ancestry in the vocal chanson, he is concerned here with the sonorous possibilities of three contrasting sound blocks, undoubtedly meant to be dispersed for spatial effects. The piece begins with all parts together, then the three choirs separate, and phrases, motives, and cadential patterns are exchanged and echoed from choir to choir. There is some polyphonic motion of the parts, but massive chordal sounds predominate, and the music is broken into segments that end in strongly tonal harmonic cadences. The last part is a repetition of the opening materials, with all of the instruments playing together once again at the close.

Don Carlo Gesualdo, Prince of Venosa (Italy, *c.* 1560–1613). Gesualdo, a nobleman from Naples, achieved notoriety by having his first wife and her lover murdered. A lutanist, composer, and patron of the arts, Gesualdo published six volumes of five-part madrigals and also wrote some sacred motets. The madrigals carried Mannerism to its most audacious extremes. Gesualdo seems to have been concerned primarily with expressing the emotions of the texts, and his style is based on the shock effect of abrupt contrasts in texture, rhythm, and harmonic color. Tone color is controlled through voice registers. In the harmonies, all twelve tones in the octave are used freely (a technique called *chromaticism*), often obscuring tonality. In this and in his attitude toward emotional expression, Gesualdo anticipated the music of the late nineteenth century. The text to his madrigal *"Moro lasso"* is full of emotionally charged words, such as *moro* ("I die"), *ahi* ("ah!"), *vita* ("life"), and *morte* ("death"). At the beginning, slow-moving chromatic chords in the lower four voices seem to wander aimlessly; then, in sudden contrast, all five voices enter in fast imitation, with a rapid turn on the word *vita*. The motion stops, there are widely dispersed cries of *ahi*, and gasps of silence break

14-64
HANS HOLBEIN THE YOUNGER, "The Old Man" from *The Dance of Death*, 1526. Engraving. The Metropolitan Museum of Art, New York. The figure of Death is playing a psaltery.

the lines, as though in disbelief. At the end, the words *ahi* and *morte* sound over and over in a texture of coloristic harmonies.

Suggestions for Further Study

Blume, Friedrich. *Renaissance and Baroque Music: A Comprehensive Survey.* trans. M. Herter. New York: W. W. Norton, 1967.

Boyd, Morrison C. *Elizabethan Music and Musical Criticism,* 2nd ed. Westport, Conn.: Greenwood, 1973.

Brown, Howard M. *Music in the Renaissance.* Englewood Cliffs, N.J.: Prentice-Hall, 1076.

Einstein, Alfred. "Narrative Rhythm in the Madrigal." *Musical Quarterly,* Vol. 29 (1943), pp. 475–84.

Fellowes, E. H. *William Byrd,* 2nd ed. London: Oxford University Press, 1948.

Grout, Donald Jay. *A History of Western Music,* rev. ed. New York: W. W. Norton, 1973. Chapters VI–VIII.

Haar, James, ed. *Chanson and Madrigal 1480–1530,* 2nd ed. Cambridge, Mass.: Harvard University Press, 1964.

Kenton, Egon F. "The Late Style of Giovanni Gabrieli." *Musical Quarterly,* Vol. 48 (1962), pp. 427–43.

Pattison, Bruce. *Music and Poetry of the English Renaissance.* New York: Da Capo, 1970.

Reese, Gustave, *Music in the Renaissance,* rev. ed. New York: W. W. Norton, 1959.

Suggestions for Further Listening

Byrd, William. Mass for five voices.

Gabrieli, Giovanni. *"In Ecclesiis."* (Motet.)

Josquin des Prez. *Pange Lingua.* (Mass.)

————. *La Bernadina.* (Instrumental canzona.)

Lassus, Roland de. *"Tristis est anima mea."* (Motet.)

Morley, Thomas. "Cease mine eyes." (Madrigal.)

————. "Sing we and chant it." (Madrigal.)

Rore, Cipriano de. *"Anchor che col partire."* (Madrigal.)

————. *"Dalle belle contrade."* (Madrigal.)

Wilbye, John. "Cease sorrows now." (Madrigal.)

————. "O Care thou wilt dispatch me." (Madrigal.)

Chapter *15* Art

Baroque Art:
1600–1700

The term *Baroque* has dual sources and has been used with varied meanings. The Italian word *barocco* grew out of the language of Medieval logic and by the seventeenth and eighteenth centuries had come to mean any system of thought that was contorted, irrational, or untrue; in Portugal, the word *barroco* referred to a rough, imperfect pearl. Both words seem to have been sources for the French word *baroque*, which originally meant an imperfect pearl and by extension something irregular or bizarre, and hence was applied to an artistic style that did not conform to accepted rules of proportions but rather to individual whim. "*Baroque*" was used by eighteenth-century writers as a disparaging term for such artists as Giovanni Lorenzo Bernini, Francesco Borromini, and Pietro da Cortona and for writers who showed an appetite for novelty or untraditional forms. In the nineteenth century, "*Baroque*" was used more objectively to denote a historical period and certain stylistic characteristics. In the narrowest sense, the period was the seventeenth century, but many writers today prefer the broader dates of 1600 to 1750. However, since Baroque qualities persevere in many important works until the end of the eighteenth century, we will use the even broader dating of 1600 to 1800 and treat each century in a separate chapter.

This period developed a wider variety of styles than we have seen in earlier centuries, and it is necessary to consider a broad range of characteristics under the concept of Baroque styles. Complexity, contrasts, bold effects of gradation and climax, overwhelming vastness or unexpected intimacy in scale, deliberate lack of clarity, illusionistic effects, and calculated surprise were used together or in various combinations. The roots of this art are found in the work of Michelangelo, in Mannerism, and especially in the Proto-Baroque.

The seventeenth century was one of bold contrasts within and between ideological systems: The parliamentary system developed in England while absolutism developed on the Continent, particularly in France; Catholicism struggled with Protestantism, and religious truth had to be reconciled with newly discovered scientific truths. Seventeenth-century science replaced the old concept of a finite and fixed universe with the more awesome vision of infinite space and ceaseless motion. The new view was paralleled in art by a preference for vast spaces and the effect of constant movement in much of the architecture, painting, and sculpture of the seventeenth and early eighteenth centuries.

In art, the prevailing system of values was promulgated by the French Royal Academy, established in the seventeenth century to provide acceptable standards. Effective at first, the Academy later became dogmatically restrictive, and many artists rebelled against it.

PAINTING IN ITALY AND SPAIN

Rome was the international center where the major stylistic tendencies of seventeenth-century painting were formed. Early seventeenth-century Italian painting reveals three major currents: a continuation of sixteenth-century Mannerism, a reappraisal, led by Annibale Carracci, of High Renaissance styles, and a pioneering trend led by Michelangelo da Caravaggio. The attitude of Carracci and his followers was conservative in that it sought to incorporate selected qualities from certain High Renaissance and Late Renaissance paintings. Clarity in parts, in expressive gestures, and in focus was joined to strong compositional structure and massively solid, ideal human form. The Carracci group was the strongest camp in Rome at the beginning of the century, and its stylistic character sometimes called *Restrained Baroque* or *Baroque Classicism*—was influential during the remainder of the century. The Caravaggio trend sacrificed clarity for dramatic light effects and complex natural detail. As the seventeenth century unfolded, all three trends contributed to full Baroque painting, which exploited illusionistic effects on a grand scale, dramatic value contrasts, active, irregular forms suggesting constant change rather than stability, compositions with a minimum of stabilizing vertical and horizontal lines and a maximum of diagonals or undulating curves, and ideal figures of heroic proportions. It attempted to break through the limits of the frame, making the painted scene a more overwhelming experience because it appears to be a part of the spectator's real world.

The seventeenth century produced a distinct division of painting into different types of subject matter with greater specialization by many artists. During the early seventeenth century, landscape painting in Rome was led by German and Flemish painters and tended to ally itself with either the Carracci or the Caravaggio group. Later, it was dominated by two French expatriates, Nicolas Poussin and Claude Lorrain, both in the Carracci camp. Genre painting gained popularity with private patrons. The genre painters, called *Bamboccianti*, were led by Dutchmen living in Rome and were scorned by the critics of the Carracci persuasion, partly because of the commonness of genre subjects and partly because

15-1 EL GRECO, *St. Jerome, c.*
1595–1600. Oil on canvas,
43½" x 37½". Frick Collection, New
York.

many genre painters rejected ideal form for the realistic detail and bold lighting of Caravaggio. Still-life painting was indebted to Dutch and Flemish art for its intense study of details and textures and to Caravaggio for its lighting.

Several other cities in addition to Rome were important for seventeenth-century painting. Venice continued in the tradition of its sixteenth-century masters, and Venetian color was a significant influence throughout the century. In Milan, a tradition of sixteenth-century Mannerism was modified by influences from the art of the Flemish painters Rubens and Van Dyck, both of whom, in turn, owed much to the art of Caravaggio. Genoa enjoyed the stimulus of numerous foreign visitors; the Flemish, especially Rubens, were leaders, and both the Caravaggio and the Carracci trends were represented. Bologna was the stronghold of the Carracci Academy, established before Annibale Carracci went to Rome. Florence, however, played a relatively minor role in seventeenth-century Italian painting.

In Spain, Seville and Madrid were the important centers. Early seventeenth-century painting there shows a strong Caravaggesque influence, and painting of the latter part of the century is marked by the soft fleshiness, undulating forms, and dramatic light of Rubens and Van Dyck.

Domenikos Theotocopoulos, called **El Greco** (Spain, 1541–1614). El Greco came from Crete to Spain by way of Italy, working first in Venice, where he was impressed by the chiaroscuro of Titian and the active compositions of Tintoretto, and then briefly in Rome, where he became acquainted with the art of Michelangelo. He settled in Toledo in 1576 or 1577. There he received numerous commissions for portraits and religious subjects. The Prado *Crucifixion* (Plate 8) is typical in the bold value contrasts, the jagged highlights, and the elongated figures with undulating contours. The crackling, flame-like energy of the stormy sky, the billowing garments, dramatic foreshortening, and the hovering weightless figures all express ecstatic religious experience. While some of his contemporaries sought a physical reality in their art, El Greco revealed the power of the spirit with an electric intensity that seems to illuminate forms from within. Even El Greco's portraits seem to transcend the physical world; the bodies, the garments, and the large eyes seem to shimmer like a mirage. In style as in actual chronology, El Greco holds a position between Late Renaissance Mannerism and the seventeenth-century Baroque.

Annibale Carracci (Bologna and Rome, 1560–1609). Carracci began his career as a Mannerist but turned more and more to High Renaissance and Proto-Baroque characteristics. His famous frescoes in the Farnese Gallery in Rome, of which *The Triumph of Bacchus and Ariadne* (Fig. 15-2) is the center, depict the loves of the classical gods and employ the heavy muscular figures seen in the art of Michelangelo and in the late work of Raphael. Carracci used an ideal facial type with full cheeks, straight, flat-planed nose, and broad forehead; his work often has strong value contrasts and compressed compositional activity. For color, his idols were first Correggio and later Titian. Annibale Carracci, his brother Agostino, and their cousin Ludovico opened an art school in Bologna before Annibale went to Rome in the 1590's. The teaching was eclectic, urging a combination of the best qualities from various masters.

Michelangelo da Caravaggio (Rome and Naples, 1573–1610). While Annibale Carracci and his followers led the conservative tendency in early Baroque painting, Caravaggio represented the more innovative spirit. He went from Milan to Rome about 1590 and, at first, earned a precarious living by painting still lifes with one or two half-length figures, sometimes with references to classical myths. These works have remarkably precise details and distinct local colors. About 1597, he received his first commission for a church (Contarelli Chapel, San Luigi de' Francesi), and from then on his subjects were usually religious. The style that made Caravaggio well known is evident in his *Conversion of St. Paul* (Fig. 15-3). All the traditional accessory figures have been omitted. We see an armored man lying on his back with arms outstretched, while his nervous

15-3 MICHELANGELO DA CARAVAGGIO, *The Conversion of St. Paul,* 1601–02. 90½" x 69". Cerasi Chapel, Santa Maria del Popolo, Rome.

15-4
PIETRO DA CORTONA, *Glorification of Pope Urban VIII's Reign*, central composition on the ceiling of the Gran Salone, Barberini Palace, Rome, 1633–39.

horse and mystified companion look on. The scene is pushed into the immediate foreground so that we have a startlingly close view. A flesh-and-blood reality is stressed by precise physical detail, yet there seems to be something extraordinary about the event. The strong spotlight that illuminates the objects against the dark background can hardly be natural light. Its source is outside the picture and remains a mystery to us, but its effect is to dramatize rather than to clarify. The few forms are broken into many parts by the light and shadow, making the composition complex and hard to comprehend immediately. This use of chiaroscuro to transcend physical reality is typical of Caravaggio's mature style and forecasts later Baroque painting. *Tenebroso* (murky) is a term often applied to Caravaggio's predominantly dark compositions. His followers are sometimes called *tenebristi*. Caravaggio's career was cut short by malaria.

Pietro da Cortona (Florence and Rome, 1596–1669). Pietro was one of the major seventeenth-century artists in both painting and architecture. He represented the full Baroque rather than the conservatism of the Carracci school. His best-known painting, the *Glorification of Pope Urban VIII's Reign* (Fig. 15-4), contains boiling masses of clouds and figures soaring up through an illusion of an architectural frame that seems to surround an opening into the sky. Light and shadow play over the forms, breaking them into complex parts. There is a strong focus on the central figure, Divine Providence, who points to a group of bees, a symbol taken from the Barberini coat of arms. The allegorical-mythological scenes at the sides refer to the piety, justice, and prudence of the Barberini Pope. The elaborate program of symbolism was worked out not by Pietro but by a poet in the Pope's circle. Pietro's dazzling production included frescoes in the Pitti Palace in Florence, in Santa Maria in Vallicella in Rome, and in the Palazzo Pamphili in the Piazza Navona in Rome. Unlike some of his contemporaries, Pietro restrained his illusionism to the extent of maintaining a clear division between painted areas and the stucco architectural framework. In his late easel paintings, he stabilized the compositions with firmer vertical and horizontal lines and contained the figures in more rigid groupings, thus rejecting his earlier dynamism.

Diego Velázquez (Seville and Madrid, 1599–1660). Seville was a center of Caravaggesque influence in Spain. Velázquez's early work, such as *The Waterseller of*

15-5 DIEGO VELÁZQUEZ. *The Waterseller of Seville,* 1619–20. Oil on canvas, approx. 3'6" x 2'8". Wellington Museum, London. Courtesy, Wellington Museum, London.

Seville (Fig. 15-5), sparkles with the brilliant detail and bold value contrasts that enchanted the followers of Caravaggio. At the age of twenty-three, Velázquez was appointed painter to the court of Philip IV, and he retained this position for the remainder of his life. His mature style exploits glazing and impasto to produce rich color and textural effects. *The Maids of Honor* (Plate 9) demonstrates his interest in the play of direct and reflected light on a variety of textures. Close observation reveals that details have been softened by brushwork that is much freer than in his early painting, and light bathes the forms like a palpable liquid, suggesting a source of nineteenth-century Impressionism. *The Maids of Honor* presents an enigma in compositional arrangement. Velázquez and the Infanta look out toward the spectator, who can see the faces of the king and queen in a mirror on the back wall. Either the spectator is placed in the position of the royal couple or the mirror is reflecting part of the picture the artist is painting.

SCULPTURE IN ITALY

At the beginning of the seventeenth century, sculpture in Italy was dominated by the style of Giovanni da Bologna, with its Mannerist poses and its Proto-Baroque irregularity and openness of form. Full Baroque sculpture developed after 1618, when the expression of greatest vitality was sought in poses, multiple and overlapping planes were employed, and deep undercutting produced dramatic shadows planned to provide gradation and climax from a fixed point of view. The sculpture of this period often breaks through the boundaries of its architectural frame or extends beyond the private spatial environment suggested by the base, so that the composition seems to inhabit the spectator's world of space and action. Such efforts to overwhelm the spectator or to draw him into the work of art are analogous to the illusionistic mural and ceiling compositions or to the intimate views found in the painting of the period. Full Baroque sculpture, like painting, used realistic details, complex parts, and lavish color. Varieties of colored stone were combined with bronze, but the leading sculptors did not use colored materials merely to counterfeit nature. Polychrome backgrounds and frames were used for contrast with figures in white stone or bronze. Special lighting, sometimes from hidden windows of colored glass, often intensified dramatic effects. As in painting, there were both full Baroque and conservative trends in sculpture, but the distinction is less clear because the influence of Bernini's full Baroque was so pervasive. After Bernini's death in 1680, the many French sculptors who had come to Rome after the founding of the French Academy in Rome in 1666 made French leadership a significant force in Roman sculpture.

Gianlorenzo Bernini (Rome, 1598–1680). Bernini, the greatest genius of the Italian Baroque, considered himself to be primarily a sculptor, but he was also architect, painter, and poet. His prodigious abilities as sculptor were demonstrated by an early series of statues done for Cardinal Scipione Borghese between 1618 and 1625. The series included *The Rape of Proserpina, David,* and *Apollo and Daphne,* all in the Borghese Gallery in Rome. The open twisting poses, the complex silhouettes, and the realistic detail make the works intensely alive. Although the Baroque is the antithesis of the serenity of much Greek sculpture, Bernini's admiration for Greek art is evident in such features as the modified Greek profiles used for Apollo and Daphne. From Bernini's middle years came the Tomb of Urban VIII (1628–47, St. Peter's), with its exuberant forms in various marbles and in bronze. In the same period, he did the Cornaro Chapel, which contains *The Ecstasy of St. Teresa* (Fig. 15-6), in Santa Maria della

15-6
GIANLORENZO BERNINI, *The Ecstasy of St. Teresa,* 1645–52. Marble, life size. Cornaro Chapel, Santa Maria della Vittoria, Rome.

Vittoria. The members of the Cornaro family are sculpted as spectators in boxes on the side walls of the chapel, and the space between the walls belongs both to the world of the spectator and to the architectural-sculptural composition, deliberately blurring the boundaries of the work of art. Multicolored marble and lavish architectural details lead to the climactic group within an undulating, concave-convex frame. White marble figures with rippling garments and lively, open silhouettes are suspended in space behind the frame and in front of a dark background. A hidden yellow glass window lights the group from above. Bernini's abilities as an organizer enabled him to assemble a large studio with many helpers to develop his ideas for the commissions that were showered on him, and it is often hard to distinguish between works executed by Bernini and those executed by assistants.

ARCHITECTURE IN ITALY AND SPAIN

Baroque architecture ran the gamut from restrained composition to dynamic complexity. Full Baroque architecture tended to exploit painting and sculpture as well as materials of different colors for a compelling total effect with strong focal emphasis. Masses were composed in complex parts and in many layers of depth; the effect of movement was obtained not only by receding and projecting parts, with their concomitant value contrasts, but also by wall surfaces of concave-convex alternations and by rhythmic variations of spaces, walls, piers, columns, and pilasters. Each layer of a multilayered wall may have a rhythmic scheme of its own, giving a fuguelike complexity to the total effect. Accordingly, architectural space was molded to express dynamic rather than static form. Converging streets, façades, or walls focus on the façade of a major building. Interiors reveal a preference for oval plans rather than the more static circular plan, and alternations of expanding and contracting spaces urge the spectator to change position constantly in order to experience the architecture completely. Characteristically, neither the masses nor the spaces have easily or simply perceived limits. Light was manipulated for focus; it often alternates with darkened areas or spaces to create movement or gradation and climax.

In Spain, a special style called the *Churrigueresque*, after a family of designers, developed in the second half of the seventeenth century; it is characterized by an extraordinary richness of decoration.

15-7
PIETRO DA CORTONA, San Martina
e Luca, Rome, 1635–50.

Pietro da Cortona. Pietro's art exemplifies the Baroque tendency to fuse painting, sculpture, and architecture for a powerful total effect. His first major commission in architecture was the church of San Martina e Luca, which came in 1635 while he was working on the Barbarini frescoes. He gave movement to the façade (Fig. 15-7) in two ways: first, by using a convex center that seems to bulge out in response to the pressure of projecting wings at the sides; and second, by creating an elaborate play of light and shadow through the use of many layers of pilasters, engaged columns, and panels. While the exterior uses the Ionic order below and Corinthian above, the interior (Fig. 15-8) is re-

15-8
Interior of San Martina e Luca.

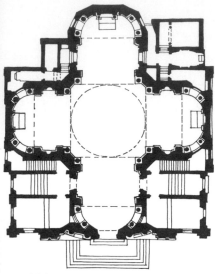

15-9 Plan of San Martina e Luca.

stricted to the Ionic. The Greek cross plan (Fig. 15-9) is opened up and given flexibility by the interior walls, which are built up in layers of panels, pilasters, and columns that create a rhythm of projecting and receding elements; the wall is transformed into undulating systems of supports. In the vaults and dome, Pietro used a great deal of architectural ornament. A strong unifying feature of the interior is the unusual restriction of color to white. His other church designs include Santa Maria della Pace and Santa Maria in Via Lata, both of which exploit deep porches or balconies for dramatic shadows and bold focus. Broken pediments—pediments whose frames have been opened up or cut into projecting and receding parts—are important features of Pietro's architecture and of the Baroque period in general.

Gianlorenzo Bernini. Bernini's activity as an architect began earlier than Pietro da Cortona's. His *baldacchino* for St. Peter's, the canopy shelter over the tomb of St. Peter, done between 1624 and 1633, fuses architecture and sculpture to produce a focal center for the vast interior. Over twisted, vine-covered columns, he placed a canopy of sweeping scroll curves flanked by restless

15-10
GIANLORENZO BERNINI, Sant' Andrea al Quirinale, Rome, 1658–70.

angels and topped by an active receding and projecting entablature. Bernini also designed the keyhole-shaped piazza in front of St. Peter's (see p. 212). The enclosing colonnades shape the piazza into an expanding and contracting space that demonstrates the preference for active spaces in Baroque art. Between 1658 and 1670, Bernini designed the small church of Sant' Andrea al Quirinale in Rome (Figs. 15-10–15-12). Concave walls focus upon the convex porch with its rounded broken pediment and ornate coat of arms. Behind the porch, actively curving scroll buttresses support the drum, which, in turn, supports the dome. From the entrance, one looks across the width of the oval interior to the high altar set deeply within an architectural frame with a concave, rounded, and broken pediment. In the opening of the pediment, the twisting figure of Sant' Andrea is shown ascending into heaven, the irregular white shape of the saint contrasting boldly with its surroundings and creating a powerful focal point. Below, the set-in altar receives dramatic illumination from a hidden window. Elsewhere, the walls are opened to form deep niches and secondary altar spaces that enrich the lighting and the spatial effect of the interior. Exuberant architectural ornament and multi colored marble complicate the wall surfaces, while the dome achieves its effect through a contrast of white and

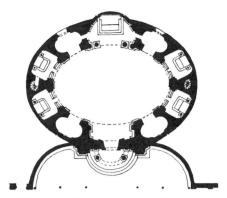

15-12 Plan of Sant' Andrea al Quirinale.

15-11 Interior of Sant' Andrea al Quirinale.

gold. Bernini's fame led to an invitation from Louis XIV in 1665 to come to Paris to suggest plans for the completion of the Louvre Palace, but the more restrained taste of the French and the jealousy of French architects led to the rejection of all of Bernini's proposals. His architecture did, however, influence the work of French architects.

Francesco Borromini (Rome, 1599–1667). From a carver of architectural ornament, Borromini moved to the position of architectural draftsman for Maderna and Bernini and finally became an architect after 1633. His first major work was the dormitory, refectory, and cloisters for the monastery of San Carlo alle Quattro Fontane (Figs. 15-13–15-15). He planned the church itself, using undulating walls and a complex rhythmic spacing of wall panels, niches, and engaged columns for the interior. The entablature has projecting and receding parts that accentuate the active design of the wall and tie together the various parts. Overhead, pendentives support an oval dome cut into deep hexagonal, octagonal, and cross shapes. The exterior façade was added by Borromini much later (1665–82) and presents an undulating multilayered composition. In the bottom half, engaged columns connect two floors, divide the façade into concave and convex areas, and support an entablature that unifies the verticals and emphasizes the movement of the whole. Above, the third floor and attic are grouped by columns, the center area becomes an oval *pavilion* (part of a building projecting from the main part and often emphasized with ornament) to provide a transition from the convex area below, and the entablature is broken to embrace a medallion that becomes the climax of the upper section. The moldings, balustrades, sculpture, and niches with small framing columns all add richness and value contrast. The tower and the lantern over the dome repeat the in-and-out movements of the façade. Borromini's other works include Sant' Ivo della Sapienza (begun in 1642, Rome) and much of Sant' Agnese in Piazza Navona (1653–63, Rome), a church that had been started by Girolamo Rainaldi and his son Carlo. Borromini frequently used surprising combinations of curves and angles to produce directional forces. His inventive and unorthodox approach led him to squeeze proportions and thereby produce tensions, to create sudden contrasts in shapes and directions, and to provide rapid variations on thematic forms. The source of some of these tendencies is found in Mannerist architecture of the preceding

15-13 FRANCESCO BORROMINI, San Carlo alle Quattro
Fontane, Rome, 1635–67.

15-14 Interior of San Carlo alle Quattro Fontane (view toward
altar), approx. 53' x 34'.

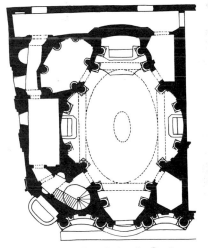

15-15 Plan of San Carlo alle Quattro
Fontane.

century. Bernini and his followers felt that Borromini went too far, and there was antagonism between these two leaders in full Baroque architecture.

PAINTING IN THE NORTH

Seventeenth-century painting in the North was influenced by Italian art, since many Northern artists studied in Italy. For French painting, Caravaggesque lighting and the realism of Bamboccianti subject matter were important during the first half of the century. A restrained style, derived from the Carracci, but emboldened by Caravaggesque lighting, was brought to France when the Frenchman Simon Vouet returned to Paris from Rome in 1627 and acquired a large following. One of his pupils, Charles Lebrun, became director of the French Royal Academy of Painting and Sculpture in 1663. The records of the Academy meetings reveal a conflict between advocates of the restrained Baroque and those of the full Baroque; as in Italy, the hero of the conservative attitude was Poussin, while the idol of the full Baroque was Rubens.

In Holland, the prevalence of Protestantism limited the demand for religious subjects, but the merchant class provided a market for portraits, landscapes, cityscapes, interiors, genre painting, and still lifes. A number of Dutchmen returned from Rome to Utrecht and created a center of Caravaggesque painting that reached its height about 1620. In the 1640's, more Caravaggesque influence in the form of Bamboccianti painting emanated from Haarlem. There were both Italianate and Flemish strains in seventeenth-century Dutch landscape painting; the first stemmed from Annibale Carracci, Claude Lorrain, and the German Adam Elsheimer; the second came from the tradition of the Flemish painters Joachim Patinir and Pieter Bruegel. Low horizons and vast, cloudy skies are typical of Dutch landscape painting. Still life tends toward lavish displays of colors, textures, and detail in foods and utensils or toward prodigious bouquets of flowers. Sensory experience is dramatized in such work by the intensity and luxury of shapes, colors, textures, and light effects. Flanders also developed outstanding still-life and genre painting, but the prevailing Roman Catholic religion encouraged religious subjects. In Holland, the major painter of the century was Rembrandt; in Flanders, Rubens dominated.

English seventeenth-century painting was dominated by foreigners, particularly Rubens and his pupil, Van

Dyck. German and Austrian painting of the period reveals no school of real national character; there was considerable dependence on Italy and Flanders.

Peter Paul Rubens (Flanders, 1577–1640). Rubens, the leading Flemish painter of the seventeenth century, received a broad classical education and was accepted as master painter by the Antwerp Guild in 1598. In 1600, he traveled to Italy and for eight years served the Duke of Mantua as both painter and diplomat. In this capacity, he brought gifts—including many of his own paintings—to King Philip III of Spain. Spanish painting was widely influenced by the Rubens paintings that became part of the royal collections. Rubens was also active in Florence and in Rome, where he copied works by Michelangelo, Caravaggio, and others. By 1608, he was reestablished in Antwerp and was soon appointed court painter to Archduke Albert and the Archduchess Isabella. Rubens' early painting, particularly before 1620, included some relatively quiet compositions, but the majority of his work shows a remarkable assimilation of the violent action and dazzling light of Tintoretto, the massive figures of Michelangelo, the spotlighting of Caravaggio, and the warm color of Venetian painting. The *Coup de Lance* (Fig. 1-23) employs the heroic proportions, the fleshy figures, the dynamic opposition of diagonal forces, the activity, and the intimate view that are characteristic of his Baroque style. Con-

15-16 PETER PAUL RUBENS and assistants, *The Reception of Marie de' Medici at Marseilles, 3 November 1600,* 1622–25. Oil on canvas, 155″ x 116″. Louvre, Paris.

tours tend to twist and undulate; faces tend to have large eyes, delicate flaring nostrils, and small Cupid's-bow mouths; hands and feet are small and tapering. As his style developed, Rubens used loose, fluid brushwork and paint textures ranging from heavy impasto to delicate transparent glazes. His international renown brought him many students and a number of large commissions, including the series of allegorical compositions depicting the dramatic life of Marie de' Medici (Fig. 15-16 and Plate 10). Many assistants were necessary, but Rubens' letters to patrons indicate clearly which paintings of a given group were done by his own hand and which were done mainly by helpers. His well-organized workshop made possible an enormous productivity in spite of Rubens' time-consuming but historically important diplomatic missions to England and to Spain.

Frans Hals (Holland, 1580–1666). Hals was born in Antwerp but is thought of as Dutch because he made his career as a portrait painter in Haarlem. His bohemian life and huge family made him the subject of constant lawsuits for debt and, in his later years, a recipient of assistance from the paupers' fund. From vigorous local colors and a detailed execution, Hals's style changed slowly toward grays and blacks rendered in freer brushwork. *The Banquet of the Officers of St. George* (1616, Frans Hals Museum, Haarlem) exemplifies his early work. Its casual grouping, active poses, and sweeping diagonal forms helped to loosen up the traditionally rigid compositions of Dutch group portraits and prepare the way for Rembrandt's *Night Watch*. Unlike Rembrandt, Hals took care to give almost equal illumination to each face. The *Malle Babbe* (*Mad Babbe*) (Fig. 15-17) reveals the dazzling impasto brushwork of his late style. The even later *Women Guardians of the Almshouse* (1664, Frans Hals Museum, Haarlem) uses somewhat more restrained execution to express a more contemplative mood. Hals's late painting was less popular than his early work; old age brought him increasing troubles and fewer commissions.

Nicolas Poussin (France and Rome, 1593/4–1665). From a peasant village in Normandy, Poussin traveled to Rouen and then to Paris, seeking instruction in art. In 1624, he carried a Mannerist style with him to Rome, where he worked in the studio of Domenichino, one of the chief pupils of the Carracci. Poussin apparently disliked the large scale required by most major commissions; his paintings are relatively small, and he depended on a small group of private patrons. His

15-17

FRANS HALS, *Malle Babbe* (*Mad Babbe*), c. 1650. Approx. 30" x 25" Staatliches Museen, Berlin.

15-18
NICOLAS POUSSIN, *Orpheus and Eurydice,* 1659. Oil on canvas, approx. 4' x 7'. Louvre. Paris.

subjects are usually religious, allegorical, or mythological, but the landscape settings often dwarf the subject matter. His early works, in their largeness of mass, dark tree silhouettes, and coloring, reveal the influence of Titian and Veronese. Later, his composition became more formal, with a stable structure of vertical and horizontal elements and an alignment of the main objects with the picture plane. For example, in his *Orpheus and Eurydice* (Fig. 15-18), the groups of trees, the hills, the buildings, and the river are all parallel to each other and to the surface of the painting. Gradation and climax are provided by lighting and by bright color in the foreground figures. Poussin believed that the spectator should read the gestures and symbols in the painting and that the content should be expressed logically and clearly by effective gestures and composition. Painting was to appeal to the mind more than to the senses. Poussin's method consisted in making a rough sketch of the subject and then setting up the composition with little wax figures and linen drapery in a stagelike box in which lighting could easily be controlled. Changes were made with the figures and lighting until the composition was decided on. Poussin said that he did not paint directly from live models because he wanted to preserve idealism in the forms. The sources for his concepts of ideal form were Raphael, Raphael's follower Giulio Romano, Annibale Carracci, and Greek and Roman sculpture. With the exception of a sojourn in Paris between 1640 and 1642, Poussin made his career in Rome. His work exemplifies the conservative Baroque that started with the Carracci School. His painting was an important source for artistic theory as taught in the French Royal Academy from the mid-seventeenth century until the French Revolution.

Claude Lorrain (France and Rome, 1600–82). Claude of Lorraine or Claude Gellée is often linked with Poussin, not only because they were contemporary French expatriates in Italy, but also because they both represent the conservative Baroque. By 1627, Claude had established himself permanently in Rome. His style owed much to German and Flemish landscape painters who had settled there. Landscapes and seascapes provided the real subjects for his paintings; their Christian or mythological subjects were, even more than in Poussin's painting, merely *staffage*—that is, an intellectual or literary excuse for the landscape and a means of establishing scale or providing nostalgia for the past. Claude's major interest was in the poetic qualities of landscapes or seaports seen in late afternoon light. Unlike Poussin's horizontally anchored planes with sharp edges and clear spatial relations, Claude's landscapes suggest no such flat stage-platform base but glide easily along rolling hills and meadows, while the trees shimmer in the breeze and present soft lacy silhouettes against the light. A composition like *A Pastoral* (Fig. 15-19) is less closed in depth than those of Poussin; the vistas give the effect of infinite space. The dazzling, gilt-hued seaport scenes, such as *The Embarkation of St. Ursula* (1641, National Gallery, London), often have the spectator looking directly into a setting sun that dissolves the

15-19
CLAUDE LORRAIN, *A Pastoral*, c. 1650. Copper, 15⅞″ x 21⅝″. Yale University Art Gallery, New Haven, Connecticut. Leonard C. Hanna, Jr., Fund.

details of architecture and ships on either side. The great demand for Claude's work encouraged forgery, and he was obliged to make a book of drawings, the *Liber Veritatis*, that recorded all his authentic paintings.

Rembrandt van Rijn (Holland, 1606–69). Rembrandt, the son of a Leiden miller, studied in Leiden and Amsterdam with minor masters. Although he admired Italian art and eventually collected a number of Italian works, he never traveled to Italy. His early style, characterized by theatrical, spotlighted areas and massed shadows, reveals the influence of Caravaggio's lighting, perhaps by way of the Utrecht painters. He broke with the conventionally even lighting and formal grouping of Dutch group portraits; his celebrated *Night Watch* (Fig. 15-20), which was originally larger, subordinates some of the company of Captain Frans Banning Cocq to shadowed areas. The dramatic value contrasts, the glowing color, the subtle organization of the active figures into the form of an "M" extending into depth, and the rich variety of personality all help make this painting the outstanding Baroque group portrait in the North. From the 1640's on, Rembrandt's art acquired a deeper gentleness; the drama became less physical and more psychological. The *Supper at Emmaus* (Plate 11) has the deeper chiaroscuro, the softer light, the suppression of local color, the reduction of physical movement, and the portrayal of intense human relationships that characterize his later work. Detail has been sacrificed to the fluidity of heavy impasto in the lighted areas and deep glazes in the shadows. Rembrandt produced many of his major etchings between 1650 and 1669. The velvet-

15-20 REMBRANDT VAN RIJN, *The Shooting Company of Captain Frans Banning Cocq* (*The Night Watch*), 1642. Oil on canvas, approx. 12'8" x 16'6". Rijksmuseum, Amsterdam.

rich blacks—often reinforced with drypoint—and the quick, telling character of the lines have made these works masterpieces in the history of printmaking. Although portraits were an important source of income for him, he painted an unusually large number of religious subjects, many of them done, like his self-portraits, for his own satisfaction. Like Caravaggio, but unlike Rubens, Rembrandt visualized Biblical events in terms of common people with unheroic proportions and individual features, although he did occasionally use exotic costumes for accessories. Rembrandt's landscape paintings make striking use of stormy skies, areas of luminous foliage, dramatic cloud shadows, and architectural ruins. Rembrandt acquired several students and some wealth, but the death of his wife in 1642 marked the beginning of a period of poor financial management that finally drove him to bankruptcy. His last years were probably unhappy ones, for his fame had been eclipsed in his own country by the successes of younger men.

Jacob van Ruisdael (Holland, 1628?–82). Within the development of landscape painting in seventeenth-century Holland, Ruisdael's works are among the richest and most varied in technique and emotional depth. His early subjects were views of the coast near Haarlem done in simple compositions with active skies, low horizons, and dark diagonal masses leading from foreground to middleground. Colors are predominantly cool with warm local accents. After a trip to Germany made about 1650, Ruisdael produced, in addition to the flat Dutch landscapes, wild mountainous views with rushing torrents, melancholy skies, and, occasionally, architectural ruins. Some of these works seem to be allegories of mortality and decay. They suggest an

15-21 JACOB VAN RUISDAEL, *Windmill at Wijk*, 1665. Oil on canvas, approx. 2'9" x 3'5". Rijksmuseum, Amsterdam.

analogy to Dutch *vanitas* paintings, still lifes in which a skull or snuffed-out candle may be contrasted with objects of material wealth and luxurious living to point up the homiletic moral of the transience of earthly life. Ruisdael's more violent landscapes were very popular with nineteenth-century Romantic painters. *Windmill at Wijk* (Fig. 15-21) has subtler drama. Towering clouds cast shadows on the land and water, expressing the power of weather. Dark land masses zigzag back into space, and the mill works in tension with the sailboat and the dark clouds on the left. The windy freshness, expansive depth, and grand scale all evoke the excitement of human contact with natural forces.

Jan Vermeer (Holland, 1632–75). Little is known about the life of the greatest of the Dutch painters of interiors. He made a precarious living as a painter and picture dealer and left his widow with a large family and numerous debts. Thirty-six paintings or less are now attributed to him, but his limited output seems to have found a ready market. Although Vermeer was a genre painter, he is more readily thought of as a painter of interiors because the quiet human activity in his pictures is usually subordinated to the structure of the composition and to the play of light on colors and textures. As in Poussin's landscapes, most of the larger objects in Vermeer's interiors are parallel to the picture plane, and we experience the picture space in a measured progression from one parallel to another. Occasionally, diagonal forms accelerate the transitions between the parts. The shapes also build a system of interlocking rectangles whose sides are often aligned with the sides of the painting, further emphasizing the static serenity of an all-pervasive order. In such works as *Young Woman with a Water Jug* (Plate 12), the underlying geometry is given relief by the curves and irregular forms of people and drapery. Light and shadow are used to group objects and to subordinate large areas of a composition in order to focus on others; light seems to wash the spaces and reveal textures and colors with gentle softness. This effect comes from minute pearl-like globules of paint and from the softening of the shadow areas with reflected light.

15-22 JAN VERMEER, *Head of a Girl in a Turban, c.* 1660–65. Oil on canvas, approx. 18″ x 16″. Mauritshuis, The Hague.

SCULPTURE IN THE NORTH

France was the major center of seventeenth-century sculpture in the North. During the first half of the century, however, France was represented by men of competence rather than genius. Style in portraiture tended toward much heavy detail, while allegorical, mythological, and religious subjects received some idealization of form. Objects were clearly defined, and drapery was simpler and less active than in Italian full Baroque work. Essentially, the French sculptors were conservative. The second half of the century saw more inspired sculpture, much of it done under the auspices of the French Royal Academy for the enormous palace at Versailles. Bernini was a major influence, but the restraint of French sculptors tempered their borrowings from Italy.

François Girardon (France, 1628–1715). Girardon subscribed to the taste and theory of the French Academy, worked closely with its director Lebrun, and established his career with the commissions for Versailles. Girardon was very interested in ancient sculpture; his famous *Apollo Tended by the Nymphs* (Fig. 15-23) shows the influence of Greek art in the profiles of the faces, the serene poses, and the relatively calm drapery. The original arrangement of the statues was more symmetrical than the present one. Similarly quiet contours and smooth transitions from part to part can be seen in Girardon's tomb of Richelieu (1675–77, Sorbonne, Paris). Girardon represents the restrained Baroque attitude that was shared by such artists as Poussin.

ARCHITECTURE IN THE NORTH

France, like Italy, developed city planning as an adjunct to seventeenth-century architecture. Parisian squares

15-23

FRANÇOIS GIRARDON, *Apollo Tended by the Nymphs, c.* 1668. Marble. Park of Versailles.

and circular places utilized converging avenues for focal emphasis on a special building. The triumph of the age was Versailles, the court palace of Louis XIV, where vast gardens and enormous buildings collaborate in an all-encompassing geometric plan. French churches of the period show the restraint, as well as the Italian influence, seen in French sculpture. A distinctly French town house evolved in the *hôtel particulier*, a central structure that had side wings embracing a court with an entry gate facing the street.

English architecture had imported Renaissance details in the sixteenth century, but not until the seventeenth century did the total effect of plan, structure, and detail become Renaissance in attitude, largely through the influence of the sixteenth-century Italian Andrea Palladio. The great fire of London in 1666 allowed a fresh start to be made in city planning and architecture. More squares were created, helping to open up the dense city. The rebuilding of churches provided England's first Baroque architecture; the style was influenced mainly by Italy but showed considerable restraint.

In the Low Countries, Holland was inspired by Palladio, but Flanders produced an architecture of strident Italianate Baroque with a special Flemish insistence on fantastically ornate gables.

In German and Austrian architecture, Italy provided the models for churches, while Versailles was the model for palaces. Italian architects were frequently employed, and on several occasions German and Austrian architects were sent to Paris to have their plans approved by leading French architects.

Inigo Jones (England, 1573–1652). We know little of Jones's background, but he traveled in Italy, gained a reputation in England as a designer of stage sets, accompanied the Earl of Arundel on a European trip, and was appointed to the highest architectural office in England—Surveyor of the King's Works. It was Jones who finally brought to England a classical attitude in the total design of a building. The austere formality of his Queen's House (Fig. 15-24) depends on stark simplicity of plan and elevation, precise symmetry, and a crystalline clarity in all the parts. The rigid equilibrium of quiet, unbroken lines and plain wall surfaces suggests the work of Palladio, Jones's major inspiration. Jones's best-known building, the banqueting hall at Whitehall Palace (1619–22, London), has slightly more activity in its three-dimensional variation and in deco-

15-24 INIGO JONES, south front of Queen's House, Greenwich, 1616–35.

rative elements. His first ecclesiastical building was the Queen's Chapel, St. James Palace (1623–27, London), where the flat wall surfaces of a rectangular box are broken only by severely simple window frames and limited by sharply defined *quoins* (especially bold stonework used to emphasize the corners of a building), corbeled cornices, and a corbeled pediment. A Palladian window is used at the east end. Jones's architecture inspired a number of followers and was the major source for the eighteenth-century architectural trend in England called the Palladian movement.

François Mansart (France, 1598–1666). Mansart was one of the most competent French architects of the seventeenth century, but his independence and his difficult disposition apparently limited the number of his commissions. Just as Inigo Jones set the key for the general conservatism of English architecture, so Mansart represents the restraint of French designers. The most complete surviving work by Mansart is the Château of Maisons (1642–51), which consists of a rectangular main structure flanked by two wings. The main building has very clear vertical and horizontal lines and a relatively shallow buildup of layered masses around the frontispiece. The classic succession of orders was used. Inside, the crisply carved ornament is unified by the exclusive use of white stone, without color or gilt paint. Mansart also planned the Val-de-Grâce in Paris (Figs. 15-25–15-27) and was responsible for construction up to the second story of the façade and up to the vaults of the nave. The second story, the vaults, and the dome were completed by Jacques Lemercier. The plan is that of a Latin cross basilica with a chapel added to the rear of the apse, all quite simple and stable compared with plans by an architect like Borromini. The nave is divided from the side aisles by Roman arches and piers with Corinthian pilasters; the entablature is simple, and the richest ornamentation is saved for the vaulting. On the exterior, the façade employs the Corinthian order. On the first level, the façade moves from corner pilasters to engaged columns and then to the freestanding columns of the porch. Above, Lemercier reversed the effect by making the engaged columns at the sides come forward while the center pulls back, taking the horizontal molding of the upper pediment with it. The large scroll buttresses at the sides of the upper level are indebted to Italian architecture.

Sir Christopher Wren (England, 1632–1723). Wren started his remarkable career as an astronomer and inventor of practical devices of all kinds. His first architectural work of significance was the Sheldonian Theater at Oxford (1662–63), a design inspired by the Roman Theater of Marcellus as described in one of Serlio's books. In 1665, Wren traveled in France and visited many major works of architecture. His great opportunity came the following year when the London fire destroyed eighty-seven parish churches. As one of the Commissioners for Rebuilding the City of London, and as Surveyor-General of the Royal Works, Wren designed many of the new churches. Like many of the architects of his day, Wren learned much from the designs of the ancient Roman Vitruvius and was aware of seventeenth-century Italian architecture. Nevertheless, the London churches show considerable originality. Their most Baroque qualities are found in the

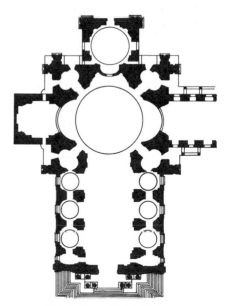

15-27 Plan of Val-de-Grâce.

15-25
FRANÇOIS MANSART and JACQUES LEMERCIER, Val-de-Grâce, Paris, 1645–66. 133' high.

15-26
Interior of Val-de-Grâce.

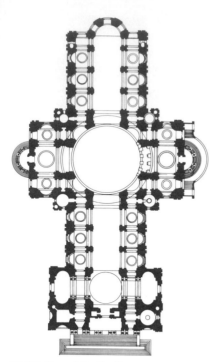

15-28 Plan of St. Paul's.

steeples. The best-known example of Wren's work is St. Paul's Cathedral (Figs. 15-28–15-30), which developed from an early design in central form to a Latin cross basilica with Baroque complexity in the many-layered façades. The west façade employs deep porches for dramatic shadow and lavishly ornamented towers that recall Borromini's Sant' Agnese in Piazza Navona. A deep colonnade provides sharp value contrasts at the base of the drum from which the great dome springs. Inside, colors and materials are varied, but the basic form of the interior space is relatively simple. This most Baroque of Wren's churches seems conservative in comparison with full Baroque design in Italy.

15-29 Interior of St. Paul's.

15-30
SIR CHRISTOPHER WREN, St. Paul's Cathedral, London, 1666–1717.

Suggestions for Further Study

Bazin, Germain. *The Baroque: Principles, Styles, Modes, Themes*. Greenwich, Conn.: New York Graphic Society, 1968.

Bergström, Ingvar. *Dutch Still-Life Painting in the Seventeenth Century*. Translated by Christina Hedström and Gerald Taylor. New York: Thomas Yoseloff, 1956.

Blunt, Anthony. *Art and Architecture in France: 1500–1700* (Pelican History of Art). Baltimore: Penguin Books, 1953.

Châtelet, Albert, and Jacques Thuiller. *French Painting from Fouquet to Poussin*. Translated by Stuart Gilbert. Geneva: Skira, 1963.

Downes, Kerry. *English Baroque Architecture*. London: Zwemmer, 1966.

Friedländer, Walter. *Nicolas Poussin: A New Approach*. New York: Abrams, 1964.

Gerson, Horst, and Engelbert H. ter Kuile. *Art and Architecture in Belgium: 1600–1800* (Pelican History of Art). Translated by Oliver Renier. Baltimore: Penguin Books, 1960.

Gudiol, José. *El Greco*. Translated by Kenneth Lyons. New York: Viking Press, 1973.

Haak, Bob. *Rembrandt: His Life, His Work, His Time*. New York: Abrams, 1969.

Hempel, Eberhard. *Baroque Art and Architecture in Central Europe: Germany, Austria, Switzerland, Hungary, Czechoslovakia, Poland* (Pelican History of Art). Baltimore: Penguin Books, 1965.

Pope-Hennessy, John. *Italian High Renaissance Sculpture, Part III: An Introduction to Italian Sculpture*. 3 vols. New York and London: Phaidon Press, 1963.

Rosenberg, Jakob. *Rembrandt*. 2 vols. Cambridge, Mass.: Harvard University Press, 1948.

————; Seymour Slive; and E. H. ter Kuile. *Dutch Art and Architecture, 1600–1800* (Pelican History of Art). Baltimore: Penguin Books, 1966.

Stechow, Wolfgang. *Dutch Landscape Painting of the Seventeenth Century*. London: Phaidon, 1966 and Greenwich, Conn.: New York Graphic Society, 1968.

Summerson, John. *Architecture in Britain: 1530–1830* (Pelican History of Art). Baltimore: Penguin Books, 1953.

Swillens, P. *Johannes Vermeer: Painter of Delft, 1632–1675*. Translated by C. M. Breuning-Williamson. Utrecht: Spectrum, 1950.

Trapier, Elizabeth du Gué. *Velázquez*. New York: Hispanic Society of America, 1948.

Waterhouse, Ellis. *Painting in Britain, 1530–1790* (Pelican History of Art). Baltimore: Penguin Books, 1953.

Whinney, Margaret. *Sculpture in Britain, 1530–1830* (Pelican History of Art). Baltimore: Penguin Books, 1964.

White, Christopher. *Rubens and His World*. New York: Viking Press, 1968.

Wittkower, Rudolf. *Art and Architecture in Italy, 1600–1750* (Pelican History of Art). Baltimore: Penguin Books, 1958.

————. *Gian Lorenzo Bernini: The Sculptor of the Roman Baroque*. London: Phaidon Press, 1955.

Wittkower, Rudolph, and Irma B. Jaffe, eds. *Baroque Art: The Jesuit Contribution*. New York: Fordham University Press, 1972.

Chapter 15 Music

Baroque Music: 1600–1700

For music historians, *Baroque* refers to the music of the period 1600 to 1750. The invention of a new dramatic style and its immediate application in musical dramas, called *operas*, had far-reaching influence. Grandiose and spectacular elements dominated operatic staging, while the musical ideal was to enhance the emotional impact of the drama.

Older attitudes about the nature and function of music vied with contradictory new trends. Seventeenth-century musicians worked to reconcile old and new styles. They also tried to create new forms and media from the prevailing chaos of disparate practices. By the end of the century they were working with rather well-defined forms and media in uniform and accepted styles.

In the seventeenth century, conscious states of emotion, called *affections*, or *passions*, were regarded as separate from bodily processes. It was assumed that music was capable of moving the affections and that this was its essential function. The new dramatic style grew out of the desire of composers to arouse extreme emotional states appropriate to the literal, implied, or symbolic meaning of the dramatic text. This attitude became central to Baroque musical aesthetics. Theorists systemized and categorized various melodic and rhythmic figures corresponding to specific affects, modeling their system on the ancient art of rhetoric. These figures were applied to instrumental as well as vocal music, and the system prevailed throughout the Baroque period.

In general, seventeenth-century scientific and philosophical ideas were not reflected in the Baroque musical style, but rather in the eighteenth-century *Classical* style that followed. Psychological and aesthetic theories regarding music were mostly unaffected by the new mathematical physics.

Except for public opera houses, mostly in Venice, music was created for ruling aristocrats, city governments, churches, and private associations called "academies." Italian music dominated all of Europe, though the French began to develop a national style in the latter part of the seventeenth century.

Musical Styles and Media

Baroque music began in Italy around 1600 with the development of a new way of writing called *monody*, or *representative style*. Composers wished to represent musically the extreme emotions of a dramatic text, and the immediate result was the creation of *opera*, an entire drama set to music. The equal-voice vocal polyphony of the Renaissance was replaced in the new style by a solo singer supported only by a bass line, plus appropriate harmonies improvised on a keyboard, lute, or other chord-playing instrument. This system of accompaniment—called *thorough bass,* or *continuo bass*—is a common feature of most music from the Baroque period. Elaborate solo parts, as well as coloristic, often dissonant harmonies, were designed to represent the affective meaning of the words. The soloist's part was a kind of speech-song, called *recitative,* which was derived from the rhythms and inflections of rhetorical speech, moving freely against the accompaniment, except on important syllables and at phrase endings. This made possible bold, unconventional harmonies particularly suited for reinforcing the expressive power of the words; at the same time, the early recitative lacked musical unity. Though the new style was anticipated in the Manneristic madrigals of the late Renaissance, heated arguments arose over the relative merits of the "old" practice and the "new," reflecting different attitudes toward the nature and purpose of music. Renaissance musicians had achieved formal integrity through unified textures and harmonies. Although they became quite skilled in the subtle expression of madrigal and chanson texts, their treatment of the words was subordinated to musical considerations. In the new style the words ruled the music, determining the choice and treatment of the rhythms, harmonies, and melodic materials.

Musicians used both styles, as well as the concerted style of the Venetian composers (see p. 278). They were faced with a profusion of conflicting forms, styles, and techniques, which they eventually fused into unified and consistent practices. They achieved musical coherence in the recitative by means of recurring passages or sections, and they transformed the bass line into an active, independent melodic part, which controlled the harmonies. A comprehensive system of tonality was de-

15-31
Woman playing the harpsichord. Early seventeenth century.

15-32
Scene from a Baroque opera. Early opera was performed on huge stages; here they have live elephants on stage.

veloped that, with the supporting bass line, eventually governed the structure in all Baroque music. This tonal system was particularly adaptable to the concerted style, in which the harmonies aleady tended to control the texture.

Early attempts to represent the individual words in a text gave way to the ideal of representing a single, static affective state throughout a movement. As a result, musical figures representing *basic affects* permeated entire movements, providing a powerful source of unity. These figures now governed the music, so that the music once again ruled the words.

Baroque composers exploited the qualities and capabilities of specific instruments and voices, and they elevated instrumental music to a position equal to vocal music. Characteristic styles were developed for the solo voice, chorus, keyboard instruments, and for the violin family, which began to be used as the nucleus of the orchestra.

The development of opera raised solo vocal music to a prominent position, and the history of Italian Baroque opera is the triumph of solo song. In the earliest operas the more dramatic passages were set to recitative, with choruses, dances, and instrumental refrains used for musical variety and coherence. After the establishment at Venice in 1637 of the first public opera house, the popularity of opera spread rapidly throughout Europe. Typical operas in the Venetian style were extravagant spectacles in which solo singing competed with choruses, dances, and elaborate staging and scenery. Italian opera soon turned from these grand productions to greater emphasis on the solo voice. *Arias*, or operatic songs, developed separately from the recitative and became stylized into several types, ranging from elaborate and demanding solo pieces to a simple version called an *arioso*. The recitative was used to move rapidly through dialogue passages, thus connecting the arias.

During the latter part of the eighteenth century French and English musicians began to develop their own operatic styles. The first truly French operas were created by Jean-Baptiste Lully. These works, which established a long tradition, combined the conventions of French theatre, court ballets, and a conception of dignified grandeur appropriate to the court of Louis XIV. In England incidental music enlivened many plays, but only one work each by John Blow and Henry Purcell can be called true operas. These works combined elements of the English choral tradition with Italian and French operatic influences.

15-33
One of the muses playing the viola da gamba.

15-34
ABRAHAM BOSSE, *Auditus, c.* 1615.
Copper engraving.

Italian solo madrigals and pieces in recitative style were extremely popular during the early Baroque. The recitative with continuo bass, aspects of the concerted style, and the harmonic boldness of the late Renaissance madrigals were combined in the *continuo madrigal*. By the middle of the seventeenth century such pieces had evolved into the solo recitative and the aria, as in the opera. A particularly popular result was the *cantata*, a sort of miniature operatic scene performed by one or two soloists in a small room or chamber, without staging, and consisting musically of two or three recitatives and arias or ariosos, accompanied only by continuo instruments.

Early Baroque composers of sacred music developed the *oratorio*, in effect a concert opera based on a Biblical or other religious text, which used the operatic musical forms, but was sung without staging, costumes, or scenery. A special type of oratorio was the *Passion*, a setting from one of the Gospels of the Passion and death of Christ.

Baroque instrumental music had its direct antecedents in Renaissance practices. Dance music was especially popular for social occasions. By the middle of the seventeenth century, groups of four or five dances were formalized into *dance suites*. Sectional and continuous variation forms were also popular. Most of these were derived from dance music, but German organists also created *chorale preludes*, variations in which elaborate musical figures were woven around the notes of familiar Lutheran hymn tunes. Other types of organ music included improvisatory *fantasias, toccatas,* and *preludes,* as well as stricter *fugues* (see p. 47).

One of the most important instrumental forms of the Baroque was the *sonata*. Composers altered the Renaissance canzona to include a continuo bass and one or more soloists, and, after the middle of the seventeenth century, such works were called "sonatas." Those for one or two violins and a continuo were especially popular, and music particularly suited to the violin became a common feature of the sonata style. Sonatas were divided into several contrasting sections, or movements, often including dance music; in fact, many were dance suites for small instrumental groups.

The orchestra had its beginnings in opera and ballet music, where large instrumental groups were needed to support grand spectacles and entertainments. The violin family, plus one or more continuo instruments, became the core of the Baroque orchestra. Lully's orchestra at the French court set a high standard of disciplined playing, which was universally admired. His orchestral dances often were assembled into suites and performed as concert pieces.

During the latter part of the seventeenth century, Arcangello Corelli and other Italian composers began to apply the concerted style to sonatas. They created contrasting sonorities by reinforcing the continuo and solo parts in places with a full orchestra. Such pieces, called *concertos*, developed into the most important form of late Baroque orchestral music. The passages with full orchestra, called *tutti*, became recurring refrains. They were used especially to confirm key centers at cadences, while the solo passages provided contrast. A three-movement structure—fast-slow-fast—eventually became standard.

Claudio Monteverdi (Italy, 1567–1643). Monteverdi sang in the cathedral choir of his native Cremona from an early age, and he later entered the service of the Duke of Mantua. During the last thirty years of his life he was Master of Music for the Republic of Venice and became influential throughout Europe. He produced Masses and madrigals in the late Renaissance style, as well as operas, solo cantatas, and madrigals in the new dramatic style. Monteverdi's late madrigals are characterized by the harmonic boldness and melodic and rhythmic freedom of the dramatic recitative. Many of them call for a continuo bass. They range from dramatic scenes for one or two soloists to highly expressive polyphonic settings. For instance, he made a five-part madrigal setting of the famous *"Lament"* from his opera *Arianna*, originally a passage in solo recitative. The words govern the rhythms and melodic lines so that none of the affective expression of the text is lost. Monteverdi's *Orfeo* (1607) was the first opera by a major composer. Using not only the new recitative style, but also strophic songs, madrigal choruses, and

15-35
Musicians playing the guitar and bagpipes.

instrumental dances, he unified the whole with frequent returning passages, both instrumental and vocal. He set a precedent by specifying the instruments to be used in most passages. Throughout the opera, Monteverdi maintains basic affective states for long passages, even whole acts, thus presaging the Baroque ideal of a single affect governing a movement or major section of a work. Orpheus's lament on his loss of Euridice (Act II) is a famous example of the early recitative style. The singer's line, as well as the harmonies, are governed by the meaning of the words. Short phrases and silences depict shock and despair. Affective words such as "dead," "life," "deep abysses," "in the company of the dead," "stars," "heaven," and "sun," are set apart musically. The bass line is simple, often sustained, and merely supports the accompanying chords. The harmonies are rich in unexpected dissonances, subtle shifts, and a sense of aimless wandering, and the passage does not begin and end in the same key.

Heinrich Schütz (Germany, 1585–1672). Schütz was born in Kösterlitz, Saxony, and was a choirboy at the court chapel in Cassel. He studied in Italy with Giovanni Gabrieli and Claudio Monteverdi. In 1615 he became music director at the Elector's court in Dresden, later traveling and conducting in Copenhagen, Brunswick, and Hanover. He introduced the dramatic recitative and concerted techniques into German religious music, while retaining the polyphonic tradition. The resulting synthesis of styles determined the future of German Baroque church music. His musical settings of the German language were masterful. His religious works include three oratorios, three Passions, and several collections of motets, in both Latin and German. His best-known works are his oratorio, *"The Seven Words of Christ on the Cross,"* and his three sets of concerted motets, the *Symphoniae Sacrae.* Part III of the *Symphonie Sacrae* contains his dramatic setting of the conversion of St. Paul, *"Saul, Saul, was verfolgst du mich,"* taken from the New Testament, with the text limited to the words of Christ. The score calls for a solo group of six voices, two four-voice choruses, two solo violins, and a continuo bass for the organ. It is quite likely that instruments also played the voice parts in performance. The piece exhibits a remarkable unity. Schütz makes good use of Gabrieli's concerted techniques and Monteverdi's affective word representations. The drama of Saul's sudden vision is realistically portrayed by the cries of "Saul, Saul," which rise initially from the bass voices. The soloists develop Christ's warning, interrupted by further cries of "Saul, Saul." These words become a persistent refrain, which is the last dying echo heard as the confrontation ends.

Jean-Baptiste Lully (France, 1632–87). Of humble Italian parentage, Lully became a page at the French court, where his musical and dancing ability soon caught the attention of Louis XIV. He became the king's principal musician and eventually headed the Royal Academy of Music, with exclusive rights to produce operas in Paris. Through this institution, which remains today as the Paris *Opéra*, he created the first truly French operas, called *tragédies lyriques*. The quality and discipline of Lully's orchestra was famous throughout Europe. His *French overture*, which became a standard Baroque orchestral form, was developed as an opening piece for his ballets and operas. The usual overtures began with a slow, stately section characterized by short-*long* rhythms, followed by a fast section in imitative polyphony, and they sometimes ended with a slow passage similar to the first section. In his operas Lully departed from the Italian style with his frequent use of ballets, choruses, and solo group scenes, but he was most typically French in his dramatic recitatives. Without sacrificing a lyric vocal line, he set his recitative texts to the rhythms of the French language as it was spoken in the theater, giving the singer freedom for effective pauses, drawn out words and phrases, exclamations, and loud-soft contrasts. At all times he insisted on clarity of the words. His solo *airs* were generally short, simple, pleasant, and songlike, with no elaborate vocal displays. In his choruses he set the words one note per syllable, with all parts moving in the same rhythm. Some of his most popular scenes were lavish spectacles

15-36

A performance of Lully's *Alceste*.

utilizing soloists, chorus, dancers, and orchestra. Though Lully's works are rarely heard today, operas such as his *Alceste, Amadis,* and *Armide* served as models for French musicians for nearly a century.

Arcangello Corelli (Italy, 1653–1713). Corelli was born near Bologna, where he received some of his early training, but he spent most of his adult life in Rome as a successful composer, conductor, and virtuoso violinist. His fame spread throughout Europe, and many excellent musicians came to Rome to study with him. Corelli established the basis for modern violin technique. His compositions became models for solo and orchestral string music, and his solo sonatas were used as standard studies for violin students. His style is based on the capabilities of the stringed instruments. The music is restrained and displays considerable clarity and economy. His published works, all for strings and harpsichord or organ, include forty-eight trio sonatas, twelve solo sonatas, and twelve concertos. Corelli's trio sonatas call for two solo violins and a cello, forming a three-part polyphonic texture, with an organ or harpsichord doubling the essential bass tones of the cello and adding appropriate chords at the discretion of the player (the continuo bass). They are structured in a series of contrasting sections, often consisting of stylized dances. Corelli's concertos are essentially trio sonatas, reinforced part of the time by a small string orchestra. The sonata instruments (two violins, cello, and keyboard) constitute a group of soloists called the *concertino,* and the orchestra as a group is called the *concerto grosso* (the whole work is also called a *concerto grosso*). Both groups together are called the *tutti.* The orchestra and the solo group typically share the same material, so that variety results from simple alternation between the groupings. His *Concerto Grosso,* Opus 6, No. 3 begins with a slow, stately section dominated by a short-*long* rhythm, with persistent alternation between the thin-textured solo group and the denser combined groups. After a pause on an incomplete cadence, a faster, fuguelike passage begins. The initial motive permeates this passage, often repeated at successively higher or lower pitches—a Baroque technique called *sequence.* At the cadences the fast triple groupings typically shift to half speed, another common Baroque technique. The *tutti-concertino* alternation continues despite the fugal texture. A brief slow ending completes this section, which is in fact Corelli's version of Lully's French overture. The next section begins with a slow passage, all tutti, in a dense polyphonic texture rich in dissonances and chromatic

15-37
A performer playing the violin.

lines. Another incomplete cadence leads to a fast, dancelike passage, featuring a continuously moving bass and persistent tutti-concertino "echo" effects. The last section, with its meter of fast triple groups, follows the general form and style of a *gigue*, a frequent final dance in Baroque suites. Although temporary modulations occur as the music proceeds, there are no significant changes of key in the whole concerto.

Henry Purcell (England, 1659?–95). Purcell became a choirboy at the Chapel Royal in 1669, and he worked as a musician there and at Westminster Abbey during the remainder of his short life. His principal teacher was Dr. John Blow, whom he succeeded as organist at Westminster Abbey in 1679. Purcell was the most gifted English musician of his time. His compositions include considerable church music, works for stage and chamber entertainments at court, and pieces for festive occasions. He adapted the recitative style to the English language, and he realized a near perfect union of words and music in his vocal works. He was particularly skilled at representing word meanings through melodic figures and harmonic color. He added French and Italian influences to English musical traditions, and his choral writing in his anthems and festive works served later as a model for George Frideric Handel. Purcell was particularly noted for his theater music. He wrote overtures, airs, and instrumental dances for forty-nine plays, as well as one complete opera. His opera, *Dido and Aeneas*, was written for amateur performance at a boarding school for girls. Though it was conceived on a small scale—the only instruments are strings and harpsichord—it nevertheless represents one of the greatest achievements in this medium. French influence is evident in the form of the overture and in Purcell's free use of choruses and dances, but his sensitive word settings and assured sense of tonality show his Italian side. Dido's farewell lament and death in the final scene is a recitative followed by an aria. The recitative, "Thy hand, Belinda," is accompanied only by the harpsichord, and bears a close resemblance to the early monodic style of Monteverdi. Sensitive harmonic shadings spiced with dissonances support the affective meaning of the words, but harmonic motion is controlled by definite tonal centers. The voice line works its way downward in small steps toward the word "death," and "darkness" is set to an embellished dissonant tone. Dido's aria, "When I am laid in earth," is sung over a five-measure ground bass that descends slowly to a cadence with each repetition. The voice moves in short, unequal phrases interspersed with silences, and it is out of phase with the bass melody much of the time. The persistent, yet restrained, movement of the repeated bass, the stately melodic line, and the power of the dense, often dissonant string texture all combine in a moving expression of Dido's resigned acceptance of her fate.

Suggestions for Further Study

Anthony, James R. *French Baroque Music.* New York: W. W. Norton, 1973.

Boyden, David D. *The History of Violin Playing from Its Origins to 1761 and Its Relationship to the Violin and Violin Music.* London: Oxford University Press, 1965.

Bukofzer, Manfred F. *Music in the Baroque Era.* New York: W. W. Norton, 1947.

Grout, Donald J. *A History of Western Music,* rev. ed. New York: W. W. Norton, 1973. Chapters IX–XI.

————. *A Short History of Opera,* 2nd ed. 2 vols. New York: Columbia University Press, 1965.

Mellers, Wilfrid. "John Bull and English Keyboard Music." *Musical Quarterly,* Vol. 40 (1954), pp. 365–83 and 548–71.

Newman, William S. *The Sonata in the Baroque Era,* 3rd ed. New York: W. W. Norton, 1972.

Palisca, Claude V. *Baroque Music* (Prentice-Hall History of Music Series). Englewood Cliffs, N.J.: Prentice-Hall, 1968.

Pincherle, Marc. *Corelli: His Life, His Work.* Translated by Hubert E. M. Russell. New York: W. W. Norton, 1968.

Schrade, Leo. *Monteverdi: Creator of Modern Music.* New York: W. W. Norton, 1969 (reprint of 1950 edition).

Zimmerman, Franklin B. *Henry Purcell 1659–1695: His Life and Times.* New York: St. Martin's Press, 1967.

Suggestions for Further Listening

Corelli, Arcangello. *Sonata da chiesa,* Opus 3, No. 7.

————. *La Follia,* Opus 5, No. 12.

Frescobaldi, Girolamo. Selected organ music from *Fiori musicali.*

Lully, Jean-Baptiste. Overture to *Alceste.*

————. Overture to *Armide.*

Monteverdi, Claudio. Selections from the opera, *The Coronation of Poppea.*

————. Selections from the *Eighth Book of Madrigals.*

Purcell, Henry. Ode, *Hail Bright Cecilia.*

Schütz, Heinrich. *The Seven Words of Christ on the Cross.*

Torelli, Giuseppe. *Concerto,* Opus 8, No. 7.

————. *Concerto,* Opus 8, No. 8.

Chapter 16 Art

Later Baroque, Rococo, and Neoclassic Art: 1700–1800

Baroque stylistic tendencies continued in much eighteenth-century art; however, two other major trends developed and acquired labels. *Rococo* art retained the complexity of the Baroque but sacrificed power for refined elegance and a delicate, light profusion of forms. *Neoclassicism* was, in part, a reaction against Baroque and Rococo characteristics. Neoclassic theory, promulgated by the German archaeologist and art historian Johann J. Winckelmann, was stimulated by the discovery and excavation of two Roman cities that had been buried by a volcanic eruption in 79 A.D.: Herculaneum and Pompeii. The increasing importance of Neoclassic art after 1750 has led some scholars to consider that date as the end of the Baroque period. One aspect of the Baroque that developed during the eighteenth century was an aesthetic concept called the *sublime*. This was presented in works like Edmund Burke's essay "The Sublime and Beautiful" (1756), which distinguished between the beautiful and the sublime in that the latter could include the ugly. While much eighteenth-century effort sought to unravel the systematic order of nature and bring it under man's control, the lovers of the sublime gloried in the mysterious power of nature over man. The sublime could be frightening, painful, or astonishing; it stimulated the emotions and the imagination. The concept of the sublime was fostered by Goethe and the *Sturm und Drang* movement, which emphasized the struggle of the individual against the world. It was the interest in the sublime that provided a basis for the broad nineteenth-century attitude called *Romanticism*.

The eighteenth century saw French art assume the position of leadership that Italian art had enjoyed previously; and French institutions, such as the Royal Academy, were imitated by other countries.

The late seventeenth and the eighteenth centuries are often called the *Age of Enlightenment*. Major scientific discoveries were made, but the term refers especially to a spirit of rationalism, empiricism, and skepticism in social and political thought. Locke, Voltaire, Rousseau, and Diderot criticized existing society and spread ideas about human rights that laid the basis for the American and French revolutions. Also basic to these revolutions was the rise of the bourgeoisie to a position of power from which it could challenge the aristocracy. Bourgeois power, like the concepts of mercantilism and colonial expansion, developed as a result of accelerating growth of commerce and industry. This environment affected, directly or indirectly, much of the art of the period.

French painting continued to be dominated by the Royal Academy until the time of the Revolution. The older Academy of St. Luke, which had grown out of the guild system, was held down to a secondary role. No painter could paint and sell pictures unless he was a member of one of these academies. The Royal Academy acquired a virtual monopoly on exhibitions; its *Salon*, a periodic exhibition named for its location (after 1725) in the Salon Carré of the Louvre, had royal sanction. Until 1748, all members could exhibit in the Salon; after that time, a jury of academicians screened submitted works. Academic teaching used various methods, from apprenticeship under a master to copying accepted masterpieces from sixteenth-, seventeenth-, and eighteenth-century painters, drawing from plaster casts of Greek and Roman sculpture, and drawing from live models. Prizes were given for the best work in anatomy, perspective, facial expression, and other categories. The most important prize was the *Prix de Rome*, which since its establishment in the seventeenth century has given selected students the opportunity to study at the French Academy in Rome. Leading academicians gave periodic discourses on theory and principle. In the seventeenth century, a hierarchy was established for subject matter; history painting—religious, historical, allegorical, or mythological subjects—was the highest category, and only painters of history could become professors. Following history painting came portraiture, genre painting, landscape (including seascapes and city views), animal painting, and still life. Early in the century, another category, that of the *fête galante* (an elegant outdoor entertainment), was added to sanction the popularity of Watteau's work. The style of history painting owed much to Rubens and to sixteenth- and seventeenth-century Italian masters. The conflict between *Poussinistes* and *Rubénistes* in the Academy was won by the *Rubénistes* early in the century, but the full Baroque styles gave way increasingly to the lighter colors and playful intricacy of the Rococo. Mythological subjects became more intimate than heroic, more gay than dignified. Genre painting gained in popularity during the period of Louis XV and often shows Rococo characteristics. Portraiture became more casual and livelier in pose and expression. Pastel portraits enjoyed great vogue. Landscape was often combined with battle scenes or with ruins, the style varying from repetitive formulas to the freshness of direct observation from nature. The major source for landscape, animal painting, and still life was seventeenth-century Dutch, Flemish, and Italian painting. The reign of Louis XVI and the revolutionary period that followed reemphasized history painting and introduced the Neoclassic style. Simplicity in accessories, clarity of contours, and rigid organization supplanted the billowing power of the Baroque and the tinkling delicacy of the Rococo. The French leader of Neoclassicism was the painter Jacques Louis David, who will be considered at length in the following chapter.

In England, a royal academy was not founded until 1768. Although its first president, Sir Joshua Reynolds, stressed in his famous discourses the superiority of history painting, he and other English painters found portraiture to be more rewarding financially. The glory of eighteenth-century English painting is its portraiture, ranging from heroic poses, idealized faces, and pompous settings to casual poses, candidly recorded faces, and unassuming environments. Genre painting and satire were also significant in England, and style ran the gamut from caricature to tentative and humble faithfulness to natural detail. Although seventeenth-century Dutch landscape and seventeenth- and eighteenth-century Italian landscape were popular with English collectors, English landscape painters were not given great encouragement at home. Despite this situation, Englishmen produced some outstanding landscape painting that varied from the delicate detail of John Crome's watercolors to the broadly brushed, sparkling watercolors of Alexander Cozens, and from the deliberate rendering of Richard Wilson's ideal landscape to the filmy brushwork of Gainsborough. In the realm of animal painting, George Stubb's carefully rendered horses appealed to a major interest of the aristocracy. Neither Rococo nor Neoclassic stylistic qualities were developed in England as fully as on the Continent.

In German regions during the eighteenth century, the northern areas were influenced by Holland and France; southern areas were inspired by Italy. Imported painters strengthened such influence, but a vigorous native Rococo style developed in the religious paintings of the German C. D. Asam and in the work of the Austrian Franz Anton Maulbertsch. German painters living abroad, such as Anton Raffael Mengs and Asmus Carstens, were leaders in developing Neoclassic art.

Antoine Watteau (France, 1684–1721). Of the three major eighteenth-century French painters whose art represents the Rococo style, Watteau is the earliest. He came from the Franco-Flemish city of Valenciennes to

Paris, where he found an international market for his work, partly through the help of several wealthy patrons. His painting was so successful that in order to accommodate it the French Academy created a new category of subject matter: the *fête galante*. Although Watteau painted religious works, portraits, and scenes with soldiers, the majority of his works depict characters or scenes from theatrical comedy or from the French aristocracy at leisure. His procedure was to paint directly on the canvas without elaborate preparatory drawings, but he composed by selecting figures from a large collection of sketches made from life. Thus his compositions are not so much records of a particular event as they are imaginative constructions. The famous *Embarkation for Cythera* (Fig. 16-1) is derived from a play and depicts a gay company about to sail for the legendary island of love. The painting is typical of Watteau in its soft, dreamlike landscape, luxurious costumes, dainty slender figures, and rich silvery colors. Its seeming casualness in composition and its softness in form contrast sharply with the paintings of Poussin. Indeed, the French Academy's acceptance of Watteau in 1717 represents one of the triumphs of the *Rubénistes*. Watteau's idol was Rubens; the delicate pointed noses, small mouths, and tapering hands of Rubens' people reappear with slender bodies and more restrained sensuality in the art of the Frenchman. Watteau also learned from the Rubenesque painters in Paris and from the art of sixteenth-century Venice. He chose not to portray important historical actions; instead he depended on the spectator's associations or emotional responses to lyrical variations on the themes of theatrical entertainment and a leisurely aristocracy in natural settings. Sometimes it is difficult to distinguish between actor and aristocrat, between theater and *fête galante.*

William Hogarth (England, 1697–1764). The famous eighteenth-century satirist began as an apprentice to a silver-plate engraver but soon turned to painting and produced a number of *conversation pieces*—group portraits posed as an informal gathering with a suggestion of typical activity or anecdote. In 1731, Hogarth painted six works that were engraved and distributed the following year under the general title of *The Harlot's Progress.* The moralizing story of the downfall of a young woman in the big city was immediately successful and inspired a number of unauthorized copies. Hogarth then promoted the Copyright Act for Engravers (1735) to secure his market and proceeded to make engravings of a similar series, *The Rake's Progress,* eight scenes portraying the dissolution of a young man. (The third scene is shown in Figure 16-2.) Such work was far more lucrative than the history painting that was Hogarth's ambition; yet the artist did occasional history paintings and continued with portraiture while he produced paintings for the engravings that were both moralizing and satirical. His satire was aimed at all classes, striking sometimes at topical events, sometimes

16-2

WILLIAM HOGARTH, *The Orgy,* Scene III from *The Rake's Progress.* Metropolitan Museum of Art, New York.

at specific facets of British society, and sometimes at universal human weaknesses. His remarkable visual memory was aided by a mnemonic system that he devised for remembering the positions and gestures of principal characters in a witnessed event. Hogarth formed his own St. Martin's Lane Academy for teaching art and became a governor of the Foundling Hospital, where he arranged for picture exhibitions; he also found time to write a theoretical treatise, *The Analysis of Beauty* (1753), urging the aesthetic values of asymmetry, intricacy, and the serpentine line. Although the proportions, intricacy, and frequent intimacy of his paintings link him with the Rococo, he was indebted to seventeenth-century Dutch genre painting and to the fifteenth- and sixteenth-century art of Bosch and of Bruegel the Elder. Hogarth was the predecessor of such satirical artists as Goya and Daumier.

Jean-Baptiste Siméon Chardin (France, 1699–1779). After working as an assistant to the painter Noël Coypel, Chardin was accepted by the Royal Academy in 1728 as a "genre painter of animals and fruit." In the tradition of seventeenth-century Dutch genre and still life, he painted quiet interiors with single figures or groups and still lifes composed of humble objects such as *Clay Pipes and Earthenware Jug* (Fig. 16-3). His art is outstanding in its subtlety of color, light, and texture. By 1740, Chardin enjoyed critical acclaim and an international demand for his paintings as well as for the engravings done after them. He spent considerable time copying his own works to satisfy collectors. By 1755, he was treasurer of the Academy and in charge of hanging exhibits. In his later years, when public favor had shifted from his still-life painting to the more moralizing and anecdotal art of others, Chardin turned to portraiture in pastels, where the crosshatching of color used in his oils is amplified.

Fançois Boucher (France, 1703–70). Boucher was the second major representative of French Rococo art. He was admitted to the Academy in 1734 and became first painter to King Louis XV in 1765. As a favorite of Madame de Pompadour, the mistress of the king, Boucher received many commissions, was made director of the Gobelins Tapestry Works, and designed tapestries as well as figures for the Royal Porcelain Factory at Sèvres. Boucher's subjects ranged from the religious to landscape, but the most frequent are allegory and mythology presented with dainty sensual figures in powder-puff landscapes that suggest stage settings. A typical example is *The Captive Cupid* (Fig. 16-4). The pretty faces, coy poses, sweet colors, delicate accessories, and lilting lines all relate Boucher to the Rococo decorations of his early master, François Lemoyne. To appreciate such art, we must not demand depth or monumentality; Boucher's graceful facility was employed to create a pleasant, carefree world that ignores the problems of real life.

Thomas Gainsborough (England, 1727–88). Gainsborough started as an assistant to an engraver who had studied under Boucher. As a restorer of seventeenth-century Dutch landscape paintings, Gainsborough acquired a love for landscape but found portraiture more profitable. His landscapes from the Ipswich and Bath periods tend to be detailed and solid in form. In the 1770's, they became softer, more loosely-brushed, and more obviously creations of imagination. After his move to London in 1774, the figure paintings had a similar development: from detailed, solid forms to light, freely brushed backgrounds, rather insubstantial bodies, and fairly solid heads, as in *The Morning Walk* (Fig. 16-5). The gauzelike background and the fluffy forms recall Watteau, whose works Gainsborough had copied. Although the full-blown Rococo never found a footing in England, Gainsborough began what has been called English Rococo portraiture. Late in life, he also developed what he called "fancy pictures," genre scenes combining pretty, unsophisticated children and rustic nature. From 1761 on, Gainsborough exhibited with the London Society of Artists, and he was one of the origi-

16-4

FRANÇOIS BOUCHER, *The Captive Cupid*, 1754. Wallace Collection, London.

16-5
THOMAS GAINSBOROUGH, *The Morning Walk*. 1785. Lent by Lord Rothschild to the Birmingham Art Gallery.

nal members of the British Royal Academy at its founding in 1768.

Jean-Honoré Fragonard (France, 1732–1806). The third major representative of the Rococo lived through the French Revolution and beyond his own era. Fragonard left Chardin's instruction for the studio of Boucher, where the student copied the master so skillfully that it is sometimes difficult to distinguish between their works. In 1752, Fragonard won the Prix de Rome and, during his stay in Italy, was deeply impressed by the work of Pietro da Cortona and Giovanni Battista Tiepolo. His other idols were Rubens and Rembrandt. Although Fragonard offered a history painting as his acceptance work for the Academy, he chose as his role the development of the subjects and the Rococo style of Watteau and Boucher. His subjects ranged from noble groups and portraits to humble genre scenes and landscapes. With dazzling technical facility, Fragonard endowed the *fête galante* with glowing pools of light and color; glazes are contrasted with impasto. One thinks of Rembrandt, but Fragonard's lightness of touch, the dainty proportions of the figures, the breaking up of the forms, and the fluttery, rippling line are all thoroughly Rococo. Like Boucher, Fragonard often painted panels

16-6 JEAN-HONORÉ FRAGONARD,
The Rendezvous, 1773.
Frick Collection, New York.

to be used as part of wall decorations in Louis XV interiors. Well-known examples are the panels on the theme of love (Fig. 16-6), which Fragonard executed for Madame du Barry, the lady who succeeded Madame de Pompadour as the mistress of Louis XV.

SCULPTURE IN THE NORTH

As in painting, the three general trends in sculpture were (1) a continuation of the seventeenth-century Baroque, ranging from stereotyped forms to a robust naturalism; (2) a Rococo style, emphasizing lilting, playful curves, intricate details in accessories, and slender proportions; and (3) a Neoclassic tendency toward simplification, quiet equilibrium, and long sweeping curves. Neoclassicism was especially important in the second half of the century. France was the most prolific producer of sculpture, but after the death of Louis XIV in 1715 the number of commissions for Versailles declined. The nobles were less attached to the court; they built town houses in Paris and furnished them with small sculptures in the Rococo style. Statuettes of porcelain and terra cotta were produced at the Sèvres workshops, a special interest of Louis XV's favorite, Madame de Pompadour. Baroque and Neoclassic styles were preferred for public monuments and other large works. Some sculptors modified their style to suit the commission.

In German areas, demand was greater for small sculpture than for monumental works. Meissen porcelain inspired the manufacture of France's Sèvres; but northern Germany imported French sculptors and French influence, while southern Germany and Austria were influenced by Italian sculpture, particularly in the stucco sculpture for their ornate Rococo churches.

Sculpture was meager in eighteenth-century England. French Baroque influence was brought to England by the sculptor Louis François Roubillac. Italian influence came from several leading Englishmen who studied in Italy. John Flaxman, for example, sent designs and sculpture from Italy to Wedgwood in England. The resulting Wedgwood ware is Neoclassic in the manner of Robert Adam decoration, that is, with a touch of Rococo delicacy. Otherwise, the Rococo did not take root in English sculpture.

Cosmas Damian and **Egid Quirin Asam** (Bavaria, 1686–1739 and 1692–1750). The Asam brothers were trained by their father, Hans G. Asam, and had the benefit of a year in Rome (1712), where they were impressed by the works of Giovanni Lorenzo Bernini, Giovanni Battista Gaulli, Andrea Pozzo, and Pietro da Cortona. The brothers formed a partnership but also worked separately. Cosmas Damian specialized in fresco painting and Egid Quirin in stucco ornament and sculpture. Their early collaborations include *The Assumption of the Virgin* (Fig. 1-27) above the high altar in the monastery church at Rohr, near Regensburg. In this overwhelming demonstration of Baroque dramatics, the sculpted figures of the gesticulating Apostles are gathered around the sarcophagus, while Mary ascends toward sculpted clouds and metallic rays that partially eclipse the architecture. The highly colored sculpture of the Madonna and the supporting angels presents a light, active, irregular group that contrasts with a darker curtain suspended in the background. The avoidance of framing and the concentrated lighting from above and from the sides are typically Baroque. The complexity, activity, and richness of the forms indicate a continuation of seventeenth-century sculptural-architectural combinations. The more delicate forms of the Rococo had not yet sapped the boisterous strength of Baroque composition. The later work of the brothers, however, became more Rococo.

16-7 JEAN ANTOINE HOUDON, *Voltaire,* 1781. Comédie Française, Paris.

Jean Antoine Houdon (France, 1741–1828). Houdon studied under the Baroque sculptors Jean-Baptiste Pigalle and Michel-Ange Slodtz, won prizes as a youth at the Academy, and spent the years from 1764 to 1768 at the French Academy in Rome. His thorough study of anatomy was demonstrated in the *Écorché* (c. 1766, École des Beaux Arts, Paris), a statue of a man without skin. Copies of this work served as study aids for anatomy classes in art schools. However, Houdon decided early on portraiture as a specialty and received many commissions from the nobility. His portrait style was one of keen characterization and precise detail. He used neither the delicate forms of the Rococo nor the generalization of the Neoclassic. Between 1771 and 1789, Houdon undertook a series of portraits of great men, including Voltaire (Fig. 16-7). His fame spread, and the esteem of Benjamin Franklin and Thomas Jefferson led to the commission for the full-length statue of George Washington (1785) in the State Capitol of Virginia, at Richmond. Houdon adopted a more Neoclassic style in a number of lesser-known works with mythological or allegorical subjects. He lived beyond the Revolution and continued to receive commissions, although he did not enjoy the favor of David, the leader of the Neoclassicists, or the patronage of Napoleon.

ARCHITECTURE IN THE NORTH

Eighteenth-century French architecture displayed a very restrained Baroque stylistic tendency that continued through most of the century and received the official sanction of the Academy. During the reign of Louis XV, the Rococo style was popular for interiors; bold surface projections were flattened, and pilasters and engaged columns were replaced by encrustations of dainty floral ornament and fluttering ribbons that break through any restraining geometric frames. Curves obscure, soften, and complicate the straight structural lines. Large halls gave way to small apartments and intimate rooms. Occasionally the Rococo was used for an exterior. The discovery of the buried Roman cities of Herculaneum (found in 1719) and Pompeii (found in 1748) provided inspiration for Neoclassicism, which developed in several directions after 1750. Simpler interiors with uninterrupted lines, rectangular rigidity, and more dependence on Roman ornament appeared in the work of Jacques-Germain Soufflot. With architects like Charles Nicolas Ledoux, however, simplicity and Greco-Roman elements were combined with jolting contrasts, grandiose scale, and surprisingly imaginative forms. The Revolution slowed building but strengthened the preference for the Neoclassic, partly because it was associated with the republican governments of certain periods in Greek and Roman history.

German eighteenth-century architecture developed a variety of styles within the general trends of Baroque, Rococo, and Neoclassicism. Some of the leading architects studied in Italy and France, and designers from these countries were brought to Germany. Churches of the early eighteenth century show the influence of the Italian Baroque. By mid-century, southern Germany and Austria were creating churches with rich Rococo interiors. Palaces were inspired by both Italian and French examples. Exteriors are often quite reserved, with decoration in low relief that does not obscure the basic masses; interiors could be lavishly Rococo. Winckelmann's influence was important in the second half of the century, and Neoclassicism waxed strong, particularly in Berlin. Neoclassic interiors often resemble those by Adam in England and suggest faint echoes of the delicacy of the Rococo.

The eighteenth century in England opened with the reserved Baroque that had developed in the previous century. After 1710, this tendency was challenged by the *Palladian Revival*, a movement espousing a return to the simpler Roman forms of the sixteenth-century Italian Palladio. A third tendency is evidenced by the occasional designs in Romanesque or Gothic styles. The ruins of Medieval architecture could be appreciated, as could Roman ruins, for their *picturesque* qualities of rough, irregular, and varied forms, and for their *sublime* qualities, which evoked nostalgic enjoyment of man's smallness and of the transitory character of his achievements in the face of nature's vastness and power. Furthermore, Gothic ornament could be appreciated for having some Rococo qualities. Neoclassic architecture developed in the second half of the century under the leadership of Robert Adam, Sir William Chambers, and Sir John Soane. It is notable that a given architect might work in several of these four trends.

Johann Bernhard Fischer von Erlach (Austria, 1656–1723). After his training in Rome, Fischer von Erlach returned to Vienna, where he became a leader in seventeenth- and eighteenth-century Austrian architecture. His church of St. Charles Borromaeus (Figs. 16-8–16-10) provides a strong focus on the main altar, which is placed in an extension at one end of an elliptical interior space. At the opposite end, a wide narthex is placed at a right angle to the elliptical center section. The

16-8
JOHANN BERNHARD FISCHER VON ERLACH,
St. Charles Borromaeus, Vienna, 1716–37.

exterior façade of this narthex consists of a Corinthian porch connected by two concave wings to towers at the sides. Within the concave areas at each side of the porch stand two tall columns with spiral reliefs in the manner of the ancient column of Trajan in Rome. Above the impressive façade looms a high dome set over the elliptical interior. The total effect both inside and out is one of dramatic contrasts between parts, but there is greater restraint in ornament than in many Italian Baroque churches.

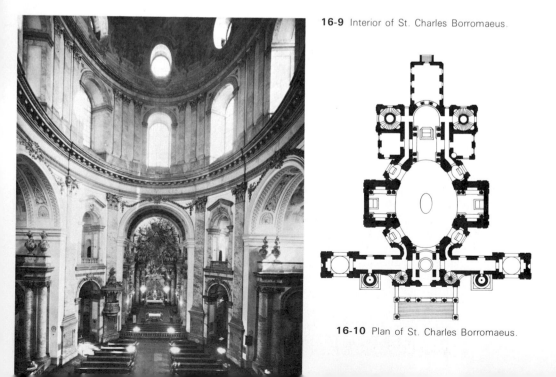

16-9 Interior of St. Charles Borromaeus.

16-10 Plan of St. Charles Borromaeus.

Balthasar Neumann (Germany, 1687–1753). Neumann was trained by the Würzburg bronze caster Sebald Kopp, and in addition gained considerable experience as a military engineer-architect. In 1720, he was given responsibility for the building of the Episcopal Residence at Würzburg and, in 1723, was sent to Paris to study French architecture. The Residence, like so many other eighteenth-century palaces, owes much to Versailles. French influences were important in the development of Neumann's Rococo style, which left a strong imprint on the architecture of southern Germany. Of his many buildings, the most celebrated church is that of Vierzehnheiligen (The Fourteen Saints, Figs. 16-11–16-13). Here, the façade pushes forward in a convex center framed by engaged columns and broken pediments; the twin towers become more complex and bolder in value contrasts as they rise. Rococo touches can be seen in the lilting curves of pediments and window frames, but the real drama is in the interior. Neumann's basilica plan was based on ovals and circles, producing even more restless wall planes than those of Borromini's San Carlo alle Quattro Fontane. The activity of the walls is intensified by the profusion of vinelike, irregular ornament that seems to crawl over the surfaces. The lavish colors, the delicate details, and the amazing effervescence of the interior make it an outstanding example of German Rococo.

16-11
BALTHASAR NEUMANN, Vierzehnheiligen
(The Fourteen Saints), near Banz,
1743–72.

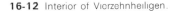
16-12 Interior of Vierzehnheiligen.

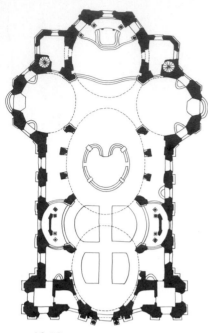

16-13 Plan of Vierzehnheiligen.

Anges-Jacques Gabriel (France, 1699–1782). Gabriel came from a family of architects and studied with his father. As architect for Louis XV, he produced both independent buildings and large building groups. His feeling for gradation and climax was expressed with spatial vistas leading to a building, central colonnaded pavilions, and occasional four-sided domes and concentrations of sculpture, as in his *Military School* (Paris, 1751). Gabriel's typical reserve is better demonstrated in the pair of palaces in the Place de la Concorde (1757–75), formerly the Place Louis XV. Rusticated and arcaded bases support colossal Corinthian orders that carry an entablature, balustrades, and corner pediments. Although the seventeenth-century east front of the Louvre inspired Gabriel's design, he used more three-dimensional variation and value contrast in the base. The simplest of his buildings is the Petit Trianon at Versailles (Fig. 16-14), an almost square structure with a symmetrical arrangement of interior spaces. While the interior has some traces of Rococo decoration, the exterior is remarkably austere. Three façades use slightly projecting pavilions marked by columns or pilasters framing the tall windows of the main floor and the square windows of the attic. The blocky form is topped by an entablature and a balustrade. It has been claimed that Gabriel was influenced by the publication, in 1758, of J. D. LeRoy's *Ruins of the Most Beautiful Monuments of Greece*, but the natural reserve of Gabriel's style came basically from the traditional restraint of French architecture in the preceding two centuries.

Robert Adam (England, 1728–92). Robert Adam was born in Scotland and attended the University of Edinburgh. From 1754 to 1758 he toured Italy, joined the artist's Academy of St. Luke in Rome, became a friend of Piranesi, and measured and drew the ruins of the palace of the Roman Emperor Diocletian at Spalato.

16-14
ANGES-JACQUES GABRIEL, Petit Trianon, Versailles (façade on the Jardin Français), 1762–68.

16-15
ROBERT ADAM, music room of No. 20,
Portman Square, London, 1777.

Upon his return to England, he formed an architectural
office with his brothers James and William. In 1761,
Robert Adam was appointed one of the two Architects
of the King's Works. He and his brothers designed
whole houses, reconstructions, interiors, and furnishings. Stylistically, their work was among the most significant done in the England of the 1760's and 1770's,
and their influence was international. The Adam style
may be called, with qualification, Neoclassical. Floor
plans such as that of Syon House, Middlesex, have
balanced symmetry and were inspired by specific
Roman or Greek buildings. Façades range from the massive stately south front of Kedleston Hall, Derbyshire,
with its Roman triumphal arch motif, to the delicate,
crisp, miniature character of the Adelphi Houses in
London. The Adams' greatest influence was on interiors.
Their preference was for slender pilasters, Grecian urns,
and architectural moldings borrowed from Rome and
Greece and used with rich profusion in very slight relief
with sharp contrasts in value or color. The result has
some of the delicacy of the Rococo but much more rigid
geometric structure, as shown in No. 20, Portman
Square (Fig. 16-15). In speaking of architecture, Robert
Adam emphasized "movement," the rise and fall, the
advance and recession of parts that is a facet of the
Baroque love of strong gradation and climax.

PAINTING IN ITALY

Major centers for eighteenth-century Italian painting were Naples, Bologna, Rome, and Venice; many Italian painters also found employment in other countries. As elsewhere, there was increased specialization in subject matter. Style in history painting was based on the work of the Carracci, Pietro da Cortona, Rubens, Titian, Tintoretto, and Veronese. The shimmering color of Veronese can be seen as one source for Italian Rococo, which was developed independently by Giovanni Battista Tiepolo. Loose brushwork and ragged, fluttering shapes created light, spacious compositions that maintain more breadth and grandeur of scale than French Rococo. Foreign painters were responsible for Neoclassic work in Italy. Portraiture was abundant in both the Baroque and the Rococo styles. Paintings of city views, ruins, landscapes, and imaginative combinations of all three found a wide international market. Not only were many north Italian palaces decorated with such subjects, but travelers collected them as souvenirs. Style varied from precise, dry detail, natural light, and documentary accuracy to fluid brushwork, dramatic lighting, and exaggerated scale. Genre painting followed the traditions of the Bamboccianti and that of the upper-class interiors from seventeenth-century Dutch painting.

Giovanni Battista Tiepolo (Venice, Lombardy, Würzburg, and Madrid, 1696–1770). Tiepolo's rise to fame began during his study under a secondary master in Venice. Commissions for wall and ceiling frescoes eventually led him from one city to another. The heavy forms and powerful value contrasts of his early work, like *The Sacrifice of Abraham* (1715-16, Church of the Ospedaletto, Venice), show the influence of Titian and of Tintoretto, but Tiepolo then turned to lighter and more open composition. In the Church of the Gesuati in Venice, he did the ceiling painting of *St. Dominic Instituting the Rosary* (1737-39), a composition that recalls the illusionistic architecture in Veronese's *Triumph of Venice*. Yet Tiepolo reduced the proportion of heavy solids and increased the proportion of sky. The thin, fluffy clouds, the fluttering airborne figures, and the light colors and shadow areas produce a buoyant effect. Between 1750 and 1753, he decorated the Episcopal Residence at Würzburg. The ceiling painting of the throne room depicts *Apollo Conducting Beatrice of Burgundy to Barbarossa* (Fig. 16-16) and goes further than earlier work in lightening and opening the composition. Architecture is reduced to a small structure

16-16 GIOVANNI BATTISTA TIEPOLO, *Apollo Conducting Beatrice of Burgundy to Barbarossa*, ceiling of the throne room of the Episcopal Residence, Würzburg, 1750–53

in the lower left, and the figure groups present fluttering irregular shapes like leaves blown in the wind. The sweeping clouds are thin overlapping veils with delicately scalloped edges. Around the painting, a gilded stucco frame consists of compound curves and lacy edges, broken in several places by painted forms that seem to spill over it in typical Baroque illusionistic fashion. From 1762 until 1770, Tiepolo worked in Spain, decorating the Royal Palace at Madrid. The jealousy of rivals and the growing preference for Neoclassicism led to a decline in his popularity and may have hastened his death. Tiepolo's painting presents the fullest expression of the Rococo in Italian art.

Giovanni Antonio Canal, called **Canaletto** (Venice, Rome, and London, 1697–1768). Canaletto studied first with his father, a painter of theatrical scenery. In 1719, the young artist traveled to Rome, where he saw Giovanni Paolo Pannini's paintings of ruins and the Bamboccianti paintings of everyday life in the city. After his return to Venice, Canaletto specialized in painting views of the city (*vedute*) and obtained numerous commissions from Englishmen making the grand tour of the Continent and wishing to take home souvenirs. Canaletto painted Venice in sharp linear detail, sweeping spaces, and vast

16-17
CANALETTO, *Piazza San Marco, c.* 1760.
Courtesy of the Trustees of the National
Gallery, London.

16-18
GIOVANNI BATTISTA PIRANESI, scene from
the *Carceri* series, 1744–45. Etching.
Metropolitan Museum of Art, New York.

gentle skies, as in the *Piazza San Marco* (Fig. 16–17).
The popularity of his art led to the publication of a
series of engravings of his paintings that was used as
a catalogue by his clients and an aid by his imitators.
It is probable that he visited Rome again in 1740. Between 1742 and 1743, he painted a series of scenes
depicting Roman ruins. Canaletto did not always limit
himself to documenting particular spots; he occasionally created imaginary scenes, sometimes containing
well-known buildings. Much of the period from 1745
to 1755 was spent in England, where his reputation was
already well established. The visit was a great success,
although the English collectors were, at first, discon-
certed by the *caprices*—imaginary scenes—that the
painter produced along with many views of London.
Commissions were so plentiful that Canaletto employed
assistants. Cityscapes and landscapes were considered
inferior subject matter by academic standards, however,
and in spite of his international success Canaletto was
not accepted into the Venetian Academy until 1763.

Giovanni Battista Piranesi (Rome, 1720–78). Piranesi's
engravings and etchings demonstrate the growing
eighteenth-century interest in Greco-Roman art and the
appreciation of the picturesque. Piranesi began his career in Venice as a student of architecture but established himself in Rome in 1740. There he turned to

engraving and etching prints of ruins and views of modern Rome. His etching of the Great Hall of the Baths of Caracalla indicates his love of grand scale, often exaggerated by depicting tiny human figures next to ragged, crumbling architecture eaten away by time and vegetation. Etching needles of different sizes made for rich diversity of line. Piranesi's best prints show a wide variation of grays and deep blacks. He documented and interpreted ancient Rome in his views of that city, but the range of his imagination is shown in his *Carceri* series (Fig. 16-18), imaginary interiors of prisons in fantastic scale and structural elaboration based vaguely on Roman architecture. A comparison of the art of Piranesi with that of David indicates the wide range of style that could be inspired by intense interest in ancient Greco-Roman art. In an effort to describe Piranesi's particular attitude and style, some writers have used the rather awkward term *Romantic Classicism.*

Suggestions for Further Study

Downes, Kerry. *English Baroque Architecture.* London: Zwemmer, 1966.

Fosca, François (pseudonym for Georges de Traz). *The Eighteenth Century. Watteau to Tiepolo* (Great Centuries of Painting). Translated by Stuart Gilbert. Geneva: Skira, 1952.

Gerson, Horst, and Engelbert H. ter Kuile. *Art and Architecture in Belgium: 1600–1800* (Pelican History of Art). Translated by Olive Renier. Baltimore: Penguin Books, 1960.

Hempel, Eberhard. *Baroque Art and Architecture in Central Europe: Germany, Austria, Switzerland, Hungary, Czechoslovakia, Poland* (Pelican History of Art). Baltimore: Penguin Books, 1965.

Irwin, David. *English Neo-Classical Art.* London: Faber and Faber, 1966.

Kalnein, Wend Graf, and Michael Levey. *Art and Architecture of the Eighteenth Century in France* (Pelican History of Art). Translation of Part II by J. R. Foster. Baltimore: Penguin Books, 1972.

Morassi, Antonio. *Tiepolo: His Life and Work.* New York: Phaidon Press, 1955.

Rosenberg, Jakob; Seymour Slive; and E. H. ter Kuile. *Dutch Art and Architecture, 1600–1800* (Pelican History of Art). Baltimore: Penguin Books, 1966.

Summerson, John. *Architecture in Britain: 1530–1830* (Pelican History of Art). Baltimore: Penguin Books, 1953.

Waterhouse, Ellis. *Painting in Britain, 1530–1790* (Pelican History of Art). Baltimore: Penguin Books, 1953.

Whinney, Margaret. *Sculpture in Britain, 1530–1830* (Pelican History of Art). Baltimore: Penguin Books, 1964.

Wittkower, Rudolf. *Art and Architecture in Italy, 1600–1750* (Pelican History of Art). Baltimore: Penguin Books, 1958.

Chapter 16 Music

Music
in
the
Eighteenth
Century

Composers continued writing Baroque music during the first half of the eighteenth century, and many of the finest examples come from this period. The Baroque style was replaced, after about 1750, by a distinctly new style now called *Classical.* Though it represented a reaction against Baroque music, the Classical style in music was not a revival of any earlier style. It had its origins in the ideas of the Enlightenment and in mannered court life, especially in France. The grandeur and complexity of the Baroque were replaced by simplicity and sentiment; "reasonable," "natural," and "pleasant" became criteria of good music. The ideal was simple beauty without excessive ornamentation, an art with universal appeal.

With the rise to power of an educated bourgeoisie, the arts gained new popularity, and public concerts began to provide a new means of supporting musicians. The first literary journals appeared in England, Germany, and France, and they often included music criticism.

Italy remained the musical center of Europe during most of the eighteenth century, and Italian opera flourished everywhere, to be seriously challenged only by the French. German composers gained increasing importance throughout the century, especially in the fields of orchestral and keyboard music. French music was strongly influenced by the fashions of the Court. Toward the end of the century leading cities such as Paris, London, and Vienna developed a rich and varied concert life based on strong middle-class support. The best practitioners of Classical music considered Vienna to be their cultural center, and the style is sometimes called *Viennese Classicism.*

Late Baroque Music

Baroque composers of the early eighteenth century worked mostly with accepted styles, forms, and techniques inherited from their predecessors, and their music was the product of over a century of consolidation. Instrumental music now held an important place, and melodies were written to suit the capabilities of specific instruments, rather than the human voice. Typically, these melodies were constructed out of one or two unifying motives, which were developed or spun out through repetition and variation. Rhythm patterns were repetitive and based on simple metrical systems. Modulation from key to key within a clear tonal sys-

16-19
ANTOINE WATTEAU, *Mezzetin*, 1715–20.
Oil on canvas, 21¾" x 17". The
Metropolitan Museum of Art, New York.
Munsey Fund.

tem, together with motivic development, gave composers the means for creating large formal structures. Except in solo keyboard works, practically all late Baroque
music utilized a continuo bass, which controlled the
tonal system.

Typical textures in late Baroque works included two
or three soloists with continuo (sonata texture), many
parts in complex polyphony, contrasts between large
and small groups (concerted style), imitative polyphony
(fugal texture), and the dramatic recitative and aria.
Baroque forms ranged from strict two-part dance forms
(such as *allemande, saraband, minuet, gigue*) to free,
improvisatory forms (*toccata, prelude, fantasia*).

Late Baroque musical style was so well integrated
that techniques, forms, and textures were transferred
freely from one medium to another. Fugues were written for chorus, orchestra, and keyboard. The textures of
organ variations and instrumental sonatas appeared in
works for voices with instruments, and sonata texture
appeared in pieces for the organ. Both sectional and
continuous variations were used in a variety of media.

Keyboard forms for organ, harpsichord and clavichord included fugues (usually coupled with a toccata,
prelude, or fantasia), sonatas, dance suites, and variations. The most important late Baroque orchestral form
was the concerto. It was also a common practice to play

16-20

A French chamber music trio.

suites of dances from French court ballets at orchestral concerts. These usually began with a French overture and were called *overtures*, or *orchestral suites*. For small instrumental groups, the principal types of music were dance suites and sonatas.

Vocal music during the late Baroque was dominated by the dramatic styles. Oratorios and Passions were created extensively in Latin as well as in the vernacular languages. Lutheran church composers also wrote miniature oratorios, called *sacred cantatas*. These ranged in style from variations on the words and melody of a chorale to recitatives, arias, and duets similar to operatic practice.

Italian operas and secular cantatas were popular throughout most of Europe, except in France, where operas in the tradition of Lully were still composed. Italian serious opera in the late Baroque (*opera seria*) became overly stylized. The plots were based on standard Roman or Greek subjects. They were set almost exclusively to alternating solo recitatives and arias, with the orchestra in a subordinate role. The recitatives usually were accompanied by the harpsichord, though sometimes by the orchestra. The arias were accompanied by the orchestra and were constructed according to fixed conventions. This rigid stylization encouraged displays of vocal acrobatics by the singers, to the detriment of the drama, and led eventually to demands for operatic reforms.

Reaction against excessive pomp and stylization in Baroque serious operas helped stimulate the development of several types of comic, or light opera: *opera buffa* in Italy, *opéra comique* in France, *ballad opera* in England, and *Singspiel* in Germany. The characters and scenes were from everyday life, and the music, sung in the national language, was generally light in character, frequently making use of popular songs of the day. All forms except the Italian used spoken dialogue instead of recitative.

Antonio Vivaldi (Italy, 1675/1678–1741). Vivaldi spent most of his career as composer and music director at the Conservatory of the Pietà in Venice. Though he is known today for his many concertos, he also wrote sonatas, church music, and numerous operas. His concertos are stylistically halfway between the earlier concerto grosso and the later solo concerto. His *Concerto Grosso*, Opus 3, No. 11 calls for two violins and a cello as soloists, plus a string orchestra with continuo bass. Vivaldi's choice and grouping of instruments is like Corelli's, but his originality shows in the independent roles he gives to the soloists. There is an introduction by the soloists, then a fast fugue in which the soloists and full orchestra exchange material. The slow middle movement features an accompanied violin solo, and the fast final movement pits the soloists against the full orchestra. The order of movements—fast-slow-fast—was standardized by Vivaldi.

16-21
An eighteenth-century advertisement for Jean-Philippe Rameau's opera *Castor and Pollux*, as well as for an Italian *opera buffa*. Operas appealed to a wide audience.

Jean-Philippe Rameau (France, 1683–1764). Rameau formulated the modern theories of harmony. His most important compositions were several stage works produced between 1833 and 1839. These were operatic spectacles with choruses, ballets, lavish scenery, and a minimum of drama—an extension of the French opera traditions established by Lully. Rameau gave the same close attention to word rhythms and declamation as Lully, but his harmonies and use of instruments were richer and more varied than Lully's. His opera *Castor et Pollux* is generally regarded as his greatest work.

Johann Sebastian Bach (Germany, 1685–1750). Bach was the most illustrious of a long line of German musicians of that name. The major part of his career was spent in successive positions as court organist and concertmaster at Weimar, court music director at Cöthen, and church music director and cantor of St. Thomas's school in Leipzig. With the exception of opera, his works include most kinds of late Baroque music. His sacred cantatas are the supreme achievement in this form. His superb craftmanship, grandeur of conception, and unrivaled contrapuntal skill represent the ultimate fusion of Baroque musical styles and techniques. Bach's music is marked by incisive melodic ideas, a powerful rhythmic flow, and terse polyphony governed by a clear harmonic plan. Formal integrity is maintained at every level, from the smallest detail to the structure of whole works, resulting in a consistent and intense emotional power. His Fantasia and Fugue in G Minor (BWV 542) sums up more than a century of organ music. The fantasia is constructed like older works of the same name. Free improvisatory passages, with a single line moving in elaborate patterns and figurations over sustained tones, alternate with sections of dense polyphony. At the same time the harmonies in the fantasia are firmly rooted in late Baroque tonality. The fugue begins typically, with the subject imitated by four voices in descending order. The melodic character of the subject commands attention, and motives derived from it permeate the whole piece. The four opening entries, as well as the next three, are all imitative, while almost all the rest are single entries, alternating with short episodes. (See the discussions of Ex. 2, Minuet, Trio I, Polacca, and Trio II from the first Brandenburg Concerto, Chs. 1, 2, and 4.)

Domenico Scarlatti (Italy, Portugal, and Spain, 1685–1757). Domenico Scarlatti was the son of Alessandro Scarlatti, a prominent Italian opera composer. He spent

16-22
Organ in St. Thomas' Church, Leipzig, where Bach created many of his cantatas and organ works.

the latter half of his life as musician at the royal courts of Portugal and Spain. His fame rests on his more than five hundred sonatas for solo harpsichord. He explored the sonorous and technical possibilities of the instrument so exhaustively that his sonatas still constitute some of the most challenging works for harpsichordists. Scarlatti's sonatas follow a two-part formal scheme, but his particular way of handling key contrasts and modulation anticipated Classical sonata form. His Sonata in C Major, K. 159 is one of his best known works and typical of his style. Its light texture and the fragmentation and ornamentation of the melodies are characteristic of the musical Rococo.

George Frideric Handel (Germany, England, 1685–1759). Handel played in the Hamburg opera orchestra and later studied and traveled in Italy. In 1711 he went to London, where he spent the rest of his life, primarily as composer, conductor, and theater manager of Italian operas, and later of English oratorios. He was a master of the Italian opera seria. He also composed many works for solo voice, some church music, orchestral suites and concertos, instrumental sonatas, and solo works for organ and harpsichord. His greatest works were his twenty-six English oratorios, mostly written during the latter part of his life. These were theatrical dramas, without costumes, acting, or scenery, created through a fusion of the forms of the opera seria with English choral music, and performed in English. Most, though not all, were on sacred subjects. His best-known oratorio is the *Messiah*, a setting of various Biblical texts illustrating the Christian concept of Christ as Messiah. It opens with a French overture, written for two violin parts, violas, and continuo. The texture is essentially three-part polyphony in the manner of Corelli, while the form is Lully's; but the lengthy development of the fast, fugal part is typical of Handel. The following recitative and aria ("Comfort Ye" and "Every Valley") are typical of the Italian opera seria style. A small orchestra of strings and continuo accompanies the solo tenor, who must command considerable vocal power and agility. Handel's choruses were the distinguishing feature of his oratorios. For the first chorus in the *Messiah*, "And the Glory of the Lord," he assigns different melodic ideas to each of four segments of the text. The instruments and the four voice parts present these ideas in textures which alternate between single lines, imitative polyphony, simultaneous chordal movement, fast lines against slow or sustained parts, and passages with instruments alone.

Classical Music

During the early eighteenth century, Baroque musical style in France gave place to a musical equivalent of the Rococo, which reflected the tastes of the aristocracy. What was expected was entertainment and diversion—simple, pleasant, restrained, and delicate, with many frills and ornaments. Typical works were short pieces for the harpsichord suitable for the fashionable Paris salons. German composers soon adopted most features of the French style, but they generally emphasized emotional expression over ornamentation. They strove for depth of feeling, with a minimum of frills and ornaments, while keeping their music simple, pleasant, and restrained.

During the latter half of the eighteenth century, Joseph Haydn and Wolfgang Mozart created the Classical style out of a merger of these French and German predecessors, and, in Mozart's case, this was done with considerable Italian influence. Their music was international, cosmopolitan, and immediately appealing; it provided depth of expression without needless complexity, and it was elegant in its poise, balance, and formal clarity.

Classical composers mostly rejected the polyphonic complexities and motivic unity of the late Baroque style. Expression of a variety of moods replaced the Baroque system of a single affect persisting throughout a piece, and the continuous bass line of the Baroque disappeared. The Classical orchestra became standard-

16-23
GABRIEL ST. AUBIN, *Le Concert*, 1774. Engraving, 8⅞'' x 15⅜''. The Metropolitan Museum of Art, New York. Harris Brisbane Dick Fund.

ized. About two dozen strings formed the nucleus, with the most basic woodwind and brass instruments, in pairs, providing some variety—a total of about thirty-five players. The harpsichord was no longer used in the orchestra.

In Classical style the melodies usually are prominent and easy to grasp, but they tend to break up into motives that are extended and developed. Textures are relatively simple, and there is a good deal of melodic and textural contrast from phrase to phrase. All elements of the music usually contribute to the formal design, which is based primarily on the tonality scheme and on development of the melodic and rhythmic ideas. The Classical style is best represented by the symphony, string quartet, solo concerto, and solo sonata. All of these are instrumental works in three or four separate movements. The first and last movements are fast, with a slow movement in between, and often there is a minuet in addition.

The structure of the first movement (and often other movements) is called *sonata form*. This form is based on the contrast of two opposing key centers. In the first part, called the *exposition*, there are three distinct processes; (1) establishment of the initial tonic, (2) modulation to a contrasting key, and (3) consolidation of this new key. The two keys usually are set apart by distinctive melodies, rhythms, and timbres. They are called, respectively, the first and second *themes*, and the modulating passage is called the *transition*. In the second part, called the *development*, materials from the exposition are expanded, altered, and transformed. In the third part, called the *recapitulation*, the entire expositon returns, except that the second theme returns in the same key as the first theme. The structure may conclude with an elaborate ending, called a *coda*, and it may begin with a separate, slow introduction.

SONATA FORM

Slow introduction (optional)	
Exposition	Theme 1—original key Transition—modulation Theme 2—new key
Development	Material from the exposition, freely expanded and altered
Recapitulation	Theme 1—original key Transition—returns to original key Theme 2—original key
Coda (optional)	

16-24

Illustration of the minuet from a dance text of 1735. Crown Copyright. Victoria and Albert Museum, London.

The slow movement in classical instrumental works may be a theme and variations or a sonata form, but it usually is lyrical and contemplative, and it often resembles an operatic aria transferred to instruments. The last movement is most often either in sonata form or in a modified version of sonata form.

The minuet was a courtly dance in triple meter, a holdover from the Baroque dance suite. The usual practice was to combine two minuets so that the first one returned after the second one was played: first minuet–second minuet–first minuet. The second minuet came to be called a "trio," hence the term, *minuet and trio* form. By speeding up the minuet, Ludwig van Beethoven created a new form that he called *scherzo,* which usually was combined with a trio to form a *scherzo and trio.*

The solo concerto usually pitted a solo instrument against an orchestra. It retained the three movements of the Baroque concerto grosso, but with the Classical sonata form and related structures. Typical middle movements showed off the lyrical qualities of the solo instrument. Any or all movements might contain a solo *cadenza,* an elaborate improvisation by the soloist just before the final orchestral flourish.

During the latter half of the eighteenth century the older Baroque styles of Italian and French serious opera were attacked as obsolete. Some composers, most notably Christoph Willibald Gluck, worked to fuse a new kind of serious opera out of the best features of the old styles. However, it was in the comic and light operas that the Classical spirit found its natural place.

From its beginnings the French national opera held the exclusive royal privilege of performing opera in Paris. The *opéra comique*, using spoken dialogue and limited musical resources, developed as a means of circumventing this privilege. Though many early productions had been simple parodies of serious opera, the opéra comique had become a significant art form by the end of the eighteenth century.

Opera buffa originated in comic interludes performed between the acts of the Italian opera seria. It was relatively free from the conventions of serious opera, and the comic ensemble, or group scene, became its most notable feature. In Germany the *Singspiel* was a mixture of German popular traditions, with borrowings from the French and English comic opera styles. Mozart raised both the opera buffa and the singspiel to unprecedented heights in works such as *The Marriage of Figaro* and *The Magic Flute*.

16-25

Scene from Mozart's *Magic Flute*, depicting Papageno, the bird catcher.

Christoph Willibald Gluck (Germany, Italy, Austria, and France, 1714–87). Gluck received thorough training in operatic composition while spending several years in Italy. After producing a number of conventional Italian operas he became the leader of the movement to reform Baroque operatic practices. Working in Vienna and Paris, he created successful operas in which conventional forms and displays of singing skills were replaced by music designed to serve the drama. Utilizing the best of Italian, French, and German traditions, he mingled solo arias, choruses, and dances in unified dramatic scenes, and he enhanced the role of the orchestra. His operas were truly Classical in their international style, elegance, dignity, and simple beauty. His first opera in the new style was *Orpheus and Euridice*, set first in Italian and later in French. Orpheus's lament after his final loss of Euridice, *"Che faro senza Euridice?,"* is one of Gluck's best known arias. The melody is simple, with large portions repeated. The singer is given no opportunities to show off vocal skills, but when it is well performed the aria is deeply expressive through its very simplicity.

Franz Joseph Haydn (Austria, 1732–1809). Haydn was born in Rohrau, in eastern Austria. From age eight until his voice changed he was a choirboy in Vienna. In 1761 he was appointed music director for the Hungarian noble family of Esterházy, in whose employ he remained for the rest of his life. Working mostly at the family's magnificent country estate of Esterháza, he supervised the extensive musical activities, rehearsed and conducted the performances, and composed all of the music. He achieved international fame with two highly successful trips to London in the 1790's. Because of his long life, the number and quality of his compositions, and his wide fame and reputation, Haydn did more than any composer to perfect the Classical style. He created the string quartet, and he made major contributions to the style of the Classical Symphony. His String Quartet, Opus 76, No. 3 is typical of his later quartet style. There are four separate movements, the first and last being fast, the second slow and lyric in a contrasting key, and the third a minuet and trio. There is great textural variety throughout, and, although the first violin frequently plays a solo melody, all of the instruments are given a good deal of interesting, independent material. The first movement is a sonata form whose separate parts are blurred by the continuous development of the ideas; there is a false recapitulation and a substantial coda. The second movement is a set of variations on Haydn's own song, "God Sustain the Emperor Franz," which became the Austrian national anthem. The complete theme is presented, followed by four variations. The variations consist mainly of countermelodies accompanying the original, with the density of the texture increasing with each variation. The third movement is a standard minuet and trio. The texture is simple throughout, with the first violin mostly playing an accompanied melody. The last movement is a display of contrasting textures and continuous development of ideas, organized through sonata form. The entire movement is built out of the ideas presented in the first two phrases. Textures include dense chords, accompanied melody, equal-voice polyphony, and simultaneous scale movement in all four parts. Rapid changes in the texture are emphasized by loud-soft contrasts. The minor mode at the beginning changes to major at the end of the recapitulation, and the movement ends in major.

Wolfgang Amadeus Mozart (Austria, 1756–91). Mozart received his education and musical training from his father, Leopold Mozart, a competent and well-known musician. He displayed such a brilliant and prodigious aptitude for music at a very early age that his father took him on numerous concert trips throughout Europe, starting at the age of six. After first seeking a career in Paris, he spent the last ten years of his life in Vienna, producing many of his greatest works, and he died in poverty at the age of thirty-five. He composed operas, symphonies, chamber music, church music, sonatas and concertos for piano and for violin, and lighter music for social occasions. In all of these he brought the Classical style to its peak of perfection, combining Italian elegance and lyricism with German depth of expression and dramatic intensity. The early piano was just being perfected in Mozart's day, and he was the first major composer to create concertos for solo piano and orchestra. His Piano Concerto in C Minor, K. 491 begins with a powerful orchestral theme that is intensified by falling chromatic lines. Both orchestra and piano present and exchange a number of melodic themes, and the key structure closely resembles sonata form. In the second movement the piano alone plays a slow, lyric melody, which returns twice as a refrain after contrasting orchestral material. The fast final movement consists of a theme and seven variations, with the piano and orchestra variously taking

16-26

Mozart (seated, at age seven) performing in concert with his father and sister.

16-27

Court orchestra in typical Rococo setting.

turns with the material. Mozart's operas are some of the finest ever created. He perfected the ensemble scenes and finales in Italian comic opera, and he displayed a masterful gift for delineation of character through the music. The *Marriage of Figaro* is an example of his best opera buffa. The lively action is a maze of improbable subterfuge and plots and counterplots, but the real drama is in the very human interaction of the characters. In the latter part of Act II (just after Antonio's entrance) the principal character, Figaro, is caught in a lie but manages to invent an alibi just in time to turn the tables on his accusor, Count Almaviva. As each new bit of the conversation among the characters subtly alters the situation, the accompanying music modulates to a new key, and, as the tension mounts, these modulations occur more often. Just as Figaro springs his alibi the final modulation leads back to the original key, the tension breaks, and all of the characters join in a four-way commentary. Three new characters enter and a loud argument ensues, with everyone holding forth at once. Each of the seven characters expresses separate opinions or reactions, and the music becomes as complex as the stage action. As the interchange grows more intense the music speeds up through metrical changes. In this way the second act comes to a rousing finish, with the argument still raging.

Ludwig van Beethoven (Germany and Austria, 1770–1827). Beethoven grew up in Bonn, where his father made cruel attempts to exploit his obvious talent for music. His early teachers were mediocre, and he was mostly self-taught until age twelve, when he began working with Christian Gottlob Neefe, the organist at the Bonn court. Until he was twenty-two he also played viola in the court theater orchestra, taught lessons, and he befriended several influential people. In 1792 he went to Vienna to study with Haydn and remained there for the rest of his life, living on income from concerts, publications, and subsidies by wealthy patrons. He composed works in almost every medium, but his greatest works were his symphonies, string quartets, concertos, and piano sonatas. He represents both the culmination and the dissolution of the Classical style. Beginning with the accepted forms and media, he experimented with new tonal and key relationships, new techniques of motivic and thematic development, and new uses and combinations of instruments. He modified standard structural procedures, particularly through expansion of connecting and developmental passages and through such formal experiments as the mixing of variations with sonata form. In most of his music, Beethoven's power and force of expression places him clearly outside the Enlightenment ideals of simplicity and moderation, and in this respect he was a precursor of the Romantic attitude. His Fifth Symphony follows the general outline of earlier Classical symphonies, but certain distinctive features of orchestration, thematic invention and development, and formal structure bear the mark of the composer's individuality. For the first three movements he calls for a standard Classical orchestra plus two clarinets; however, he adds a piccolo, a contrabassoon, and three trombones for the last movement, and there are prominent solos for horn, oboe, bassoon, flute, trombone, cellos, and even double basses. The first and last movements are in sonata form, with elaborate codas, but the second movement is constructed out of two themes, one of which returns as variations, while the other recurs intact as a refrain. The third movement proceeds as a scherzo and trio, but the reprise of the scherzo disintegrates into a passage of sustained dissonance that builds expectancy for and leads directly into the final movement. The rhythm of the motive which begins the first movement—short-short-short-*long*—appears in some form in all four movements. (The use of common themes among movements and the direct connection of one movement to the next were favorite tactics of several later composers.) Beethoven sought power of expression rather than elegance, and in this his style is no longer Classical. One of his favorite devices was repetition of rhythms, notes, chords, or motives, and much of his thematic development proceeds by this means. The resulting rhythmic drive may be forcefully interrupted by sudden pauses; or repeated dissonances, coupled with a buildup of loudness, may produce a powerful sense of motion toward a goal, as in the passage linking the third movement to the fourth. During the coda to the last movement the beats are speeded up to form background groupings, and the symphony concludes in a great burst of speed. (See the discussions of Ex. 1, Seventh Symphony, second movement, Chs. 1, 2, and 4.)

Suggestions for Further Study

Bukofzer, Manfred F. *Music in the Baroque Era.* New York: W. W. Norton, 1947.

David, Hans T., and Arthur Mendel, eds. *The Bach Reader,* rev. ed. New York: W. W. Norton, 1966.

Einstein, Alfred, *Gluck* (Master Musician Series). Translated by Eric Blom. New York: Octagon Books, 1955.

————. *Mozart: His Character, His Work.* Translated by Arthur Mendel and Nathan Broder. New York: Oxford University Press, 1965.

Forbes, Elliot, ed. *Thayer's Life of Beethoven,* rev. ed. 2 vols. Princeton, N.J.: Princeton University Press, 1967.

Geiringer, Karl, and Irene Geiringer. *Haydn: A Creative Life in Music,* rev. ed. Berkeley: University of California Press, 1968.

Grout, Donald Jay. *A History of Western Music,* rev. ed. New York: W. W. Norton, 1973. Chapters XII–XV.

Kirkpatrick, Ralph. *Domenico Scarlatti,* rev. ed. Princeton, N.J.: Princeton University Press, 1953.

Landon, H. C. Robbins. *Essays on the Viennese Classical Style: Gluck, Haydn, Mozart, Beethoven.* New York: Macmillan, 1970.

Lang, Paul Henry, ed. *George Frideric Handel.* New York: W. W. Norton, 1966.

Pauly, Reinhard G. *Music in the Classic Period,* 2nd ed (History of Music Series). Englewood Cliffs, N.J.: Prentice-Hall, 1973.

Pincherle, Marc. *Vivaldi: Genius of the Baroque.* New York: W. W. Norton, 1962.

Rosen, Charles. *The Classical Style: Haydn, Mozart, Beethoven.* New York: W. W. Norton, 1972.

Suggestions for Further Listening

KEYBOARD

Bach, Johann Sebastian. Passacaglia and Fugue in C Minor (BMV 582).

———. Preludes and fugues from the *Well-Tempered Clavier,* Book I, Nos. 1, 2, 15, and 16.

Beethoven, Ludwig van. Sonata, Opus 53.

Mozart, Wolfgang Amadeus. Sonata in F, K. 332.

Scarlatti, Dominico. Selected harpsichord sonatas.

CONCERTO

Bach, Johann Sebastian. Brandenburg Concerto, No. 2.

Beethoven, Ludwig van. Piano Concerto in G, Opus 58.

———. Violin Concerto in D, Opus 61.

Handel, George Frideric. One of the Concertos from Opus 6.

Mozart, Wolfgang Amadeus. Piano Concerto in D Minor, K. 466.

Vivaldi, Antonio. Concerto, Opus 3, No. 8.

———. Concertos, Opus 8, Nos. 1–4.

ORCHESTRA

Bach, Johann Sebastian. One of the Orchestral Suites.

Beethoven, Ludwig van. Symphony No. 7.

Haydn, Joseph. Symphony No. 104.

Mozart, Wolfgang Amadeus. Symphony No. 40, K. 550.

OPERA

Gluck, Christoph Willibald. Act II, Scene 1, from *Orfeus and Euridice.*

Handel, George Frideric. Selections from *Giulio Cesare.*

Mozart, Wolfgang Amadeus. Selections from *Don Giovanni.*

———. Selections from *The Magic Flute.*

VOCAL-CHORAL MUSIC

Bach, Johann Sebastian. Cantata No. 4.

———. Cantata No. 140.

CHAMBER MUSIC

Beethoven, Ludwig van. String Quartet, Opus 132.

Haydn, Joseph. String Quartet, Opus 77, No. 2.

Mozart, Wolfgang Amadeus. String Quartet in C, K. 465.

Neoclassic Through Post-Impressionist Art:

1800–1900

Modern art is often dated from David's rebellion against the Baroque and Rococo styles in the late eighteenth century (see p. 252). Rebellion against tradition, even an immediately preceding one, and the rapid change of form and content are important characteristics of modern art. With these characteristics in mind, we can consider the nineteenth century to be the first major period in the history of modern art. The development of archaeology and art history as disciplines seems to have led to greater self-consciousness about individual style and to an increased awareness of stylistic movements and group identities. For some artists, however, the interest in these disciplines led to more precise borrowing from the art of the past. These divergent tendencies, along with changing ideas in philosophy and science, help to explain why different concepts of artistic "truth" are implicit in the different styles in art and in the writings of art critics during the nineteenth century.

The most important geographical area for developments in painting and sculpture was France. In architecture, England played a significant role, especially since her leadership in the Industrial Revolution encouraged pioneering in the use of iron and glass as building materials.

During the first half of the nineteenth century, the various styles tended to express one of two major attitudes, Neoclassicism or Romanticism. The distinction between the two is not always sharp since there were considerable overlapping and mutual influence. Nineteenth-century Neoclassicists borrowed more specifically from Greek and Roman art than did their eighteenth-century predecessors. Underlying the many Neoclassic styles is the search for an absolute beauty based on the perfection of nature and in accordance with preconceived ideal types. Clarity of parts, stable equilibrium, and proportions inspired by Greek and Roman art are basic to Neoclassic work. The attitude called Romanticism produced such a wide range of styles that it is more difficult to characterize; generally there is an insistence on the freedom of the individual and the importance of individual experience. Individual characteristics—the unique form rather than the ideal type—are stressed, and restrictive traditions are rejected. In the famous preface to his play *Cromwell* (1827), Victor Hugo provided a manifesto for Romanticism. He attacked academic dogma and argued that the Christian concept of the worth of the individual makes possible a new kind of pity, *melancholy*. He stated that the individual, indeed all of nature, contains the ugly as well as the beautiful, evil as well as good. Art should therefore dramatize the dual nature of reality, stress the worth of the individual, and evoke the profound sentiment of melancholy. Romantic artists found subject matter in the works of Lord Byron and Sir Walter Scott and inspiration in the appeal to emotional and mystical experience by writers like François René de Chateaubriand and Wilhelm H. Wackenroder. Christian pietism frequently reinforced the Romantic attitude and created an interest in the Middle Ages; the Romantic could turn to any period in the past, however, since he appreciated the exotic and the remote in time or place.

After the middle of the nineteenth century, the Neoclassic and Romantic attitudes gave way to tendencies that have been described as a *positivistic reaction* and that are reflected in some of the pioneering literature, painting, and sculpture of the period. The continuing desire to upset conventional ideas was joined by an interest in treating all aspects of everyday life in styles that were labeled *Realistic* or *Naturalistic*. Such art was linked with the growing enthusiasm for science, and artists began to investigate even the chaotic incidental nature of human events and the impressionistic character of our experience of the physical world. Toward the end of the century, however, the realization grew that science and progress would not solve all the ills and mysteries of the world. The *Symbolist movement* in literature and art emphasized the enigma of existence and the subjective nature of reality. In the 1890's, a stylistic trend called *Art Nouveau* in France and *Jugendstil* in Germany spread across Europe and America, bringing into art and product design a preference for flat shapes and undulating, plantlike contours.

PAINTING

In France, the late eighteenth and early nineteenth centuries saw the triumph of Neoclassicism under the leadership of Jacques Louis David. During the early years of the nineteenth century, however, Neoclassic stylistic qualities were temporarily supplanted, in the work of many artists, by more irregular masses, deliberate merging and obscuring of some compositional parts, more individualistic details in anatomy, and more specific and contemporary details in accessories. These features, some of which recall seventeenth-century Baroque art, were particularly evident in the painting of Napoleonic history and were further developed, during the years after the fall of Napoleon, in much of the painting that has been called Romantic. The immediate ancestry of Romantic art can be found in the eighteenth-century enjoyment of the picturesque and in the sentimentality of such eighteenth-century painters as the Frenchman Jean Baptiste Greuze. Delacroix was considered to be the leader of Romanticism, while Ingres led academic art in the search for the ideal truth of Neoclassicism. The Salon of 1824 provided a confrontation of works by the two leaders, and it is from this date that the conflicting and overlapping attitudes of Neoclassicism and Romanticism assume major importance in French art.

Academically approved "classic landscape" painting, exemplified by Poussin's work, was superseded during the first half of the century by the art of certain French painters who turned to more direct experiences of nature. These *Barbizon painters* did much painting outdoors, in the forest of Fontainebleau near the village of Barbizon. Although the works were usually finished in the studio, they retained the freshness of firsthand experience in more casual, varied, and free compositions than those of academic landscape. The Barbizon painters made their debuts around 1830 but were not widely accepted until the second half of the century. Their delight in sensitive interpretation of the moods of nature, ranging from lyrical reverie to dramatic storm, links them with Romanticism, and their ancestry may be found in seventeenth-century Dutch landscape painting.

The mid-century was marked not only by political revolution but also by a new movement in French painting, *Realism*, which treated all facets of daily life in a style that showed frank enjoyment of the natural shapes, textures, and colors of things and a delight in the manipulation of the paint itself. In comparison with Realist work, the painting of the Barbizon artists and the exotic subjects, grand passions, glowing colors, and dashing brushwork of Delacroix became much more acceptable to conservative critics, and Realism succeeded Romanticism as the rebel of the period. The leader of the Realists, Gustave Courbet, was rebuked for the vulgarity in form and subject matter in his work.

The hegemony of the French Academy suffered a blow in 1863 when the outcry against the severity of the Salon jury caused the emperor to order an exhibition of rejected works, called the *Salon des Refusés*. Although the public tended to agree with the jury's decisions, the artist's right to exhibit outside the Salon was taken more seriously than before.

After about 1860, certain French artists, notably Édouard Manet, began to intensify their pictorial images by using patches of color relatively unbroken by internal modeling. An important inspiration for this trend was the Japanese woodblock print. The intensification of vision assumed another form in the stylistic movement called *Impressionism*, which made its formal debut in the exhibit of the *Société anonyme des artistes, peintres, sculpteurs, graveurs, etc.* in 1874. The momentary visual impression of a world of light and color in constant change became the major interest of Impressionist leaders like Claude Monet and Auguste Renoir, who went one step further than the Barbizon painters by finishing their paintings outdoors, working directly from the subject. Their patient study of the effects of light and color has been linked with the scientific study of optical phenomena, but they intensified the effects of shimmering light, reflected colors, and simultaneous contrasts, re-forming the visual world into a luminous matrix of small strokes of rich color. Their scientific objectivity seems to have been qualified by sensuous enjoyment of visual experience. By the 1890's, Impressionist work was grudgingly accepted by academic juries and even awarded occasional prizes.

Meanwhile, attitudes in academic painting had undergone changes. The fall of Napoleon had not stopped Napoleonic history painting, and the taste for specific details and local color that had been inspired by Napoleonic history was strengthened by an interest in the developing scientific methods in archaeology and history and by the exactitude of photography. Neoclassic painting was continued by some painters, but after mid-century, academic painters turned increasingly to precise, carefully researched details, and the truth of Neoclassic ideal form was supplanted in academic work by this documentary or archaeological truth.

In the 1880's and 1890's, a number of pioneering young painters who had tried Impressionist painting early in their careers came to feel that Impressionism sacrificed too much solidity of form and compositional structure for the sake of color and light. They therefore turned to very different styles in their mature painting. The most important of these men were Seurat, Van Gogh, Cézanne, and Gauguin. They have been called *Post-Impressionists*, and their styles forecast significant directions in the painting of the twentieth century.

German painting at the beginning of the nineteenth century was molded by the doctrines of Winckelmann and the influence of the Frenchman David. Rome was the training ground for many of the leading German painters, just as it had been for David (see p. 276). A group known as the *Nazarenes* sought new purity of religious content through a self-consciously simple, linear style inspired by Italian Renaissance art like that of Perugino and Raphael. Members of the Nazarene group later obtained positions of leadership in German academies at Düsseldorf, Munich, and Berlin. German Romanticism was expressed in styles that incorporated more precise detail than did those in France; evocations of nostalgia about the brevity of man's existence, the mysterious forces of nature, and the secret life of the individual recur frequently in paintings by Philipp O. Runge and by Caspar David Friedrich. Realism developed in the work of several Germans and was inspired either by Courbet or by the concept of documentary truth. Impressionism had a belated emergence in Germany.

In Italy, as in France and Germany, the major academies were dedicated to Neoclassicism in the early part of the century. A Romanticism that rejected Neoclassic ideal form for individualistic details made its appearance in Milan. By mid-century, a group of Roman painters called the *Macchiaiuoli* ("painters of spots") were employing bold patterns of color patches that forecast the style of Manet in France several years later. Documentary history painting became important in the second half of the century.

In England, the opening years of the nineteenth century were dominated by several of the great eighteenth-century portrait painters. As the century unfolded, genre painting found a wide market. Landscape painting was led by Constable, whose free brushwork influenced Delacroix, and by Turner, who exploited dramatic effects of light and color in both real and imaginary landscapes. In 1848, the *Brotherhood of Pre-Raphaelites* united several precocious young painters whose moralizing zeal was combined with a yearning for mystical experience, a love of involved literary symbolism and feverishly bright detail, and a desire to return to the style of art before Raphael. Carefully staged and precisely rendered history painting came from the brushes of academicians. Impressionism did not develop in England as it did in France. The American expatriate James McNeill Whistler was fascinated by Oriental art, and his muted, misty riverscapes of scenes along the Thames combine the broad patterns of Manet's art with Impressionistic interest in atmospheric effects. Whistler's English student, Walter Sickert, used more broken color, but his heavy, earthy style is quite unlike French Impressionism.

During the nineteenth century in the United States, patrons became increasingly more sophisticated and developed interests in a wider range of subject matter and style. Portraiture remained the type of painting in greatest demand, and style ranged from the facile brushwork of Thomas Sully to the sparkling detail of Thomas Eakins. Genre and landscape painting expressed a patriotic enthusiasm for the local customs and natural beauty of a rapidly growing America. The *Hudson River School*, a group of landscape painters dedicated to depicting Arcadian river views, might be compared with the Barbizon painters in France. During the second half of the century, a romantic nostalgia for grandeur and overpowering scale is evident in some landscape paintings. The mystery of nature was expressed in the glowing, somber landscapes and seascapes of Albert P. Ryder; the Impressionistic interest in natural light and color came only in the last decade of the century.

Francisco Goya (Spain, 1746–1828). While Goya's love of fantasy has led some historians to consider him a Romantic, his expository portrayal of human personality has inspired the term Realist. The latter designation seems more accurate in that even his imaginative work stresses the realistic acceptance of the role of the irrational in human experience; yet Goya's art is far different from that of the French Realists of the mid nineteenth century. Goya's teachers were minor masters, who had less influence on his art than did the paintings of Tiepolo and Velázquez. In his mature work, Goya used a dazzling variety of textures; his style ranges

17-1
FRANCISCO GOYA, *May Third, 1808*, 1814–15. Oil on canvas, approx. 9' x 11'. Prado, Madrid.

from harsh light and simplified forms to soft light and the effect of mass and detail seen through dense air. In *May Third, 1808* (Fig. 17-1), which shows Spanish citizens being shot by Napoleonic soldiers, a harsh style underscores the painting's social comment. The grouping of shapes into simple areas of light and dark intensifies the gestures of the subjects and the total impact of the composition; Goya here forecasts the art of Manet. Social commentary is implicit in some of Goya's portraits as well. *The Family of Charles IV* (1800, Prado, Madrid) candidly reveals the homeliness or viciousness of the different personalities and contrasts these with the luxurious costumes. Goya's frankness makes his official success surprising, for he became painter to the king and president of the Spanish Royal Academy. The most macabre and enigmatic of his works are the so-called *black paintings,* done on the walls of his house in the 1820's. His strongest social commentary and his most unrestrained fantasy are found in his prints. *The Caprices* (Fig. 4-3), a series of eighty-two aquatint etchings, depict man as unreasonable, petty, self-indulgent, and sadistic. *The Disparates,* a set of twenty-two aquatint etchings, reveal Goya's extraordinary imagination in a sequence of grotesque visions; they are frequently ambiguous in meaning, but the total effect is one of fascination and horror in the observation of man. Inhumanity and viciousness are the essence of *The Disasters of War,* a series of eighty-three aquatint etchings presenting a catalogue of barbaric cruelties in Spain during the period of Napoleonic control.

Jacques Louis David (France, 1748–1825). David lived through some of the most violent periods in French history, and his art spearheads one of the most drastic stylistic changes in French painting. As a student at the Paris Academy, David won a Prix de Rome in 1774 with a history painting done in the Baroque manner. During his sojourn in Rome, he changed his style in works like *The Oath of the Horatii* (Fig. 17-2), which caused great excitement. This composition is starkly simple; the figures form triangular or rectangular groupings, and the main elements are aligned with stable verticals and horizontals as well as with the picture plane. While the light is dramatic, it does not obscure the rigid structure of the painting. There is no softening effect of sfumato in the sharp contours of the forms. David's inspiration came from certain Greek and Roman works, from his teacher Joseph Vien, and from the theories of Johann J. Winckelmann, who praised the noble simplicity and calm grandeur of ancient Greek art. David's

17-2 JACQUES LOUIS DAVID, *The Oath of the Horatii*, 1784. Oil on canvas, approx. 10' x 14'. Louvre, Paris.

style, in its simplicity and strength, seemed the very antithesis of the aristocratic art of the Rococo, and David was adopted as the artist of the developing Revolution. Not only the style but also the subject of *The Oath of the Horatii* acquired political implications. Three Roman brothers, the Horatii, pledge to fight for Rome against three brothers, the Curiatii, from the city-state of Alba, to decide which city will rule the other. The wife of one of the Horatii is sister to one of the Curiatii, and one of the Horatii's sisters is betrothed to another of the Alban champions. Fatherland above family was the message carried by the painting. After the Revolution, David became a veritable dictator of the arts. His Neoclassical style was the order of the day, and he was powerful enough to have the Royal Academy abolished. However, David's painting changed in the early years of the nineteenth century. David and others were inspired by Napoleonic history, and Greco-Roman subjects gave way to dramatic contemporary events. The austere rigidity of David's early style softened to suggest more dramatic movement and more detailed accessories. For example, the *Bonaparte Crossing the Alps* (1800, Kunsthistorisches Museum, Vienna) employs unsupported contrasting diagonal forms quite unlike the stable triangular arrangements in David's earlier works. The search for timeless ideal human form changed to an interest in topical detail, as demonstrated by *The Coronation of Napoleon* (1805, Louvre, Paris). After the fall of Napoleon, David went into exile in Belgium, where he continued to produce portraits and also painted mythological subjects, which he treated in a less dramatic manner than that of his earlier style.

William Blake (England 1757–1827). Blake was an engraver, painter, poet, and visionary. He illustrated his own poems with hand-colored engravings. *The Creation of Eve* (Fig. 17-3), from Milton's *Paradise Lost*, is a watercolor incorporating typically linear, ideal, Neoclassic figures into a very personal vision. A flaming nimbus surrounds the body of Adam, and the light figures are set against a delicate foliage pattern, a black sky, and a crescent moon. His most famous works include twenty-one illustrations for *The Book of Job* (1820–26) and 102 illustrations for Dante's *Divine Comedy*. Blake's late style became more extraordinary in imagination, more extreme in figure proportions, and less clear in spatial relations. He drew inspiration from Medieval and Renaissance art. Some of his work was based on a mythology of his own, infused with personal mysticism. His art provides a link between Neoclassic form and the subjective dream world of many Romantics in the following generations. Blake also influenced Art Nouveau (see p. 271).

17-3 WILLIAM BLAKE, *The Creation of Eve,* from the *Paradise Lost* series, 1808. Pen and watercolor on paper. 19¾″ × 15¾″. Museum of Fine Arts, Boston. Gift by subscription.

Caspar David Friedrich (Germany, 1774–1840). Friedrich studied at the Academy of Copenhagen and moved to Dresden in 1798, where he joined a circle that included the Romantic writers Ludwig Tieck and Novalis and the painters Philipp Runge and Ferdinand von Olivier. In 1805, Friedrich's sepia drawings won a prize in a competition judged by Goethe. Friedrich's subjects tend to show a single person or a small group dwarfed by the vastness of nature. He loved grand scale, sweeping vistas, effects of sunrise or moonlight, and a mood of

17-4 CASPAR DAVID FRIEDRICH, *Cloister Graveyard in the Snow,* 1810. Approx. 47″ x 70″. Staatliche Museen, Berlin. (Now lost.)

17-5 JOSEPH MALLORD WILLIAM
TURNER, *Burning of the
Houses of Parliament,* 1834.
Oil on canvas, 36½" x 48½".
The Cleveland Museum of Art,
Bequest of John L. Severance.

solitude, meditation, or melancholy. He is identified with
Romanticism in Germany, as was Delacroix in France,
but there are wide differences between the styles of the
two men. Friedrich loved precise detail and patterns
formed by delicate silhouettes. His *Cloister Graveyard
in the Snow* (Fig. 17-4) is typical. The painting evokes
a powerful mood of melancholy. Although it has none
of the vigorous brushwork and apparent spontaneity
of Delacroix's art, it contains a similar suggestion of
man's tragic and ephemeral existence.

Joseph Mallord William Turner (England, 1775–1851).
Turner was first a watercolorist, adding color washes
to drawings by Thomas Girtin, but in the 1790's he
began painting landscapes in oil, his major sources of
influence being seventeenth-century Dutch landscape,
Claude Lorrain, and Nicolas Poussin. During walking
tours of England and France, he made thousands of
drawings that became the bases for many of his paintings. Turner worked in two styles: One recorded nature
in faithful detail and was the basis for his acceptance
by a part of his public; the other, thought of today as
the typical Turner, intensified the vast scale of nature
and the effects of light and atmosphere. Solid forms
dissolve in a shimmer of mist, glowing light, and iridescent color. *Rain, Steam, and Speed* (Plate 13) exploits
a combination of rain and the steam of a locomotive
for these effects. Sunrise, sunset, storm, and the clearing
after a storm were favorite moments for Turner. He

frequently used mythological subjects or motifs based on actual situations: a slave ship jettisoning its cargo or a grand old warship being towed to the scrapyard by a dirty tug. Because many of his works sacrifice detail for effects of light and color, Turner has been considered a source of French Impressionism, which developed in the latter half of the century (Fig. 17-5). But Turner's more imaginative paintings are visions that magnify the mystery and grandeur of nature; in this respect, they reflect the Romantic attitude.

John Constable (England, 1776–1837). Constable began life as the son of a country miller but in 1799 was admitted as a student to the Royal Academy in London. His mature style was considered to be crude and unfinished by some critics. *The Hay Wain* (Fig. 17-6), one of his best-known landscapes, was exhibited in 1821. Although considerably more detailed than a full-sized oil sketch of the subject (Victoria and Albert Museum, London), the final work has sparkling color and buttery paint application that create an effect of dewy freshness. The composition reflects the influence of Constable's idols, Claude Lorrain and Thomas Gainsborough, as well as of seventeenth-century Dutch landscape painting. *The Hay Wain* was exhibited in the Paris Salon of 1824. French critics, like the English, had mixed responses, but painters were impressed by the vigor and

17-6

JOHN CONSTABLE, *The Hay Wain*, 1821. Oil on canvas, approx. 4' x 6'. Courtesy of the Trustees of the National Gallery, London.

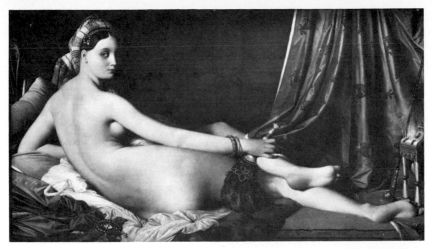

17-7 JEAN AUGUSTE DOMINIQUE INGRES, *Grande Odalisque,* 1814. Oil on canvas, approx. 35″ x 64″ Louvre, Paris.

freedom of the execution. Delacroix is said to have repainted the background of his 1824 Salon entry after having seen Constable's painting. Along with Turner, Constable helped to open the way for the freer interpretation of landscape later in the nineteenth century.

Jean Auguste Dominique Ingres (France, 1780–1867). David's replacement as leader of academic Neoclassicism did not emerge immediately. The early work of Ingres, a pupil of David, was criticized for the distortions of anatomy and complexities of drapery that the young artist created in the interests of rhythmic line. Ingres was happy, therefore, having won a Prix de Rome with a carefully constructed academic exercise, to leave France in 1806 for Florence and Rome. This first sojourn lasted eighteen years. The *Grande Odalisque* (Fig. 17-7) reveals Ingres's Neoclassic training, his love of Raphaelesque ovoid forms, his use of arbitrary human proportions, his contrast of smooth flesh with complex drapery, and his highly finished paint surfaces. His portraits, done in paint and in pencil, display great linear elegance. In 1824, his Salon contribution, *The Vow of Louis XIII,* was so successful that he returned to Paris as the leader of academic painting and became president of the École des Beaux-Arts. Academic teaching under Ingres's leadership was very dogmatic; he insisted that drawing was the basis of art, and he stressed sharply defined contours and smooth finish. He was considered to be the leader of Neoclassicism and the foe of Romanticism; at the Paris International Exposition of 1855, the most lavish representation in the exhibit of French painting was accorded the paintings of Ingres and Delacroix.

17-8 J. A. D. INGRES, *Portrait of Count Antoine Apponayi,* 1823. Graphite and white chalk on paper, 17¹³⁄₁₆″ x 13⅝″ Courtesy, Fogg Art Museum, Harvard U., Grenville L. Winthrop Bequest.

17-9 CAMILLE COROT, *Democritus and the Abderites*, 1841. Oil on canvas, approx. 4'11" x 3'11". Musée des Beaux-Arts, Nantes.

Camille Corot (France, 1796–1875). Corot was born in Paris and trained by painters of classic landscape in the tradition of Poussin. During a sojourn in Italy in the 1820's, Corot developed landscapes with bold masses and simplified areas of light and dark, usually grouped around a horizontal or vertical axis, as in *Democritus and the Abderites* (Fig. 17-9). In the 1840's, he turned to the silvery, cloudlike foliage and poetic delicacy typified by *Souvenir de Mortefontaine* (Plate 14). Small flecks of light-colored flowers float against deep shadows; light filters through the leaves, and hazy banks of foliage step back into space. Although Corot occasionally peopled his landscapes with Grecian nymphs, his scenes are more earthbound than those of Turner. Corot's landscapes are based on a lifetime of outdoor drawing and painting; he was associated with the Barbizon painters. Until the twentieth century, Corot's figure paintings were less appreciated than his landscapes. Most are portraits of anonymous people whom Corot painted in subtle colors and solid forms and with quiet dignity, using some of the broad simple areas of value and color that are typical of his early work. Corot was awarded the Legion of Honor in 1846 and lived to see his works forged to meet a growing demand by collectors.

Eugène Delacroix (France, 1798–1863). For Delacroix, the most important qualities in painting were vitality and the sensuous appeal of color. Although his teacher was the academic painter Guerin, his real inspiration was the art of Michelangelo and Rubens; Delacroix was a descendant of the *Rubénistes*. While his subjects usually came from literature, as did those of Ingres, Delacroix's painting seemed violent, crude, and unfinished to Ingres and his followers. *The Lion Hunt* (Plate 15) recalls similar subjects by Rubens and reveals Delacroix's love of dramatic action and exotic settings; a trip to Morocco in 1832 and the reading of Byron's *Childe Harold* had fired his enthusiasm for the Near East. The writhing entanglement of hunters, horses, and lions suggests the eternal struggle between man and his environment, a theme dear to Delacroix and to Romantic art and literature. The explosive energy of the composition is organized within an oval of light. The blurred edges, the *lost and found* (discontinuous) outlines, rapid brush strokes, vigorous paint texture, and touches of bold color all make the action more convincing. Delacroix did not seek the timeless ideal form and precise sleek finish of Ingres's painting, nor did he employ the heroic proportions of Rubens' figures. The sense of immediate, everyday reality in Delacroix's treatment of literary themes comes in part from his use

17-10 EUGÈNE DELACROIX, *The Abduction of Rebecca.* 1846. Oil on canvas, 39½" x 32¼". Metropolitan Museum of Art, New York. Purchase, 1903, The Wolfe Fund.

of ordinary human proportions, like those of the people in the paintings of Rembrandt. It is not surprising that Delacroix's painting is often described as emotional and that of Ingres as intellectual; yet Delacroix's *Journals* indicate that he had a calculating nature, while Ingres's emotional nature was well known. The apparent freedom and spontaneity of Delacroix's canvases were achieved with deliberation and method. He learned much from the dynamic compositions of his fellow student Théodore Géricault and from the English painter Constable, who often placed colors side by side rather than blending them smoothly together. Delacroix's use of complementary colors to obtain liveliness within shadow areas forecasts the practices of the Impressionists. In spite of official opposition to his work, Delacroix received a number of important mural commissions and was finally granted membership in the Academy in 1857.

Honoré Daumier (Paris, 1808–79). Daumier's keen powers of observation and his remarkable ability as a draftsman compensated for his lack of formal training. He earned a meager living as a cartoonist, using woodcuts for book illustrations and lithography for political journals like *La Caricature* and *Le Charivari*. The bourgeoisie, the law courts, and the government all provided material for Daumier, but his main protests were against the shortcomings of human nature on all

17-11
HONORÉ DAUMIER, *Behind in the Rent,* 1847. Lithograph, 10⅛'' x 7½''. Courtesy of the Boston Public Library, Print Department.

17-12
HONORÉ DAUMIER, *The Third-Class Carriage, c.* 1865. Oil on canvas, 25¾'' x 35½''. Havemeyer Collection, Metropolitan Museum of Art, New York, Bequest of Mrs. H. O. Havemeyer, 1929.

17-13
GUSTAVE COURBET, *The Rock Breakers,*
1849. Formerly in the Staatliche
Kunstsammlungen, Dresden (painting lost
during Second World War)

social levels (Fig. 17-11). His work ranges from brutal caricature to gentle humor and warm appreciation of life. Daumier was essentially an optimist endowed with the grace of liking people in spite of their failings. Unlike Goya, he was realistic without being bitter. Daumier's oil paintings were relatively unknown until his first exhibition, which was in 1878, the year before his death. While the prints rely on line reduced to its most essential and expressive gesture, the paintings depend on starkly simple masses modeled in strong chiaroscuro. *The Third-Class Carriage* (Fig. 17-12) retains the sensitive line characteristic of his lithography; yet the use of light and mass is typical of his oils.

Gustave Courbet (France, 1819–77). While various aspects of realism are basic to the art of Goya and of Daumier, the artist who chose the term Realism for his battle standard was Courbet. He came from a farm to Paris and had several of his early works accepted by the Salon. His notoriety and his leadership in French painting began with the Salon of 1850, where his *Rock Breakers* (Fig. 17-13) and *Funeral at Ornans* (Louvre, Paris) were attacked as unartistic, crude, and socialistic. His early works had been admitted to the Salon because their moody chiaroscuro fitted the now acceptable qualities of much Romantic painting. His mature work stresses the physical reality of the everyday world and the artist's enjoyment of paint textures. Neither the polite veil of the acceptable ideal form of Ingres nor the exotic dramatic subject matter of Delacroix appealed to Courbet, who preferred subjects from his own experience and painted them with an obvious enjoyment of the texture of the paint itself, which he applied with brush and palette knife. The epithet "socialistic" came partly from the combination of style and subject that made *The Rock Breakers* look like ragged workers doing a miserable task—the wrong kind of content for a bourgeoisie still frightened by the socialist uprising that occurred after the Revolution of 1848—and partly from the perennial tendency of some critics to ascribe any deviation from conventional standards in the arts to the latest unpopular political movement. Courbet was adopted as a standard-bearer by the socialist philosopher Proudhon, but his painting continued to be a fresh appreciation of the people and the landscape around him. During the International Expositions of 1855 and 1867 in Paris, Courbet built his own pavilions of Realism and held private showings of his work, thus helping to establish the artist's right to have privately organized exhibitions.

Édouard Manet (France, 1832–83). The most shocking painting in the Salon des Refusés of 1863 was the *Luncheon on the Grass* (*Déjeuner sur l'Herbe*) (Fig. 17-14) by Manet. Earlier work by the painter had been accepted; Manet had come from a wealthy family and had studied under the academic painter Couture. He had even won an honorable mention in the Salon of

17-14
ÉDOUARD MANET, *Luncheon on the Grass* (*Déjeuner sur l'Herbe*). 1863. Oil on canvas, approx. 7' x 9'. Galerie du Jeu de Paume, Paris.

17-15
ÉDOUARD MANET, *The Bar at the Folies-Bergère*, 1881–82. Oil on canvas, 37" x 51". Courtauld Institute Galleries, London.

1861. Neither the subject nor the style of the *Luncheon on the Grass*, however, was considered proper by the public or by many critics. Manet had taken the basic idea from Giorgione (Plate 6) and had borrowed the poses of the main figure group from an engraving of a Raphael painting of the *Judgment of Paris*, but he had omitted the mythological context and shown a nude woman in the company of two well-dressed contemporary Frenchmen. Further, the forms are reduced to large simple areas of color and value; few highlights or shadows break up the shapes. The brushwork is bold and rejoices in the texture of the paint. Frans Hals and Rembrandt, not to mention Delacroix, had used bold brushwork, but without such drastic simplification of form. After 1874, Manet's style changed; the large forms were broken more and more into small areas of bright color, and he increasingly depicted outdoor scenes and effects of light. His late work is represented by *The Bar at the Folies-Bergère* (Fig. 17-15). Here the intensity of vision is different from that in the early work. The shimmering light and color partially fuses the forms and suggests a momentary glimpse during an ebb and flow of constant change. Manet owed this vision to the young Impressionists.

Edgar Degas (France, 1834–1917). Manet's friend Degas also came from a family of means. Degas admired Delacroix but idolized Ingres and studied under one of Ingres's pupils. Line was the most natural medium

17-16
EDGAR DEGAS, *Foyer de la Danse,* 1872.
12½" x 18⅛". Camondo Collection, Louvre,
Paris.

of expression for Degas, but he was not interested in adopting the ideal forms of Neoclassicism. He found his favorite subjects in the streets of Paris, the cafes, races, theaters, and women's boudoirs. The *Foyer de la Danse* (Fig. 17-16) is typical of Degas' unconventional composition and reflects the influence of Japanese prints. An irregular, diamond-shaped spatial disposition is made by the dancer on the far left, the background dancers, the group around the ballet master, and the foreground chair. Architecture supports the figure arrangement through the placement of the arch, the corner of the room, the open door on the left, and the practice bar. The center of the composition contains only the psychological tension between the ballet master's group and the dancer receiving his correction. Such focus of attention helps the lone figure on the left counterbalance the greater weight of objects on the right. Unlike Manet, Degas often chose to depict the marginal event, the wings of the stage, as though the essential meaning could best be seen in those watching or waiting to perform. It is this "keyhole" vision, inspired partly by Japanese prints, that gives the impression of a momentary glimpse in Degas' particular kind of Impressionism, which differed sharply from that of the Impressionist leader Claude Monet. Degas did not subscribe to the soft form and vague edges in Monet's

Plate 17
PAUL CÉZANNE, *Mt. Ste.-Victoire from Bibemus Quarry,* c 1898. Oil on canvas,
25½″ x 32″. Baltimore Museum of Art, Cone Collection.

Plate 18
CLAUDE MONET, *Rouen Cathedral*, 1894. Oil on canvas, approx. 39¼'' x 25⅞''. National
Gallery of Art, Washington, D.C.

Plate 19
AUGUSTE RENOIR, *Little Blue Nude, c.* 1880. Oil on canvas, 18¼'' x 15⅛''. Albright-Knox
Art Gallery, Buffalo. General Purchase Funds.

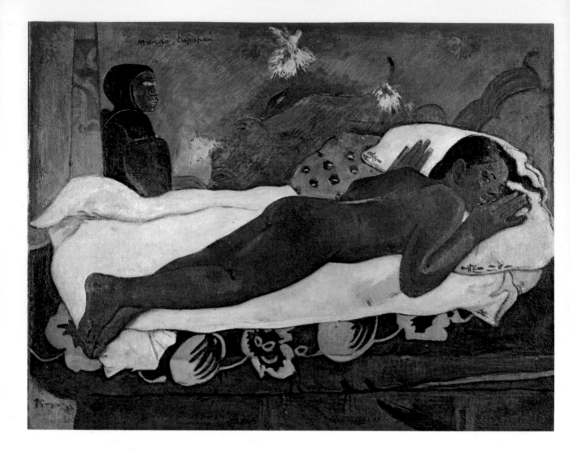

Plate 20
PAUL GAUGUIN, *The Spirit of the Dead Watching*. 1892. Oil on canvas, 28¾″ x 36¼″.
Albright-Knox Art Gallery, Buffalo. A. Conger Goodyear Collection.

Plate 21
VINCENT VAN GOGH, *Enclosed Field*, 1890. Oil on canvas, 28½" x 36¼." State Museum Kröller-Müller, Otterlo.

Plate 22
GEORGES SEURAT, *Sunday Afternoon on the Island of La Grande Jatte*, 1884–86. Oil on canvas, approx. 8′9″ x 10′. Art Institute of Chicago, Helen Birch Bartlett Memorial Collection.

Plate 23
VASSILY KANDINSKY, *Painting with White Form, No. 166*, 1913. Oil on canvas, 47″ x 54⅜″. The Solomon R. Guggenheim Museum, New York.

Plate 24
PIERRE BONNARD, *The Palm,* 1926. Oil on canvas, 44″ x 57½″. The Phillips Collection, Washington, D.C.

Plate 25
HENRI MATISSE, *Decorative Figure on an Ornamental Background*, 1927. Oil on canvas, approx. 48″ x 36″. Musée National d'Arte Moderne, Paris.

Plate 26
GEORGES ROUAULT, *The Old King*, 1916–38. Oil on canvas, approx. 30¼ x 21¼''.
Collection, Museum of Art, Carnegie Institute, Pittsburgh (Patrons Art Fund).

Plate 27
PABLO PICASSO, *Three Musicians,* 1921. Oil on canvas, 80″ x 74″. The Philadelphia Museum of Art: The A. E. Gallatin Collection.

Plate 28
JOAN MIRÓ, *Dutch Interior, I,* 1928. Oil on canvas, 36⅛ x 28¾". Collection, The Museum
of Modern Art, New York. Mrs. Simon Guggenheim Fund.

Plate 29
HANS HOFMANN, *Bird Cage, Variation II*, 1958. Oil on canvas, 60'' x 48''. Collection of
Mr. and Mrs. Saul Z. Cohen, Larchmont, New York.

Plate 30
MARK ROTHKO, *Brown and Black on Plum,* 1958. Oil on canvas, 80″ x 82″. Private
Collection, Zurich.

Plate 31
WILLEM DE KOONING, *Woman I*, 1950–52. Oil on canvas, 6'3⅞'' x 58''. Collection, The
Museum of Modern Art, New York. Purchase.

Plate 32
VICTOR VASARELY, *YMPO*, 1970. Acrylic on canvas, 67'' x 99½''. Galerie Denise René,
New York.

work until late in his career. While Monet saw human forms merely as objects reflecting light and color, Degas showed strong interest in the character of individuals. In his later work, Degas abandoned oil for pastels; soft light and glowing, broken colors are combined with firm anatomical structure and the softened but ever-present contour (Plate 16). His relatively traditional use of line enabled Degas to exhibit frequently at the Salon. Although he disliked the term Impressionism, he participated in most of the eight Impressionist exhibits. Degas modeled wax and clay statuettes of dancers and horses, many of which have expressive poses and rough surfaces that produce multiple highlights, making the sculptures comparable to some of his drawings and paintings.

Winslow Homer (United States, 1836–1910). Homer's early work in magazine illustration emphasized bold massing of values and incisive characterization. He made a sensational debut as an oil painter with Civil War subjects. His paintings of genre scenes show a keen interest in outdoor light and atmospheric effects. He turned increasingly to elemental subjects of man and nature: the lone hunter, the struggle of boats in rapids, and the violence of the sea. His watercolors range in technique from broad sweeping brush strokes with sparkling transparent washes to small areas of

17-17
WINSLOW HOMER, *The Artist's Studio in an Afternoon Fog,* 1894. Rochester Memorial Gallery, University of Rochester.

overlapping washes and careful detail. Both in water-colors and in oils Homer subordinated detail to large areas of contrasting values that strengthen the visual impact of the composition. This aspect of his style is exemplified in *The Artist's Studio in an Afternoon Fog* (Fig. 17-17), an oil study in browns that has satisfying variations in its simple proportions. Certain angles in the roofs echo the powerful middle-ground diagonal plane, which seems to express the conflict of land and sea; this darkest area is set against the small patch of water and foam that receives the brightest highlights in the painting and outshines the veiled sun. Homer's method of working was apparently instinctive, for he denied that he modified nature for the sake of art.

Paul Cézanne (France, 1839–1906). One of the most celebrated of the Post-Impressionist painters was Cézanne, who came from Aix-en-Provence to Paris and studied at the Académie Suisse, an unusual institution that provided models and working space but no instruction. The young artist admired Delacroix and Courbet but also several of the academic painters. Cézanne's early work is characterized by dark values, bold awkward forms, and thick paint handled in such a way as to suggest powerful feelings. In the 1870's, he turned to Impressionist painting and exhibited the *House of the Hanged Man* (Fig. 17-18) in the first Impressionist show in 1874. He came to feel, however, that Impressionism sacrificed too much solidity and structure, and in the 1880's he changed to the style for

17-18
PAUL CÉZANNE. *The House of the Hanged Man.* 1873–74. Oil on canvas, 22¼'' x 26¾''. Louvre, Paris.

which he is well known today. Cézanne's portraits, still lifes, and landscapes all reduce objects to basic planes and masses that are brought into subtle complementary relationships on the canvas. The *Mt. Ste.-Victoire from Bibemus Quarry* (Plate 17) is typical in the small groups of parallel brush strokes that suggest massive form in mountain, in foliage, and even in sky. Lost and found outlines define the masses but allow them to flow into each other at various points, and the planes and angles of the forms are echoed and modulated throughout the canvas. All the forms acquire a structural unity—a family resemblance—in this way. Roundness is achieved not only with light and shadow but also with advancing and receding colors. Yet all forms are obviously constructed with paint, and there is a paradoxical suggestion of mass and depth and at the same time of a flat painted surface. In contrast to Impressionist painting, Cézanne's mature work emphasizes a static structure that largely excludes motion or the changing effects of light and weather. His link with the past can be found in the art of Poussin. Cézanne's importance for the future was summed up in his advice to a young painter to paint nature in terms of the cylinder, the sphere, and the cone—that is, the basic geometric forms. This is generally what was done in Cubist art, which began in 1907, a year after Cézanne's death and the same year as his first large retrospective exhibition.

Odilon Redon (France, 1840–1916). Redon came from Bordeaux to Paris in 1864. He devoted much of his time to charcoal drawings and albums of lithographs, but he also worked in oils and pastels. His titles, referring to dreams, the works of Edgar Allan Poe and Goya, the Temptation of St. Anthony, and Baudelaire's *Fleurs du Mal*, indicate Redon's concern with fantasy. *The Cyclops* (Fig. 17-19) reveals a dream world of iridescent color and floating forms. His monsters, spiders, and ghostly faces seem more playful or melancholy than frightening. Many of his flower paintings are simply delicate, ethereal bouquets; others contain apparitions of faces. His gentle, mysterious work was discovered by the French Symbolist writers in the 1880's, and Redon was labeled a Symbolist and admired by the painters known as the *Nabis* (see p. 295).

Claude Monet (France, 1840–1926). Monet came from Le Havre to Paris and studied at the Académie Suisse and in the studio of the academic painter Gleyre, where

17-19
ODILON REDON, *The Cyclops*, 1900–05. 25¼″ x 20″. Rijksmuseum Kröller-Müller, Otterlo.

17-20 CLAUDE MONET, *Impression: Sunrise,* 1872. Oil on canvas, 19⅝'' x 25½''. Musée Marmottan (Collection Donop de Monchy), Paris.

he met Renoir and several other young men who would later participate in the Impressionist movement. In Le Havre, Monet early acquired a love of painting outdoors, partly through the example of his older friends Eugène Boudin and Johan Jongkind. His early style was bold in color and vigorous in brushwork. Large unbroken areas recall the art of Manet; yet the Salons of 1865 and 1866 accepted some seascapes and a portrait by Monet and praised him as a "naturalist." However, as he went further in his studies of the effects of light on color and as his forms became less clearly defined, Monet was continually rejected by juries. In 1874, his *Impression: Sunrise* (Fig. 17-20) caused the label "Impressionism" to be attached to the exhibition by critics. The smoldering light of the rising sun coming through mist and shimmering on the surface of the water is rendered in loose brush strokes and vague forms, a technique meant to distill the total visual impression of a particular moment. For many critics this appeared to be sheer incompetence. Seeking more subtle distinctions in changing light and color, Monet sometimes worked in series, painting the same subject—a haystack, a railway station, or the cathedral of Rouen—in various kinds of light. *Rouen Cathedral* (Plate 18) employs the complementary colors blue and orange in separate brushstrokes to create a vibrating mirage-like image that sacrifices solid form for intensity of visual experience. Had the blues and oranges been blended by the brush, they would have neutralized rather than intensified one another. Where the brush strokes are small enough to allow the spectator's eyes to "mix" the colors when viewing the painting at a distance (*optical mixing*), the effects range from intense color to lively grays. The Impressionist process of applying colors separately in order to exploit their effects on each other is called the technique of *broken color*. By the 1890's, Monet's series paintings had met with considerable success; his approach could be appreciated as scientific, although scientific interest is not a satisfactory explanation of his work. There is an intensification or exaggeration of natural color and light effects—typified in Plate 18—that comes from the artist's sensuous enjoyment of such phenomena. The subject of Monet's last great series, spread over the latter years of his life, was a pond with water lilies. Here the imaginative quality of his art grew more evident, and the paintings became increasingly abstract.

Auguste Renoir (France, 1841–1919). Renoir, Monet's friend and fellow Impressionist, began as an apprentice to a porcelain decorator and then studied with the academic painter Gleyre. His early work consists of rather tightly detailed landscapes and earthy, solidly painted nudes that show the influence of Courbet. Renoir was accepted by the Salon in the 1860's and occasionally thereafter. Like Monet, he turned increasingly to broken color and the evanescent effects of light.

17-21 AUGUSTE RENOIR. *The Swing*. 1876. Oil on canvas, 35¾" x 28". Louvre, Paris.

He managed to obtain a number of portrait commissions, and these were usually executed with more detail than his other subjects. During his travels in the 1880's, his encounter with Raphael's paintings in Italy led him to return temporarily to sharper outlines and curved forms in flowing, rhythmical relationships. In the work that followed, the interest in curving forms remained, but contours were softened. Woman is the main subject, and Renoir gave her his personal concept of ideal form: soft masses of flesh in delicate, luminous colors. In *Little Blue Nude* (Plate 19), color and light suggest full volumes while paradoxically dissolving solid form. The impersonal treatment of the human figure in earlier work here gives way to a mystical reverence for woman as a symbol for the fecundity and glory of nature.

Thomas Eakins (United States, 1844–1916). Eakins first studied at the Pennsylvania Academy of Fine Arts in Philadelphia and then went to Paris in 1866, right after the stormy Salon des Refusés and during Manet's notoriety. Eakins studied with the French academic painter Jean L. Gérôme, however, and his art shows little influence of the young French painters of the day. He seems to have been more sympathetic to the art of Velázquez and Ribera, which he saw during a trip to Spain. Upon his return, Eakins settled in Philadelphia and spent the rest of his career painting the people and the life around him. His major interests were the individual character of a human face, the anatomical structure of the body, and the rich variety of textures and

17-22 THOMAS EAKINS, *The Agnew Clinic*, 1889. Oil on canvas, 6'2'' x 10'10''. Courtesy of the University of Pennsylvania.

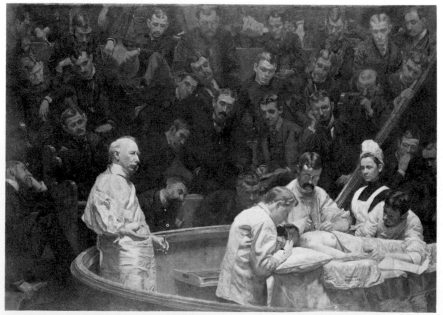

details in all things. *The Agnew Clinic* (Fig. 17-22) is typical of his detailed observation of contemporary life. The dramatic focus in the painting stems from sharp tonal contrasts, actual and suggested diagonal forces in the background, the curved rail, and the separated and distinctive figure of the speaker.

Paul Gauguin (France, 1848–1903).   As a young man, Gauguin developed a promising career in a brokerage firm, collected Impressionist paintings, and painted as a hobby. This hobby eventually led him to leave his secure situation and seek a career as a full-time painter. Partly to live less expensively and partly because he was fascinated by primitive societies, he went to Brittany (first to Pont-Aven and then to Le Pouldu). His early work there was Impressionistic; but under the influence of Cézanne, Manet, Japanese prints, and the young painter Bernard's use of flat shapes, Gauguin slowly turned away from broken color and began to use outlines around areas of closely modulated color. The color areas became more closed, suggesting flat textile patterns, and color contrasts became bolder. Several young men joined Gauguin in Brittany and accepted him as their leader. These Pont-Aven artists chose the word *synthesism* to describe their painting. Later the term *symbolist-synthesist* was used frequently as Gauguin became acquainted with some of the Symbolist writers. Two of the Pont-Aven painters joined the *Nabis* (Hebrew for prophets), a group that derived some of its symbolism from the mysticism of Theosophy, but Gauguin maintained an independent attitude. His symbolism expresses the mystery and the imaginative life of primitive peoples. In 1891 he traveled to Tahiti, where he produced such works as *The Spirit of the Dead Watching* (Plate 20). Here resonant hues of yellows, purples, oranges, and blues join the flat patterns that set off the ponderous, solid body of the frightened girl lying on a bed. The spirits of the dead, represented by small flashes of light, and a ghost, represented by a woman in profile, watch from above and behind. His sculptures and woodcuts from this period were influential in early twentieth-century expressionistic art. Gauguin returned to Paris for a short time (1893–95) and rapidly spent a small inheritance. He was soon back in Tahiti, where his health began to fail. His last two years were spent in the Marquesas Islands.

Vincent Van Gogh (Holland and France, 1853–90).   Van Gogh was a Dutchman, but most of his painting was done in France during the last four years of a short

17-23 PAUL GAUGUIN, *The Moon and the Earth*, 1893. Oil on burlap. 45" x 24½". Collection, The Museum of Modern Art, New York, Lillie P. Bliss Collection.

17-24 VINCENT VAN GOGH, *The Potato Eaters*, 1885. Oil on canvas, 32¼″ x 44⅞″. Municipal Museum, Amsterdam, V. W. Van Gogh Collection.

but intense life. After abortive attempts at working for art dealers (in The Hague, London, and Paris), studying theology, and preaching evangelism among coal miners, Van Gogh turned to painting in 1880. Millet, Daumier, and Rembrandt were the idols of his early period; in works like *The Potato Eaters* (Fig. 17-24), poverty-stricken workers are compassionately portrayed with heavy blunt forms and dark brownish color. In 1886, Van Gogh settled in Paris with his brother Theo. Study with the academic painter Cormon soon gave way to enthusiasm for the Impressionists. Under the encouragement of Camille Pissarro, Van Gogh's colors became brighter and lighter, and he began to use broken color; yet his brush strokes have a writhing liveliness unlike those in most Impressionist work. While in Paris, Van Gogh became acquainted with Japanese prints, such as those shown in the background of his portrait of *Père Tanguy* (1887–88, Collection of Stavros Niarchos, Athens). In 1888, Van Gogh left Paris for Arles in southern France. His compositions began to employ more powerful colors, often clashing complementaries; thick paint textures that seem to be sculpted with the brush or the palette knife; and shapes whose abruptly changing contours express a convulsive energy. Van Gogh was subject to occasional epileptoid seizures, and these led to a year's residence in the asylum at Saint-Rémy. The *Enclosed Field* (Plate 21) is a work typical of this period in its glowing colors and in the dancing, twitching rhythm that activates earth and sky.

Paint is applied in short, choppy strokes that seem to sculpt edges and surfaces. From Saint-Rémy, Van Gogh went to Auvers, near Paris, to receive treatment from Dr. Gachet, a friend of Pissarro, and it was at the small village of Auvers that he committed suicide. His imaginative use of color, his expressive distortion of natural forms, and the emotional force of his art made him an important source for many trends in twentieth-century painting, particularly Fauvism and Expressionism. His letters to his brother Theo are, with Delacroix's journal, among the richest documents of modern art.

17-25 VINCENT VAN GOGH. *Portrait of Dr. Gachet,* 1890. Oil on canvas, 26″ x 22½″. Anonymous New York collection.

Georges Seurat (France, 1859–91). The last Impressionist exhibition, in 1886, was marked by dissension; Monet and Renoir were both absent. A central problem was the new approach represented by Seurat and his followers. Their works were displayed in a separate room and their style, generally subsumed under the label of Post-Impressionism, came to be called *Neo-Impressionism*. The intensity of light and color in Impressionist work appealed to Seurat, but he felt—as did Cézanne—that mass and compositional structure had been unduly sacrificed; so he set out to systematize the broken color of Impressionism and to clarify its forms. On the basis of the color theories of Michel Chevreul and Charles Henry, Seurat applied colors in uniformly small dots in specific quantities to create particular effects when the spectator experienced optical mixing. Seurat's technique was called *pointillism* in regard to the paint application and *divisionism* in regard to the systematically broken color. The suggestion of constant change and movement found in much Impressionist work was replaced, in Seurat's painting, by more rigid organization and static form. In his *Sunday Afternoon on the Island of La Grande Jatte* (Plate 22 and Fig. 17-26) the shadows, trees, and figures form static horizontals and verticals; the clearly edged and simplified forms become standard rather than individual objects; and there is a quality of geometric order, of inflexible balance, and of calculated method. In 1884 Seurat became one of the founders of the *Salon des Indépendants*, which provided exhibition opportunities without jury selection and thus answered one of the basic needs that had inspired the Impressionist exhibitions between 1874 and 1886.

17-26

GEORGES SEURAT. detail from *Sunday Afternoon on the Island of La Grande Jatte,* 1884–86. Oil on canvas, approx. 7′ x 11′. Art Institute of Chicago.

James Ensor (Belgium, 1860–1949). After studying at Ostend and Brussels, Ensor became a painter and printmaker; he worked with still-life, landscape, marine, religious, and mythological subjects, ranging from

everyday scenes to frightening grotesqueries involving men, animals, and monsters. His early art employed gentle lighting and subtle colors, although the paint was often applied vigorously with a palette knife. In the course of the 1880's, fantasy invaded his subject matter, and paint application became increasingly nervous and complex. *Masks Confronting Death* (Fig. 17-27) is typical in its combination of delicate color and grotesque subject. It recalls late Medieval prints depicting the Dance of Death. Ensor's etching *The Vengeance of the Hop Frog* (1898) combines cruelty with a Bosch-like imagination. In his most macabre works, Ensor mixed religious and scatological elements; yet at the same time, he continued to paint still-life, landscape, and marine subjects like those of the early period. While some of his more conventional paintings owe much to Impres-

sionism, the highly imaginative compositions are more closely related to the Expressionist art of the late nineteenth and early twentieth centuries.

Gustav Klimt (Austria, 1862–1918). Klimt both studied and worked in Vienna. In 1897, he became the first president of the Vienna Secession, an organization of artists opposed to conservative art. In *Death and Life* (Fig. 17-28) Klimt used two-dimensional shapes, stressed undulating contours, and exploited intricate, abstract patterns based on geometric and plant motifs for symbolic purposes. His art can be seen as a significant contribution within the introspective and symbolic tendencies of the late nineteenth and early twentieth centuries and within the stylistic trend of Art Nouveau.

Edvard Munch (Norway, 1863–1944). A government grant for study in Paris from 1889 to 1892 and a controversial exhibition of his work in Berlin in 1892 were major events in the formation of Munch's style and his recognition as a leading figure in the modern movement. During the Paris sojourn, his style changed from a boldly painted, factual presentation modified by Impressionist light to stronger, simpler, and more arbitrary colors and shapes. Toulouse-Lautrec and Gauguin were major influences. The Berlin exhibit was closed as a result of pressure by conservatives, and Munch became a celebrity among young German painters and an important influence on the *Brücke* group (see p. 347). *The Cry* (Fig. 17-29) employs dissonant colors, undulating shapes, and violent perspective to express the tension and anxiety characteristic of Munch's art. He intended many of his works to be part of a *Frieze of Life*, a series that was never finished.

Henri de Toulouse-Lautrec (France, 1864–1901). The extreme dissoluteness of Toulouse-Lautrec's life, his aristocratic ancestry, and his dwarfed and crippled body have made dramatic material for biographies. In spite of the dissipated life he led, however, his short career was remarkably productive. After training in the studio of an academic painter and working in an Impressionistic vein, Toulouse-Lautrec formed a style closely related to that of Degas. His *At the Moulin Rouge* (Fig. 17-30) is a casual passing glimpse of the cabaret life that provided many of his subjects. The large areas of color function as bold patterns and reveal the influence of Japanese prints and the paintings of Degas. As in Degas'

17-29 EDVARD MUNCH, *The Cry.* 1893. 33" x 26½". Nasjonalgalleriet, Oslo.

17-30
HENRI DE TOULOUSE-LAUTREC, *At the Moulin Rouge*, 1892. Oil on canvas, approx. 48⅜'' x 55¼''. Helen Birch Bartlett Memorial Collection, Art Institute of Chicago.

work, movement is expressed by the contours of active shapes, the sweeping asymmetrical diagonals, and the extension of major figures beyond the edges of the composition. Like Degas, but unlike many of the other Impressionists, Toulouse-Lautrec was interested in human personality. His depictions of Paris dandies and prostitutes show a sensitivity that neither condones nor criticizes but mercilessly reveals the monotony, the frantic efforts to live fully, the cynicism, the lust, and the gaiety of a certain stratum of international society. His famous posters for several of the cabarets are brilliant demonstrations of lithography applied to advertising art. Toulouse-Lautrec never became a member of the Impressionist group; he belongs more properly with the Post-Impressionists.

SCULPTURE

Nineteenth-century sculpture was less inventive than painting, and stylistic trends are less distinct. After the Revolution, France gave preference to the clear sweeping lines and ideal forms of Neoclassic sculpture. Napoleon supported this preference and commissioned portraits from the Italian Neoclassicist Antonio Canova. The Romantic attitude in sculpture became apparent in the Salons of 1833 and 1834, when rough surfaces, individualized features, and entangled forms were used to accentuate active subjects, as in the work of Antoine Barye and François Rude. The second half of the century saw more precise anatomical and costume detail. The major figure in French sculpture of the late nineteenth and early twentieth centuries was Rodin, who combined an interest in lively, rippling surfaces with expressions of man's aspirations and of conflicts between mind and body.

During the first half of the century Italy was the center of Neoclassic sculpture, which was led by Antonio Canova. During the second half of the nineteenth century, the tendency toward increasingly naturalistic detail was international.

Antonio Canova (Italy, 1757–1822). Canova was trained in Venice and developed an early style that combined naturalistic detail with late Baroque composition. When he moved to Rome in 1779, however, and studied Roman ruins and ancient sculpture, his style changed to the simplified anatomy, long sweeping curves, and quiet compositions that became representative of the Neoclassic aesthetic. The *Pauline Borghese as Venus* (Fig. 17-31) presents an idealized portrait of Napoleon's sister in a serene pose with clear stately contours in a static alignment of vertical and horizontal elements. The composition seeks an absolute beauty outside the reach of motion, change, or time.

François Rude (France and Belgium, 1784–1855). Rude studied in Dijon and came to Paris in 1807. After a successful beginning and a twelve-year sojourn in Belgium, he returned to Paris and won the Legion of Honor in the 1833 Salon. Of his many commissions,

17-31 ANTONIO CANOVA, *Pauline Borghese as Venus*, 1805–08. Marble, life size. Galleria Borghese, Rome.

17-32

FRANÇOIS RUDE, *The Departure of the Volunteers of 1792.* 1833–36. Approx. 42' x 26'. Arc de Triomphe, Paris.

the best known is *The Departure of the Volunteers of 1792* (Fig. 17-32), a 42-foot-high relief on the Arch of Triumph in Paris. This bristling composition depicts young and old warriors, allegorically dressed in an imaginative version of Roman armor, setting off for battle. Above them, the winged goddess of war surges forward. The frantic complexity of the group sets it apart from Neoclassic concepts, and Rude was linked with Romanticism.

Auguste Rodin (France, 1840–1917). The Frenchman Rodin dominated Western sculpture in the late nineteenth and early twentieth centuries. He was trained as a sculptor's helper and as a carver of architectural ornament. A voyage to Italy in 1875 opened his eyes to the expressive power of Donatello and Michelangelo; he was particularly impressed by the pulsating life suggested in the rough surfaces of Michelangelo's unfinished work. Exhibited in the 1877 Salon, Rodin's *Age of Bronze* (Rodin Museum, Paris) gains its vitality from surfaces broken into a flickering complexity of highlights while preserving some of the malleability of clay, his favorite material. In 1879, Rodin began planning *The Gates of Hell* for the Museum of Decorative Arts in Paris. Although the project, initially in-

17-33
AUGUSTE RODIN, *The Thinker*, 1889. Bronze, 70½" high
including base. Metropolitan Museum of Art, New York
(gift of Thomas R. Ryan, 1910)

spired by Dante's *Inferno*, was never finished, the constantly evolving plan for the work served as a source
from which Rodin took figures for other sculptures. *The
Thinker* (Fig. 17-33) was first conceived as part of the
reliefs for *The Gates of Hell* but gained fame as an
individual figure. The bronze presents a convincing
muscular and skeletal structure, but details have been
omitted or softened, and the surfaces are both rough
and lively. Like many of Michelangelo's figures, *The
Thinker* implies that physical power does not hold the
solution for man's most challenging problems. Because
of such expressive distortions, Rodin's *Monument to
Balzac* (Fig. 17-34) was refused by the society that had
commissioned it. Although he also produced stone
sculpture, Rodin's style is best seen in his bronzes,
which catch the essence of the artist's work in clay;
assistants did much of the stone carving. The effect
of agitated surfaces in Rodin's work has caused him
to be called an Impressionist in sculpture. Such a
designation ignores the powerful emotional expression

17-34
AUGUSTE RODIN, *Monument to Balzac*,
1891–98. Bronze, 79" high. Musée
Rodin, Paris.

in his art, a quality not basic to Impressionism in painting but most important to French Fauvism and to German Expressionism.

ARCHITECTURE

Nineteenth-century architecture has been described as the "Battle of the Styles" because of the prevailing tendency to borrow forms from various periods of the past. This eclecticism had begun in the eighteenth century, especially in England, where the work of a single architect would frequently include buildings in the Greek, Roman, Romanesque, Gothic, and Renaissance styles. Eclecticism became international during the nineteenth century, and the word *revival* is often used to indicate the close dependence of a particular style on its historical prototype. Iron could be cast into different kinds of ornamental details, but it could also be used inventively for strikingly new architectural forms such as those of the Crystal Palace, built as an exhibition hall for the London International Exhibition of 1851. In the last quarter of the century, steel frames were used in monuments like the Eiffel Tower and in the development of skyscrapers. During the second half of the century, England developed the so-called *Victorian Gothic* (Italianate Gothic with polychrome stripes) and imported the Second Empire Style from France. The British arts and crafts movement urged efficient, practical design and was an indirect influence on twentieth-century art and theory.

France began the century with dreams of creating an empire rivaling that of ancient Rome. Napoleonic plans provided for vast Greco-Roman monuments, like the Arch of Triumph and the Church of the Madeleine, many of which were finished long after the Battle of Waterloo. Renaissance revival designs were also popular. The *Second Empire Style*, named for the empire of Napoleon III, is characterized by *mansard* roofs (steeply pitched roofs with a flat or almost flat platform at the top) and highly decorated dormer windows. Walls were treated with ornate sculptural richness, in a style often described as *Neo-Baroque*. French and Belgian architecture of the 1890's led in the international style called *Art Nouveau*, which turned away from eclecticism and exulted in a profusion of irregular, curving, linear ornament inspired by plant life.

Outside of France and England, the revival styles were equally current in Germany, Italy, and the United

States. The reaction against eclecticism began with the work of Louis Sullivan and Frank Lloyd Wright.

Thomas Jefferson (United States, 1743–1826). One of the stylistic phases of postcolonial architecture in the eastern United States is often called the *Federal Style*. Thomas Jefferson's home, Monticello (Fig. 17-35), is a fine example of this Roman phase of the Neoclassic. Of the many amateur architects of his day, Jefferson produced some of the most influential buildings, even while he was engaged in a variety of other activities. Monticello is based on Palladio's Renaissance interpretation of Roman architecture. Jefferson used strict symmetry, a pedimented porch with a semicircular Roman window, Roman-inspired Tuscan columns, a low Roman dome on an octagonal base, severely simple ornament, and the single-story effect of a Roman temple. His designs for the Capitol Building at Richmond, Virginia (1785–89), were based on the Maison Carrée (Fig. 11-2). Jefferson's architecture, however, shows a flexibility and inventiveness in the application of Roman forms that is a refreshing contrast to the more imitative pedantry of many Neoclassic designers.

17-35 THOMAS JEFFERSON, Monticello, Charlottesville, Virginia, 1796–1808.

Sir John Soane (England, 1753–1837). One of England's most original Neoclassicists was Sir John Soane. During a visit to Italy, he studied the antique world of Piranesi's imaginative prints, actual Roman ruins, and Renaissance buildings. In 1788, he was appointed architect for the Bank of England. He used Roman domes and arches, but instead of the ponderous mass of Roman work, Soane used linear ornament. The total effect, as in the Consols Office of the bank (Fig. 17-36), is one of crisp precision with thin, taut surfaces. His own house in London—No. 12, Lincoln's Inn Fields (now a museum)—provided more opportunity for experiment. Canopylike cross-vaulted ceilings cover spaces that continue over screening walls which stop short of the ceiling. From low dark spaces, one is drawn toward high, brightly lighted areas. Mirrors help to convey light and to emphasize the continuity of space. The variety of spaces and light effects and the variety of Soane's collection of art objects lead one to expect surprises around every corner. It is here, rather than in the austerely simple surfaces and restrained linear ornament of his larger buildings, that we see Soane's kinship with Piranesi.

17-36

SIR JOHN SOANE, Consols Office of the Bank of England, London, 1797.

17-37 KARL FRIEDRICH VON SCHINKEL, Old Berlin Museum, 1824–28.

Karl Friedrich von Schinkel (Germany, 1781–1841). Germany's leading architect in the first half of the nineteenth century began, like Inigo Jones, as a designer of stage sets; but his architecture began as Greek revival and eventually employed Roman domes and arches. A good example of his early work is the New Guardhouse in Berlin (1816–18), with an authentically proportioned Doric order and the severe simplicity of parts that is characteristic of much Greek revival architecture. His Old Berlin Museum (Fig. 17-37) masks the two-story interior with a huge Ionic stoa and hides the interior Roman dome behind a simple rectangular attic. Von Schinkel was also active as a painter and city planner.

Sir Charles Barry (England, 1795–1860). Barry's career demonstrates the various enthusiasms of nineteenth-century architects and their patrons. Barry began by designing Gothic revival churches but turned to Renaissance revival as his major interest. In 1836 he won the competition for the new Houses of Parliament (Fig. 17-38) with a Gothic design, forecasting the wide popularity of Gothic in the Victorian period. In the same year, A. Welby Pugin's book *Contrasts* appeared, arguing that the Gothic style should be used exclusively. It was Pugin who designed the details for the Houses of Parliament; late Gothic was used because its more complex ornament was considered to be richer and more picturesque for a skyline as prominent as that of Parliament.

17-38
SIR CHARLES BARRY and A. WELBY PUGIN,
Houses of Parliament, London, begun 1835.

17-39
HENRI LABROUSTE, Bibliotèque Sainte-Geneviève, Paris,
1843–50.

17-40 Reading room of the Bibliotèque Sainte Geneviève.

Henri Labrouste (France, 1801–75). Labrouste's masterpiece is the Bibliothèque Sainte-Geneviève in Paris (Fig. 17-39), a design based on Italian Renaissance palaces but handled with sensitivity in its proportions and inventiveness in the application of iron in the interior. The reading room (Fig. 17-40) gains spaciousness from the slender iron columns, which support a ceiling of plaster panels between round arches of perforated iron. Labrouste added a reading room to the Bibliothèque Nationale in Paris (1862–68), where he again used thin iron columns, this time supporting light terra cotta domes. The book-stack areas that he designed for the same building are of iron and glass. With respect to both design and materials, Labrouste was an important leader in mid-nineteenth century French architecture.

Antonio Gaudi y Cornet (Spain, 1852–1926). After studying architecture in Barcelona, Gaudi made his career there, aided by many commissions from the industrialist Güell. Gaudi's inventive mind utilized Medieval masonry vaults, Moorish forms, and contrasting materials to develop a unique style related to Art

17-41
ANTONIO GAUDI Y CORNET. Casa Milá,
Barcelona, 1907.

Nouveau in its irregular, constantly curving surfaces. His thin, laminated vaults of tile and mortar, his warped surfaces—such as hyperbolic parabolids (see p. 46) —and his inclined supports all forecast later twentieth-century architecture. The Casa Milá (Fig. 17-41) presents a constantly undulating wall surface of hammered stone. Windows and doors suggest grotto openings, and balcony railings are explosions of foliagelike ironwork. The irregular rise and fall of the roof line and the twisting forms of certain chimneys and ventilators offer a bizarre silhouette. Interior rooms are irregular, with curving walls and spaces that seem flexible and flowing. The building was originally intended to be a base for an enormous statue of the Virgin.

Louis Sullivan (United States, 1856–1924). America's most pioneering architect in the late nineteenth century was Louis Sullivan, who was trained at the Massachusetts Institute of Technology and at the École des Beaux-Arts in Paris. At a time when architecture was deriving inspiration from the past, Sullivan insisted on a fresh approach to form and decoration. His concept that *form follows function* (suggested earlier in the century by Horatio Greenough) argued that design should express the use, structure, and materials of a building. Sullivan, a Bostonian, came to Chicago in 1873, and from 1879 to 1895 he worked in partnership with Dankmar Adler. Sullivan's early work is represented by the Chicago Auditorium Building (Fig. 17-42). In the lower floors, the granite masonry is handled with bold roughness and deep shadows, emphasizing the base and creating an effect of vast scale and strength. Above, the smooth stone façade is unified by tall arches with groups of windows that decrease in size as they approach the final cornice. Sullivan here shows the influence of Henry Hobson Richardson, an older architect noted for his sensitive interpretation of Romanesque forms. Other Chicago architects were more advanced

17-42
LOUIS SULLIVAN and DANKMAR ADLER.
Chicago Auditorium Building, 1889.

17-43 LOUIS SULLIVAN, Wainwright Building, St. Louis, 1890–91.

than Sullivan in exploring new structural methods and materials, particulary the steel frame, but these new techniques were hidden behind facings of columns and pilasters. It was only in 1890 and 1891 in St. Louis that Sullivan used the steel frame in a design independent of past styles. In his Wainwright Building (Fig. 17-43) the idea of form following function resulted in large-windowed shops at the base, a central section of offices treated as a framed area, and a crowning band of floral ornament beneath the projecting cornice. The steel frame is expressed in the large windows and slender brick-covered piers; it is obvious that the steel skeleton, not the wall, supports the building. Sullivan believed that a tall building should look tall, so he made the vertical piers rise through the contrasting horizontal floors with their panels of rich ornament. The ornament is composed of geometric and plant forms in intricate profusion. Though there is no direct reference to past styles, the total effect recalls Celtic art or the looser, more asymmetrical Art Nouveau in Europe. Sullivan's commissions for large buildings declined as eclecticism increased in commercial architecture during the late nineteenth and early twentieth centuries. His ideals gained fuller acceptance after his death, when they were carried on in the work of his former employee, Frank Lloyd Wright.

Suggestions for Further Study

Badt, Kurt. *The Art of Cézanne.* Translated by Sheila Ann Ogilvie. Berkeley: University of California Press, 1965.

Courthion, Pierre. *Edouard Manet* (The Library of Great Painters). New York: Abrams, n.d.

Dowd, David L. *Pageant-Master of the Republic: Jacques Louis David and the French Revolution.* Lincoln: University of Nebraska Press, 1948.

Elsen, Albert. *Rodin.* New York: Museum of Modern Art, 1963.

Fernier, Robert. *Gustave Courbet.* Translated by Marcus Bullock. New York: Praeger, 1969.

Gaunt, William. *Impressionism: A Visual History.* New York: Praeger, 1970.

Hamilton, George Heard. *Nineteenth and Twentieth Century Art.* New York: Abrams, 1971.

Hitchcock, Henry Russell. *Architecture: Nineteenth and Twentieth Centuries* (Pelican History of Art). Baltimore: Penguin Books, 1958.

Huyghe, René. *Delacroix.* Translated by Jonathan Griffan. New York: Abrams, 1963.

Licht, Fred. *Sculpture, Nineteenth and Twentieth Centuries* (History of Western Sculpture). Greenwich, Conn.: New York Graphic Society, 1967.

Rewald, John. *The History of Impressionism.* New York: Museum of Modern Art, 1946.

———. *Post-Impressionism from Van Gogh to Gauguin.* New York: Museum of Modern Art, 1956.

Rosenblum, Robert. *Jean-Auguste-Dominique Ingres* (The Library of Great Painters). New York: Abrams, 1967.

Sloan, Joseph C. *French Painting Between the Past and the Present.* Princeton, N.J.: Princeton University Press, 1951.

Sullivan, Louis. *Kindergarten Chats and Other Writings.* Edited by Isabella Athey, rev. 1918. New York: Wittenborn, 1947.

Sutter, Jean, ed. *The Neo-Impressionists.* Translated by Chantel Deliss. Greenwich, Conn.: New York Graphic Society, 1970.

Chapter *17* Music

Music in the Nineteenth Century

The same intellectual and cultural forces affected both music and the visual arts in the nineteenth century, with results that were in some respects parallel, but widely divergent in others. Musicians talked and wrote about rebelling against tradition, but they based their music on an extension of attitudes and practices from the past. There was an increased shift toward more personalized expression, but most of the music displays common stylistic traits. The music of the whole century is often called Romantic, but this term can be misleading because the Romantic attitude influenced what people thought and said about music much more than it influenced the music itself.

Throughout the nineteenth century German and Austrian music dominated most of Europe. Concerts and operas were available to a large middle class audience in Vienna, London, and most of the other major European cities. Italy continued its venerable operatic tradition but produced little else of note. Paris maintained its position as a leading cultural center in Europe, but until the latter part of the century much of its best music was produced by composers from other nations, especially Germany and Italy.

Political, economic, and technological revolutions brought about a shift of power and wealth to a relatively unsophisticated middle class, many of whom nevertheless extensively patronized painters, poets, musicians, writers, and other creative people. Musicians enjoyed a considerable elevation in their social status, and they became involved in the general ferment of artistic ideas. They were strongly influenced by the other arts, especially literature, which led various musicians to attempt to incorporate some of the ideals of Romanticism into their musical expression. Some musicians, for both economic and egotistical reasons, encouraged the popular myth that the composer or performer was the helpless captive of his own genius or "daemon," creating in intuitive flashes of inspiration without substantial recourse to any learned skill or craftmanship. This separation of creativity from craftmanship originated during the Renaissance, but it became a major tenet of Romanticism.

In fact, the musical styles as well as the musical aesthetics of the nineteenth century were essentially culminations of the Baroque and Classical traditions, modified and extended to meet the needs of the time. The prevailing musical aesthetic resembled the Baroque "doctrine of the affections" by assuming that specific musical ideas evoked fixed emotions or images and that

17-44
MARY CASSATT, *A Woman in Black at the Opera,* 1880. Oil on canvas, 32″ x 26″. Museum of Fine Arts, Boston. Charles Henry Hayden Fund.

the evocation of such responses was the purpose of music. The public expected music to "say" something. Composers met this demand through a combination of associative stimuli—musical, verbal, theatrical, and otherwise. A story or poem often was provided in the printed program as a means of reinforcing the listener's response to the music. Program music usually employed familiar musical effects in order to assure the presence of musical associations. Composers tended to emphasize elements that evoked emotional associations and conditioned responses, concerning themselves in particular with melodic associations and with the expressive effects of momentary sound combinations. They used increasingly complex chord structures and were especially inclined to a highly sophisticated exploitation of instrumental timbres. Manipulation of timbres was considerably advanced by improved instrument-making techniques.

Rising nationalism, which surged through Europe during the nineteenth century, provided fertile ground for musical expression, and many composers, especially during the latter part of the century, turned for inspiration to musical materials and subject matter identifiable with a particular people and their culture. Musical *Nationalism* occurred in almost every country in Europe, but was especially prominent in Russia, Bohemia, and the Scandinavian countries, often in reaction against German and Italian influences. Aside from occasional outright use of folk or popular melodies, Nationalism's main musical manifestations were in melodic, rhythmic, and harmonic idioms derived from these national or cultural sources.

Toward the end of the century, Realist, Impressionist, and Post-Impressionist art, and Symbolist literature influenced the style of certain composers. One important result was a musical style called *Impressionism*, a kind of nonspecific program music related in part to Symbolism and Post-Impressionism. Realist literature was paralleled by a brief operatic movement in Italy called *Verismo*, which took violence among ordinary people as its subject.

Musical Styles and Media

Romantic concern with the individual moment, thing, or experience found musical expression in an emphasis on momentary effects and variety of coloristic detail. It led to a diminished rhythmic drive (less moment-to-moment connection among the sounds) and episodic rather than integrated formal structures. During the early part of the century many composers, especially in Germany, were strongly influenced by Romantic writers, and they consciously sought ways to incorporate Romantic ideals into their music. These composers took the late works of Beethoven for their musical models, and they drew heavily from literary sources for inspiration. In general, the new musical forms and media were influenced by literary or other extramusical sources. At the same time many older forms were retained, which incorporated the newer harmonic, textural, and coloristic techniques.

During the nineteenth century new music was created chiefly for public performance in concert halls and opera houses and for private gatherings in salons and parlors. Public performances required operas, and orchestral or solo works featuring brilliant technical display, while smaller, more intimate works for soloists or chamber groups better served private occasions. The piano, which was much improved acoustically and mechanically early in the century, proved ideally suited for both the concert hall and the parlor. The nineteenth century is the great period for solo piano music. Many composers wrote sonatas, concertos, and variations, which more or less followed Classical models; some,

notably Franz Liszt, wrote virtuoso display pieces for
concert audiences. The works most typical of the period, though, are small, unpretentious, often simple
character pieces. Their titles were often whimsical or
suggestive, with no precise meaning, such as Franz
Schubert's *Impromptus* and *Moments Musicaux*, Felix
Mendelssohn's *Songs Without Words*, Robert Schumann's *Papillons* and *Carnaval*, Frédéric Chopin's *Preludes* and *Nocturnes*, Johannes Brahms's *Capriccios* and
Intermezzos, and Claude Debussy's *Suite bergamasque*
and *Images*. Liszt demonstrated the limits of virtuoso
piano performing technique, and Chopin in particular
exhaustively explored and exploited the expressive
possibilities of the instrument.

The earliest, and one of the most obvious, means for
merging Romantic literature with music was the art
song (German *Lied*; French *chanson*), a solo song for
voice and piano. Earlier composers, including Beethoven, wrote art songs, but Schubert brought the medium
to perfection by combining a sensitive vocal melody
with a complementary and equally important piano
part. The result was not merely an accompanied melody, but rather a musical expression of a poetic text by
both voice and piano. Principal composers of art songs
in Germany after Schubert were Schumann, Brahms,
and Hugo Wolf; in France, Gabriel Fauré and Debussy;

in Russia, Modest Mussorgsky. Gustave Mahler and Richard Strauss wrote art songs for solo voice with orchestra.

Expanded and improved instruments, plus the widespread taste for coloristic detail, led to works that exploited the varied tone colors of a large orchestra. In Classical practice the woodwinds were blended with the strings, and the trumpets, horns, and kettledrums were used to add weight and loudness to the full orchestra. In contrast, nineteenth-century composers sought to realize the potential of individual instruments and to develop new collective sonorities. They specified more instruments and treated the woodwinds, brasses, and strings as separate families or "choirs." They began to combine unlike instruments and to add new instruments, including percussion. Melodies were associated with particular instruments, often alone or in combinations. Expansion of the orchestra made it possible to subdivide the string, brass, and woodwind choirs and finally to develop acoustical effects similar to the mixing of organ stops, so that harmonic and instrumental colors merged into a single web of diverse timbres. The great innovators in the art of orchestration were Hector Berlioz, Richard Wagner, Nicolas Rimsky-Korsakov, Mahler, and Debussy, two of whom—Berlioz and Rimsky-Korsakov—wrote important treatises on the subject. Other composers quickly assimilated the new techniques, and a general concern for instrumental and

17-46
EDGAR DEGAS, *The Musicians of the Orchestra,* 1868–69. Oil on canvas, 22" x 18". Galerie du Jeu de Paume, Paris.

17-47
Scene from the last act of Verdi's opera *Aida*.

harmonic color pervades most nineteenth-century orchestral music.

The principal works for orchestra can be divided into two broad categories: standard Classical forms, such as symphonies, concertos, and variations; and experimental forms, most often with programmatic associations, such as *symphonic suites, program symphonies, symphonic poems,* and some *concert overtures.* Experimental works often were organized as a series of episodes linked through common melodic ideas rather than through tonal relationships and thematic contrast and development. Schubert, Mendelssohn, Schumann, and, especially, Brahms wrote important works in the standard Classical form, while the orchestral works of Berlioz, Liszt, Rimsky-Korsakov, Debussy, and Richard Strauss generally fall in the second category. Peter Ilyich Tchaikovsky wrote works of both kinds, and Mahler attempted to fuse both categories in his grandiose symphonies.

During the nineteenth century, Italy, France, and Germany each had its own distinct operatic style. The Italians continued, with only minor modifications, their centuries-old tradition of human emotions expressed through solo song. Their most important composers were Gioacchino Rossini, Giuseppe Verdi, and Giacomo Puccini. In France, *grand opéra* often degenerated into a series of crowd-pleasing spectacles featuring choruses, ballets, lavish scenery, and elaborate staging, while music and drama became incidental. By contrast, the humbler opéra comique, emphasizing drama and spoken dialogue, became a well-balanced art form using effective music complimented by effective drama, as in Georges Bizet's *Carmen*. In Germany, which had no significant operatic tradition of its own, Wagner developed the *music drama*. In this form he attempted to unify the diverse elements of drama, staging, scenery, and music through the expressive power of the orchestra. Richard Strauss was the principal heir to Wagner's operatic innovations.

Except for piano music and songs, chamber music during the nineteenth century was mostly based on Classical models, such as string quartets, quartets plus one or two more instruments—especially the piano (*quintets* and *sextets*)—and sonatas for piano plus another instrument. The style was essentially conservative—no program music and no real departures from the older forms. Schubert, Mendelssohn, Schumann, Brahms, and César Franck were the leading composers in this realm.

Although many short choral pieces were written during the period, it was in several large concert works for chorus and orchestra, especially those by Rossini, Berlioz, Verdi, and Brahms, that nineteenth-century choral music found its most characteristic expression. These works tended to be grandiose, often dramatic, with the combined expressive powers of solo singers, chorus, and orchestra utilized to their fullest.

Franz Schubert (Austria, 1797–1828). Schubert began composing in his early teens, and, after a brief attempt to follow his father's profession as a school teacher, he devoted the remainder of his short life to music. Most of his works were composed in the accepted Classical forms, including symphonies, chamber works, sonatas and short pieces for the piano, choral and stage works, and art songs. These works displayed an incomparable melodic invention and a subtle harmonic freshness involving both coloristic harmonies and surprising shifts of tonal center. Applying these qualities to the German poetic song, or *Lied*, Schubert in effect created the nineteenth-century art song. He also transferred the characteristics of his songs to the solo piano in the sets of short pieces called *Moments Musicaux* and *Impromptus*, which became models for many later character pieces. In all, Schubert composed more than six hundred songs. *Der Erlkönig*, his first published song, is a setting of a dramatic poem by Goethe. Narrative stanzas at the beginning and end describe the scene, in which a father rides desperately through the night with his sick and dying son in his arms. The music depicts the three-way conversation between the father, son, and Death (the Erlking), who wins in the end. With each stage of the conversation the music modulates to a higher key, underlining the successive changes of mood and creating an ever-increasing tension. After the child's last anguished cry the key returns to the original minor tonic as the father arrives home with his dead son. The fears of the father and the child, as well as the sound of the galloping horse, are expressed by the frantic, throbbing, repeated octaves and rapid runs in the piano part during the introduction, the narrative stanzas, and the cries of the child. Even though the underlying triple pulsations never cease until near the end of the final narrative stanza, changes in the melody and the piano figurations depict the contrasting moods and characters in the drama. The text is typically Romantic, and the form and musical materials of the song are designed to express its poetic content rather than simply to outline its strophic and metrical structure.

Richard Wagner (Germany, 1813–83) Wagner showed keen literary and dramatic interests during his schooling in Dresden and Leipzig. His musical training was haphazard until age eighteen, when he began to study composition seriously, but at twenty he began a long and successful career as a theater and concert conductor, composer, and writer. Wagner's greatest works were his music dramas, a special operatic form that he

17-48
AUGUSTE RENOIR, study for a painting of Wagner's *Tannhauser*, c. 1879. Oil on canvas, 20⅝" x 25⅞". Sterling and Francine Clark Art Institute, Williamstown, Massachusetts.

developed according to his own dramatic, aesthetic, and literary theories. Opera, Wagner believed, should be a *Gesamtkunstwerk* (total art work), in which music, poetry, acting, scenery, and staging unite as equal elements to express the drama. Ancient Germanic myths were preferred as the dramatic vehicle because they were ideal abstractions of the human condition. Although his works call for extravagant scenery and stage effects, and great demands are made on the singers, the music of the orchestra dominates and carries the weight of the drama. Today some scenes are even performed as orchestral concert pieces, without the singers. Instrumental resources are richly exploited, including unique timbres and mixtures, and the addition of special instruments is often required. Singers are treated as additional instruments in the orchestra. The music flows continuously, urged on by uncompleted cadences, abrupt tonal shifts, and harmonic ambiguities. Wagner's most important music dramas were *Tristan und Isolde*, *Parsifal*, *Die Meistersinger von Nürnberg*, and *Der Ring des Nibelungen*, a cycle of four dramas ("*Das Rheingold*," "*Die Walküre*," "*Siegfried*," and "*Götterdämmerung*") based on ancient Nordic and German legends concerning the mortal hero Siegfried, and the predestined doom of the gods. "*Siegfried's Rhine Journey*" is an orchestral connecting passage between the Prologue and Act I of "*Götterdämmerung*." It depicts Siegfried's departure from Brünnhilde and his journey to the Rhine River. It is a popular concert piece, with a forceful overall energy shape, unified through repetition, growth, and development of musical ideas. The effect of program music is conveyed through a succession of motives having specific meanings: Fate (first three notes, low brasses); Dawn and Sunrise (long melody, low strings); Siegfried the Man (brasses); Brünnhilde the Woman (clarinet, then strings); Siegfried (martial passage)—agitation to leave; Brünnhilde—acquiescence in his departure; Siegfried's Horn Call, plus Brünnhilde—he is on his way—followed immediately by Brünnhilde's Love (full orchestra); the Horn Call, combined with a motive from "*Die Walküre*" in a sort of "promenade"; the Rhine (rising notes in the brasses), plus Death of the Gods (descending version of the Rhine motive); the Rhine Maidens (full orchestra, then mostly woodwinds); and the Rhinegold (upward leaps, brasses).

Giuseppe Verdi (Italy, 1813–1901). Verdi studied with local teachers until he was sixteen, when a friend agreed to finance his further study in Milan. There he worked diligently under private tutelage and at twenty-six had his first opera successfully performed at La Scala opera house. Several more early successes secured his reputation, and he devoted the remainder of a long and distinguished career almost exclusively to the composition of operas. Although Verdi was well aware of the French and German operatic trends, including the innovations of Wagner, he was firmly independent and chose to extend and refine the Italian operatic tradition rather than to break with it. Verdi's best works are unsurpassed in their economy of means, subtlety of characterization, dramatic unity, and melodic invention. In his later works he increasingly employed expressive harmonic and orchestral color, but in all of his operas the solo human voice dominates, and the drama concerns real people and their emotions. His last opera, *Falstaff*, is based on Shakespeare's *Merry Wives of Windsor*. The voices always carry the drama, yet the orchestra is no mere accompaniment; it enhances the changes of mood and sentiment, it "comments" on what is sung, and it keeps the action moving. Every subtle shift in the characters' perceptions is instantly reflected by an appropriate instrumental gesture, including explicit commentary, as in Act II, Scene I, when the orchestra repeats the refrain, *"dalle due alle tre,"* emphasizing the idea of an amatory rendezvous in Falstaff's consciousness. This scene has two parts: Falstaff's meetings with Mistress Quickly and then with Ford, both delineated by brief orchestral passages at the beginning, middle, and end. The same music ends both parts, and the middle passage also begins and ends Falstaff's "Go, old Jack." Dame Quickly enters and leaves to the same music (*"Reverenza"*), and the refrains *"dalle due alle tre"* and *"povera donna"* recur in symmetrical order in this part, with extreme comic effect. *"Dalle due alle tre"* returns in the second part, when Falstaff tells the jealous Ford of his imminent rendezvous with the latter's wife. Much of the music parodies Italian opera, as in Ford's monologue, which mimics the standard vengeance aria, and when he and Falstaff make a joke of his "madrigal." The music condenses traditional expressions of mood and sentiment from arias or sections to mere phrases or words in a unity of drama and music that rushes continually forward.

Johannes Brahms (Germany and Austria, 1833–97). Brahms was born in Hamburg, where he demonstrated an early proficiency as a child pianist. Although he

17-49
Sketch of Brahms at the piano.

worked for some time in various German cities, he
spent much of his career, including his last years, in
Vienna. His works for orchestra, chamber groups,
piano, choruses, and the solo voice reflect his preference for the older, established forms of pure music,
such as variations and sonata. Brahms's music exhibits
an elaborate variety of textures, timbres, harmonies,
and rhythmic complexities. Unlike many of his contemporaries, Brahms showed no interest in dramatic
music, program music, or any of the formal experiments generated by extramusical inspiration and associations. The final movement of his *Fourth Symphony* is
typical. In this portion of the work he created thirty
variations based on repetitions of the opening succession of eight chords, together with the eight-note melody that rises in small steps as the top notes in these
chords. This succession of chords sets up a repeated
harmonic time cycle that persists almost to the end of
the movement, except for three times when it occurs at
half speed, and the harmonies are structured so that
their forward propulsion always turns back on itself to
repeat the cycle. The tones of the eight-note melody are
present in each cycle, but much of the time they are
buried in the complex texture or obscured by more
prominent melodies. Although the original eight-cord
set retains its essential components, Brahms incorporates into the texture every chromatic inflection possible
short of destroying the underlying tonal center. The

resulting richness of detail is enhanced by an abundance of lyric melodies, extensive exploitation of orchestral timbres, and cross meters and shifting accents
that tend to produce a metric blur. Persistence of the
cycle produces a slow, eight-count metrical frame,
while the successive variants merge into several large-
scale divisions, marked off by slow passages and the
return of the opening cycle.

Claude Debussy (France, 1862–1918).   After some private study, Debussy was admitted to the Paris Conservatory at the age of eleven, where he won several prizes,
including, after graduation, the Grand Prix de Rome.
Influenced by contemporary Russian composers and
Javanese music, he translated into musical terms the
aesthetic attitudes of Symbolist writers and Impressionist or Post-Impressionist painters. Debussy's piano
music consists mostly of character pieces, and the orchestra music includes several symphonic poems. The
piano and orchestral pieces generally have suggestive or
descriptive titles, but no specific programs. His one
opera, *Pelléas et Mélisande*, is a unique setting of a
Symbolist play by Maurice Maeterlinck. His style,
often called musical Impressionism, is in reality a logical extension of an attitude that seeks truth in the
unique fact or event. Thus, traditional processes of
motivic and thematic development and other cause-

17-50
THOMAS EAKINS, *The Pathetic Song,*
1881. Oil on canvas, 45" x 32½".
Corcoran Gallery of Art, Washington, D.C.

effect formal relationships are replaced by moment-to-moment effects. Chords and melodic figures are utilized for their unique colors and sonorous qualities, often without regard for traditional dissonance-consonance relationships. Principally through this and through his masterful, subdued control of loudness and timbres, Debussy created music that focuses attention on momentary, often fleeting effects of melody, harmony, and tone color. *"La cathédrale engloutie"* (*"The Sunken Cathedral"*), from his first book of *Préludes*, is typical of his Impressionistic style applied to the piano. The title refers to the cathedral of Ys which, according to an old Breton legend, rises periodically from beneath the sea. Debussy evokes the aura of mystery, the fluidity of the sea, and the suggestion of cathedral bells through subtle shadings of piano tone. Widely spaced chords move in parallel streams over sustained sounds. The texture becomes denser and the loudness increases as the cathedral bells toll, then the process reverses as the cathedral sinks once more into the sea. (See the discussions of Ex. 3, *Prelude to the Afternoon of a Faun*, in Part One, Chs. 1, 2, 3, and 4.)

Suggestions for Further Study

Abraham, Gerald. *Chopin's Musical Style.* London: Oxford University Press, 1939.

Barzun, Jacques. *Berlioz and the Romantic Century,* 3rd ed. 2 vols. New York: Columbia University Press, 1969.

Brion, Marcel. *Schumann and the Romantic Age.* Translated by Geoffrey Sainsbury, New York: Macmillan, 1956.

Brown, Maurice J. E. *Schubert: A Critical Biography.* New York: St. Martin's Press, 1958.

Calvocoressi, Michel D. *Mussorgsky.* New York: Macmillan, 1962.

Einstein, Alfred. *Music in the Romantic Era.* New York: W. W. Norton, 1947.

Geiringer, Karl. *Brahms: His Life and Work,* 2nd ed., rev. and enl. Translated by H. B. Weiner and Bernard Miall. New York: Oxford University Press, 1947.

Grout, Donald Jay. *A History of Western Music,* rev. ed. New York: W. W. Norton, 1973. Chapters XVI–XIX.

Lockspeiser, Edward. *Debussy: His Life and Mind.* 2 vols. New York: Macmillan, 1962, 1965.

———. *Music and Painting: A Study in Comparative Ideas from Turner to Schoenberg.* London: Cassell, 1973.

Newman, Ernest. *Life of Richard Wagner.* 4 vols. New York: Knopf, 1933–1946.

Riedel, Johannes. *Music of the Romantic Period.* Dubuque, Iowa: William C. Brown, 1969.

Walker, Frank. *The Man Verdi.* New York: Knopf, 1962.

Suggestions for Further Listening

PIANO

Brahms, Johannes. *Three Intermezzi,* Opus 117.

Chopin, Frédéric. *Nocturnes.*

————. *Preludes.*

Debussy, Claude. *Images.*

————. *Children's Corner.*

Schumann, Robert. *Carnaval.*

ART SONGS

Brahms, Johannes. Selected songs.

Debussy, Claude. *Trois Ballades.*

Mussorgsky, Modest. *Songs and Dances of Death.*

Schubert, Franz. *Die Schöne Müllerin.*

Schumann, Robert. *Frauenliebe und Leben.*

ORCHESTRA

Berlioz, Hector. *Symphonie Fantastique.*

Brahms, Johannes. One of the symphonies.

Debussy, Claude. *La Mer.*

Mendelssohn, Felix. *"Hebrides" Overture.*

Strauss, Richard. *Till Eulenspiegel's Merry Pranks.*

OPERA AND MUSIC DRAMA

Bizet, Georges. *Carmen.*

Mussorgsky, Modest. *Boris Godunov.*

Verdi, Guiseppe. *Otello.*

Wagner, Richard. *Die Meistersinger von Nürnberg.*

CHORAL MUSIC

Brahms, Johannes. *German Requiem.*

CHAMBER MUSIC

Brahms, Johannes. Piano Quintet in F Minor, Opus 34.

Schubert, Franz. Quintet in A Major, "The Trout."

Chapter 18 Art

Photography and Motion Pictures

Photography and motion pictures (film), as we know them, began in the nineteenth century and have grown to special prominence in the twentieth. At first art forms in their own right, they later joined with other forms in intermedia works to expand the definition of art.

Photography's greatest initial impact came from its documentary function in recording the likeness of a sitter or of important events and topography. Although photography was occasionally used as an aid by artists, it generally competed with documentary painting and graphics, which had provided artists with an income. It was not long, however, before photography began developing aesthetic criteria of its own that were separate from its recording function. As the aesthetics of photography developed so too did its technology. Part of that developing technology was the invention of motion pictures, which in turn generated a new aesthetic involving time as well as space. Eventually, visual images in motion were brought from the public theater into the private living room by means of television.

Visual images engage the viewer more directly and convey information more quickly than does the printed word. Photography and film have surrounded us with visual images, generating in part the information explosion of the twentieth century. Film and television shrink distances and tend to jump language barriers, making possible what Marshall McLuhan has described as the "global village."

PHOTOGRAPHY

It is no accident that our word camera comes from the Italian word for room. The *camera obscura* (dark room) described by Renaissance Italian writers was a darkened chamber with a small hole in one wall. This hole projected an inverted image of a brightly lit exterior on the opposite wall of the darkened room. Later the term "camera obscura" was applied to various kinds of boxes, some of them portable, with lenses for sharpening the focus and ground-glass screens onto which the image was projected. These boxes were used during the seventeenth and eighteenth centuries as an aid to artists in drawing from nature (Fig. 18-1). The desire to make projected images permanent, without the labor of tracing them from a transparent screen, led, after considerable experimentation, to photography—the fixing of images on a surface by means of chemicals sensitive to light or other radiant energy.

In France between 1816 and 1829, the inventor Nicéphore Niépce succeeded in fixing an image on

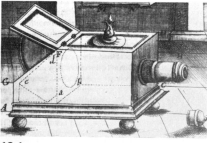

18-1
Camera obscura with reflex lens, Germany, invented by Johann Zahn, 1685.

pewter by using bitumen of Judea. He called his process heliography but did not live to perfect it. Photography later became available to the public through the work of Niépce's partner, the painter and showman Louis Jacques Mandé Daguerre, who developed the *daguerreotype*. Copper plates coated with iodide of silver were exposed to light and the resulting image was then developed by mercury and made permanent by a salt or hyposulfite-of-soda solution. A tiringly long exposure was necessary, and there was no negative; the original plate became the sole print (Fig. 18-2). Nevertheless, daguerreotype studios sprang up in many countries after the process was announced in the summer of 1839. At the same time in England, William Henry Fox Talbot produced paper negatives from which any number of prints could be made. His findings were also announced in 1839, and the prints came to be called *calotypes* (Fig. 18-3). They were soft and grainy, lacking the sharp detail of daguerreotypes. In 1851, the Englishman Frederick Scott Archer discovered that the *wet plate*, glass coated with wet collodion and silver nitrate, gave faster and superior results, though the wet plate had to be developed immediately (Fig. 18-4). By 1878, the *dry plate*, glass coated with a bromide emulsion in gelatin, made possible faster exposures and eliminated the need for immediate development. After 1889 celluloid was used for roll film. Shorter exposures became increasingly possible as more sensitive chemical emulsions that reacted more quickly to light were made on film.

Progress in film was accompanied by improvements in two other vital elements of the camera: the shutter and the lens. The shutter is a windowlike device that opens for a precisely controlled amount of time, such as $\frac{1}{500}$ of a second, to allow light to enter the camera and strike the film. Early cameras had simple metal flaps or lens caps that were removed and then replaced after the necessarily long exposures. Later in the century the flap or cap was replaced by a shutter. In addition to the shutter, an adjustable *diaphragm* controls the amount of entering light (measured in *f* stops). In dim light, fast film, a wide-open diaphragm, and a slow shutter speed are used in order to let maximum light enter the camera. For dim light, the photographer also needs a fast lens. The lens is a single- or multiple-glass assembly that gathers and focuses light. Fast film, fast shutters, and fast (wide, light-gathering) lenses have made possible photographs of fast-moving objects. When a fast lens is used with a wide diaphragm opening and focused on foreground objects, the *depth of field* (range of depth in which objects are sharply defined) becomes

18-2
PHILIP HAAS, *John Quincy Adams*, 1843. Daguerreotype.

18-3
DAVID OCTAVIUS HILL and ROBERT ADAMSON, *Fishwife, Newhaven, Scotland, c.* 1848. Calotype.

18-4
NADAR, *Eugene Delacroix*, 1855. Wet plate, or collodion, print.

shallow. To obtain *deep focus* (acceptable definition in foreground and distant objects), the diaphragm aperture must be reduced and the exposure time lengthened. Early photographers used flash powder for taking photographs in dim light. In 1929, Johannes Ostermeier patented the flashbulb. Today, pocket-sized, rechargeable electronic flash units can be attached to small 35 mm cameras.

Enlarging is a darkroom process whereby light is projected through the developed film (*negative*) onto chemically-coated photographic paper, thus producing a photographic *print*. A print that is not enlarged but is the same size as the negative is called a *contact print*. Enlarging was difficult until late in the nineteenth century; therefore, camera sizes varied according to the desired size of the finished contact print. Improvements in the enlarging apparatus made possible the popularity of the 35 mm camera from the 1920's to the present.

The lack of color in photography was considered a drawback from the beginning, and some daguerreotypists hand-colored their work. Experiments with color were made continually, however, and, in the 1930's, Kodak in America and Agfa in Germany began manufacturing color film with three layers of emulsions: one for each of the primary colors of light—red, blue, and green. According to the type of film used, either color transparencies (slides) or color prints (opaque color on photographic paper) can be made, and transparencies can be used to produce color prints. In 1963, color film was finally developed for Polaroid cameras, which use special film sheets that develop into finished prints within seconds after exposure.

Early photography was used mainly for city views, landscapes, and—as exposure time shortened—portraiture. At that time the role of photography was thought to be documentary, sharply focused reportage (Fig. 18-5). As photography progressed, some photographers posed models, arranged sets, and created storytelling, allegorical, and moralizing pictures in imitation of much nineteenth-century painting. In these "artistic" photographs, retouching and *soft focus* (blurred forms) could be used for "painterly" effects, and several negatives might be assembled to make *combination prints*. One of the most famous of such prints is Oscar G. Rejlander's allegory, *The Two Paths of Life* (Fig. 18-6), which interprets a young man's choice between a life of industry and one of sensual pleasures. This sort of manipulation of subject and form was referred to as *pictorial* photography.

By the 1850's, the virtues of pictorial versus direct or

18-5
ALBERT SANDS SOUTHWORTH
and JOSIAH JOHNSON HAWES,
The Boston Athenaeum, 1853.

documentary photography became the subject of heated controversy. One place these debates occurred was the Photographic Society of London, founded in 1853, where such debates were visually represented in its annual exhibitions. In 1893 a photographic group called the Linked Ring was formed in England, and its annual salons claimed to stress the "artistic" (pictorial) rather than the "scientific" (documentary) aspect of photography. Both aesthetic positions are revealed in the annual issues of *Photograms of the Year,* begun in 1895. Similar magazines and photographic societies appeared in the major cities of many countries. In New York, Alfred Stieglitz edited *Camera Work* (1902–17), a photographic quarterly open to the avant-garde of all

18-6
OSCAR G. REJLANDER, *The Two Paths of Life,* 1857. Combination print.

the arts. His 291 Gallery exhibited both direct and manipulated photographs, as well as avant-garde drawing and painting. As the technology of photography progressed, the distinction between direct and manipulated work became less evident or significant. Today different lenses and filters make possible a great variety of images in exposure without the need for retouching the negative or manipulating light in printing.

As in painting and sculpture, twentieth-century photography has also developed abstract and nonobjective trends, but these have not become dominant as they did in the other arts. After 1918, Dada photographers and painters produced *photomontages* (combination prints or cut-and-pasted photographs). They also created photographs without cameras by placing objects on or suspending them over photosensitive paper to create nonobjective compositions. Man Ray, Dada photographer and painter, called these *Rayographs*; Lászlo Moholy-Nagy, a painter-designer who taught at the Bauhaus in Germany, called them *photograms.* In contrast to abstract experiments, the *New Objectivity* movement produced obsessively detailed, recognizable images. This movement arose in photography, as in painting, during the 1920's and spread from Germany to other countries. Social commentary and direct photography of precise detail from the everyday world were stressed, although magnification of small details sometimes resulted in rich patterns but unidentifiable forms. Today, the influence of the New Objectivity style may be seen not only in documentary photography but also in abstract work by photographers who do not believe in altering the image after exposure.

Since the end of World War II the range and possibilities of photography have expanded greatly. Extraordinary shapes have been obtained in microscopic photography, while infrared photography has produced unusual dark-light contrasts in black and white film and unexpected hues in color film. Experimentation in the darkroom has taken many forms. Images can be broken up and recombined in photomontage; distortion can be induced by tilting the paper under the enlarger or by making the paper concave or convex during enlargement. The photographer can lighten areas of a print by masking them or shading (dodging) them during exposure under the enlarger. High-contrast photographic paper can be used to eliminate details and half-tones, thus producing bold contrasts between major shapes. Negative prints reverse dark and light values; and negatives can be modified before printing. For example, partial reexposure of film during its development can result in part negative, part positive prints with luminous effects, a process called *solarization*. In the *cliché verre* technique, glass is drawn or painted on and then used as a negative to make photographic prints. A whole new field for photography exists in *holograms*, three-dimensional photographic images projected into space by laser beams.

The following are only a few of the outstanding photographers thus far in our century.

Alfred Stieglitz (United States, 1864–1946). Stieglitz grew up in New York and went to Germany to study engineering, where he changed his field of study to photography and, after eight years abroad, returned to New York in 1890. As his career developed, he produced photographs of his immediate surroundings that reflected remarkable patience and a subtle sense of tonal values and design. Although he did not retouch, enlarge, or manipulate effects, Stieglitz defended pictorial, or manipulated, photography because his major interest was in the aesthetic potential of formal elements. Many of his photographs, moreover, convey great sensitivity to the character of a place. In *The Terminal* (Fig. 18-8), an initial sense of numbing cold and steaming horseflesh is portrayed within a subtle range of grays and a design that sets the diagonal of the car and the taut curves of the rails against the white of the piled snow and the angles of the architecture. Through his own photography as well as his editorship of *Camera Work* and his leadership of the 291 Gallery, Stieglitz achieved international importance in the history of art.

18-7
DOUG PRINCE, Untitled, 1975. Solarization print. Courtesy, Light Gallery, New York.

18-8
ALFRED STIEGLITZ, *The Terminal*, 1893.

Imogen Cunningham (United States, 1883–1976). After studying chemistry in the United States and Germany, Imogen Cunningham turned to professional photography. Upon her return to the United States she opened a portrait studio and quickly gained a steady clientele. She continued her portrait photography, on both commercial and artistic levels, for the rest of her life. Always concerned with the carefully designed image, she also photographed people in a wide variety of compositions, plants in tight closeups, and architectural elements in virtually abstract compositions. Although devoted to the principles of direct photography espoused by the f/64 group, Cunningham also used various techniques to manipulate her images. But the works for which she is primarily noted are straight photographs of people and plants. Her *Self-Portrait on Geary Street, 1958* (Fig. 18-9) combines the several qualities characteristic of her photography. Although an example of direct photography, the picture gives one the impression of being a multiple image created in the darkroom. This is achieved by the discontinuity in spatial relationships created by the vertical mirror. On

18-9
IMOGEN CUNNINGHAM,
Self-Portrait on Geary Street,
1958.

18-10
EDWARD WESTON, *Dunes, Oceano, California,* 1936.

the level of abstract form, however, there is considerable continuity throughout the image. The verticals of the mirror's edges are paralleled by the verticals of the architectural details, such as the doorways and the supporting post; the rectangles of the back wall are continuous with rectangles reflected behind Cunningham in the mirror; the diagonal edge of her cloak in the mirror echoes the diagonal axes of the panels leaning against the side wall on the porch. An intense awareness of the interaction of light, tone, form, and design is present throughout all her work.

Edward Weston (United States, 1886–1958). From his youth, Weston planned to be a photographer. He earned his living by portraiture, but he established his reputation as an artist with photographs of landscapes and architecture, and close-ups of shells, fruits, and vegetables. Weston quickly earned awards for soft-focus pictures and then changed to sharp detail during the growth of the New Objectivity movement in the 1920's. His favorite instrument was an 8" x 10" view camera (a camera with a removable back that allows the photographer to see on ground glass the image that will be received on the plate of film that is then inserted; the camera also has bellows that are extendable, allowing the use of a wide variety of lenses). Weston worked directly, usually without enlargement. In 1932 he helped found f/64, a group of California photographers dedicated to direct photography (f/64 refers to a small-diaphragm aperture that produces sharp focus). Between 1937 and 1939, he received two Guggenheim grants and produced fifteen hundred pictures, many of which were later published in *California and the West*, a record of a photographic trip, produced jointly with his wife. *Dunes, Oceano* (Fig. 18-10) is typical of his later work in its rich textural detail, bold patterns, and dramatic rhythmic sweep.

18-11
DOROTHEA LANGE, *Migrant Mother, Nipomo, California,* 1936. Dorothea Lange Collection, The Oakland Museum.

Dorothea Lange (United States, 1895–1965). After studying photography at Columbia University, Lange set out at age 20 to work her way around the world as a photographer. She got no farther than San Francisco, however, where she opened a portrait studio in 1916. Photography became for her a means of understanding human beings in specific situations, a way of enticing the viewer to appreciate the lives of others. During the Depression in the 1930's, she and the economist Paul Taylor were employed by the State of California, and later by the federal government, to report on the conditions of American workers. Their published reports and photographs of the unemployed and dispossessed awakened the sympathy of the country. *Migrant Mother* (Fig. 18-11) conveys anxiety and maternal concern without posing or dramatic lighting. Lange was able to catch people in naturally expressive moments that demand we consider their fate as humans. She tried not to pose or to influence her subjects, and she sought a sense of place and time. Her factual and masterful work reveals rather than preaches. She is among the best photographers in the documentary tradition.

Ansel Adams (United States, 1902–). Adams put aside a promising career as a concert pianist after publishing successful portfolios of photographs between 1923 and 1930. His favorite subjects have been the people and the landscapes of California and the Southwest. In 1932 he helped to establish Group f/64 and exhibited his work in a one-man show in the De Young Museum in San Francisco. Alfred Stieglitz was enthusiastic about Adam's work and exhibited it in New York in 1936, a year after Adams had published his first book on photographic technique. In *Sierra Nevada from Lone Pine, California* (Fig. 18-12), the delicate trees and the horse emphasize awesome scale. Contrast in values and contours expresses the grandeur of the peaks; the dark, softly curved hills mediate between the frozen, jagged heights and the fertile, life-supporting valley.

18-12
ANSEL ADAMS, *Sierra Nevada from Lone Pine, California,* 1944

Henri Cartier-Bresson (France, 1908–). Cartier-Bresson gave up painting for photography in 1930. Traveling throughout the world, he has searched out representative human situations. He uses only a 35 mm camera, eschewing flash equipment, any form of posing or manipulation, and unusual angles. This severe limitation of means allows his sure sense of design and subtle recognition of the expressive moment full play. The *Allée du Prado, Marseilles* (Fig. 18-13) exploits symmetry and perspective to focus attention on the man's head and reinforce the formal dignity of his bearing. The man's simple silhouette presents a marked contrast to the jagged trees and, with its forceful impact, suggests the power of his personality. Cartier-Bresson also made documentary films of the Spanish Civil War and, during the Second World War, served with a French army film unit. After the defeat of France he was imprisoned by the Germans and escaped after three attempts to work with the underground, for which he organized a photographic unit that took pictures of the occupation and retreating Nazi armies. His exhibitions and books of photographs have earned him an international reputation.

Duane Michals (United States, 1932–). "Everything is quite extraordinary but we use all our energies to make things ordinary," Michals has said. Like some Surrealist painters, he wants to reveal the mystery of common objects and events. He turned to photography in 1960

18-13
HENRI CARTIER-BRESSON, *Allée du Prado
Marseilles,* 1932.

after having worked as a free-lance designer in New
York. The portrait photographer, he argues, should
never impose his own personality upon that of the
subject; technique should be simple and geared only
toward capturing the most telling qualities of the subject. To express the character of our environment,
Michals photographed a series of generally well-popu-
lated places that were empty of people, including a
subway car, barbershop, office, bus, theater, and laundro-
mat. In 1968 he began to use groups of photographs in
narrative sequences. For example, in *The Human Condition* (Fig. 18-14), the first picture shows a young man
standing on a subway platform; the second shows him
dissolved in an aura of light, and the last two scenes are
views of the heavens, which suggest that the individual
has been absorbed into the vastness of the universe.
Michals's images represent an interior reality dealing
with the unusual in life and the mystical in death.

MOTION PICTURES

The most distinctive, typical, and influential art form of the twentieth century is the motion picture. Film employs visual images in time and space, elements that imitate more closely than the traditional art forms our common experience of reality. Because the viewer is seated in a dark interior before a screen with a vast range of visual and auditory effects, film is less vulnerable to distractions and more completely absorbing than many other arts. While any art can become infinitely complex, film has complexities derived from the elements of the other arts, such as plot development, pictorial composition, acting, music, and dance. The filmmaker must integrate these elements and anticipate the results of the camera operator and film editor as he or she attempts to visualize the finished work.

The basic structural units of motion pictures are the *shot*, an uninterrupted camera view that may be close up, medium, or long, and the *sequence*, a combination of shots that is produced by *editing* (cutting and splicing). A sequence may develop around a *scene*, during which action occurs in one time and place; it may take the form of a *montage*, which is a rapid succession of images and/or sounds, often used to build emotional intensity. Because of editing, film has the ability to shift time and space, move back and forth between past, present, and future, or alternate between reality and unreality. Editing may also abbreviate narrative, suggest connections between events, and show different points of view. Many of these effects are achieved by various types of *cutting*, changing from one shot to another. *Cross-cuts* are rapid switches from one scene to another to present simultaneous actions, as with alternating views of the pursued and the pursuer. A shot may *fade out* (slowly disappear from the screen) sometimes to be replaced by another. A *dissolve* simultaneously superimposes the new shot as the former image fades. Fade outs are often used to conclude a film. When cuts make large jumps in space and time, the filmmaker must ensure against spectator confusion—unless ambiguity is desired. Transitions between narrative events are some-

18-14
DUANE MICHALS, *The Human Condition,* 1969.

times needed: Cutting back to previous events (*flashback*), as with the memories of a character, can provide the necessary connections and is often used to provide the exposition or background information for a film. Transitions can also be achieved by use of similar shapes or sounds: An oval-shaped face might dissolve into the oval of a baseball stadium; a thundering waterfall might merge into the sound of stampeding horses. By manipulating his or her shots, as in accelerating or slowing the experience of time in a sequence, the editor can create rhythm, gradation, and climax in a film.

The expressive content of a film depends on camera work as well as on effective editing. The camera angle can evoke the emotional overtones of a character or a setting (see the discussion of perspective angles on pp. 6–7). *Framing* (composing) the shot within the rectangle of the film involves many of the pictorial elements and design functions discussed in Part I of this book, but with the complicating addition of actual movement. The use of the wide screen has made vast scale possible but has produced problems in framing. These problems are prominent when one or two characters are shown on a wide rectangular screen that includes a large amount of setting. In such situations, soft focus can be used to keep the background from competing with foreground action. The motion-picture camera may be stationary during a shot, or it may be attached to some form of *dolly*, a mobile platform that can be as simple as an extension arm on a tripod, or as complex as a wheeled platform on tracks and a boom (a platform device on a truck-attached fire ladder), which allows the camera operator to hover over the subject. A *pan* (sweeping) shot is effective for panoramic vistas. A *dolly* shot can, for example, follow a group traveling through a landscape, or can move toward or away from a subject to express isolation or intimacy.

Other elements that affect the expressive content of a film are makeup, costuming, set design, lighting, color, and the quality of sound, in other words, volume or harshness. Each of these elements can utilize the design functions discussed in Part I, such as repetition, theme and variation, gradation, and climax.

Film's ancestry goes back to the magic lantern, a primitive slide projector invented in the seventeenth century. By the 1830's, a number of toys had been invented that produced the illusion of moving images. In one of these, a series of figures in varied poses was painted around the outside of a disk, the circumference of which was notched with slots (Fig. 18-15). The user held the painted side toward a mirror, spun the disk slowly, and viewed the reflected figures through the slots. Rather than a blur of forms, a distinct image was seen in apparent motion. By the 1850's, a magic lantern was used to project such images onto a wall. In the 1870's, two experiments advanced the analysis of motion through photography: Eadweard Muybridge arranged a row of cameras along a race track and produced a series of photos showing the sequential positions of a galloping horse, and the movement of the planet Venus was recorded by the French astronomer Pierre Jules César Janssen, who used a clockwork photographic device to take pictures at intervals (*chronophotography*). In the 1890's motion pictures were projected from film by inventors in France, the United States, Germany, and England. By passing film—consisting at first of hundreds, and later of thousands, of still photographs (*frames*)—through a projector, the illusion of motion was produced on the screen. Although each frame occupies the screen for only a fraction of a second, the image is retained somewhat longer by the retinas of our eyes, causing each image to merge with the next. Since the position of a moving object is slightly different in each frame, the rapid sequence of merged frames produces the sensation of moving objects. After the 1890's, development of films was swift.

18-15
Phenakistiscope.

Borrowing tested plots from the popular stage, early directors created films characterized by violent action, exaggerated pantomime, strong contrasts in emotions, and polar opposites in good and evil. The result was melodrama. Live music, usually provided by a piano, was added in the theater to accompany a film and to stress action and mood. Early silent films were made with a stationary camera recording uninterrupted action, like that of a stage play. The narrative time of the film was confined to the actual time it took to photograph the scene. At first, films were only several minutes in length and recorded special events or provided amusement with pantomimed comic episodes. As technical improvement occurred, directors freed themselves from the space-time and static-spectator limitations of the early films as they developed the expressive potential of a mobile camera and film editing. Changes in narrative time and space were pioneered by the French director Georges Méliès in his science-fiction films *The Vanishing Lady* (1896) and *A Trip to the Moon* (1902). In America, Edwin Porter began to alternate close-up and medium-distance shots, as well as interior and exterior scenes, to build his story in *The Life of an*

American Fireman (1902) and *The Great Train Robbery* (1903).

The greatest early filmmaker was the American D. W. Griffith, who toned down overacting, used electric lighting for dramatic effects, employed double and triple exposures, tinted his film, and made camera work and editing as expressive as acting. Simultaneously, Charles Chaplin was directing and acting in comic masterpieces of his own creation. Somewhat later, documentary films were established in America with Robert Flaherty's *Nanook of the North* (1922), which explored the life of the Eskimo.

One of the trends in the filmmaking of Germany after the First World War was *Expressionism*, a cinematic style that bore some resemblance to German painting, poetry, and drama known by the same label. *The Cabinet of Dr. Caligari* (1919–20), by Hans Janowitz, Carl Mayer, and Robert Wiene, depicted various states of mind by employing artificial light, abstract sets designed by German painters, unusual camera angles, sudden shifts of scene, stylized acting, and a complex plot (Fig. 18-16). Germany and Austria, however, also produced a *Realistic* film trend that, although related to Expressionism, dealt with simple, ordinary situations involving individual and social tensions. *The Joyless Street* (1925), directed by G. W. Pabst, portrayed the economic and moral decline of the Austrian middle class during the inflationary period following World War I. Film Realism parallels the New Objectivity movement in photography and in German painting of the 1920's.

In marked contrast to the German and Austrian cinema, Russian films of this period combined epic scale and social commentary. Its development began right after the October Revolution of 1917 and was led by Sergei Eisenstein, who used editing to create powerful contrasts and symbolic parallels between nature, objects, and people. His actors were often nonprofessionals. Each shot was carefully composed to exploit its abstract relations of masses, shapes, and values; narrative conflict was often reinforced by contrasting movement in the images of successive shots. Eisenstein's preeminent cinematic device was montage, which he used to heighten the dramatic intensity, symbolic force, and ideological persuasiveness of his films. The small Russian film industry was put under government control after 1919, and thereafter films served a propagandistic function.

In France and Germany after 1919 significant film experiments were undertaken by the *Dada* movement,

18-16

HANS JANOWITZ, CARL MAYER, and ROBERT WIENE, *The Cabinet of Dr. Caligari,* 1919–20.

which lasted from 1916 to 1923, and the *Surrealist* movement, which began in 1924. These movements, largely in literature, painting, and sculpture, were inspired by the Freudian theory of the unconscious and by an increasing appreciation of nonrational thought processes and of the subjective nature of reality (see Chapter 19). Dada and Surrealistic films employed surprising combinations of images to reproduce the effects of dream experience in order to stimulate the viewer's imagination. Leaders in Germany were Hans Richter and Raoul Haussmann; in Paris, they were the American painter-photographer Man Ray, the French artist Marcel Duchamp, the Spanish filmmaker Luis Buñuel, and the Spanish painter Salvador Dali. Their films pioneered in the use of sudden, disjointed contrasts in images, and their influence is important in contemporary cinematography.

After more than thirty years of experiment with synchronized records and other devices, sound tracks for film became available in the 1920's. The first major sound film in America was *The Jazz Singer* (1927). At first, actors had to stay close to a microphone and the noisy camera had to be enclosed in a soundproof booth, resulting in severe restriction of movement. Greater freedom came with the development of quieter cameras and of more sophisticated microphones suspended on booms (cranes) near the actors.

Sound was exploited immediately in the animated films made by Walt Disney. Animated films are made by photographing thousands of drawings, each one with slight variations in the position of the object to be represented in motion. When the film passes through the projector, the illusion of movement is produced in the same way as with frames photographed from living actors.

Color was attempted early in film history. At that time monochromatic tints were used: for example, green for landscapes, red for dramatic violence. By 1935 a wide range of colors was available to the filmmakers, but for some years these colors were often garish and lacking in nuances. Today filmic color can provide a subtle display of nuances in hue and tone. The serious filmmaker is now able to use either color or black and white, according to his aesthetic needs.

During the 1930's and '40's, filmmaking in Hollywood became big business, resulting in huge studio organizations that deprived the director of total control by interposing special departments for music, sound, writing, producing, directing, and editing. Artistic quality often suffered. In its place, dependable formulas for

18-17
ORSON WELLES, *Citizen Kane*, 1941.

box-office success were evolved for musicals, westerns, comedies, detective stories, and fantasies. Good usually triumphed over evil, and daydream over reality. Both inside and outside these Hollywood formulas good works were produced when depth and subtlety of content or strength of cinematic techniques rose above stereotypes. Among war films, Lewis Milestone's *All Quiet on the Western Front* (1930) was a deeply moving antiwar statement that benefited from its striking episodes and effective editing. Alfred Hitchcock's mystery films, such as *The 39 Steps* (1935), were original in their mixture of suspense, surprise, mystery, and whimsy. John Huston's *The Maltese Falcon* (1941) was unusually strong in its combination of humor, tension, violence, and surprise. Landmarks in filmmaking included Orson Welles's *Citizen Kane* (1941), which was brilliant in its sociological interpretation, compositional complexity, and technical innovation, and John Ford's *Grapes of Wrath* (1940), wherein fine acting and editing did justice to John Steinbeck's powerful novel about the tragedy of the dust bowl. In comedy, outstanding acting overcame unimaginative or stereotyped plots in Charlie Chaplin's films, such as *The Great Dictator* (1940), and in W. C. Fields's films of the 1930's.

In France during the 1930's and '40's filmmakers gained from the Surrealist experiments of the 1920's and from powerful psychological studies such as Carl-Theodore Dreyer's *The Passion of Joan of Arc* (1928). René Clair's *À Nous la Liberté* (1931) combined fantasy with harsh comment on the dreary lives of mass-production workers. Visual metaphors, creative use of sound, and symbolic action are outstanding. Moral decadence in the French upper class furnished the theme for Jean Renoir's *The Rules of the Game* (1939), while Marcel Carné and the poet Jacques Prévert collaborated in films such as *Port of Shadows* (1938) that explored the problems of individual freedom within a social system. The union of aesthetic subtlety and social realism caused the term "poetic realism" to be applied to these films.

England also experienced a great expansion in film technology, audience support, and organization within the filmmaking and film-distributing industry in the 1930's and '40's. Alfred Hitchcock directed mystery films, and Anthony Asquith's *Tell England* (1931) was the first effort to interpret World War I with historical perspective. Along with a wealth of documentary films on such themes as weather warning systems and sea rescue, there were realistic dramas like Carol Reed's mining story, *The Stars Look Down* (1939). The English film industry, which was relatively small even in its period of greatest expansion, produced many elaborate costume epics based on historical figures such as *Catherine the Great*, directed by Paul Czinner in 1934, and on literary classics such as Shakespeare's *As You Like It*, directed by Czinner in 1936. The further development of British films was inhibited from 1941 until 1945 by World War II.

German films of the 1930's suffered under restrictive Nazi pressures. After an imaginative mountaineering film called *The Blue Light* (1932), the woman director Leni Riefenstahl turned to filmed glorification of Hitler in *The Triumph of the Will* (1936). G. W. Pabst scorned the heroics of militarism in *Westfront, 1918* (1930) and was forced to flee to Paris. Max Ophuls also incurred the wrath of the Nazi regime with his *Liebelei* (1933) and left Germany in 1933.

Government control continued to hamper the creativity of Russian filmmakers in the 1930's and '40's; nevertheless, impressive films were produced. Eisenstein believed that sound should not be used merely to record the speech of the actors but rather to add a distinctly different and often opposing element, which is evident in parts of *Alexander Nevsky* (1938). But the Soviet government film control committee felt that Eisenstein was too esoteric for the masses and accused him of "formalism." Similarly accused was Vsevlod Pudovkin, a leading director of Soviet films (*Deserter*, 1933), who preferred smoother, less abrupt editing than that of Eisenstein. Stunning pictorial composition within the frame and a sense of fantasy characterize the work of Alexander Dovzhenko (*Ivan*, 1932). The Soviet leader in documentaries was Dziga-Vertov (*Three Songs of Lenin*, 1934).

The Second World War brought about a significant break in the history of serious film. After the war, many countries needed years to regain momentum in their film activities. Moreover, postwar television changed the nature of movie audiences. In the United States, especially, home television provided the relaxation formerly found in motion pictures. Those who attend the movies today tend to come from the younger and more educated segments of the population and are more demanding than moviegoers of the past. Contemporary films contain a "new intellectualism" that is very appealing to this younger audience. The old formulas, however, are still used for television, while many of the huge studios of prewar Hollywood have closed or have dispersed their activities.

Postwar French films continued their earlier empha-

18-18
ALAIN RESNAIS, *Last Year at Marienbad*, 1961.

sis on elaborate formal structure at the expense of naturalness. Surrealist experimentation inspired the writer Jean Cocteau to make films. Max Ophuls made his major films in France during the 1950's; his films minimize narrative and use a series of situations to comment on conflicts between sexual obsessions and social mores. Jacques Tati's few but carefully made films established him as a brilliant director and actor of comedy. The most distinctive postwar French movement was *la Nouvelle Vague* (the New Wave), which began in 1959. The films of this movement are stylistically identifiable by ambiguity, surprise, and abrupt changes in space, time, and mood. Of the leaders, Alain Resnais uses the most calculated effects. His *Last Year at Marienbad* (1961), from the script by Alain Robbe-Grillet, retains a slow, contemplative pace even while blurring distinctions between past, present, and future. François Truffaut employs more spontaneous leaps in time and space in conjunction with abrupt changes in shooting style, ranging from long nostalgic shots to abruptly comic ones, as in *Jules and Jim* (1961); Jean-Luc Godard switches from rational to irrational actions and encourages the viewer to remain detached from filmic illusions.

Other directions have also been explored since the 1950's. The Swedish director Ingmar Bergman employs elaborate symbolism and allegory to deal with life, death, and human strivings. England's postwar films have included polished adaptions of literary classics, elegant Robert Hamer comedies for Alec Guinness, "Angry Young Men" portrayals of life at various levels of British society—especially the working class—and suspense films of military or political conflict. From a strictly cinematic point of view English films have been very conservative.

In reaction against the technical slickness and banality of films of the late 1930's and '40's, especially those of Hollywood, the postwar moviegoing public found special satisfaction in the loosely plotted, commonplace dramas of survival presented by Italian Neorealist films, such as Roberto Rossillini's *Open City* (1945) and Vittorio De Sica's *The Bicycle Thief* (1947). Nonprofessional actors were often used. Such films expressed the ideas of one person, the filmmaker, and led, in Europe, to the "auteur" (author) approach to film criticism, which developed in the mid-1950's and treated the film as a work of art made by one individual rather than by a group, as in Hollywood. The auteur approach is less suited to big Hollywood films, which are often the product of a collective effort, are written to fit the talents of specific stars, and are conceived as works of entertainment rather than as works of art.

Two of the most influential filmmakers of the 1960's and '70's, Michelangelo Antonioni and Frederico Fellini, produced their early works in the Neorealist style. Antonioni's art has moved from the effects of social situations on individuals to evocations of states of mind. Fellini's development has been toward lavish richness and multiplication of images loosely connected by a narrative line. He portrays the frustration of the body and the decay of the spirit in a corrupt society.

Revolutionary political content characterizes many of the contemporary films made in Cuba, South America, and the communist or socialist countries. The most creative work, however, is usually less specific in its political message and more involved with the broader aspects of human experience. In spite of a strong nationalistic trend, Cuban films have shown imagination, humor, and versatility; Tomás Gutiérrez Alea and Manuel Octavio Gomez have been the important directors. In Brazil, Glauber Rocha has written on film theory and directed experimental films that combine folklore with urgings for social reform. In Hungary, Miklós Jancsó's films, such as *Silence and Cry* (1968), often deal with the confusion that follows a war, with arbitrary acts of cruelty, with shifting political power, and with opposing groups that are neither good nor bad, right nor wrong. His style consists of long shots taken by a constantly moving camera; cuts are used mainly to show a change of time or place. In Yugoslavia, Dusan Makavejev used brilliant editing in his *WR: Mysteries of the Organism* (1971) to unite a kaleidoscopic array of materials into a hilariously erotic political comedy.

In India, the films of Satyajit Ray have portrayed tensions between traditional social forms and modern developments in society by focusing on individuals and select details. His major work has been the Apu trilogy: *Pather Panchali* (1954), *Aparajito* (1956), and *The World of Apu* (1959). In Japan, Akira Kurosawa has been a leading filmmaker for the past thirty years. Although he has been influenced by such western authors as Dostoevsky, Kurosawa addresses himself primarily to social and human issues within the distinctive context of Japanese culture. His *Rashomon* (1950) and *Seven Samurai* (1954) made western viewers aware of Japanese filmmaking. In *Rashomon*, he used tracking shots with great effectiveness to express moods, personalities, and the uncertainty of perception. In *Seven Samurai* intercuts, panning shots, and zoom shots were used to create the illusion of frantic action and the terror of battle. Kurosawa's carefully composed frames have been appreciated as poetic and powerful. *Seven Samurai* has an international reputation as one of the best post-war films.

In America, Neorealism had some impact on works such as Stanley Kramer's and Fred Zinnemann's *High*

18-19

AKIRA KUROSAWA, *Seven Samurai*, 1954.

Noon (1952), Otto Preminger's *Exodus* (1960), and Elia Kazan's *On the Waterfront* (1954). *Bonnie and Clyde* (1967) by Arthur Penn went further than earlier films in using sudden changes in mood, abrupt contrasts of humor and brutality, and antiheroes. Imagination and vast scale were joined in Stanley Kubrick's *Dr. Strangelove* (1964) and *2001: A Space Odyssey* (1968). *Bonnie and Clyde* and Kubrick's films utilize ambiguity, but the space-time and causal relationships remain generally more conventional than in the most pioneering films of Fellini, Antonioni, or Resnais. Underground films, however, have been the freest vehicles of experimentation in America. Directors like Andy Warhol have reverted to simple, even crude, methods and equipment, using a static camera to portray an almost eventless scene or a continuous shot to study explicit sexual behavior. Other underground filmmakers use hand-held cameras, while still others use complex equipment. Stan Brakhage, for example, produced dizzying superimpositions of astronomical, anatomical, and microscopic images in *Dog Star Man* (1959–64).

The avant-garde films made since World War II have tended to express the uncertainty of our experience of reality, especially our ability to distinguish illusion from reality, by rejecting or modifying traditional narrative sequences and causal relationships. These films represent emotional states or responses to the environment through random, often disconnected episodes. Transitions between scenes may be minimized for effects of jarring discontinuity, as in some contemporary poetry. Dialogue and background music have sometimes been reduced or entirely eliminated. As in the other arts, such as painting, literature, music, and dance, avant-garde films have revealed a need to defy traditional rules and values. They demand a fresh vision, heightened awareness, and continuous sympathy from their limited audience. Above all, avant-garde filmmakers have sought freedom to use all aspects of the human experience in their work.

The following directors represent a very incomplete list of outstanding talents in twentieth-century filmmaking.

David Wark Griffith (United States, 1875–1948). After a childhood in Kentucky, Griffith went to New York, where he acted in Edwin S. Porter's films. By 1908 Griffith was directing short melodramas for the rapidly multiplying nickelodeon theaters. Between 1908 and 1913 he experimented with camera and editing in these short, innovative films. His insistence on rehearsals, an

18-20
DAVID WARK GRIFFITH, *Intolerance*, 1916.

extravagance in the eyes of his employers, led to improved acting. Griffith's films always had a melodramatic quality, in part because he was a moralizer who stressed the virtues of peace, courage, motherhood, fidelity, home, and family. In 1914 he produced his first epic, *The Birth of a Nation*, based on Thomas Dixon's novel *The Clansman*. It concerns the South in the periods before, during, and after the Civil War. The racist portrayal of blacks mars the film, but its stupendous scale, innovative camera work, and imaginative editing made it a commercial success and an object of international study. His next spectacle was on an even grander scale (Fig. 18-20). *Intolerance* (1916) was intended as a rebuke to those critics who had censured *The Birth of a Nation* for its bigotry. The basic theme of the film is that narrow-mindedness results in evil. *Intolerance* was not a commercial success. Griffith's moralizing and his melodramatic compulsions eventually made his films seem old-fashioned. After 1931 he ceased making films and spent his last seventeen years watching others develop an art in which he had been a pioneer.

Robert Flaherty (United States, 1884–1951). The documentary films made by Flaherty are a form of realism dealing with the human battle for survival against nature. His first use of a movie camera was to document an exploration of Hudson Bay in Canada. In 1920 he persuaded a French fur company to sponsor him in producing a film about one year in the lives of a typical Eskimo family. For sixteen months he shared their precarious existence and returned with *Nanook of the North* (1922). The camera was stationary, using only pans and tilts, and the editing was simple; but the frames were effectively composed and the stark presentation was impressive. Unlike Griffith or Eisenstein, Flaherty used very simple and direct techniques in his early works. Despite this simplicity of method, he leads us to understand his subjects and their values. *Man of Aran* (1934), filmed in the stark Aran Islands off Ireland, again centered on the life of a representative family wresting a living from the meager land and the violent sea. Bolder dark-light contrasts were used with increased sophistication in editing. Flaherty's documentaries ignore modern influences in the lives of his subjects. He wanted to record their primitive customs even when some of these had to be relearned and staged for the camera. Such staging raises questions about the truth that documentaries seek.

Charles Chaplin (United States, 1889–). In 1913 Chaplin was lured away from vaudeville by the Keystone Studios, where he was directed by Mack Sennett. Sennett, however, emphasized superficial silliness, and Chaplin, who had spent two years of his boyhood in a workhouse for the poor, wanted to use comedy to reveal human aspirations and weaknesses. He therefore left Keystone for Essanay so that he could write and direct his own films. In works like *The Tramp* (1915) and *The Gold Rush* (1925), he portrays a tragicomic loner, excluded from most human fellowship and from the good life—at least until the climactic end of the plot. Through his character types, especially his clown figure, the Little Tramp, he comments on social values. Chaplin was also ingenious in exploiting objects as instruments of comedy and using variations on themes to unify his plots. His early sound films, such as *Modern Times* (1936), used synchronized scores but not speech. His later works contain a large portion of pathos and social comment. *Limelight* (1952) revives the circus theme, which he had used earlier in *The Circus* (1928), to present clowns as symbols of the tragicomic duality of human behavior.

18-21
CHARLES CHAPLIN, *Modern Times*, 1936.

Jean Renoir (France and the United States, 1894–   ). Renoir, the youngest son of the renowned painter, wrote his first script and directed his first film in 1924. The financial failure of his early works forced him to produce conventional, commercially viable films during the rest of the silent period. With sound, however, he began to create works that were both artistically significant and profitable. International attention came with *La Grande Illusion* (1937), which uses a World War I prison to reveal stratification and change in European society. In microcosm we are shown the decline of aristocracy and the rise of the working and middle classes. *The Rules of the Game* (1939) depicts the corrupt and ritualistic behavior of the upper class. Here Renoir was a pioneer in the use of deep focus to contrast foreground with background actions for purposes of tension. Tracking shots of long duration contrast with the fast action of the plot, which develops during a weekend house party at a country estate. Conventional behavior patterns are seen to apply to adultery as well as to a brutal hunt. Much of the film's power derives from parallel action. The hunt of the animals by the weekend guests is echoed in the "hunt" of the women by the men and the hunt of an "enemy" by a jealous husband. Rhythmic editing and subtle use of the camera help express the mood of the characters and the world they inhabit; comic touches abound. The film was banned by the French government. Renoir spent the years of the Second World War working in the United States. His postwar films, among them *The Golden Coach* (1953), have been more abstract in allegory, more delicate in image, and lighter in mood than his earlier work. Protest has given way to benevolence.

Sergei M. Eisenstein (Russia, 1898–1948).   Viewing Griffith's *Intolerance*, Eisenstein changed his interest from stage to screen, and his first picture, *Strike*, was made in 1924. A scarcity of camera film is thought to have led Russian directors to use sequences of brief shots that imply much more than is actually shown. Under the film teacher Lev Kulshov, and through study of Griffith's work, Eisenstein learned to use editing to build narrative, suggest ideas, and evoke emotion. In his films shots jump ahead, flash back, or crosscut to represent simultaneous actions. Parallel shots of a priest tapping his crucifix and an officer tapping his sword in *Potemkin* (1925) suggest the oppression of the people by church and state. In the same film, a shot of a sailor smashing plates forecasts a mutiny. Far more subtly than for Griffith, editing works for Eisenstein in several ways to create mood: *tonally*, by moving gradually or suddenly from light to dark; *rhythmically*, by varying the length of shots to suggest slowing or quickening of tempo; *formally*, by exploiting the difference or similarity of shapes for unity or contrast; and *directionally*, by repeating or contrasting movement. A textbook demonstration of such devices can be found in *Potemkin*, an interpretation of a mutiny that is supported by the people of Odessa and, in Eisenstein's hands, becomes an epic representation of the Russian Revolution. Eisenstein did not use professional actors for his films, choosing instead untrained local people to fill the roles. His process of selection reflected his interest in social groups and types rather than in individuals. As his career developed, Eisenstein wrote many books on film theory that provide unusual insights into the creative process of filmmaking.

Rene Clair (France, 1898–   ).   Clair came to filmmaking by way of acting and film criticism. His first film established the character of his style. *Paris qui dort* (1923), or *The Crazy Ray*, deals with the effects of a ray that puts the Parisian population to sleep, paralyzed in the midst of their activities. When the ray is turned off, action is first frenetic and then depicted in slow motion. The narrative line of *Entr'acte* (1924) is less logical. The film ranges from fantasy to slapstick and reveals the influence of Dada and Surrealist art. Cinematic trickery abounds. *The Italian Straw Hat* (1927), usually considered the best of Clair's silent films, adds satire of bourgeois manners to wild whimsy. The economic crisis of 1930 may, in part, explain the harsher social comment in *À Nous la Liberté* (1931), in which two escaped convicts find that neither management nor labor has freedom in a production-oriented society. Parallel shots of prison and factory activities are effective. The pessimism of the message is lightened by bits of Chaplinesque humor. During the Second World War, Clair worked in Hollywood and has since made a number of elegant films.

Luis Buñuel (Spain, United States, Mexico, and France, 1900–   ).   Buñuel's disapproval of the Spanish government led him to move to France in 1925. *Un Chien Andalou* (1927) and *L'Age d'Or* (1930), made by Buñuel and Salvador Dali, are early classics of Surrealist cinema. Shocking in their illogical contrasts, sexual references, and sadistic violence, these films represent a world subject to the chaotic demands of the subconscious. *Un Chien Andalou*, for example, contains an

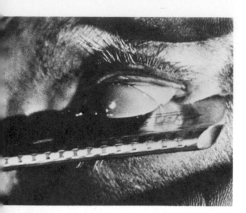

18-22
LUIS BUÑUEL and SALVADOR DALI, *Un Chien Andalou*, 1927.

unforgettable shot of a razor slicing the eye of a young woman. Buñuel used a more documentary approach in *Los Hurdes* (1932) and *Los Olvidados* (1950) to show the degradation of extreme poverty in Spain and Mexico. The intensity of action and image makes a powerful and pessimistic statement about society. While Buñuel's repertory includes comedy, his dominant themes emerge from a sardonic view of human weakness. *Belle de Jour* (1967) presents a typically jolting contrast of beautiful photography and brutal action and a blurring of distinctions between the worlds of reality and fantasy. A young doctor's wife, through boredom or frustration, becomes a daytime prostitute in a brothel. After erotic adventures with a wide range of clients, she is so desired by one that he shoots and cripples her husband, whom the wife then apparently nurses. The closing scene, however, suggests that much of the preceding story might have been fantasy. The film's light touches do not soften Buñuel's basic view of human nature as ambivalent and easily corruptible.

Vittorio De Sica (Italy, 1902–). A well-known actor in the 1930's, De Sica turned to directing in 1939. His films were the inspiration of the Neorealist movement between 1944 and 1952. His most admired work, *The Bicycle Thief* (1948), involves the search by a father and son for a stolen bicycle that is necessary to a newfound job (Fig. 18-23). In desperation the father finally steals a bike but is caught and shamed before his son. De Sica's filming of all scenes on location rather than in the studio, his use of nonactors for major roles, and his

18-23
VITTORIO DE SICA, *The Bicycle Thief*, 1948.

emphasis on demeaning social conditions are typical of Neorealism. Simple editing and use of medium shots support an effect of objectivity that reinforces the realism of the film.

Michelangelo Antonioni (Italy, 1912–). Antonioni's early films were documentaries. His first full-length picture, *Cronaca di un Amore* (1950), contains elements of his later films: the special emphasis on women and a tendency to emphasize the feelings of his characters more than the events of his stories. This film, like *Le Amiche* (1955) and *Il Grido* (1957), portrays frustrated, isolated lives and allies itself with Neorealism. A change is evident in *L'Avventura* (1960), the film that won Antonioni international acclaim. During an excursion a girl disappears; she is never found, but, in the process of searching for her, her fiancé and friends experience complex changes in their relationships to each other. Transitions between scenes are slow, and the meager narrative events are overshadowed by Antonioni's study of their mental consequences. As in earlier films, the human situation is characterized by boredom, self-centeredness, ambivalence, and loneliness; yet in this work some communion is finally apparent between the two main characters. The end of the film suggests a trace of hope for the future. Alienation is also a major theme in the two films that followed: *La Notte* (1961) and *Red Desert* (1964). In Antonioni's films, the human problem is to break out of one's solitude, to communicate with others. This theme is evident in *Blow-Up* (1967), which in its fast action, jumpy editing, and blurring of fantasy and reality is related to the New Wave films in France. In *Zabriskie Point* (1970), shot mainly in Death Valley and dealing with American youth, Antonioni develops greater looseness of narrative links between beautifully photographed kaleidoscopic parts than he had previously.

Ingmar Bergman (Sweden, 1918–). Bergman began writing and directing professionally for stage, radio, television, and films in 1944, after studying at Stockholm University and working in amateur theater. International recognition came in the 1950's with three films: *The Seventh Seal* (1956), *Wild Strawberries* (1957), and *The Magician* (1958). The first film uses moody symbolism to explore the human quest for meaning in a brutal world. A disillusioned knight returns from years of crusading to find Sweden ravaged by the plague and by moral corruption. The figure of Death appears, and

18-24
MICHELANGELO ANTONIONI, *L'Avventura,* 1960. Courtesy Janus Films.

18-25
INGMAR BERGMAN, *The Seventh Seal,*
1956. Courtesy Janus Films.

the knight challenges him to a game of chess in order to gain time to seek knowledge of God and to do some worthy act. The knight, who seeks God, and his squire, a cynical, practical materialist, are contrasted in their sophistication with a family of young actors whose simple love is unburdened by profound questions or the cynicism of worldly experience. The knight distracts death, losing the chess match but saving the lives of the actors, and thus accomplishes a positive moral act. At the end of the film all but the actors are forced to join Death in a dancing procession that moves out along a high ridge silhouetted against the sky (Fig. 18-25). The basically simple plot is complicated by the symbolic overtones of every action and detail. Bergman treated theological questions within an allegorical framework, yet the power of his presentation and the universal import of his content appeal to a wide modern audience. Although his editing is not unusual, his composition within each frame is striking and has gained him wide acclaim. *Persona* (1966), a title taken from the Latin word for an actor's mask or the Jungian term for the role an individual plays in life, is freer in narrative style and cinematic technique than Bergman's earlier films. Attention is called to the film medium itself when cinematographer and director are photographed and when, at a moment of great tension, the face on the screen dissolves as the film is burned away. Bits and pieces of consciousness are presented from different and uncertain points of view in time and space, as the film seems to present a struggle for identity between a nurse and her patient as well as the conflicts between dream and reality, life and art. Equally concerned with aesthetic distance, *The Passion of Anna* (1970) explores psychological conflicts and the search for love. The film has a complex structure that uses interviews with actors to promote viewer detachment. Sound, color, and composition within the frame are remarkably expressive.

Federico Fellini (Italy, 1921–). Fellini is concerned with alienation from a moral point of view. Neorealism is evident in *I Vitelloni* (1953). By 1954, with *La Strada*, his insistence on private feelings represented a break with Neorealism. The success of *La Strada* opened the way for *La Dolce Vita* (1958–60), a vast, convoluted, and fragmented work that became the subject of international controversy. Fellini wanted to show the moral condition of humanity and the rootlessness of modern culture. Fellini says that autobiographical material was used in this film and in $8\frac{1}{2}$ (1962), where divisions between reality and dream are less distinct. In this work, a film director goes to a health spa to rest, and the arrival of first his mistress and then his wife (Fellini's spouse) triggers memories and fantasies in a lavish profusion of images. Dialogue is relatively unimportant. In *Satyricon* (1969), the orchestration of forms and colors reaches a zenith. The source of the film is the fragmented work of literature attributed to Petronius, a Roman of the first century A.D. The original story consists of a series of episodes, often disconnected in time and space and rarely complete in themselves, that occur in the life of a beautiful youth. His adventures run the gamut of sexual perversities and debauchery in a Roman society that has lost its faith, values, and stability. Fellini hewed closely to the episodic structure of the original, created an astounding variety of grotesque human characters, and added a mélange of languages. Action is sometimes recounted in dialogue rather than being shown; at other times, dialogue is hardly more than background sound to the action and images. Fellini has said that he wanted *Satyricon* to suggest the idea of fragments excavated from the debris of the past. He also intended an analogy with society today.

18-26
FREDERICO FELLINI, *La Dolce Vita,*
1958–60

Jean-Luc Godard (France, 1930–). Godard's first major film, *Breathless*, appeared in 1959 as part of the New Wave in France. His films are self-conscious comments on reality rather than imitations of it; a director's philosophical statement rather than a revelation of characters. The audience is never allowed to lose itself in a story. Sudden jumps, shifts, digressions, fragmented images, and editorial comments are used to create distance between the audience and the film events. Like many twentieth-century painters and sculptors, Godard wants his spectators to appreciate the art medium not as an imitation of life but as a separate but related world. The mystique of the woman and the individual's involvement in violent human relations and class politics are basic themes developed with increasing complication in films ranging from *Le Petit Soldat* (*The Little Soldier*) of 1960 to *The Weekend* (1968). After the French student revolts of 1968, Godard withdrew from the established film industry and joined the *Dziga Vertov* group, named after a Soviet filmmaker of documentaries, to direct indoctrination films for political-action organizations. In 1972 Godard returned to making films meant for commercial distribution with *Tout Va Bien* (*All's Well*), which investigates the role of the intellectual in the revolution of the working class. In this film, Godard points to a lack of leadership and coordination in the various aspects of the class struggle. Both the Communist party and the New Left are presented as inadequate. The audience is left to ponder the sources of new leadership and the tripartite social division between workers, bourgeois, and intellectuals. Godard's film style has been described as illogical, careening, and anarchic, yet he is considered one of the most important innovators of the 1960's.

Lina Wertmuller (Italy, 1932–). Wertmuller's international reputation developed suddenly in the 1970's. She had written scripts and directed for television, theater, and short films before 1963, when Federico Fellini chose her to assist him with his film *8½*. He had previously helped her find financial backing for her first full-length film, *The Lizards* (1962), which won an award at the Locarno Film Festival. Her films show the influence of Fellini's overwhelmingly profuse imagery and of Italian Neorealism.

18-27
LINA WERTMULLER. *Seven Beauties*. 1975.

Although she has been described as belonging to the New Left, Wertmuller's films cannot be described as political propaganda; they deal with individuals trapped and denied by social systems of all types. *All Screwed Up* (1973) portrays young people forced into dehumanizing roles in order to survive in an urban situation. *Swept Away* (1974) is a modern treatment of an old theme: the reversal of roles when master and servant are shipwrecked on a deserted island. A wealthy woman behaves arrogantly to a deckhand on her yacht only to become his slave and mistress after they are marooned. In *Seven Beauties* (1975), a petty hoodlum employs a wide range of survival techniques when he counters a murder conviction with a successful insanity plea and maneuvers from a mental hospital to the

Italian army in the Second World War and finally to a German concentration camp. There, he turns in desperation to the seduction of the camp commandant, a frozen-faced Nordic amazon. Wertmuller's penetrating interpretations of human relationships gain vitality from fast-paced, rich, explosive sequences of images. She has explained that she does not have a clear concept of the film until the parts are composed in the editing room. Comedy, vulgarity, cruelty, humanity, and contradictory behavior are all part of her fascinating pattern.

Suggestions for Further Study

Armes, Roy. *Film and Reality; An Historical Survey.* Harmondsworth, Eng.: Penguin Books, 1974.

Arnheim, Rudolph. *Film as Art.* Berkeley: University of California Press, 1957.

Casty, Alan. *Development of the Film.* New York: Harcourt Brace Jovanovich, 1973.

Coke, Van Deren. *The Painter and the Photograph.* Albuquerque: University of New Mexico Press, 1964.

Cowrie, Peter. *A Concise History of the Cinema.* 2 vols. London and New York: A. Zwemmer, 1971.

Fulton, Albert R. *Motion Pictures: The Development of an Art from Silent Films to the Age of Television.* Norman: University of Oklahoma Press, 1960.

Gernsheim, Helmut, and Alison Gernsheim. *The History of Photography from the Camera Obscura to the Beginning of the Modern Era.* 2nd ed. New York: McGraw-Hill, 1969.

Kyrou, Ado. *Luis Buñuel: An Introduction.* Translated by Adrienne Foulke. New York: Simon and Schuster, 1963.

Leprohon, Pierre. *Michelangelo Antonioni: An Introduction.* Translated by Scott Sullivan. New York: Simon and Schuster, 1963.

Mast, Gerald. *A Short History of the Movies,* New York: Bobbs-Merrill, 1971.

Metz, Christian. *Film Language: A Semiotics of the Cinema.* Translated by Michael Taylor. New York: Oxford University Press, 1974.

Newhall, Beaumont. *The History of Photography.* New York: Museum of Modern Art, 1949.

Pollack, Peter. *The Picture History of Photography.* Rev. ed. New York: Abrams, 1969.

Sarris, Andrew. *Interviews with Film Directors.* Indianapolis: Bobbs-Merrill, 1967.

Scharf, Aaron. *Art and Photography.* Baltimore: Penguin, 1968.

Simon, John. *Ingmar Bergman Directs.* New York: Harcourt Brace Jovanovich, 1972.

Solomon, Stanley J., ed. *The Classic Cinema: Essays in Criticism.* New York: Harcourt Brace Jovanovich, 1973.

Tyler, Parker. *Underground Film: A Critical History.* New York: Grove Press, 1969.

Chapter 19 Art

*Modern
Art:
1900
to
the
Present*

The twentieth century, even more than the nineteenth, has been characterized by international and individual rather than regional styles and by a diversity that makes generalization difficult. Not only new materials and techniques but a rapidly changing world view have influenced art. The increasing importance of the machine seems to be reflected in some styles and reacted against in others, and psychology and physics have reshaped the artist's conceptions of man and the physical world. The complex interaction of factors that form the artist's style, however, does not encourage simple or easy explanations, especially since many artists have moved through a number of stylistic trends.

One widespread tendency in twentieth-century art has been to place the highest value on purely formal qualities—for example, the coherence, variety, subtlety, and uniqueness of forms—rather than to stress the interpretation of subject matter. This tendency accompanied perforce the rise of abstract and nonobjective art, but it has since affected attitudes toward representational art as well. Most artists and critics have used the language of pure form to evaluate the cityscapes of Hopper as well as the personal revelations of De Kooning and the calculated structures of Mondrian.

Sometimes allied with and sometimes opposed to the emphasis on formal qualities has been a tendency to stress subjectivity, the individual's reaction to his world, his exploration of the realm of fantasy, or his creation of new worlds without familiar objects.

More pervasive than either of these has been the tendency to attack conventional ideas about the nature and value of art, even when such ideas have only recently played a revolutionary role themselves. For example, the emphasis on formal values has been challenged as being too limited in its concept of art as good taste embodied in a precious object. The challenge appeared as early as 1913, with Duchamp's exhibition of factory-produced articles as art, and was continued by *Pop Art*, which blurs the division between art and mass-media images or mass-produced objects; by *Conceptual Art*, which presents idea as art; and by those *Minimal* artists who claim to present objects liberated from formal relationships. The concern with subjective experience and personal style has been challanged by Pop Art and Minimal Art, which are sometimes mass produced, by team-produced art, and by Photo-Realism. The traditional concept of art as a precious object to be merchandised and collected has been further attacked through sculpture that destroys itself in a dramatic performance, through some earth works, and through *Happenings*, artist directed theatrical events employing crudely made properties and improvised action. Happenings were replaced in the 1970's by *Performance Art*, which is less improvisational and, in turn, has various forms. *Video Art* has documented performances planned specifically for video tape. Categories have overlapped and multiplied in art criticism as a result of the complex and swiftly changing situation. Some trends of the 1960's and '70's have at first scorned the "art establishment" of critics, dealers, collectors, and museums. However, these institutions, as well as a portion of the public, have moved quickly to underwrite and absorb new developments whenever possible, and many of the disaffected artists have accepted this encouragement and returned to the fold.

Geographically, the United States has become much more important since the Second World War; New York now rivals Paris as a creative center, although in very recent years art has tended toward decentralization, with new developments taking place in San Francisco, Tokyo, and London.

In this chapter, we depart occasionally from the method of discussing individuals in order of birth so as to consider them in the period of their most important work.

1900–1945

PAINTING

The first major event in twentieth-century western painting occurred at the Paris Salon d'Automne in 1905, when a number of French painters, including Derain, Vlaminck, Marquet, Rouault, and Matisse, exhibited paintings with such intense color, free brushwork, and expansive shapes that a critic called the painters *Fauves* (wild beasts). *Fauvism* was a short-lived movement, lasting only about three years and never formally organized; while its influence was widespread in later twentieth-century painting, only a few of its members, notably Matisse, continued to paint in the style. The immediate sources of Fauvism were Van Gogh and Gauguin, and its bursting vitality and instinctive spontaneity give it an expressionistic quality.

The year 1905 also marked the first exhibition of a group of German painters that called itself *Die Brücke* (The Bridge). The group, centered about Karl Schmidt-Rottluff, Emile Nolde, Ernst Ludwig Kirchner, Erich Heckel, and Max Pechstein, lasted from 1905 until

19-1

MAURICE DE VLAMINCK, *Portrait of a Woman*, 1905–06. Oil on canvas, 24⅛'' x 18''. A painting from the Fauve period. Collection of Mr. and Mrs. Nathan Smooke.

1913. These men, whose headquarters was in Dresden, were inspired by the paintings of the Fauves and the Norwegian painter Munch and by Medieval German woodcuts. They used harsh, brutally simplified forms and strong, often clashing colors in a heavy, expressionistic manner. Some of the Bridge group were absorbed by *Der Blaue Reiter* (The Blue Rider), a group formed in Munich in 1911 by Vassily Kandinsky that encompassed a variety of styles, ranging from Kandinsky's gay, buoyant, nonobjective paintings to the moody, geometric abstractions of Franz Marc. The Bridge and Blue Rider groups provided the basis for the broad trend known as *German Expressionism*, which is still evident today.

Meanwhile, *Cubism* developed in France during the period from 1907 to 1914 under the leadership of Pablo Picasso and Georges Braque. Its early phase, often called *Analytical Cubism*, sought to reduce nature to its basic geometric shapes while viewing objects from several sides simultaneously. This simultaneity of vision implies a summation of visual experience from different moments and different positions in space and suggests an intriguing parallel to the theories of relativity that Einstein was proposing in the same period.

Analytical Cubism employed restrained colors, limited space, and a limited repertory of geometric shapes; it may be understood partly as a reaction to the spontaneous freedom and lively color of Fauvism. The second phase of Cubism has been called *Synthetic*, because it is a more imaginative reconstruction of or improvisation on the forms of natural objects. Color and space are less limited, and shapes are less restricted to basic geometry. Synthetic Cubism employed *collage*, the pasting of actual objects, such as pieces of newspaper, to the surface of the painting.

French Cubism inspired the Russian painter Kasimir Malevich, who proclaimed a movement called *Suprematism* in 1915. Malevich's geometric compositions evolved from Cubism to nonobjectivism. A broader movement, which embraced both painting and sculpture, was *Constructivism*, the manifesto of which was drawn up in Moscow in 1920 by the brothers Antoine Pevsner and Naum Gabo. Constructivist painting employed precise geometric forms in generally nonobjective compositions. French Cubism also inspired the Dutchman Mondrian to seek even greater austerity in compositions of rectangles and primary colors. In Holland, Mondrian helped form a group in 1917 that is generally known by the name of its magazine, *De Stijl*. The influence of Cubism may be seen in the Italian movement called *Futurism* (c. 1909–15), which used multiple contours, diagonal lines, and swirling curves to express the dynamism of the machine age.

19-2
KASIMIR MALEVICH, *Suprematist Composition: White on White*, 1918. Oil on canvas. 31¼'' x 31¼'' Collection. The Museum of Modern Art, New York.

The tendency to apply a severe geometric system of order to an objective or a nonobjective world has been widespread in twentieth-century art and has produced a wide variety of styles. A very different tendency has developed concurrently since 1916, when *Dada* was founded in Zurich, Switzerland. Dadaism was a nihilistic rejection of rationality and order. Arising from the disillusionment of the First World War, Dada sought to destroy through ridicule the old ideas about the character, aims, and standards of art and to build a new standard with an appreciation of fantasy and the irrational. Dadaists used sculpture, painting, and photomontage (compositions made up of various photos or of their fragments) to present extraordinary combinations of ordinary objects, thereby destroying the conventional meaning of the objects and opening the way for new interpretations by the spectator. Dadaism reflected the growing appreciation of the role of the irrational as revealed by psychiatry. It spread quickly to Cologne, Berlin, Paris, and New York. Its organized life was short (1916–22), but its influence can be seen in much contemporary painting and sculpture. Many Dadaists joined the *Surrealist* movement, which announced its aims in a Paris manifesto in 1924 and which continues as one influence on painting today. Some Surrealist work, like that of René Magritte, attempts to depict hallucinatory or dream experiences in which recognizable forms appear in surprising combinations. Other Surrealists, like Joan Miró, produce compositions with lighter, more humorous fantasies. A major source of both Dadaism and Surrealism was the works of Giorgio de Chirico, who was painting haunting, dreamlike landscapes as early as 1910.

In the 1920's and '30's, while Surrealism, Expressionism, and various kinds of geometric abstraction developed, there was also much painting with social commentary being done in Europe and the Americas. The cynicism that grew out of the First World War encouraged not only the Dada movement but also a trend that in Germany was called *The New Objectivity* (*Die Neue Sachlichkeit*). Here realistic detail was used more specifically than in Dadaism to point out the horrors and corruption of people and society. There were counterparts to the New Objectivity in other countries. In the United States, the vigorous life of crowded cities, particularly that of the slum areas, provided subject matter for the so-called *Ash Can School*, or *The Eight*, which played an avant-garde role from 1908 until 1913. After the 1913 New York Armory Show, which jolted Americans into awareness of advanced trends in European art. American patrons became more sympathetic to abstract art. A generation of American artists, many of whom had studied in Paris during the crucial years of Fauvism and Cubism, had become pioneers in American abstract painting. However, in the late 1920's there was a tendency to move away from abstraction and toward painting the American scene. The Depression of the 1930's encouraged such art to depict not only the face of America but also the tragedy and suffering caused by economic crisis. In Russia after 1921 the Communist government forced into exile those artists who would not turn to a propagandistic realism in support of its political ideas. Mexico produced three of the most powerful artists of social commentary in the 1920's and '30's, José Orozco, Diego Rivera, and David Alfaro Siqueiros, whose mural paintings protest the viciousness of humanity and the oppression of the weak by the strong.

Vassily Kandinsky (Russia, Germany, and France, 1866–1944). Kandinsky was born in Moscow but settled in Munich; he became the leader of the Blue Rider group in 1911. Earlier he had abandoned a career in law and had turned to Fauvist painting and, eventually, to increasingly abstract forms. It may have been as early as 1910, depending on the disputed date of a watercolor, that he developed nonobjective art. His treatise *Concerning the Spiritual in Art*, published in 1912, urged that painting can approach the state of pure music—that is, that line, color, and form may be used like sounds to evoke emotional response without the help of subject matter. He often used titles such as "fugue" or "improvisation" to stress the correspondence with music. *Painting with White Form* (Plate 23) is typical of his early nonobjective paintings. Cloudlike forms, angular and wavy lines, and rainbow colors expand spirally from a nucleus of smaller, brighter, denser, and more sharply contrasting parts. The activity is buoyant and spontaneous in effect but carefully controlled within the limits of the picture. From the 1920's on, Kandinsky also composed with rigid, precise, geometric shapes or combinations of geometric and freer forms. Occasionally, recognizable objects appear in his work. In 1934, Kandinsky settled in Paris, where he spent much of the remainder of his life. His art has been a major influence in twentieth-century painting.

Pierre Bonnard (France, 1867–1947). In the 1880's, Bonnard joined the *Nabis* (prophets), a small group of French painters who believed that lines, shapes, and colors can evoke within the spectator a certain state of mind. In their view, the real content of the work of art was the spiritual result of its physical forms. Following the lead of the poets Charles Baudelaire and Stéphane Mallarmé, the Nabis spoke of mystical correspondences between the physical and the spiritual worlds and of the possibility of using one sensory experience, such as sight, to evoke another, such as sound or taste (synesthesia). Critics linked the Nabis with the Symbolist movement in literature. In painting, Gauguin was the Nabis' idol; his flattened forms and imaginative colors demonstrated that a painting was an expressive and symbolic object not to be confused with an imitation of nature. They also found these qualities in Japanese wood-block prints. Of the Nabis, Bonnard especially, throughout the 1880's and '90's, used flat, softly edged shapes with occasional undulating, Art Nouveau curves and muted colors, and therefore was often called "the Japanese Nabi." His works of this period portray people in parks and interiors; the mood of these paintings is meditative, almost sacramental. Critics coined the term *intimiste* to describe the emotional tone of his art. Bonnard also did lithographic illustrations for *La Revue Blanche* and designed posters, sets, and costumes for Lugné-Poë's experimental Théatre de l'Oeuvre and Paul Fort's Théatre d'Art. By 1911, Bonnard had heightened his palette, using more intense and sometimes dissonant colors sensitively organized on the picture surface. In *The Palm* (Plate 24), small ovoid color spots produce smoldering contrasts. The drawing seems at first unsure and the proportions clumsy, yet the total composition is very effective. The curves of the palm branches, the soft geometry of the houses, and the colors focus with great intensity on the figure. The result goes beyond Impressionism to suggest a visionary experience. Although he played an avant-garde role in the late nineteenth century, Bonnard's popularity came in the twentieth century, after Fauvism had paved the way for his use of stronger colors. Historically and stylistically, his art links very different movements: Impressionism, Symbolism, and Fauvism.

Henri Matisse (France, 1869–1954). The study of law failed to satisfy the young Matisse, and his brief period as a student of the academic painter Adolphe Bouguereau was equally frustrating. After this, he studied with the lenient Gustave Moreau. Matisse's early work revealed an interest in Impressionism and in Seurat's pointillism. Matisse then became enthusiastic about the work of Cézanne and Gauguin. By 1905

19-3
HENRI MATISSE, *The Green Line* (Portrait of Mme. Matisse), 1905. Oil on canvas, 16″ x 12¾″. Statens Museum for Kunst, Copenhagen.

Matisse's art had developed large areas of relatively unbroken color, often chosen quite independently of nature, and shapes manipulated to intensify their directional forces. In the Salon d'Automne of 1905, Matisse was seen as the leader of the Fauve group. *The Green Line* (Fig. 19-3), a portrait of Madame Matisse, indicates by its title the artist's concern with color. Vibrating complementaries—greens and reds, yellows and violets—achieve a dynamic equilibrium and a life of their own. Such gymnastics with color continued to be typical of Matisse's style, but in his later works he tended to use thinner paint and to create looser forms. *Decorative Figure on an Ornamental Background* (Plate 25) is one of the more tightly constructed works from the 1920's, yet the solid rigidity of the figure contrasts with the exuberance of the patterns and colors. The exhilarating effect of ease and spontaneity masks the continual repainting and the deliberation that went into Matisse's painting. In *Notes of a Painter*, published in 1908, Matisse describes his dream of an art of balance, purity, and serenity devoid of troubling or depressing subject matter. No elaborate theories guided him; he relied on his instinct as he worked and reworked a composition according to his conviction that everything—shapes, spaces between shapes, colors, lines—should contribute to the total expression. In the 1940's

Matisse developed a special technique: *papiers collés*. He painted sheets of paper, cut them into shapes, and pasted them on a background. The result was crisp, lively patterns in striking contrasts of hue and value.

John Marin (United States, 1870–1953).   Marin started his career in painting late, after a serious attempt at architecture. Following his studies in Philadelphia and New York, he spent most of the years from 1905 to 1911 in Europe, where he produced etchings and watercolors and exhibited in the Paris salons. While in Europe, he began a lifelong friendship with Stieglitz. Marin first exhibited in Stieglitz's 291 Gallery (see p. 318) in 1909. Once back in New York, Marin produced watercolors with slashing, angular strokes that expressed his feelings about the dynamism of New York in a style related to Cubism and Futurism. After 1914, his subjects were New York in the winter and Maine in the summer. In landscapes and seascapes, Marin's sense of conflicting forces in nature was realized within a conception of the picture plane as a field of forces. Pencil lines and brush strokes construct intricate geometric shapes that preserve the flat plane of the paper while suggesting natural forms like rocks or water, as in *Sailboat in Harbor* (Fig. 19-4). Dry-brush strokes contrast with watery washes of delicate hues in this watercolor. While the painting may suggest deep space and solid objects in the natural world, it also presents a formal structure with its own laws and drama. Marin is known primarily as a watercolorist; his oils utilize similar forms but exploit the thick textures possible to that medium.

19-4
JOHN MARIN, *Sailboat in Harbor*, 1923. Watercolor on paper, 13½″ x 17″. Collection, The Columbus Gallery of Fine Arts, Columbus Ohio. Gift of Ferdinand Howald.

Georges Rouault (France, 1871–1958). Rouault's training consisted of an apprenticeship to a maker of stained glass and the study of painting with Gustave Moreau. By 1905, Rouault was painting with the slashing brushwork and urgent scumblings seen in the *Head of Christ* (Fig. 19-5). Although his works were not exhibited in the same room with those of the Fauves during the Salon of 1905, he seemed Fauvist in the expressive violence of his forms and was often identified with this movement. Rouault's content, however, which deals more with the pathos, tragedy, and corruption of humankind, links him with German Expressionism. Frequent subjects are prostitutes, sorrowful clowns, evil judges, and the head of Christ. His deep religious convictions owed much to the writings of Léon Bloy; his sense of social justice recalls the art of Daumier. As Rouault's style matured, contours became rigid containers for islands of thick glowing color. *The Old King* (Plate 26) has the radiance of a stained-glass window or a Byzantine icon. His genius as a printmaker is revealed in the lithography and intaglio prints that he executed as book illustrations under the patronage of his dealer, Ambrose Vollard, from 1916 to 1927, and which he eventually published as the *Miserere*.

Piet Mondrian (Holland, 1872–1944). Mondrian, even more than Kandinsky, was the exponent of nonobjective painting. Mondrian studied at the Amsterdam Academy and began as a painter of landscapes in bright Fauvist colors. After moving to Paris in 1912, his style was strongly influenced by Cubism and became in-

19-5
GEORGES ROUAULT, *Head of Christ*, 1905. Oil on paper mounted on canvas, 38¾″ x 24½″. Chrysler Museum at Norfolk. Gift of Walter P. Chrysler, Jr.

19-6
PIET MONDRIAN, *Composition*, 1913. Oil on canvas, 34⅝″ x 45¼″. Ryksmuseum Kröller-Müller, Otterlo.

creasingly abstract. *Composition* (Fig. 19-6) indicates that by 1914 he was reducing subject matter to intricate flat rectangular systems limited to a few colors. Mondrian returned to Holland in 1913 and remained there during the First World War. In 1917, he and a circle of friends founded the magazine *De Stijl*, whose name was subsequently attached to their group. He remained the major spokesman for the group and the only faithful follower of the strict principles he enunciated, which he termed *Neo-Plasticism*. He stated that the new plastic idea would seek universal harmonies using the pure forms of straight lines and primary colors. He saw subject matter as an impurity that limited the universality of the painting by tying it to a particular time and place. *Composition with Blue and Yellow* (Fig. 3-3) exemplifies Mondrian's mature style; a certain intensity of warm yellow and a certain intensity of cool blue are adjusted in quantity to form an equilibrium within the simple gridwork of black lines. This search for absolute order makes an interesting parallel with the Neoclassic artist's effort to find an absolute beauty that would last through the changes of time and place. In 1919, Mondrian returned to Paris and stayed there until 1938, when the impending Second World War forced him to move to London for two years and then to New York. His art has had a wide influence on painting, sculpture, architecture, and commercial design.

Kasimir Malevich (Russia, 1878–1935). The Kiev School of Art and the Moscow Academy of Fine Arts provided Malevich with his formal training. By the time of his first exhibition, in 1909, his art revealed the influence of Vuillard, Bonnard, and Matisse. Between 1911 and 1913, he came under the spell of Cubism and Futurism. The desire to purify and reduce painting to essential elements led him, in 1913, to paint *Black Square* (Russian Museum, Leningrad), a black rectangle in the center of a white canvas. This was followed by other geometric compositions, sometimes in only one color, with simple shapes floating against white backgrounds. Only in 1915 did Malevich announce a name and a program for this kind of painting: Suprematism. *White on White* (Fig. 19-2) reached an ultimate in his search for purity; the white square can be distinguished from its white background only through faint value differences. Suprematism paved the way for the broader movement of Constructivism.

Paul Klee (Switzerland and Germany, 1879–1940). Klee grew up in Bern, Switzerland, but studied in the Acad-

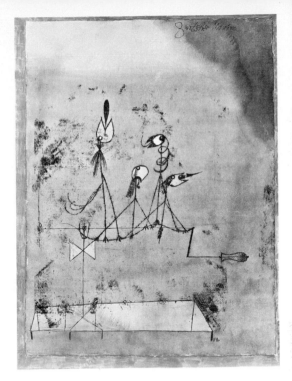

19-7
PAUL KLEE, *The Twittering Machine*, 1922.
Watercolor and pen-and-ink, approx. 16¼" x 12".
Collection, The Museum of Modern Art,
New York. Purchase.

emy at Munich. After traveling in Italy, he painted and
did etchings in Bern until 1906, when he moved back to
Munich. In 1912, he participated in the second Blue
Rider exhibit there. Although his studies included a
firm academic grounding in life drawing and perspective, Klee early developed a preference for abstractions
done in small scale with subtle color and delicate line.
His intellectual attitude was very sophisticated, but his
writings show a desire to join adult understanding and
experience with the freshness of vision and the delight-
ful fantasy usually left behind with childhood. Many of
his landscapes of the 1920's employ delicate rectangles
of color and softly emerging shapes of trees and birds.
The quality of intimate personal fantasy is all-pervasive. Klee's sly sense of humor and sensitivity of line
are evident in works like *The Twittering Machine* (Fig.
19-7). During the 1930's, the shapes tend to become
bolder, the line heavier, and the colors more opaque.
From 1920 to 1930, Klee taught at the Bauhaus, the
pioneering German school of design. During these
years, he published many of his ideas in the *Pedagogical
Sketchbook*. After teaching at the Dusseldorf Academy
from 1931 to 1933, Klee was dismissed by the Nazi
government; he returned to Bern, where he worked
until his death.

Ernst Ludwig Kirchner (Germany, 1880–1938). In
Dresden in 1905, Kirchner and Nolde, along with sev-

19-8
ERNST LUDWIG KIRCHNER, *Street, Berlin,*
1913. 47½" x 35⅞". Collection, The
Museum of Modern Art, New York.
Purchase.

eral others, founded *Die Brücke*, a group dedicated to
the "renewal of German art." The dating of Kirchner's
early paintings and prints is uncertain, but they seem to
reflect the character of Art Nouveau and the influence
of Munch. Under the influence of Medieval German
woodcuts and African and Oceanic art, Kirchner's work
became more abrupt, angular, and dissonant. The
color became more brilliant and clashing, and distortions more extreme. In 1911, Kirchner moved to
Berlin, where the life of the city provided a theme for
a series of paintings and woodcuts. Some of the latter
were used in the avant-garde publication *Der Sturm.*
Street, Berlin (Fig. 19-8), one of the paintings in the
series, demonstrates the conflict of angles, the splintered forms, and the spatial tensions common to Kirchner's work before 1920. From the time of his military
service (1914 to 1915) and concomitant nervous disor-
ders, Kirchner's style slowly changed. In the 1920's,
shapes began to be more clearly separated and to contain less active brushwork. Kirchner went to Switzerland,
where he spent the remainder of his life, and took
much of his subject matter from the Swiss Alps. Like
many pioneering artists, he was vilified by the Nazis as
a degenerate. This contributed to the discouragement
that led to his suicide.

19-9
PABLO PICASSO, *Les Demoiselles d'Avignon*, 1907. Oil on
canvas, 8' x 7'8''. Collection, The Museum of Modern Art,
New York. Acquired through the Lillie P. Bliss Bequest.

19-10
PABLO PICASSO, *The Aficionado*, 1912. Oil
on canvas, 53¼'' x 32⅜''. Kunstmuseum,
Basel.

Pablo Picasso (Spain and France, 1881–1973). After a
triumph as a precocious academic student, Picasso went
from Spain to Paris and quickly began experimenting
with the revolutionary styles of the recent past. From
early attempts at Impressionism, he moved to the first
of many personal stylistic developments: his Blue Period (1901–04), during which he used blues and grays to
depict people who seem spiritually and physically ex-
hausted. In 1905 and 1906 he turned to warm tans and
reds, circus subjects were frequent in this Rose Period.
Slowly the forms stiffened and the faces became
masklike. Picasso had become interested in the primitive formal power of African Negro and ancient Spanish
sculpture. A major milestone is *Les Demoiselles
d'Avignon* (Fig. 19-9), in which five female figures with
masklike faces and flat, angular body forms become
part of a sequence of splintered planes with lost-and-
found edges. The painting is often seen as the starting
point for Cubism. An example of Analytic Cubism is
Picasso's *The Aficionado* (Fig. 19-10), while Synthetic
Cubism is exemplified by the *Three Musicians* (Plate

19-11
PABLO PICASSO, *Weeping Woman*, 1937. Oil on canvas, approx. 21″ x 17½″. Private Collection, London.

27). Here, the effect of collage is produced with paint, and the liveliness of the composition is achieved within a more severe discipline than is found in Fauvist work. The drawing of Dr. Claribel Cone (Fig. 1-1), done in the same period, presents an entirely different stylistic discipline. It employs the massive simplified forms seen in many of Picasso's paintings done mainly during the 1920's. These works have been called Neoclassical because they have some of the qualities of Greek sculpture. From the next decade, the best-known work is the *Guernica* mural, done for the Spanish government building at the Paris World's Fair of 1937. The painting is a violent but controlled expression of the horror evoked by the bombing of the town of Guernica during the Spanish Civil War. Interest in dissonant forms—shapes with much internal conflict in their directional forces—had been building in his work before *Guernica* and became prevalent in his art (Fig. 19-11). The stylistic variety continued, however, and ranged from precise portraits to ebullient patterns in strident colors.

Georges Braque (France, 1882–1963). Braque went from Le Havre to Paris and, by 1906, was painting Fauvist works. In the following year he became enthusiastic about the art of Cézanne, and some of Braque's offerings to the Salon d'Automne of 1908 were refused because of his startling use of lively geometric form applied to landscape subjects. The critic Louis Vauxcelles wrote of "Cubism" in describing Braque's work, thus naming for the first time one of the most important movements in twentieth-century art. Picasso had already initiated this trend in 1907, and he continued to provide the inventiveness and drive for Cubism, while his friend Braque went through fewer drastic changes of style and worked more methodically in exploring stylistic possibilities within a limited range. The shallow depth, restrained color, and many-faceted order of Analytical Cubism are evident in Braque's *The Portuguese* (Fig. 19-12). After his service in the First World War, Braque worked in the realm of Synthetic Cubism but employed unique, low-keyed, sonorous color harmonies. In the 1920's, he painted a number of nudes with delicate wavering outlines, thin washes of paint, and monumental proportions like those in some of Picasso's figure compositions from this period. At the same time, Braque continued to work out the sensitive modulations of shape, texture, and color in still-life paintings. More playful arabesque curves and lighter colors appear in some of the work done during the 1930's, and the 1940's saw a series of compositions on the theme of the *atelier* (studio). These paintings reach a new height in complexity and control; textures, textile patterns, and transparent and opaque shapes move back and forth within labyrinthine spatial relationships.

19-12
GEORGES BRAQUE, *The Portuguese,*
1911. Oil on canvas, approx. 46" x 32".
Kunstmuseum, Basel.

Edward Hopper (United States, 1882–1967). Commercial art provided Hopper's living for years while he studied painting with Robert Henri and absorbed European art in museums and on trips abroad. From 1908 until his death, he lived in New York and spent summers in Maine. Hopper's subjects include New England houses

19-13
EDWARD HOPPER, *Night Hawks,* 1942. Oil on canvas, 30" x 60". Art Institute of Chicago. Friends of American Art Collection.

and coast scenes, but he is best known for paintings of the city. Works like *Early Sunday Morning* (1930, Whitney Museum of American Art, New York) and *Night Hawks* (Fig. 19-13) utilize bold patterns of light, shadow, and color to distill the character of buildings and to express the monotony and the drama of daily life. A poignant loneliness frequently haunts the mute façades. Hopper's paintings of the American scene help us find significance in the commonplace; one senses the isolation of the individual within the group, the ageless cycle of life and death; his drab buildings assume the expressive burden of man's condition.

Umberto Boccioni (Italy, 1882–1916). Boccioni's painting drew from Seurat's divisionism but employed featherlike brush strokes that evoke forms in violent motion. Boccioni was one of the authors of the *Technical Manifesto* of Futurist painting in 1910, which stressed the destruction of material bodies by movement and light and called for painting that expressed universal dynamism and metamorphosis. These convictions are powerfully conveyed by *The Dynamism of a Soccer Player* (Fig. 19-14), in which objects sacrifice much of their solidity and take on the appearance of colorful whirlwinds. Boccioni's sculpture, like his painting, evokes a sense of violent motion and interpenetration of mass and space.

José Orozco (Mexico, 1883–1949). After training in the Academy of San Carlos in Mexico City, Orozco painted murals depicting themes of revolution, pillage, suffering, and cruelty in huge, massive forms. At the New School for Social Research in New York, he painted the

revolution of the proletariat; and, in the Baker Library
at Dartmouth College, he interpreted American history.
The Dartmouth paintings include one of the most overwhelming of Orozco's compositions: *Christ Destroying
His Cross* (Fig. 19-15). Having lost patience with humankind, Christ has repudiated his sacrifice, chopped
down the Cross, and stands facing us with an ax in one
hand and the other hand raised in a clenched fist.
Christ's wrath is awesome as he stands with enlarged
eyes, blue-shadowed face, reddish beard and hair, a
torso of blue, orange, green, gray, and purple, and
partially flayed legs. In 1934, Orozco returned to Mexico to paint his most furious condemnations of war in
murals for the Palace of Fine Arts in Mexico City and
for the University, the Government Palace, and the
Hospicio Cabañas in Guadalajara.

Amedeo Modigliani (Italy and France, 1884–1920). After
conventional art training in Italy, Modigliani arrived in
Paris in 1905 or 1906 and became associated with Pablo
Picasso and Constantin Brancusi, as well as other
avant-garde artists. By 1908, his painting showed the
influence of Fauvist brushwork and the muted colors of
Picasso's Blue Period. His subjects were mainly portraits and nudes. Enthusiasm for the sculpture of
Brancusi and of Africa, as well as for the painting of
Cézanne, led Modigliani to develop simpler forms and
harmonious relationships between the curves and angles in his figures and backgrounds. Contours assumed
great importance. In the portrait of Anna Zborowski,
the wife of his patron (Fig. 19-16), the diagonal upper
body and the contrasting diagonals of her dress and
right arm divide the background into three shapes that

19-16
AMEDEO MODIGLIANI, *Anna Zborowski*,
1917. Oil on canvas, 51¼" x 32".
Collection, The Museum of Modern Art, New
York. Lillie P. Bliss Collection.

are highly dynamic. Forming wedges that thrust against the figure, their dynamism is reinforced by active brushwork. These shapes, as well as those of the dress, hands, neck, and face produce a shallow, flattened space. The overlapping or tilting planes suggest that edges have been lifted slightly from the painted surface, an effect utilized in Cubism during the preceding ten years. Long, graceful curves relate the different parts of the composition. Theme and variations ease the taut conflict of figure and ground. The head is typical of Modigliani's images: Its elongated ellipse is repeated in the eye sockets, eyes, mouth, and neck. Remarkably, the individuality of Modigliani's subject is always retained in these masklike faces. The suave harmony of elliptical shapes contains a faint echo of Raphael's art. Modigliani's colors are quiet, but there are lush combinations of complementaries, such as terra-cotta reds and oranges against greens and blues, or somber harmonies in tans, red browns, grays, and blacks. Between 1909 and 1915, he carved masklike heads and *caryatids*—kneeling female nudes supporting a segment of architecture.

Max Beckmann (Germany and the United States, 1884–1950). The Weimar Art School provided training for the young Beckmann, whose early style was a boldly brushed Impressionism. During military service in the ambulance corps in the First World War, he developed compositions of greater dissonance and intensity, like his *Self-Portrait with Graver* (Fig. 1-2). As a leader in the German New Objectivity movement, he depicted the poverty, corruption, and hopelessness of his era. *Departure* (Fig. 19-17) assumes the traditional triptych format of an altarpiece. The harsh angles, the pinched and twisted forms, the conflict between two-dimensional and three-dimensional forms, and the spatial compression are found, to some extent, in much of his work. The side panels depict scenes of torture and of burden-bearing or constraint; the center is relatively tranquil. At one time, Beckmann said that the woman bound with a man, on the right, symbolized the individual searching through life but tied to the burden of past failures; that the center depicts triumph over the tortures of life and attainment of freedom; and that the title referred to departure from the illusions of life. However, he also said that each spectator must understand the painting in his or her own way. Unlike Medieval symbolism, Beckmann's symbols, as many in twentieth-century art, are personal, enigmatic, and de-

19-17

MAX BECKMANN, *Departure,* 1932–33.
Oil on canvas, triptych central panel
7'3¾'' x 3'9⅜''. Collection, The
Museum of Modern Art, New York (given
anonymously).

mand completion by each spectator. Beckmann left
Germany for Amsterdam during the Second World
War. In 1947 he moved to the United States, where he
taught painting in St. Louis and in New York. His art is
one of the most powerful expressions of concern for the
anguish and suffering of twentieth-century humankind.

Oskar Kokoschka (Austria and Switzerland, 1886–   ).
African art, Oceanic art, and Japanese woodcuts fascinated Kokoschka even before his training at the Vienna
School of Arts and Crafts. His early paintings (*c.* 1908–
10) included many portraits from a circle of friends,
among them Arnold Schönberg, Gustav Mahler, and
Anton von Webern. Kokoschka scraped and rubbed a
thin layer of paint onto the canvas and then often
scratched lines into the paint with his brush handle.
The worried paint surface, the delicate color, and the
gauntness of the figures all suggest a hypersensitive,
fragile, anxious world. In 1910, Kokoschka moved
toward thicker, darker, and more iridescent paint. By
1914, in *The Tempest* (Fig. 19-18), an expression of the
painter's passion for Alma Mahler, the brush strokes
are sweeping, and the forms are conceived as active
forces. By this time, Kokoschka had sojourned in Ber-

19-18
OSKAR KOKOSCHKA, *The Tempest,* 1914. Oil on panel,
40¼'' x 75¼''. Kunstmuseum, Basel.

19-19
MARCEL DUCHAMP, *The Large Glass or the
Bride Stripped Bare by Her Bachelors, Even,*
1915–23. Oil and wire on glass,
34¾'' x 21½''. The Philadelphia Museum of
Art. Bequest of Katherine S. Dreier.

lin, done art work for *Der Sturm,* and influenced some
of the Brücke painters there. Between 1938 and 1947,
he stayed in England; since 1947 he has lived in Switzerland. His style since 1924 has tended to combine active
line and brushwork with luminous color. Kokoschka is
one of the leading painters within the many-faceted trend
called Expressionism.

Marcel Duchamp (France and the United States, 1887–
1968). Duchamp has been one of the most publicized
exponents of the irrational in art. He studied at the
Académie Julian in Paris and painted under the influence first of Cézanne and then of the Fauves. By 1912,
he had formed a personal style and painted the *Nude
Descending a Staircase* (Arensberg Collection, Philadelphia Museum of Art) which became the focus of attention in the New York Armory Show of 1913. The
concern with motion and its expression through multiple contours or repeated shapes suggests the influence
of Cubism, photography, and the Italian Futurist movement. The same year, Duchamp produced the first of
his "ready-mades," a bicycle wheel mounted upside
down on a stool. By exhibiting a common, machine-
made article as art, he challenged traditional definitions
and values. In 1915 he came to the United States, where
he spent most of the remainder of his life. *The Large*

19-20
GIORGIO DE CHIRICO, *The Mystery and Melancholy of a Street*, 1914. Oil on canvas, 34¼" x 28⅛". A private collector.

Glass or the Bride Stripped Bare by Her Bachelors, Even (Fig. 19-19) has been the subject of much interpretation. Some critics have restricted their interpretation to a sexual one, based on the implications of the title; others view the work as an attack on the mechanization of modern man. The composition relates readily to Dada art, and Duchamp was, from 1915 on, the center of a New York group that was Dada in character and, eventually, in name. In the 1920's, his activities as an artist gave way to his interest in chess, although he did help to organize the 1942 Surrealist exhibition in New York.

Giorgio de Chirico (Italy and France, 1888–). The precursor of the Surrealists, De Chirico was trained in Athens and in the Munich Academy, where he grew to admire the art of the Swiss painter Böcklin, the German painter Klinger, and the German philosopher Nietzsche. For De Chirico, Böcklin's fantasies, painted with realistic detail, may have expressed the reality underlying the physical world. *The Mystery and Melancholy of a Street* (Fig. 19-20) exemplifies the style that made De Chirico famous during his stay in Paris from 1911 to 1915. The empty arcades of two buildings, each seen from a different eye level, and a long human shadow provide a disquieting environment for the small girl playing with a hoop. Colors are somber and the paint is applied thinly. There is an almost hypnotic effect of loneliness and quiet. De Chirico's deserted cities, echoing arcades, and vast spaces suggest the world of dreams, and he was later appreciated by the Surrealists in Paris. After being called into the Italian army in 1915 and stationed in Ferrara, De Chirico found time to paint. He and Carlo Carra, a former Futurist, established the *Scuola Metaphysica*, a small group of painters who were influenced by De Chirico's style. In 1918 De Chirico returned to Rome and changed his style slowly toward more conventional work in a Neoclassical vein. The Surrealists eventually attacked him for having deserted their camp; the critics lost interest in his work, and the unfortunate De Chirico was reduced, on occasion, to copying or imitating works in his earlier style.

Marc Chagall (Russia, the United States, and France, 1889–). Chagall's early style was formed during his residence in Paris from 1910 to 1914, when he was introduced to Cubism. Memories of his childhood in Vitebsk, Yiddish folklore, and Cubist geometry are freely combined without regard to time, space, or scale in *I and My Village* (Fig. 19-21). Back in Russia between 1914 and 1923, Chagall served as Commissar of Fine Arts at Vitebsk and designed murals and stage sets for the Jewish State Theater in Moscow. The *Double Portrait with Wine Glass* (Fig. 19-22), from this period, portrays Chagall seated on his wife's shoulders drinking

19-21

MARC CHAGALL, *I and My Village*, 1911. Oil on canvas, 21¾" x 18¼". The Philadelphia Museum of Art. Gift of Mr. and Mrs. Rodolphe M. de Schauensee.

to the future while his young daughter hovers over his head. The monumental figures dwarf the cityscape beneath them, and bright colors combine with sudden angles, rippling curves, and anatomical transformations to provide an ecstatic vision. In the 1920's, geometric elements faded from his art, and softer, more sensuous shapes appeared.

Max Ernst (Germany and France, 1891–1976). In 1919, Ernst, a student of philosophy, became known as a leader of Dada art in Cologne. A 1920 exhibition of his work in Paris was a sensation, and he moved there in 1922, joining the Surrealists in 1924. As a child he had been introspective, sensitive, and imaginative. As a young man he was haunted by obsessive images, interested in the art of mental patients, and inspired by the work of De Chirico, Chagall, and Kandinsky. Ernst developed several of the popular Dada and Surrealist devices for exploring the realms of fantasy. One of these devices is *psychic automatism*, the Surrealist term for nonobjective or vaguely recognizable images that are brought forth from the imagination, or from nonrational thought. Another was photomontage, including fragments of engravings, which he used as a means to create surprising combinations of ordinary objects that upset rational

19-22
MARC CHAGALL, *Double Portrait with Wine Glass*, 1917. Oil on canvas, 91¾'' x 53½'' Musée National d'Arte Moderne, Paris.

19-23
MAX ERNST, *Napoleon in the Wilderness*, 1941. Oil on canvas, 18¼'' x 15''. Collection, The Museum of Modern Art, New York. Acquired by exchange.

expectations and stimulated the imagination. He also produced extraordinary images by rubbings of objects placed under paper (*frottages*); the forms that emerged were then elaborated upon. Another of Ernst's devices was *decalcomania*, a work of art produced by painting the surface of an object and pressing it onto a canvas to transfer an image. The resulting textures and shapes were then developed by the artist, as in *Napoleon in the Wilderness* (Fig. 19-23). Ernst also scraped, spattered, and smoked the surface of a canvas to produce hallucinatory images of animals, plants, machinery, and persons. After the period of the Second World War, which he spent in the United States, Ernst lived in France. Although he had broken with the Surrealist group in 1938, his work continued to be Surrealist in character. After 1945 his colors were more intense and luminous. Ernst was also a major Surrealist sculptor, combining such forms as snakes, bottles, and horned disks to tempt our imagination.

Joan Miró (Spain and France, 1893–   ). Miró was born in Barcelona and trained in the La Lonja School of Fine Arts. His early work consisted of landscapes and portraits done in lively colors, patterns of repeated shapes, and occasional delicate detail. After 1919, Miró spent much of his time in Paris, and in 1924 he associated himself with the Surrealists. By that time, his work had developed a combination of reality and fantasy that evoked the quality of dream experience so interesting to the Surrealists. The *Dutch Interior, I* (Plate 28) presents a preposterous collection of brightly colored objects wriggling buoyantly in an architectural interior. Many of Miró's works are more abstract than this, but some identifiable objects are usually present. Frequently, the soft, undulating, amoebalike shapes change color where they overlap. Miró often dribbles or splashes paint onto a new canvas, employing accident to suggest the start of a composition. Renown has brought him a number of important mural commissions, such as that for the graduate center at Harvard University (1950–51). After devoting much time to ceramics between 1955 and 1959, he produced two ceramic murals for the UNESCO Buildings in Paris.

Stuart Davis (United States, 1894–1964). Davis received his early training in New York. The famous Armory Show of 1913 introduced him to Cubist and Fauve painting. During a year in Paris (1928–29), he produced a number of street scenes with delicate line and rectan-

19-24
JOAN MIRÓ, *Woman and Birds in the Night,* 1968. Oil on canvas, 18″ x 10⅝″ Collection, Victor K. Kiam VI, New York.

19-25
STUART DAVIS, *Something on the Eight Ball*. 1953–54. Oil on canvas, 56" x 45". The Philadelphia Museum of Art. Purchased. The Adele Haas Turner and Beatrice Pastorius Turner Memorial Fund.

gular patterns. After his return to New York, his compositions were still lifes, bustling city street scenes with garish advertising, and harbor scenes—all done with the aggressive shapes, jangling colors, and bits of letters or words that have come to characterize his mature style. *Something on the Eight Ball* (Fig. 19-25) is typical in the jerky curves and angles that weave a loose dynamic structure.

René Magritte (Belgium, 1898–1967). With the exception of his mother's suicide in 1912, Magritte's life was remarkably uneventful. His excitement came from mental adventures: the search for mystery in ordinary objects. He studied at the Brussels Academy of Fine Arts and had his first exhibition in 1920. The Cubist character of his early work changed after he saw reproductions of the painting of Giorgio De Chirico. Magritte's interest in the elusive nature of reality dates from this event in the 1920's. From 1927 until 1930 he lived in Paris and had intermittent contacts with the Surrealists. He was uninterested in the leftist political concerns of their leader, André Breton. Magritte admired Max Ernst but was not interested in Ernst's technical experimentation, in psychic automatism, or in dream experience. *Euclidean Promenades* (Fig. 19-26) invites us to consider the ambiguity between the physical world and representations of it. He used the picture-within-a-picture theme for many paintings; it had been used earlier in De Chirico's art. Occasionally,

Magritte made his point by using words within the picture. *The Use of Words I* (1928–29, Collection of William M. Copley) is a meticulously painted image of a pipe above the sentence *Ceci n'est pas une Pipe* ("This is not a Pipe"). Magritte felt that an image, work, or symbol is vastly different from its referent, although the differences are not always clearly understood. This simple point has profound implications for daily life, in which we depend constantly upon interpretations of images, words, and symbols. For Magritte, painting was not an end in itself; it was a means of exploring mental processes and of giving images maximum significance. His images acquire a peculiar intensity through their elusive and paradoxical meanings. While most Surrealists have relied upon startling combinations of unrelated objects, Magritte often used related objects but changed their scale relationships (a rose blossom fills a room), their substance (a stone fish lies on a rocky shore), their dependence upon gravity (a rock floats beside a cloud), or their separateness (a pair of shoes turns into feet). Magritte's mature painting reveals little stylistic change. His manner was methodical and meticulous except for two brief periods. During the Nazi occupation of Belgium in the 1940's, Magritte turned to a soft, colorful Impressionistic style that he said was in opposition to the oppressive political situation. In 1947 his *vache* (cow) paintings employed violent brushwork and deliberate crudeness in a parody of Fauvism.

19-26
RENÉ MAGRITTE, *Les Promenades d'Euclide,* 1955. Oil on canvas, 64⅛'' x 51⅛''. The Minneapolis Institute of Art. The William Hood Dunwoody Fund.

SCULPTURE

During the first half of the twentieth century, sculpture often reflected movements that occurred first in painting. As the twentieth century has unfolded, especially notable characteristics of sculpture have been: (1) a tendency to find inspiration in primitive art; (2) the rejection of mass by many sculptors; (3) the consideration of space as a positive compositional element; (4) the use of actual movement in sculptural compositions (kinetic sculpture); (5) the increasing use of welded metal and a variety of synthetic materials; (6) the tendency to create sculpture by assembling objects that have been worn out or cast aside by our culture.

In the early years of the century, the mobile surfaces of Rodin's art were countered by the stable massiveness of Aristide Maillol's work. Revolutionary portents emerged in the simplified forms and aggressive three-dimensionality of sculpture done by the Fauve painter Matisse. Equally expressionistic work was produced in Germany by sculptors like Ernst Barlach. Cubist sculpture, like Cubist painting, practiced disciplined analysis and free improvisation on natural forms. The Russian-instigated movement of Constructivism produced much nonobjective sculpture, created a pioneering example of kinetic sculpture, and provided a significant statement in the form of the *Realist Manifesto* (1920), which asserted the importance of space and time, rather than mass, as elements from which art should be built. The few pieces of sculpture created by Futurists are important three-dimensional expressions of the artists' obsession with speed and constant change. The Dada movement carried further the technique of *assemblage* that had been initiated by Cubist collage and first realized in sculpture by Picasso in 1912. Dada sculptures, sometimes called objects of non-art by their creators, were efforts to ridicule the world of convention and reason. The Dada blurring of distinctions between painting, sculpture, and commercially manufactured objects was portentous for later art. Surrealist sculpture has been more methodical in its effort to investigate the nonrational and to stimulate fantasy and free association by creating surprising combinations.

Aristide Maillol (France, 1861–1944). Maillol and Rodin were major influences in early twentieth-century sculpture. In the 1890's, Maillol developed a mature style that remained essentially unchanged throughout his career. Unlike Rodin, Maillol preferred ponderous masses and broad simple surfaces; his poses are usually

19-27
ARISTIDE MAILLOL, *The
Mediterranean*, 1902–05. Bronze,
41″ high, at base 45″ x 29¾″.
Collection, The Museum of Modern
Art, New York. Gift of Stephen C.
Clark.

static. In *The Mediterranean* (Fig. 19-27), the back and the raised knee and arm create a large stable triangle that is reinforced by the smaller triangular forms of the raised leg and the arm supporting the head. Geometric stability is strengthened by the simple, massive body forms, but the stony monumentality of the work is softened by slight undulations in contour. This sturdy female body appears throughout Maillol's work, ranging from blocky hardness to active musculature.

Ernst Barlach (Germany, 1870–1938). The key to Barlach's style may be found not so much in his studies in Hamburg and Dresden as in an early trip to Paris in 1895, where he saw and admired the massive peasants in Jean François Millet's paintings, the expressive force of Van Gogh's art, and the enduring strength of the workers sculpted by Constantin Meunier. From early work in clay, Barlach turned to wood as a favorite material. He reduced the human body and its costume to large simple masses, often unified by a common texture of gouge marks, emphasizing lines of force that express powerful feelings. His *Man Drawing a Sword* (Fig. 19-28) rises from the lines of tension in the skirt to the sweeping flare and bold shadows of the cape, which call attention to the hands drawing the sword. Tense urgency and vitality emanate from the simple forms.

19-28
ERNST BARLACH, *Man Drawing a Sword,*
1911. Wood, 29½″ high. From the
Collection of the Galleries of the Cranbrook
Academy of Art, Bloomfield Hills, Michigan.

Constantin Brancusi (Rumania and France, 1876–1957). Brancusi studied at the Academy of Fine Arts in Bucharest and, after settling in Paris in 1904, at the École des Beaux-Arts. His first exhibit in 1906 revealed the influ-

ence of Rodin. By 1908, Brancusi was finding his way toward greatly simplified forms with slight but important surface variations. A series of heads gains monumentality from sweeping planes and the reduction of facial features to grooves and ridges. These works indicate Brancusi's debt to African sculpture and his influence on the sculpture and painting of Amedeo Modigliani. By 1910, Brancusi had pushed simplification still further in *The Sleeping Muse* (Fig. 19-29). The head is reduced to an egg shape, with slight ridges for nose, lips, and ear. This reduction to geometric forms must be distinguished from that of Cubism; Brancusi was not interested in a multiplicity of views or a plane-by-plane analysis. He sought form that would be both visually exhilarating in its absolute simplicity and significant in its symbolism. *The New-Born* (1915, Museum of Modern Art, New York) is a sleek bronze egg form that is sliced by a plane and interrupted by a ridge. Where flat surface meets curved surface, the resulting edge gives a more precise idea of the nature of the curved surface. In addition to satisfying formal elegance, the work has subject matter that can be discerned with the help of its title. The egg not only refers to the beginning of life but also suggests the head of an infant, the anonymous face of a child whose personality is yet to be shaped by experience. Brancusi's preference for ovoid form is evident in the series of heads entitled *Mlle. Pogany,* done in many versions over a period of years, or in the versions of the *Fish* (one in the Museum of Modern Art, New York, done 1918–28), where the sleek, blade-shaped form is poised over a flat surface. Polished

19-30
CONSTANTIN BRANCUSI, *Caryatid,* early 1940's. Wood, 90⅛'' high. Musée National d'Arte Moderne, Paris.

forms were sometimes set on bases of roughly carved wood. His late work included pieces done entirely in wood, with choppy surfaces and abrupt transitions between the parts. These have the character of tribal gods. Brancusi remained aloof from the various groups and movements in twentieth-century art, yet the influence and appreciation of his sculpture have been international.

Jean (Hans) Arp (France, Germany, and Switzerland, 1887–1966). When Arp exhibited with the Blue Rider artists in Munich in 1912, he had already studied in Weimar and Paris and had shown an early tendency toward abstraction. From 1916 to 1919 he produced painting, sculpture, and poetry as a member of the Dada group in Zurich. Some of his nonobjective collages seem to have been arranged according to the laws of chance, reflecting the Dadaist rejection of rational order. With the exception of some rectangular compositions, Arp preferred irregular curves that suggested animal life. His shapes were sawed from planks, superimposed in two or more layers, and painted in usually contrasting hues to form polychrome sculpture. His first free-standing sculptures came only in the 1930's. Arp was a member of the Cologne and Paris Dada groups as well as of the Zurich one. When Dada ideas and artists were absorbed into the Surrealist movement in 1924, Arp was in Paris to contribute to their first exhibition in 1925. In all his work, a sly humor is present in the relationships of irregular curves and unexpected angles. The subject of *Aquatic* (Fig. 19-31) eludes clear identification, but in the sculpture lurks the hint of a rollicking seal, or perhaps a penguin that has stumbled. Like Brancusi, Arp sought forms with broad symbolic overtones and subtle relationships between the parts, yet Arp's work is more complex and more playful. It seems to be a cele-

19-31

JEAN ARP, *Aquatic,* 1953. Marble, 13'' high, 9'' deep, 25½'' long. Collection, Walker Art Center, Minneapolis.

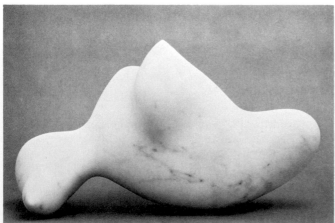

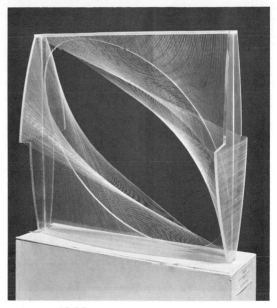

19-32
NAUM GABO, *Linear Construction.*
1942–43. Plexiglas, 24¼" x 24¼". The
Phillips Collection, Washington, D.C.

bration of the vitality and ceaseless metamorphosis that he felt to be present in nature.

Naum Gabo (Russia, Germany, France, England, and the United States, 1890–   ).   Gabo's Russian parents sent him to study medicine in Munich, but his interests turned toward science and sculpture. Acquaintance with Kandinsky, travels in Italy, and visits with his brother Antoine Pevsner, then a painter in Paris, all strengthened Gabo's interest in art. He began to use wood, metal, and celluloid to create forms that were open spatial volumes rather than masses. In 1917, Gabo returned with his brother to Russia, and in 1920 they spoke for the Constructivist group in publishing the *Realist Manifesto*, which called on art to express the new realities of space, time, and motion. Soon the Soviet government became hostile to abstract art, and Gabo and Pevsner were among the many artists to leave Russia. Gabo's *Linear Construction* (Fig. 19-32) is typical of his mature style. Nylon string and plastic sheets form gracefully curving planes that are subtly adjusted to the square edges of the composition and frame a central opening. Light and space permeate the transparent composition, and space participates as a positive element, providing the major theme in the form of the central opening. Gabo's work continues to embody most of the principles of the 1920 *Manifesto*. Using transparent planes, he imposes order on space. Time is organized by motion, but motion is expressed by flowing rhythmic continuity rather than by actual movement. Since his first experiment with motorized kinetic

sculpture in 1920, Gabo has felt that represented movement, rather than actual movement, is more effective for his sculpture. Since 1946, he has lived in the United States.

Jacques Lipchitz (Lithuania, France, and the United States, 1891–   ). Lipchitz left his Russian section of Lithuania in 1909 and came to Paris. His early work shows a tendency toward stolid equilibrium and heavy simplified anatomy similar to that in the art of Maillol. Soon, however, Lipchitz became involved with the concepts of Cubism. The *Sailor with Guitar* (Fig. 19-33) has the cascading sequences of planes found in Cubist painting. Lipchitz's art was to become more open in form. After doing a series of relief plaques in a Cubist style, he moved toward freer-flowing curves. A series of *transparencies*, as he called them, abandoned the traditional mass of sculpture for thin perforated planes, straps, and wiry forms. During the 1930's, the forms regained some of their mass and became knotted and muscular. In *Prometheus Strangling the Vulture II* (Fig. 19-34), the forms become convulsive in their energy. Primarily a modeler, Lipchitz makes the malleable clay burst with a life force. He has attempted to exploit the spontaneity of accident by blindly forming a mass of clay and then improvising with the result. He calls such works *semiautomatics*. Although most of his subjects can be recognized, their expressive and symbolic character is not always easy to define; the forms seem laden with suggestions of fecund plant and animal life, of male and female elements, and of the mystery of creation. After 1941, Lipchitz made his home in the United States.

19-33
JACQUES LIPCHITZ, *Sailor with Guitar,* 1914. Bronze, 31'' high. The Philadelphia Museum of Art. Given by Mrs. Morris Wenger in memory of her husband.

19-34
JACQUES LIPCHITZ, *Prometheus Strangling the Vulture II,* 1949. 7'9'' high, 7'8'' wide. The Philadelphia Museum of Art. Purchased: The Lisa Norris Elkins Fund.

Alexander Calder (United States and France, 1898–1976). Although Gabo experimented with moving motor-driven sculpture, Calder is acknowledged internationally as the most important pioneer in kinetic sculpture. Calder was born in Philadelphia; he studied engineering before he enrolled at the Art Students' League in New York. In Paris, in 1926 and 1927, he used wire to create toy circus performers and caricatures. From this, he turned to more abstract compositions of wire, metal shapes, or wood forms that were activated by electric motors or hand cranks. His acquaintance with the work of Mondrian led him to use color on some parts. Since 1932, he has felt that natural air currents are the best means of activating mobile or kinetic sculptures. *Red Petals* (Fig. 19-35) is typical in the lively curved metal shapes attached to the ends of delicately hinged and balanced wires. The flat metal pieces, like those of a weather vane, react to air currents, and the composition bobs and turns. Such sculpture renounces the traditional importance of mass; the open compositions participate actively in time and space. Calder has also done many *stabiles*, in which the motionless forms acquire liveliness from the directional forces within the cutout sheet-metal pieces.

Henry Moore (England, 1898–   ). England's most renowned twentieth-century sculptor studied at the Leeds School of Art and had his first one-man show in 1928. His early work is simple, massive, and blocky, reflecting an enthusiasm for ancient Mexican sculpture. By 1932, he was piercing the masses with openings treated as shaped spaces. The *Reclining Figure* (Fig. 19-36) has

19-35
ALEXANDER CALDER, *Red Petals,* 1942. Painted metal, stabile-mobile, 102'' high, petal span, 3' x 4'. Collection of the Art Club of Chicago.

19-36 HENRY MOORE, *Reclining Figure,* 1935. Wood, 19'' x 35''. Albright-Knox Art Gallery, Buffalo.

19-37
HENRY MOORE, *Helmet Head No. 1,* 1950. Bronze, 13½" high. The Tate Gallery, London.

such positive spaces; the female figure acquires the broad undulating hills and valleys of a landscape. As in so many of Moore's reclining figures, there is the suggested symbolism of the great earth mother, source of all life. During the 1930's, he did a number of string figures, in which string is threaded through the masses to form groups of lines that define spaces. Meanwhile, the reclining figures became increasingly open. During the bombings of London in the Second World War, Moore made drawings of Londoners sleeping in subway tunnels; war had driven people back into the womb of the earth. The cavernous openings within the figures suggest a relationship with their cavernous environment. It was also during the war that Moore began his series of *Helmet Heads* (Fig. 19-37), helmetlike metal shells into which one of a number of bony core forms could be fitted. Although very abstract, the results produce the uncanny effect of a frightened being looking out of a sheltering helmet. In the 1950's he produced a number of sparse skeletal figures with a regal, if occult, bearing, and several mutilated warriors, timeless expressions of humankind's self-destruction. Moore's sculptures, like those of Lipchitz, rely not on precise conventional symbols but on forms that suggest partly hidden truths about the nature of humankind and its relation to the universe.

Alberto Giacometti (Switzerland and France, 1901–66). Giacometti settled in Paris in 1922. His early work was inspired by Cubism, but from 1929 until 1934 he was a member of the Surrealist group and produced such sculpture as *The Palace at 4 A.M.* (1932–33, Museum of Modern Art, New York), a cagelike structure inhabited by skeletal forms. After 1934, he turned to more defi-

19-38
ALBERTO GIACOMETTI, *City Square,* 1948. Bronze, 8½" x 25⅜" x 17¼". Collection, The Museum of Modern Art, New York. Purchase.

nite human figures, employing drastically elongated proportions. The fragile, isolated, phantom beings in the *City Square* (Fig. 19-38) suggests that human society offers no escape from man's alienation from his fellows.

Barbara Hepworth (England, 1903–75). One of England's foremost sculptors, Hepworth received her training in England and Italy during the 1920's, at which time she also held her first exhibitions. Her early sculptures were figures in simplified masses and rhythmic harmonies that reflect the influence of Brancusi and Arp. In 1931 she produced a piece of sculpture in which a hole served as the focus. This work led the way, in British sculpture, for the positive use of empty space. The following year Henry Moore moved in the same direction. Since then, he has used space as a cavernous interior volume, while Hepworth retained the sense of a pierced opening communicating between two sides of a mass. From 1934 on, she turned predominantly to nonobjective forms, preferring for several years a very rigid geometry. During the 1930's, she was a member of the Seven and Five Society, Unit One, and Circle groups, which produced abstract and nonobjective art. Inspiration for this abstract movement came from the temporary presence in England of Gabo, László Moholy-Nagy, and Mondrian. By 1938 Hepworth had returned to freer, more irregular forms. At this time she frequently used paint on the interior surfaces of her sculpture and occasionally used strings to define her open spaces. In *Pendour* (Fig. 19-39), painted blue and white surfaces contrast with the openings and natural color of the wood to produce delicate shadows that delineate the complex movements and rhythms of the forms. In 1950 Hepworth represented England in the Venice Biennale, an international cultural event. In 1956, she began to use metal, first by cutting metal sheets directly and then by working with plaster and wood from which castings were made. Severe rectan-

19-39
BARBARA HEPWORTH, *Pendour*, 1947.
Painted wood, 10⅜″ x 27¼″ x 9″.
Hirshhorn Museum and Sculpture Garden,
Smithsonian Institution, Washington, D.C.

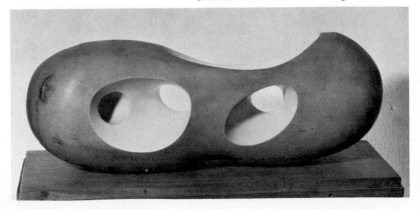

gles and circles reappeared among the wide repertory of forms in her later work.

ARCHITECTURE

Twentieth-century architecture has lost almost all vestiges of regional style and has been characterized by broad international trends. Eclecticism and Art Nouveau continued as rival stylistic tendencies in the early years of the century. The relatively new materials—steel and reinforced concrete—were usually disguised by traditional forms in eclectic work; their structural potential was demonstrated more clearly in the organic curves of Art Nouveau. An architectural style that exploited the advantages of reinforced concrete had its beginnings in buildings by the Frenchman Auguste Perret. The simplicity of Perret's work provided refreshing contrast to the crowded surfaces and self-conscious ornament of both eclecticism and Art Nouveau. Simplification was carried further by several Viennese architects, notably Adolf Loos. After 1910, the severe cubic forms of Loos's work were echoed in other countries and came to be known as the *International Modern Style*. The austere geometric buildings of this style were designed by Walter Gropius, Ludwig Mies van der Rohe, and other architects who worked at the *Bauhaus*, Germany's famous school of design during the 1920's, and by Le Corbusier in France. A secondary trend developed between 1910 and 1925 in Holland and Germany, where certain architects designed buildings with sudden curves or exaggerated streamlining. Effects ranged from playfulness and whimsy to overpowering

19-40
FRANK LLOYD WRIGHT, Robie House, Chicago, 1909.

animated or machinelike forms. The architecture has been described as expressionistic.

In the United States, Frank Lloyd Wright followed his master, Louis Sullivan, in rejecting eclecticism, and Wright's use of uninterrupted interior spaces, asymmetrically expanding plans, long horizontal lines, and interlocking masses influenced the early work of Gropius, Mies van der Rohe, and several of the Dutch architects, all of whom learned of Wright's work through German publications. In place of severe geometric simplicity, however, Wright preferred proliferation of masses and the enrichment of surfaces with contrasting textures and colors. Wright has had great influence in residential design, while Gropius and Mies van der Rohe have shaped the prevailing styles in skyscraper design.

The principles of modern architecture and urban planning found their major support in *CIAM* (*Congrès International d'Architecture Moderne*, or the International Congress of Modern Architecture), which lasted from 1928 until 1956. *CIAM's* most influential members were Le Corbusier, Gropius, Alvar Aalto, and José Luis Sert.

Frank Lloyd Wright (United States, 1867–1959). Wright, America's leading architect in the first half of the twentieth century had two years of engineering training at the University of Wisconsin before going to Chicago and joining the firm of Adler and Sullivan. Unlike Sullivan, Wright designed few large public buildings. He acquired from Sullivan a love of mass, a hatred of imitation, and the convictions that form should be determined by function and that decoration should emphasize structure. The low, widespread, asymmetrical ranch house has its ancestry in Wright's early *prairie houses*, the best known of which is the Robie House (Figs. 19-40 and 19-41). The asymmetrically arranged spaces are interrupted as little as possible and flow around the central chimney mass. Wright believed that walls should be opened up by large groups of windows to achieve the greatest sense of spaciousness, but he loved to contrast large window areas with unbroken masses of wall. He felt that the exterior should seem to be part of the building's site. The long low lines of the Robie House echo the flat earth plane and were originally punctuated by greenery in planters, so that the house seemed to be a part of nature. The wide overhanging eaves are typical expressions of Wright's conviction that the sheltering function of a roof should be emphasized. Concrete, brick, stone, and natural wood

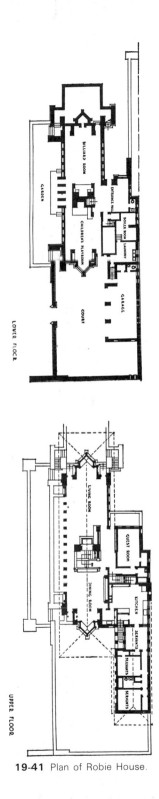

19-41 Plan of Robie House.

19-42
FRANK LLOYD WRIGHT, Guggenheim
Museum, New York, 1946–59.

were used for contrasts of color and texture. Wright
often elaborated on interlocking structures; throughout
his work, masses, spaces, and the smallest details inter-
penetrate to express the unity of the whole. Wright's
favorite term for such unity of site, structure, and decoration was *organic architecture*. His designs are remarkably original, though he learned much from Japanese
architecture, and though some of his more massive
buildings have a similarity to ancient Mayan architecture. His greatest technical triumph was the design of
the Imperial Hotel in Tokyo (1915–22), which was
planned to be earthquake-proof and was undamaged by
the terrible earthquake of 1923. The houses of his later
years sometimes employ a polygonal, circular, or triangular thematic shape as a unifying module for floor
plans, for built-in furniture, and even for gardens. A
circular module was the basis for the most controversial
large building of his career, New York's Guggenheim
Museum (Fig. 19-42).

Adolf Loos (Austria and France, 1870–1933). Loos was
one of the architects who rebelled against both eclecticism and ornament. He spent three years (1893–96) in
the United States, and returned to Vienna to pursue a
career in architecture, teaching, and writing. The Steiner
House (Fig. 19-43) of 1910 illustrates his preference for
starkly simple, boxlike geometric forms that rely completely on proportions for their aesthetic effect. Loos
first acquired an international reputation through his
writing, which was published in Vienna and then repub-
lished in Berlin and Paris. His most controversial essay
was "Ornament and Crime" (1908), in which he
equated ornament with crime and argued that culture

advances as ornament decreases. Loos, like many of the International Style architects, was an avid admirer of engineers and machines. After 1923, he was active in Paris.

Auguste Perret (France, 1874–1954). Perret was trained as an architect in the École des Beaux-Arts. He is especially important as a pioneer in the use of reinforced concrete. For his Rue Franklin Apartments (1902–03, Paris) he used a ferroconcrete framework protected on the exterior by tile. Dramatic openness was arranged in the Garage Ponthieu (1905–06, Paris), where the stark concrete frame is filled in with glass. Perret's basilica church of Notre Dame Le Raincy (Figs. 19-44 and 19-45), has canopies of ferroconcrete vaults supported by slender columns. The walls, which are not needed to support the vaulting, consist of concrete blocks perfo-

19-44
AUGUSTE PERRET, Notre Dame Le Raincy, 1922–23.

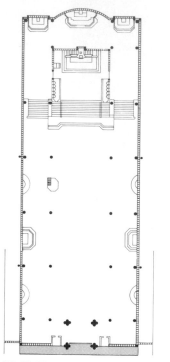

19-45 Plan of Notre Dame Le Raincy.

rated with designs and filled with stained glass. The buoyant, light-filled interior thus uses new means to achieve some of the qualities of Gothic architecture. He often mixed color aggregates with concrete in order to vary the color and minimize weather staining.

Walter Gropius (Germany and the United States, 1883–1969). Mies van der Rohe, Le Corbusier, and Gropius were the major leaders in the trend toward austere simplicity from about 1920 until 1940. Of these, Gropius is the one whose theories have been most influential, through his architecture, his teaching, and his writing. In 1918, after several years of private practice as a Berlin architect, he was appointed Director of the Grand Ducal Saxon School of Applied Arts and the Grand Ducal Academy of Arts in Weimar. He united the two schools under the name *Staatliches Bauhaus* with the aim of joining the creative energies of artists and product designers. Like Loos, Gropius was enthusiastic about the possibilities of the Machine Age and deplored the use of applied ornament as a kind of cultural cake frosting. Gropius' buildings have been consistent with his theory. His first major work (in collaboration with Adolf Meyer), the Fagus Factory (Fig. 19-46), employed steel supports, concrete floor slabs, and screen walls of glass. He used glass curtain walls again with dramatic effect in the new Bauhaus buildings at Dessau in 1926 (Fig. 19-47). In the Stuttgart Werkbund Housing Exhibition of 1927, where Le Corbusier and others demonstrated their advanced ideas, Gropius submitted a prefabricated house using a metal frame with asbestos and cork walls. In 1934, Gropius was forced by Nazi policies

19-46
WALTER GROPIUS and ADOLF MEYER,
Fagus Factory, Alfeld, 1910–14.

19-47
WALTER GROPIUS, Bauhaus shop, Dessau, 1925–26.

to leave Germany. He first went to England and, in 1937, came to the United States, where he taught at Harvard and formed TAC (The Architects' Collaborative).

Ludwig Mies van der Rohe (Germany and the United States, 1886–1969). Like Gropius, Mies van der Rohe worked with the architect Peter Behrens before starting independent practice in Berlin. The extent of his vision was evidenced in his project for an office building for Friedrichstrasse in 1919. He proposed a steel frame with cantilevered floors and curtain walls of glass. His design for a brick country house (1923) has low spreading lines, grouped windows, and asymmetrical spaces that suggest the influence of Frank Lloyd Wright. Mies directed the Werkbund Exhibition of 1927 in Stuttgart. Two years later, for the German Pavilion at the International Exhibition at Barcelona, Mies produced one of the landmarks of twentieth-century architecture (Fig. 19-48). The small building consisted of marble panels, steel supports, and glass walls. Spaces were defined without being isolated from each other or from the exterior. The spaciousness, the long low lines, the reflecting pools, and the steel, glass, and marble materials all created an effect of serene elegance. These stylistic features were incorporated in the famous Tugendhat House (1930, Brno, Czechoslovakia). The exterior of the house is starkly simple, employing blank walls and translucent glass on the street side and curtain walls of transparent glass on the garden side. Within, slender steel columns support the roof, and the minimal number of dividing walls creates a maximal sense of space. In 1933 Mies, who was then its director, closed the

19-48

LUDWIG MIES VAN DER ROHE, German Pavilion,
International Exposition, Barcelona, 1929.

19-49

LUDWIG MIES VAN DER ROHE, Seagram
Building, New York, 1956–58.

Bauhaus because of political pressure, and in 1939 he
came to Chicago to head the architectural school of the
Armour Institute, which later became the Illinois Institute of Technology. The buildings that he designed for
I.I.T. became Mies's manifesto in America. The simple
rectangular forms were made of steel cages constructed
on a 24-foot module and filled in with brick or glass.
The Seagram Building (Fig. 19-49) was planned in 1956.
The interior floor space gained by the height of the
building enabled the architect to leave a large open area
at the base for outdoor pools and gardens set into a
pink granite platform, thus relieving the congestion at
street level. The amber gray glass and bronze tower that
forms the main part of the building extends beyond the
steel piers on which it is raised, emphasizing its lightness and openness. The vertical bronze beams, partly
structural and partly decorative, stress the soaring
height and provide a delicate linear pattern in relief.

Charles Édouard Jeanneret, called **Le Corbusier** (Switzerland
and France, 1888–1965). Charles Édouard Jeanneret,
who took the name Le Corbusier to avoid confusion
with his cousin, the architect Pierre Jeanneret, was born
in Switzerland but made his career in France. He studied with Perret, learning about ferroconcrete and inher-
iting Perret's admiration for engineering and the efficiency of machines. Le Corbusier's Dom-ino multiple
housing project, planned in 1914 and 1915 but never
built, used ferroconcrete frames that reduced walls to
weather screens have no weight-bearing function. The
projects for the Citrohan House (1919–22) were a more

complete exposition of his aims. Standardized parts were used wherever possible, and the severely simple boxlike form was of plain ferroconcrete, with no effort to vary texture. A wall of windows at one end illuminated a two-story high living room; bedrooms were on a balcony and a third floor, and a recreation area was provided on the flat roof. A second version raised the whole house on concrete piers. Like Frank Lloyd Wright, Le Corbusier was a leader in opening up interior space with grouped windows and a minimum of partition walls. Although his houses were criticized as bleak machines, Le Corbusier often sacrificed the practical for the aesthetic—the huge window areas and two-story living rooms, for example, are very costly to heat. Le Corbusier's sense of the beautiful was inspired by machines, and his buildings have the look of machinelike efficiency, but they are designed to satisfy his love of spaciousness and light. Many of his projects were never built, but the Citrohan idea was realized in a house built for the Stuttgart Werkbund Exhibition of 1927. Only in the latter years of his career did Le Corbusier have the opportunity to realize his urban planning theories. The most notable design is that for Chandigarh. After 1940 Le Corbusier's architecture developed a very different character. The rigid boxlike forms gave way to irregular curves and deep openings in wall surfaces, producing a more sculptural effect. Notre-Dame-du-Haut at Ronchamp (Figs. 19-50–19-52)

19-50
LE CORBUSIER, Notre-Dame-du-Haut, Ronchamp. 1950–55.

19-51
Interior of Notre-Dame-du-Haut.

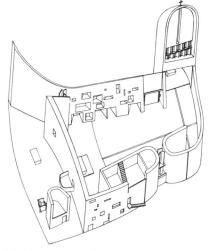

19-52 Plan of Notre-Dame-du-Haut.

is an outstanding example, and it is one of the most controversial church designs of our time. The billowing vitality of the roof, the sweeping curves of the walls punctuated by deep irregular windows, and the spotlighting effects on the interior dramatize the experience of worship.

1945–1960

PAINTING

Between World War II and 1960 an international trend toward abstract and nonobjective art enjoyed dominance. Many European artists were driven by the war to the United States, bringing with them quantities of talent and new ideas. It was in New York, under the leadership of Jackson Pollock, Franz Kline, and Willem de Kooning, that the first major movement in postwar painting developed—*Abstract Expressionism.* This painting is sometimes abstract and sometimes nonobjective, but it is usually explosive in the activity of its forms. The impact of the work is often magnified by large scale. The quality of expressed activity—often cathartic in its violence—led American critics to describe much Abstract Expressionist art as *Action Painting.* A less violent trend within Abstract Expressionism has been called *Color Field* painting because it relies for its impact on large areas of intensely interacting colors. Although the term Abstract Expressionism was applied first to American painting of this type during the 1940's, similar work has been done in other countries. It has its ancestry in Fauvism, German Expressionism, and the Surrealist emphasis on instinct and fantasy. More than previously, however, Abstract Expressionist painters produced series of works that were intended to be experienced as a whole. The way was paved for compositions of total environments that were to become common especially after 1960.

Toward the end of the 1950's, young British and American artists were laying the basis for Pop Art, which utilized mass-media images. Geometric abstraction also continued. In France, Victor Vasarely was experimenting with the optical illusions that were to become essential to *Op Art* in the next decade.

Hans Hofmann (Germany and the United States, 1880–1966). From Impressionist painting produced while a student, Hofmann turned to Cubism during his stay in Paris from 1903 to 1914. After his return to Munich, he quickly gained a reputation as an art instructor. This led to summer teaching jobs in California and to permanent residence after 1932 in New York, where he taught at the Art Students' League and later opened his own school. His art and teaching form a major link between European Expressionism and New York Abstract Expressionism. In his paintings, he ranged stylistically from free forms done with poured, spattered, or violently brushed paint to hard-edged, rectangular planes. Often the two kinds of forms are combined in one painting, as in *Bird Cage, Variation II* (Plate 29). Textures in the paintings vary from thin washes to puttylike thicknesses. Hofmann argued that vitality in art arises from movement and tension between opposing elements, which he termed "push-pull." In painting, this comes from the contrasting directions of overlapping planes, the opposing movements of line and the immediate juxtaposition of soft and hard edges, quiet and aggressive brushwork, and—most of all—advancing and receding colors (see pp. 16–17). The illusionary spaces between colors are charged, he felt, with energy. He wanted to preserve the sense of the flat surface of the canvas even while the illusion of depth was generated by his jockeying of forms in space. The central red orange plane in *Bird Cage, Variation II* floats forward but is tied to the surface by colors that overlap and diffuse its edges. The green bar in the lower left pulls away from the yellow background at its left edge but is overrun by thick strokes of paint on its right; no area of the composition is allowed to be empty. In Hofmann's theory even the smallest area, active or passive, should

19-53
JOSEF ALBERS, *Homage to the Square: Apparition,* 1959. Oil on board, 47½" x 47½". The Solomon R. Guggenheim Museum, New York.

have interest or substance. The relatively passive white areas have sparks of color, delicate modulations of value, and textural weight. At the upper left, the variegated whitish mass surges in front of the blue rectangle. For Hofmann, a painting was a field of forces to be controlled and manipulated by the artist in achieving the utmost vitality.

Josef Albers (Germany and the United States, 1888–1976). Albers taught in elementary schools and produced lithographs and *linocuts* (linoleum block prints) before entering the Bauhaus as a student in 1920. By 1923, he had become an instructor there, teaching glass painting, which is a form of stained glass. His nonobjective works in this medium were made at first from scavenged bottle-glass of irregular shapes. Then he turned to precise, rectangular forms in milk glass with color overlays. At the same time, he made linocuts and woodcuts, occasionally creating ambiguous spatial effects with overlapping shapes. When the Bauhaus closed in 1933 Albers came to the United States, where he taught at Black Mountain College in North Carolina, at Harvard, and at Yale. He spent his career investigating the perception of line and color. His best-known series, *Homage to the Square* (Fig. 19-53), painted from 1949 until the end of his life, employs symmetrically arranged squares of pure colors and unvarying textures. With the exceptions of pink and rose, the colors are used directly from commercial tubes of oil paint and noted on the back of each Masonite panel. Colors and proportions are selected to create effects of vibration, translucency, changing saturation, and movement up and down or back and forth in illusionary space. In our perception, color changes according to its environment. Albers' aim was to make us more sensitive to color phenomena; he was a forerunner in the development of Op Art.

Jean Dubuffet (France, 1901–   ).   Enraged spectators slashed some of Dubuffet's paintings in 1946 at his second one-man exhibition. Undaunted, he became one of the leaders in the international avant-garde of the 1950's. He used tar, cement, glue, bark, sponges, driftwood, steel wool, and butterfly wings to produce images of startling energy, brute force, and childlike directness of vision. Dubuffet has long been interested in folk art and in the art of the mentally disturbed, which he collected and exhibited under the title *l'Art Brut* (unrefined art)—a term which has been applied to his own work as well. He tends to produce paintings in series on such subjects as female figures, landscapes, city scenes, tables (Fig. 19-54), and portraits of friends. Even in his portraits, personal features are less important than the suggestion of a type. Often a major form within a composition is so expansive in proportion to the surface area that it threatens to burst the pictorial boundaries. On a technical level, his preference has been to use heavy pastes composed of ingredients like zinc oxide and varnish, which are troweled onto panels. Cut-and-pasted shapes, impressions of kitchen utensils as well as other objects, and incompatible paints all

19-54
JEAN DUBUFFET, *Work Table with Letter,*
1952. Oil paint in Swedish putty on
composition board, 35⅝'' x 47⅞''.
Collection, The Museum of Modern Art, New
York. Gift of Mr. and Mrs. Ralph F. Colin.

contribute to the wrinkled and lacerated forms of his images. For Dubuffet the crudeness of his materials serves to intensify his forms while providing resistance to the facile recognition of his images. The shock of finding images in such crude materials evokes within the spectator fresh imaginative responses. In recent years, Dubuffet has used more delicate textures in such series of works as *Texturologies* and *Beards*. Many of these works have employed shapes like those of jigsaw puzzles. In spite of his anti-intellectual position, Dubuffet's talks and writings are highly sophisticated and articulate.

Mark Rothko (Russia and the United States, 1903–70). In 1933, at the time of his first one-man show, Rothko was using subtle colors and flat shapes to depict isolated figures in urban settings. In the 1940's, he changed to wide bands of thinly painted color containing delicately drawn forms that suggest plant or animal fossils. By 1950, he had turned to large, nonobjective compositions of several soft-edged rectangles aligned with the canvas surface, as in *Brown and Black on Plum* (Plate 30). Rothko chose colors that would produce luminous intensity where the shapes meet. The blurred, resonant edges make the shapes and their position in space elusive. While the shapes seem to be absorbed in the canvas surface, they also appear to float in a veiled space, creating a tension between surface and depth. Their power and size tend to overwhelm or engulf the spectator, especially when the work is viewed at close range. Because color is more important than shape in his work, Rothko is considered a Color Field painter.

Willem de Kooning (Holland and the United States, 1904–). De Kooning worked as a commercial artist during the day and studied art in night classes, first at the Academy in Rotterdam, later in Belgium, and, after 1926, in New York. In 1935, he became a full-time painter, and during the 1940's he made his reputation in New York. His early style, in the 1920's and '30's, often combined recognizable objects with geometric shapes. Forms are solidly modeled in some parts and flattened in others, and there is a constant shifting from mass to plane and from flatness to depth. Colors develop around pinks, yellows, and light blues, sometimes in vibrating contrasts. In the 1940's, he produced a series of abstract and nonobjective works in black and white, with sprightly curving planes and active lines. These paintings composed the major part of his first one-man show in 1948, which immediately established his reputation.

During the 1950's, color was added to the slashing brushwork and explosive energy of his earlier works, as is evident in the series called *Woman*. Plate 31 is typical of this group; the work seems to have emerged from a violent encounter between the artist and his materials to become a record of action and spontaneous decision. In the late 1950's and early '60's, de Kooning painted many nonobjective works; in the mid-1960's, he once more began painting the human figure, this time with more fluid brushwork than before.

Victor Vasarely (Hungary and France, 1908–). Vasarely came to Paris in 1930 after study in a Budapest school patterned after the German Bauhaus. For a time he worked as an advertising designer and did noncommercial designs in his free time. In 1944 he first exhibited his "free-graphics" and left commercial art. His early geometric abstractions occasionally used optical illusions of change and movement in patterns and colors, and after 1955 Vasarely became a pioneer in the exploitation of these kinetic effects, which he calls *cinétisme* and which is exemplified by *YMPO* (Plate 32). The physiological basis for such illusions is retinal fatigue. Vasarely was a source of inspiration for such groups as *NTrc* (*Nouvelle Tendence recherche continuelle*) and *GRAV* (*Groupe de Recherche de l'Art Visuel*), which developed in the 1960's as part of the international spread of Kinetic and Op Art (see p. 406).

Francis Bacon (Ireland and England, 1909–). Although he began to paint in the 1930's, it became Bacon's chief

19-55
FRANCIS BACON, *Number VII from Eight Studies for a Portrait*. 1953. Oil on canvas, approx. 60″ x 46⅛″. Collection, The Museum of Modern Art, New York (gift of Mr. and Mrs. William A. M. Burden).

activity only in 1945. Even after the violence of the Second World War, the public was unprepared for the images he thrust upon it: Half-effaced, dislocated, humanoid forms seem to be screaming through the walls of transparent boxes (Fig. 19-55). His later works depict even more violent contortions and a sense of urgent metamorphosis achieved with swirling brushwork and paint applied with rags or thrown onto the canvas. Bacon feels that portraiture is the most challenging subject today. He prefers to work largely from photographs because it is easier to do "injury" to the image when the subject is not watching, although he is not deliberately creating horror images or commenting on the human situation. Rather, he wishes to record intensely some aspects of human behavior and to remake images irrationally. Bacon feels that life is an accident without purpose or reason, but also that one can derive satisfaction from a profound experience and an awareness of different levels of reality. His interest in controlled accident and instinctive or irrational painting is indebted to Surrealism. In this way he evokes a special mood of crisis, of physical and mental vulnerability, that reflects some of the anxiety explored by post–World War II existentialism. Intentionally or not, Bacon's work seems to reveal contemporary humans as changeable, molded by contingency, and possibly self-contradictory.

Franz Kline (United States, 1910–62). Kline, one of the leaders of the Abstract Expressionist movement, was born in Pennsylvania. He established himself in New York in 1938, teaching at Pratt Institute and working as a commercial artist to earn a living. During the 1930's and '40's, he painted portraits, landscapes, and cityscapes. In 1950, the same year of his first one-man show, he saw some of his small drawings enlarged by an opaque projector. The power of the forms thus magnified inspired Kline to turn to broad sweeping strokes in nonobjective compositions. For several years, he used only black and white, but in the mid-1950's he began to employ color again. Kline did brush drawings on newspapers and the pages of telephone books. These sketches were then framed with different-sized rectangles or cut into fragments. Once the plan was established in this way, it was enlarged on canvas and painted with large brushes. *Le Gros* (Fig. 19-56) is typical in the slashing power of the black strokes, which establish a horizontal shape poised on a vertical one. Prolonged observation, however, calls into question the

19-56
FRANZ KLINE, *Le Gros,* 1961. Oil on canvas, 41⅜" x 52⅝". The Sidney and Harriet Janis Collection. Gift to the Museum of Modern Art, New York.

relationship between the black figure and the white background, for the artist dragged white paint over the black in certain areas to keep the white from being simply empty. It takes little effort to reverse the figure-ground relationship and see the white shapes as positive forms in black space.

Jackson Pollock (United States, 1912–56). Pollock studied in Los Angeles and New York and eventually settled on Long Island. His painting became increasingly abstract after 1940. From convulsive linear shapes that sometimes acquire the character of humans, animals, or

19-57
JACKSON POLLOCK, *Pasiphaë,* 1943. Oil on canvas, 56⅛" x 96". Collection, Lee Krasner Pollock.

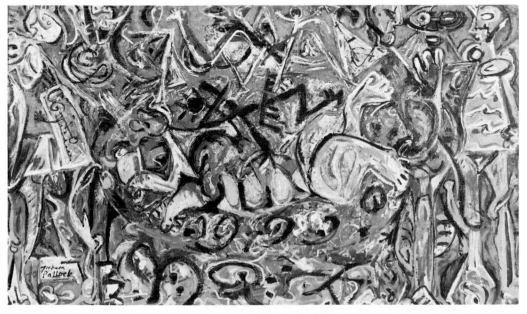

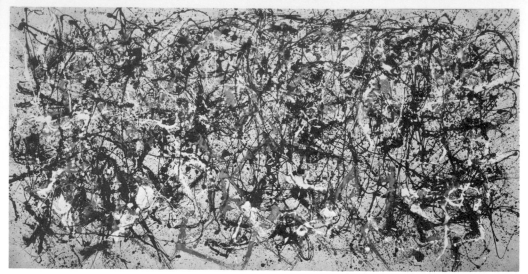

19-58
JACKSON POLLOCK, *Autumn Rhythm*,
1950. Oil on canvas, 105″ x 207″. The
Metropolitan Museum of Art. George A.
Hearn Fund.

cryptic symbols, as in the *Pasiphaë* (Fig. 19-57), he
turned by 1948 to intricate, nonobjective networks of
swirling, colored line. *Autumn Rhythm* (Fig. 19-58) is
typical of his late works, sometimes called drip paintings because they were done by dripping paints of
different thicknesses from cans onto canvas stretched
flat on the floor. Pollock's painting career was cut short
by his death in a car accident, but he has a wide influence as a leader of Abstract Expressionism and action
painting.

Robert Motherwell (United States, 1915–). Research
on the art theories of Delacroix, Baudelaire, and the
French Symbolists prepared Motherwell to appreciate
the subjective character of Surrealist art. Motherwell
used paint and collage to create large, irregular shapes

19-59
ROBERT MOTHERWELL,
*Elegy to the Spanish
Republic XXXIV*, 1953–54.
Oil on canvas, 80″ x 100″.
Albright-Knox Art Gallery,
Buffalo, New York. Gift of
Seymour H. Knox.

and areas of texture and pattern in his early work that recall Miro's art in their animation and representational implications. A sweeping oval above tapered legs becomes Pancho Villa; wavering vertical bands and sharply edged rectangles become a Spanish prison. The symbolic potential of psychic automatism or psychic improvisation was important to Motherwell, who knew French Surrealists in exile in New York during the Second World War and whose art was taking form during the early phase of Abstract Expressionism. The major theme of his career came from childhood memories of news reports about the Spanish Civil War. He began his *Elegies to the Spanish Republic* series in 1949 (Fig. 19-59). Large canvases present threatening oppositions of black with white and of violently brushed verticals with ovoid forms. These ominous polarities suggest symbolic conflicts of life and death or the heavy rhythm of funereal drum beats. Greater automatism is evident in the *Lyric Suite* (1965), a series of compositions made with ink that was poured and spattered on rice paper. The *Open* series (1967–69) developed very different forms. Subtle modulations within a single color hint at the possibility of atmospheric depth on the flat canvas surface. Thin lines suggest a window shape that appears to be more closed than open. These gentle enigmas continued in some work of the 1970's, but there has also been a return to active brushwork and aggressive shapes with bold value contrasts. Automatic forms characterize much of his work in lithography, silk-screen, and etching. Motherwell is a major theoretician of contemporary painting; his editing, writing, and teaching have made an important contribution to the continuing dialogue about the nature and role of art in the twentieth century.

Robert Rauschenberg (United States, 1925–). After trying a variety of approaches, including blank white canvases and compositions in black and white, Rauschenberg turned to assemblages of found objects and objects combined with vigorously brushed painting, such as *The Bed* (1955, Collection of Mr. and Mrs. Leo Castelli), which consists of quilt, pillow, and paint. By 1961, exhibits in New York and Paris had established Rauschenberg as a daring and prolific talent. *Tracer* (Fig. 19-60) indicates a flattening tendency in that no actual objects are attached to the canvas surface. The work's photomontage profusion was obtained by transfer of magazine images to silk screens that the artist then used to print on the canvas. The energy and scale of the

19-60
ROBERT RAUSCHENBERG, *Tracer*, 1962. Approx.
17'9" x 12'8". Collection of Mr. and Mrs. Frank
Titelman, Altoona, Pennsylvania.

brushwork links such a painting with Abstract Expressionism; the unexpected combinations of common objects recall Dada photomontage.

SCULPTURE

The sculptural counterparts to Abstract Expressionist painting are rough, jagged forms, often constructed by welding, and given color and texture by chemicals; energetic and spontaneous effects are prized. Assemblages of found objects add to the symbolic and imaginative possibilities of sculpture. An alternative was offered by continuing geometric styles, which suggested strict control and deliberate calculation. New methods of construction have allowed for easier experimentation than did traditional methods such as carving and casting. During the 1945 to 1960 period, sculpture gained a new momentum, which has grown subsequently and given sculpture great importance.

Louise Nevelson (Russia and the United States, 1899–   ). Nevelson's early work dealt with the human figure treated in simplified cubic masses and lively angles. Bronze, terra cotta, and occasional marble pieces were produced from the late 1920's into the '40's, but in 1944 she exhibited for the first time her compositions assembled from scrap wood, the type of sculpture that was to make her reputation. These totemic compositions recall Russian Constructivism, with the added wit of Dada and the ambiguity of Surrealism. In the 1950's she began to create works composed of found objects and scraps of wood assembled in boxes that were then combined in compartmentalized groups that filled whole walls. Nevelson then unified the rich diversity of parts in these works by spray-painting each composition a single color; from flat black, she turned to pure white and then to gold (Fig. 19-61). In 1965 she was one of the artists chosen to represent the United States at the Venice Biennale. At about the same time she began to use aluminum or Plexiglas to create forms of a precise, machinelike quality. In the late 1960's and early '70's she produced some pieces from aluminum scraps and weathering steel, which allows controlled rusting for color and texture. Her favorite material, however, continues to be wood, painted black and arranged in compartmentalized structures.

David Smith (United States, 1906–65). Smith studied painting in Washington, D.C., and New York during the 1920's. In 1931, inspired partly by Picasso's welded sculpture, he began attaching found and shaped wooden objects to his paintings; and in 1932 he began making welded sculpture. Rough-edged geometric

19-61
LOUISE NEVELSON, *Royal Tide II*, 1961–63. Painted wood, 94½'' high, 126½'' wide, 8'' deep. Collection of The Whitney Museum of American Art, New York. Gift of the artist.

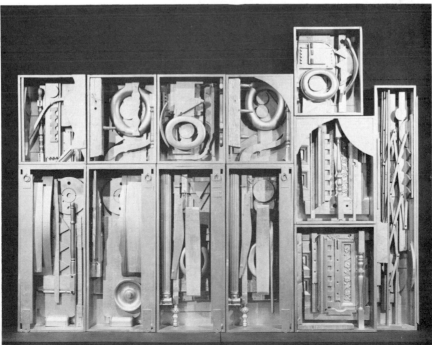

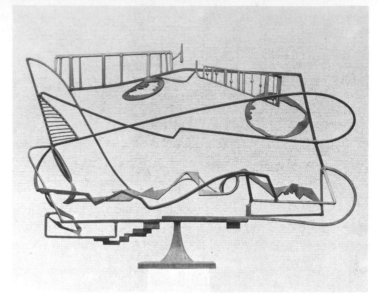

19-62
DAVID SMITH, *Hudson River Landscape*, 1951. Steel, 101¾" high, 33" wide, 20½" deep. Collection of The Whitney Museum of American Art, New York.

19-63
DAVID SMITH, *Cubi XVIII*, 1964. Polished stainless steel, 9'7¾" high. Museum of Fine Arts, Boston. Anonymous Centennial Gift.

planes and masses were combined and painted in compositions like *Suspended Cube* (1938, Estate of David Smith). Social comment appears in the *Medals of Dishonor*, silver and bronze reliefs pointing out unjust or inhuman aspects of the Second World War. Smith's inventiveness ranged from such unlikely subjects as *Hudson River Landscape* (Fig. 19-62) and *Banquet* (1952, private collection, New York), both linear steel hieroglyphs in space, to a pure geometry of burnished or painted steel in the *Zig* and *Cubi* series. *Cubi XVIII* (Fig. 19-63) is a daring and "momentary" poise of shimmering geometric solids, a visual statement with the authority of a trumpet call.

Theodore Roszak (United States, 1907–   ). Roszak was born in Poland and came to Chicago in 1909. He settled in New York in 1931 and created geometric nonobjective sculpture in the manner of the Constructivists. In 1945 came the stylistic change that led to his mature style, a bristling, explosive combination of jagged, torn forms and rough textures. The *Whaler of Nantucket* (Fig. 4-6) has the elusive symbolism of *Moby Dick*. The welded steel assumes threateningly violent forms that refer obliquely to the snout of a whale, the thrust of a harpoon, and the prow of a boat. Such active, powerful form links Roszak's art to Abstract Expressionist and Action Painting.

ARCHITECTURE

The post-World War II period has been characterized by extensive rebuilding, expansion, technological progress, and affluence in the industrialized western countries. Architects and critics, like Lewis Mumford in the United States, have become increasingly concerned with the sociological, political, and technological aspects of architecture, sometimes at the expense of aesthetic concerns; city planning has gained importance. The prevailing tendency has been to tear down existing structures and replace them with tall buildings that allow for high density at the same time that they provide open spaces for the community; in city planning the tendency has been to separate activities for maximum efficiency. Opponents of this trend, like Jane Jacobs in the United States, argue that such bulldozer schemes sacrifice cultural roots, diversity, individuality, and human scale; they feel that the old should be selectively restored and that planning should link the past with the future. The destruction of existing structures was not necessary for two exciting new cities: Chandigarh, the new capital of Hariana and the Punjab, designed by Le Corbusier, and Brasília, the new capital of Brazil, designed by Oscar Niemeyer. The planners of both cities have attempted, with mixed success, to separate social and economic activities.

This period also saw the late work of the "first-generation" leaders: Wright, Gropius, Mies van der Rohe, and Le Corbusier, all but the latter working in the United States. With the exception of Mies's work, the style of these men changed from an early austerity toward a complexity in form and richness in texture and color. Some critics saw this development as "neohistoricism" or "decorated modern," but nevertheless it

19-64
LOUIS KAHN, Richards Medical Research Building, University of Pennsylvania, Philadelphia, 1957–61.

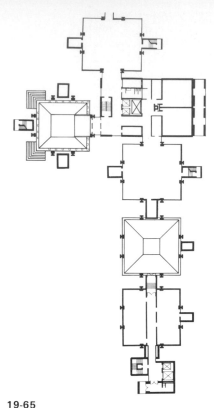

19-65
Plan of Richards Medical Research Building.

19-66 TWA Terminal.

influenced the second-generation leaders. Mies's expression of structure and Le Corbusier's use of massive, rough concrete were basic to an international inclination toward fortresslike proportions and rough surfaces that has been termed the *New Brutalism.*

Louis Kahn (United States, 1901–74). Kahn received his degree from the Architecture School of the University of Pennsylvania in 1924 and worked as assistant to other architects until 1934. His early work, involving city planning and housing projects, revealed an admiration for Gropius in its flat-roofed, wide-windowed horizontality. In 1947, Kahn joined the architecture staff of Yale University and began to design more buildings that expressed his individual concepts rather than those of a team. Kahn's work has emphasized revealed structure and spaces that are more separate than continuous. The Richards Medical Research Building (Figs. 19-64 and 19-65) clearly separates the massive service-utility towers from the glass-walled laboratories. Although the whole form is complex, the stark simplicity of its individual parts and the bold contrast of upright and horizontal, transparency and opacity, projection and recession, give a total effect of variety and monumentality. Stylistically, this, and many other Kahn designs, may be included in the New Brutalism movement.

Eero Saarinen (Finland and the United States, 1910–61). After moving with his family to the United States in 1923, Saarinen studied in Paris and at Yale before joining the architectural firm of his father, Eliel Saarinen. His developing concept of architecture led to a separation from his father in 1948. Eero Saarinen's firm designed the huge General Motors Technological Center near Detroit (1951–57), using a severely rectangular architecture influenced by Mies van der Rohe. Unlike Mies, he enlivened his forms with red, blue, yellow, and orange walls. From this colorful outgrowth of the International Modern Style, Saarinen, like Le Corbusier, turned to a more complex, animated style. In the University of Chicago Law School (1956–60), he employed glass in vertical accordion pleats as deliberate embellishment. Although his former restraint occasionally returned, his late trend is strikingly exemplified in the TWA Terminal at Kennedy Airport (Figs. 19-66 and 19-67). Here the convoluted ferroconcrete forms are notable for their absence of stabilizing horizontal and vertical lines. The interior space is restlessly enveloped

19 67
EERO SAARINEN, Interior, TWA Terminal, Kennedy Airport, New York, 1956.

by ebbing and flowing masses; the exterior suggests a giant bird with lifted wings.

Paolo Soleri (Italy and the United States, 1919–). Soleri came from Italy to join Frank Lloyd Wright's community of architects at Taliesin West, in Arizona, from 1947 until 1949. After a visit to Italy, Soleri settled in Arizona, where he makes varied ceramic and bronze bells. His drawing-board projects for visionary cities have gained increasing attention. Evolution occurs through increasing complexity and through miniaturization, Soleri argues; he feels these two principles should be basic to urban planning. His designs for towering and intricate single-building cities (megastructures) achieve high population density with minimum energy expenditure for transportation, manufacturing, environmental control, and waste disposal. Automated manufacturing functions are usually located deep in the base of the building near the major energy source; community, business, and cultural areas are in the center; living quarters, sports areas, gardens, promenade decks, and heliports are on the outer surface. *Babeldiga* is designed for 1,200,000 inhabitants and a population density of 665 people per acre. His theory is called *arcology*, a combination of the words architecture and ecology. Soleri bases his ideas not only on socioeconomic efficiency, but on a conviction that controlled environments will help humankind attain a more compassionate value system and a more aesthetic life.

Architecture students have been flocking to Soleri's Arizona headquarters to contribute volunteer labor in the construction of a small city, *Arcosanti* (Fig. 19-68), that is planned as an experimental model.

19-68
PAOLO SOLERI. Plans for Arcosanti, Arizona, begun in 1970 (1969 design).

1960 to the Present

PAINTING, SCULPTURE, AND INTERMEDIA

Since 1960 the dominance of Abstract Expressionism has been challenged by a variety of international trends initiated by Pop Art, Op Art, and Minimal Art. Pop Art first developed in England during the 1950's and then blossomed in the United States in the next decade. Images derived from the mass media, advertising, and comic strips were presented in bizarre combinations, distortions, or exaggerations. Op Art was a development within the broad category of geometric abstraction and nonobjective painting; it employed precise shapes and optical illusions to achieve literally dazzling effects of movement and ceaseless change. Some Op Art works overlap Minimal Art, a movement toward the reduction of a work of art to few shapes and colors or to a single shape and color.

More ephemeral works were also produced during the 1960's, such as some of the kinetic sculptures of the Swiss artist Tinguely that were designed to destroy themselves by fire and explosion in a predetermined sequence. Similarly unique but temporary occurrences were the *Happenings*, nondramatic events in time and space, organized by Allan Kaprow and others. Other artists, equally interested in the problems of time in art, have used neon and fluorescent lights to create spatial and temporal environments through which the spectator moves. The terms *systemic art* and *serial art* have been applied to some of these neon or fluorescent pieces and to some geometric sculpture and painting that elaborate combinations of one or two basic modules. This modular approach to art has been encouraged by systems analyses in socioeconomic studies.

Beginning in the 1960's artists have exploited modern technology. Some avant-garde artists have employed a mixture of several media, such as painting, sculpture, light, film, and sound, in producing their works. These pieces are called *multimedia* or *intermedia*. Electronic technology has become available to the artist and has created vast new possibilities for aesthetic experience. For example, sound can be fed into laser equipment to create three-dimensional projections of colored forms in space, and computers have been used to produce drawings. *Cyborg*, or *cybernetic*, works allow feedback, which is the mutual response of and interaction between the work of art, its environment, and its spectators. Here there is a continuation of the earlier interest in chance or unpredictability. Computer information systems and recent linguistic theories have led to a new emphasis on art as communication, but the concern for communication has now resulted in questioning the role of art and in demonstrating the processes of nature or human thought.

Along with the interest in modern technology is a renewed interest in the individual and society. *New Realism* or *Photo-Realism* are both terms applied to a recent tendency to document minutely the surface effects of a visual experience. In painting, subjects cover the traditional range from landscape to portraiture, but special interest is shown in commercial urban street scenes and interiors. Highly reflective surfaces are prevalent. Photographs are often used by the artists as aids. Photo-Realism has grown out of Pop Art and has the same mechanical, impersonal nature. In sculpture, life-sized nudes, race riots, or tourists acquire the eerie effect of wax museum counterfeits. Concern for social integration has also stimulated art forms that involve participation in group experiences and the study of relationships between people, their socioeconomic systems, and their environment. Huge, inflated plastic balloons have been used for a variety of purposes: for sound and film projections, for groups of people to roll about on, and for walking on water (inside a large balloon, a person can walk forward, pushing and rolling the balloon on the water). While the balloons could be considered giant playthings, one creator of such *air structures* has said that their aim is to explore individual behavior in groups and to lower social barriers. In addition to the direct concern with social phenomena, an interest in space, time, and constant change has led to *Performance Art*, which can be exemplified by the public gesture of releasing a piece of plastic to float in the wind or by a person lying wrapped in a blanket on the floor of an art gallery. Performance Art owes much to the Happenings of the 1960's. Related to Performance Art is *Body Art*, in which the artist may mark his or her body or place it in jeopardy to demonstrate ideas, processes, or relationships between people, animals, and objects.

Today art takes many forms and has broken through many barriers. For example, it can create a new environment for the spectator-participant. Interiors much like stage sets have been exhibited with accompanying written descriptions (*scenarios*) of social situations to fit the set. Life-sized mannequins or plaster casts of humans have been combined with actual objects, such as automobiles or lunch counters, in compositions that provide the entire environment. Total floor areas of galleries have been used as the compositional frame for fluorescent light arrangements or for *floor pieces* that may be scattered objects or rigidly geometric patterns. *Earthworks* may be mammoth bulldozer projects in desert areas so remote that only photos are available to spectators, or they may consist of piles of stone on a gallery floor. *Field pieces* are outdoor works that may be permanent or impermanent. Compositions in the "field" have been created by cutting designs in grass or by arranging bales of hay in the countryside. Concrete or steel forms installed in a landscape, however, provide an art form that is more traditionally permanent. The growing awareness of change and interaction between elements has led to *Process Art*, an example of which is the exposure of chemicals to the air so that oxygen acts upon them to produce visible changes. The rebellion against viewing works of art as precious objects has culminated in *Conceptual Art*, in which words or graphs may be used to present the idea of a work rather than the finished work itself as art. This dematerialization of art often leaves little that can be sold or collected, although indefatigable collectors have sought to purchase the ideas or plans for concept pieces.

The most recent developments in contemporary art indicate a growing concern for extra-aesthetic or non-formal matters. In contrast to the aesthetic attitudes in earlier twentieth-century art, the avant-garde works produced today seem concerned with the human problems generated by our postindustrial society: the relationship of the individual to a diminished sense of self, to the threatening dominance of technology, and to the dangers of ecological imbalance. As a result of this new social orientation, there is an interest in modifying or creating complete environments, as well as an impatience with the traditionally rigid divisions between art media and with what is now perceived as a false separation of art and life. Much contemporary art seems to challenge even the most recent conventions and to force a constant reevaluation of our established ideas.

While modern technology, with its emphasis on group production, is exploited for a variety of purposes in much present-day art, other developments, such as the crafts revival, stress the uniqueness of individual, handmade objects. Other artists have returned from abstract modes to more traditional forms, as in some contemporary painting that echoes the flat color and unified tones found in the early work of Monet and Manet. Still other young artists are continuing, in their own manner, the established styles of the twentieth century, such as Abstract Expressionism, Surrealism, and geometric abstraction. The multifaceted aspects of contemporary art seem to be expanding in accordance with the complexity of modern perceptions. Most current forms have roots in the past, but they are opening up vast possibilities for the future.

Nicolas Schöffer (Hungary and France, 1912–). Schöffer studied at the Budapest Art Academy before coming to Paris in 1936. At the time of his first one-man show, in 1948, he was still a painter; but in 1950 he presented an exhibition of kinetic sculpture. In 1954, with the financial and technical aid of the Phillips Corporation, he created his first spatiodynamic tower. The tower was an open metal frame with moving, colored, rectangular blades and loudspeakers emitting taped music composed of electronic and environmental sounds. Since then, other towers have combined sound, light, projected images, and motion, expressing Schöffer's belief that art should utilize the essential elements of space, time, light, and change. *CYSP I* (Fig. 19-69), whose

name stands for cybernetic-spatiodynamic construction, was done in 1956, again with the help of the Phillips Corporation. The piece is mobile and sonic. Darkness and silence cause it to move and to produce loud sounds; brightness and noise cause it to become still and quiet; the presence of different colors produces varying degrees of reaction. A ballet was created by Maurice Béjart using *CYSP I,* dancers, and electronic music.

Joseph Beuys (Germany, 1921–). Beuys has been described as the most controversial artist and the most sought-after teacher in Germany. Reflecting the influence of Dada art objects from the 1916–22 period, his work employs clay, gauze, fat, and bloodsoaked cloth to suggest decay and the impermanence of organic life. He has earned much of his notoriety with *actions* (performances). For one of these, which took place in 1974, he flew to New York, was wrapped in felt blankets before leaving the airport, came directly to his art gallery in an ambulance, and spent three days in a fenced-off area there with the following properties: a live coyote, a stack of *Wall Street Journals* (renewed each day), a pile of hay, a pan of water, a cane, two felt blankets, and a constantly burning flashlight. He played with the coyote, talked to friends, smoked, and occasionally wrapped himself in one of the felt blankets, with only the cane protruding. After bending and swaying, he would topple over and lie still for a time. Periodically, he would strike a triangle hanging from his vest. This signaled the playing of fifteen seconds of deafening tape recordings of industrial noises. At the end of three days, he departed for Germany in the manner in which he had arrived. In spite of his involvement with nonpermanent art, Beuys has repeatedly stressed the importance of the art object as a palpable thing that can provide spiritual nourishment. He also believes that art and life are identical; thus he considers his political convictions as part of his art. Beuys has influenced a generation of art students in Germany.

Ellsworth Kelly (United States, 1923–). Kelly's paintings in the early 1950's sought maximum visual impact with stripes, grids, or panels in dazzling black and white contrasts or in a few brilliant colors. By 1955, he had begun to do painted reliefs and freestanding sculpture of simple metal shapes painted in highly saturated colors. In both painting and sculpture, a single intense color often suffices to give one or two shapes great energy. In *Blue-White* (Fig. 19-70), two swelling fields of

19-69
NICOLAS SCHÖFFER, *CYSP I.* 1956. Steel and aluminum, 70⅞'' x 63''. Galerie Denise René, Paris.

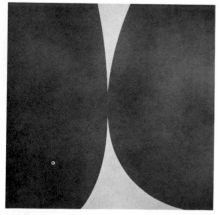

19-70
ELLSWORTH KELLY, *Blue-White,* 1962. Oil on canvas, 8'7'' x 8'10''. Collection, Brandeis University Art Collection, Rose Art Museum, Gevirtz-Mnuchin Purchase Fund, Waltham, Massachusetts.

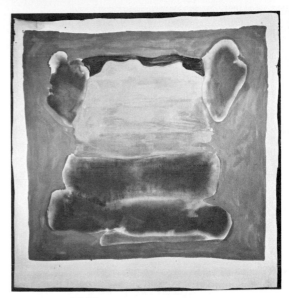

19-71
HELEN FRANKENTHALER, *Buddha's Court,*
1964. Acrylic paint on canvas. 98" x 94".
Private collection, Andre Emmerich Gallery.

powerful blue meet in the center, cutting in two the
white buffer between them. Though he is linked with
the tradition of geometric abstraction, Kelly has been a
leader in Minimal Art.

Helen Frankenthaler (United States, 1928–). Thin
paints poured onto flat canvas produce the fluid, free
forms that have made Frankenthaler's painting internationally known. Her New York background included
training by some of the major Abstract Expressionists
of the 1940's and '50's. While retaining their freedom of
form, she moved away from impasto in the early 1950's
and used instead thin oil on raw canvas. The resulting
stained, flowing forms seem to unite with the background into which they are literally absorbed, yet an
ambiguous illusion of deep space often seems to con-
tradict this unified surface. Her paintings of the 1950's
often allude to natural objects. Turning to acrylics after
1962, she later painted in a darker palette, with firmer
edges to her shapes, and simpler, quieter, more compact
and nonobjective forms. *Buddha's Court* (Fig. 19-71) came
early in this development. In contrast to the traditional
respect for the original format of a painting to which the
artist adjusts his or her composition, Frankenthaler
often crops a work after it is finished, thus composing
"after the fact."

Donald Judd (United States, 1928–). Judd studied
painting at the Art Students' League and at Columbia
University before turning to three-dimensional form. In

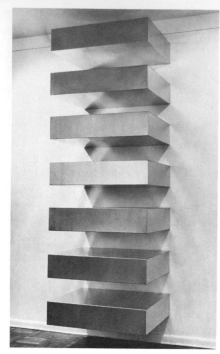

19-72
DONALD JUDD, untitled construction, 1965. Galvanized iron and aluminum, 33" x 11'9" x 30". Leo Castelli Gallery, New York.

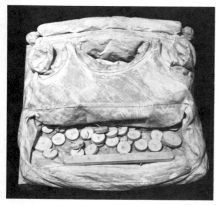

19-73
CLAES OLDENBURG, *The Soft Typewriter*, "Ghost" version, 1963. Canvas, kapok, wood, liquitex, 9" x 27½" x 26". Karl Stroher Collection, Darmstadt.

the early 1960's, he produced reliefs of painted wood and metal and made his first boxlike floor constructions of metal and Plexiglas. Judd states that he wants to rid his art of illusions, compositional relationships, and rational implications; the work should be experienced as a single whole without reference to ideas beyond itself. This position has been taken by other Minimal artists and has been related to phenomenological philosophy. The untitled construction from 1965 (Fig. 19-72) is a series of identical masses and spaces whose reflecting surfaces and complex shadows produce effects of sensuous richness and severe order.

Claes Oldenburg (United States, 1929–). After studying English and art at Yale, Oldenburg enrolled at the Chicago Art Institute. His first one-man show, in New York, was in 1959 and consisted of assemblages of street materials painted only in gray, white, or black. In 1961, he created an environment of store objects in a rented storefront. After the exhibit closed, the store became "The Ray Gun Theater," where Oldenburg produced *Happenings*. *The Store* was his first critical success; its second version, in the Green Gallery in 1962, contained an enormous hamburger and a slice of cake, both made of brightly colored stuffed canvas. *The Soft Typewriter* (Fig. 19-73), though modest in size, was produced during this phase. A common object is presented with a change in one basic characteristic, a change that makes the viewer perceive the object in a new way. Pop Art, in which Oldenburg is a leader, has tended to depict objects or images from our consumer culture. In the late 1960's, he planned large public monuments based on such common objects as lipsticks. Unlike many Pop artists, Oldenburg sometimes implies satire; he has said that humor is a useful tool in a dissolving world.

Jasper Johns (United States, 1930–). Since his first one-man show in 1958, Johns has been a leader in painting and sculpture. His early work involved stained surfaces, collage, and assemblages in boxes. During the 1950's, he initiated most of his major themes: targets, flags, numbers, and letters, all of which came from fixed, conventionally symbolic images. His media have been encaustic, oil, collage, and sculptmetal (a metallic plastic), sometimes combined with plaster casts and actual objects. Clearly defined commonplace objects and symbols are robbed of their clarity and dependable meanings, acquiring an ironical allusiveness. Johns subverts the usual clarity of his chosen images by submerging them in collage and layers of dripping, impetuously brushed paint. For example, the primary colors—red, yellow, and blue—have been sabotaged in a series of paintings. In *By the Sea* (Fig. 19-74), four separate canvases within one frame present the words *red*, *yellow*, and *blue*, and a fourth "word" that is an amalgamation of the first three. With word mixing, Johns seems to parody the color mixing learned by all beginning art students. We look in vain, however, for a pure red, yellow, or blue in the composition. Each letter of each word is produced by a complex and subtle mixture of the three primary colors. The letters almost lose their identity and merge with the equally rich surface around them. The entire work was painted with spontaneous brushwork, eroding the objective clarity of the standard letter shapes and the three basic colors. The obvious becomes elusive as Johns uses contradiction, disjunction, and paradox to throw doubt on our conventional symbols and the logic of language.

Andy Warhol (United States, 1931–). Warhol, one of the leaders of Pop Art, was raised in Pittsburgh and trained at the Carnegie Institute of Technology. He began a career in advertising art and window display and later employed the images of advertising in his paintings. Since 1961, his subjects have included cola bottles, soup cans, Brillo boxes, and the actress Marilyn Monroe. The Brillo boxes are plywood boxes on which labels have been silk-screened; they belong more to the realm of sculpture than do the other subjects, which are depicted on flat surfaces. Repetition is an important characteristic of Warhol's art. Frequently his compositions consist of one subject repeated many times, sometimes with slight variations. Figure 19-75 is one of a group of four Campbell's soup cans that differ from one another only in color. Warhol has verbally expressed a conviction that individuality is on the wane; his art celebrates the impersonal nature of a machine-oriented culture.

Carl Andre (United States, 1935–). After studying painting and filmmaking in the 1950's, Andre traveled abroad and then settled in New York. From poetry and painting, his focus shifted to geometric sculpture in Plexiglas and wood; Andre's major inspiration came from the work of Brancusi. Compositions of rough lumber, notched and stacked, gave way in the mid-1960's to stacks of Styrofoam slabs and floor pieces of bricks arranged in rectangular units related proportionally to the room in which they were placed. His

19-74
JASPER JOHNS, *By the Sea*, 1961.
Encaustic on canvas, (4 panels),
72" x 54½". Private Collection, New York.

19-75
ANDY WARHOL, *Campbell's Soup*, 1965.
Oil, silk-screened on canvas, 36⅛" x 24⅛".
Collection, The Museum of Modern Art, New York. Elizabeth Bliss Parkinson Fund.

Spill, consisting of eight hundred plastic blocks scattered from a canvas bag onto the floor, revealed an interest in chance. The *Plain* is one of many floor pieces constructed of commercially made metal plaques. Variations in color and texture are used to create patterns that are often sensuously rich and intricate. In his recent work, Andre has used rods and bands of industrial materials such as plastic, steel, and iron in parallel and random distributions. They occupy the room completely, producing an environment filled with multidirectional forces that contrast with the static geometry of the otherwise empty room.

Richard Estes (United States, 1936–). Work experience in advertising and illustration gave Estes the technical background for paintings like *Nedick's* (Fig. 19-76). This work is typical of the New Realist, or Photo-Realist, movement. While paintings such as *Nedick's* are related to Pop Art, they are less concerned with the amplification of simple mass-media images and more obsessed with the literal depiction of surface details. Sharp-focus photography is an influence and a tool. There is a preference for reflective, synthetic surfaces in complex urban scenes. The New Realists often work from photographs, sometimes projecting them onto the canvas and rendering them with an airbrush. Sharpness of focus is often manipulated by the painter. Estes achieved intensification of physical data by equally sharp focus in foreground and background. Perhaps in reaction to subjective trends in twentieth-century art, the New Realists, like the Pop artists, value a cool, neutral effect. Estes's painting is so intensely descriptive that the

19-76
RICHARD ESTES, *Nedick's,* 1969–70. Oil, 48'' x 66''. Collection of Mrs. Donald Pritzker.

physical character of glass, metal, and concrete acquires an almost hypnotic quality. We are presented with a heightened and immediately accessible physical reality.

Judy Chicago, formerly **Judy Gerowitz** (United States, 1939–). Judy Chicago's first one-woman show, in a Los Angeles gallery in 1966, revealed her interest in geometric structures, delicate color, and rearrangeable environments. In the same year she was also represented in the New York Jewish Museum exhibition that established *Primary Forms* (a sculptural term for Minimal Art) as a movement in sculpture. Her entry consisted of six diagonal beams, each painted a different pastel color, that related to the architectural structure of the room. Chicago's art has ranged from plastic domes sprayed with lush, pearlescent acrylic colors to series paintings of geometric forms on flat plastic. In all her work, her intention is to express the values and attitudes of a woman seeking recognition in a male-dominated arena. For her *Reincarnation Triptych* themes, she chose three women of special accomplishments: Madame de Staël, Virginia Woolf, and George Sand (Fig. 19-77). In each composition, Chicago has written a commentary on her subject. Concerning the *George Sand* composition, she later explained that the radiating center repressed by the enclosing squares symbolizes a phase in women's history as well as a phase in Judy Chicago's development.

Richard Serra (United States, 1939–). Serra studied sculpture in California and at Yale. In the Documenta V exhibition in Kassel, Germany, in 1972, his interest in structuring complete environments was shown in a work consisting of four upright steel slabs arranged in an X, thus dividing a room into four parts. He has chosen an open-air setting and a larger scale for field pieces like *Shift* (Fig. 19-78), a composition of six concrete slabs, each 8 inches thick, arranged in two sets, one for each of two hills. The valley between the sets is about 120 feet wide. The directional alignment of each slab corresponds to the sharpest drop of the land, and the downhill end of each slab is beveled to relate to the direction of the next slab. The length of the slabs varies from 90 to 240 feet. Each piece begins flush with the ground and extends horizontally until the ground has dropped 5 feet. Thus, the length and direction of each slab are determined by the topography of the land. Walking into the composition provides a succession of changing views; as the zig-zag forms are seen from

19-77
JUDY CHICAGO, *Reincarnation Triptych-2* "George Sand," 1973. Oil on canvas, 5' x 5'. Private Collection.

19-78
RICHARD SERRA, *Shift*, 1970–72. 6
rectilinear cement sections, total length,
815'. King, Ontario.

different angles, they appear to compress or extend
space. Their horizontal top edges establish bases for the
contours of the land above and behind them, while the
bottom of each piece defines and is shaped by the
curvature of the hill. Each slab acts as a template to
reveal the profile of the earth mass. The geometry of the
slabs contrasts with the irregularity of the site. As with
ancient monuments, one feels that nature has been
modified by the presence of the human mind.

Vito Acconci (United States, 1940–). Acconci gained
critical attention starting in 1970. In work which is often
referred to as body art, he has tried to erase the distinction between the artist and the work of art. *Step Piece*
(1970) was a work in which the artist stepped up and
down on an eighteen-inch stool at the rate of thirty
steps a minute beginning at 8:00 A.M. and continuing for
as long as he was able without stopping. In *Security
Zone* (1971), Acconci's hands were tied and he was
blindfolded. He then allowed a stranger to spin him
around and let him wander dangerously near the edge
of a pier. In this and other pieces, he attempts to make
himself vulnerable, to put himself at another's mercy.
In this way he seeks to open up closed systems and to
break through conventional behavior in order to break
down barriers between people.

Michael Heizer (United States, 1944–). In the 1960's
Heizer turned from painting to earthworks. His *Dis-*

19-79

MICHAEL HEIZER, *Double Negative*, 1970. 240,000 ton removal on Virgin River Mesa, Nevada. 1600' x 30' x 50'.

sipate (1968) consists of five shallow trenches, each twelve feet long, in a fifty-foot-square area of Black Rock Desert, Nevada. Heizer determined the positions of the trenches by throwing toothpicks on a tabletop. His most publicized earthwork is *Double Negative* (Fig. 19-79), from 1969 but reworked in 1970, on the Virgin River Mesa, Nevada. In the 1970 version, 240,000 tons of earth were displaced to produce a trench (1,600 feet long, 50 feet wide, and 30 feet deep); it consists of two parts that notch the sides of an indentation in the wall of the mesa. The straight gouge is a startlingly human mark on the desolate landscape. Heizer prefers relatively inaccessible sites, and his earthworks are known mainly from documentary photographs.

Joseph Kosuth (United States, 1945–). Kosuth studied painting at the School of Visual Arts in New York during the 1960's and became interested in the gap between the physical world and language. His *Table* (1965-67), includes an actual table, an enlarged photograph of the table, and an enlarged photocopy of a dictionary definition of a table. His *Fifteen Locations, Art as Idea* (1969-70), occurred when he published selected entries from a thesaurus in the advertising columns of newspapers and magazines all over the world. The *Ninth Investigation, Proposition I* of 1972 consisted of looseleaf notebooks containing photocopied pages from philosophical writings on science and linguistics; enlarged photocopies of selections from each notebook were keyed to the work and hung on the facing wall. Drawing inspiration from such contemporary thinkers as Claude Lévi-Strauss, Ludwig Wittgenstein, Noam Chomsky, and A. J. Ayer, Kosuth believes that works of art are analytical systems with their own logic and no meaning outside the context of art. For Kosuth, the physical art object is little more than a historical curiosity; the actual work of art is the idea.

ARCHITECTURE

Architects, as well as other artists, in the late 1960's and in the '70's have shown an increasing awareness of the problems created by rapid change, social dislocation, and ecological ignorance. As a result, there has been a growing trend toward nonspecialized, multipurpose, easily transformable buildings. In schools of architecture, the traditional concern for individual buildings is now rivaled by an interest in environmental design. Among younger architects, the belief that architecture is a social art that creates environments for human situations has gained wide acceptance. Versatility and flexibility are being sought not only for a changing technology but also for the changing human patterns that go with it. Some architects have pointed to an increasing freedom and variety in life styles and have argued that environmental design must plan for this. The swift rate of change, especially in cities, has encouraged the argument that aesthetically satisfying buildings are less important than urban structures that can be modified quickly to meet changing needs. Architects have projected cities with movable or changeable parts that plug into a framework that has attachments for energy, water, and disposal systems. There have also been proposals for cities, or city "frames," and energy centers that could move on rails.

Architects still concerned with visual effect have made much use of abrupt contrasts of cubic, cylindrical, and triangular forms. In contrast, the maverick of American architecture, Robert Venturi, has manipulated clichés from low-budget commercial buildings and mass-market homes in an effort to avoid elite taste and find a common architectural idiom.

Robert Venturi (United States, 1925–). Venturi graduated from Princeton in 1950 and worked first with Saarinen and then with Kahn. A controversial figure, Venturi has argued that complexity and contradiction are suited to the richness and ambiguity of modern

19-80
ROBERT VENTURI and JOHN RAUCH,
Architects and Planners, with assistance of
GEROD CLARK. Residence, Mr. and Mrs.
Nathaniel Lieb, Loveladies, New Jersey,
1967.

experience and are necessary to architecture today. He finds most contemporary buildings dull and void of content. As with many innovators, few of his major designs have been executed; an outstanding example, however, is his Lieb beach house (Fig. 19-80 and 19-81). The elevations present jolting contrasts; forms constantly crowd, intersect erratically, or interrupt each other. The plan also contains dissonance and surprise. Although the house appears to be square, the plan reveals it to be trapezoidal. Venturi describes the house as an ordinary shed with conventional elements, such as asbestos shingles with imitation wood grain. Yet the conventional elements behave unconventionally; the forms are blatant on one level and subtle on another. Venturi has maintained that mainstreet is almost all right. The elements that others have equated with visual and auditory pollution, Venturi desires for perceptual excitement relevant to an "autoscape." Architecture, for him, is a system of communication, and he feels the iconography and mixed media of roadside commercial architecture provide the "language" suited to our needs. Popular art forms, he believes, are valid; they are a kind of aesthetic realpolitik. Not surprisingly, Venturi's work has been called pop architecture.

Kisho Noriaki Kurokawa (Japan, 1934–). Kurokawa received his training at the Kyoto School of Architecture and at Tokyo University during the 1950's. He belongs to the *Metabolist* group of Japanese architects, which sees architecture and city planning as life-support systems with aesthetic qualities. Space is

FIRST FLOOR

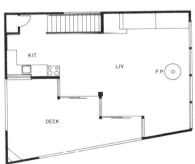

SECOND FLOOR
19-81
Plan of Lieb beach house.

19-82
KISHO NORIAKI KUROWKAWA, Takara Furniture Group
Pavilion, Expo '70, Osaka.

thought of as an information network, and information is seen to include people, things, and energy in effective circulation—like nourishment in a blood stream. Just as the metabolism of organisms involves constant transformation, the Metabolists argue, so architecture must be changeable, with multipurpose spaces and variable components. The Metabolist term "group form" refers to units of many buildings and to individual buildings with many changeable parts. Kurokawa's *Takara Furniture Group Pavilion* for Expo '70, in Osaka, is a deliberately dramatic presentation of Metabolist theory (Fig. 19-82). Prefabricated, six-armed crosses are bolted together to form a many-celled frame into which rooms can be inserted. The frame is painted white, the display rooms are stainless steel, and the exterior service pipes are painted vivid red and blue. The transformable and expandable nature of the structure is emphasized by its unfilled spaces and the projecting arms that await additions. Kurokawa has also proposed one city in the form of a curving wall and another in the form of a stepped helix. His boldest plans, however, have thus far remained on the drawing board.

Suggestions for Further Study

Amaya, Mario. *Pop Art . . . And After.* New York: Viking Press, 1966.

Banham, Reyner. *The New Brutalism: Ethic or Aesthetic.* New York: Reinhold, 1966.

_____. *Theory and Design in the First Machine Age.* New York: Praeger, 1960.

Battcock, Gregory, ed. *Idea Art.* New York: Dutton, 1973.

_____, ed. *Minimal Art: A Critical Anthology.* New York: Dutton, 1968.

Cook, Peter. *Architecture: Action and Plan.* New York: Reinhold, 1967.

Crespelle, Jean Paul. *The Fauves.* Translated by Anita Brookner. Greenwich, Conn.: New York Graphic Society, 1962.

Gropius, Walter. *Scope of Total Architecture* (World Perspectives). Edited by Ruth N. Anshen. New York: Harper & Row, 1955.

Haftmann, Werner. *Painting in the Twentieth Century.* 2 vols. Translated by Ralph Manheim. New York: Praeger, 1960.

Hamilton, George Heard. *Painting and Sculpture in Europe: 1880–1940* (Pelican History of Art). Baltimore: Penguin Books, 1967.

Jean, Marcel. *The History of Surrealist Painting.* Translated by Simon Watson Taylor. New York: Grove Press, 1960.

Jeanneret-Gris, Édouard. *Le Corbusier, 1910–1965.* Edited by W. Boesiger and H. Girsberger. New York: Praeger, 1967.

Kirby, Michael. *Happenings.* New York: Dutton, 1966.

Lippard, Lucy. *Six Years: The Dematerialization of the Art Object from 1966 to 1972.* New York: Praeger, 1973.

Meyer, Ursula. *Conceptual Art.* New York: Dutton, 1972.

Neumann, Erich. *The Archetypal World of Henry Moore.* Translated by R. F. C. Hull. New York: Pantheon Books, 1957.

Norberg-Schulz, Christian. *Intentions in Architecture.* Cambridge, Mass.: M.I.T. Press, 1965.

Read, Herbert, and Leslie Martin. *Gabo: Constructions, Sculpture, Paintings, Drawings, and Engravings.* Cambridge, Mass.: Harvard University Press, 1957.

Richter, Hans. *Dada Art and Anti-Art.* New York and Toronto: McGraw-Hill, 1965.

Rickey, George. *Constructivism: Origins and Evolution.* New York: Braziller, 1967.

Rosenblum, Robert. *Cubism and Twentieth-Century Art.* New York: Abrams, 1960.

Selz, Peter. *German Expressionist Painting.* Berkeley: University of California Press, 1957.

Seuphor, Michel (Ferdinand Louis Berckelaers). *The Sculpture of This Century.* Translated by Haakon Chevalier. New York: Braziller, 1960.

Venturi, Robert. *Complexity and Contradiction in Architecture.* New York: Museum of Modern Art, 1966.

_____. *Learning from Las Vegas.* Cambridge, Mass.: M.I.T. Press, 1972.

Wall, Donald. *Visionary Cities: The Arcology of Paolo Soleri.* New York: Praeger, 1971.

Wright, Frank Lloyd. *An American Architecture.* Edited by Edgar Kaufmann. New York: Horizon Press, 1955.

Chapter 19 Music

Music in the Twentieth Century

Parallels between music and the visual arts have been more pronounced in the twentieth century than in any other period. The deliberate search for individual styles has erased national and regional distinctions and created an international, often eclectic diversity. Older techniques have been extended, while the use of new sound materials has vastly increased available possibilities. New modes of communication have made all types of music widely available, electronics technology has provided a whole new means for creating and performing music, and changing conceptions of human nature and physical reality have led to changes in the relation of musicians to their subject matter of time and sound.

The nineteenth-century concern with symbolic and subjective musical expression has generally been replaced by abstract, nonreferential music based on pure form and process. Composers have returned to older, abstract formal practices, as well as devising various systems, often mathematical, for ordering the compositional process. Some composers, however, have extended subjective associations to include the expression of anxiety, isolation, alienation, and the subconscious forces controlling human behavior.

Going even further, some recent composers have attacked long accepted ideas about the very nature and purpose of music. The concept of music as form and process, the expression of subjective and personal experience, and the composer's role as a creator who determines the musical outcome all have been challenged by music in which some aspects are determined by chance, by performer choices, or by the performance situation. Some composers, especially of electronic music, have so completely controlled their materials that the performer is eliminated. Distinctions between "musical" and "nonmusical" sounds have disappeared, so that even chance environmental "noises" may be accepted as part of a musical event. Music as idea is reflected in ordered systems, often mathematical, which may not necessarily be heard, and also in *antimusic*, which rejects traditions of musical performance and recreation of "masterworks" (the precious art object). Signs of a new synthesis of these conflicting attitudes and techniques have appeared in the recent works of some composers.

Since the Second World War many musical innovations, experiments, and new techniques have originated in the United States, though musicians throughout the world have been quick to adopt them, and a number of

19-83
KEES VAN DONGEN, *Modjesko Soprano
Singer,* 1908. Oil on canvas, 39⅜″ x 32″.
Collection, The Museum of Modern Art, New
York.

European centers have encouraged performances of
new music.

1910–1945

MUSICAL STYLES AND MEDIA

From the Renaissance to the early twentieth century,
European composers assumed that music developed in
a logical succession analogous to human speech and
thought and that its essential materials were melodies,
harmonies, and textures, determined by the organization of pitches and metric rhythms. Logical flow and
formal integrity were maintained above all through
dissonance-consonance fluctuations within a tonal system. Late nineteenth-century composers accepted a
moral obligation to communicate their subjective perceptions through musical associations; at the same time,
they were approaching limits in the expressive use of
traditional materials. In the music of Wagner and his
German and Austrian followers, traditional tonality was
extended to include frequent, ambiguous shifts of key
center, with free use of all available tones. Fluctuations
in texture and harmonic dissonance largely replaced
metric rhythms in sustaining the logical flow, while

19-84
ERNST LUDWIG KIRCHNER, *The Flute Player*, 1922–23. Oil on canvas, 46½″ x 35″. Private Collection.

melodies and harmonies were closely linked with the expressive play of orchestral timbres. In France Debussy used delicate nuances of tone color to express the unique moment, with a minimum of logical development.

During the early twentieth century Arnold Schoenberg and his followers pursued the logical consequences of late German Romanticism, and in so doing destroyed the style from within. Their interest in subconscious forces and irrational experience was the basis for musical *Expressionism*. In this style, total pitch freedom destroyed tonality and rendered harmonic dissonance meaningless. Pitch became merely one factor in the ebb and flow of sound aggregates, with variety of timbres and textures paramount. Unwilling to abandon a pitch-based logical flow, Schoenberg established the *twelve-tone system* in the early 1920's. This compositional method enabled him to order the pitches in atonal music. He continued to unify his works through the development of melodic ideas. Anton von Webern, on the other hand, used twelve-tone procedures to produce delicate, abstract structures of sounds in time, with little regard for expressive, referential meanings or logical development. He thus rejected both the style and the aesthetic of late Romanticism and prepared the way for *abstract serialism*, which followed the Second World War.

19-85
MAX ERNST, *Upside Down Violin*, 1920. Collage on paper mounted on paperboard, 5¾″ x 3⅞″. Galerie Brusberg, Hanover.

Other musicians, especially in France, who were less concerned with "historical necessity" and the need for theoretical justification of their actions, began early in the century to challenge both the means and the accepted purpose of music. Eric Satie in particular attacked the traditions of "serious" music (partially anticipating Dadaism), deliberately avoided conventions of logical succession, created forms from a montage of disparate elements, and did some pioneering work in intermedia. Following the First World War, composers such as Darius Milhaud, Francis Poulenc, and Sergei Prokofiev abandoned subjective expression, creating music full of rhythmic surprises and fresh sound combinations. During the 1920's Paris became the center of *Neoclassicism*, a movement led by Igor Stravinsky and characterized by a return to older forms and techniques, tonality and pitch-based structures, and an objective attitude toward the musical materials. Stravinsky developed new concepts of rhythm and sonority, and he regarded music as a process of ordering sounds in time to create forms, with no expressive purpose. In Germany, Paul Hindemith adopted similar views, but saw himself as a craftsman creating music for specific use (*Gebrauchsmusik*).

Many composers sought new materials in folk music, in exotic music of other cultures, and in experiments with nonmusical sounds. Béla Bartók in Hungary and Ralph Vaughan Williams in England both made extensive studies of folk music; American jazz and ragtime influenced Stravinsky, Milhaud, and others.

After the First World War American musicians began to free themselves from the dominance of European traditions. Charles Ives, Henry Cowell, and Harry Partch experimented with incongruous sound combinations, clusters, "noise," new pitch relationships, new instruments, and new sounds from old instruments. Too revolutionary to be accepted at the time, their ideas have recently influenced a number of composers.

Beginning in the 1920's many American composers studied in France and were strongly influenced by French ideas and the Neoclassicism of Stravinsky. Essentially conservative composers such as Walter Piston, Roger Sessions, Elliott Carter, Roy Harris, and Aaron Copland sought to create truly "American" music by incorporating suggestions of jazz rhythms, folk melodies, or the general spirit of a region. American music was further influenced by several prominent European composers who moved to the United States, including Hindemith, Schoenberg, and Stravinsky. Edgard Varèse, who came in 1915, conceived of music as "organized sound" and experimented with structures of time and timbre while others were still writing pitch-based music. His ideas were not accepted until after World War II, when electronics made their realization possible for the first time. The economic and political crises of the 1930's led the governments of Germany and Russia to suppress controversial or experimental music in favor of music with mass appeal that served the needs of the state. In the United States many composers also wrote for the new mass audiences created by the radio, cinema, and phonograph.

Arnold Schoenberg (Austria, Germany, and the United States, 1874–1951).   One of the pivotal figures of twentieth-century music, Schoenberg served as a link between the highly expressive style of the late nineteenth century and the abstract serialism of the late twentieth century. At various times, Schoenberg was a composer and a conductor and teacher in Vienna, Berlin, and after the Nazis came to power, in California. He also was a painter and a member of Kandinsky's Blue Rider group. There are striking similarities between Kandinsky's move to nonobjective art and Schoenberg's development of new, abstract techniques for structuring music. In his works prior to the First World War, Schoenberg sought alternatives to the style of late German Romantic music and became the leader of musical Expressionism. His search for unhampered expression led him away from traditional harmonies toward a free use of

19-86

VASSILY KANDINSKY, *Improvisation with Green Center*, 1913. Oil on canvas, 43¼'' x 47½''. The Art Institute of Chicago.

pitch aggregates as elements of time-sound structures. In these early years he rejected tonality as an unnecessary restriction and sought to unify his music through the continual variation of a single melodic idea. Schoenberg's radical experiments with harmonic complexities, new timbres, and formal systems elicited considerable opposition. After World War I he worked out a "system of composing with twelve tones," by which the twelve pitches in the octave are prearranged in a unique set or series that determines the order of pitches throughout a given composition. A new pitch set is invented for each new piece. By systematically working through the series he could avoid tonality, since all of the tones are equal. His influence was far-reaching, eventually finding international support. Schoenberg's most important atonal works before World War I were *Five Pieces for Orchestra*, Opus 16 and *Pierrot Lunaire*, Opus 21, an Expressionistic work exploring psychotic fantasies. After 1920, the twelve-tone organization characterized almost all of Schoenberg's works. These include solo piano works, the third and fourth string quartets and other chamber works, a concerto each for piano and violin, orchestral variations, and an uncompleted opera, *Moses and Aaron*. In his *Five Pieces for Orchestra*, Opus 16 (1909) Schoenberg controls the ebb and flow of energy through contrasts in loudness and tone colors. He treats pitch as an aspect of timbre, so that dissonance, consonance, and tonality are no longer relevant. Most of the pieces are characterized by considerable polyphonic and rhythmic complexity and especially by continuous variation of melodic ideas. The third piece in the set, "Summer Morning by a Lake: Colors," is a study in subtly shifting timbres. Recurring aggregates of sound oscillate between different instrumental combinations. The instruments come and go without accent, producing delicate changes of timbre. The chords change subtly both in their pitch structures and in their instrumentation, so that the harmonic changes function as an integral part of the changes in timbre. The gentle sounds provide a kind of background of color, against which flutes, clarinets, a harp, and other instruments play tiny, fragmentary motives. In spite of its static quality, an overall shape can be discerned in the piece, consisting of four segments of about fifty, seventy, thirty, and sixty seconds, respectively. The regular oscillation of sounds continues through the first part, with solo instruments only, there is a pause, then the oscillation resumes, with enriched timbres from additional instruments; new sounds enter

19-87
MARC CHAGALL, *The Green Violinist,*
1923–24. Oil on canvas, 78″ x 42¾″.
The Solomon R. Guggenheim Museum, New
York.

and all activity increases; there is another pause, and the last part combines the instrumentation of the second part with a reversal of the oscillating chords from the first part.

Béla Bartók (Hungary and the United States, 1881–1945). Bartók held the post of professor of piano at the Royal Academy of Music in Budapest, Hungary, from 1907 until 1934. He became an internationally known concert pianist and composer but was slow to gain recognition in his own country. Bartók's interest in folk music led him to collect thousands of field recordings of folk music from many East European and North African cultures. In his own music he blended folk elements with Classical forms, polyphonic techniques, and twentieth-century harmonies, timbres, and rhythms. Though he based his harmonies on tonal centers, his music abounds in harsh dissonances, cluster sounds, and chords derived by unconventional means. Folk elements show most clearly in his melodic styles, patterns of meter and accent, and extreme rhythmic vitality. His best-known works include his six string quartets, several orchestral works, three piano concertos, one violin concerto, considerable solo music for piano, and several works for unusual instrumental combinations. His String Quartet No. 4 (1928) is in five movements, with the four outer movements arranged in complementary pairs. The first and fifth movements are based on transformation and development of the same motive, and both feature harsh, dense textures and driving rhythms. The second and fourth movements are lighter in texture. Both are polyphonic, with furious running lines in the second movement, and an insistent metrical drive in the fourth movement. In the central third movement, dense textures are sustained as accompaniment to rhapsodic solo lines. Bartók calls for several special effects, including pitch slides (first and second movements), muted strings (second movement), plucked strings (fourth movement), and the striking of the strings with the wood of the bow (fourth and fifth movements). (See the discussions of Ex. 5, *Music for String Instruments, Percussion and Celesta*, first movement, in Part One, Chs. 2 and 4.)

Igor Stravinsky (Russia, France, and the United States, 1882–1971). Stravinsky was the son of a famous singer at the Imperial Opera in St. Petersburg, and he received a thorough musical education as a child at home. He studied law for five years but also began serious study of music composition at the age of twenty. Between the two World Wars he lived most of the time in France, and after 1939 he lived in California. His reputation was established with his early ballets, especially *The Rite of Spring* (1913), written in Paris for Sergei Diaghilev and the Russian Ballet. Writing much for the ballet as well as other kinds of music, Stravinsky became, in the 1920's the recognized leader of Neoclassicism, a movement that was in opposition to the atonal style of Schoenberg and his followers. After Schoenberg's death in 1951, however, Stravinsky wrote several works using the twelve-tone technique, most notably *Canticum Sacrum* (1955) and *Threni* (1958). Though he created works in almost every medium, the essence of his style remained constant despite many superficial differences: an almost obsessive concern with rhythm and timing, especially in complex metric structures and repeated patterns; brilliant use of variegated timbres and instrumental combinations; use of chords for timbre and sonority, but usually with some tonal focus; melodic motives or ideas repeated but not developed; and forms created through carefully timed sectional episodes. Stravinsky is considered Neoclassical not only because of his penchant for borrowing materials, techniques, and forms from the past, but rather because of his aesthetic attitude. For him, composing was an act of problem solving, the process of organizing sounds in time to create forms. He rejected the validity of any

19-88

PABLO PICASSO, *Portrait of Igor Stravinsky,* 1920. Drawing. Private Collection.

associational or expressive meaning outside of the music itself, thus rejecting the aesthetic assumptions of nineteenth-century music. His *Symphony of Psalms* (1930) is a setting, for chorus and orchestra, of selected passages from the Latin version of the Psalms. The orchestra requires two pianos and large brass and woodwind sections, but no clarinets, no violins or violas, and only timpani and a bass drum for percussion. The style is Neoclassical; sounds are organized to create rational forms, using ordered pitches and conventional media as primary materials. Timing and speed are the controlling elements, while carefully chosen timbres underline static qualities. Part III is a setting of Psalm 150. Consonance, dissonance, and tonality are vital to the structure, but they are effected through unconventional pitch relations. Static repetition of a few pitches throughout most of the piece creates a strong tonal focus, which coalesces into a clear tonic at crucial cadences. Rhythm patterns, pitch patterns, and words are repeated and reiterated throughout, especially the words and rhythm of *Laudate Dominum* (Praise God). The overall form and structural divisions are created through speed and timing and through contrasts between static and dynamic passages. Beginning with a solemn *Alleluia—Laudate Dominum*, the first verse of the Psalm is presented at the slowest speed, followed by the second and third verses at the fastest. The rapid motion suddenly is interrupted by the slow *Alleluia* from the beginning, then resumes as the words and rhythm of *Laudate Dominum* are elaborated. From here—about halfway through—the speed progressively slows through the fourth and fifth verses, and the piece ends as it began, with the same *Alleluia—Laudate Dominum*. At the end of the third and fourth verses a slow buildup of textural density creates mounting tension, which is released by a sudden decrease in loudness and speed. The fifth verse is a stately dance of exultation in which the sung parts move in a slow triple meter over a four-note bass pattern, creating two meters that move in and out of phase.

Anton von Webern (Austria, 1883–1945). Webern rigorously pursued Schoenberg's twelve-tone technique to its logical consequences and in so doing made a complete break with the German Romantic style. He began studying composition with Schoenberg in 1904 and remained his fervent disciple for life. Webern sought extreme clarity and economy in all of his works, and he rejected the excessive musical rhetoric of the Wagnerian

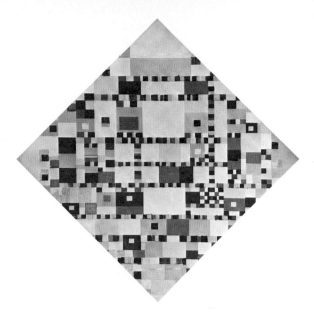

19-89
PIET MONDRIAN, *Victory Boogie Woogie,*
1943–44. Unfinished oil on canvas with
colored tape and paper. Collection of
Mr. and Mrs. Burton Tremaine, Meriden,
Connecticut.

tradition. He abandoned tonality, and he anticipated
Schoenberg's twelve-tone system as early as 1911.
Webern adopted that system without compromise in all
of his later works, and he applied a similar kind of
precise control to other aspects of his music. The
twelve-tone series determined rhythms, textures, registers, timbres, and forms, as well as the pitches. His
works are delicate miniatures of extreme brevity. Individual pitches tend to be scattered over a wide range,
and each separate tone often has its own unique duration, timbre, and articulation. This style, sometimes
called *pointillism*, was the starting point for the post–
World War II serialists, such as Pierre Boulez, Karlheinz
Stockhausen, and Milton Babbitt. It also provided the
aesthetic basis for much early electronic music. Webern
went beyond Schoenberg in creating a music of structured sounds and silences with no referential meaning
outside itself. His *Symphony, Opus* 21 (1928), for a
chamber orchestra, is in two movements, lasting about
six and a half and two and a half minutes, respectively.
Both movements are constructed entirely from a single
pitch series in which the twelve tones are divided into
two symmetrical six-tone sets, each the reverse of the
other half an octave away. This means that the whole
series, or tone row, sounds the same backwards, pitched
half an octave higher or lower. In the first movement the
tone row proceeds simultaneously in two versions, each
of which is also imitated in contrary motion, making

four polyphonic "lines." These lines, however, are obscured by the wide dispersion of pitches, frequent silences, and rapid changes of timbre (pointillism). In general the listener will perceive neither the actual pitches of the tone row nor the polyphonic imitations. The pointillist texture creates a random effect, with a lack of pitch-directed movement and a kind of static symmetry. At the same time, there are subtle but perceptible contrasts and clearly audible repetitions of formal sections. The first movement is in two parts, both repeated, with the second part nearly twice as long as the first. Higher pitches, more use of violins, louder sounds, and shorter durations add to the levels of contrast in the second part. The musical energy of the whole movement is directed to a high point just before the end. The pointillism is modified by fewer silences and more sustained sounds until, at the energy peak, several sounds occur at once. The second movement is a theme and seven variations with a short ending, or coda added. The theme is about fifteen seconds long. It is symmetrical, the second half being a reversal of the first half, with a pivotal center. Furthermore, the last three variations are based on a reversal of the first three, with the fourth acting as a pivot, and the coda balancing the opening theme, so that the form and materials of the whole movement are derived from the nature of the tone row.

1945 to the Present

ADVENTURES IN SOUNDS AND IDEAS

In Europe since the Second World War, the performance of new music has been encouraged and supported by national and local governments—especially through the state radio systems—and by activities such as the special summer courses at Darmstadt, Germany, as well as by various festivals of new music. Many European musicians came to the United States just before and during the war, and their influence has helped to create an international musical climate in America. Some of the most radical new ideas and experiments have originated with the post-war generation of American composers, many of whom work at or near university centers.

The challenges to accepted musical traditions that

occurred earlier in the century coalesced after 1945 into several specific attitudes and techniques, with considerable cross-influence. Composers have expanded their search for new sound materials, sought alternatives to the older concepts of continuity and logical flow, and altered the relationship between composer and performer by redefining who controls the musical process.

The movement in music toward nonreferential sounds in time, which began early in the century, became dominant after World War II. Influenced by Webern, many composers during the early 1950's sought total control in their works through serialization of the various elements. Their concern with control of processes represented a complete rejection of referential associations. The search for new sounds intensified, and the use of clusters, sound masses, new kinds of instrumental sounds, and heretofore unacceptable "noises" became commonplace. At about the same time electronics technology made available an incredible variety of sounds that could be stored, altered, combined, and arranged with near total control. Many composers immediately saw in this medium the answer to their search for new sounds, new techniques, and new means of control. Rapid technical advances have made inexpensive synthesizers widely available, and the use of electronics has spread to include the fields of popular and commercial music. Considerable interest has developed in the combination of live with electronic sounds, and recent experiments with computer assisted musical composition have opened a whole new area of unexplored possibilities.

Composers of serial music typically have sought to avoid any logical flow of ideas in the traditional sense, and the same attitude is evident in much electronic music. The resulting sound complexes sometimes can be heard as generalized gestures, but they often take on the character of random events on which the listener is free to impose his or her own order. Composers such as Cage, Boulez, Stockhausen, and Iannis Xenakis have achieved similar results by introducing random selection, chance, or statistical probability into the musical process. Also, in their search for new sounds, composers have given more creative responsibility to performers, often specifying only the limits within which improvised actions are to take place. Some composers employ chance operations in predetermining a specific result, while others specify actions in which the element of chance causes indeterminate results. The composer thus becomes a programmer who specifies a set of actions or possibilities.

Interest in the visual element in creative performance, the need for visual action to accompany electronic sounds, and experimentation with spatial effects have encouraged inclusion of theatrical elements in musical performance. These new aspects, combined with the acceptance of chance and indeterminancy all have contributed to the development of *happenings* and *intermedia.*

19-90
LARRY WILLIAMS, *Untitled,* 1974. Photo emulsion and pencil on music paper. 9'' x 11½''. Collection of the Artist.

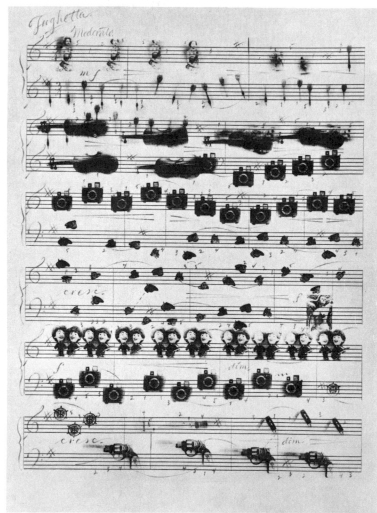

Indeterminancy represents the total acceptance of music as process, instead of the predetermined product of the composer's will. It rejects the concept of music as art object, since each performance is a new set of events, and in so doing it challenges most of the traditions of Western art and thought. Some composers (or noncomposers) have carried the challenge so far as *antimusic*, a sort of neo-Dada doctrine of the absurd that results in musical "works" that cannot be performed.

Many composers have continued to reject some or all of these new techniques and concepts, choosing to work in more traditional ways. Most of the recent works that have gained wide acceptance, by composers such as Luciano Berio, George Crumb, György Ligeti, and Krzysztof Penderecki, represent a judicious synthesis of old and new techniques chosen to achieve a particular effect. In a similar way, the broad category of popular music called *rock* represents a sophisticated synthesis of many diverse materials, styles, and techniques, including blues and jazz improvisation, folk music, electronic manipulation, experiments with new sounds, and considerable emphasis on the creative process in performance. Most serious rock musicians reject the separation of art from life, and regard their works more as processes than as fixed art objects.

Edgard Varèse (France and the United States, 1885–1965). Varèse prepared to study engineering, but turned to music at the age of twenty-one. In addition to composing, he spent much of his life organizing and conducting concerts in Europe and the United States, living mainly in the United States after 1915. He was the first to define music simply as organized sound. This view of music led him to explore new sound sources and to accept any sound as appropriate musical material. Lacking adequate means for realizing his ideas, Varèse anticipated and fought for electronic music years before it became a practical reality. *Ionisation* (1931) calls for thirty-seven percussion instruments with thirteen players. It is structured through loudness, timbre, and time only, with no recourse to melody or harmony. The high and low quality of the pitched instruments (sirens, piano, celesta, and chimes) is treated as an aspect of timbre. Sounds and patterns are developed logically in a carefully timed cumulation and flow of energy that builds to a climax, then subsides to a cadence. The phases of this process are marked by contrasts in qualities of sounds and by the presence or absence of metric patterns. The rhythm patterns change continuously yet maintain a degree of regularity, providing continuity while creating a sense of expectancy. Sensitive shadings of loudness enhance the energy flow, and individual timbres stand out clearly. Following the Second World War, Varèse's penchant for using any sounds as musical raw materials gained wide acceptance, and pitchless music emphasizing sounds as sounds became common. In his *Étude for Two Pianos, Percussion, and Mixed Chorus* (1954), taped industrial sounds alternate with live instrumental sounds. His *Poème Électronique* (1958) was created as an intermedia work combining spatial distribution of sounds with projected visual images within a special architectural environment. A pavilion was provided with 425 loudspeakers arranged so that the sounds seemed to come and go throughout the interior space. Varèse chose and organized his sounds for maximum contrast; at the same time, each sound tends to appear in some rational pattern or shape, often repeated or grouped in numerical sets, and some return later in the piece. A sense of motion in space is created by the formation, combination, and dissipation of the sounds. Only some of the sounds have precise pitch, but these are carefully controlled. Some are combined as pure harmonic intervals, and there is a rising three-note motive that recurs later in various guises. Human vocal sounds are introduced near the center of the piece, and the final section is set off by ten seconds of silence.

John Cage (United States, 1912–).   Cage's ideas have been very influential among contemporary artists, writers, and musicians. Much of his early work was done with dance, theater, and percussion ensemble groups. Since the 1940's he has worked with the dancer Merce Cunningham, eventually becoming musical director of the Cunningham Dance Company. In 1952, together with Earle Brown, Morton Feldman, and Christian Wolff, he organized the Project of Music for Magnetic Tape, a pioneering American effort in electronic music. Most of Cage's music is untraditional and unique. He has been a leader in the free use of sounds, intermedia, live electronic music, and, especially, in the application of chance to composition and performance. From his work with percussion he developed an interest in the duration and time-scale of events and the properties of sound and silence. Between 1934 and 1956 he followed a path similar to Varèse—the organization of sound using percussion instruments, then exotic instruments,

19-91
Merce Cunningham and Dance Company in
Second Hand (1970). Music by John Cage,
costumes by Jasper Johns.

and finally electronics. During the 1940's he received
considerable attention for his invention of the "prepared piano," a means of achieving percussive effects
by inserting various objects between the strings of the
piano to alter its timbres. While such experiments extended the possibilities of conventional instruments,
they also emphasized actions for the players to take so
that the results were partially indeterminate. *Theater
Piece*, first performed in 1952 by the Cunningham dance
group at Black Mountain College, North Carolina,
probably was the first intermedia happening staged in
the United States. It involved music, dance, lectures,
poems, paintings, and projected movies and slides,
randomly juxtaposed. Influenced by Eastern philosophy, especially Zen, Cage came to the idea that art is
inseparable from life and that it imitates the random
operations of nature. Further, realizing that there is no
silence for the human ear, he concluded that all sounds,
intended or not, are equally acceptable, and the choice
of sounds by the composer is not necessary. The original score of his *4'33''*, "for any instrument or combination of instruments," consists of six pages containing
only six vertical lines, with timings, marking the beginnings and endings of its three parts. The blank space is
scaled horizontally to represent the indicated durations.
The performer is expected to follow the timings across
the pages precisely, but to make no sounds in the
process. Cage has thus completely controlled timing,
but left to chance the kinds of sounds that will occur
during performance. The sounds come from the audi-

ence, from chair scrapings, coughs, the rustle of clothes, and the like. The performer is silent. Hence, the random sounds produced by the environment actually constitute the musical experience. Frequently the sequence and combination of events or the details of performance are determined by chance, so that Cage's pieces become processes with no predetermined beginnings or endings that can be realized in many ways and even combined with each other. Between 1967 and 1969 Cage collaborated with Lejaren Hiller to produce *HPSCHD*, using the computer facilities and the Experimental Music Studio at the University of Illinois. Its name is the word *harpsichord* reduced to the six digits allowed in the computer program. There are fifty-one computer-generated sound tapes and seven harpsichord solos, each of about twenty minutes in duration and each capable of beginning at any time and being combined in any order. Cage and Hiller determined the overall procedures while the computer specified the precise details, basing its decisions on chance. Also included with each of the recordings of this piece (Nonesuch H-71224) is one of ten thousand different versions of a program called *KNOBS*, which specifies a random series of settings for the volume, treble, and bass controls on a playback amplifier, allowing the listener to "play" the knobs. By relinquishing control of the music to chance, Cage has rejected the ideas of logical sequence and the composition as an art object as well as of the composer as an elite creator. For Cage, music and art should be life-affirming activities that encourage individual freedom of choice.

Pierre Boulez (France, 1925–). Boulez is a well-known and influential composer, author, and conductor and has been a frequent guest conductor throughout Europe and America. In 1971 he was appointed conductor for the New York Philharmonic orchestra. The style of Webern led Boulez to control all aspects of time and sound through ordered sequences such as the pitch series in twelve-tone music. In 1950 and '51 he created works in which pitches, durations, loudness, attacks, and timbres all were serialized. He soon moved away from total serialization and has allowed performer choices in some of his later works. Most of Boulez's music combines mathematically rigorous structures with extremely expressive effects and is particularly notable for clear, distinct timbres. He uses voices and conventional instruments for the most part, though he also has worked with electronics. In addition to works in these media, there are pieces for piano, string quartet, orchestra, and unique instrumental combinations. His *Le marteau sans maître* (1954–57) is built around three Surrealist lyrics from a cycle of poems by René Char. The work, for a small group of solo instruments and a contralto singer, is in nine movements. The titles of the poems are *"L'artisanat furieux," "Bel édifice et les pressentiments,"* and *Bourreaux de solitude."* The settings of the texts each have one or more associated movements, all juxtaposed in a sort of Surrealist mix. The first three movements will serve as a representative sample of the work. The first movement calls for alto flute, vibraphone, guitar, and viola. Rapid changes of texture produce a kaleidoscope of colors, but an overall continuity of sound surges and ebbs in a series of free-flowing gestures, marked by periodic pauses, speed changes, and a lack of metric rhythm. A strong sense of order prevails, despite the seemingly random relationships of pitch and time. The alto flute, xylorimba (a marimba with modified resonators), side drum, and muted viola begin the second movement very quietly in a precisely metered, pointillistic texture, which contrasts markedly with the continuous gestures of the first movement. The flute drops out following a conspicuous trill, and bongos replace the side drum in a contrasting loud section in which speed changes and frequent pauses all but obliterate the sense of meter. The flute and side drum return near the end. The third movement, for flute and voice, illustrates a speech-song technique, first developed by Schoenberg, which requires the singer to move in wide, awkward intervals, with frequent slides and ornaments, in an exaggeration of speech inflections. The flute holds equal place with the voice, the two timbres mixing remarkably well.

Luciano Berio (Italy and the United States, 1925–). Berio studied at the Music Academy in Milan, where he graduated in 1951. In 1955 he helped found the electronic music studio at the Italian Radio in Milan, and he has been a contributing composer and lecturer at the Darmstadt summer courses. Berio came to New York in 1962, where he teaches composition at the Juilliard School. Except for the use of electronic tapes, all of his music utilizes standard instruments, including the voice, in widely varied combinations. He used serial techniques in most of his works through 1957, then began to experiment with electronic treatment of sounds and performer choices (indeterminacy). Many of his works explore the rich timbres of the human voice. Since 1962 he has used serial procedures, indeterminacy, and live and prerecorded sounds variously chosen to suit each individual work in a synthesis of contemporary procedures. His *Sinfonia* (1968) presents live instrumental and vocal sounds in ways typical of electronic treatment. (See the discussions of Ex. 4, *Sinfonia*, Section I, in Part One, Chs. 1, 2, 3, and 4.)

Earle Brown (United States, 1926–). Brown studied mathematics and engineering as well as music. He was one of the members of the Project of Music for Magnetic Tape in New York. His first works were serialized, with a mathematical basis, but his association with John Cage quickly led him to experiment with conductor and performer choices, chance concurrences, and indeterminacy. He has frequently acknowledged his debt to the painter Jackson Pollock and the sculptor Alexander Calder. Brown seeks to create an environment in which the musical outcome will be determined by the needs of the moment. As in Calder's mobiles, there are basic units that may be subjected to many different relationships or forms, with the performers participating ac-

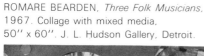

19-92
ROMARE BEARDEN, *Three Folk Musicians,*
1967. Collage with mixed media,
50″ x 60″. J. L. Hudson Gallery, Detroit.

lively in the creation of the work. The result is music with *open form*, the components of which may be arranged in any order. A work retains its identity through the character of the basic events, yet no two performances will achieve the same formal result. In some cases the sounds are specified, with the performers choosing the sequence; in others, the sequence is predetermined but the specific sounds are not. His *Available Forms 2*, "For Large Orchestra, Four Hands" (1962), is an open form work in which two conductors each direct half of the musicians in a full orchestra of ninety-eight, who are seated together rather than in two separate groups. Thirty-eight different sound events, which the conductors may interpret in several ways, are written on separate pages. The conductors choose the sequence and timing of the events, and the performers have considerable freedom for interpretation. The separate events are rehearsed, but the combinations are not. Since neither conductor knows what event the other will choose, the juxtaposition of events depends partly on chance and partly on the conductors' responses to each other's choices. Brown has provided elaborate performance instructions, including a precise set of conducting signals. Of course, no two recorded performances of this work will sound the same.

Krzystof Penderecki (Poland, 1933–). Penderecki graduated from the Music Academy in Cracow and has recently taught at Yale University. He used serial procedures in some early works, but soon began writing music characterized by the interplay of blocks, bands, and various configurations of sound, ranging from subtle shadings to harsh contrasts and dense masses. Time and motion are controlled through gradual changes in sound production, configuration, or combination. Though he has created some electronic tapes, he more often achieves similar effects through new uses of voices or conventional instruments. He sometimes allows performer choices within strict limits, so as to produce a statistically predictable yet slightly indeterminate result. Much of the music is illustrative and dramatic, and, except for some chamber music and electronic pieces, most of the works are vocal or orchestral. The vocal works typically require soloists, chorus, instruments, and a narrator, and many of the instrumental pieces are for a string group. The sustained intensity of his *To the Victims of Hiroshima: Threnody* (1961) reflects the associational meaning of its title (a *threnody* is a lament for the dead). All of the sounds are created by a standard orchestral string section of fifty-two players, who use both conventional and unconventional playing techniques and are required part of the time to improvise together. There are no recurring sounds or rhythm patterns. The duration of events is given in seconds and timed with a clock, so that a sense of motion and change is created through the duration and succession of sounds, sudden contrasts, and the phasing in and out of different kinds of events. Sustained sound masses dominate the work, ranging from precisely defined bands to massive clusters, which alternate with "clouds" of seemingly random sounds.

Suggestions for Further Study

Austin, William W. *Music in the Twentieth Century from Debussy through Stravinsky.* New York: W. W. Norton, 1966.

Cage, John. *Silence: Lectures and Writings.* Cambridge, Mass.: M.I.T. Press, 1966.

Cope, David. *New Directions in Music,* 2nd ed. Dubuque, Iowa: William C. Brown, 1976.

Cowell, Henry, and Sidney Cowell. *Charles Ives and His Music.* New York: Oxford University Press, 1969.

Hansen, Al. *A Primer of Happenings and Time-Space Art.* New York: Something Else Press, 1965.

Kolneder, Walter. *Anton Webern: An Introduction to His Works.* Translated by Humphrey Searle. Berkeley: University of California Press, 1968.

Meyer, Leonard B. *Music, the Arts, and Ideas: Patterns and Predictions in Twentieth-Century Culture.* Chicago: University of Chicago Press, 1967.

Peyser, Joan. *The New Music; The Sense Behind the Sound.* New York: Dell, 1972.

Reich, Willi. *Schoenberg: A Critical Biography.* Translated by Leo Black. New York: Praeger, 1971.

Salzman, Eric. *Twentieth-Century Music: An Introduction,* 2nd ed. Englewood Cliffs, N.J.: Prentice-Hall, 1974.

Schwartz, Elliott and Barney Childs, eds. *Contemporary Composers on Contemporary Music.* New York: Holt, Rinehart and Winston, 1967.

Schwartz, Elliott. *Electronic Music: A Listener's Guide.* New York: Praeger, 1973.

Slonimsky, Nicolas. *Music Since 1900,* 4th ed. New York: Scribner's, 1971.

Stevens, Halsey. *The Life and Music of Béla Bartók,* rev. ed. New York: Oxford University Press, 1967.

Stravinsky, Igor. *An Autobiography*. New York: W. W. Norton, 1962.

Varèse, Louise. *Varèse: A Looking-Glass Diary*, Vol. I (1883–1928). New York: W. W. Norton, 1972.

Vinton, John, ed. *The Dictionary of Contemporary Music*. New York: E. P. Dutton, 1974.

Yates, Peter. *Twentieth Century Music: Its Evolution from the End of the Harmonic Era into the Present Era of Sound*. New York: Pantheon Books, 1967.

Suggestions for Further Listening

Bartók Béla. Third *String Quartet*.

Berg, Alban. *Wozzeck*.

————. *Concerto for Violin*.

Berio, Luciano. *Thema: Omaggio a Joyce*.

————. *Visage*.

Britten, Benjamin. *War Requiem*.

Cage, John. *Aria with Fontana Mix*.

Carter, Elliott. Second *String Quartet*.

————. *Eight Etudes and a Fantasy*.

Copland, Aaron. *Appalachian Spring*.

Crumb, George. *Ancient Voices of Children*.

Hindemith, Paul. Orchestral suite of *Mathis der Maler*.

Ives, Charles. *Three Places in New England*.

Ligeti, György. *Atmosphères*.

Partch, Harry. *And on the Seventh Day Petals Fell in Petaluma*.

Penderecki, Krzystof. *Passion According to St. Luke*.

Schoenberg, Arnold. *Pierrot Lunaire*.

————. Fourth *String Quartet*.

Stockhausen, Karlheinz. *Kontra-Punkte*.

————. *Hymnen*.

Stravinsky, Igor. *Rite of Spring*.

————. *L'histoire du soldat*.

————. *Canticum sacrum*.

Webern, Anton von. *Piano Variations*, Opus 27.

Wuorinen, Charles. *Times Encomium*.

Xenakis, Iannis. *Pithoprakta*.

Picture Credits

Art

Photo credits

Chapter 1 p. 7, top, Scala New York/Florence; 9, Alinari-Art Reference Bureau; 13, Bildarchiv Foto Marburg; 16, Herschel Levit

Chapter 2 p. 36, Marburg-Art Reference Bureau; 37, Alinari-Art Reference Bureau

Chapter 4 p. 78, top right, Bildarchiv Foto Marburg

Part Two Opening p. 96, Scala New York/Florence

Chapter 6 p. 101, Trustees of the British Museum; 105, Editorial Photocolor Archives; 107, bottom, and 108, bottom, Oriental Institute, University of Chicago

Chapter 7 p. 113, bottom, George Gerster, Photo Researchers, Inc.; 114, 115, Hirmer Fotoarchiv, Munich; 117, top, and 118, top, Metropolitan Museum of Art, New York; 119, éditions d'Art Albert Skira, Geneva; 120, top, Hirmer Fotoarchiv, Munich; 121, Eliot Elisofon; 123, top and bottom, Hirmer Fotoarchiv, Munich; 124, Oriental Institute, University of Chicago; 125, Egyptian Expedition, Metropolitan Museum of Art, New York

Chapter 8 pp. 132, 133, top and bottom, 134, 135, Hirmer Fotoarchiv, Munich

Chapter 9 p. 139, top and bottom right, Alinari-Scala; bottom left, Hirmer Fotoarchiv, Munich; 141 and 143, top, Scala New York/Florence; 143, bottom, and 144, bottom, Hirmer Fotoarchiv, Munich; 145, 146, left, Alison Frantz; 146, bottom right, Alinari-Art Reference Bureau; 147, top right, Alinari-Art Reference Bureau; bottom, Hirmer Fotoarchiv, Munich; 148, Caisse Nationale des Monuments Historiques, Paris; 149, bottom, Marburg-Art Reference Bureau; 150, top, Alinari/Scala; bottom, Courtesy of the Trustees of the British Museum; 152, Editorial Photocolor Archives; 153, top, Alinari-Art Reference Bureau; bottom, Hirmer Fotoarchiv, Munich; 154, top and bottom, Hirmer Fotoarchiv, Munich

Chapter 10 p. 160, Gabinetto Fotografico Nazionale, Rome; 161, Deutsches Archäolo-gisches Institut; 162, Fototeca Unione, Rome; 163, Scala New York/Florence

Chapter 11 p. 166, top, French Embassy Press and Information Division; 167, 168, bottom, 169, 170, Alinari-Art Reference Bureau; 173, top, G. E. Kidder Smith; 174, 175, 176, 177, bottom, Alinari-Art Reference Bureau; 178, top left, éditions d'Art Albert Skira, Geneva; top right, Alinari-Art Reference Bureau

Chapter 12 p. 183, Pontifica Commissione Centrale per L'Arte Sacra in Italia; 184, 186, top, Scala New York/Florence; 186, center and top, Anderson-Art Reference Bureau; 187, top right and left, 188, top and bottom, Hirmer Fotoarchiv, Munich; 189, bottom, Alinari-Art Reference Bureau; 190, Anderson-Art Reference Bureau; 191, Alinari-Art Reference Bureau; 193, Anderson-Art Reference Bureau

Chapter 13 p. 197, Courtesy of the Trustees for the British Museum; 198, top, Trinity College Library, Dublin; 200, top left, Dr. Harald Busch, Frankfurt; 201, bottom, Hermann Wehmeyer; 202, top, Marburg-Art Reference Bureau; bottom left, Bildarchiv Foto Marburg; 203, bottom left and right, Jean Roubier, Paris; 204, top and bottom, Alinari-Art Reference Bureau; 205, bottom, Scala New York/Florence; 206, top left, A. F. Kersting; 207, Hermann Wehmeyer; 208, Marburg-Art Reference Bureau; 209, top, H. Roger-Viollet, Paris; bottom, Bayerische Staatsbibliothek, München; 210, Bulloz; 212, top left and right, Jean Roubier, Paris; 213, bottom left and right, Clarence Ward; 214, bottom left, Edwin Smith; right, National Monuments Record, England; 215, top left and right, Deutscher Kunstverlag; 216, Photographie Giraudon, Paris; 217, James Austin; 218, top, Marburg-Art Reference Bureau; bottom, Bildarchiv Foto Marburg; 219, Archives Photographiques, Paris. Reproduced by permission of Caisse Nationale des Monuments Historiques, Paris; 220, Rapho-Guillumette Pictures; 222, top and bottom, Scala New York/Florence

Chapter 14 p. 231, top, Copyright A.C.L., Brussels; bottom, Museo Nacional del Prado; 232, Walter Steinkopf; 233, Alinari-Art Reference Bureau; 235, Scala New York/Florence; 236, top, Alinari-Art Reference Bureau; bottom, Alinari-

Scala; 237, Copyright Frick Collection, New York; 238, top, Scala New York/Florence; bottom, and 239, Alinari-Art Reference Bureau; 240, Bayer, Staatsgemäldesammlungen, Munich; 241, 242, 243, 244, Alinari-Art Reference Bureau; 245, Anderson-Giraudon; 246, top left and right, Anderson-Art Reference Bureau; 247, bottom, Brogi-Art Reference Bureau; 248, top left, Alinari-Art Reference Bureau; right, Photo Researchers, Inc.; 249, bottom, and 251, Alinari-Art Reference Bureau; 252, Alinari-Scala; 253, top, and 254, Alinari-Art Reference Bureau; 255, top, Alinari-Scala; bottom, Alinari-Art Reference Bureau; 256, top and bottom, 258, 259, Scala New York/Florence; 260, Alinari-Art Reference Bureau; 261, bottom, Anderson-Art Reference Bureau; 262, top, Alinari-Art Reference Bureau; 263, Metropolitan Museum of Art, New York; 264, top, Alinari-Art Reference Bureau; 268, top, Scala New York/Florence; 270, top, Photographie Giraudon, Paris, bottom, Bulloz

Chapter 15 p. 286, Copyright, The Frick Collection, New York; 287, top, Scala New York/Florence; bottom, Alinari-Scala; 288, Scala New York/Florence; 291, Alinari-Art Reference Bureau; 293, top and bottom, 294, bottom, Scala New York/Florence; 295, bottom, Anderson-Scala; 297, top, Anderson-Art Reference Bureau; bottom, Alinari-Art Reference Bureau; 299, Cliché des Musées Nationaux, Paris; 300, Walter Steinkopf; 301 and 306, Photographie Giraudon, Paris, 308, British Crown Copyright, reproduced with permission of the Controller of Her Brittanic Majesty's Stationery Office; 309, bottom left and right, Marburg-Art Reference Bureau; 310, bottom left, Crown Copyright, National Monuments Record; right, Edwin Smith

Chapter 16 p. 325, Scala New York/Florence; 327, Cliché des Musées Nationaux, Paris; 328, Reproduced by permission of the Trustees of the Wallace Collection; 329, © Birmingham Art Gallery; 330, Copyright, The Frick Collection, New York; 332, Photographie Giraudon, Paris; 334, top and bottom left, Scala New York/Florence; 335, top and bottom, Marburg-Art Reference Bureau; 336, bottom, Archives Photographiques, Paris; 337, Courtauld Institute of Art, Reproduced by permission of Country Life, London; 339, Hirmer Fotoarchiv, Munich

Chapter 17 p. 363, Museo del Prado, Madrid; 365, Photographie Giraudon, Paris, 369, top, Alinari-Art Reference Bureau; 370, Photo by Studio Madec, Nantes; 373, Bruckmann-Art Reference Bureau; 374, Cliché des Musées Nationaux, Paris; 376, 378, 380, Photographie Giraudon, Paris; 381, Cliché des Musées Nationaux, Paris; 386, bottom, Galerie Welz, Salzburg; 387, Oslo Kommunes Kunstamlinger, Munchmuseet; 389, Alinari-Art Reference Bureau; 390, Photographie Giraudon, Paris; 391, bottom, Art Reference Bureau; 393, Thomas Jefferson Memorial Foundation; 394, Radio Times Hulton Picture Library; 395, Marburg-Art Reference Bureau; 396, top, Louis H. Forhman; bottom, Photographie Giraudon; 397, Marburg-Art Reference Bureau; 398,

Foto Mas, Barcelona; 399, Wayne Andrews; 400, Missouri Historical Society

Chapter 18 p. 416, The Gernsheim Collection; 417, top, The Metropolitan Museum of Art, New York, Gift of I. N. Phelps Stokes, Edward S. Howes, Alice Mary Howes, Marion Augusta Howes, 1937; bottom, George Eastman House; 418, Bibliothèque Nationale, Paris; 419, top and bottom, George Eastman House; 421, top, Courtesy of Light Gallery, New York; bottom, The Alfred Stieglitz Collection, The Art Institute of Chicago; 422, The Imogen Cunningham Trust; 425, George Eastman House; 426, top, Magnum Photos; 429, George Eastman House; 430, 434, 436, 438, 439, 442, top, Photo Courtesy of Museum of Modern Art/Film Stills Archive; 432, RKO Radio Pictures, a Division of RKO General, Inc./Photo Courtesy of Museum of Modern Art/Film Stills Archive; 442, bottom, © 1976 Richard Feiner and Company, Inc./Photo Courtesy of Museum of Modern Art/Film Stills Archive; 443, 444, 445, Photo Courtesy of Museum of Modern Art/Film Stills Archive; 446, Cinema 5 Ltd.

Chapter 19 p. 450, Photo Courtesy The Museum of Modern Art, New York; 462, Photo by John Webb, F.R.P.S., Brompton Studio; 469, Photo Courtesy The Museum of Modern Art, New York; 471, top, Scala New York/Florence; 477, bottom, Cliché des Musées Nationaux, Paris; 484, Chicago Architectural Photo Co.; 487, top, Photoatelier Gerlach, Wein; bottom, Chevojon Frères, Paris; 488, bottom, and 489, Photo Courtesy of The Museum of Modern Art, New York; 490, top, © Dr. Franz Stoedtner, Dusseldorf; bottom, © Ezra Stoller; 491, George Holton, Photo Researchers, Inc., 492, top, from *The New Churches of Europe* by G. E. Kidder Smith; 499, bottom, Courtesy, The Marlborough Gallery, New York; 505, Malcolm Smith Studio; 506, bottom, and 507, © Ezra Stoller; 508, Reproduced by permission of Cosanti Foundation, Scottsdale, Arizona; 514, bottom, Photo by Geoffrey Clements, Staten Island; 515, top, Photo Courtesy of Leo Castelli Gallery, New York; 519, Gianfranco Gorgoni; 521, top, Photo by Steven Hill; 522, Sekai Bunka Photo

Color Section Plates 1, 3, 5, 6, 7, 8, Scala New York/Florence; Plate 2, by permission of The Board of Trinity College, Dublin; Plate 9, Copyright by Kodansha, Ltd., Tokyo; Plate 11, Photographie Giraudon, Paris; Plate 25, Bulloz; Plate 27, Photo by Alfred J. Wyatt; Plate 29, Photo by Malcolm Varon; Plate 30, Photo by Walter Dräyer

Permission S.P.A.D.E.M. 1977 by French Reproduction Rights, Inc. for the following: Plates 16, 18, 19, 24, 25, 26, 27. Pp. 379; 380; 450; 455; 457, top and bottom; 459; 461, top and bottom; 462; 467; 468, top; 471, bottom; 476, top; 477, top and right; 487, bottom; 491.

Permission A.D.A.G.P. 1977 by French Reproduction Rights, Inc. for the following: Plates 23, 28. Pp. 463, top; 466; 470; 471, top; 472; 481, top; 482, bottom; 493.

Illustration credits

P. 101 (by permission of The Trustees of the British Museum); 108, top, and 117, bottom (from Banister Fletcher); 129; 130, top and bottom; 144, top; 146, top; 159; 173, bottom; 182; 189, top; 200, top right; 203, top; 205, top; 206, bottom left; 212, bottom left; 214, top left: From *Gardner's Art Through the Ages*, 6th ed., revised by Horst de la Croix and Richard G. Tansey, © 1975 by Harcourt Brace Jovanovich, Inc. and reproduced with their permission.

P. 107, top: From R. Ghirshman, village perseachéménide, Mem. de la Mission Archeologique d'argent à l'èpoque achéménide, Athēna, 1956

P. 117, bottom; 130; 247, top: After Sir Banister Fletcher, *History of Architecture*, 18th ed. Athlone, London, 1975.

P. 128, Hirmer Fotoarchiv, Munich

P. 209, top, and 210, top: From *Art and Architecture in Italy* by Rudolph Wittkower. Penguin Books, Ltd. 1958.

P. 310, top: From *Architecture in Britain* by John Summerson. Penguin Books, Ltd., 1963.

P. 488, top: From *Nineteenth and Twentieth Century Architecture*, 2nd ed. by Henry R. Hitchcock. Penguin Books, Ltd., 1963.

Drawings Felix Cooper, Vantage Art, Inc., Ira Graboff, Bert Schneider

Music

Photo credits

Chapter 1 p. 23, Lynda Gordon; 24, Marjorie Pickens

Chapter 2 p. 42, Ginger Chih from Peter Arnold; 47, Print Division, The New York Public Library, Astor, Lenox and Tilden Foundations; 52, The Bettmann Archive; 54, Gerhard E. Gscheidle from Peter Arnold

Chapter 3 p. 63, top, Hubert Josse/Bibliothèque de l'Arsenal; 64, *Sinfonia* by Luciano Berio, © - Copyright 1972 Universal Edition, London. Used by permission of Associated Music Publishers, Inc.

Chapter 4 p. 84, Marjorie Pickens; 86, Barbara Pfeffer from Peter Arnold; 90, The Bettmann Archive

Chapter 9 p. 161, Jan Lukas-Editorial Photocolor Archives

Chapter 13 pp. 228, 229, The Bettmann Archive; 230, Bibliothèque Nationale, Paris

Chapter 14 p. 273, Photo courtesy of the Music Division of The New York Public Library at Lincoln Center, Astor, Lenox and Tilden Foundations; 280, The Bettmann Archive

Chapter 15 p. 313, top and bottom, Bibliothèque Nationale; 314, Kunstsammlungen der Veste Coburg; 315, The Bettmann Archive; 316, Germanisches Nationalmuseum; 318, The New York Public Library, Astor, Lenox and Tilden Foundations; 319, Barenreiter-Bildarchiv

Chapter 16 p. 343, The Metropolitan Museum of Art, Munsey Fund; 344, Barenreiter-Bildarchiv; 345, Roger-Viollet; 346, The Bettmann Archive; 348, The Metropolitan Museum of Art, Harris Brisbane Dick Fund; 350, Victoria and Albert Museum; 351, 353, 354, The Bettmann Archive

Chapter 17 pp. 407, 412, The Bettmann Archive

Chapter 19 p. 533, Photograph, courtesy of The Museum of Modern Art, New York; 536, Photograph, courtesy of Light Gallery, New York; 539, James Klosty

Permission S.P.A.D.E.M. 1977 by French Reproduction Rights, Inc. for the following: p. 41; 50; 406; 409; 525; 526, bottom; 531

Permission A.D.A.G.P 1977 by French Reproduction Rights, Inc. for the following: p. 63, bottom; 403; 528; 530

Illustration credits

p. 25, 26, 27, 28, Reproduced by permission of Harcourt Brace Jovanovich, Inc. from *Music: A Design for Listening*, Third Edition by Homer Ulrich. © 1957, 1962, 1970 by Harcourt Brace Jovanovich, Inc.

Drawings Vantage Art, Inc.; Joyce Biegeleisen

Index

Italicized numbers refer to illustrations

Art

Archaic period: Egyptian, (continued)
111–16; Etruscan, 159; Greek, 137–41
Archer, Frederick Scott, 417
arches, 76–77, 164, 165, 201
architectural design, 76–80
architectural materials, 76. See also reinforced concrete
architrave, broken, 247
arcology, 507
Arcosanti, 508
Arena Chapel (Padua), 222
armature, 73
Armory Show of 1913, 452–53, 468, 472
Arnolfini and His Bride (Van Eyck), 56, 230, PLATE 4
Arp, Jean, 478–79
art criticism, 92–94
art history, 358
Art Nouveau, 359, 366, 387, 392, 397–98, 454, 484
art patronage, 228–29
Artemision Statue, 145, 147
artistic truth, 358
artist's proofs, 67
Artist's Studio in an Afternoon Fog, The (Homer), 377, 378
As You Like It (Czinner), 433
Asam, Cosmas Damian (ä'zäm, koh'zmäs), 5, 9, 12, 14, 15, 39, 324, 331
Asam, Egid Quirin (ēg'ed), 5, 14, 331
Asam, Hans G., 331
Ascension window, 210
Ash Can School, 452
Asquith, Anthony, 432
assemblage, 475, 514
Assumption of the Virgin, The (Asam), 5, 12, 14, 331
Assumption of the Virgin, The (Titian), 253
Assurbanipal Killing a Lion, 105
Assyrian art, 98, 99, 103–06
asymmetrical balance, 34, 38
At the Moulin Rouge (Toulouse-Lautrec), 387, 388
atelier theme, 463
Athenian mixing bowl, 148
atmospheric perspective, 15
atrium, 165, 181
Augustus, 166, 167
Austrian architecture, 307, 333–34, 486–87
Austrian films, 430
Austrian painting, 264, 324, 387, 467–68
Austrian sculpture, 331
authentication, 97
Autumn Rhythm (Pollock), 500
axial balance, 34, 36, 38, 139, 141, 170
axial planning, 141–42

Babeldiga, 507
Bacon, Francis, 497–98
balance, 34–35, 36, 38, 139, 141,

170
Ballerina and Lady with a Fan (Degas), PLATE 16
Bamboccianti painting, 285, 298, 338, 339
Banquet (Smith), 504
Banquet of the Officers of St. George, The (Hals), 300
Baptism of Christ, The (Verrocchio), 244
Bar at the Folies-Bergère, The (Manet), 375
Barbarian architecture, 198–99
Barbarian metalwork, 197
Barbarian painting, 197–98
Barbizon painters, 360, 361, 363, 370
Barlach, Ernst (bär'läkh), 475, 476
barocco, 284
Baroque architecture, 292–98, 306–10
Baroque Classicism, 285
Baroque painting, 285–90, 298–305
Baroque sculpture, 290–92, 305–06
barrel vault, 77
Barry, Sir Charles, 395, 396
Bartolomeo Colleoni (Verrocchio), 244–45
Barye, Antoine (bä rē', än twän'), 388
basilica, 163: domed, 187, 189; double-ender, 199, 201, 202; Early Christian, 199, 201; hall church form, 201; Norman, 203; pilgrimage church type, 201, 203
Basilica of Constantine, 173
baths, Roman, 171
battered sides, 112
Battista Sforza, Duchess of Urbine (Piero), 236
Battle of Greeks and Amazons (Scopas), 150
Battle of the Centaurs, The (Michelangelo), 258
Bauhaus, 459, 484, 488, 494
Bauhaus buildings, 488, 489
bays, 78
Beards (Dubuffet), 496
Beatus Commentary on the Apocalypse, 208
Beauvais Cathedral, 211
Beckmann, Max, 4, 5, 466–67
Bed, The (Rauschenberg), 501
Behind in the Rent (Daumier), 372
Behrens, Peter (bär'ənz), 489
Belle de Jour (Buñuel), 442
Bellini, Giovanni (bel lē'nē, jo vän'nē), 237, 252, 253
Bellini, Jacopo (yä'ko pō), 237
Belvedere Court, 261
Belvedere Torso (Michelangelo), 258
bent-axis approach, 100, 106
Bergman, Ingmar, 434, 443–45
Berlin Museum, 394, 395

Bernini, Giovanni Lorenzo (bər nē'nē, jo vän'nē lo ren'dzō), 261, 284, 291–92, 294–96, 298, 306, 331
Bertoldo, Giovanni (bər'tol dō), 250
Beuys, Joseph, 512
Bibliothèque Nationale, 396
Bibliothèque Saint-Geneviève, 396, 397
Bicycle Thief, The (De Sica), 435, 442
binder, 70, 72, 116: synthetic, 72
Bird Cage, Variation II (Hofmann), 493–94, PLATE 29
Birth of a Nation, The (Griffith), 438
Birth of Spring, The (Botticelli), 239
Birth of Venus, The (Botticelli), 239
Bishop Bernward, 201–02, 207
Bison, 96
black-figure vase painting, 138, 139
black paintings (Goya), 364
Black Square (Malevich), 458
Blake, William, 366
blind arcades, 200, 203
Blow-Up (Antonioni), 443
Blue Light, The (Riefenstahl), 433
Blue Rider group, 450, 453, 459, 478
Blue-White (Kelly), 512
Boccioni, Umberto (bōt chyō'neh, ōōm ber'tō), 464
Body Art, 510
Bonaparte Crossing the Alps (David), 365
Bonnard, Pierre (bô'nar'), 453–54
Bonnie and Clyde (Penn), 437
Book of Job, The (Blake), 366
Book of Kells, 198 (detail), PLATE 2
Book of Pericopes of Henry II, 209
books, 182–83. See also manuscript illumination
Borromini, Francesco (bor ō mē'nē, frän ches'kō), 284, 296–98, 310
Bosch, Hieronymus (bosh; Dutch bos, hē ro'ni mus), 233, 234, 327
Boston Athenaeum, The (Southworth and Hawes), 419
bottega, 229
Botticelli, Sandro (bot i chel'ē, sän'drō), 239–40
Boucher, François (bōō shā', frän swä'), 328, 329
Boudin, Eugène (bōō'dan, eu zhen'), 380
Bouguereau, Adolphe (bōōgə rō'), 454
Brakhage, Stan, 437
Bramante, Donato (brə män'teh, do nä'tō), 260–61
Brancusi, Constantin (bräng kōō'zē; Rumanian bräng kūsh'), 476–78
Braque, Georges (bräk, jorj;

Die Brücke, 387, 449–50, 461
Die Neue Sachlichkeit. *See* New Objectivity movement
Dioskourides of Samos, 169
dipteral plan, 140, 151
Diptych of Anastasius, 194–95
Diptych of Melun (Fouquet), 232
Dipylon grave vase, 138, *139*
direct axial plan, 100
direct photography, 418–20, 422, 424
direct sand casting, 75
Disasters of War, The (Goya), 364
Discus-Thrower (Myron), 146, 147
Disney, Walt, 431
Disparates, The (Goya), 364
Dissipate (Heizer), 518–19
dissolve, 427
divisionism, 385, 464
Dixon, Thomas, 438
Documentary truth, 361, 362
Dog Star Man (Brakhage), 437
Doge's Palace, 255
Dogon tribesman, 5
dolly, 428
domed central plan, 185
Domenichino, Il (dō mā nə kē'nō, ēl), 300
domes, 80: Byzantine, 185, 189
Dom-ino multiple housing project, 490
Donatello (don ə tel'ō), 236, 238, 244, 245, 390
Doric order, 112, 141, 142, 151, 171, 260
dormer windows, 392
Double Negative (Heizer), *519*
Double Portrait with Wine Glass (Chagall), 470–71
Dovzhenko, Alexander (dəv cheng'kō; *Russian* dōv zhen'kō), 443
Dr. Claribel Cone (Picasso), 4, 10, 66, 462
Dr. Strangelove (Kubrick), 437
drapery panels, 209
drawing, 66–67
Dreyer, Carl-Theodore, 432
drip painting, 500
dromos, 128
dry brush drawing, 67
dry plate, 417
drypoint process, 69
Dubuffet, Jean, 495–96
Duccio de Buoninsegna (dōō'chyō; *Italian* dōō'chō de bwō nēn se'nyä), 220, 222
Duchamp, Marcel (dü shän'), 431, 448, 468–69
Dunes, Oceano, California (Weston), *423*, 424
Dürer, Albrecht (dür'ər, äl'brekht), 265–67
Durham Cathedral, 200, *205–06*
Dutch architecture: Baroque, 307; twentieth century, 484–85

Dutch Interior, I (Miró), 472, PLATE 28
Dutch painting: Baroque, 286, 298–99, 300, 303–05; nineteenth century, 383–85; Renaissance, 233, 234; twentieth century, 448, 457–58, 496–97
Dynamism of a Soccer Player, The (Boccioni), 464

Eakins, Thomas, 363, 382–83
Early Christian architecture, 180–82
Early Christian mosaics, 182, 183
Early Christian painting, 182–83
Early Christian sculpture, 184–85
Early Renaissance, 228
Early Sunday Morning (Hopper), 464
Earth Goddess with Snakes, 133–34
Earthworks, 510, 517–19
easel paintings, 249
eclecticism, 392, 393, 484
Écorché (Houdon), 332
Ecstasy of St. Teresa, The (Bernini), *291*, 292
edition, 67, 69
effigies, 161
Egyptian architecture: Archaic period, 111–14; Middle Kingdom, 117; New Kingdom, 120–22; Old Kingdom, 111–14
Egyptian painting: Amarna style, 123; Archaic period, 115–16; Middle Kingdom, 119; New Kingdom, 123–24; Old Kingdom, 115–16
Egyptian sculpture: Archaic period, 114–15; Middle Kingdom, 118–19; New Kingdom, 122–23; Old Kingdom, 114–15
Eight, The, 452
Eisenstein, Sergei M., 433, 440–41
Elegy to the Spanish Republic XXXIV (Motherwell), *500*, 501
elevation: in architecture, 76; in sculpture, 115
El Greco, 286–87
Elizabeth of Austria (Clouet), 268
Elsheimer, Adam, 298
Embarkation for Cythera, The (Watteau), *325*
Embarkation of St. Ursula, The (Claude), 302–03
empathy, 35
encaustic painting, 72, 168, 182
Enclosed Field (Van Gogh), 384–85, PLATE 21
engaged columns, 78, 107
English architecture: Baroque, 307–08, 309–10; eighteenth century, 333, 336 37; Gothic,

214; nineteenth century, 392, 394, 395, 396; Romanesque, 205–06
English films, 432–33, 434–35
English painting: eighteenth century, 324, 326–27, 328–29; nineteenth century, 362, 366, 367–69; Renaissance, 265, 267–68; twentieth century, 467–68, 493, 497–98
English sculpture: eighteenth century, 331; twentieth century, 479–80, 481–82, 483–84
engraving, 229, 267: Copyright Act for, 326; Cretan, 133; metal, 69; wood, 68
enlarging, 418
Enlightenment, Age of, 322
Ensor, James (en'sōr), 385–87
entablature, 141, 165
entasis, 142
Entr'acte (Clair), 441
environment, art and, 322
Episcopal Residence at Würzburg, 335, 338
Erasmus (Holbein), 267
Erechtheum, *143*
Erlach, Johann Fischer von. *See* Fischer von Erlach, Johann
Ernst, Max, 471–72
Estes, Richard, 516–17
etching, 68, 69, 303, 340–41, 364
Étienne Chevalier and St. Stephen (Fouquet), *232*
Etruscan architecture, 159–61
Etruscan painting, 162–63
Etruscan sculpture, 161–62
Eugene Delacroix (Nadar), *417*
Eworth, Hans, 264
Exekias (eks ē'kē as), 139
exhibitions. *See* Salon exhibitions
Exodus (Preminger), 437
Expressionism, 385, 387. *See also* Abstract Expressionism; German Expressionism
expressionistic architecture, 485
ex-votos, 132

Façade (Mondrian), 458
fade out, 427
Fagus Factory, *488*
faïence, 133
Fallen Warrior, 144, 145
false door, 112
Family of Charles IV, The (Goya), 364
Farnese Gallery, 287
Fauves, 449, 450
Fauvism, 385, 391, 449, 453, 454, 457, 468, 475, 493
Feast in the House of Levi, The (Veronese), 256, 257
Federal Style, 393
Fellini, Federico, 435, 436, 446
ferroconcrete. *See* reinforced concrete
fête galante, 323, 325, 326, 329
field pieces, 510

monochrome landscapes, 177, 178
monotype process, 70
montage, 427
Monticello, *393*
Monument to Balzac (Rodin), *391*
Moon and the Earth, The (Gauguin), *383*
Moore, Henry, 481–82, 483
Moreau, Gustave (moh ro'), 454
Morning Walk, The (Gainsborough), 328, 329
mortuary chapel, 112
mosaics: Byzantine, 189–91; early Christian, 181, 182, 183; Roman, 169
Mother's Advice, The (Chardin), 327
Motherwell, Robert, 500–01
motion: in architecture, 337; in line, 6; in sculpture (*see* kinetic sculpture); in shapes, 10
mounds, 100
Mountain Landscape with Sheep (Gainsborough), 328
Mr. and Mrs. Andrews (Gainsborough), 328
Mt. Ste.-Victoire from Bibemus Quarry (Cézanne), 379, PLATE 17
mud brick buildings, 99–100, 103
mud plaster painting, 103
multimedia, 509
multiple-point perspective system, 7
mummies, 179
Munch, Edvard (mūngkh), 387, 450
Muybridge, Eadweard (moi'-brij, ēd'wärd), 429
Mycerinus and His Queen, 9, 11, 115, 123
Myron, 144, 146, 147
Mystery and Melancholy of a Street, The (De Chirico), *8* (diagram), 469–70

Nabis, 379, 383, 453–54
Nadar, 417
Nahash Threatening the Jews at Jabesh, 221
Nanook of the North (Flaherty), 430, 439
Napoleon in the Wilderness (Ernst), *471, 472*
narthex, 181
Naturalism, 330, 359, 379, 388
nave, 78
Nazarenes, 362
Neapolitan Fisherboy (Rude), 389
necropolises, 112, 159, 160
Nedick's (Estes), *516*
Nefertiti, 123
negative, 418
Neithardt-Gothardt, Matthias (nīt'härt goht'härt). *See* Grünewald
Neo-Baroque, 392

Neoclassicism, 93, 322, 324, 330, 331, 332, 333, 337, 338, 358, 359–62, 365, 366, 369, 388–89, 392, 394, 424, 462, 470
Neo-Impressionism, 385
Neo-Plasticism, 458
Neorealism, 435, 436–37, 443, 445
Neumann, Balthasar, 335
Nevelson, Louise, 502–03
New-Born, The (Brancusi), 477
New Brutalism, 506
New Guardhouse (Berlin), 395
New Kingdom, 110, 120–24
New Objectivity movement, 420, 423, 430, 452, 466
New Realism. *See* Photo-Realism
Nicholas Chapel, 236
Niemeyer, Oscar, 505
Niépce, Nicéphore, 416–17
Night Hawks (Hopper), *463, 464*
Night Watch (Rembrandt), 300, *303*
nike type sculpture, 154
nimbus, 254
Ninth Investigation, Proposition I of 1972 (Kosuth), 519–20
No. 12, Lincoln's Inn Fields, 394
No. 20, Portman Square, *337*
Nolde, Emile (nōl'deh, ā'mēl), 449–50, 460–61
nonobjectivism, 61, 451, 453, 457, 483, 492, 494, 496, 500
Norman architecture, 204, 205
Norwegian painting, 387
Notes of a Painter (Matisse), 455
Notre Dame Cathedral, 211–*12*
Notre-Dame-du-Haut, 12, 15, *491, 492*
Notre Dame Le Raincy, *487–88*
Nouvelle Vague, la, 434
Noyon Cathedral, 211
NTrc, 497
Nude Descending a Staircase (Duchamp), 468
Number VII from Eight Studies for a Portrait (Bacon), *497, 498*

Oath of the Horatii (David), 364, *365*
obelisk, 121
objectivism, 93–95
obvious balance, 34, 35, 36, 38
occult balance, 34, 35, 38
Oceanic art, 460, 467
Octopus Vase, 132, *133*
oculus, 173
Odo of Metz, 199
Odyssey Landscapes, The, 168, 169
oil painting, 70, 71–72
Old Basilica of St. Peter's, *181*
Old Berlin Museum, *395*
Old Guitarist, The (Picasso), 424
Old King, The (Rouault), 457, PLATE 26
Old Kingdom, 110, 111–16
Oldenburg, Claes (klous'), 514

Olympic games, 136
On the Waterfront (Kazan), 437
one-point perspective system, 7
Op Art, 493, 495, 497, 508
Open City (Rossellini), 435
open form, 12
Open series (Motherwell), 501
Ophuls, Max, 433, 434
optical mixing, 381
order, 34, 36, 38: absolute, 458
orders: colossal, 262–63; Greek, 141, 142; Roman, 170–71, 260; Tuscan, 170, 171
organic architecture, 486
Orgy, The (Hogarth), 326
Orozco, José Clemente (o ros'kō, ho zā' kle men'teh), 453, 464–65
Orpheus and Eurydice (Poussin), *301*
orthographic projections, 76
Osiris cult, 117
Ostermeier, Johannes, 418
Ottonian art, 207, 208

Pabst, G. W., 430, 433
painting techniques, 70–72: prehistoric, 96–97
Painting with White Form, No. 212, (Kandinsky), 453, PLATE 23
paints, 70–71
Palace at 4 A.M., The (Giacometti), 482
Palace at Knossos, *128–29,* 131–32
Palace of Francis I, 269
Palace of the Senators, 262
Palace Style, 131
palaces: Achaemenian, 106–07; Assyrian, 103, 105; Cretan, 127; Egyptian, 111; Italian Renaissance, 247; Sumerian, 100
Palazzo Pamphili, 289
Palazzo Thiene, 264
Palazzo Vecchio, 247
Paleolithic Age, 96–97
palettes, 72, 115
palisades, 199
Palladian motif, 264, *265*
Palladian movement, 308
Palladian Revival, 333
Palladian window, 308
Palladio, Andrea (päl lä'dyō), 263–64, 307, 393
Palm, The (Bonnard), 454, PLATE 24
pan, 428
Pannini, Giovanni Paolo (pän nē'nē, jō vän'nē pä'o lō), 172, 339
Pantheon, *172,* 173, 258, 393
paper: for drawing, 66; for watercolor, 70
papier collés, *455,* 456
papyrus, 115
parchment, 183, 192, 197
Paris Academy, 217
Paris Cathedral, 211

Music

dance music: Baroque, 315, 316, 343; Renaissance, 277
"Das Rheingold" (Wagner), 410
David Playing for Saul (Leyden), 277
"De plus en plus" (Binchois), 227
Debussy, Claude (deb yōō se', klaud; French də beu sē, klōd), 23–24, 25, 31–32, 41, 42, 45, 53, 62–63, 83, 405, 407, 413–14
Degas, Edgar, 406
Delicate Joy (Kandinsky), 63
density, 43, 47, 54
Der Erlkönig (Schubert), 408–09
Der Ring des Nibelungen (Wagner), 410
development, 42, 83, 349, 352, 353, 355, 356
Dido and Aeneas (Purcell), 320
Die Meistersinger von Nürnberg (Wagner), 410
"Die Walküre" (Wagner), 410
diminution, 46, 48
dissonance, 50–51, 55, 85, 226, 273, 275, 313, 317, 320, 321, 356, 414, 525, 526, 529, 530
drama, music, 408, 409–10
drums, 27, 276
Dufay, Guillaume (deu fā', gē yōm'), 226, 227, 272, 274
Dunstable, John, 225–26
duple groups, 21
duration, 20, 23–24

Eakins, Thomas, 413
electronic music, 29–30, 55, 524, 528, 533, 535, 536, 537, 538–39, 541–42, 543
Ernst, Max, 526
ethos, 156–57
Étude for Two Pianos, Percussion, and Mixed Chorus (Varèse), 538
expansion, continuous, 83–85
exposition, 47, 349
Expressionism, 526, 529

Falstaff (Verdi), 411
fantasia, 277, 315, 343
Fantasia and Fugue in G Minor (Bach), 346
Fauré, Gabriel (fō rā', gä brē el'), 405
Feldman, Morton, 538
Fifth Symphony (Beethoven), 355–56
First Brandenburg Concerto (Bach), 22, 25, 32, 42, 45, 52–53, 63–64, 85, 93
Five Pieces for Orchestra, Opus 16 (Schoenberg), 529–30
flute, 25, 27, 28, 31–32, 41, 63, 83, 280, 355
Flute Player, The (Kirchner), 526
folk music, 527, 530, 537
form, 3, 82: common, 83–85; open, 543; sonata, 85; 349–50, 352, 353, 355; texture and,

47–48; three-part, 84; time and, 25; two-part, 84–85
4'33" (Cage), 539–40
Fourth Symphony (Brahms), 412–13
Franck, César (fränk, sā zär'), 408
French horn, 25, 27, 28, 29
fugato, 47, 88
fugue, 47, 315, 343, 345, 346

Gabrieli, Andrea (gä brē e'lē, än drā'ä), 281
Gabrieli, Giovanni (jo vän'nē), 281–82, 317
Garden of Earthly Delights, The (Bosch), 275
Gebrauchsmusik, 527
Gesualdo, Don Carlo (je zōō äl'do), 282–83
gigue, 320, 343
Gloria, 225
Gluck, Christoph Willibald (glōōk, kris'tot vil'i bält), 351, 352
"God Sustain the Emperor Franz" (Haydn), 353
Goethe, Johann Wolfgang von, 408
"Götterdämmerung" (Wagner), 410
Green Violinist, The (Chagall), 530
ground bass, 87, 320–21
guitar, 86, 316

half step, 49
half tone, 49
Handel, George Frideric (hand'əl, jorj frid'ə rik), 320, 347
happenings, 536, 539
Harmonice Musices Odhecaton A, 273
harmony, 48: chords, 49–50; coloristic, 53–54; consonance, 50–51; dissonance, 50–51; medieval, 224; modes, 49; musical style and, 54–55; scales, 48–49; tonality, 51–53
harp, 276
harpsichord, 27–28, 52, 276, 277, 281, 313, 319, 320, 343, 344, 347, 349
Harris, Roy, 527
Haydn, Franz Joseph (hīd'ən, fränts yō'zef), 348, 352–53
Hiller, Lejaren, 540
Hindemith, Paul (hin'də mith, pōl; German hin'də mit, poul), 527
Holbein, Hans the Younger, 282
homophonic, 44, 275, 281
Hosanna, 225, 279
HPSCHD (Cage and Hiller), 540

idea, musical, 62, 83, 86, 89
imitation, 46, 47–48, 272, 274, 275, 279, 280, 281, 282

Impressionism, 404, 413–14
Impromptus (Schubert), 405, 408
Improvisation with Green Center (Kandinsky), 528
indeterminacy, 537, 539, 542
Ingres, Jean Auguste Dominic, 87
intermedia, 536, 539
Intermezzos (Brahms), 405
interval, 40, 41, 44, 46, 49
inversion, 46, 48
Ionisation (Varèse), 537–38
Ives, Charles, 527

jazz, 23, 87, 527, 537
Johns, Jasper, 539
Josquin des Prez (zhos kan dā prā'), 272, 274–75

Kandinsky, Vassily, 63, 528
kettledrum, 27, 28
keyboard instruments, 27, 28, 280–81, 313, 314, 315, 343
Kirchner, Ernst Ludwig, 526
KNOBS, 540
krummhorn, 276
Kyrie, 225

La cathédrale engloutie (Debussy), 414
"La nuict froide et sombre" (Lassus), 279–80
Lady at the Piano (Renoir), 41
Lassus, Roland de (läs'ōōs, rō'länt də), 275, 279–80
Le Concert (St. Aubin), 348
Le marteau sans maître (Boulez), 541
Leyden, Lucas Van, 277
Lied, 405, 408
Ligeti, György (lig et'ē, dyor'dē), 537
Liszt, Franz (list, fränts), 405, 407
loudness, 25–26, 30–33, 51
Lully, Jean-Baptiste (leu lē', zhän bä tēst'), 314, 316, 318–19, 344, 346, 347
lute, 225, 276, 277, 280, 313
lyre, 157

Machaut, Guillaume de (mä shō', gē yōm' də), 225, 226
madrigal, 275–76, 279, 282, 313, 315, 316
Maeterlinck, Maurice, 413
"Ma fin est ma commencement" (Machaut), 225
Magic Flute, The (Mozart), 351
Mahler, Gustave (mä'lər, gōōs'taf), 406, 407
Mallarmé, Stéphane, 62
Mandolin and Guitar (Picasso), 50
Mannerism, 276, 282, 313
marimba, 27
Marriage of Figaro, The (Mozart), 351, 354–55
mass: medieval, 225, 227; Ren-

Sanctus, 225, 279
saraband, 343
Satie, Eric, (sä tē', er'ik; *French* e rēk'), 527
"Saul, Saul, was verfolgst du mich" from *Symphoniae Sacrae* (Schütz), 317–18
saxophone, 27
scales, 48–49
Scarlatti, Alessandro (skär lät'tē, ä les sän'droh), 346
Scarlatti, Domenico (doh meh'nē koh), 346–47
scherzo, 350: and trio, 350, 355
Schoenberg, Arnold (sheun'- bərg; *German* scheun'- berkh, är'nəlt), 526, 528–30, 532, 533, 541
Schubert, Franz, 405, 407, 408–09
Schumann, Robert, 405, 407, 408
Schütz, Heinrich (sheuts, hīn'rikh), 281, 317, 318
score, musical, 64, 89, *90*
"Se la face ay pale" (Dufay), 227
Second Hand (Cage), 539
sectional addition, 83–85
sequence, 319
serial music, 526, 534–35, 540, 541, 542
Sessions, Roger, 527
Seurat, Georges, 405
"Seven Words of Christ on the Cross, The" (Schütz), 317
Seventh Symphony (Beethoven), 20–22, 23, 25, 31, 41, 42, 44–45, 47, 53, 63–64, 87–89
sextet, 408
shawm, 276
"Siegfried" (Wagner), 410
Sinfonia (Berio), 23–24, 25, 32–33, 42–43, 45, 53, *64*, 90–91, 93, 542
Singspiel, 345, 351
snare drum, *27*
sonata: Baroque, 315, 316, 319, 343, 344, 345, 347; Classical, 349; nineteenth century, 404, 408, 412
Sonata in C Major (Scarlatti), 347
Songs Without Words (Mendelssohn), 405
Soprano Singer, The (Van Dongen), *525*
sound: envelope, 30; new sources of, *29* 30; traditional sources of, 27–29
speech–song technique, 541
spinet, *276*
Stockhausen, Karlheinz (stok'- hou zən; *German* shtōk'hou zən, kärl'hīnz), 533, 535
Strauss, Richard (strous; *German* shtrous, rikh'ärt), 406, 407
Stravinsky, Igor (strə vin'skē,

ē'gor; *Russian* strä vēn'ski, eh'gor), 527, 530–32
stretto, 47, 48
string bass, 27, 28
string instruments, *26*, 27, 28, 406
string quartet, *24*, 349, 352–53, 408, 530
String Quartet, Opus 76, No. 3 (Haydn), 352–53
String Quartet No. 4 (Bartók), 530
strophic songs, 84
style, concept of, 97
subbeat, 21–22
subgroup, 21–23
subject, 47
subjectivism, 94
subjectivity, 92–93
suite: dance, 315, 343, 344, 347; orchestral, 344; symphonic, 407
Suite bergamasque (Debussy), 405
Suitor's Visit, The (Ter Borch) 88
Symphoniae Sacrae (Schütz), 317–18
symphony, 349, 352, 355, 407, 408, 412, 532, 534
Symphony, Opus 21 (Webern), 533–34
Symphony of Psalms (Stravinsky), 532
syncopation, 23
synthesizer, *29*–30, 535

Tallis, Thomas, 280
tambourine, 27
Tannhauser (Wagner), *409*
Tchaikovsky, Peter Ilyich (chī kof'skē, il'yich; *Russian* chī kohf'ski, pyoh'tər il'yēch), 407
tempo, 24
Ter Borch, Gerard, 88
texture, 43: form and, 47–48; varieties of, 43–45
Theater Piece (Cage), 539
theme, 349; and variations, 86–87
thorough bass, 313
"Three Blind Mice," 48
Three Folk Musicians (Bearden), 542
Threni (Stravinsky), 531
timbre, 25–27, 30–33, *51*, *62*, 83
time: durational structures, 23–24; form and, 25; measures, 20–22; meter, 21–23; musical movement, 24–25; rhythm, 20–24, 25, 51, 62, 83
To the Victims of Hiroshima: Threnody (Penderecki), 543–44
toccata, 277, 315, 343
tonality, 51–53, 55, 82, 83, 282, 313, 320, 346, 349, 525, 529, 532, 533
tone, 40
tonic, 51

tragédies lyriques, 318
transition, 349
transposition, *46*, 48
triad, 49–50, 226, 227, 273
triangle, *27*
trio. *See* minuet; scherzo
triple groups, 21
Tristan und Isolde (Wagner), 410
"Tristis est anima mea" (Lassus), 279
trombone, 25, 27, 28, 355
trumpet, *25*, 27, 28, 276
tuba, 27, 28
tutti, 316, 319
twelve-tone system, 526, 529, 531, 532, 533–34, 540

Untitled (Williams), *536*
Upside Down Violin (Ernst), *526*

value judgment, 92–95
Van Dongen, Kees, 525
Varèse, Edgard (vä rez', ed gär'), 527–28, 537–38
variation, 85–89, 342, 343, 344, 350, 353, 355, 404, 407, 412, 529, 534
Vaughan Williams, Ralph, 527
Verdi, Giuseppe (ver'dē, jōō sep'peh), 407, 408, 410–11
verismo, 404
Victory Boogie Woogie (Mondrian), *533*
viol, *276*, *280*
viola, *26*, 27, 28
viola da gamba, *314*
violin, *26*, 27, 28, 316, *319*, 353
virginal, 281
Vivaldi, Antonio (vi väl'dē, an tō'nē o; *Italian* vē väl'dē, än toh'nyo), 345

Wagner, Richard (väg'nər, rikh'ärt), 406, 408, 409–10, 525
Watteau, Antoine, 343
Webern, Anton von (vā'bərn, än'tōn fōn), 526, 532–34, 535
whole step, 49
Williams, Larry, 536
wind instruments, 27, 28, 276–77
Wolf, Hugo (vohlf, hōō'gō), 405
Wolff, Christian, 538
Woman in Black at the Opera, A (Cassat), *403*
wood blocks, 27
woodwind instruments, *25*, 27, 28–29, 349, 406

Xenakis, Iannis (zə näk'ēs, yä'nēs), 535
xylophone, 27

zink, 276

7
B 8
C 9
D 0
E 1
F 2
G 3
H 4
I 5
J 6